A KABBALAH AND JEWISH MYSTICISM READER

The Jewish Publication Society expresses its gratitude for the generosity of the sponsors of this book.

PATRONS

In gratitude for the leadership of Rabbi Horwitz
The Stein Family of Houston, Texas

FRIENDS

In memory of Evelyn (z"l) and John (z"l) Horwitz
Nancy T. Beren and Larry S. Jefferson

In honor of our children, grandchildren, and
great-granddaughter
Shirley and Leon (z"l) Cooper

JPS ANTHOLOGIES
OF JEWISH THOUGHT

UNIVERSITY OF NEBRASKA PRESS

Lincoln

A Kabbalah and Jewish Mysticism Reader

Daniel M. Horwitz

THE JEWISH PUBLICATION SOCIETY
Philadelphia

All rights reserved. Published by the
University of Nebraska Press as a
Jewish Publication Society book.
Manufactured in the United States of America.

Library of Congress
Cataloging-in-Publication Data
Names: Horwitz, Daniel M., author.
Title: A Kabbalah and Jewish mysticism
reader / Daniel M. Horwitz.
Description: Philadelphia: Jewish Publication
Society; Lincoln: University of Nebraska Press,
2016 | Series: JPS Anthologies of Jewish Thought
| Includes bibliographical references and index.
Identifiers: LCCN 2015047971
ISBN 9780827612563 (pbk.: alk. paper)
ISBN 9780827612860 (epub)
ISBN 9780827612877 (mobi)
ISBN 9780827612884 (pdf)
Subjects: LCSH: Cabala. | Mysticism—Judaism.
Classification: LCC BM525 .H67 2016 |
DDC 296.7/12—dc23 LC record available
at http://lccn.loc.gov/2015047971

Set in Lyon by M. Scheer.
Designed by Rachel Gould.

Contents

Illustrations

Preface

What drew me into the study of Jewish mysticism? In the middle of my life, after about fifteen years as a rabbi and thirty years into my serious involvement with Judaism, rather than simply continuing what I was doing I asked myself: what has made Judaism work for *me*? Why has it provided the level of intensity that elicited my commitment to the God of Israel as I came to understand Him, and to the traditional pattern of Jewish life?

It was about this time that I first took a serious look at a book called *Shnei Luhot ha-Brit*, [The two tablets of the covenant], authored in 1625 by my ancestor Rabbi Isaiah Horowitz. It is a vast collection of teachings on all things Jewish, all of them understood through a kabbalistic lens, expressing a passionate desire for intimacy with God. Through this and other mystical texts, I began to consider issues I had never studied or understood.

At about the same time, as part of a doctoral program I had recently entered, I participated in a seminar with Moshe Idel, generally considered to be the leading scholar on Jewish mysticism. Idel introduced me to the theme of *deveikut*, "cleaving" to God, through a variety of texts, most entirely new to me.

In the same period, I reread some of the work of the great twentieth-century Jewish mystical teacher Abraham Joshua Heschel, including newly republished essays, and began to understand how he had integrated many Jewish mystical concepts into his writings.

These were primary elements of the journey that became the impetus for this book. They led me to understand not only the power of the mystical path, but the necessity of including its energy within any Judaism that would be viable and meaningful for me.

Here I offer a single example of a mystical teaching, a sixteenth-century interpretation of a scriptural verse, which reflects one person's desire to connect with his Creator.

> **"Like a bird wandering from its nest, is a man who wanders from his home" (Prov. 27:8). When the bird wanders from its nest, it longs to return. Similarly with man, who has a soul within him; when he wanders from his destiny and from his plane, which is among the higher beings, he perforce longs continually to return to it. (Meir Ibn Gabbai, introduction to *Avodat ha-Kodesh* [The service of the Holy One])**

Most readers would naturally understand the verse from Proverbs as saying: don't stray from your home, from your family, from your people. The mystic looks at it and says: the soul longs to return to its mysterious Source on high.

Some people naturally see most things in life as matter of fact, prosaic. They get up in the morning, eat breakfast, do carpool, go to work, do all the normal things people do . . . and they never wonder where their soul comes from. They never feel a need to connect with that mysterious Source. They may be good citizens, loving husbands and wives, devoted parents . . . but if their children *do* want to connect with that Source, they are often totally discombobulated, as if their children were suddenly speaking a foreign language.

All religions deal with a very basic problem, the gap between God and human beings. Much of Jewish life does not concern itself with this problem, but Jewish mysticism does; it attempts to bridge the gap. This book is a partial record of what Jews have done to bridge that gap, to connect with their Source. I am not here to convince you that such intimacy with God is possible for you, only to show you that many Jews *did* and *do* believe it is possible. And I encourage you, as you read, to imagine what it would be like to believe in and even experience this kind of God. My hope is that the texts and commentary here will resonate with you on some level, add to your understanding of Judaism, answer some of your questions, and lead you to new ones.

This book aims to provide a serious yet accessible, text-based introduction to the Jewish mystical tradition. It is designed to introduce the basic concepts and teachings of Jewish mysticism, ground these ideas within the broader framework of Judaism, and show how they are still relevant today for many Jews.

In the pages that follow you will find writings on a variety of important themes in the Jewish mystical tradition as well as brief introductions to some of the major figures in its history. Together with the commentaries that accompany them, these texts trace the development of Jewish mystical thinking and practice, from the biblical times to today.

Chapter 1 defines mysticism and Jewish mysticism and briefly introduces five different types of Jewish mysticism, with subsequent chapters presenting texts across the spectrum of types. This provides a compromise between the need students frequently express for something resembling a chronological development (which, if presented rigidly, would not accurately portray the subject) and the typological approach. Thus the subject development is, for the most part, in chronological order, but all subjects include one or more of the five types, and material from different eras is frequently included under one subject.

In transliterating Hebrew words and phrases, I have generally followed the Jewish Publication Society guidelines. Bible passages are usually from the NJPS translation, but frequently the context of the material required an alternative. I have benefited from the various translations available for many of the selected texts (as mentioned in the footnotes), while adjusting the language as I deemed appropriate.

A work of this nature obviously has serious limits. I have chosen to omit a great many significant figures in the history of Jewish mysticism, usually because they had limited influence on Jewish life beyond their time. For those interested, the suggestions for further reading at the end of the book provide additional direction.

Naturally, a work such as this requires the assistance and cooperation of many individuals. First, I am very grateful to Kathleen Bloch, collections manager of the Spertus Library, and her staff, who have ably assisted with my many requests for books and articles during the course of my doctoral studies at the Spertus Institute of Jewish Leadership and Learning. Their great patience, particularly in the face of difficult conditions caused by the library's relocation, is very much appreciated.

Many thanks to those individual scholars who have been kind enough to answer various questions: Morris Faierstein, Pinchas Giller, Daniel Matt, Mark Verman, Aryeh Wineman, and Elliot Wolfson. My apologies for any inadvertent omissions.

I have been fortunate to be able to teach classes on aspects of Jewish mysticism to groups of enthusiastic students in two communities where I have served as rabbi. I am most grateful for the opportunity to study together with students in the Melton Adult Mini-School in both communities and with members of Congregation Ohev Sholom in Prairie Village, Kansas, and Congregation Beth Yeshurun in Houston. They have helped me to approach much of the material and successfully confront some of its challenges. I am especially thankful for the help of Abby Rotenberg at Beth Yeshurun for her patient and skillful assistance along the way.

I am grateful to my friend and teacher Rabbi Joseph Radinsky of Houston, with whom I have had the privilege to study on a regular basis for the last several years. I humbly thank him for sharing his time, his learning, and his regular encouragement.

Special thanks to Carol Hupping and Rabbi Barry Schwartz of the Jewish Publication Society, for their faith in the value of this book and for helping me to make it as useful as possible. Michele Alperin's close reading of the text helped improve it considerably, and I appreciate her patience with the text and with my own idiosyncrasies. Ultimately, of course, I am responsible for any errors, and I hope that readers will contact me through JPS with their thoughts.

Sadly, I never had the opportunity to study together with Rabbi Abraham Joshua Heschel. His books and ideas have informed my rabbinate, my personal commitments, and my work on this project. But I *have* had the great direct benefit of the advice and direction of his student Dr. Byron Sherwin, who consistently provided inspiration and assistance. I do not believe I could have completed such a project without them, and I will always be grateful for all they have added to my life, as well as for what they have enabled me to provide to my students. Dr. Sherwin's death is a great loss to all of us who have studied with him, but his life set an example for all who sought to combine Jewish commitment with the highest commitment to scholarship.

Finally, I am most grateful to the members of my family who have encouraged me throughout the development and completion of this book. They regularly remind me what matters most. Thank you

> to my children, Dina and Joey Carr (with our granddaughter Emmy), Sarit, Shaye, and Eliana Horwitz;
>
> to their grandparents, Leon (*zikhrono livrakha*) and Shirley Cooper, and John and Evelyn Horwitz (*zikhronam livrakha*);
>
> and, most especially, to my wife, Tobi Cooper, for the many hours she has had to deal with the demands of the present tense while I lingered in some earlier century.

Landmark Dates and Key Figures
in Jewish Mysticism

UNTIL 165 BCE
Biblical era
Prophetic experiences
Early apocalyptic views

SECOND CENTURY BCE TO SECOND CENTURY CE
Postbiblical era
Temple experiences
Early Rabbinic mysticism

SECOND TO SEVENTH CENTURY
Rabbinic era
Heikhalot (*Merkavah*) mysticism
Sefer Yetzirah

TWELFTH TO THIRTEENTH CENTURY
Hasidei Ashkenaz in Germany
First appearance of Mainline Kabbalah
Sefer ha-Bahir (~1180)
Various schools in southern France, Spain
Nahmanides (1194–1270), Joseph Gikatilla (b. 1248)
Zohar (~1280); Moses de Leon

Meditative system of Prophetic (or Ecstatic) Kabbalah; Abraham Abulafia (b. 1240)

SIXTEENTH CENTURY

Flourishing of Kabbalah in Safed, including Joseph Karo (1488–1575); Moses Cordovero (1522–70); Isaac Luria (1534–72); and Hayyim Vital (1542–1620)

Judah Loew of Prague (~1520–1609)

SEVENTEENTH CENTURY

Spread of Lurianic Kabbalah

Isaiah Horowitz (~1565–1630)

Kabbalah turns to messianism

EIGHTEENTH CENTURY–PRESENT

Hasidic and non-Hasidic Kabbalah

Ba'al Shem Tov (d. 1760)

Among the next generations: Dov Ber, the Maggid of Mezeritch (1710–73); Levi Yitzhak of Berditchev (1740–1809); Nahman of Bratslav (1772–1811); Shneur Zalman of Liady, the first Chabad rebbe (1745–1812); Jacob Isaac Horowitz, the Seer of Lublin (1745–1815); Jacob Isaac, the "Holy Jew" (1765–1814); Simha Bunim (1765–1827); Menahem Mendel Morgenstern, the Kotzker Rebbe (1787–1859); and Mordecai Joseph Leiner (1800–1854)

TWENTIETH CENTURY–PRESENT

Adaptations of Kabbalah for Zionism and non-orthodox Jews; academic study of Jewish mysticism

Dozens of Hasidic groups appear, Chabad the largest and most prominent; Menahem Mendel Schneerson II, the seventh Chabad rebbe (1902–94)

Other prominent twentieth-century mystics: Abraham Isaac Kook (1865–1935); Kalonymous Kalman Shapira (1889–1943); and Abraham Joshua Heschel (1907–72)

Part 1
The Roots of Jewish Mysticism

1
What Is Jewish Mysticism?

Mysticism is the process of striving for an intense relationship with God, sometimes going so far as to achieve an altered state. This striving has the effect of adding energy and intensity to religious life. Hence, mysticism has been defined by Bernard McGinn as "the ongoing search for a heightened consciousness, or awareness, of the presence of the living God—the God who makes a difference not only in what believers think, but also in how they struggle to live."[1]

A key word here is "search"; mystical experience does not usually come without effort, and it often requires using certain techniques as well as acquiring knowledge. Another important idea here is "presence." Those with a much more abstract notion of God, a God who does not address the personal situations of individuals, are likely to assume that the mystical quest is impossible or irrelevant. If this is your understanding of God, I hope you will suspend that for the time being and imagine what it would be like to believe in and even experience a different type of God. Imagine sensing that, as the Prophet Isaiah saw it, "the whole world is filled with His glory."[2] Imagine that all we need to have this experience, to bridge the gap between God and human beings, is to refine our senses, acquire some knowledge and techniques, and sharpen our ethical sensitivities.

The mystic search for some form of union with the Divine is described by the twentieth-century theologian Abraham Joshua Heschel:

> The universe, exposed to the violence of our analytical mind, is being broken apart. It is split into the known and unknown, into the seen and unseen. In mystic contemplation all things are seen as one. The mystic mind tends to hold the world together: to behold the seen in conjunction with the unseen, to keep the fellowship with the unknown through the revolving door of the known, "to learn the higher supernal wisdom from all" that the Lord has created and to regain the knowledge that once was in the possession of men and "that has perished from them." (Heschel, *Mystical Element in Judaism*, 603)[3]

Many would consider this goal extremely dangerous. To mention one obvious concern, what would result from "union with God"? Could one possibly return from it? We will encounter ample evidence of such concerns throughout this book. Nonetheless Heschel insists that the mystical experience is the pinnacle of religion, revealing a truth beyond words, beyond what is visible to us.

> The power of expression is not the monopoly of man. Expression and communication are, to some degree, something of which animals are capable. What characterizes man is not only his ability to develop words and symbols, but also his being compelled to draw a distinction between the utterable and the unutterable, to be stunned by that which is, but cannot be put into words. . . .
>
> What smites us with unquenchable amazement is not that which we grasp and are able to convey but that which lies within our reach but beyond our grasp; not the quantitative aspect of nature but something qualitative; not what is beyond our range in time and space but the true meaning, source and end of being, in other words, the ineffable. (Heschel, *Man Is Not Alone*, 4-5)

There will be a good deal on this subject that is difficult, if not impossible, to convey; this remains one of the chief challenges, even when the experienced mystic endeavors to tell us about the mystical experience.

Nonetheless, the one who believes in a truth beyond what is visible will likely understand the world differently from others, and may, like many Jewish mystics, seek the tools that will help him or her interpret that truth.

While there are common experiences among all mystics, they pursue and convey the experience in terms consistent with their own religious traditions. There is no such thing as a "generic" mysticism, and Jewish mystics do not suddenly have visions focused on the cross or hear the voice of Mohammed. Jewish mysticism involves Jewish rituals and symbols.[4]

Does this limit Jewish mystical experience? For instance, since the Torah tells us that we cannot "see" God, would the visual aspect of mystical experience be less frequent for Jews? We will see that the visual is not only a common theme, but in some periods one of the most frequent.[5]

While Jewish mystics seemed to oppose what passed for normative Judaism in various eras, they firmly believed that their goals and experiences represented the most essential part of Judaism; they did not reject Rabbinic Judaism, but saw themselves and their practices as its fulfillment. The early Jewish mystics did not even have a concept such as "mysticism" and never thought their experiences so abnormal as to require a special term. Indeed Hebrew has no word for the mystical experience.[6]

The texts in this book, taken from different eras, illustrate five different categories of Jewish mysticism. We will see later what techniques each of these types employs to achieve its goals, as well as how they work and more about how they developed.[7]

Normal Mysticism

Ongoing Jewish activity maintains awareness of God's Presence, without any sort of paranormal activity. In mindfully fulfilling a precept or reciting a brief prayer, one consciously and simply acknowledges that Presence. Normal Mysticism turns common events like these into moments for a brief recognition of God. By creating such occasions, "an awareness of

God seeps into all the activities of human life until this unseen Presence is taken as the true foundation of being."[8] Jewish life offers continual ritual opportunities that can stimulate such awareness when they are carried out with proper intention. Such an experience involves no great intensity and indeed no such intensity is desirable for the average Jew. Anything beyond Normal Mysticism is intended only for an elite.

Deveikut, "Cleaving" to God

The root of the word *deveikut* appears in Gen. 2:24: "Hence a man leaves his father and mother *v'davak b'ishto,* and cleaves to his wife, so they become one flesh." This suggests for the mystic an intimate closeness with God. For some mystics, the ultimate religious experience is this intense sense of closeness with God, a radically transformative experience that involves a sweeping attempt to eliminate the gap between God and man. Complete *deveikut* may exist in intimate communion, or even union or reunion. The goal is to maintain intense intimacy as much as possible, and for the mystic who desires it the purpose of Jewish practice is to foster it.

Teacher and storyteller Yitzhak Buxbaum gives an excellent illustration of how this should work in daily life: "Consider what a person does when driving a car. He can turn the radio channel with one hand, adjust the speed with his foot, and, at the same time, carry on a conversation with a friend in the front seat; but all the while, his attention is firmly fixed on the road to see that he stays in his lane, and his second hand is on the wheel to steer the car. That is a matter of life and death. So can you do the things you have to do in the world while the greater part of your attention is fastened on God."[9]

Mainline Kabbalah

The basic teaching of this form of Jewish mysticism is that what we do can affect God's inner life, and that by doing so we make a great difference for all life. This teaching is sometimes described as "theosophical," which means: having to do with mystical insights into the nature of God.[10] As

Heschel taught: "This is the pattern of Jewish mysticism: to have an open heart for the inner life of God. It is based on two assumptions: that there is an inner life in God, and that the existence of man ought to revolve in a spiritual dynamic course around the life of God."[11]

It may seem strange to suggest we could have such knowledge of God's inner life, but much of the Jewish mystical tradition is based on this assumption. Mainline Kabbalah is also sometimes described as "theurgical," relating to the mystic's beneficent involvement in God's inner life, in order to accomplish goals on that level (which may incidentally benefit this world).[12] Several chapters in this volume are devoted to the terminology Kabbalah uses in explaining what these goals are and how the mystic achieves them.

Affective Kabbalah

Affective Kabbalah is related to Mainline Kabbalah, but with one important difference. Action in this world still stimulates action in a higher world, but here the action is for human benefit, not for God's sake. This is human-centered mysticism, meant to address communal or personal needs. Jewish magic falls into this category, as it seeks to draw down and channel the divine powers toward certain goals. Specific deeds, holy or otherwise, promote or obstruct the divine flow that sustains our world. Frequently in this form of mysticism emphasis is placed on the role of the tzaddik, the spiritual master who is able to maintain a relationship with God, serve as a channel for divine grace, and improve conditions for us.[13]

Prophetic, or Ecstatic, Kabbalah

Here, the highest goal is to achieve some form of union with God, but in a way that will enable an individual to reach the peak of his spiritual potential, achieve revelation through mystical experience, and even attain a level of prophecy. This level of enlightenment is a different kind of intimacy with God; it has additional purposes, such as learning the secrets of the Torah and God's decrees for the future, the prayers of the angels, and other supernatural knowledge.

The Historical Development of Jewish Mysticism

This book traces the history of the five types of Jewish mysticism described above as they manifest in several different categories over the last two thousand-plus years:

1. Mysticism in the Bible, both before and after the Second Temple, is addressed in chapter 2.

2. The Rabbinic period (first to eighth century CE), including not only the mainstream Rabbinic literature such as the Talmud and Midrash but also a variety of texts dealing with mystical experience, is covered in chapters 3 through 6.

3. Hasidei Ashkenaz (German pietists, eleventh to thirteenth century) and their form of mystical moralism are examined in chapter 7.

4. Early Kabbalah (twelfth to fifteenth century), the development of its main ideas in the Zohar, and the alternate path of Abulafia are covered in most of chapters 8 through 15.

5. Lurianic Kabbalah (sixteenth to seventeenth century), which was centered in the mystical community of Safed and greatly expanded upon existing kabbalistic practices, is the focus of chapters 16 through 18. (Chapters 19 through 22 examine specific concepts within Jewish mysticism and how they were interpreted during different periods.)

6. Hasidism (eighteenth century to the present) is the great revivalist movement founded in Eastern Europe that brought a kabbalistic view and practice to a much larger group of Jews than ever before. Selected Hasidic thinkers and ideas can be found in chapters 23 through 26, and three twentieth-century mystics are discussed in chapter 27.

7. What lies beyond the present? How did we get to the Judaism of today, and how might Jewish mysticism affect the Judaism of the future? These questions are dealt with directly in chapter 28 and indirectly in a number of other chapters.

This is not a guidebook for experiencing Jewish mystical heights, but it will give you a sense of what such experiences are like through the descriptions and teachings of those who claim to have had them. You will develop a sense for the impact of the mystical impulse on all aspects of Jewish life and why so many Jews in diverse times and places saw it as the central force and purpose of Judaism. And you will also understand the challenge it posed to Jewish leaders as it developed different forms. Finally, you will appreciate the joys and ecstasies—and also the potential dangers—experienced by those who pursued Jewish mystical experiences.

2
Mysticism in the Bible

The Hebrew Bible describes many meetings between God and human beings. We see the exceptional access granted to Moses and the Patriarchs. The prophets are given messages to transmit, and occasionally intense visions. Psalms frequently speak of the longing to experience and to dwell in God's Presence. When examining the mystical experiences recorded in the Bible, it is important to see not only the quality of these experiences but how they were understood in succeeding generations. Later mystics were inspired particularly by two visions, one of Isaiah and the other of Ezekiel.

Isaiah lived in the eighth century BCE; here he describes God's throne room, a divine parallel to the earthly Temple in Jerusalem.

> In the year that King Uzziah died, I beheld my Lord seated on a high and lofty throne; and the skirts of His robe filled the Temple. Seraphs stood in attendance on Him. Each of them had six wings: with two he covered his face, with two he covered his legs, and with two he would fly. And one would call to the other, "Holy, holy, holy! The Lord of Hosts! His presence fills all the earth!"
>
> The doorposts would shake at the sound of the one who called, and the House kept filling with smoke. I cried, "Woe is me; I am lost! For I am a man of unclean lips and I live among a people of unclean lips; yet my own eyes have beheld the King Lord of Hosts." Then

one of the seraphs flew over to me with a live coal, which he had taken from the altar with a pair of tongs. He touched it to my lips and declared, "Now that this has touched your lips, your guilt shall depart and your sin be purged away."

Then I heard the voice of my Lord saying, "Whom shall I send? Who will go for us?" And I said, "Here am I; send me." And He said, "Go, say to that people: 'Hear, indeed, but do not understand; see, indeed, but do not grasp.'" (Isa. 6:1–9)

The mystical experience described here is not just about the message God gives the prophet; it's also about the prophet's reaction. By assigning this Isaiah passage as the haftarah to be read with the Torah reading (in Exodus 20) about God giving the Ten Commandments, the Rabbis made clear that they saw Isaiah's individual mystical experience of revelation as parallel to what the Israelites experienced at Sinai.

The opening verse suggests that Isaiah is within the temple courts. He suddenly has an ecstatic vision of God, similar to other biblical scenes of God's throne (such as in 1 Kings 22:19–23 and Dan. 7:9–14). A form of the word "fill" (*malei*) is repeated three times in the first four verses, emphasizing the overwhelming Presence of God.[1] Angelic beings pay tribute to God, and Isaiah has an overpowering sense of his own impurity in this holy realm; one of the angels brings him a purifying coal, after which he is able to withstand the moment and bring a message from the higher realm to his people. Isaiah does not seem to have done anything to prepare for this experience; it is simply granted to him—or, more accurately, forced upon him. He does go up to the Temple in Jerusalem, but he is clearly raised up to a higher court.[2] This is the mystical experience of the prophet; its goal is simply to prepare him to receive and transmit God's word.

What do the angels mean when they say that God's Presence (*Kavod*; sometimes translated as "glory") fills all the earth? What is this *Kavod*? It seems to be a visible manifestation of God's glory.[3] If you are troubled by such anthropomorphisms (the attribution of human form or behavior to God), you are in good company; Maimonides and other medieval philosophers wrestled with this as well.[4] We will see many other such expressions here and later, because they are common in mystical expression.

Now we turn to Ezekiel, who was carried from Jerusalem into exile in Babylonia, where he experiences this astonishing, even bizarre revelation:

> In the thirtieth year, on the fifth day of the fourth month, when I was in the community of exiles by the Chebar Canal, the heavens opened and I saw visions of God. On the fifth day of the month—it was the fifth year of the exile of King Jehoiachin—the word of the Lord came to the priest Ezekiel son of Buzi, by the Chebar Canal, in the land of the Chaldeans. And the hand of the Lord came upon him there.
>
> I looked, and lo, a stormy wind came sweeping out of the north—a huge cloud and flashing fire, surrounded by a radiance; and in the center of it, in the center of the fire, a gleam as of amber. In the center of it were also the figures of four creatures. . . . Each had four faces, and each of them had four wings; the legs of each were [fused into] a single rigid leg, and the feet of each were like a single calf's hoof; and their sparkle was like the luster of burnished bronze. They had human hands below their wings. The four of them had their faces and their wings on their four sides. . . .
>
> Each of them had a human face [at the front]; each of the four had the face of a lion on the right; each of the four had the face of an ox on the left; and each of the four had the face of an eagle [at the back]. Such were their faces. As for their wings, they were separated: above, each had two touching those of the others, while the other two covered its body. And each could move in the direction of any of its faces; they went wherever the spirit impelled them to go, without turning when they moved.

. . . With them was something that looked like burning coals of fire. This fire, suggestive of torches, kept moving about among the creatures; the fire had a radiance, and lightning issued from the fire. Dashing to and fro [among] the creatures was something that looked like flares.

. . . As for the appearance and structure of the wheels, they gleamed like beryl. All four had the same form; the appearance and structure of each was as of two wheels cutting through each other. And when they moved, each could move in the direction of any of its four quarters; they did not veer when they moved. Their rims were tall and frightening, for the rims of all four were covered all over with eyes. And when the creatures moved forward, the wheels moved at their sides; and when the creatures were borne above the earth, the wheels were borne too. Wherever the spirit impelled them to go, they went—wherever the spirit impelled them—and the wheels were borne alongside them; for the spirit of the creatures was in the wheels. . . .

Above the heads of the creatures was a form: an expanse, with an awe-inspiring gleam as of crystal, was spread out above their heads. . . .

Above the expanse over their heads was the semblance of a throne, in appearance like sapphire; and on top, upon this semblance of a throne, there was the semblance of a human form. From what appeared as his loins up, I saw a gleam as of amber, what looked like a fire encased in a frame; and from what appeared as his loins down, I saw what looked like fire. There was a radiance all about him. . . . That was the appearance of the semblance of the Presence of the Lord. When I beheld it, I flung myself down on my face. And I heard the voice of someone speaking. And He said to me, "O mortal, stand up on your feet that I may speak to you." As He spoke to me, a spirit entered into me and set me upon my feet; and I heard what was being spoken to me. He said to me, "O mortal, I am sending you to the people of Israel, that nation of rebels, who have rebelled against Me. They as well as their fathers have defied Me to this very day; for the sons are brazen of face and stubborn of heart. I send you to them, and you shall say to them: 'Thus said the Lord God'—whether they listen or not, for they are a rebellious breed—that they may know that there was a prophet among them."

. . . Then a spirit carried me away, and behind me I heard a great roaring sound: "Blessed is the Presence of the Lord, in His place." (Ezek. 1:1–2:5, 3:12)

This prophetic vision is not only outside the Temple; it is outside the Land of Israel entirely. However, it is the vision of a *Kohen*, a priest who almost certainly participated in the temple service. And much of its imagery is based on different aspects of the Temple: the cherubim (creatures part human and part animal), the Ark of the Covenant below them, and the Holy of Holies containing them (as per Exodus 25 and 37). However, by virtue of the fact that this mystical experience takes place in exile, it suggests that intense experience of God's nearness need not be limited to the Land of Israel. It is the most detailed and puzzling of all the biblical visions of God, or His *Kavod*, including not only the divine throne but also a heavenly chariot, or *Merkavah*. (Though this word does not appear in the text, the experience of Ezekiel is often referred to as "seeing the *Merkavah*.") So mysterious and confusing did the Rabbis find this text that many would not allow it to be included as one of the public readings (*haftarot*) from the books of the Prophets. Ultimately it did become the standard haftarah for the first day of Shavuot, when the Ten Commandments are read from the Torah.[5]

What does one make of Ezekiel's experience? Here are interpretations of some portions of this challenging text:

1. The number four is significant: there are four creatures, each with four faces and four wings. These correspond to the four cherubim surrounding the Ark,[6] and the four horns of the temple altar (see Exod. 27:2). These may represent the four directions, with God's Presence at the center of the universe (i.e., in the Temple). Thus

these sets of four evoke a special sense of closeness to the Divine.[7] Finally, the four wheels are able to move in all four directions. What is the "spirit" (*ruah*) propelling these creatures?

2. The Hebrew makes frequent use of the word *demut*, often translated as "likeness," as in Gen. 1:26: "Let us make man in our image, after our likeness." What is a "likeness"? It appears to be something, but actually is not. Thus, this account of Ezekiel claims to see things as they appear to be, while recognizing that they may actually be something different. This is one of the frequent themes in Jewish mysticism: that which appears to be is not necessarily real. Similarly, the word "like" is frequently used in one form or another, suggesting that the description is necessarily inexact.

3. Something that looked like flares approached the throne, then dashed away. Perhaps these beings sought closeness with the divine power and then became frightened, quickly backing off. This is similar to the experience of the Israelites who came to Sinai but were afraid to approach, leaving Moses to go forward alone to receive God's revelation.

4. In the English translation the throne appears "like sapphire." (Actually, the modern form of sapphire was unknown in the ancient Near East, and this *sappir* refers to the deep blue lapis lazuli.)[8] Discussion of the next text will delve into this more. Perhaps the author wished to suggest that God shines like precious stones.[9]

5. Ezekiel's vision of the "semblance" of the *Kavod*, the Divine Presence, is so powerful that he feels compelled to prostrate himself. This would have been a natural reaction for a *Kohen* who served reverently in the temple precincts and knew of the prostrations that took place in the Holy of Holies. But it is at this point that the vision gives way to the words.[10] "Seeing God" is not the point of the journey.

6. Finally, just as Isaiah's divine court spoke of God's holiness,

Ezekiel hears a roaring sound: "Blessed is the Presence of the Lord, in His place" (*Barukh k'vod Adonai mimkomo*). This phrase also became part of daily prayer, in the core of the "Kedushah." Its meaning is unclear, but Plaut suggests "it is best to see it as a parallel to Ps. 135:21, which has a similar phrase: "Praised be the Eternal from Zion," meaning, "God is praised by those who are in Zion." For Zion is God's place, and—says Ezekiel—when the exiles will return to it, God's Presence will once more be praised *from its place*."[11] Ezekiel is outside of the Land of Israel, but the point is not clear: does the vision intend to suggest that God reveals himself in foreign lands or that God is associated only with the Holy Land?[12]

Why were the prayer of the angels in Isaiah and the closing line from Ezekiel adapted into the "Kedushah" of the daily service? Perhaps its creators believed that some vision of God's Presence, or at least a sense of that Presence, was or ought to be available to every Jew. Alternatively, the liturgists may have wanted to emphasize the importance of this mystical experience, even if most Jews would not experience it.

All in all, the prophet's remarkable experience serves to prepare him (as it did Isaiah) for the task of prophecy. We shall shortly see another example of this.

Since Moses was considered the greatest of the prophets, we would expect to find that he has extraordinary encounters with God, and we will examine a few.

Then Moses and Aaron, Nadab and Abihu, and seventy elders of Israel ascended; and they saw the God of Israel: under His feet there was the likeness of a pavement of sapphire, like the very sky for purity. Yet He did not raise His hand against the leaders of the Israelites; they beheld God, and they ate and drank. (Exod. 24:9–11)

Here, a substantial group of Israelites ascend and "see" the God of Israel, complete with "feet" on the likeness of a pavement of lapis lazuli, which seems to be the foundation of the throne of God.[13] Ancient Ugaritic literature mentions the decorative use of this element within a palace, and it may have been natural for the biblical author and characters to imagine God's throne as contained within a palace.[14] The deep blue also would be appropriate imagery for human beings looking up at the sky, the "throne" of God. "By focusing on what was *under His feet*, it seems to suggest that the leaders did not see God directly but from below, through a transparent . . . colored pavement."[15]

How is this to be interpreted? Most traditional authorities do not take it at face value. One suggestion was that the experience of God substituted for eating and drinking, as was the case for Moses during his forty days on Sinai.[16] Maimonides held that the experience of Moses and the elders was an intellectual perception of God, not a sensory experience.[17] Abraham ibn Ezra understood it as part of a prophetic vision like those of Isaiah and Ezekiel.[18] But the text literally does say that the people *saw* God.

> Now Moses, tending the flock of his father-in-law Jethro, the priest of Midian, drove the flock into the wilderness, and came to Horeb, the mountain of God. An angel of the Lord appeared to him in a blazing fire out of a bush. He gazed, and there was a bush all aflame, yet the bush was not consumed. Moses said, "I must turn aside to look at this marvelous sight; why doesn't the bush burn up?" When the Lord saw that he had turned aside to look, God called to him out of the bush: "Moses! Moses!" He answered, "Here I am." And He said, "Do not come closer. Remove your sandals from your feet, for the place on which you stand is holy ground. I am," He said, "the God of your father, the God of Abraham, the God of Isaac, and the God of Jacob." And Moses hid his face, for he was afraid to look at God. (Exod. 3:1–6)

Initially, Moses is unaware that any holiness is attached to this place. (Recall the experience of Jacob: "Surely God is present in this place and I, I did not know"; Gen. 28:16, where the notion of sanctified space first appears.)[19] But when Moses sees that the bush is not consumed by the fire, his attention is aroused. Initially, the text says: "An angel of the Lord appeared to him in a blazing fire"; why would God appear in fire? As Jeffrey Tigay notes, fire evokes the Divine "because it is insubstantial yet powerful, dangerous, illuminating, and purifying."[20]

Moses is told to remove his shoes, which indicated respect and humility in that time and place. This is a significant aspect of Muslim worship, and traditional synagogues also retain a remnant of this practice in the ceremony performed by the *kohanim* when they remove their shoes to bless the congregation during the festival *Musaf* service (and, in Israel, at the daily morning service).

What does Moses do when he realizes God is speaking to him? He hides his face. He is afraid to look. This may seem to be a natural reaction, but the point is that *there is something to look at*. Some of us might take such passages as metaphors, but would we really be so afraid of a metaphor? And the previous text suggests that under certain circumstances not only can people see God, but they need not be afraid of doing so.

The Lord would speak to Moses face to face, as one man speaks to another. And he would then return to the camp; but his attendant, Joshua son of Nun, a youth, would not stir out of the Tent.

Moses said to the Lord, "See, You say to me, 'Lead this people forward,' but You have not made known to me whom You will send with me. Further, You have said, 'I have singled you out by name, and you have, indeed, gained My favor.' Now, if I have truly gained Your favor, pray let me know Your ways, that I may know You and continue in Your favor. Consider, too, that this nation is Your people." And He said, "I will go in the lead and will lighten your burden." And he said

to Him, "Unless You go in the lead, do not make us leave this place. For how shall it be known that Your people have gained Your favor unless You go with us, so that we may be distinguished, Your people and I, from every people on the face of the earth?"

And the Lord said to Moses, "I will also do this thing that you have asked; for you have truly gained My favor and I have singled you out by name." He said, "Oh, let me behold Your Presence!" And He answered, "I will make all My goodness pass before you, and I will proclaim before you the name Lord, and the grace that I grant and the compassion that I show. But," He said, "you cannot see My face, for man may not see Me and live." And the Lord said, "See, there is a place near Me. Station yourself on the rock and, as My Presence passes by, I will put you in a cleft of the rock and shield you with My hand until I have passed by. Then I will take My hand away and you will see My back; but My face must not be seen." (Exod. 33:11–23)

Moses asks to be shown God's *Kavod*, God's Presence. We have seen that this may refer to some kind of physical manifestation of God, and that is the apparent meaning here. Moses, now much more accustomed to God than he was at the burning bush and already privileged with "face-to-face" communication (and we might well ask about what *this* means!), wants to have a visual experience, a more intense knowledge of God. Normally, the visible *Kavod* is a group experience, at a time and place chosen by God, and somewhat distant from those observing.[21] Moses asks for an exception. God tells him: I'll give you part of what you desire, but no individual may have all of it. Actually seeing God would be too powerful an experience for any individual; even Moses cannot prepare adequately for it. God provides a screen ("I will . . . shield you with My hand") and shows Moses His "back" . . . perhaps, as Nahum Sarna suggests, "the traces of His presence, the afterglow of His super-natural effulgence."[22] But even though Moses is not entitled to see the *Kavod*, the text does not deny that such a visible form exists.[23] Indeed, as

Moshe Weinfeld has proposed, the warning about the danger of seeing God usually affirms the possibility of such an experience![24]

But what exactly is this *Kavod*, the Presence? In the thirteenth century Nahmanides (Ramban, Rabbi Moshe ben Nahman) suggests that Moses wanted to see the visible Divine Presence through a clear speculum (a mirror or prism). This refers to a Rabbinic teaching suggesting that "all the prophets saw [God] through an unclear glass . . . but Moses saw through a clear glass."[25] In other words, Moses had the most perfect, direct "view" of God possible, even though it could not be complete. Nahmanides's view of the text is emphatically not metaphorical, unlike those mentioned on Exodus 24 above. As we shall see, this is consistent with the views of many other Jewish mystics.[26]

Among the other books of Scripture, Daniel is also filled with visionary experiences. Although the book of Daniel is set in the early exilic period—sixth century BCE—scholars regard it as a product of the period leading into the Maccabean Wars of the second century BCE.

In the third year of King Cyrus of Persia, an oracle was revealed to Daniel, who was called Belteshazzar. That oracle was true, but it was a great task to understand the prophecy; understanding came to him through the vision.

At that time, I, Daniel, kept three full weeks of mourning. I ate no tasty food, nor did any meat or wine enter my mouth. I did not anoint myself until the three weeks were over. It was on the twenty-fourth day of the first month, when I was on the bank of the great river Tigris, that I looked and saw a man dressed in linen, his loins girt in fine gold. His body was like beryl, his face had the appearance of lightning, his eyes were like flaming torches, his arms and legs had the color of burnished bronze, and the sound of his speech was like the noise of a multitude.

I, Daniel, alone saw the vision; the men who were with me did not see the vision, yet they were seized with a great terror and fled into hiding. So I was left alone to see this great vision. I was drained

of strength, my vigor was destroyed, and I could not summon up strength. I heard him speaking; and when I heard him speaking, overcome by a deep sleep, I lay prostrate on the ground. Then a hand touched me, and shook me onto my hands and knees. He said to me, "O Daniel, precious man, mark what I say to you and stand up, for I have been sent to you." After he said this to me, I stood up, trembling. He then said to me, "Have no fear, Daniel, for from the first day that you set your mind to get understanding, practicing abstinence before your God, your prayer was heard, and I have come because of your prayer. However, the prince of the Persian kingdom opposed me for twenty-one days; now Michael, a prince of the first rank, has come to my aid, after I was detained there with the kings of Persia. So I have come to make you understand what is to befall your people in the days to come, for there is yet a vision for those days." (Dan. 10:1-14)

This vision includes a heavenly being who shares some characteristics of the being in Ezekiel, but is not presumed to be God Himself. Receipt of this vision required extensive preparation by Daniel. While it offers him the understanding that he had requested, it certainly is not as direct an experience of the Divine as occurs in the Isaiah and Ezekiel texts.

But it is still physically draining, creating a markedly different and intense "state" for Daniel. Jewish mystics later invented a term for this state in which one is prepared to receive divine messages: *mohin d'gadlut*, or "higher consciousness."

The book of Psalms, the collection of devotional hymns, also contains examples of anonymous authors who sought intimate contact with God.

Protect me, O God, for I seek refuge in You.
I say to the Lord: "You are my Lord, my
    benefactor; there is none above You."
As to the holy and mighty ones that are in the land,
    my whole desire concerning them is that those who
    espouse another [god] may have many sorrows!

I will have no part of their bloody libations;
　　their names will not pass my lips.
The Lord is my allotted share and portion; You control my fate.
Delightful country has fallen to my lot;
　　lovely indeed is my estate.
I bless the Lord who has guided me; my
　　conscience admonishes me at night.
I am ever mindful of the Lord's presence; He is at
　　my right hand, I shall never be shaken.
So my heart rejoices, my whole being exults,
　　and my body rests secure.
For You will not abandon me to Sheol, or
　　let Your faithful one see the Pit.
You will teach me the path of life. In Your presence is perfect
　　joy; delights are ever in Your right hand. (Ps. 16)

What is meant by "I am ever mindful of the Lord's Presence," or, more literally, "I have always set the Lord before me"? The Psalmist could be saying he consistently follows God's guidance, and since he does the right thing, he has faith he will not be abandoned. Or, he could mean: I constantly focus on God's Presence, and that is what gives me security and joy.[27] Many Jewish mystics chose to read the psalm this way, and made it their business always to "set God" before them. Many synagogues (and some individual Jewish homes) contain a plaque that serves as a meditative device, called a *shiviti* (the Hebrew word for "I have set" or "I am mindful"), containing the Four-Letter Name from this verse—so that one literally sets God's Name out as a visual focus.

The great twentieth-century scholar Gershom Scholem, who established the academic study of Jewish mysticism, rejected the idea of biblical mysticism. He believed that religion went through three stages: (1) pagan faith, a mythical (prebiblical) epoch where people experienced the world as full of gods "whose presence can be experienced without recourse to ecstatic meditation"; (2) the period when institutional religion arises (for Jews, the biblical period) and God and man are separated by a gulf "which can be crossed by nothing but the *voice*; the voice of God, directing and law-giving in His revelation, and the voice of man in prayer"; (3) the romantic period of established religion (for Jews, the Rabbinic era), where mysticism begins to develop in order to overcome the abyss through direct experience of God.[28]

Even though Scholem's scheme of three developmental stages of religion still carries some weight in the field, his assumptions are widely questioned. It is logical to include these biblical experiences as mystical because the impulse behind them has so much in common with what follows. And we shall see many of the same elements, particularly altered states and visions of God, in the earliest forms of Jewish mysticism that follow the time of the Hebrew Bible.

Part 2
Early Mystical Pursuits

3

Mysticism in the Talmud

ENTERING THE *PARDES*

A major theme in the classical Rabbinic period, the first six centuries CE, has to do with the lure, and the dangers, of mystical experience. Uncertain about the appropriate role for mystical exploration, the sages set limits on it in this early text, where it is grouped with another realm where scholarly discussion is delimited—forbidden marriages.

> **The subject of forbidden incestuous marriages may not be expounded in the presence of three, nor the work of Creation [*ma'aseh Bereshit*] in the presence of two, nor the work of the chariot [*ma'aseh Merkavah*] in the presence of one, unless he is a sage who understands on his own.**
>
> **Whoever speculates on these four matters, it would have been better if he had never come into the world: what is above, what is below, what came before, and what will come after. And whoever has no regard for the honor of his Creator, it would have been better if he had never come into the world. (M. Hag. 2:1)[1]**

An investigation of why the Rabbis limited legal discussion of forbidden marriages will throw light on their attitude toward mystical speculation. In addition to the prohibition of adultery in the Ten Commandments (Exod. 20:12), Leviticus 18 prohibits sexual relations with a variety of close relations. These are the "forbidden incestuous marriages" that are the initial subject of the Mishnah, an early part of the Talmud that provides the raw material for the extended discussions in the Gemara.

Why would the Rabbis have placed limits on this topic? For one thing, discussions of marriage and sexuality can be an awkward topic even today, let alone nearly two thousand years ago. While the Rabbis did teach abundantly about these matters as they created Jewish law, or *halakhah*, they limited certain aspects as being improper for public discussion. Furthermore, they might have been concerned that such discussions would lead to inappropriate thoughts and personal confusion. Finally, such marriages would lead to serious problems for their offspring as well as consequences for their identity as functioning members of the Jewish community. The Rabbinic teacher, however, had to teach his students, future Rabbis who would have to rule on the permissibility of certain relationships, all the details of matters whose consequences would have such serious implications.

Even more limited than discussion of forbidden marriages is that of *ma'aseh Bereshit*, which literally means "the work of Creation." But more specifically the term refers to all the details left out of, and questions raised by, the Gen. 1–2:5 account of Creation. Given the early sages' familiarity with how surrounding cultures had dealt with questions about the origin of the universe and humanity's place within it, they felt the need to develop their own approach based on Scripture as they understood it.[2]

Here are some questions the sages ask about the Creation story:

What does "In the beginning" really mean? Beginning of what?
Just how does God create everything? All we are told is "and He said." Were there any preexisting elements?
What exactly is meant by God's "saying"?
Why does God create this universe? For that matter, why does God create at all? Did God have any "helpers"?
Some things listed are not mentioned as being "created." Why not? And why is there no mention of them?
What exactly is meant by the "image of God"? What are the common elements between God and humanity?[3]

Generally, unclear issues in the Torah are fair game for discussion. So why would the Mishnah limit conversation about the Creation to a private audience between one teacher and one student? One reason may lie in the difficulty of the subject, thus rendering it problematic for a class discussion. Further, since it is not a matter of law or given knowledge, the teacher has to gear his responses to the individual. However, as we see from the continuation of the Mishnah, other concerns *are* at work. Because *Ma'aseh Bereshit* is speculative, and with speculation there might be no end to the matter, most of the sages in this period generally did not want to be involved in such conjecture; their focus was on more practical matters.[4] Finally, this area of speculation was loaded with many ideas from foreign sources and indeed considered foreign to many of the sages.[5] So there were several reasons for the Rabbis to place limitations upon this area of study. But we shall see that their efforts were not completely successful.

The sages' concerns about *ma'aseh Merkavah*, the "work of the chariot" as depicted in Ezekiel 1, were even greater than those about *ma'aseh Bereshit*; as we read in chapter 2, many opposed having this read as a haftarah. Ezekiel 1 deals with the *Merkavah*, the chariot of God that has been a focus of mystical experience. When the above text speaks about the "work of the chariot," it is referring to the interpretation and meaning of the Ezekiel chapter. Because *ma'aseh Merkavah* provided so many details and such precision in its view of the supernal world, many Jews deliberated over it at length and expounded not only the specific items brought forward in Ezekiel, but also its potential underlying meaning, its *derash*. (Biblical commentator Avivah Zornberg is reported to have said that *peshat*, the plain, contextual meaning of the text, is what you tell your therapist; *derash* is what the therapist hears.)

What is meant by "a sage who understands on his own"? Presumably he has a certain amount of background that he has acquired on his own initiative. Therefore he does not need a great deal of explanation, and the teacher will not be called on for extensive details. Perhaps it was felt that in such cases, the teacher could not be effective if the student was incapable of grasping these matters on his own, at least to some degree. Or, as Heschel suggested, "the student does not embrace this knowledge; this knowledge rather embraces the student."[6] Finally, a student who truly understands the material should also understand the need for discretion in sharing it publicly.

This concern is echoed in a much later midrash: "Matters concerning *ma'aseh Merkavah* are kept secret, because they are *k'vod Elohim* [God's honor]."[7] But immediately afterward the opposite is suggested: real *k'vod Elohim* is when one *does* occupy oneself with such mysteries. Perhaps the tension is intentional: one must keep God's concealed chambers secret from others, but the qualified and devoted sage still must peer into them. We shall shortly meet Rabban Yohanan ben Zakkai; what he said (in a different context) well expresses the predicament of the sage: "Woe to me if I say it; woe to me if I do not say it!"[8]

What is the problem with the four areas of speculation that the text warns the sages against studying? Presumably that it is just speculation, with no practical use. But we often do love to speculate about these matters: above and below (meaning "heaven" and the netherworld) and before and after (what preceded the biblical Creation story and what will happen in the end of days). This portion of the Mishnah is much more stringent than the first segment; while the opening allows for some study of these matters, here it says: better never to be born than to engage in them. (It is possible that this latter part of the Mishnah comes from a different source.)[9] Partly as a result of this teaching, Rabbinic Judaism suppressed much of this kind of discussion.

What does the last sentence, about having "no regard for the honor of his Creator," mean? Why is it here? Perhaps it suggests that the "honor of his Creator" requires a degree of privacy, which is a much deeper concern than merely discouraging speculation. It starkly warns us: do not pry into His concealed matters; they are not intended for you. You've been given the account in the Torah, and that is all you are meant to know.[10]

It is not our destiny to meddle with the most sensitive and difficult parts of the Bible that affect the honor of the Creator; if you do enter these realms, know that you put yourself at grave risk.

In contrast to the position that all knowledge should be available to everyone, this material is considered "classified"!

Our next text concerns the first-century CE sage Rabban Yohanan ben Zakkai, who preserved Jewish life after the destruction of the Second Temple by developing a school for scholars in Yavneh. He was not only a scholar in matters of law but also interested in mystical issues, though his own teachings on mysticism are not well preserved (which is not surprising considering the Mishnah text we just read). Eleazar ben Arakh is one of his best students.

> Our Rabbis taught: Once Rabbi Yohanan ben Zakkai rode on a donkey when going on a journey, and Rabbi Eleazar ben Arakh followed him. The latter said to the former: Master, teach me a chapter of this work on the chariot. Rabbi Yohanan answered: Did not the sages teach: "nor the work of the chariot [*ma'aseh Merkavah*] in the presence of one, unless he is a sage who understands on his own"? Rabbi Eleazar said to him: Master, will you permit me to say something on my own? Say it, he replied. When Rabbi Eleazar ben Arakh began his discourse on the work of the chariot, Rabbi Yohanan ben Zakkai descended from the donkey, saying, it is improper that I listen to a discourse in honor of my Creator while I ride on a donkey.
>
> They seated themselves under a tree. A fire descended from heaven and encompassed them; the ministering angels danced before them as the attendants of a wedding canopy do to bring rejoicing to a groom. One angel called out of the fire: The work of the chariot is indeed in accord with your exposition, Eleazar ben Arakh. At once all the trees opened in song: "Then shall all the trees sing before the Lord" (Ps. 96:13). When Rabbi Eleazar completed his discourse

on the work of the chariot, Rabbi Yohanan ben Zakkai stood up and kissed him on the head and said: Praised be the Lord God of Abraham, Isaac, and Jacob who has given Abraham our father a wise son who knows how to expound the work of the chariot. (Y. Hag. 2:1)[11]

When Yohanan ben Zakkai gets down from his donkey, we know this is a serious event.[12] He realizes that his student is not just going to "say something," but he's going to give a real piece of mystical Torah. And it turns out to be no ordinary lesson! (It has been suggested that some of these "special effects" evoke those associated with the revelation at Sinai discussed in Exod. 19:18–19 and Deut. 5:4.)[13]

Strikingly, although we are given specific information about the parties involved and the conversation between them, as well as the supernatural results, this text tells us *nothing* about the content of Eleazar ben Arakh's teaching. Normally a talmudic story would emphasize the specific lesson included, but here that is withheld from us. Nonetheless it is clear that the sages involved believed in the power of mystical experience.

One postscript to this story: Eleazar ben Arakh separated from his colleagues—possibly persuaded by his wife[14]—and we see no significant sign of him, his teachings, or his students after that time.

The next piece is one of the most famous Jewish mystical texts, the more so for the involvement of Rabbi Akiva, one of the greatest sages. We are presented with a parable of a *pardes*, an "orchard" (the word is taken from Songs 4:13). This word should not be confused with "paradise" (*gan Eden*),[15] although the two are conceptually related:[16] in the Garden of Eden, an angel with a flaming sword is posted at the gate (Gen. 3:24), and the *pardes* contains something dangerous as well.

Many Rabbis in this period believed that Jewish men should follow Jewish law and study Torah with few limitations. However, the small circles of Jews who did practice contemplation of the *ma'aseh Bereshit* and even the *ma'aseh Merkavah* were considered beyond the pale. They used meditational techniques unsanctioned by the Rabbis, attempting to have an experience or vision of the *Merkavah*, the divine body or glory. Such efforts are extremely dangerous; you can pay a high price for tinkering with the ultimate Power. So when the tradition discusses them, they are an ideal, but the ideal is always combined with a warning against its pursuit, restricting that pursuit to a very small elite.

It is widely believed that one should not engage in the study of Kabbalah until after age forty. But the institution of this as a formal requirement came fairly late in Jewish history[17]—in the eighteenth century—as a result of the Sabbatean and Frankist heresies.[18] Many great Jewish mystics were either unaware of such a directive or simply ignored it, because some of the most prominent did much of their work before that age. Two of the greatest, about whom we will later learn much more, lived in Safed, Israel, in the sixteenth century. One, Moses Cordovero, wrote his magnum opus when he was in his midtwenties.[19] The other, arguably the most important of all, the Ari (Lion), Isaac Luria, died before he turned forty. So forty was no magic number.

This directive did reflect a general attitude among the Rabbis that a person had to be sufficiently mature and firmly rooted in reality to pursue the study of mysticism. Maimonides expressed it well: "It is not proper to walk in the *pardes* without being filled with bread and meat, to know what is permitted and forbidden and the like."[20] In other words, knowledge of the law and the Talmud provides stability; it roots one in the physical world and the performance of its commandments, to which we should always return.

Although the four sages discussed in this text did live at approximately the same time, it should not be taken as a report of historical events but as a collection of traditions about the effects of entering the *pardes*. Rather than reading this as biographical, we should read it as a *typological* account, describing types of experiences and their potential consequences.[21] And so it became a general way of expressing the danger zones of religious experience. In the Rabbinic view, Normal Mysticism is to be preferred because of the risks involved with paranormal experience and because other forms would potentially divert participants from community needs. Needless to say, this remains a major concern, perhaps as much today as for those tempted to enter into the *pardes* in antiquity.

> **Our Rabbis taught. Four entered an orchard: Ben Azzai, Ben Zoma, *Aher* [Elisha ben Abuyah] and Rabbi Akiva. Rabbi Akiva said to them: When you reach the stones of pure marble, do not say, "Water, water!" For it is said, "He who speaks falsehood shall not be established before my eyes" (Ps. 101:7).**
>
> **Ben Azzai gazed and died. Of him Scripture says: "Precious in the sight of the Lord is the death of His saints." (Ps. 116:15) Ben Zoma gazed and was stricken. Of him Scripture says: "If you find honey, eat only what you need, lest you be overfilled with it and throw it up." (Prov. 25:16) *Aher* cut down the shoots. Rabbi Akiva departed in peace. (B. Hag. 14b)[22]**

Ben Azzai and Ben Zoma are actually Shimon ben (son of) Azzai and Shimon ben Zoma; they were considered sages, but were never ordained as Rabbis. (Some suggest that they were not called by their full names because it would have seemed insulting to refer to them as such without the title of Rabbi.[23]) *Aher* means "Other" and refers to the fact that he, Elisha ben Abuyah, became a nonbeliever—this is the meaning of the phrase "cut down the shoots," to deny the fundamentals of Judaism—presumably because of the confusion caused by this experience.

What are the "stones of pure marble" that can be mistaken for water, and why is that considered to be such a critical "falsehood"? The answer requires a brief introduction to *Heikhalot* literature, which contains the next major branch of Jewish mysticism and is explained in detail in chapter 4. *Heikhalot*, which literally means "palaces," refers to attempts to visit the divine throne through mystical contemplation. Some of these texts describe the soul's mystical ascent through seven halls to reach the divine throne. The sixth hall contains an illusion: pure marble that looks like dancing waves of water. It contains no water, just the sparkle of the marble. But an illusion is still a falsehood, and at such a high level in the divine realm, the guardians of the throne cast out any trace of falsehood. Hence one who falls prey to this illusion risks critical danger. This esoteric path for a select few uses "magical names and incantations designed to overcome the many dangerous impasses that lie in wait for the mystical aspirant."[24]

What do we make of Ben Azzai's journey, which ended in death? Read positively, we might understand his death as the final cleaving to God from which no one returns, not an accident but actually bridging the gap between God and man. As Exodus 33 said, "you cannot see My face, for man may not see Me and live." Ben Azzai's death is the consequence of being given a vision of the *Merkavah*, or the divine radiance, which no human being can bear. "He died the way many saints want to die, that is, while having a beatific vision of God."[25] Once you enjoy a certain level of union with God, even if it were possible to return, you might not want to do so! This is supported by Ps. 116:15, which suggests that Ben Azzai was a saint. And some *Heikhalot* texts associate him with Rabbi Akiva, who alone emerged from the *pardes* unharmed.[26]

The second interpretation suggests that Ben Azzai was in some important way unprepared for this experience and should not have undertaken it. *Heikhalot* texts portray him as having made the fatal mistake of perceiving the marble as water.[27] Furthermore, the tradition tells us he had failed to fulfill a key mitzvah that would have more firmly rooted him in this world: though he was indeed a pious and learned sage, he never had children[28] and no clear tradition exists that he even married.[29] Marvin Sweeney provides a negative interpretation of Ps. 116:15, which says: "Precious in the sight of the Lord is the death of His saints." "The term precious, *yakar*, is best translated as 'costly,' and indicates that ben Azzai's lack of children at his death cost the world dearly in lost potential."[30]

How was Ben Zoma understood? He "was stricken" with madness, perhaps a kind of posttraumatic stress syndrome. Having progressed to a certain level, he was not ready to go any higher. Forcing himself upward caused him to become mentally disturbed, or damaged by the powerful forces that protect those higher levels. Ben Zoma also is lacking a key qualification: apparently, he "never completed his full education in *halakhah*."[31] (All three of the sages who are damaged were not ordained rabbis.) When he is later described by Rabbi Joshua as "outside,"[32] it may have meant he was outside the bounds of interpretation, that his analysis of Scripture crossed the boundary of accepted rules. Alternatively, it may have meant that his behavior was unacceptable and that he had become too oblivious to his social and religious obligations due to his immersion in thoughts about his journey.[33]

Ben Azzai and Ben Zoma are damaged physically and psychologically by their visit to the *pardes*; and Elisha ben Abuyah is understood to be spiritually damaged. However, some suggest that in ben Abuyah's case, at least part of the damage preceded the experience, in the sense that he was insufficiently committed to the prescribed regimen of Jewish law. One must be fully respectful of the Owner of the orchard before reaching and appreciating such heights. Because of this, not only is he not granted a full understanding of the *pardes*, but he is led further astray into outright heresy. Although it is of peripheral importance to our study here, there are other explanations of how Elisha ben Abuyah became a heretic. Most notably, it is said that he witnessed a young boy die during the fulfillment of a particular mitzvah (Deut. 22:6–7, shooing away the mother bird before taking her fledglings), which specifically promises long life to those who fulfill it.[34] Much interesting material exists about Elisha ben Abuyah within Rabbinic literature, a good deal of it a "constructed image" probably added long after his death.[35] Presumably this is why he is referred to as *Aher*, the "Other," the one who has stepped outside the accepted bounds. After all, no one is so useless that they can't serve as a bad example!

Only Rabbi Akiva was qualified, sufficiently mature, or had properly practiced the various aspects of the journey; only such a person was able to handle the experience and come back. Akiva may also have possessed qualities that the other sages lacked to some degree. Akiva is properly involved in all aspects of the world, whereas, as Byron Sherwin puts it, "being overly preoccupied with individual spiritual fulfillment is seen as diverting our attention away from social life and communal needs, away from the continuity of Judaism and the Jewish people."[36] Later mystics suggest that one who aspires to this experience must be willing to approach a "curtain of fire" to merit consideration for admission to the inner sanctum.[37]

It has also been proposed that the problem with Rabbi Akiva's colleagues was that they were entering the *pardes* for their own personal experience and benefit, rather than for some need beyond their own. This anticipates the kabbalistic notion of the *tzorekh gavoha*, which will be explained in chapter 11, and suggests that a truly great deed is accomplished only if done for God's benefit.

There are some additional significant details in the account of the *pardes* and the related literature of the late talmudic period. Clearly, the discipline needed for ascent requires a master who will teach it to a disciple and certify his knowledge. While it is presumed that the disciple is himself a sage, the journey involves meditational practice, not knowledge of Torah. Also, it is said that Rabbi Akiva "entered [the *pardes*] in peace and he exited in peace." This same phrase is applied to the *Kohen Gadol* (High Priest) after the annual pronunciation of God's Ineffable Name in the Temple on Yom Kippur.[38] This carried particularly strong connotations among the priestly elite of the Second Temple period and beyond, and must have evoked similar if not equally powerful feelings among those who witnessed and recalled it. (See chapter 5 for further investigation of the importance of the Temple in the development of Jewish mysticism.)

Many early scholars of Judaism believed that Rabbinic Judaism was generally not open to the kinds of mystical formulations discussed in this chapter and that the *pardes* story (and other references to "mythological" material) was a way to strip unwanted characteristics from Judaism. Later scholars, including most of the leading scholars of Jewish mysticism today, suggest that the subject is much more complex, and that the Rabbis of this period were not as hostile to mystical views as had been believed.[39] Nonetheless it is fair to say they preferred that most Jews focus their efforts on this world rather than the upper worlds.

Early Jewish mysticism emerges in three phases. The first includes sources speculating about the meaning of the *ma'aseh Merkavah*. A second attempts to interpret Song of Songs and alludes to esoteric practices similar to what is suggested in the story of the *pardes*. Finally, the *Heikhalot* texts more fully illustrate the process of "ascent" to the divine throne, including discussion of magical formulas and powers. We shall see more of these in subsequent chapters. The *Heikhalot* literature, over many centuries, eventually became incorporated into later forms of Jewish mysticism and laid the foundation for the next mystical awakening in the High Middle Ages.[40]

4

Song of Songs and *Ma'aseh Merkavah*

The next phase of Jewish mysticism became much more complex, involving intricate techniques designed to assist the mystic on his way. To understand how this came about, we will initially view biblical texts that were understood to allude to the intimate connection between human beings and God.

Although the Song of Songs (*Shir ha-Shirim*) was not written as a mystical book, the sages chose to read it as such for reasons we will explore here.

> **The Song of Songs, of Solomon.**
> **Oh, give me of the kisses of your mouth,**
> **For your love is more delightful than wine.**
> **Your ointments yield a sweet fragrance,**
> **Your name is like finest oil—**
> **Therefore do maidens love you.**
> **Draw me after you, let us run!**
> **The king has brought me to his chambers.**
> **Let us delight and rejoice in your love,**
> **Savoring it more than wine—**
> **Like new wine they love you!**
>
> **I am dark, but comely,**
> **O daughters of Jerusalem—**

Like the tents of Kedar,
Like the pavilions of Solomon.
Don't stare at me because I am swarthy,
Because the sun has gazed upon me.
My mother's sons quarreled with me,
They made me guard the vineyards;
My own vineyard I did not guard. (Songs 1:1-6)

On the face of it, this is simply about physical love. But then how did a book of poetry about physical love find its way into the Bible? The Rabbis taught it as a parable of the love between God and Israel, building a large body of interpretation around this understanding. Thus it became regarded not only as a sacred work, but it was, according to Rabbi Akiva (see chapter 3), "the Holy of Holies," an intimate view into sacred realms from which we are normally barred.[1] The mystical premise behind this is that what we see—the text of this biblical book, or the physical attraction and experiences of love—is just a vessel holding a much greater, invisible reality. More simply, the apparent is not the real; the Rabbis took these expressions of physical love and interpreted them as references to a much higher love.

The Rabbis included Song of Songs in the liturgy on two occasions: It is recited on Shabbat during Passover, the holiday that celebrates the strongest evidence of God's love for Israel: God's taking the Israelites out of slavery. And it is recited in Sephardic and a few Ashkenazic congregations prior to *Kabbalat Shabbat*, the service welcoming the Sabbath. A well-known tradition teaches that marital relations are particularly encouraged on Friday night, most especially for the sages and their wives.[2] But Song of Songs is not just included to celebrate marital love; it signifies a supernal love. And we shall see later (in chapter 14) how the erotic became very significant in Jewish mysticism for this reason.

Studying a text such as Song of Songs, which so intimately connects us to God, may itself be a mystical experience. Thus, study of Torah is not only an intellectual appreciation of God's will; it is also a means of approaching and obtaining knowledge of God. This will be elaborated in chapter 13.

Let us now examine some selections from the book of Daniel, in which we meet a few of the angels who play an important role in the higher realms.

> Then I heard a holy being speaking, and another holy being said to whoever it was who was speaking, "How long will [what was seen in] the vision last—the regular offering be forsaken because of transgression; the sanctuary be surrendered and the [heavenly] host be trampled?" He answered me: "For twenty-three hundred evenings and mornings; then the sanctuary will be cleansed." While I, Daniel, was seeing the vision, and trying to understand it, there appeared before me one who looked like a man. I heard a human voice from the middle of [the] Ulai [river] calling out: "Gabriel, make that man understand the vision." He came near to where I was standing, and as he came I was terrified, and fell prostrate. He said to me, "Understand, O man, that the vision refers to the time of the end." When he spoke with me, I was overcome by a deep sleep as I lay prostrate on the ground. Then he touched me and made me stand up, and said, "I am going to inform you of what will happen when wrath is at an end, for [it refers] to the time appointed for the end." (Dan. 8:13-19)

> I, Daniel, kept three full weeks of mourning. I ate no tasty food, nor did any meat or wine enter my mouth. I did not anoint myself until the three weeks were over. It was on the twenty-fourth day of the first month, when I was on the bank of the great river—the Tigris—that I looked and saw a man dressed in linen, his loins girt in fine gold. His body was like beryl, his face had the appearance of lightning, his eyes were like flaming torches, his arms and legs had the color of

burnished bronze, and the sound of his speech was like the noise of a multitude. I, Daniel, alone saw the vision; the men who were with me did not see the vision, yet they were seized with a great terror and fled into hiding. So I was left alone to see this great vision. I was drained of strength, my vigor was destroyed, and I could not summon up strength. I heard him speaking; and when I heard him speaking, overcome by a deep sleep, I lay prostrate on the ground. Then a hand touched me, and shook me onto my hands and knees. He said to me, "O Daniel, precious man, mark what I say to you and stand up, for I have been sent to you." After he said this to me, I stood up, trembling. He then said to me, "Have no fear, Daniel, for from the first day you set your mind to get understanding, practicing abstinence before your God, your prayer was heard, and I have come because of your prayer. However, the prince of the Persian kingdom opposed me for twenty-one days; now Michael, a prince of the first rank, has come to my aid, after I was detained there with the kings of Persia. So I have come to make you understand what is to befall your people in the days to come, for there is yet a vision for those days." (Dan. 10:2-14)

"At that time, the great prince, Michael, who stands beside the sons of your people, will appear. It will be a time of trouble, the like of which has never been since the nation came into being. At that time, your people will be rescued, all who are found inscribed in the book. Many of those that sleep in the dust of the earth will awake, some to eternal life, others to reproaches, to everlasting abhorrence. And the knowledgeable will be radiant like the bright expanse of sky, and those who lead the many to righteousness will be like the stars forever and ever. But you, Daniel, keep the words secret, and seal the book until the time of the end. Many will range far and wide and knowledge will increase." (Dan. 12:1-4)

The book of Daniel was probably written close to the time of the

Maccabean War (168–164 BCE). The work's late origin may be why Daniel is not considered a prophet and why this book is not included among the books of the Prophets but with the Writings in the Hebrew Bible. The book offers encouragement to those battling for Jewish independence and the rededication of the Holy of Holies, in what they are told is "the time appointed for the end" (Dan. 9:24). Here we meet Gabriel and Michael, two guardian angels of the Israelite people, who interpret Daniel's visions and forecast the future as if they were prophets. But there is a crucial difference between "ordinary" prophecy about the future, and prophecy about the end of time, which requires a higher level of prophecy. Thus, these visions require the participation of these high-ranking celestial figures.

As explained in chapter 3, matters concerning the *ma'aseh Merkavah,* the work of the heavenly chariot, were not widely shared; we only have many fragments, and it is likely that other such texts have been lost to us. Other documents in the *Merkavah* tradition, however, describe the physical size of God, which is counter to what most of us educated as Jews were taught—that God has no physical body, that God is "spirit," and so forth. But at some point in this era the book *Shi'ur Komah* [Divine dimensions] appeared; scholars have great difficulty dating it, but its nucleus, if not the full text, may well go back to the second or third century CE).[3] It is "apparently inspired by the description of the masculine 'lover' found in Song of Songs, chapter 5."[4] According to this book, God is *very large.* For instance, the author states that each of God's fingers measures 150 million *parsa'ot.* Each *parsah* measures ninety thousand *zerotot,* making God's finger thirteen-and-a-half trillion *zeratot.* So what is a *zeret* (singular for *zerotot*)? He says: "This refers to His little finger, and His little finger is the entire universe, as it states: 'Who has measured the waters in the hollow of his hand, and meted out heaven with the *zeret*' [Isa. 40:12]." In other words, each of God's fingers is thirteen-and-a-half trillion times the size of the whole world![5]

God's size is immense beyond our ability to comprehend, but the above text implies that God is measurable. However, when God is described in such huge terms, the emphasis is on God's difference from us, God's transcendence, and not on the theoretical limitations that these "measurements" place upon Him. This book may fit into a pattern of attributing immense size to the gods in Near Eastern traditions.[6] There is a great deal we do not know about *Shi'ur Komah*, but it clearly comes from the realm of the *Merkavah* mystics.

The next set of *Merkavah* texts should be read with several factors in mind:[7] (1) Every experience in this set grows out of the study of Ezekiel 1; David Blumenthal calls it the "springboard" into the *Merkavah* literature. (2) During this period, other writings and other cultures talk of similar heavenly beings and dangerous trips. Among them are apocalyptics and visionaries, both Jewish and Christian, whose writing appears even in the later books of the Bible (such as Daniel) and who sought to describe the "end of time." Also the Jewish and Christian Gnostics,[8] who believed in a universe created by two powers and who claimed to have secret knowledge about the nature of God and of creation, were very active during the period of *Heikhalot* literature (see below), although their influence extended well beyond this time, for almost a thousand years. (3) The Rabbis in the early centuries of the Common Era have a particular view of the universe. For them, all reality is ordered by God, as He expresses it in the Torah. The *Merkavah* mystics generally share this view, even though they may not feel bound by every limitation Rabbinic Judaism places upon their pursuits.[9] Although the word *merkavah* generally means "chariot," in this literature it is used to mean "throne."[10]

Heikhalot comes from the term *heikhal*, the entrance hall to the Holy of Holies in the Jerusalem Temple. As for the actual dating and geographic origin of these texts, scholars have not arrived at a consensus but increasingly propose that most were edited in Babylonia between the third and eighth centuries CE.[11]

The next text we will treat below—a significantly abbreviated portion of a segment of *Heikhalot Rabbati* [The greater treatise on the Palaces]—and similar *Heikhalot* texts have two primary purposes: to describe the upper kingdom in as much detail as possible and to teach the mystic how to get there (and return) safely.[12] Originally, the leading mystics may not have wanted to write down such materials, fearing they would fall into the hands of those who might not be worthy. However, as with other sacred writings—many of which, after all, originated as part of the oral tradition—concerns developed that the entire process might be lost, particularly in periods of persecution (to which the beginning of the next text alludes). Some parts of these texts are still not well understood; scholars continue to debate many details.

While many issues can be raised about these texts, two require special attention. The first is how one prepares for such an experience, which presumably requires extensive grounding and training. The beginning of the text deals with some of the prerequisites. The second question is what is *really* happening here. Many have suggested that the "ascent" described is simply a contemplative exercise taking place within the individual's consciousness. Those who participated in such experiences were described as *yordei Merkavah* (those who *descended* to the chariot); Gershom Scholem suggests that the expression designated "those who reach down into themselves in order to perceive the chariot."[13] The term is frequently repeated in our text.

Finally, the text is set during or just before the Bar Kokhba rebellion, about 120–35 CE, but this should not be taken as historical fact. Rabbi Nehunya ben ha-Kannah was an actual sage whose teachings are cited in Rabbinic literature, but many mystical traditions later became attached to his name. We see at the outset a "historical" justification for his revealing these matters.

Rabbi Ishmael said, When Rabbi Nehunya ben ha-Kannah saw that wicked Rome was planning to destroy the mighty of Israel, he at once revealed the secret of the world as it appears to one who is worthy to

gaze on the King and His Throne in His majesty and His beauty: the *hayyot* of holiness, the cherubim of might, and the wheels of the *Shekhinah* as lightning mixed with awesome electrum; the beauty that is around the Throne; the bridges and the growing chains that rise between the bridges; the dust, smoke, and wind that raise the dust of the coals, for they conceal and cover all the chambers of the place of Aravot-Rakia with the clouds of their coals; and Surya, the Prince of the Countenance, the servant of Totarkhiel-YHVH, the proud one.

What is it like [to know the secret of *Merkavah*]? It is like having a ladder in one's house upon which he ascends and descends, and there is no creature that can hinder him, if he is innocent and free from idolatry, sexual offenses, bloodshed, slander, false oaths, profanation of the Name, impertinence, and unjustified enmity, and who observes every positive and negative mitzvah. (*Heikhalot Rabbati*, 198–99)[14]

The sages, the "mighty of Israel," are endangered, and so these secrets must be revealed.[15] Rabbi Ishmael was not only one of the mystical circle, but also the son of the *Kohen Gadol*, the "High Priest," and perhaps even functioned as such himself, and so he is considered of exceptional importance in many *Heikhalot* texts.[16] Rabbi Nehunya ben ha-Kannah is understood to be the leader of the mystical circle described. We see the images used in Ezekiel 1: the *hayyot* (creatures), the cherubim, the *ofanim* (wheels), the awesome electrum (brilliant gleam). The throne, the object of much speculation and the goal of these visions, is God's dwelling place. The "chains" are not actually chains, but flames; we see coals that nourish the fire. This is a visionary ascent; we shall see evidence that it is not a physical journey.

What are the meanings of the strange names listed here? First, both Aravot and Rakia have to do with parts of heaven; when combined, they refer to heaven's highest, most concealed part.[17] Two angels are mentioned here, representing two separate groups of angels. One is Surya, whose name apparently comes from *sar*, "prince," and who is described as *sar ha-panim*, "prince of the [divine] countenance." Totarkhiel is a combination of *tetra*, "four"—representing the power of the Four-Letter Name—and *El*, another of God's Names. To this is appended the *actual* Four-Letter Name (YHVH), a common practice within this group of angels. All these Divine Names clearly suggest the immense power placed under angelic authority. The angels are not God, but they are God's agents and possess plenty of clout.[18]

If you meet the requirements for becoming one of these mystics, you will have "a ladder in your house." You will have effortless access to the heavenly realms and to heavenly knowledge, including the prayers of the angels and knowledge of the Torah.[19] (See chapter 13 for an important example of this last idea.) You will also have knowledge of the future, including God's decrees. In short, you will be a master of the *Merkavah*, no longer a mere student. While the gap between the mystic and God is reduced, its elimination does not seem to be a primary goal of such journeys.

Such information is clearly not meant for everyone. The text makes clear the extensive moral, ritual, and intellectual qualifications for the mystic.[20] (We will read below of a very distinguished inner circle of sages chosen to receive this experience, while others stand in an outer circle; not many are worthy.) Later mystical groups had similar expectations of their members. There is no suggestion here that one had to have reached a certain age; that would be far too simple. Finally, the last phrase—because women are generally exempt from positive time-bound mitzvot—makes it clear that this is an exclusively male enterprise.

Then there came Rabban Shimon ben Gamliel, Rabbi Eliezer ha-Gadol, Rabbi Eleazar ben Damah, Rabbi Eliezer ben Shamua, Rabbi Yohanan ben Dahavai, Hananyah ben Hanihai, Yonatan ben Uziel, Rabbi Akiva, and Rabbi Yehudah ben Bava. We came and sat before him while the mass of companions stood on their feet, for they saw that pans of fire and torches of light formed a barrier between them and

us. Rabbi Nehunya ben ha-Kannah sat and expounded for them all the matters of the *Merkavah*: the descent to it and the ascent, how one who descends should descend, and how one who ascends should ascend.

When anyone would want to "go down to the *Merkavah*," he would call upon Surya, the Angel of the Presence, and make him swear one hundred and twelve times in the name of Tootruseah-YHVH who is called Tootruseah Tzortak Totarkhiel Tofgar Ashrooleah Zevoodiel and Zeharariel Tandiel Shoked Hoozeah Dahivoorin and Adiridon-YHVH, Lord of Israel.

He may not do it more than one hundred and twelve times, or less, for he who adds or subtracts: his blood is on his head.[21] Rather, one's mouth brings forth the names and one's fingers count one hundred and twelve times. He then immediately goes down and masters the *Merkavah*. (*Heikhalot Rabbati*, 203–5)

The sages mentioned here were contemporaries, although, again, this should not be taken as a historical account; however, the portrayal of an inner circle and an outer circle may well have corresponded not only to the sages but also to the mystical groups of the time. We are not told directly about the supernatural phenomena here, or whether the "ascent and descent" relates to the mystical ladder itself or the techniques required to use it. Presumably this is an ascent of the soul, not a physical ascent. Light is a major theme in this literature,[22] and part of the reason for this may be that Rabbinic Jews, including the mystics, believed in the existence of a primordial light stored away for the righteous in the world to come.[23] (This is based on the Creation story, where light is created on the first day, but the celestial bodies such as the sun are only created on the fourth day.)

Why the number 112? One must ascend through seven palaces, each with two gates, and each gate has four guards, which makes a total of 56. But you have to go down as well as up, and so the number is doubled. This means there are 112 guards whose power must be defused; thus, the mystic must administer 112 oaths to Surya, who swears that he will protect the mystic throughout the journey. All this must be done very precisely, as the heavenly dominion allows no falsehood or impurity[24] and will cast down the mystic if he is inaccurate to the tiniest degree. Furthermore, as we shall see further in the next chapter, names have creative power. If any Name of God is misused, not only can it harm the mystic, it can also cause cosmic rupture.

Some of these names defy explanation, but a few *are* understood. Like Totarkhiel, Tootruseah is a compound of *tetra*, but with a Greek suffix, *ousion*, which means "essence." Thus Tootruseah means "the essence of the Four-Letter Name." Zevoodiel likely comes from the root meaning *zeved*, a "choice gift,"[25] combined with *El*. Zeharariel derives from *zohar*, meaning "radiance," again combined with *El*. Adiridon is from *adir*, "mighty."

We do not see in the text the precise oath administered to the angel.[26] But when it is completed, the mystic "masters the *Merkavah*," meaning that he both enters the altered state in which he is ready for this experience and achieves power over these realms. "Mastering" the *Merkavah* is, in other words, the execution of magic that rules realms beyond our normal limits.

The next reading skips ahead to the dangers at the sixth palace, after the mystic has completed all the trials up to that point.

> **The guards of the sixth palace make a practice of killing those who "go and do not go down to the *Merkavah* without permission." They hover over them, strike them, and burn them. Others are set in their place and others in their place. The mentality [of those killed] is that they are not afraid nor do they question: "Why are we being burned?" [The mentality of the guards is not to ask:] "What profit do we have, that we kill those who go and do not go down to the *Merkavah* without permission?" Nevertheless, such is the mentality of the guards of the sixth palace. (*Heikhalot Rabbati*, 224)**

At this stage, the danger increases and the guards have the potential for much more irrational behavior. All this is very difficult to comprehend, and so the guards decide to bring back Rabbi Nehunya ben ha-Kannah from his trance; a segment that we omit then tells how they touch him with something that has a minute amount of impurity, wrapped in a protective case. This confirms that he had remained with them and that his vision was solely a mental experience, an ascent of the soul. The segment below tells of the question the group asks upon his return.

> **Then we asked him [Rabbi Nehunya ben ha-Kannah]: Who are those who are among those who descend to the *Merkavah* and those who are not? He said to us, Those are the men whom those who do go down take with them, whom they then establish above and in front of them, and to whom they say, "Look carefully, see, hear, and write all that I say and all that we hear in the presence of the Throne of Glory." These men, if they are not worthy of the task, are those who are attacked by the guards of the sixth palace. Be cautious, therefore, to choose men who are fit and tested companions. (*Heikhalot Rabbati,* 228)**

The "legitimate" mystic can make and manage the trip. However, some of the students are "along for the ride," possibly because they want (but are not ready) to share the experience, or because they are there to record it; this too presents serious dangers. The answer is not fully clear, and scholars continue to debate its full meaning.[27]

The mystic frequently longs for the special knowledge that comes with a successful journey. For the *Heikhalot* mystics, the Bible (particularly the vision of Ezekiel) was accepted as absolute truth, so much so that these speculations and practices developed from it and pointed to the acquisition of a higher wisdom. But over and over we find warnings of the catastrophe that will come to those inadequately qualified and prepared for the journey.

Perhaps it would be safer, or the destination would be closer, if there were a special place to experience God directly? That is the subject of the next chapter.

5

The Temple

THE MEETING PLACE FOR GOD AND HIS PEOPLE

For many Jews today, the Kotel, or Western Wall—what remains of the Temple in Jerusalem—is still a space of special holiness, the place where God is most accessible. What would have made this location special in the first place?

> **A song of ascents. Now bless the Lord, all you servants of the Lord, who stand nightly in the house of the Lord. Lift your hands toward the sanctuary and bless the Lord. May the Lord, maker of heaven and earth, bless you from Zion. (Ps. 134)**

> **God, You are my God; I search for You, my soul thirsts for You, my body yearns for You, as a parched and thirsty land that has no water. I shall behold You in the sanctuary, and see Your might and glory. (Ps. 63:2–3)**

> **You shall slaughter the passover sacrifice for the Lord your God, from the flock and the herd, in the place where the Lord will choose to establish His name. (Deut. 16:2)**

The Temple had a powerful effect on those who visited it. Zion was a source of blessing because it housed the Temple. And the Temple was the place where God, or at least God's "might and glory," could be "seen."[1] A modern commentator on the Psalms has a telling thought: "The light of

God will shine forth from the Holy of Holies . . . if those gathering in the Temple court can draw it out."[2] The connection is available; one simply has to know how to plug into it. Even after the Temple had been in ruins for many centuries, the power of this imagery affected one of the most important figures in the history of religion, Mohammed. He had a vision of a nighttime journey on his horse to Jerusalem, and when he arrived at the Temple Mount, he stood on the rock and soared up to heaven. (Thus the name of the mosque at this site, the "Dome of the Rock.")

Deuteronomy—which scholars understand to have been written during the late First Temple period—tells of "the place where the Lord will choose to establish His name." Whereas people at that time understood God to have established His Name and Presence in the Temple, today we are more distant from that notion and do not literally believe that God lives in the synagogue or even at the site of the Temple in Jerusalem. But many of us do believe certain places have more holiness than others.

Frequently, as in the next text, the specific holiness of the place is expressed literally; this is the place God has established as His home, even though the whole "earth is the Lord's."

> **The earth is the Lord's and all that it holds,**
>> **the world and its inhabitants.**
> **For He founded it upon the ocean, set it on the nether-streams.**
> **Who may ascend the mountain of the Lord?**
>> **Who may stand in His holy place? —**
> **He who has clean hands and a pure heart, who has not**
>> **taken a false oath by My life or sworn deceitfully.**
> **He shall carry away a blessing from the Lord, a**
>> **just reward from God, his deliverer.**
> **Such is the circle of those who turn to Him,**
>> **Jacob, who seek Your presence. *Selah*.**
> **O gates, lift up your heads! Up high, you everlasting**
>> **doors, so the King of glory may come in!**

Who is the King of glory?—the Lord mighty and
   valiant, the Lord, valiant in battle.
O gates, lift up your heads! Lift them up, you everlasting
   doors, so the King of glory may come in!
Who is the King of glory?—the Lord of hosts,
   He is the King of glory! *Selah.* (Ps. 24)

This psalm was likely connected to some kind of dedication (or rededication) ceremony for the Temple in Jerusalem.[3] We see that the doors do not open sideways, but upward. This suggests a more celestial Temple, corresponding to the possibility of communion with God, and perhaps a vision of God.[4]

What exactly is it that makes this place God's "home" on earth?

David gave his son Solomon the plan of the porch and its houses,
. . . and the plan of all that he had by the spirit: of the courts of the
House of the Lord and all its surrounding chambers, and of the
treasuries of the House of God . . . the weight of refined gold for the
incense altar and the gold for the figure of the chariot—the cherubs—
those with outspread wings screening the Ark of the Covenant of
the Lord. "All this that the Lord made me understand by His hand
on me, I give you in writing—the plan of all the works." (1 Chron.
28:11–12, 18–19)

What is meant by "the plan of all the works"? The Temple attempts to model God's dwelling place on high here on earth. This illustrates a frequent theme in Jewish mysticism: as it is above, so it should be below. We will see many instances of such "mirroring" as we encounter Jewish mystics. And once again we see the cherubim as mystical, heavenly figures; they are not God of course, but they are God's angelic representatives.

Indeed, this was a place of intimate access to God, sometimes expressed in most startling fashion, as in this talmudic passage:

It was taught: Rabbi Ishmael ben Elisha said, "I once entered the innermost part [of the Temple] to offer incense, and I saw Akatriel-Yah the Lord of hosts sitting on a high and exalted throne. He said to me: 'Ishmael, My son, bless Me!' I responded: 'May it be Your will that Your mercy overcome Your anger and Your mercy prevail over your other attributes, so You deal with Your children compassionately and be more gracious to them than the law demands.' He nodded His head to me." We learn from this that the blessing of an ordinary individual should not be taken lightly. (B. Ber. 7a)[5]

Akatriel-Yah means "Crown [*Keter*] of God." Thus, this purports to be a vision of God Himself. No angel would have referred to humanity as "children," nor do angels—generally considered to be mere servants of God—possess the attribute of compassion.[6] The event described in the text takes place in the Holy of Holies at the center of the Temple and thus could only have been performed by the *Kohen Gadol*, the "High Priest." However, no record exists attesting to a *Kohen Gadol* by the name of Ishmael ben Elisha (although there was an Elisha and a sage named Ishmael ben Elisha). There also exists a parallel *Heikhalot* text,[7] which probably stems from no earlier than the third century CE, and the Talmud was edited much later than that. Thus, this text appears to originate in post-Temple days.[8] Nonetheless, it is directly associated with the Temple; as Elliot Wolfson notes, "The Holy of Holies, in which the Ark of the Covenant was enshrined, was the seat of the divine Presence, and hence the locus for the visualization of God."[9]

One aspect of this text also fits with the fundamentals of Mainline Kabbalah, in which the mystics are able to affect the inner life of God. Ishmael ben Elisha here influences God's qualities, and his action in doing so is not only desired but requested by God! So we see here a precursor of much later kabbalistic activity.

The *Kohen Gadol* was believed to have great potential for such a meeting with God, even in this earthly location:

For forty years Shimon the Just served Israel as *Kohen Gadol*. The last year, he said to them: "This year I will die." They said to him: "No! How do you know?" He told them, "Every year, when I have entered into the Holy of Holies, there was an old man dressed and wrapped in white who entered and exited with me. But this year, he entered with me, but did not exit with me." . . . Rabbi Abbahu told them: "He said it was a man, but I say it was the Holy One, Blessed be He." (Y. Yoma 27a)[10]

With the prophets and the mystical visions treated in earlier chapters, the mystical moment took place in or was aimed at the upper world, at God's throne. But now God is experienced visibly in some form—at least by the *Kohen Gadol*—here on earth. Again, the meeting place is the Temple.

But what makes the Temple such an access point for a meeting with God? *Ha-Makom*, "The Place," is one of the many names for God in Jewish tradition. Why is *this* place the *Makom*, the Place where God is so intensely found?

Rabbi Shimon ben Yehotzadak asked Rabbi Samuel bar Nahman: "Since I have heard you are a master of *aggadah*, from where was the [original] light created?" He replied: "[The verse] teaches us that the Holy One, Blessed be He, wrapped himself in it as in a robe and irradiated with the luster of His majesty the whole world from one end to the other." Now he had answered him in a whisper; Rabbi Shimon said to him: "There is an explicit verse [to that effect], 'Who is wrapped in a robe of light' (Ps. 104:2), yet you say it in a whisper!" He answered him: "Just as I heard it in a whisper, so I told it to you in a whisper." Rabbi Berekhiah said, "If Rabbi Yitzhak had not expounded [it] in public, it would be impossible to say it."

Before this, what did [the sages] say [on this matter]? Rabbi Berekhiah said in the name of Rabbi Yitzhak: "The light was created from the place of the Temple, as it is written: 'And behold, the glory of the God of Israel came from the east, [with a roar like the roar of mighty waters, and the earth was lit up by His glory].' (Ezek. 43:2) And 'His glory' always refers to the Temple, as it is said, 'O Throne of Glory exalted from of old, our Sacred Shrine.'" (Jer. 17:12) (*Midrash Bereshit Rabbah* 3:4)

This text offers one clue that can help us understand the central meaning of the Temple—it is located in the place from which the divine light was born, the place of God's glory, God's throne on earth; that is why the Temple is placed there and the light continues to shine from it. That throne, that place on earth, is the model for God's supernal dwelling place. It is where God can be seen.[11] This being taught in a whisper stresses that the rabbis do not play around with these issues; they are not for public consumption.

But if this is so, how did this teaching make it into the text of a major midrashic work? We could ask the same question of other such mystical texts in the Talmud. The answer is probably that even when such matters are not widely taught, they creep in all the same. You cannot keep mysticism out completely, even in its most explosive forms. The mystical impulse does have to be kept under control, but ultimately it is a natural, if not essential, feature of religion.

Current scholarship on the significance of the Temple in Jewish mysticism is rather preliminary, but we will look at one theory about some of its implications. Rachel Elior notes that the Israelites saw heaven and earth as unified, with the Temple being the place where heaven's order was maintained, an order "in which the laws of nature were harmonized with sacred time, sacred place, and sacred service."[12] To make things "work right" in this world, the way heaven intends, there has to be something here that mirrors the world above. A very precise cycle of Sabbaths and festivals must be observed, not only because the Torah says so or because human beings require them, but because they mirror a divine order. And we have already seen evidence of this principle in Jewish mysticism.[13] The Temple is the place that serves this purpose, the place where heaven and earth match and touch.

How was this sense of order preserved after the Second Temple was destroyed? Certainly the development of synagogue life was one attempt to do this. The synagogue served as a mini-sanctuary preserving temple rituals through traditions relating to the language of hymns and songs of praise and the use of holy names (sometimes associated with angels and priests). And in the synagogue it was possible (and essential) to pray for the restoration of the Temple and the *real* sacred service. Temple traditions that carried over into synagogue life included recitation of biblical passages describing the sacred incense (still found in Orthodox prayer books), the formal recitation of the priestly benediction (still proclaimed on the festivals in traditional synagogues, and daily in Israel), and recitation of the "Kedushah," which is an imitation of the angels, complete with the reminders from Isaiah 6 and Ezekiel 1. Even prostration was carried over into synagogue life, although now it only takes place on Rosh Hashanah and Yom Kippur.

Not everyone was satisfied with this "second-best" maintenance of the Temple's sacred service. According to Elior, aspects of the *Heikhalot* and *Merkavah* literature were attempts to express a sense of that service, to show and even experience it . . . but in the heavenly sanctuary, not on earth.[14] We shall see other texts giving evidence that Jews had not abandoned the belief that the Temple would be rebuilt yet again. To provide some background for this, we need to look at another segment from Ezekiel.

> **I could see that there were four wheels beside the cherubs, one wheel beside each of the cherubs. . . . And when they moved, each could move in the direction of any of its four quarters; they did not veer as they moved. . . . Each one had four faces; one was a cherub's face, the second a human face, the third a lion's face, and the fourth an**

eagle's face. . . . Each one [of the cherubs] had four faces and each had four wings, with the form of human hands under the wings. (Ezek. 10:9, 11, 14, 21)

Much of this is similar to the vision in Ezekiel 1, in which the number four recurs. What is the significance four in Judaism, in life? There are four directions. The cycle of a woman's ovulation lasts four weeks. And there are four seasons, each of which lasts approximately thirteen weeks ($4 \times 7 \times 13 = 364$, almost corresponding to the number of days in a solar year).[15] Additionally, the four seasons each last three months. This is significant because twelve also is an important number in Judaism. Twelve is the number of tribes, and thus the breastplate of the *Kohen Gadol* had twelve stones.

In addition to the number four, we also know that the number seven plays a critical role in Judaism. Seven represents the holy Sabbath. For certain forms of impurity (see Lev. 12:2, 13:2–5), seven days are required for purification. Seven also plays a critical role in the Temple, where, in addition to the items mentioned above, the menorah has seven branches and the *Kohen Gadol* has seven priestly garments. Also critical is the cosmic order of Sabbaths as understood in the Creation story, as well as what was believed to be the cosmic order of seven firmaments and seven levels of heaven. Corresponding to this was the ritual of priestly service during the seven days of the week and pauses of seven weeks between the harvests.[16]

So when the *kohanim* set up the observance of the Temple, they likely did so along an axis of holiness where the numbers four and seven played a critical role. The Sabbaths were divided into four seasons, four quarters of thirteen Sabbaths each. At some point, during a seven-month period from Nisan to Tishrei, seven festivals were celebrated. "In this 28-week period, there were four festivals of first fruits at intervals of 7 Sabbaths (the first two coinciding with the biblical festivals of Omer and Shavuot): the Festival of the First Barley (26 Nisan), the Festival of the First Wheat

(15 Sivan), the Festival of the First Wine (3 Av), and the Festival of the First Olive Oil (22 Elul). They were always celebrated on a Sunday and involved pilgrimage to the Temple; they are detailed in the Temple Scroll and [*Miktzat Ma'asei ha-Torah*],"[17] two scrolls of the Dead Sea Scrolls. The Temple is thus intended to reflect both the cosmic order of nature and a fixed order of ritual roughly corresponding to the solar calendar.

In the Holy of Holies in the Temple, there were cherubs—angelic, childlike figures—over the Ark. Their significance is discussed in the Talmud and explained in the classical commentary on the Talmud by Rashi (Rabbi Shlomo Yitzhaki, eleventh c.).

> **Talmud: Whenever Israel came on pilgrimage on festivals [to the Temple in Jerusalem], the curtain would be removed for them and the cherubs were shown to them, whose bodies were intertwined with one another, and they would be thus addressed: "Look! You are beloved before God as the love between man and woman."**
>
> **Rashi: The cherubs are united one with the other, and cleaving to each other and intertwining one with the other as a male hugs a female. Intertwining is a language of conjugal union. (B. Yoma 54a, and Rashi's commentary)[18]**

The cherubs are a fertility symbol; that is the secret of the touching wings. As Elior explains, "this description echoes a mythical mystical tradition associating the implied intimacy of the cherubs with the act of pilgrimage; the tradition is most probably very early and refers to the First Temple, for in the Second Temple the Chariot Throne of the cherubs was no more than a mythical memory."[19] Possibly the festival intended is Shavuot, which later mystical tradition treats as the celebration of the marriage between God and Israel, another kind of sacred union. Just as a couple in (what was regarded as normal) sexual intercourse would be face to face, the cherubs are face to face, as if to emphasize the intimacy between God and Israel associated with this place.[20] (The role of the erotic in Jewish mysticism is discussed in greater depth in chapter 14.)

Biblical texts testify that the cherubs also form part of God's throne: King Hezekiah prays, "O Lord of Hosts, enthroned on the Cherubim" (Isa. 37:16)! Ezekiel has a vision (10:20) in which he learns that the creatures who carried the *Merkavah* in his first vision are cherubs.[21]

What exists above must be mirrored below, and the Temple was where it happened. The Temple was the mirror to the supernal Temple above. Any disturbance of such mirroring will result in unthinkable consequences. Consider one example: what if, instead of those *kohanim* who were commanded to do the work of the Temple, other people not so designated performed it? Jews of the day would have assumed this *must* create a cosmic disturbance. And, according to some sources, this is precisely what happened.

In the period leading up to the Maccabean War (168–165 BCE), the service in the Temple was interrupted. When it was restored, the Hasmonean family (also known as "the Maccabees") took over the leadership. But many believed that they were not even *kohanim*, or at least were not the proper ones to conduct the service, and may not even have known the proper Temple procedures for the various offerings.[22]

Consequently, there developed a group of *kohanim* (Elior refers to them as the "secessionist priesthood") who preserved the proper traditions, even though they no longer controlled the Temple. They saw the Temple as desecrating and violating the hallowed rules of purity and considered it so defiled that they would no longer participate in its service.[23] Those who believed this wrote about it, and their writings were found among the Dead Sea Scrolls, at the caves at Qumran, beginning in 1949.[24]

The first of these, *Miktzat Ma'asei ha-Torah* [From the works of the Torah], written at the beginning of the Hasmonean epoch, deals with the laws of purity in the Temple and the various sins that brought about the Temple's defilement. The *Commentary on Habakkuk* is believed to have been written later, in the second half of the first century BCE, but appears to refer to characters in the early Hasmonean period.

[And you know that] we have separated from the mass of the people and from mingling with them in these matters and from being in contact with them in these matters. And you [know that no] treachery or lie or evil is found in our hands. (*Miktzat Ma'asei ha-Torah*)

"Because of the blood of men and the violence done in the land, to the city, and to all its inhabitants" (Hab. 2:7). This concerns the Wicked Priest whom God delivered into the hands of his enemies, because of the iniquity committed against the Teacher of Righteousness and the men of his Council, that he might be humbled by means of a destroying scourge, in bitterness of soul, because he had done wickedly to His elect. (*Commentary on Habakkuk*)[25]

The "Wicked Priest" designated here was very likely Jonathan, the Hasmonean, the son of Mattathias and one of the brothers of Judah Maccabee.[26] In mainstream Jewish history, the Hasmoneans were heroes, but to these authors and their followers (and many others, as we shall see), they were considered villains. So if the Hasmoneans were the villains, who were the true heroes? According to Elior, they were the priests of the House of Zadok, who carried the Ark in the time of King David and anointed his son as king. They are the ones who will set everything straight in the ideal priesthood of the future, and the secessionist priesthood claims descent from the House of Zadok.

Not all scholars agree with the full analysis of Rachel Elior,[27] but the basic theory is difficult to dispute. There were Jews who rejected the "fake" priesthood of the Hasmonean family and returned to earlier models of the Temple and its correspondence with the "heavenly" Temple. Elior writes: "On the evidence of the scrolls, the members of the Community scrupulously observed the cyclic order of Sabbaths and festivals according to the solar calendar, shared the cyclic celebrations of the sacred rites with the angels, and meticulously adhered to the stringent laws of purity and impurity that made it possible for them to keep angelic company."[28]

Incidentally, the fact that the Psalms were chanted in the Temple was also regarded as having special consequence, because the Psalms were attributed to King David. He was a figure of mystical significance as a seventh son, and as (according to 1 Chronicles 2) a fourteenth-generation descendant of Abraham.[29] Even the number of any psalm chanted during the year was considered of particular importance.

What follows is an excerpt from the book of Jubilees (second c. BCE). It is not clear who or what group authored this book, but we know that the same people who preserved the Dead Sea Scrolls also revered this, because fifteen Jubilees scrolls were found in the caves at Qumran. Jubilees is sacred scripture in the Ethiopian Orthodox Church.

> **And on the first of the first month and on the first of the fourth month and on the first of the seventh month and on the first of the tenth month are the days of remembrance and they are the days of appointed times in the four parts of the year. They are written and inscribed for an eternal witness. . . . And they set them upon the heavenly tablets. Each one of them is 13 weeks from one to another of the remembrances, from the first to the second, and from the second to the third, and from the third to the fourth. And all of the weeks which will be commanded will be 52 weeks of days, and all of them are a complete year. Thus it is engraved and ordained on the heavenly tablets, and there is no transgressing in a single year, from year to year. And you, command the children of Israel so that they shall guard the years in this number, 364 days, and it will be a complete year. And no one shall corrupt its appointed time from its days or from its feasts because all [of the appointed times] will arrive in them according to their testimony. . . .**
>
> **And there will be those who will examine the moon diligently because it will corrupt the [appointed] times and it will advance from year to year ten days. Therefore, the years will come to them as they corrupt and make a day of testimony a reproach, and a profane day**

a festival, and they will mix up everything, a holy day profaned and a profane day for a holy day, because they will set awry the months and Sabbaths and feasts and jubilees. (Jub. 6:23-32, 36-37)[30]

Again we see the solar calendar, in the form of the 364-day year, as the prevailing pattern of sacred time, beginning from Creation. Again, the "correct" Temple service can only be performed in this way and no other, by the proper individuals and no others. But the second paragraph tells us that there are those who *want* a lunar calendar, which contradicts the pattern of sacred time that the secessionist priesthood upheld.

How did all this affect the future development of Judaism? For the most part, not at all. The Hasmoneans, and the sages and Rabbis of later generations, won; the Judaism that developed in succeeding centuries—with variations in time and place—was essentially their Judaism. But without the Temple it may have been quite natural for Jews to turn to those who had been busy perpetuating the "proper" temple traditions, or at least to some of their practices.[31] And the priests who served in the Temple—like Ezekiel—functioned as divine assistants, virtual angels, who caused heaven and earth to touch through performing the service precisely in the prescribed fashion.[32] So this opposing group may have had some influence,[33] as they created their own prayers and developed their own mystical approaches to maintain closeness with God in the way they believed essential. Most especially, the "Kedushah," inserted into the "Amidah" that Jews have recited since the Rabbinic period, has as its foundation the key verses from Isaiah's vision of the divine throne room and Ezekiel's vision of the *Merkavah*.[34]

As Heschel points out,[35] there was a dispute among the sages as to the function of the Temple. Rabbi Ishmael taught: "It is a testimony to one and all,"[36] meaning that it was built to serve a human need. Rabbi Shimon bar Yohai taught that "the sanctuary below faces the sanctuary above,"[37] and it serves a divine, cosmic need. We shall see that this is a recurring theme in the history of Jewish mysticism.

For many Jews today, the Kotel, the Temple's Western Wall, is sacred, a representation of the great holiness and potential for mystical experience associated with the ancient Temple. But when the Temple was destroyed, some believed that its remains could no longer bridge the gap between God and humans, and they sought other substitutes. In Christianity, which emerged after the destruction of the Second Temple, Jesus served that purpose. And we will eventually see how Hasidism developed a different way for individuals to eliminate the gap.

Our next text comes from the Zohar, a vast and complex discussion of verses, ideas, and themes in the Torah that is discussed in much greater detail in later chapters. Scholars believe it was created in the thirteenth century, although many details of its authorship are subject to debate. This brief excerpt shows how, long after it was destroyed, the Temple was believed to have functioned in the mystical imagination.

> **When the first Temple was built, another Temple was erected throughout all worlds, illumining all worlds. The world became fragrantly firm,[38] and all supernal windows opened, radiating. There has never been such joy in all the worlds as on that day. Then those above and those below opened, uttering song, namely Song of Songs—song of those musicians who play for the Holy One, Blessed be He.[39] (Zohar 2:143a)[40]**

Once again we see the theme of parallel worlds, with the Jerusalem Temple corresponding to a heavenly Temple that joins with the world below. This brings about a cosmic union benefiting both worlds.

Even after the Temple was destroyed, its location was believed to facilitate a more intense connection between Jews and God. Prayers for the reestablishment of the Temple contain this subtext—that the connection will be as strong in the future as it was in the past. But how did the mystical impulse continue to develop for Jews after they accepted the fact that the Temple would not be rebuilt, at least not for the foreseeable future? This is taken up in the next chapter.

6

Ma'aseh Bereshit, Sefer Yetzirah, and Sefer ha-Bahir

THE ROOTS OF KABBALAH

The Rabbis taught that "the world was created by ten utterances,"[1] nine of which are introduced in the opening chapter of Genesis by the phrase *Vayomer Elohim* ("And God said"). They also considered the word *Bereshit* ("In the beginning [God created the heaven and the earth]") as an utterance, as if to say: Let there be heaven and earth. Since God presumably could have created the entire universe with one utterance (or without any "speech" at all), the Rabbis found it instructive that He did it with ten.

Why is this of particular interest? Because it refers to what we have already called *ma'aseh Bereshit*, the creation of life. The Torah only says that creation took place through divine speech; God spoke and it was so. But this does not tell us how divine speech brought about the Creation.

So what is the secret of creative power? If we knew the secret, could *we* do it? It seems impossible, but there is a classic Jewish story of such creation: the golem legend. In its most famous version, the creation of a golem is attributed to Rabbi Judah Loew of Prague (ca. 1525-1609), although the story was only ascribed to him a century after his death.[2] However, stories from much earlier also deal with the artificial creation of life, including the following excerpt from the Talmud that involves teachers from the third and fourth centuries. The story illustrates the wonder-working skills many sages were believed to possess, as well as the mindset that created Affective Kabbalah, the will to draw down God's power for our benefit.

Rava said: If they wished, the righteous could create a world, for it says: "Your sins have separated you from your God" (Isa. 59:2)

Rava created a man. He then sent him to Rabbi Zeira. Rabbi Zeira spoke to him, but the man did not answer. Rabbi Zeira then said: "You are from the *hevra* [i.e., the society of sages, created by one of them]; return to your dust."

Rav Hanina and Rav Oshaya would sit every Friday afternoon and deal with *Sefer Yetzirah*, and they created a third-grown calf and ate it [i.e., for their Shabbat meal]. (Sanh. 65b)

This text presumes that human beings can accomplish divine deeds of creation. But here, unlike within the Mainline Kabbalah approach, this power is used not for God's benefit, but for human needs. The creation of a golem (a being artificially constructed in the form of a human and given life) is presumably for his own or his community's benefit. The creation of an animal is for a human meal, not for an offering to God. Because Rava and the other creative sages mentioned are presumably sinless and possess mystical knowledge, they are able to achieve this creation. However, Rava couldn't quite match God's power; His golem, after all, had certain limitations; for one, he lacked the power of speech.

Although *deveikut* (cleaving to God; see chapters 1 and 10) is a mystical tactic of its own, separate from Rava's approach, it is frequently considered a prerequisite for such creative abilities. His use of *deveikut* here is not because he is trying to achieve an ecstatic experience, and Rava is certainly not trying to strengthen God. Rather, he suggests that if we are truly sinless, we can share in certain aspects of God's power. And this text gives no indication that the sages disapproved of such wonder-working. Even though Judaism forbids many magical activities, nowhere does it say that what Rava did was forbidden. And the text makes clear that he was not the only sage believed to be capable of doing this.

So how did he do it? Rashi assumes that Rava used the same source that other wonder-workers possessed, the *Sefer Yetzirah* [Book of

Creation], "where he learned how to combine the letters of the Name of God" in order to accomplish this. However, what remains of this book contains only theoretical principles of creation.

As we have seen, the biblical Creation story raises more questions than it answers about how the Creation was accomplished. *Sefer Yetzirah* attempts to answer some of these questions. Similarly to the texts in chapter 4, it sees the biblical text as deliberately leading us to ask such questions and interpret accordingly. It also adopts the Rabbinic view of the world—that it is a realm meant to be governed by the Torah. This book accepts other ideas common in late antiquity, such as the notion that numbers and letters are not just symbols but have a central importance and great power.[3] As Racher Elior puts it, *Sefer Yetzirah* "introduced the interesting idea that creation is an ongoing, creative linguistic process, whereby language and divine creativity are shared by humans and God."[4]

In the process of explaining the Creation story, *Sefer Yetzirah* also seeks to teach about creative magic. Of course when God creates we don't generally call it "magic." Human beings using divine-like powers are often described as magicians; today, of course, genetic surgery, cloning, and other creative acts taking place in laboratories may also seem like magic! (Other material on magic in Jewish mysticism is discussed in chapter 20.)

We do not know who wrote *Sefer Yetzirah* or for whom it was intended. Even the time of its authorship is widely debated. If the talmudic text is to be accepted at face value, the two sages referred to as using *Sefer Yetzirah* lived in the fourth century CE. But that remains unproven at best; we cannot say for sure whether sages actually used or tried to use the book. We simply don't know enough about it to say whether the version we possess was written in the second century, or the seventh century, or anywhere in between.[5]

Most of the excerpts here come from the first of six chapters in this very short book. The second chapter of *Sefer Yetzirah* describes the origin and the functions of the twenty-two letters of the Hebrew Alef Bet, and the third through fifth chapters deal with different types of letters and their role in the Creation. The sixth chapter concludes the book but does not provide the ending that the reader would be hoping for: the actual prescription for the creation of life.

> *Yah*, the Lord of Hosts, the God of Israel, the living God, God Almighty, merciful and gracious, "high and exalted, dwelling forever, and Holy is His Name" (Isa. 57:15), engraved thirty-two wondrous paths of wisdom, creating the universe in three entities [*sefarim*]: boundary [*sefer*], number [*saffar*], and language [*sippur*]. (*Sefer Yetzirah* 1:1)[6]

The plethora of Divine Names is typical of many Hebrew texts of the Rabbinic period. But once we get past those Names, we are left with a few very significant points. Why was the universe created with thirty-two paths of wisdom? The "thirty-two" paths comprise the twenty-two letters in the Hebrew Alef Bet and the ten digits, 0 to 9. It is assumed that these thirty-two tools are created by God, but we are not told where they come from, only what they are used for. Of course Jews in antiquity believed that Hebrew was the original, divine language; as Joseph Dan puts it, "God created the universe by saying '*y'hee or*' and not by saying 'Let there be light.'"[7]

What are the three entities the text discusses? Some suggest they are three principles operating throughout creation, but each with a reality of its own. The pun in the Hebrew terms, which share the same Hebrew root, cannot really be translated adequately, but it expresses the common ground and purpose shared by these three entities. They are brought into being by the power of the letters and numbers. Again, in antiquity letters and numbers were not just signs and symbols as we tend to think of them; they had real existence, sanctity, and power.[8]

God creates *sefer*, "boundedness," using the thirty-two letters and numbers to give shape to the world and make it finite.[9] (*Sefer* can also mean "book," made of pages bound together and set apart from other pages.) God—singular, One—creates *saffar*, "number," bringing multiple options into the world. And God creates *sippur*, "language," words that give life and multiple levels of meaning to the individual letters and that *m'saper*, "tell," of God's nature.

In any case, the author makes it clear that God created His world with these thirty-two paths. This is not a symbolic statement, nor a description of Genesis 1; as Joseph Dan has written, it is "a *scientific statement*, that a certain combination of these thirty-two paths brings about the creation. . . . Thus whoever knows the secret of the thirty-two paths can possibly participate in the process of creation, either of a world or of a creature."[10]

> **There are ten intangible [*belimah*] *sefirot* and twenty-two letters as a foundation: three are Mothers, and seven double, and twelve simple. (*Sefer Yetzirah* 1:2)**

The term *belimah* is obscure, but probably should be read as a conjunction of two Hebrew words, *beli* and *mah*, "without what." Job 26:7 uses this word: "He stretches the north over chaos and suspends the earth over *belimah*," presumably referring to a cosmic void or emptiness (parallel to the word *tohu*, "chaos"). Chapter 1:8 of *Sefer Yetzirah* (see below) repeats this word and follows it with the term *belom*, "to restrain," "to bridle"; it tells the reader to "restrain your mind from imagining, your mouth from speaking." It is translated here as "intangible," but it could also simply mean "incomprehensible."[11] The significance of "Nothingness" in Jewish mysticism and the illusion of physical reality is dealt with beginning in chapter 8 on the *Ein Sof*.

This text marks Jewish mysticism's earliest use of the term *sefirot*, a word that becomes critically important in Kabbalah, although here it merely signifies the ten numbers and the source of the mathematical relationships known in the world. If they are *belimah*, one cannot really comprehend them. Perhaps the simplest (and admittedly inadequate) way to explain this is that while God is really infinite, God is somehow constricted into these ten *sefirot*, these numerical concepts. Later sources will relate this to the word *sapir*, "sapphire" or "gem," and to the mystical verse quoted in chapter 2: "And they saw the God of Israel: under His feet there was the likeness of a pavement of sapphire [*sapir*], like the very sky for purity" (Exod. 24:10).

By "foundation," the text might be referring to the twenty-two basic letters (excluding the five final-letter forms), or to the idea that all these letters serve as the foundation, the roots, of creation. The latter seems a more likely explanation because *Sefer Yetzirah* 2:2 says that the letters were used to depict all that was or ever would be formed.

The twenty-two letters of the Alef Bet are divided into three groups. "Single" letters are those that are pronounced the same wherever they appear. "Doubles" are those whose pronunciation changes when, for grammatical reasons, they have within them a *dagesh*, a dot: sometimes this changes the letter's pronunciation more significantly (as when the letter *veit* becomes *beit* and its sound is changed from "V" to "B"), whereas in other cases, the sound of the letter is only lengthened but not altered.[12] Twelve other letters can have no *dagesh* within them and so are dubbed the "simple" or "single" letters. Three remaining letters *alef*, *mem*, and *shin*, are singled out; they are associated with three elements: *mem* stands for *mayim*, "water"; *shin* is related to the word *eish*, "fire"; *alef* stands for *avir*, "air," which mediates between fire and water.

In short, the source for everything below exists above, and all is within the power of the letters. The conclusion of *Sefer Yetzirah* underscores how these three basic elements come from the three Mother letters, the seven planets from the seven double letters, and the twelve constellations of the Zodiac and months of the year from the twelve single letters.

There are ten intangible *sefirot*, corresponding to the ten fingers, five opposite five, and in the center is set the covenant of unity,[13] in the word of the tongue [*b'milat ha-lashon*] and in circumcision [*b'milat ha-ma'or*].

There are ten intangible *sefirot*, ten and not nine, ten and not eleven. Understand in wisdom, be wise in understanding. Examine them, investigate them. Clarify matters completely, and restore the Creator to His abode. (*Sefer Yetzirah* 1:3-4)

The "covenant of unity" includes both speech, which creates words, evidence of the spirit within human beings, and the generative organ, which creates life itself. Thus these two covenants—united linguistically through the pun on the Hebrew word *milah*, which can mean either "word" or "circumcision"—are the building blocks of civilization and provide cosmic significance to the body; as David Blumenthal notes, "the sex organ and speech are (also) the metaphors par excellence for the creative process."[14] Ten corresponds to the five fingers on each hand, which have the tongue in the middle; likewise, there are five toes on each foot, and the circumcised organ between them. So it *must* be "ten and not nine, ten and not eleven," otherwise the practitioner will not succeed.

What does it mean that the reader is told to "examine" and "investigate"? He is meant to create as God did, through attempting various combinations of letters and numbers. By doing so, he "restores the Creator to His abode." This may mean that he becomes to a degree like God, a (magical) creator, or that by discovering this divine reality he provides glory to God, confirming His Kingship.

There are ten intangible *sefirot* whose measure is ten, yet infinite [*Ein Sof*]. Depth of beginning, depth of end, depth of good, depth of evil, depth of above, depth of below, depth of east, depth of west, depth of north, depth of south. God alone, faithful Divine King, rules over them all from His holy abode unto eternity.

There are ten intangible *sefirot*, a vision flashing like lightning; their limit is infinite. His word surges within them "going to and fro" [Ezek. 1:14]; they pursue His command like the whirlwind and bow down before His Throne. (*Sefer Yetzirah* 1:5-6)

Reality has boundaries, and here *Sefer Yetzirah* defines them. In addition to the three dimensions of space (length and width expressed by the four directions, and height by above and below), there exists the dimension of time, and the dimension of good and evil, the ethical realm. All these are treated as infinite; presumably we are left with the infinite possibilities of good and evil actions.

Although the use of the term *sefirot* here should not be confused with the way it is used in kabbalistic writings, it is interesting to note that another term made popular in Kabbalah is found here, the phrase *Ein Sof*. It refers to the infinite quality of God, the idea that God is transcendent and beyond human apprehension or understanding. The meaning of *Ein Sof* is further discussed in chapter 8.

What is the "abode" of God referred to here? It seems likely that, like most Jews in antiquity, this author believed that the Temple was God's "true" dwelling place and that the location of the Temple even before it was built was the center of the cosmos from which God's creation emanated.[15]

The last paragraph in the text above, referencing the lightning and the whirlwind along with its use of the phrase "to and fro" from Ezek. 1:15, suggests Ezekiel's *merkavah*, the chariot of God. The description is similar to the terminology in *Heikhalot* texts. So while the *sefirot* here are the building blocks of creation, and expand to infinity, beyond comprehension, they are also visible, dynamic creatures who bow before the divine throne and are potentially associated with mystical experience.[16]

> **There are ten intangible *sefirot*. Restrain your mind from imagining and your mouth from speaking. If your mind races, return to the place from which you started, for it is written: "The creatures darted to and fro." (Ezek. 1:14) Concerning this a covenant was made. (*Sefer Yetzirah* 1:8)**

The thrust of this section is not to try to describe or understand the *sefirot*, but the recognition of their existence is important enough to warrant a covenant, a solemn agreement, among those initiated in this field of study and mystical experience: like others before them, they are not to speak openly of these matters.

> There are ten intangible *sefirot*. One is the spirit of the living God; "His throne is established from of old" (Ps. 93:2). May the blessed Name of the Eternal One be blessed, the voice of spirit and speech, and this is the Holy Spirit.
>
> Two is spirit from spirit. He engraved and inscribed upon it the twenty-two letters as a foundation—three Mothers, seven doubles, and twelve simple, and they are of one spirit.
>
> Three is water from the spirit. He engraved and inscribed upon it formlessness and void, mud and clay that He engraved as a type of garden. . . .
>
> Four is fire from water. He engraved and inscribed upon it the Throne of Glory, the *ofanim* and the seraphim and the holy *hayyot*, and the ministering angels, and from these three He formed His abode. (*Sefer Yetzirah* 1:9–12)

Here the text begins to reckon the *sefirot* as "stages in the process of the forming of the elements,"[17] each one a domain within which God performs a particular act of creation. The first three paragraphs, 1:9–11, correspond to three pieces of Genesis 1:

"A wind from God sweeping" (1:2)
"God said. . . ." (1:3); that is, God created by means of the letters
"Hovered over the waters" (1:2)

The fourth paragraph, 1:12, is more complicated. While no reference to fire exists in the Creation story, the Rabbis assumed that fire was created on the second day to "dry up" the firmament—based in part on their translation of Isa. 64:1: "As when the blazing fire melted and divided the waters into two." They understood this verse as referring to a fire dividing the upper and lower waters on either side of the plane that represented the firmament.[18]

The highest level of creation is the spirit of the living God, God's creative spirit, which is the source for everything else and thus the most exalted of the ten *sefirot*. The next three represent three basic elements: air (*ruah*, "spirit from spirit"), water, and fire. But they should not be confused with the elements of Greek science, which are four, including earth, and which postulated those elements as always existing. In our text, they are simply God's creations.

Sefer Yetzirah 1:10, dealing with the second *sefirah*, clearly indicates that the letters of the Alef Bet are the tools with which God builds the universe. These tools are "one spirit" in that they are created by the one spirit, that is, the first *sefirah*. The rest of this section essentially repeats what we have already been told about the letters.

In *Sefer Yetzirah* 1:10, we see that the third *sefirah* represents something created from the letters, even though it is as close as one gets to *tohu va-vohu*, "formlessness and void." The creation of water is thus that of the "formlessness and void," primeval and uncontrolled waters. In *Sefer Yetzirah* 1:12, the fourth *sefirah* refers to the heavenly beings that are regarded as "fiery"—the "Throne of Glory, the seraphim and the *ofanim* and the holy *hayyot*, and the ministering angels," most of which come from the vision of Ezekiel 1.[19] The "abode" of God is thus created from these different elements that themselves are created from fire.

All this describes what the Rabbis referred to as *ma'aseh Bereshit*, the parts of creation not recounted in Genesis 1. In *Sefer Yetzirah*, the *sefirot* are the stages prior to the first act recorded in the Creation story of Genesis 1, "Let there be light."[20]

He chose three of the simple letters, set them into His great Name [i.e., the Four-Letter Name, YHVH], and sealed through them six extremities.[21] Five: He sealed height, He turned upward and sealed it with YHV. Six: He sealed the beneath, He turned downward and sealed it with YHV. Seven: He sealed East, He turned forward and sealed it with HYV. Eight: He sealed West, He turned backward and

sealed it with HVY. Nine: He sealed South, He turned right and sealed it with VYH. Ten: He sealed North, He turned left and sealed it with VHY. (*Sefer Yetzirah* 1:13)

Instead of going on to describe the next *sefirot*,[22] we are told about the boundaries of the universe, the six dimensions of space. Using three letters—the letters that are used to form the Ineffable Name—and infusing them with spirit, God sets limits to the six spatial dimensions.

This first chapter of *Sefer Yetzirah* answers some of the questions about *ma'aseh Bereshit*.

The "formlessness and void" did not precede the creation, but came from the water. God did not literally speak; he created letters from the "air" and used them to create the world. Angels came from the "fire." And prior to creation God produced all the boundaries and the tools necessary for creation itself.

When our father Abraham came, he looked, saw, explored, understood, engraved, hewed out, and succeeded at creation, as it says, "and the souls [*nefesh*] which they had made in Haran" (Gen. 12:5); immediately, the Lord of All, Praised be He, was revealed to him; He set him in His lap, and kissed him on his head, and called him "Abraham, My beloved" (Isa. 41:8), and made a covenant with him and with his seed, as it says, "And he put his trust in God, and He reckoned it to him as righteousness" (Gen. 15:6). He made a covenant with him between the ten fingers of his hands, which is the covenant of the tongue [i.e., language], and between the ten toes of his feet, which is the covenant of circumcision. And He bound the twenty-two letters of the Torah to his tongue, and He revealed to him His mystery: He drew them through water, He burned them in fire, He shook them through the air, He kindled them in the seven [planets], He led them through the twelve constellations. (*Sefer Yetzirah* 6:7)

This final paragraph of *Sefer Yetzirah* claims that Abraham possessed these secrets and powers, and hence was able to create life. The proof-text[23] contains the word *nefesh*, here translated as "soul" but often meaning "living bodies." Generally, the Rabbis interpreted this verse as referring to those individuals whom Abraham and Sarah had "converted" from paganism to monotheism. But here it is understood to say that he literally "made" human beings! Because of this, it was widely believed that Abraham was the author of *Sefer Yetzirah*.

One might have expected God to be angry with Abraham for usurping His unique creative power, but God approves of such creation. Abraham is granted a vision of and intimate contact with God. The conclusion harks back to the beginning: the twofold covenant of tongue and circumcision in 1:3 is repeated, complete with the emphasis on ten fingers and toes, representing the ten *sefirot*.

Unfortunately, the book does not give us the actual formula for creation; it does not provide the recipe for a golem. The ultimate mystery of creative power is deliberately hidden, as if to say: *you*, the reader, are not supposed to do this magic. Only a select few—an Abraham, or those sages in the Talmud—are granted this knowledge.

The book *Bahir* (meaning "brightness") is sometimes referred to as *Midrash Rabbi Nehunya ben ha-Kannah*, because it opens with a teaching quoted in the name of this first-century sage. Written considerably later, the book first appears in the late twelfth century; the author is unknown.[24] It is a short book, though longer than *Sefer Yetzirah*. Written in the form of a dialogue between mystical master and student, it contains many parables, some of them quite difficult to understand, dealing with an earthly king, his family, his subjects, and his palace. It is largely a reflection on the opening chapters of Genesis, and its main theme is God's mysterious activity, which created and continues to create the world. It also comments on some of the statements in *Sefer Yetzirah* and the use of sacred names in magic.

The main point in the excerpts here is that *Bahir* draws on the concept of the ten *sefirot* mentioned in *Sefer Yetzirah* but portrays them quite differently: they now appear as actual qualities, attributes of God. The *sefirot* are also pictured together as a cosmic tree, the source from which all souls develop. (Chapter 9 deals in detail with the *sefirot*.) *Bahir* is the first extant book presenting a system similar to that in the body of work that has come to be known as Kabbalah.

Bahir confronts a question different from that of *Sefer Yetzirah*; instead of just imitating God and His creative capacity, the author asks: how can I narrow the gap between God and man, in order to be closer to Him?

> Rabbi Rehumei said: ... Could we infer that whatever was needed for this world, the Holy One, Blessed be He, created before the heavens? He said to him: Yes. What is this like? A king wanted to plant a tree in his garden. He examined the entire garden to find a spring with flowing water to nourish the tree, but could not find one. He said: I will dig for water, and bring forth a spring to sustain the tree. He dug and brought forth a spring flowing with living water; afterward, he planted the tree that bore fruit. It succeeded because the roots always watered it from the spring.
>
> What is this tree of which you speak? He said to him: It refers to the powers [i.e., the *sefirot*] of the Holy One, Blessed be He, ordered one above the other, and they are like a tree. Just as a tree brings forth fruit by being watered, so the Holy One, Praised be He, increases the powers of the tree through water. And what *is* the water of the Holy One, Blessed be He? It is wisdom. And this also refers to the souls of the righteous that are carried from the spring to the great channel, and ascend and are attached to the tree. Through what are they carried? Through the People of Israel. When they are righteous and good, the *Shekhinah* dwells among them and in their works, in the lap of the Holy One, Blessed be He, and He prospers and increases them.
>
> Why are they called *sefirot*? Because it says, "The heavens declare [*m'saprim*] the glory of God" (Ps. 19:2). (*Bahir* 23, 119, 125)[25]

We find a good deal of "code language" in the *Bahir*, as in other kabbalistic texts. The tree represents the fullness of the ten *sefirot*, the entire array of creation. The higher *sefirot* emanate into and develop each of those below, which in turn flow into and sustain all of creation. "Heavens" refers to a complex of six *sefirot* that are in the center of the tree. "Earth," in which the tree is rooted, is immediately below the "heavens" and is the lowest of the ten *sefirot*. The "spring" represents the third *sefirah*, which is commonly referred to in kabbalistic texts as *Binah*, "understanding." *Binah* is also sometimes referred to as a "womb," because it is the "spring" that nourishes the lower seven *sefirot*. Finally, "wisdom" refers to the second *sefirah*, *Hokhmah*, which sustains everything below it.

The *sefirot* are called *sefirot* because they *m'saprim*, they *tell*, they disclose the glory of God. We have already encountered the notion of creation through language and the idea that such creation in a lower realm, perceivable by human beings, parallels that which takes place in a higher realm. The higher realm is also alluded to in the relationship between the words *m'saprim* and *sapir*, the sapphire-like radiance of the heavens.[26] As Moshe Hallamish explains, "The Jew expresses himself in a rich language composed of twenty-two letters, and God expresses himself in the *language of the sefirot*."[27]

The next text addresses what for many Jews has been the biggest problem in maintaining faith: why do bad things happen to good people?

> **Why is there a righteous person who enjoys good, and a righteous person who suffers affliction? Because the latter was formerly wicked and now suffers punishment. But is one punished for offenses committed in one's youth? Did not Rabbi Shimon say that the heavenly tribunal inflicts punishment only for misdeeds committed after the age of twenty?[28] He replied: I do not refer to misdeeds during a person's life, but to the fact that this person preexisted prior to his present life. His colleagues said to him: How long will you mystify**

your words? He said to them: See, what is this like? A person planted a vineyard and hoped it would grow good grapes, but sour grapes grew. He saw that his planting and harvest were not successful, so he tore it out. He cleaned out the bad vines and planted again. He saw that his planting was not successful, so he tore it out and planted again. How long does this go on? He said to them: For a thousand generations, as it is written: "The matter which He ordained for a thousand generations" (Ps. 105:8). (*Bahir* 195)

If God is good, dealing fairly with individuals, and if God is all-powerful, why does God allow the righteous to suffer? Obviously one of the premises has to be rejected: either God is *not* good, or God is *not* all-powerful. Or perhaps the suffering is only apparent but not "real." The approach of the *Bahir* is not only unusual, but also new to Jewish thought. It says: Souls have unfinished business and must return to deal with it. If you are righteous but suffering unfairly, it means you have sinned in a previous life and have punishment coming to you. Many Jewish mystics taught this idea of transmigration of souls. (There is a difference between reincarnation and transmigration; with the former, the person becomes something or someone else, while the latter involves the soul maintaining his or her past self in some sense, but taking on an additional entity as well.)

Here the idea of transmigration is treated as a great mystery, so much so that the text does not even have a term for it! However, beginning in the thirteenth century, the term *gilgul* (literally, "revolving") became commonly used for this idea.[29] Some kabbalists placed a limit on the number of transmigrations through which a soul might go, suggesting that the wicked only get so many opportunities and the righteous need only so much trouble.[30] Here in the *Bahir*, however, the possibilities are essentially endless, even "for a thousand generations"; a soul is brought back over and over again, until all its sins have been rectified. Chapter 17 addresses the problem of evil more broadly, and chapter 19 deals with transmigration in more detail.

Instead of seeking to be close to God, many early Jewish mystics sought to be like God and to uncover the secrets of creation, the ability to channel divine power. They are the originators of what ultimately became what I have described as Affective Kabbalah, and their ideas reverberated powerfully in the thought of later mystics, as we will see particularly in chapter 20.

We have now examined many of the ideas from antiquity that preceded the development of Kabbalah. But before going further into Kabbalah, we turn in the next chapter to a particular Jewish society that created its own mystical approach from these prekabbalistic elements.

7

Hasidei Ashkenaz

MYSTICAL MORALISM

In Germany, primarily in the twelfth and thirteenth centuries, a group of Jewish mystics came to be known as Hasidei Ashkenaz (distinct from the eighteenth-century Hasidim). Literally "the German pietists," they were strongly moralistic, very humble, and deeply ascetic (although by no means celibate, as they were all expected to marry); and because they paid special attention to the cultivation of inner piety, they were called *Hasidim.* Although German Jews during this period experienced serious persecution, we are not sure how this may have influenced the thought of this mystical group

Their most prominent thinker was Rabbi Yehudah he-Hasid,[1] the primary author of the group's most significant literary creation, *Sefer Hasidim.* Born around 1150, about three years after the Second Crusade, he belongs to the earlier period of the Hasidei Ashkenaz, when there was a stronger, more supportive community of pietists.[2] They were familiar with some of the *Merkavah* literature (see chapter 4), and it is widely accepted that their approach was heavily influenced by one Babylonian mystic, whose works were very closely guarded, handed down from father to son, and eventually had their impact in Germany.[3] Hasidei Ashkenaz were also particularly meticulous about the exact formulae of the prayers they recited. In this they are similar to the secessionist priests discussed in chapter 5, who were very precise about key matters, although they were very different matters!

The Hasidei Ashkenaz lived an extremely austere and demanding life; their moralism required a constant emphasis on repentance for every possible misdeed. Not only did the laws of the Torah and standard Rabbinic practices explicitly express God's will, but there was also God's "implicit" will, which was hidden and unknowable; this left these Hasidim never quite knowing where they stood with God and always needing to perform acts of repentance.[4] As part of this process, one was expected be resourceful and devise new obligations!

Requirements placed on individuals might be modified based on their temperament or intellectual ability, but for the most learned and capable pietists they were very steep. While subject to some Christian influence, the Hasidei Ashkenaz found precedent for such practices in classic Rabbinic sources,[5] and some of their penances were quite severe. (Not included here are texts that describe some of the mortifications prescribed for various sins.) Equanimity was also an important virtue among them; they believed that one should be unmoved by praise or insult.[6] They saw martyrdom as a serious possibility, prizing it as the ultimate sanctification of God's Name. If life is a trial, martyrdom is the ultimate test, and it was occasionally imposed during this period, which overlapped with the Crusades.[7] In short, the Hasidei Ashkenaz have been described as "the Puritans of early European Judaism."[8]

While the Hasidei Ashkenaz certainly believed that God was invisible and nonphysical, they also held that God made Himself manifest through His *Kavod*, the visible aspect of God's glory discussed in chapter 2. This visible aspect of God is sometimes referred to as either the *Shekhinah*, the Divine Presence—a term we will see with much more powerful meaning when we examine it within the kabbalistic system—or occasionally the *Ruah ha-Kodesh*, the Holy Spirit. All the anthropomorphic references in Scripture apply to this personification of the divine majesty.[9] The learned elite, the sages, are urged to concentrate and meditate on this *Kavod*, while the ordinary folk are to concentrate on the transcendent Creator on high.[10]

The teacher in this opening text, Rabbi Eleazar ben Yehudah of Worms (d. about 1230), is best known for a halakhic work called *Sefer Rokeah*. *Rokeah* here probably means "perfumer," and this book dispensed halakhic guidance so that the ethical lives of its readers would pass a "smell" test. (Eleazar probably gave it this title because his name and the word *rokeah* have the same value in *gematria*, Jewish numerology, i.e., 308.) The text below, however, is a more directly mystical passage.

Now I shall instruct you how to love God, praised be He, and then I shall write out for you the secret of the *Merkavah*.

"Let a man always be subtle in the fear of God."[11] This means he should reflect on the subtleties and glories of the world, how, for example, a mortal king orders his soldiers to go out to do battle. Even though they know they may be killed in battle, still, they are afraid of him and obey him, even though they know that the fear of him is not everlasting, since one day he will die and perish, and they can run away to another country. How much more so, then, should man fear the King of the kings of kings, the Holy One, Blessed be He, and walk in His ways, for He is everywhere and He gazes at the wicked and the good. Whenever a man sees groups of the righteous he should attach himself to them so he should have a portion among them. He should do it for the sake of heaven and walk in the ways He has created. Whenever he recites a *berakhah*, he should concentrate on the meaning, as it says: "I have set the Lord always before me." (Ps. 16:8) That is why the Rabbis ordained that we should say in the *berakhah*, "*Barukh Atah*," [Praised are You] as if a man were conversing with his neighbor.

He should also consider that whenever a man sins, when, for example, he steals or fornicates with his neighbor's wife, how much subtlety does he display in order to prevent others knowing of it so that he should not be put to shame. How much more so should a man worship his Creator. And he should be subtle in doing good deeds. (Eleazar ben Yehudah of Worms, *Sodei Razayya*)[12]

The text opens by explaining its two purposes: it is an appeal to love God and live a pious life, and it is a mystical exercise to prepare the reader before going too deeply into the *Merkavah*, the heavenly chariot. God is portrayed here as very involved with and close to human beings, "as if a man were conversing with his neighbor,"—even though *Heikhalot* mysticism generally emphasizes God's transcendence, God's distance and difference from human beings. Psalm 16:8, "I have set the Lord always before me,"[13] is frequently cited as a directive to mystics to maintain God in one's thoughts constantly. This theme is consistent with the idea of *deveikut,* cleaving to God, examined briefly in chapter 1 and treated in more detail in chapter 10.

Although subtlety and resourcefulness in serving God is a frequent theme among the Hasidei Ashkenaz, if your whole life is a trial and you are always being scrutinized, it is logical that you put your best efforts into managing the trial.

> **The root of *hasidut* [saintliness] is for man to go beyond the letter of the law, as it says, *"v'hasid b'khol ma'asav"* ["And gracious in all His works"] (Ps. 145:17).**
>
> **The root of fear is when it is hard for a man to do the thing, as it says: "For now I know that you are a God-fearing man." (Gen. 22:12)**
>
> **The root of prayer is that the heart rejoices in the love of the Holy One, Blessed be He, as it says: "Let the heart of them rejoice who seek the Lord" (1 Chron. 16:10), which is why David played on the harp.**
>
> **The root of the Torah is to study with profundity so as to know how to carry out all God's commands, as it says: "All who practice it gain sound understanding" (Ps. 111:10). (*Sodei Razayya*, continued)**

If indeed life in this world is a trial, what is the substance of the case? The Hasid is always given tests and temptations (particularly erotic or ego pleasures) that he must resist. In response to these tests, he must direct his energy to love of God, through service to God. Although it is not stated explicitly, in this view life here is a preparation for the afterlife and dwelling in the presence of the Beloved God.

(The next sections, omitted here, deal with the roots of the mitzvot, the fear of God, the love of God, and humility.)

The root of love is to love the Lord. The soul is full of love, bound with the bonds of love in great joy. This joy chases away from his heart all bodily pleasure and worldly delight. The powerful joy of love seizes his heart so that at all times he thinks: How can I do the will of God? The pleasures of his children and the company of his wife are as nothing in comparison with the love of God. Imagine a young man who has not been with a woman for a very long time. He longs for her, his heart burns for her. Imagine his great love and desire when he cohabits with her and how when his sperm shoots like an arrow he has so much pleasure. All this is as nothing compared with his desire to do the will of God, to bring merit to others, to sanctify himself, to sacrifice his life in his love just as Pinchas sacrificed himself to slay Zimri (Numbers 25), and like Abraham who said: "I swear to the Lord, God most high, Creator of heaven and earth: I will not take so much as a thread or a sandal-strap." (Gen. 14:22–23), like Elisha who refused to take anything from Naaman (2 Kings 5). The love of heaven in his heart is like the flame attached to the coal. He does not gaze at women, he does not engage in frivolous talk, but he concerns himself only to toil to do the will of God and he sings songs in order to become filled with joy in the love of God. (*Sodei Razayya*, continued)

For the Hasidei Ashkenaz, doing God's will becomes an act of love, and the mystic's relation to God is described in highly erotic terms.[14] Similar erotic language can also be found in much of the medieval Christian mystical love poetry.

Below are excerpts from "Shir ha-Kavod" (or "An'im Zemirot," the hymn's two opening words), commonly attributed to Rabbi Yehudah he-Hasid though the actual authorship is uncertain. An excellent example of the mystical tradition's influence on the siddur, the prayer book, this hymn is sung on Shabbat in many traditional synagogues, often at the end of the service and frequently led by young children (who fortunately usually do not understand much of its content). It presents a portrait of a God who, as Arthur Green puts it, "combines the lover of the Song of Songs, the warrior of the ancient prophets, and the crowned God of the *merkavah* tradition."[15]

> **Sweet hymns shall be my chant and woven songs,**
> **For Thou art all for which my spirit longs.**
> **To be within the shadow of Thy hand**
> **And all Thy mystery to understand.**

The term *an'im zemirot* (sweet hymns) comes from 2 Sam. 23:1, where David is called the sweet singer of Israel, *na'im zemirot*. So the poet compares his song to the Psalms of David. The phrase "my spirit longs," refers to Ps. 42:2: "Like a hind crying for water, my soul cries for you, O God." This establishes a certain sensual character to the author's experience of God. "Within the shadow" is a reference to Songs 2:3: "Like an apple tree among trees of the forest, so is my beloved among the youths. I delight to sit in his shade, and his fruit is sweet to my mouth." This underscores the author's desire to be God's beloved. "All Thy mystery" uses two terms, *raz* and *sod*, both meaning "secret." *Sod* also means "council," possibly a heavenly council. Perhaps the author is a *Merkavah* mystic who hopes to be protected by God as he learns the mysteries of the heavenly host.

> **The while Thy glory is upon my tongue,**
> **My inmost heart with love of Thee is wrung.**
> **So though Thy mighty marvels I proclaim,**
> **'Tis songs of love wherewith I greet Thy name.**

"Thy glory" references the *Kavod*, the visible Glory of God. An examination of the Hebrew text will uncover numerous mentions of the *Kavod* in the next several lines, suggesting that the author not only seeks it and loves it but is virtually obsessed with it . . . that is, with God Himself. "Love of Thee," *El dodekha*, should actually be translated "for Your love," as it references Songs 1:2, "for Your love is more delightful than wine." Again, we see a clearly erotic reference.

> I have not seen Thee, yet I tell Thy praise,
> Nor known Thee, yet I image forth Thy ways.
> For by Thy seers' and servants' mystic speech
> Thou didst Thy sov'ran splendor darkly teach,

"I tell Thy praise" again refers to the *Kavod*. This is also likely a reference to Ps. 19:2, "The heavens declare the glory of God." "I image forth" may evoke from readers the complaint that Jews are not supposed to "image" God, but that is precisely what the author does, and continues to do throughout the hymn, and he bases himself on these many references to Scripture. "Servants' mystic speech" is the poet's understanding of *b'yad nevi'ekha*, which literally means "by way of the prophets." Since God has already revealed some of these images to the prophets, who then could portray God in very "human" terms, the poet certainly has the right to do so.

> To countless visions did their pictures run,
> Behold through all the visions Thou art one.
> In Thee old age and youth at once were drawn,
> The grey of eld, the flowing locks of dawn,

"Their pictures run" is based on the Hebrew *Himshilukha*, meaning literally "they made analogies about You"; the word comes from *mashal*, "parable" or "analogy," but here refers to a vision of God like that of a human being. That was the likeness that the mystic offered, though it may seem strange to those of us who were taught not to "image" God in any physical form. "In Thee old age . . . locks of dawn" responds to a Rabbinic teaching that Israel had two visions of God: one as a youth at the parting of the sea, one as an elder at Sinai.[16]

Could this be used to suggest the existence of two gods? No, say the Rabbis, for God begins revelation at Sinai with the word *Anokhi*, "I" (am the Lord your God), so as not to allow anyone else to say this. As the next line confirms, God's appearance changes, depending on what we need to see.

> **The ancient judge, the youthful warrior,**
> **The man of battles, terrible in war,**
> **The helmet of salvation on His head,**
> **And by His hand and arm the triumph led,**

Here we are given the youthful image of God, as warrior and lover. Now—after all the talk of *Kavod* and image, *demut*—the mystic gets serious about what God will do. As in subsequent sections of this hymn, we see much mention of God's head (and also frequent repetition of the word for "head," *rosh*, as if to make sure this emphasis is noticed). While the picture of God's head is not as detailed as in *Shi'ur Komah* (see chapter 4), there is a good deal of description here. Some of it is symbolic: God's helmet corresponds to His tefillin, which are cubes containing Torah parchment, worn during weekday morning servicces. God's head corresponds to our head, because the physical world is (as always, in Jewish mysticism) a reflection of the supernal world. Similarly, Rabbi Eleazar of Worms says: "It is known that the human being is the most glorious of all creatures, and the head of a human the most glorious of all limbs, and so it is above."[17] (The Hasidei Ashkenaz were well aware of the *Shi'ur Komah* and similar texts.)

The "helmet of salvation," taken from Isa. 59:17, emphasizes God's warrior-like qualities, which should be expected from a Jewish poet living after the Crusades, particularly given that his people have been in exile for a thousand years, frequently under oppressive conditions. The original text of "Av ha-Rahamim" (Merciful Father), a Shabbat morning prayer composed (mostly from biblical verses) in the same period, includes a similar and more direct call for vengeance.

> His head all shining with the dew of light,
> His locks all dripping with the drops of night.
> I glorify Him, for He joys in me,
> My crown of beauty He shall ever be!

The "dew of light" is related to Songs 5:2: "Let me in, my own, my darling, my faultless dove! For my head is drenched with dew, my locks with the damp of night." Just like that, the warrior becomes a lover ... and a passionate lover at that! Aroused, he asks his beloved to allow him to enter. "Head all shining with the dew of light" may also be a euphemism for his phallus and semen, as he approaches sexual climax.[18] The Rabbis also referred to dew as if it were a magical potion used to resurrect the dead: "When God resurrects the dead, He shakes out His locks and the dew falls."[19] They also taught that dew was present at Sinai and used to revive Israel when they passed out in ecstasy at the time the Torah was given.[20] So the author assumes that this dew has tremendous power! "I glorify Him, for He joys in me," *Yitpaer bee, ki hafetz bee*: in other words, "He is glorified with me, for He desires me." The intensity of the erotic imagery moves forward.[21] Finally, "My crown of beauty" references Isa. 28:5, where God is the crown of Israel: "In that day, the Lord of Hosts shall become be a crown of beauty and a diadem [*tzefirah*] of glory for the remnant of His people." Here Israel has a crown—God—and Israel also functions as God's crown.

> His head is like pure gold; His forehead's flame
> Is graven glory of His holy name.
> And with that lovely diadem 'tis graced
> The coronal His people there have placed.

The opening comes from Songs 5:11: "His head is finest gold, his locks are curled and black as a raven." The "graven glory of God's Name" appears to be inscribed directly on God's forehead! The "crown His people have placed there" is a reference to a midrash on Songs 3:11, "the crown that his mother gave him" (i.e., King Solomon), which suggests that the crown is made not by *immo*, "his mother," but *umato*, "his people."[22]

> His hair as on the head of youth is twined,
> In wealth of raven curls it flows behind.
> His circlet is the home of righteousness;
> May He not love His highest rapture less!

What's the image here? A virile young man with rich, thick dark hair! (*Mahl'fot*, the twined hair, is only used in the Bible to refer to Samson; see Judg. 16:13, 19). "The home of righteousness" is a term used in Jer. 31:22 to refer to Jerusalem. The author requests that God keep Jerusalem above all His beloved.

> And be His treasured people in His hand
> A diadem His kingly brow to band.
> By Him they were uplifted, carried, crowned,
> Thus honored inasmuch as precious found.

The "people in His hand" as a crown for God is a reference to Isa. 62:3, "You shall be a glorious crown in the hand of the Lord." As with much of the *Heikhalot* literature, this song is in many ways a coronation ceremony for God.

> His glory is on me, and mine on Him,
> And when I call He is not far or dim.
> Ruddy in red apparel, bright He glows
> When He from treading Edom's
>   winepress goes. *(From "Shir ha-Kavod")*

"Glory," *pe'er*, refers to tefillin; these crowns are the tefillin of God and Israel. Earlier in this chapter, a talmudic text pictures God as wearing tefillin. Here, as Ivan Marcus notes, "The poet imagines that God's tefillin box is worn on, and its straps wrapped around, the author's/Israel's head; reciprocally, the author/Israel's tefillin (or the crown made from his prayers) are worn on God's head."[23] "Ruddy in red" joins the two images of God as lover and warrior.[24] Songs 5:10 provides one part of the picture: "My beloved is clear-skinned and ruddy." Isa. 63:1–4 provides the flip side: "Who is this coming from Edom . . . why is Your clothing so red?" God answers, "I trod out a vintage alone . . . their life-blood bespattered My garments. . . . For I had planned a day of vengeance, and My year of redemption arrived." God as lover is clear skinned, but God as warrior is stained red with the blood of Edom. Edom, once code language among the Rabbis for Rome, now refers to the Christians. And the author believes that Isaiah's word is a promise to crush the Christians who oppressed our people in his time, just like the vintner stomping the grapes.

We find in this hymn a startling combination of images; a young, virile, masculine God is combined with the older traditions of the visible *Kavod*. As if in a medieval European fairy tale, the hero turns out to be a young prince, except that the prince also happens to be divine. In earlier sources, the divine is beautiful, but in the way that infinite light and angels might be beautiful; here, God is beautiful in human terms.[25] There did exist sacred and even erotic love poetry beyond that of Song of Songs (a book that only the Rabbis interpreted as referring to God), particularly in the work of the Spanish poets Solomon ibn Gabirol and Yehuda ha-Levi), and other such compositions occasionally crept into the liturgy, especially among the Hasidei Ashkenaz.[26] "Shir ha-Kavod" stands out as startlingly explicit in this regard, yet still maintains a place in traditional liturgy.

Another outstanding characteristic here is the role of the crown; we find many references to Israel not merely making or offering God a crown, but actually *being* the divine crown. That is a step up from the coronations previously noted, and the crown (and the role Israel plays in relation to it) will continue to be a significant symbol in the development of Kabbalah.

For the Hasidei Ashkenaz, prayer was formulated very precisely; they counted and calculated every word in the prayers, *berakhot*, and hymns, and they sought a reason in the Torah for the number of words in the prayers.

> **You inhabitants of France and the Islands of the Sea who err utterly and completely, for you invent lies and add several words in your prayers of which the early sages who formulated the prayers never dreamed. . . . Every blessing which they formulated is measured exactly in its number of words and letters, for if it were not so, our prayer would be like the song of the uncircumcised non-Jews. Therefore, give heed and repent, and do not go on doing this evil thing, adding and omitting letters and words from the prayers. (Pietist work, manuscript fragment)[27]**

Deviation from the inherited texts, even the prayer book, was seen as having harmful cosmic implications.[28] This would nullify the mystical correspondences between words and numerical patterns, which were only effective if you recited the exact words and the exact *number* of words in the prayers. For example, the prayer that (in Ashkenazic synagogues) today typically opens *Pesukei de-Zimra*, the preliminary section of hymns and psalms, is known as "Barukh She-amar," "Praised is He who spoke." This prayer contains eighty-seven words. In *gematria*, eighty-seven is equivalent to *peh-zayin*, which spells out the word *paz*, meaning "gold." Thus this text was considered "like gold," and not to be altered. The sage, if not the average pietist, would certainly include in his meditations reflections on the meaning of the number of words, as well as the meaning of the words themselves.[29] Here is a further example of the importance of the established liturgy:

Tik'u va-hodesh shofar, ba-keseh l'yom hageinu.
Kee hok l'Yisrael hoo, mishpat lEilohei Ya'akov.

("Blow the horn on the new moon, on the full moon for our feast day. For it is a law for Israel, a ruling of the God of Jacob." Ps. 81:4-5, a text which plays a significant role in the Rosh Hashanah liturgy.)

These verses have thirteen words, corresponding to the thirteen attributes [of mercy]. For the Holy One, Blessed be He, is filled with mercy through [the blowing of] the shofar on account of the merit of the thirteen letters in [the Hebrew names of] the patriarchs of the world [i.e., the Hebrew names of Abraham, Isaac, and Jacob total thirteen letters]. (Eleazar of Worms, from manuscript)[30]

The presumption is that the number of words has its own sanctity, over and above the fact that they happen to be located in Scripture. For Eleazar, thirteen was a number that signified God's grace.

How bad would it be to change such prayers? The answer comes from another section of the above text, which notes that some French Jews have tampered with the siddur, and so "they cause exile to themselves and their children until the end of all generations."

The Hasidei Ashkenaz were also strongly opposed to magical practice . . . most of the time.[31] But many traces of magic and superstition can be found in *Sefer Hasidim*.

The knowledge of God's Four-letter Name should be taught only to a scholar who will not make use of it.[32] But if the master thinks that utilizing the Name will be beneficial, then he should use it. However, he must be a wise man who is able to discern what is beneficial. He also should be willing to heed the advice of devout rabbis and not insist on having his way when they tell him that using the Name is not propitious. Furthermore, he should not use the powers inherent in the Name for self-promotion. (Yehudah he-Hasid, *Sefer Hasidim*, 471)

For several centuries *Sefer Hasidim* was an extremely popular work, geared to the average Jew, although it demonstrates great learning. Here it makes clear that certain kinds of mystical learning are only for an elite rank of sages, and only for what is generally beneficial and not for their own advantage. A good deal of material in *Sefer Hasidim* concerns what *should* be part of a person's Torah education;[33] this is about what should *not* be part of their curriculum.

> **A tree was found to have drops of wax on it. Sometimes it appeared as if candle drippings were trickling from it. One day, someone wanted to cut down that tree. Said the rabbi, "Be careful. You are risking your life, because Lilith convenes meetings on top of that tree. If you don't annoy a demon, it won't harm you. Also, make sure you don't leave any excrement there." (Yehudah he-Hasid, *Sefer Hasidim*, 462)**

Jewish tradition contains many stories about Lilith, a female demon who attacks newborn children and their mothers, and who causes nocturnal emissions.[34] She is later identified as Adam's first wife and eventually is seen as the female leader of the *sitra ahra*, the impure side of divine emanations. *Sefer Hasidim* is also very concerned with the dead who attempt to draw the living into their netherworld.[35]

Many of the beliefs and practices among the Hasidei Ashkenaz can be interpreted as "defense mechanisms" in a world where one is constantly on trial, but can also be seen as normal outgrowths of Jewish tradition. Those familiar with Kafka's story "The Trial" might compare it with the philosophy of the Hasidei Ashkenaz.

Most of what we have read so far is not Kabbalah, but it shares many of the same impulses as Kabbalah; some have referred to it as "proto-Kabbalah." The next chapter begins tracing the development of Kabbalah.[36]

Part 3

Basic Concepts in Kabbalah

8

The *Ein Sof*

THAT WHICH IS ENDLESS

Today Kabbalah is associated with celebrities, expensive seminars, and the broader spiritual quest. It is even seen as a shortcut to wisdom, largely disassociated from traditional Jewish life. But this is not new; at least some people have treated Kabbalah this way for a long time. The great sixteenth-century authority on Jewish law Rabbi Moses Isserles wrote of this phenomenon: "Many ordinary people run to study the subject of Kabbalah, for it is very desirable in their eyes.... Not only that the scholars should understand it, but even [ordinary] householders, who don't know their right from their left and walk in darkness, not even knowing how to explain the weekly Torah portion or a Torah passage with the commentary of Rashi, run to learn Kabbalah."[1] As it was then, so it is today; many Jews without even a basic knowledge of Jewish text seek the more advanced material, which they hope might give them guidance on critical issues.

But Kabbalah is rooted in normative Jewish religious practice; indeed, the word *kabbalah* literally means "received" and is often understood as "received tradition," that which was passed down from individual teacher to student. Beginning in chapter 3, we read that the sages regarded mystical teachings as material that should be limited to an elite group of students and that was potentially disorienting and even destructive to those who were not deeply rooted in Jewish practice or sufficiently mature to deal with its ideas. So it may be surprising to find that for many centuries Kabbalah was a central force in Jewish life and thinking.

Beginning in the thirteenth century, virtually every rabbi and many other learned Jews knew of Kabbalah. However, it was not the *base* of Jewish life; that remained the daily performance of the mitzvot. Kabbalah became a higher platform, a way to provide enhanced meaning to one's spiritual life. Thus it is difficult to imagine authentic Kabbalah outside a traditional Jewish framework, and many have warned of the consequences of detaching it from its roots. As Byron Sherwin put it, "Without Judaism, Jewish mysticism is a soul without a body, a vagabond spirit. Without mysticism, Judaism is a body without a soul."[2]

Most Jews growing up in the twentieth century were taught little, if anything, about the Kabbalah. There are two primary reasons for this. One was that most Jews knew little about Judaism, and therefore lacked the base on which to build an appreciation of Kabbalah. The other was the prevailing bias against all forms of Jewish mysticism, which is addressed in chapter 28.

Normative Jewish religious practice seeks to follow God's will as understood through the Torah and through the sages who have interpreted it. The mystic seeks not only to follow God, but to have communion with God, thereby acquiring a deeper understanding of the divine. Thus one sees more of what God sees and knows more of what God knows. Traditional Jewish practice is clearly consistent with this desire; for instance, in the "Kedushah" prayer recited daily, Jews quote the verse in Isaiah 6 that tells us *m'lo khol ha-aretz k'vodo*, the whole earth is filled with God's glory, with God's Presence. The point of such recitation is that one must be open to experiencing that Presence. Abraham Joshua Heschel (see chapter 27) wrote of our tradition's "legacy of wonder," saying: "The surest way to suppress our ability to understand the meaning of God and the importance of worship is *to take things for granted*. Indifference to the sublime wonder of living is the root of sin."[3]

The third of the three main types of Jewish mysticism, what I call Mainline Kabbalah, is an attempt to understand the mind and plan as well as the will of God, in a way that would not be dangerous for the mystic.

This assumes that God *has* such an inner life and that our existence ought to seek this life, take it into account, and assist God in the fulfillment of His purposes through our mindful actions and our meditational life. This may well seem to be a herculean task, and it is by no means simple. Several chapters are devoted here just to introducing some of the basic concepts of Mainline Kabbalah.

Falling under the rubric of "Kabbalah" are five periods and styles, although they often differ significantly and have their own goals and priorities:

1. Twelfth- through thirteenth-century Spain, including schools in Gerona and Provence
2. Beginning in late thirteenth-century Spain, the spread of the Zohar, the major work of Mainline Kabbalah
3. Thirteenth-century Spain, the school of Abraham Abulafia, which taught what became known as Prophetic Kabbalah (see chapter 12)
4. Sixteenth century, emanating from the city of Safed in the Land of Israel, the extremely complex and elaborate system known as Lurianic Kabbalah (see chapter 16)
5. From the eighteenth century to the present, the teaching of a more philosophical but less elaborate system of Kabbalah through the Hasidic movement (see chapters 23 through 26)

Although we have seen other forms of Jewish mysticism, these are the ones considered to be part of what is known as "Kabbalah." This book's approach to the most basic concepts of Kabbalah will cut across some of these periods so that you can see how they developed and affected Jewish mystical thinking.

The first of these concepts is the *Ein Sof*. Literally, *Ein Sof* means "without end" or "infinite."[4] It is not a name, but points to God's nature, in that *Ein Sof* represents the most hidden essence—the most *true* essence—of God, the transcendent aspect of God that is entirely unknowable to humans. In Kabbalah God can only be known through His emanations, the ten *sefirot*, those ten creative forces that mediate between the *Ein Sof* and our world (see chapter 9).[5]

In the Middle Ages God was frequently described as having two primary aspects, one concealed and one revealed. In this view, the real essence of God is the hidden part, and *Ein Sof* is the Jewish understanding of the concealed God who is hidden and limitless. Jews who followed a more philosophical approach to Jewish faith believed this was the *only* way to understand God. For Maimonides God was simply unknowable, and humans speaking of God could only say what He is not, but not what He is. "Know that when you make an affirmation ascribing another thing to Him, you become more remote from Him in two respects: one of them is that everything you affirm is a perfection only with reference to us, and the other is that He does not possess a thing other than His essence."[6] God is infinitely beyond anything we can say about Him or any relationship we might have with Him. For the mystics, however, this is only part of the story . . . but it is the *beginning* of the story without which everything else would be impossible.

In some respects the kabbalists go even further by describing God as *Ayin* (another form of the word *Ein*), literally, "Nothingness," that which is no thing. *Ayin* is the opposite of *Yesh*, the material, temporal world within which everything can be quantified, defined, or explained.[7] Everything material has a beginning and an end. By contrast, *Ayin* is that which is *not* material. This does not mean that it has no being, only that certain things cannot be described, defined, or bounded—those that have no beginning or end and those that we cannot change or affect. Similarly, some try to describe God's reality through the metaphor of the ocean: *Ayin* is the ocean, and *Yesh* is the waves that occasionally pop up out of the underlying unity of all being.[8]

Everything is from *Ein Sof*; nothing exists outside it.

One should avoid fashioning metaphors regarding *Ein Sof*, but in order to help you understand, you can compare *Ein Sof* to a candle

from which hundreds of millions of other candles are kindled. Though some shine brighter than others, compared to the first light they are all the same, all deriving from that one source. The first light and all the others are, in effect, incomparable. Nor can their priority compare with its priority, for it surpasses them; their energy emanates from it. No change takes place in it; the energy of emanation simply manifests through differentiation. (Azriel of Gerona, *Commentary on the Ten Sefirot*)[9]

At the level of *Ein Sof*, there is no change, no development, only infinite energy. The metaphor of a candle is necessarily inexact, for a candle eventually burns out—which can never happen with the *Ein Sof*. It is only with the image of candles lit from the "ultimate" candle that we can grasp something of their nature, and even this cannot really help us understand the *Ein Sof*, for it cannot be compared to the *sefirot*, the emanations.

How do we know of this *Ein Sof*, if it is by definition unknowable?
Know that the *Ein Sof* that we have mentioned is not referred to in the Torah, the Prophets, or the Writings, or in the words of the rabbis, but the masters of worship [i.e., the kabbalists] have received a little hint [*remez*] of It. (*Ma'arekhet ha-Elohut*, 82b)[10]

The God we encounter in the narratives or revelations within Scripture is *not* the *Ein Sof*, because the *Ein Sof* is transcendent, beyond our knowledge. What the Bible tells us about God is about His actions; it only hints at God's Self, although it does allude to God's concealment. In Exodus 3, when Moses asks God to tell him His Name, God responds by saying: "*Ehyeh Asher Ehyeh*," "I will be what I will be." God may be telling Moses: I have no bounds, no limits, not even a Name with which you can pin Me down. For the kabbalists perhaps *Ein Sof*—the infinite, the endless—is the closest possible, most legitimate Name for God. So how do we begin to describe the indescribable?

"See now that I, even I, am He, and there is no god with Me" (Deut. 32:39).[11] What is the significance of this verse? This is the cause over and above all the highest things. That which is called the "cause of causes" is the cause of [known] causes, for not one of these causes performs any act without obtaining permission from the cause that is above it, as I have explained earlier. (Zohar 1:22b, *Tikkunei ha-Zohar*)[12]

One of the philosophical terms used to describe God was "cause of causes." Indeed this was one of the earliest "proofs" for God's existence: there must be some cause of human existence, and a cause of *that* cause, and the first cause of all those causes is what we call "God." The statement made here is that anything we can call the "cause of causes" is not the ultimate, inexpressible cause. Thus, what we call the "cause of causes" must refer to the highest of the *sefirot*, but the *Ein Sof* lies still beyond that. Perhaps the verse cited here is one of the "hints" (noted in the above text from *Ma'arekhet ha-Elohut*) that the kabbalists believed they had received about the existence of the *Ein Sof*. Kabbalists often used such philosophical language about God, particularly when describing the *Ein Sof*.[13] But as the next text makes clear, no language can be adequate for the Infinite, though the *sefirot* are tools that may give us a glimpse of understanding.

He understands all, but there is none that understands Him. He is not called by the Name *Yud, Heh, Vav, Heh*, nor by any other name, except when His light extends itself upon them. And when He removes Himself from them, He has no name of His own at all.

"That which is exceedingly deep, who can find it?" (Eccles. 7:24). No light can look upon Him without becoming dark. Even the supernal *Keter*, whose light is the strongest of all the levels, and of all the hosts of Heaven, both the upper and the lower realms, is alluded to in the verse, "He made darkness His hiding-place" (Ps. 18:12), while of *Hokhmah* and *Binah* it is said, "Clouds and thick darkness surround

Him" (Ps. 97:2). This is even truer of the remaining *sefirot* (Zohar 3:225a, *Ra'aya Meheimna*)[14]

Even the Ineffable Four-Letter Name of God is not an adequate name, unless the light of the *Ein Sof* is extended to it. Later on we will see that different *sefirot* are associated with different Names of God, so that when *Ein Sof* "shines" on those *sefirot*, those Names can be used meaningfully.

This text makes reference to the first three of the *sefirot*: *Keter* (Crown), *Hokhmah* (Wisdom), and *Binah* (Understanding). For the time being I will not try to explain these individual *sefirot*, except to note the difference expressed here between them: *Keter* is the first "hiding-place" of the *Ein Sof*, the highest level of darkness, while the next two *sefirot* are concealed in "clouds and thick darkness." It should also be noted that even though these texts often stress the unity of the *Ein Sof* with the *sefirot*, the transition from *Ein Sof* to *Keter* is of tremendous importance.[15]

Zohar means "radiance." The Zohar is by far the most important and widely read kabbalistic book. It is partly narrative, partly commentary on the Torah, and partly a work of great imagination. The sages depicted within it—particularly the famous talmudic figure Rabbi Shimon bar Yohai—live in the second century CE, and the Zohar is set in the context of his wanderings with his circle of disciples, who seem to seek not simply the presence of God but a deep understanding of God. Within traditional Judaism a good deal of the Zohar's authority stemmed from the authority of Rabbi Shimon and his colleagues.[16] However, this work was only made public in Spain at about the end of the thirteenth century, and modern scholarship assumes it was authored around that time. Although for some years scholarly circles accepted that the Zohar was written by Moses de Leon, more recently it has been suggested that De Leon may have been only one member of a group of kabbalists—but possibly the editor—who wove together this vast text.[17] As we progress, we will learn more about the Zohar and its important role in Jewish life.

In our prayers, do we actually connect with the *Ein Sof*? This next text from the Zohar relates to this question in connection with the sacrifices in the Temple, for which prayer became a substitute in normative Jewish practice.

> **Rabbi Eleazar asked Rabbi Shimon: We know that the whole offering is connected to the Holy of Holies so that it may be illuminated. To what heights does the attachment of the will [to God] of the *Kohen*, the Levites, and Israel extend? He said: We have already taught that it extends to *Ein Sof*, for all attachment, unification, and completion is to be enclosed in that secret which is not perceived or known, containing the will of all wills. *Ein Sof* cannot be known, and does not produce end or beginning like the primal *Ayin* [nothing], which does bring forth beginning and end. What is beginning? The supernal point, which is the beginning of all, concealed and resting within thought. . . . But there are no end, no wills, no lights, no luminaries in *Ein Sof*. All these lights and luminaries depend on It for their existence, but they are not in a position to perceive It. That which knows, but does not know, is none but the Supernal Will, the secret of all secrets, *Ayin*. (Zohar 2:239a)[18]**

Much of the Zohar is written in code language and cannot be understood fully without a few hints. Here, for instance, the "whole offering" and the "Holy of Holies," in what seems to be a discussion of matters pertaining to the Temple, actually refer to two of the ten *sefirot*. The "whole offering" is an allusion to *Malkhut* or *Shekhinah*, the lowest of the ten *sefirot*, while the "Holy of Holies" refers to *Binah*, the third *sefirah*. This in turn suggests the connection of the lower and higher levels of the *sefirot*.[19] Also, the "primal *Ayin*" refers to *Keter*, the highest of the *sefirot*; unlike the *Ein Sof*, it *does* have a beginning and, at least potentially, an end.[20] The "supernal point" here refers to the second of the *sefirot*, *Hokhmah*, seen as the beginning of all because of Scripture's use of the phrase *reishit hokhmah* in Ps. 111:10 and Prov. 4:7. It is generally translated as "the beginning of wisdom is" but the kabbalist reader sees it as "the beginning is wisdom."

"Attachment of the will" is a way of saying that the individual bringing this offering links himself to God through his intention, through what nonkabbalists and kabbalists alike called *kavanah*. Just as Jews are supposed to pray with direction, willfulness, and mindfulness, so the offerings in the Temple were to be brought with an appropriate mental sense of purpose. The question asked in the text is, in the kabbalistic scheme, how far does a person's *kavanah* reach when he fulfills this mitzvah? Does it only reach the level of one or another of the *sefirot*? The answer given here is that even though we have no apprehension of the *Ein Sof*, appropriate *kavanah* ascends "all the way." It goes to the "will of all wills," the *Ein Sof*.

What else are we told about the *Ein Sof*? It "does not produce end or beginning," it is boundless, beyond time and space. This notion of God is consistent with all of Rabbinic Judaism; it is attested, for example, in the words of the hymn "Adon Olam" (part of our liturgy for almost a thousand years) declaring that God is *b'li reishit, b'li takhlit*, "without beginning, without end." Only when one goes to the level of the *sefirot* is there some perception of a manifestation of God available to us. Within *Ein Sof* there are "no luminaries," nothing that could suggest any form of separation. Any such separation takes place within the *sefirot*, which are supported from *Ein Sof*.

We are taught from childhood that God is *one*. But what does this actually mean for the kabbalist? If there are *sefirot* and *Ein Sof*, how do they coexist with the notion of God's Oneness?

> **Do not attribute duality to God. Let God be solely God. If you suppose that *Ein Sof* emanates until a certain point, and that from that point on is outside of it, you have dualized. God forbid! Realize, rather, that *Ein Sof* exists in each existent. Do not say: "This is a stone and not God." God forbid! Rather, all existence is God, and the stone is a thing pervaded by Divinity. (Moshe Cordovero, *Shiur Komah*, 206b)[21]**

Cordovero (sixteenth-century Safed), one of the most erudite and prolific writers in the Jewish mystical tradition, answers that God pervades everything: every person, every object, even a stone! The *Ein Sof* dwells within every aspect of the universe.[22]

What happens when we try to conceive of God in some tangible fashion?

When your intellect conceives of God . . . do not permit yourself to imagine that there is a God as depicted by you. For if you do this, you will have a finite and corporeal conception of God, God forbid. Instead, your mind should dwell only on the affirmation of God's existence, and then recoil. To do more than this is to allow the imagination to reflect on God as God is in Himself and such reflection is bound to result in imaginative limitations and corporeality. Put reins therefore on your intellect and do not allow it too great a freedom, but assert God's existence and deny your intellect the possibility of comprehending God. (Cordovero, *Elimah Rabbati*, 4b)[23]

It may be natural to try to "imagine" God. Cordovero teaches that one must resist this, because it will lead to erroneous thinking about God, making the *Ein Sof* into something limited by our own limited ability to perceive God. All we should do is to "assert God's existence," and go no further.

Isaiah Horowitz gives a basis for a particular understanding of the Infinite God that may startle many readers familiar with the source:

True and absolute faith states: "In heaven above and on the earth below, there is no other [*ein od*]" (Deut. 4:39). The meaning of this verse is not as some have said, that there is no other God than He. This much we already knew from "[Hear O Israel,] The Lord is God, the Lord is One" (Deut. 6:4)! Rather, the meaning is that there is nothing else in the world besides His Divinity. To clarify: there is nothing in the world of any kind, which has vitality, power, and movement,

even inorganic matter, which has not been emanated from Him, in accord with the verse: "You give life to all of them" (Neh. 9:6). (Isaiah Horowitz, *Shnei Luhot ha-Brit, Toldot Adam, Beit ha-Behirah*, sec. 4)

Deuteronomy 4:39 is included in the "Aleinu," part of every daily service. On the face of it, the phrase *ein od* seems to be saying that there is one God and no other. But Shelah (an acronym for this work by which Horowitz was widely known) reminds us that the Torah contains this idea elsewhere. Like other traditional rabbis, he looks for unique meaning in every part of the Torah, and in the process translates the phrase to mean: "There is nothing else." In other words, *everything* is God, or at least everything contains the *Ein Sof*, the transcendent God.

This notion also found a home among many of the Hasidic masters. Here are two examples:

[Those who seek to approach God,] who would cleave to Him in thought because of their love of Him, and linking themselves to Him with cleaving, longing and desire, likening themselves to *Ayin*, understand that were it not for the power of the Creator who continuously creates and sustains them, they would be nothing, just as they were before the creation. For indeed, there is nothing in the world except for God. (Meshullam Feivush Heller of Zbarasz, *Yosher Divrei Emet*, sec. 14)[24]

In chapter 1 we read that *deveikut*, "cleaving" to God, is a major theme in Jewish mysticism. If God is so transcendent, how can one hope to cleave to Him? The author stresses that it is important to understand that the Creator "continually creates and sustains" us. Seeking *deveikut*, seeking some form of union with God, means to approach and liken oneself to the *Ayin*, the divine nothingness. And if you think of yourself as being created by God right now, you are more able to drift into this sense of nothingness. After all, if you might not wake up tomorrow, you are transitory and thus less important than you are generally inclined to believe. By contrast, if you think of yourself as nothing within the greatness that is God, you are (as the text later puts it) like the branch of a tree that is part of a unity with the root. And the root, of course, is the *Ein Sof.* Thus, paradoxically, one arrives at a form of greatness through mentally attaching oneself to that tree.[25]

> I may not be able to see it right now, but the Holy One is the source of all reality. Being is made of God, you and I, everything is made of God—even the grains of sand beneath my feet—the whole world is utterly comprised of, and dependent upon God. I, while stubbornly insisting on my own autonomy and independence, only succeed in banishing myself from any sense of the presence of God. (Kalonymous Kalman Shapira, *B'nei Mahshavah Tovah*)[26]

Rabbi Shapira (1889-1943), the Piesetzner Rebbe, murdered by the Nazis, was one of the most formidable Hasidic thinkers of the twentieth century (see chapter 27 for more on his writings). Here he offers his students a prescription regarding how to think about themselves and God, and thereby maintain *deveikut*. It is when we assume we are independent of God that we lose the connection with God. True awareness involves the immersion of the self in the Greater Being.

Rabbi Lawrence Kushner, who has written much popular material on Jewish mysticism, offers an excellent metaphor for the *Ein Sof*.

> God—that is, the Oneness in which all being is dissolved and from which being continuously emerges—is called, in Hebrew, *Ein Sof,* literally the One "without end." This is much more than simply the arithmetic concept of infinity. *Ein Sof* is neither numeric nor mathematical. It means, instead, without boundary, without definition, without any characteristics whatsoever. Indeed, to say anything about it at all violates the essential notion of the term. *Ein Sof* is the font, the source, the matrix, the substrate, the motherlode of being. It may also be being itself. It is to being what electricity is to the letters

and words on a video computer monitor. And, as anyone who has not conscientiously backed up his or her work knows, turn off the power and the letters and words are as if they had never been. For kabbalists, therefore, creation is not some event that happened in the past but a continuous and ever-present process. When we express our gratitude for the world, it is because it has literally been created anew each day, each moment. (Kushner, "What Is Kabbalah")[27]

If the source of the power is interrupted, everything dependent on it disappears. For us, it would be as if all the oxygen were suddenly sucked out of the atmosphere. We give thanks because the *Ein Sof* continues to sustain us. Kushner also reaffirms an important lesson we have already seen about the *Ein Sof*: It defies definition or description.

If God is to be understood as either transcendent—totally separate from humankind—or immanent—near and involved with His creation—the idea of the *Ein Sof* revolves completely around the transcendent view. But in Kabbalah that is not the full story, because the mystic longs to know what aspects of God we *can* comprehend to some degree. This leads us into the next chapter, dealing specifically with the *sefirot*.

9

The *Sefirot*

PERCEIVING GOD

How can we bridge the gap between humans and God? In Mainline Kabbalah this is done through knowledge of God: that is, through understanding God's "extensions," the *sefirot*. The mystic's task is to penetrate to and participate in God's inner life through mindful concentration while performing the mitzvot, particularly through meditation and prayer. Mainline Kabbalah also deals with the mystic's beneficent involvement in God's inner life, in order to accomplish goals on that level. In other words, we affect God's inner life by what we do. As we have seen, this cannot be done with the *Ein Sof*. But what we do in this world *does* make a difference because the *sefirot* are designed to make this possible, to make God accessible to us. "Access" is a useful term here, as many of the symbols in Kabbalah as well as the *sefirot* themselves function as access codes, providing entry for relationship with God.

In Kabbalah, *sefirot* are not understood as they were in *Sefer Yetzirah*. They are more than simply emanations flowing from the *Ein Sof*; they represent ways in which God reveals His hidden Being to us to some degree and allows us to be involved with Him. The *sefirot* do not teach us anything about the *Ein Sof*; rather, they allow us to experience aspects of God that are directed toward us. As we will soon see, different theories exist about what exactly these aspects of God, or *sefirot*, are. Kabbalah shares with many other Western mystical systems the assumption of a flow of energy directed from God into the world; however, in distinction to certain philosophical schools, it views emanation as a process taking part *within God*.

The most obvious objection to the idea of the *sefirot* is the "monotheistic" issue: if God is one, how can there be ten different *sefirot*? To this we might respond: each of you is one person, one unity. But you have many different aspects and concerns. God—being God—has the capacity to incorporate different qualities and show different manifestations, often described in many ways and with many symbols, while still essentially remaining one unified God.[1]

Although many Christians understand God through the three aspects represented by the Trinity, perhaps suggesting a Christian influence on the idea of the *sefirot*, the idea of God manifesting His characteristics to us and, in so doing, making it possible for us to love Him and to feel love for Him directly is strongly rooted in both the Hebrew Bible and the Rabbinic tradition. Ultimately, every religion must provide a means to close the gap between God and humanity. In the Bible it is the faith of the prophets through which God's pathos reaches through the gap and addresses us directly.[2]

In the following midrashic teaching the sages make clear that God's power depends on human beings, and the Zohar text makes this even more explicit:

> **"So you are My witnesses, declares the Lord, and I am God"** (Isa. 43:12). **When you are My witnesses, I am God. And when you are not My witnesses, I am not God** (*Sifrei*, Ve-zo't ha-berakhah, 5).

> **Why is it written *Va'asitem otam* ["You shall do them," i.e., the commandments, Lev. 26:3, after it is written, "If you walk in My statutes and keep My commandments"]? He who fulfills the mitzvot of the Torah and walks in His paths creates Him, as it were, above. The Holy One, blessed be He, says: It is as if he made Me!** (Zohar 3:113a).[3]

Without our witness, it is as if God is not God. We actually make God, God. Thus it might also be said that God needs us in order to fulfill His role.[4] Based on two points regarding the Hebrew of the Torah verse—that the verb *asah* as used in the Bible can mean both "do" and "make," and that *otam* and *atem*, "them" and "you," are composed of the same letters[5]—the Zohar interprets the biblical verse to say that human beings create divine forces. In the kabbalistic view, by supporting the complex of *sefirot*, it is as if humans "create" God. The task of the mystic is to operate within the *sefirot* in such a way as to strengthen God, to affect these higher levels in positive ways. This does not lessen the importance of the individual; on the contrary, it offers a powerful view of human purpose and responsibility, if our task is not to help ourselves but to help God. We do receive incidental benefits, of course: divine power flows through the cosmos and provides vitality throughout. But we are here to support God's purposes, rather than the other way around.

This raises serious questions about individual prayer: When we pray, can we truly pray for individual needs, whether they are needs of others or our own? This, after all, is a significant part of prayer, but what does it have to do with "strengthening God"? The kabbalistic answer is that we *do* have petitionary prayer, but at the deepest level those needs for which we pray are not simply our own—they are also needs of God. We will see how this works and examine this idea in more detail in chapter 11.

While no visual can really describe the functions of the *sefirot*, a diagram can clarify each one's nature and their relationships to one another. Diagrams of the *sefirot*, such as the one here, commonly take the form of the human body, for, as Lawrence Fine has put it, "among the various symbolic patterns by which the *sefirot* are imagined, none is more central to Kabbalah nor more radical in its implications than the symbolism of divine Body."[6] In Jewish mysticism everything below mirrors something above; as the Zohar teaches: "This world is patterned on the world above."[7] So although this often seems an extremely radical concept, the human being, created in God's "image," also mirrors the divine.[8]

In advance of the next, detailed text, here is some very basic information about each of the *sefirot*:[9]

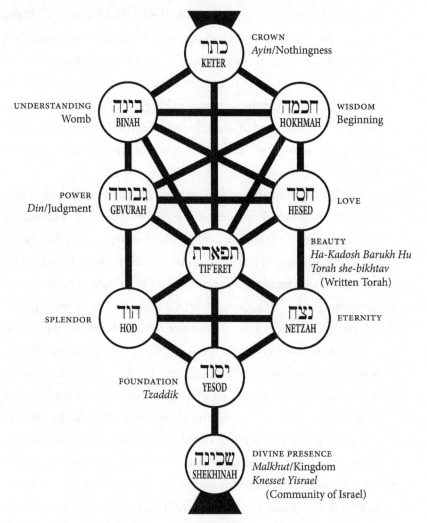

Fig. 1. The ten *sefirot*. Courtesy of Malka Levy.

1. *Keter*, "Crown," is so called not only because it is the highest of the *sefirot* but also because it is sometimes represented in the form of a body with a crown on top. The fact that it is above the head also alludes to that which is incomprehensible; for this reason it is sometimes referred to as *Ayin*, "Nothingness."[10]

2. *Hokhmah*, "Wisdom" is the stage where God's intellectual attributes begin to unfold. It is the main force in the creative process,

in accord with Ps. 104:24: "You made them all with wisdom." Many of the *sefirot* are loosely associated with male or female qualities; *Hokhmah* is masculine, providing the seed for the *sefirot* below it.

3. *Binah*, "Understanding" (including intuitive knowledge), takes the untreated wisdom, refining it and making it useful in specific ways. *Binah* is feminine and often referred to as the "womb" that gives birth to the *sefirot* below, those that are most affected by human actions.[11]

4. *Hesed*, "Love," considered a masculine realm in Kabbalah, is also identified with Abraham, one of the key biblical models of loving-kindness. The first three *sefirot* are more abstract, intellectual; *Hesed* begins the process of bringing about specific actions. *Hesed* is also associated with *middat ha-rahamim*, God's attribute of compassion.

5. *Gevurah*, "Power" (frequently referred to as *Din*, "Judgment"), considered a feminine realm, is identified with Isaac, perhaps because it requires power to restrain one's emotions, and Isaac was able to restrain himself when bound on the altar as a sacrifice. *Gevurah* is associated with *middat ha-din*, God's attribute of justice, and so at times is used to suggest the necessity of boundaries and the acceptance of responsibility. *Hesed* and *Gevurah* must be carefully balanced, as will be seen and discussed in the texts below.[12]

6. *Tiferet*, "Glory" or "Beauty," mediates the two *sefirot* above. It unifies these two qualities to maximize their potential. It is generally considered a masculine quality (with exceptions) and associated with Jacob, who is seen as the synthesis of his father and grandfather. It is also often associated with the Written Torah.[13]

7. *Netzah*, "Eternity" or "Victory," begins the level where some of the above qualities are put into practice.

8. *Hod*, "Splendor," is often portrayed with *Netzah* as the legs of the body formed by the *sefirot*, because the legs take us wherever we must go to carry out our actions. *Hod* and *Netzah* draw on the *sefirot* immediately above them; *Netzah* represents God as compassionate

King, while *Hod* is the powerful King. *Netzah* and *Hod* are also considered to be the source of prophecy and thus are associated with Moses and Aaron.

9. *Yesod*, "Foundation," is sometimes called *Tzaddik*, "Righteous," because *Tzaddik yesod olam*, "the righteous is the foundation of the world" (Prov. 10:25). *Yesod* is linked to Joseph, who is referred to as the righteous one in Rabbinic tradition; *Yesod* is associated with the sexual organ, and Joseph was one who withstood sexual temptation (see Genesis 39). This is a natural association because, in a sense, it is *Yesod* that bestows the "seed" from above to the last *sefirah*, and through it to the entire world.[14]

10. *Malkhut*, "Kingship," is often referred to as *Shekhinah*, the divine dwelling place; at this level, it is the most accessible connection to God, our link to the realm of the *sefirot*. Nonetheless, as part of God it still cannot be known fully. It is associated with the Oral Torah, i.e., the oral traditions derived from the Written Torah. Most significantly, it is understood to be feminine and must link with *Tiferet* in order for the *sefirotic* system to function properly. Their separation is also compared to the exile of the Jewish people from its home.[15] Congruent to this idea, the unification of *Malkhut* and *Tiferet* is understood to be a restoration of their proper relationship.[16] This is a good example of how, as Harold Bloom has suggested, "the *sefirot* are neither things nor acts, but rather are relational events, and so are persuasive representations of what ordinary people encounter as the inner reality of their lives."[17] Finally, because it is a "portal" between two worlds, it is associated with the Land of Israel, fundamentally holy and yet earthbound.[18] This also ties into the suggestion, based on Exod. 6:4, that it is because the Jews practice circumcision that they are worthy of the land; being associated with *Yesod*, representing the holy circumcised organ, enables them to possess the Holy Land, the realm of *Malkhut*.[19]

How do we humans relate to the *sefirot*? The analogy of "bumper cars" has been suggested;[20] we have invisible lines through which we relate to the *sefirot*, and our actions "bump" into other forces in the heavens. The bumper car is also reactive, moved by other forces. So are we, and therefore so are the supernal forces, that is, the *sefirot*.

As noted, the hero of much of the Zoharic literature is Rabbi Shimon bar Yohai. In this text, Rabbi Shimon and his colleagues are visiting the heavenly academy and are instructed by the Prophet Elijah himself.

> **Elijah opened his teaching this way: Master of Worlds, You are One but are not numbered. You are higher than the highest, hidden within all secrets, utterly incomprehensible!**
>
> **You generated ten perfections [*tikkunim*], which we call the ten *sefirot*. Through them You govern secret worlds, which are not revealed, and revealed worlds. In them, You are concealed from human beings, but You are the one who binds and unites them. Since You are within them, whoever separates one of these ten from the others, it is as if he divided You. (*Tikkunei ha-Zohar* 17a–b)[21]**

As we saw earlier, the *Ein Sof* is "one but not in number," for "in number" would imply the existence of a series of numbers. The anonymous kabbalist who authored this text consistently denies any attributes to the *Ein Sof* apart from the *Ein Sof*'s essence. *Tikkunim* here refers to the *sefirot* and their role as seen from on high—sources of perfection emanated from above to the lower realms. (More generally in Kabbalah this important term, *tikkun*, addressed in chapter 16, literally means "repair"; in the Zohar, and more intensely in Lurianic Kabbalah, the mystic takes responsibility in all his actions and meditations to repair flaws, not only within himself but within the supernal world as well.) *Ein Sof* reveals Itself, stage by stage, through the *sefirot*. Without them, we could not even apprehend a reflection of It. But the *Ein Sof* is also concealed by them; they are like garments that guard us from an impossible, unbearable encounter with infinite power.[22]

The ten *sefirot* are one unified system containing the light of the *Ein Sof*. While the text here speaks of the *sefirot* as if they were independent of the *Ein Sof*, it cautions that this is not so.

These ten *sefirot* flow forth in order: one long, one short, one in between. You are the One who guides them. But no one guides You, not from above, not from below, nor in any direction. You have prepared garments for them from which souls fly to human beings. And You have prepared various bodies for them; they are called bodies but only in contrast to the garments covering them.[23]

These bodies are named according to this arrangement: *Hesed* is the right arm; *Gevurah* is the left arm. *Tiferet* is the trunk of the body. *Netzah* and *Hod* are the two legs. *Yesod*, the completion of the body, is the sign of the holy covenant; *Malkhut* is the mouth, which we call the Oral Torah. *Hokhmah* is the brain, inner thought; *Binah* is the heart, of which it is said: "The heart understands."[24] Concerning these two, it is written: "The concealed things belong to the Lord our God" (Deut. 29:28). The supernal *Keter* is the crown of royalty [*Keter Malkhut*], of which it is said: "It declares the end from the beginning" (Isa. 46:10). It is the headpiece of the tefillin, within which are the letters of the ineffable Name of God: *Yud, Heh, Vav, Heh*,[25] which is the path of emanation, the sap of the [cosmic] tree, spreading through its arms and branches, like water drenching a tree, which then flourishes. (*Tikkunei ha-Zohar* 17a-b, continued)

There are ten *sefirot*, but this refers to three: one on each side of the picture and one mediating between them. These signify *Hesed*, *Gevurah*, and *Tiferet*. On the visual map of the *sefirot*, note several such "triangles," and three columns ordering the *sefirot*.[26] This "arrangement" speaks in terms of the structure of the human body, providing a way of understanding the *sefirot*. The holy covenant referred to in connection with *Yesod* is the covenant of circumcision. *Malkhut* represents speech, alluding to the Oral Torah, in contrast to *Tiferet* and the Written Torah. The "mouth" may also be a euphemism for the female sexual organ, which receives seed from the man's organ (i.e., *Yesod*), representing the process of divine influence.[27] *Lev meiveen*, "the heart understands," draws on the direct relationship between the words *meiveen* and *Binah*, which derive from the same root.[28] Note that the text alludes to the contrast between intellect in *Hokhmah* and more intuitive wisdom in *Binah*. But in such abstract form both are part of the "concealed things," not apprehensible to us.

Keter is the "crown of royalty," but *Malkhut*, royalty, is the last of the *sefirot*. Thus both are connected, unifying the entire *sefirotic* system. The verse "It declares the end from the beginning" also tells us that everything, the whole pattern of creation including all the *sefirot*, is planned from the beginning. *Keter* is also represented as the strap of the headpiece that surrounds the brain, *Hokhmah*. The letters of God's Ineffable Name—*Yud-Heh-Vav-Heh*—are at the root of *Keter*. Furthermore, when each of these four letters is spelled out in full (that is, *Yud* equals *Yud-vav-dalet*, *Heh* equals *Heh-alef*, *Vav* equals *Vav-alef-vav*, and *Heh* again), as they are in the Hebrew version of this text, they contain ten letters altogether, signifying the ten *sefirot* emanated from the *Ein Sof*.

Finally, the "sap of the tree" alludes to *Keter*, which is sometimes called "the root of roots." Its energy "waters" the rest of the tree. *Tiferet* is also frequently referred to as "the tree," with its arms and branches representing the lower *sefirot*, so this segment can be seen both as a general statement about the flow of support from *Keter* to all the *sefirot* and as a specific point about its support of *Tiferet*, one of the "central lines" in the scheme. As Louis Jacobs notes, "The Zohar is trying here to grapple with the great mystery of how God's creativity begins, how, as it were, the first impulse to create (from which all else ultimately follows) has its origin."[29]

We learn here two primary lessons about the world of the *sefirot*. First, they are a unity reflecting the dynamic content of God's life. Second, each one is separate and a world of its own, and as such relates to each of the others.

What do we really mean when we refer to the *sefirot*; how "real" are they? There are at least four different conceptions of how kabbalists have understood the *sefirot*:[30]

1. The *essentialist* view: The *sefirot* are actually divine powers, part of the divine essence.

2. The *instrumentalist* view: The *sefirot* are not actually divine, but serve as instruments, vessels for God through which He creates and maintains existence. Thus they are seen as God's actions, rather than God Himself.

3. The *panentheistic* view: The *sefirot* are the way to experience God within the world; they are the paths through which God's sustenance flows to the world. In panentheism, God is found in everything and everything is contained in God; similarly, here, God is within the *sefirot*, the *sefirot* are within God.

4. The *human* view: The *sefirot* represent human qualities or psychological processes.[31] We are a microcosm of the supernal world. We are created in God's image, made of the same attributes as God, sharing in His characteristics; thus we can contemplate the possibility of mystical union with God.

Most significantly, all these views resist the notion of making the *sefirot* mere symbols.[32]

The *Yud* of the Holy Name is tied with three knots. Therefore this *Yud* has one point above, one point below, and one in the middle, since there are three knots tied in it. One point is above, supernal *Keter*, the highest of the high, the head of all heads, and it stands above all. One point is in the middle, and this is another head, since there are three heads and each one of them is a head in its own right; and so the middle point is another head emerging from the point above, and it is head of all the other heads in the construction of the Holy Name, and this head is concealed from all. Another head is below, the head that

waters the garden, a spring of water, from which all the plants quench their thirst. This is the *Yud* with three knots. It is therefore called a "chain," like a chain that is interlinked, and all is one. (Zohar 3:10b)[33]

The Holy Name, of course, is the most sacred Four-Letter Name of God. The three knots are the first three of the *sefirot*, *Keter*, *Hokhmah*, and *Binah*. *Binah* is the *sefirah* that "waters the garden," providing sustenance to all the "plants," that is, the lower *sefirot*. And they are firmly linked so that the *sefirot* are unified. The *sefirot* are also associated with different Names of God and with the letters of the Four-Letter Name. *Keter* is beyond association with any of those letters, but is symbolized by the "point above," the very tip of the *Yud*.

Our next two texts address the question: how do the *sefirot* come into being?

> "In the beginning" (Gen. 1:1)—At the head of potency, the King made engravings in luster on high. A spark of impenetrable darkness flashed within the concealed of the concealed, from the head of *Ein Sof*, a cluster of vapor forming in formlessness, thrust in a ring, not white, not black, not red, not green, no color at all. As a cord surveyed, it yielded radiant colors. Deep within the spark gushed a flow, splaying colors below, concealed within the concealed of the mystery of *Ein Sof*. It split and did not split its aura, was not known at all, until under the impact of splitting, a single, concealed, supernal point shone. Beyond that point nothing is known, so it is called *reshit* [beginning]: the first command of all. (Zohar 1:15a)[34]

"The King made engravings": *Ein Sof* begins the process of implanting the "genetic code," as it were, for what later became the *sefirot*. The "luster on high" refers to *Keter*, the "concealed of the concealed," which in the Zohar is often spoken of as if it were coexistent with the *Ein Sof*. What happens at this beginning of creation? From "the head of *Ein Sof*" there flashes what the Zohar calls *botzina d'kardenuta*, a "spark of impenetrable darkness," an enigmatic turn of phrase exemplifying Jewish mysticism's use of paradox to describe experiences that defy any rational explanation. Although the spark is overwhelmingly brilliant, it is described as dark because of its concealment. As Daniel Matt puts it, this blinding spark "is the first impulse of emanation flashing from *Ein Sof* through *Keter* and proceeding to delineate the various *sefirot*."[35] It forms "in formlessness," because there are no forms as yet; the ring in which it is thrust is code language for *Keter*, the supernal crown. It does not show as the four colors mentioned here, which are associated with four of the *sefirot*, because no forms exist that can depict these colors; those *sefirot* do not yet exist. Nonetheless, we see that the potential for them is laid out and they will flow from "deep within the spark."

Incidentally, the concept of *botzina d'kardenuta* is also an excellent example of the use of paradox in Jewish mysticism. We have already seen that so much of mystical experience defies any rational explanation, and such enigmatic turns of expression often seem necessary to describe the indescribable.

The spark is also "a cord surveyed," which like a measuring line lays out the process and the boundaries of emanation. "It splits and does not split": inexplicably, indescribably, the flow of creation breaks through from the aura (*Keter*), forming the next *sefirah*, *Hokhmah*, the single concealed point that is *reshit*, the "beginning." Recall from the previous chapter that *Hokhmah* is identified with *reshit*, perhaps indicating that *Hokhmah* is the highest level in the *sefirot* that is in any way recognizable to human beings. We also saw in chapter 6 that the world was created through ten commands. The opening verse of Genesis is considered to be the first of these, the "first command of all." The kabbalists see these ten directives as symbolic of the ten *sefirot*.

In the beginning, *Ein Sof* emanated ten *sefirot*, which are of its essence, united with it. It and they are entirely one. There is no

change or division in the emanator that would justify saying it is divided into parts in these various *sefirot*. Division and change do not apply to it, only to the external *sefirot*.

To help you conceive this, imagine water flowing through vessels of different colors: white, red, green and so forth. As the water spreads through those vessels, it appears to change into the colors of the vessels, although the water is devoid of all color. The change in color does not affect the water itself, just our perception of the water. So it is with the *sefirot*. They are vessels, known for example as *Hesed*, *Gevurah*, and *Tiferet*, each colored according to its function, white, red, and green, respectively, while the light of the emanator—their essence—is the water, having no color at all. This essence does not change; it only appears to change as it flows through the vessels.

Better yet, imagine a ray of sunlight shining through a stained-glass window of ten different colors. The sunlight possesses no color at all but appears to change hue as it passes through the different colors of glass. Colored light radiates through the window. The light has not essentially changed, though so it seems to the viewer. Just so with the *sefirot*. The light that clothes itself in the vessels of the *sefirot* is the essence, like the ray of sunlight. That essence does not change color at all, neither judgment nor compassion, neither right nor left. Yet by emanating through the *sefirot*—the variegated stained glass—judgment or compassion prevails. (Cordovero, *Pardes Rimonim*, 4:4, 17d-18a)[36]

Again we see that the *sefirot* are essentially one with *Ein Sof*; however, they do have an "external" aspect that can be said to fluctuate and change from our perspective, even though (like the water in bottles of different colors) they do not actually change. This is also true with the metaphor of sunlight used at the conclusion of this text. *Hesed*, because it represents love, is seen as pure white. *Gevurah* or *Din* is red; *Tiferet*, which harmonizes these two *sefirot*, is associated with green, understood to be a color of harmony.[37]

Many kabbalists who came after the writing of the Zohar visualized a particular color to represent the *sefirah* on which they were meditating. Since one could not visualize the *sefirot* themselves, this use of colors helped to "bridge the gap" and induce a paranormal state of consciousness. Sometimes the Divine Names would be visualized with a particular color; sometimes such visualization would accompany the combining of letters.[38] Here is another text that takes this approach, and also includes the roles of certain angels.

"And, behold, three men" (Gen. 18:2). These were three angels, messengers who clothe themselves in atmosphere and descend to this world and appear there in human form. These three were modeled on the celestial pattern, because the rainbow appears with only three colors, white, red, and green, and this is really so, and these were the "three men," the three colors, the color white, the color red, the color green. The color white is Michael, because he is the right side. The color red is Gabriel, the left side. The color green is Raphael. These are the three colors without which the rainbow cannot appear. Consequently "He appeared to him" (Gen. 18:1), that is the appearance of the *Shekhinah* in these three colors. And they were all needed: one to heal [Abraham] after his circumcision, and this was Raphael, the master of healing; one to tell Sarah of her son, and this was Michael, because he is put in charge of the right side and all goodness and blessing are in his control on the right side; and one to destroy Sodom, and this was Gabriel, because he is on the left, and he is put in charge of all the judgments in the world on the left side, so that he might act and pass judgment through the Angel of Death, who is the executioner in the royal court. They all fulfill their mission, each one doing what is required, the angel Gabriel with respect to the holy soul, and the Angel of Death with respect to the soul of the evil impulse [*yetzer ha-ra*]. (Zohar 1:98b–99a, *Sitrei Torah*)[39]

In the Torah, immediately after Abraham's circumcision, three unnamed angels, disguised as humans, come to visit him. What does it mean that they are "modeled on the celestial pattern"? They represent three of the key *sefirot* that act on the *Shekhinah*: *Hesed*, *Gevurah*, and *Tiferet*. The "rainbow" is code language for *Shekhinah*, so the statement that "the rainbow appears with only three colors" is a way of saying that these three *sefirot* influence the *Shekhinah*. The (preferable) right side, *Hesed*, is displayed in white. *Gevurah*, on the left, the side of judgment, is red. *Tiferet*, the *sefirah* of harmony between *Hesed* and *Gevurah*, is green, a color of harmony. This is the color linked to Raphael (meaning, "God has healed"). The other two names of the angels are familiar to us from Daniel.[40] Michael (Who is like God?), the highest ranking of these angels, comes from *Hesed*, and so is the messenger of the good news that Sarah will bear Abraham a son. Gabriel (God is my strength) is from *Gevurah* (or *Din*), and thus is a messenger of judgment, the impending destruction of Sodom. He works as a partner with the Angel of Death; in this view, when the body dies, Gabriel takes the higher aspect of the soul, while the Angel of Death claims the lower part, which is susceptible to the person's *yetzer ha-ra* (evil impulse).

How do angels function in the *sefirotic* system? Here we will look at two Rabbinic texts about angels and see how the Zohar added a level of interpretation.

Each and every day, ministering angels are created from the fiery stream [*n'har dinur*], and utter song, and cease to be, as it says: "They are renewed every morning; great is Your faithfulness" (Lam. 3:23). (B. Hag. 14a)

When were the angels created? Rabbi Yohanan said: They were created on the second day, as it is written: "He sets the rafters of His lofts in the waters, makes the clouds His chariot [here interpreted as referring to the firmament created on the second day]. . . . He makes

the spirits His angels,[41] the fiery flames His servants" (Ps. 104:3-4). Rabbi Hanina said: They were created on the fifth day, for it is written: "And birds that fly [*y'ofeif*] above the earth" (Gen. 1:20), and it is written: "And with two wings he [i.e., the angel] would fly [*y'ofeif*]" (Isa. 6:2). (*Midrash Bereshit Rabbah* 1:3)

"Who causes the grass to grow for the beast" (Ps. 104:14). Did David speak with the Holy Spirit simply in order to congratulate the beast for having grass [to eat]? No. "Who causes the grass to grow" refers to the six hundred million angelic messengers who were created on the second day of Creation. They are all a flaming fire, and they are grass. Why "grass"? Because they grow like grass in the world. They are cut down every day, and they grow again as at the beginning. And so it is written, "Who causes the grass to grow for the beast." This is the point of: "The righteous knows the soul of his beast" (Prov. 12:10). (Zohar 3:217a)[42]

The talmudic text suggests that angels come from a fiery stream, *n'har dinur*, which can be associated with *din*, judgment. They fulfill one task and then disappear, with new ones popping up each day. The midrash, wishing to emphasize that the angels are not cocreators, brings proof-texts to show that they are created either on the second day or the fifth day of the week of Creation.

The segment from the Zohar begins with what seems to be a normal verse from a psalm of praise to God but suggests that the point of the verse is far too prosaic and must have another meaning on the supernal level. The grass is not simply food for the beast; it alludes to a vast number of angels. The midrashic text proposes that the angels were created on the second day, which in the Zohar represents *Gevurah* (or *Din*); this fits with the talmudic text about the source of the angels. Thanks to the verse from Proverbs—where the "righteous," as usual, represents *Yesod*, who knows the "soul" of *Malkhut* below it—the "beast" is interpreted as code language for *Malkhut*, with its "lower" judgment, and fire, which consumes them. So in this representation, angels of judgment are created on the second day, while other angels are created on the fifth day, satisfying both positions represented in the midrashic text.

We should note that the Zohar bears a significant resemblance to classical midrashim in the way it creatively reinterprets the biblical text. The symbolism, however, is utterly different from what one finds in other, nonkabbalistic midrash.[43]

> Rabbi Akiva said: Everything the Holy One, Blessed be He, has made, can teach us immense wisdom, as it is written (Prov. 16:4): "The Lord made all things *l'ma'aneihu*" [generally translated "for a purpose"; here, it means "concerning himself"]. Rabbi Eleazar said: [Learn it] from here, as it is written (Gen. 1:31): "God saw everything that He had made, and behold, it was very good." What is the point of "very"? Learn from it [i.e., from what He made] the supernal wisdom. Rabbi Yehudah said (Eccles. 7:14): "The one corresponding to the other God has made."[44] The Holy One, Blessed be He, has done on earth similar to the heavens; all things below are symbols of what is above. (Zohar 2:15b; *Midrash ha-Ne'elam*)[45]

The key point is the last phrase. By mirroring some aspect of God, one arouses and strengthens that aspect in the higher realms. As a later text puts it, "the tzaddik below arouses the tzaddik above."[46] Elsewhere the Zohar says: "An entity above is not aroused until there is first aroused that below on which it may abide."[47] Our text here says that the reverse is true as well, that we can learn about aspects of God from everything on earth. If there is no place and no object—and certainly no person— totally devoid of God, it falls to us to identify the aspect of God that is dominant in that spot. Even evil can be an aspect of God, a subject of chapter 17.

Following much earlier sources, this eighteenth-century Hasidic teaching treats the *sefirot* as representing the letters of God's Name:

> [Prov. 3:6 says:] "In all your ways know Him" [*da'eihu*: "acknowledge him"]. This is an important principle: *da'eihu* is an expression of joining together, i.e., joining the *heh* to the *vav*, in all your dealings, even in your physical involvements. (*Tzava'at ha-Rivash* [The testament of the Ba'al Shem Tov], sect. 94)[48]

The author of the book of Proverbs probably meant to tell his readers: in the values by which you live, acknowledge God's rule and reality. But the root of the word *da'eihu* literally means "to know." And as we have it from the story of Adam and Eve, "knowing" in the Bible does have the implication of sexual joining (see, e.g., Gen. 4:1). By dividing up the word, the Hasidic master reads it as follows: *da heh-vav*, join together the *heh* and the *vav*, the *heh* representing *Malkhut* and the *vav* (again, the sixth letter of the Alef Bet) representing the cluster of six *sefirot* around *Tiferet*. Unify these two *sefirot*, have in mind this unification, in everything you do.[49] We will also see this theme emphasized when we deal more extensively with prayer and ritual in chapter 22.

Finally, a longer text from the Zohar integrates several themes concerning angels, biblical characters and verses, and various *sefirot*:

> "In the third month after the children of Israel had left [the land of Egypt]" (Exod. 19:1). This is when Uriel was dominant, the chief officer, accompanied by 365 myriads of camps, corresponding to the number of days of the year. They all had 365 keys to the lights that radiate from the light that emerges from the supernal, innermost *hashmal*, treasured and concealed, on which depend the mysteries of the holy supernal letters of the Holy Name.
>
> This is the mystery of "a man of completion" [*ish tam*] (Gen. 25:27), master of the house, and "husband of God" [*ish ha-Elohim*] (Deut. 33:1 and Josh. 14:6). "Completion," for here is completion and the

knot of the tefillin, and Jacob was man of perfection. In his image survives the mystery of the supernal, innermost *hashmal*, treasured and concealed. He grasps all the hidden, supernal radiances, and they emerge from him. All those camps hold the keys of that light radiating from *hashmal*.

This light is comprised of two lights, and they are one. The first light is a white light, which the eye cannot apprehend; this is the light stored up for the righteous, as it is said, "Light is sown for the righteous" (Ps. 97:11). The second light is a sparkling light, flashing red. The two lights coalesce as one, becoming one.

Uriel, the chief officer, and all those camps receive this light. Because it [that month] is comprised of two, it is called "twins" (Gen. 25:24). Therefore it is ruled by the constellation called in its own mystery "twins" [Gemini], and in it the Torah was given. From there the various levels extend below, until attaining names to conduct the world. (Zohar 2:78a–b)[50]

There are four archangels, and Uriel is the third of them; presumably this is why he is ascendant in the third month of the year. There are 365 keys of light, one for each myriad of camps of angels. These keys open the supernal channels for the flow of energy that sustains life. *Hashmal*, a term from the vision of the chariot in Ezekiel 1, is a glowing, mysterious substance. Because the Four-Letter Name connected with it here is associated with *Tiferet*, it may be understood similarly.

The Zohar brings here two verses associated with *Tiferet* through their protagonists, Jacob and Moses. Jacob is described as the *ish tam*, often translated "simple man" but frequently also understood as "wholesome" or "complete." Completion, in the supernal realm, is *Shekhinah* (or *Malkhut*), which completes the *sefirotic* realm. But *ish* can also mean "husband." So Jacob, and then Moses, are understood to be the "husbands" of God, that is, completing and uniting with the *Shekhinah*.[51] The knot of the tefillin is referred to in a talmudic text discussing Exod. 33:32, where God tells Moses that he will not see God's face, but only His back; the Talmud there interprets the "back" as referring to the knot of God's tefillin.[52] Thus the Zohar interprets this knot as *Shekhinah*, which, as it were, "ties up" the end of the *sefirot*. Uriel, the third angel, is also associated with *Tiferet*,[53] and his camps send on the flow of light from above.

This central light, *Tiferet*, is composed of two lights, combining those from *Hesed* and *Gevurah*. The light from *Hesed*, from love, is the light from the opening of Creation, prior to the making of the sun and the stars, said to be set aside for the righteous in the world to come.[54] The second is red, the color associated with severe judgment. Finally, we see the reference to twins, which in the biblical context refers to Jacob and Esau,[55] but here probably refers to these two lights.[56] The month ruled by Uriel in which Jews celebrate Shavuot, which commemorates the revelation, is the third month (*Sivan*); this is ruled by Gemini. This fits in another respect; Torah is also "two lights," that is, the Written Torah and the Oral Torah (representing *Tiferet* and *Malkhut* respectively). We are also told that the supernal realm stretches downward to the constellations, which in turn rule over their own portion of the lower realms. Again the angel plays a prominent role in the ongoing cosmic drama as well as in this specific event in Jewish history.

The *sefirot* are not only the building blocks of the universe, but also the means by which we understand, meet with, and affect God. For the mystics, knowing their characteristics is the highest form of wisdom. The idea of God being subject to other forces may trouble or baffle some readers. As David Blumenthal notes, "To the traditional theologian, these are very strange ideas. To the philosopher, they are preposterous. Yet for the author of the Zohar, they are central to our understanding of God."[57] If our actions can affect God, then our lives must have more meaning than we ever imagined.

10

Deveikut

CLEAVING TO GOD

Can a faithful Jew feel close to God? The Torah assumes that one can:

> "While you who held fast [*ha-deveikim*] to the Lord your God, are all alive today."
>
> "If then, you faithfully keep all this Torah that I command you, loving the Lord your God, walking in all His ways, and holding fast [*ul'dovkah*] to Him."
>
> "You must revere the Lord your God: only Him shall you worship, to Him shall you hold fast [*tidbak*], and by His Name shall you swear." (Deut. 4:4, 11:22, 10:20)

As noted in chapter 1, the root of the word *deveikut* is also used in Gen. 2:24: "Hence a man leaves his father and mother and cleaves to his wife [*v'davak b'ishto*], so they become one flesh." *Deveikut* thus suggests strong intimacy. But if God has no body, how do I "cleave" to God? Does it mean cleaving to God's attributes? Does it mean cleaving to a way of life that testifies to God's reality? Or does it mean something more passionate, more fervent?

The Rabbis of antiquity began with the premise that if the Torah said we should cleave to God, it could be done . . . *if* we could overcome certain barriers!

Rabbi Eliezer would say: Woe unto us, for whoever cleaves to impurity, the spirit of impurity rests upon him. But one who cleaves to the *Shekhinah*, it is natural [*din hu*] that the Holy Spirit rests upon Him. So what causes this [not to happen]? "Your sins have separated you from your God" (Isa. 59:2). (*Sifrei* 173)

While this does not explain much about what *deveikut* is, it certainly suggests what prevents it. Sin creates a barrier between man and God (see chapter 6). Thus the prerequisite for *deveikut* is to minimize any kind of sin.

In his twelfth-century code of Jewish law, Maimonides discusses what it means to be constantly mindful of God, whom we are also commanded to love.

What is the way we should love God? We should love Him with an overwhelming and unlimited love, until our soul becomes permanently bound in the love of God, like one who is lovesick and cannot take his mind off the woman he loves, but always thinks of her, when lying down or rising up, when eating or drinking. Even greater than this should be the love of God in the hearts of those who love Him, thinking about Him constantly, as He commanded us, "And you shall love the Lord your God with all your heart and with all your soul" (Deut. 6:5). (Maimonides, *Mishneh Torah, Hilkhot Teshuvah* [Laws of repentance] 10:3)

For Maimonides, *deveikut* means being lovesick . . . only more so than a man might be for a woman! But he does not compare it to a man actually *being with* a woman (perhaps since God has no gender). *Deveikut* here is understood as an experience of the intellect, an intense longing to apprehend God. Anything more direct than that is not possible within our physical bodies.[1] Maimonides recommends the very moderate approach suggested in the Talmud (see below) as the proper course for most people, since they will not be able to achieve this kind of *deveikut*. But for those who are capable, this kind of intimacy with God is an appropriate goal.

Following are a series of texts that will shed light on how the kabbalists responded to and built upon the earlier Rabbinic views on *deveikut*. The first text sets out the problem.

> **Rabbi Shimon opened, saying: Two verses are written. "For the Lord your God is a consuming fire" (Deut. 4:24), "and you who cleave to the Lord your God are all alive today" (Deut. 4:4). We have established these verses in various places, and the companions have been aroused by them. (Zohar 1:50b–51b)[2]**

In this text are two biblical verses that appear to contradict each other. How can you be close to God, if God is fire? When the Zohar says, "We have established these verses in various places," this refers to the Rabbinic resolutions to the problem, two of which are offered below.

> **Rabbi Eleazar said to Rabbi Yohanan: Master, I have found for those without knowledge of Torah[3] a remedy in the Torah. [It says:] "you who cleave to the Lord your God are all alive today"; is it really possible to cleave to the Divine Presence, of which it is written: "For the Lord your God is a consuming fire?" Rather, this means: Whoever marries his daughter to a disciple of the wise, conducts business on their behalf, or benefits them from his assets, is regarded by Scripture as if he cleaves to the Divine Presence. (B. Ket. 111b)**

It seems that, for Rabbi Eleazar, only the sages can actually have such an experience. The unlearned have only indirect solutions, presumably because they would be consumed or at least harmed by more direct experiences for which they are unprepared. Just marry your daughter to a scholar, or help support a scholar, and you get credit as if you yourself had cleaved to God. This may not seem to be worth much, but it is certainly what many of the Rabbis recommended for the average Jew.[4] Indirectly, the text also suggests that Torah study is a strong form of *deveikut*, because penetrating knowledge of God's word also yields deeper closeness with the Divine.

Rabbi Hama said in the name of Rabbi Hanina: What is the meaning of "Follow the Lord your God" (Deut. 13:5)? Is it really possible for a person to follow the *Shekhinah*? Is it not also written, "For the Lord your God is a consuming fire"? Rather, it means one should follow the attributes of the Holy One, Blessed be He. Just as He clothes the naked, as it is written: "And the Lord God made garments of skins for Adam and his wife, and clothed them" (Gen. 3:21), so should you clothe the naked. The Holy One, Blessed be He, visits the sick, as it is written: "The Lord appeared to Abraham by the terebinths of Mamre" (Gen. 18:1 [shortly after Abraham's circumcision]), so should you visit the sick. The Holy One, praised be He, comforted mourners, as it is written: "After the death of Abraham, God blessed his son Isaac" (Gen. 25:11), so should you comfort mourners. The Holy One, Blessed be He, buries the dead, as it is written: "He buried Moses in the valley" (Deut. 34:6), so should you bury the dead. (B. Sot. 14a)

Although this text does not directly mention *deveikut*, it deals with the same problem others raise about *deveikut*, even using the same verse (Deut. 4:4) as an objection.[5] The answer given here is that being like God, being close to God, means doing the things God does, taking on divine qualities. This is a perfectly sensible answer, consistent with the fact that in Deut. 11:22, cleaving to God is taught along with walking in God's ways. This answer to the problem would fit very nicely with the ideal of Normal Mysticism discussed in chapter 1; while this lacks the kind of intensity often associated with mystical experience, performance of certain holy deeds can indeed lead to an enhanced feeling of closeness with God. But however praiseworthy this might be, it is not the constant *deveikut* sought by the mystics. Such ethical behavior would be considered an essential prerequisite for mystical experience, but it is not the experience itself.

Joseph Gikatilla, who lived in the thirteenth century, when the Zohar was written, responds to the Rabbis by framing *deveikut* specifically within the realm of the *sefirot,* in a systematic discussion of kabbalistic concepts.

> The ninth *sefirah* is His and the tenth is ours, for it is our inheritance and our portion. For when the tenth *sefirah* connects and unites with the ninth, then all Israel as one attaches itself to the Name, Blessed be He, as it has been said: "And you who cleave to the Lord your God." Do not be concerned over what the sages said: "Is it really possible to cleave to the Divine Presence [*Shekhinah*]?" Indeed, it is possible! Everything was revealed when they said that the verses were telling you to cleave to one of the learned among us. We know who the learned are, the students of God; without a doubt, this is the mystery of the cleaving of the tenth *sefirah* to the ninth. For whoever causes the unity of *Knesset Yisrael* [the People of Israel] with the *sefirah* of *Yesod, Yesod* cleaves to the *Shekhinah* and she cleaves to him, and both as one cleave to the Four-Letter Name. (Gikatilla, *Sha'arei Orah* [Gates of light], 166)[6]

Gikatilla's answer to the problem is that yes, you *can* cleave to the *Shekhinah*, if you think of the cleaving as the relationship between the *sefirot*. He reinterprets the directive of the Talmud (in *Ketubot*) to associate with the sages as follows: the sages are the righteous, hence they are identified with *Yesod* as in the verse "The righteous is the foundation, *Yesod*, of the world" (Prov. 10:25). *Knesset Yisrael*, "the People of Israel," is code language for *Shekhinah*, because for the kabbalists Israel is eventually intended to serve as the representative of the Divine Presence in the world. Thus when ordinary Jews cleave to the sages, they carry out in this world what is intended to happen on the supernal level.

Now we return to the text of the Zohar, to see how it resolves the contradiction:

> Come and see: "For the Lord your God is a consuming fire." The word has been discussed among the companions; there is a fire consuming

fire, consuming and devouring it, for there is a fire fiercer than fire, as they have established. But come and see: Whoever desires to penetrate the wisdom of holy unification should contemplate the flame ascending from a glowing ember, or a burning candle. For flame ascends only when grasped by coarse substance.

Come and see! In a flame ascending are two lights: one, a radiant white light; the other, a light tinged with black or blue. The white light is above, ascending unswervingly, while beneath it is the blue or black light, a throne for the white, which rests upon it, each embracing the other, becoming one. This black light colored blue, below, is a throne of glory for the white. Here lies the mystery of the thread of blue. This blue-black throne is grasped by another substance below, so it can flame, arousing it to embrace the white light. Sometimes this blue-black [light] turns red, while the white light above it never wavers, constantly white. This blue one, though, changes color: sometimes blue or black, sometimes red. This [light] is grasped in two directions: above, by that white light; below, by what lies beneath, by which it is fueled, primed to glow. This [light] constantly devours and consumes what is placed beneath it, for the blue light devours anything cleaving below, anything it rests upon, since by nature it devours and consumes. On it depends destruction and death of all.

So it devours anything cleaving below, while that white light hovering over it never consumes or devours, nor does its light waver. Therefore Moses said, "For the Lord your God is a consuming fire"— really consuming, consuming and devouring anything found below. That is why he said "the Lord your God," and not "our God," for Moses inhabited that white light above, which does not devour or consume.

Come and see: The only arousal kindling this blue light, to be grasped by the white light, is Israel cleaving below. Come and see: Although by nature this blue-black light devours anything cleaving below, Israel cleaves below and abides enduringly, as is written, "You who cleave to the Lord your God are all alive"—i.e., "to the Lord your

God," not "our God," to the Lord your God, to that blue-black light consuming, devouring whatever cleaves below—yet you cleave and endure, as it is written "alive, all of you, today."

Above the white light hovers a concealed light, encompassing it. Here abides supernal mystery. You will discover all in the ascending flame, wisdoms of the highest. (Zohar 1:50b–51b)

What is "a fire devouring fire"? This is a phrase from the Talmud, referring to the fire of *Shekhinah*, the Divine Presence, which consumes even the angels. *Shekhinah* here is another name for the *sefirah* of *Malkhut*. The Zohar is saying: if you cleave to *Shekhinah*, you are protected from the danger of being devoured. We are able to cleave to God through the *sefirot*, and the *sefirot* cleave to one another, but how is it really possible for human beings, imperfect and transitory as we are, to attach ourselves to the Divine? The Zohar tells us: it is like the flame of a candle, which actually *requires* some "coarse substance" for the flame to ascend.

White light represents *Tiferet*; *Shekhinah* is a darker light, because it only reflects the light of the other *sefirot*. Blue is significant in part because it is a mixture of all other colors; on its own, without reflected light, *Shekhinah* remains completely dark. Blue is also important because it is the color of the thread within the tzitzit, the tassels on a four-cornered garment that represent the mitzvot. A midrashic teaching attributed to Rabbi Meir declares that "whoever fulfills the mitzvah of tzitzit is considered to have greeted the face of *Shekhinah*, as it were; for blue resembles the sea, and the sea resembles the sky, and the sky resembles the Throne of Glory."[7] We are thus instructed that the blue part of a flame in the physical world is a parallel to God's throne. The "higher" flame, the white light of *Tiferet*, is on the throne. Just as the flame of a candle rests on and uses its wick and wax (or its oil), so *Shekhinah* uses the realms below in order to burn, to climb higher, and to achieve union with *Tiferet*. The "blue-black" light sometimes turns red because *Gevurah* (or *Din*), representing the quality of God's judgment, is represented by the color red; when she brings additional influence on *Malkhut*, it affects the "blue-black" of *Malkhut*.

One of the "code" terms for *Malkhut* is "death," especially when *Malkhut* is separated from *Tiferet*. *Malkhut* is closer to mortal beings. Also, death came into being when Adam and Eve ate the fruit of the tree of knowledge of good and evil, and *Shekhinah* is also associated with this tree.[8] So the "blue light" is also a source of death. Moses, the key figure of the Written Torah, is naturally associated with *Tiferet* and its white light. But when he speaks of "your" God, he is interpreted as alluding to the *sefirah* most closely associated with Israel,[9] *Malkhut*.

What brings about the unification of the blue and white lights, that is, *Malkhut* and *Tiferet*? It is the devotion of "Israel cleaving below" that provides the spark for their union. So Israel has enormous responsibility in the cosmic scheme, for this union is key to the proper functioning of the supernal world. These two *sefirot*, feminine and masculine aspects, are alienated from each other; our job is to reunite them, as is discussed further in chapter 11. An interesting feature of this text is that the emphasis is all on how we affect and assist the divine processes, and not on the experience of the mystic himself.[10]

Finally, the concealed light above the white light of *Tiferet* represents *Binah*, who gives birth to and supports all the lower *sefirot*. And this mystery prompts the author of the Zohar to reflect on how everything can be seen within this ascending flame of the candle. On this, Daniel Matt quotes the nineteenth-century physicist Michael Faraday: "There is no better, there is no more open door by which you can enter into the study of natural philosophy, than by considering the physical phenomena of a candle."[11]

Below is a view of *deveikut* penned by Judah Loew of Prague (the Maharal), an extraordinary figure in the sixteenth century: communal leader, Czech national hero, and author of many writings on virtually all aspects of Jewish thought in his day.

Scripture states: "Hear O Israel! The Lord is our God, the Lord is One. You shall love the Lord your God" (Deut. 6:4–5). Since God is one, no existing being in the world is separated from God; all things that exist depend upon and cleave to the blessed God, since He is the basis for all. It is for this reason that love applies to God. Indeed, love of God is more fitting than love of anything else. For in every kind of love that obtains between two human lovers, though they may cleave to one another, nevertheless, each retains his or her individuality. However, in the love of a human for God, a human being can completely return his spirit and soul to God to the extent that he loses his individual existence and completely cleaves to God, as it is written, "to love the Lord your God and to cleave to Him." This is complete love.

It is as Rabbi Akiva said: "All my days I have been troubled by the verse, 'You shall love the Lord your God with all your heart and all your soul,' and now that I have the opportunity, shall I not fulfill it?"[12] This is complete love—when someone surrenders one's life to God, for by so doing, one completely cleaves to God. It has been explained that love applies more to God, since a human being can give up his life for God and completely cleave to Him. This is true love. (Judah Loew of Prague, *Netivot Olam* [Eternal paths], 2:39)[13]

This text, part of a longer discussion of the implications of Rabbi Akiva's martyrdom, begins with an arresting assertion: if God is One, nothing is truly separated from God. *Deveikut* is nothing more or less than returning to our source, not simply a form of union with God but *re*-union.[14] Loving God is not only fundamentally different from any other kinds of love but superior to them. And martyrdom is the ultimate form of love, in which one completely cleaves to God.

Loew notes that some mitzvot are particularly effective for achieving a high level of *deveikut*:

One should know that the Shabbat represents the *deveikut* which exists between Israel and God. . . . The attachment and cleaving of

Israel to God represented by the Shabbat differs from that engendered by the other mitzvot. For Shabbat represents Creation. . . . [In the Talmud we learn: "Rabbi Yehudah said in the name of Rav: Had Israel kept their first Shabbat, no nation or tongue would have enjoyed dominion over them."[15]] If Israel would have observed its first Shabbat, it would have become attached to God through Creation, and whatever is related to the Creation is eternal and unchanging. (Judah Loew of Prague, *Hiddushei Aggadot* 1:56)[16]

Loew elsewhere notes that repentance and prayer (along with the service in the Temple, for which prayer was perforce a substitute) are especially helpful in attaining *deveikut*.[17] Because of the connection between Shabbat and Creation, he understands this to have a similar value. This teaching asks us: what mitzvot today, or personally, for me, might help bring about a similar sense of closeness with God?

Reshit Hokhmah is a large ethical compilation based on kabbalistic teachings, authored in Safed in the sixteenth century by Elijah de Vidas. It describes the nature of *deveikut* as a fervent desire:

A man would not delay mating with his wife when he feels passion for her, even if you gave him all the money in the world. Similarly, it is appropriate that a person feel passionately about performing the commandments, since through performing them he couples with the daughter of the King: that is, the *Shekhinah*. (De Vidas, *Reishit Hokhmah* [The beginning of wisdom], *Sha'ar ha-Ahavah* [Gate of love]), ch. 4:24)[18]

While this text does not directly mention *deveikut*, the idea of cleaving to God is implicit, since it likens "passion" for the commandments to passion for one's wife. De Vidas, like Loew, emphasizes the role of mitzvot in attaining closeness to God. However, Loew's language about *deveikut* is somewhat more removed from the kind of erotic suggestion we see here. De Vidas does emphasize elsewhere that *deveikut* involves no physical cleaving, that it ultimately involves a degree of separation from matters of this world.[19]

The text below begins by emphasizing that *deveikut* is the goal of all the commandments, the entire structure of Jewish life. Contrary to the notion common today that an experience of closeness with God inspires a person to fulfill the mitzvot, Isaiah Horowitz teaches just the reverse: one fulfills the mitzvot in order to meet God, as a natural part of the process of cleaving to God.

> "And you who cleave to the Lord your God are all alive today" (Deut. 4:4): This verse includes the whole Torah, and the deeds and characteristics and conduct of mankind, that all be for the sake of His Name and to be in *deveikut* with the Blessed God. And even when he attends to his vital physical needs, he should not waver from this *deveikut*. When he attends to his business, he should think: "I am attending to my business, and I hope in the Blessed God that I will have profit, for the Blessed One is actually the giver, and from this I will perform a mitzvah, and sustain myself, my wife and children, so that they live to maintain the service of God, and I will contribute to charity, to the study of Torah, and other such needs." And when he eats or lies down to sleep, he should intend that this strengthen his body so that he might attend to the study of Torah and the performance of mitzvah; similarly with all matters. . . . Thus a man will throughout life be continually cleaved to the Blessed God, if he follows in this path, and will merit eternal *deveikut* with the Blessed One. And the Zohar (3:138b, *Idra Rabba*) says: "Rabbi Shimon began by quoting, 'And you who cleave to the Lord your God.' What nation is so holy as Israel, of whom it is written: 'O Happy Israel, who is like you, a people delivered by the Lord?' (Deut. 33:29). For the cleaving [of Israel] in this world is to the holy Name, and in the next world [even more so], for there they are not separated from the bond of life in which the righteous are bound. This is the meaning of 'you who cleave to the

Lord': actually to the Lord!" (Isaiah Horowitz, *Shnei Luhot ha-Brit*; *parashat* Va-ethannan, *Derekh Hayyim Tokhehot Musar*)

Horowitz illustrates in detail how one maintains *deveikut* while performing mundane activities. And he brings the Zohar teaching that speaks of the reward in the next world to support the idea that this cleaving to God will continue and intensify beyond physical death. What is the reward for maintaining *deveikut* here? More *deveikut*, and more powerful *deveikut* in the afterlife. And this more passionate *deveikut* will be a true union with God. Thus this text illustrates many aspects of the mystical intimacy achieved through *deveikut*.

In this view, *deveikut* is not simply for private meditational periods, or for prayer in the synagogue. For the true mystic, *deveikut* is an ideal to be maintained at work, at home, and while active in the community; in short, at all times. Yet this does not necessarily contradict the opinion of those (like De Vidas, as mentioned) who believe that *deveikut* requires some degree of separation from the world.[20] One can be *in* the world, but not firmly attached to it.

The mystic treats the fulfillment of the mitzvot not as ends unto themselves, but as a path to stronger *deveikut*. Thus Horowitz is challenging not only those who might treat the mitzvot as expendable, but also those who perform them. Furthermore, *deveikut* in this world is a path to a more powerful *deveikut* in the next, where the obstacles of physical life are no longer present. So *deveikut* here is not union with God, but such union would be possible in the next world.

We have already encountered the word *demut*, "likeness"; the Hebrew root *d-m-h*, meaning "similar," also appears in the text below, which uses an advanced form of Hebrew numerology.

"And He called their name Adam" (Gen. 5:2): this refers to the generations of Adam and his end. If he cleaves to what is above and likens himself to the blessed One, to walk in His ways, then his name will indeed be called Adam, from the language of *edameh l'Elyon* ["I will be like the Most High," Isa. 14:14] and to "on the likeness of the throne, the likeness of man" (Ezek. 1:26). But if he separates himself from this cleaving, then he will be called Adam by the name of the earth [*adamah*] from which he is taken, for he is dust, and to dust he shall return. However, the name Adam from *edameh l'Elyon* is the essential purpose, for evil is only created for the sake of the good as I have explained. Therefore, this is the essential name of Adam, for this is also the numerical value of the *miluy* of His great Name, *Yud-Heh-Vav-Heh.* (Introduction to *Shnei Luhot ha-Brit, Toldot Adam,* sec. 3)[21]

Shelah arrives at an interesting hypothesis. The name "Adam" is generally understood to come from the word *adamah*, the earth "from which he is taken" and to which he will return. But Shelah suggests that man can go either way. If he cleaves to God (and Shelah says that this is man's "essential purpose," our intended direction in life), then he is *not*, ultimately, of the earth, but *edameh l'Elyon*, "like the Most High," belonging to the supernal realms. Through *deveikut*, by connecting to God, man overcomes his physicality and even, in some sense, overcomes the return to the earth. If so, then *deveikut* transcends death, in much the same way suggested previously. Also, *deveikut* seems to be that which makes us most fully human and enables us to fulfill our potential. Note also that Maimonides considers imitation of God to be one of the positive commandments, following Deut. 28:9, "You shall walk in His ways."[22]

Many names of God derive from the Four-Letter Name. One of these uses *miluy*, an expanded form, spelling out the four letters *Yud, Heh, Vav,* and *Heh*, as *Yud-vav-dalet, Heh-alef, Vav-alef-vav,* and (again) *Heh-alef.* When the numerical equivalents of these letters are added together, they total the number forty-five. *Adam* is spelled *alef-dalet-mem*, which also totals forty-five. To the mystics, this suggested an essential likeness between God and man, or at least a mirroring between the divine world and our own.

We have already encountered the idea that if we could avoid sin we could maintain (or create) life. For Horowitz and for the thirteenth-century Torah scholar Nahmanides (and most kabbalistic thinkers), death is not a necessity. It is not even God's intention.

> Know that those who study nature have said that death is natural for a human being, because every being perishes.... All of our sages who are enamored of Greek wisdom have been drawn to this opinion. They make bitter the judgment and intention of our Torah. But the true sages of the Torah who possess true faith [i.e., the kabbalists], our Rabbis of blessed memory, believe that death is not natural. They said that if one did not sin, he would never die. The sage of truth and kabbalist, our great Rabbi Nahmanides of blessed memory, said as follows about *parashat* Bere'shit:[23] "Know that composition does not imply decomposition, except according to the opinion of those of little faith who think creation was necessary. But according to the men of faith who say the world was created by divine desire, it is clear that its existence also depends upon Him forever, as long as this desire exists. This is a clear truth."
>
> Certainly the students of nature walk in darkness, for *deveikut* with the Blessed One is above nature, and the will of the Blessed One is that man's *deveikut* will be eternal.... We true believers hold that everything is from God's will, and His will is that man will be eternal, if he remains in *deveikut*. (*Shnei Luhot ha-Brit, Toldot Adam, Bet David,* sec. 8)

God's desire is that we walk together in His ways and in our thoughts, in ongoing *deveikut*. If we would do this, it would be His will that we be "eternal." This is the literal meaning given to Deut. 4:4, "You who cleave to the Lord your God, are all alive today." *Deveikut* in this sense may or may not quite be a total absorption into God, but it has lasting power.

In the eighteenth century, the Ba'al Shem Tov, the founder of Hasidism, reads the same verse with a different twist.

"And you who cleave to the Lord your God are all alive today" (Deut. 4:4): This means that *deveikut* is the cause of true life. When you have *deveikut* with God, the life of life, you are alive in essence. But when you interrupt your *deveikut*, you are alive only by happenstance. Just as heat is the essence of fire, but only happens to water in certain circumstances, and the heat does not remain if water is removed from a fire, [so it is with *deveikut*].

Regarding *deveikut*, the sages remarked on the verse ". . . and cleave to Him" (Deut. 11:22): "How can one cleave to Him? Is not God "a consuming fire" (Deut. 4:24)? Rather, it means to cleave to His attributes."[24] This means cleaving to Him through the Torah. The Ba'al Shem Tov also taught that when a person is occupied with prayer and Torah, which is completely composed of God's Name, he should absolutely be in a powerful state of *deveikut*. And even throughout the day he should still fulfill the verse "I have set God always before me" (Ps. 16:8) by having some measure of *deveikut*.[25]

To what may this be compared? To a candle or a burning coal. For as long as there is still a live spark within it, the flame can be revived. But if there is not even a spark remaining, the fire must be brought from a new source. . . . This is the meaning of "And you who cleave to the Lord your God are all alive today"; *deveikut* is not only a guarantee for attaining eternal life in the world to come, but also ensures life in this world, which is called today. (Ba'al Shem Tov, *Keter Shem Tov*, 1:84)[26]

It is not *deveikut* that leads to eternal life; *deveikut* is life itself. God is the "life of life," the ultimate Life, both the source of life and eternally living. By achieving *deveikut* with God, one latches onto the essence of life itself. If we are *not* in *deveikut* with God, we may happen to be alive, but we are removed from the source of life, and so are no longer alive "in essence." In this view, without *deveikut*, your life is an accident!

Cleaving to God's "attributes" is interpreted much differently here. The Torah itself is seen as a collection of God's attributes; furthermore, the Torah in its entirety is considered to be one name of God.[27] There-fore, Torah study, and the fulfillment of the Torah's mitzvot, is a means of attaining a strong sense of *deveikut* with God. The last sentence here emphasizes again that *deveikut* takes place in all of one's ordinary activi-ties. Implied is that one meditates on the Name of God contained within this particular verse (Ps. 16:8).[28] While the text does not state it explicitly, certain kinds of visualizations may also help a person achieve a signifi-cant level of *deveikut*.[29]

By maintaining *deveikut* during ordinary activities, you nurture the spark that will burn more strongly during prayer, Torah study, and perfor-mance of other mitzvot. "Today" is understood as the mundane actions of our lives; if we are in *deveikut* "today," we will certainly be able to be "alive" in *deveikut* eternally!

I close this chapter with a teaching on *deveikut* from an early Hasidic master, a student of the Ba'al Shem Tov, who deals with the question: must one maintain *deveikut* while still dealing with the needs of those who depend on us? (We will see that *deveikut* plays a critical role in Hasidic thought when we examine Hasidism directly, beginning in chapter 25.)

> The tzaddik who ascends higher and higher, from one level to another, is always in great *deveikut* with the Creator, blessed be His Name. When he is in *deveikut*, his mind is distracted from people and thus he is unable to act on behalf of people's needs, for he is in no way part of this world. Therefore, the tzaddik must sometimes let go of his *deveikut* for the sake of individual needs, so that he might act on their behalf, either through praying for their physical or financial needs, or by bringing down the divine flow of beneficence, which depends upon him. Thus, by occasionally letting go of his *deveikut*, the tzaddik performs a great mitzvah, and this [his letting go] is the will of the Creator. (Elimelekh of Lizensk, *Noam Elimelekh*, Shelah-Lekha, 264b)[30]

For Rabbi Elimelekh, the high level of the tzaddik's *deveikut* is incompatible with action in this world. Only by temporarily removing himself from this *deveikut* can he accomplish something for others . . . and he must!

Of course, one only withdraws from a *deveikut* if it is a high priority to have it at all. As Harold Kushner has written: "It is not enough to believe in God intellectually—to conclude that there is a God and that it would be prudent and proper to follow God's teachings. We must cleave to God as one cleaves to a spouse, to a lover, in response to our soul's deepest needs. Only then will our relationship with God be a source of life."[31]

11

Tzorekh Gavoha

THE DIVINE NEED

Normal Mysticism, as introduced in chapter 1, teaches that the purpose of fulfilling the Torah's laws is to make one a better person: more ethical, more sensitive, more understanding, more aware of God's Presence. In Mainline Kabbalah it is not about "me" at all. Religion, or at least the Jewish religion, exists in order to help God. Carrying out the commandments affects a higher realm, and that is more important than anything such activity does for me; God's needs matter more than my own.

Mainline Kabbalah asserts that by constantly performing all possible mitzvot with the proper *kavanah*, the appropriate intention, we stimulate the *sefirot* to move in the proper direction, with their intention mirroring our own.[1] Of course, only human beings can properly perform these mitzvot; thus, the success of the entire kabbalistic enterprise depends on us. God needs us to help bring about the completion and perfection of the universe, as the kabbalists understand it.[2] This cosmic requirement is called the *tzorekh gavoha*, the "divine need."

Miles Krassen describes this idea as follows: "The concept *tzorekh gavoha* means to fulfill the need of the High One, that is, the divine need. This entails the cultivation of unceasing awareness of all that one does, in order to make sure that nothing occurs, even inadvertently, that will be a transgression. The purpose of this constant watchfulness is to ensure that none of one's actions is performed for personal benefit, but all is done for the sake of uniting aspects of the highest world, the 'world of emanation,' which is an extension of God."[3]

This concept presents a challenge to those who see God as all-powerful, and its adherents offer three responses to their concerns. One is that God is not and never was omnipotent. Not only does the Bible never explicitly assert that God is all-powerful,[4] but the sages understand God as weeping for the suffering of His people, unable to prevent or end their pain.[5] The whole idea of God's omnipotence does not appear in Jewish thought until the Middle Ages, probably as a result of contact with Islamic thinking.[6] A second response is that the *Ein Sof* is omnipotent, but the *sefirot*, the lower manifestations of God, are not. A third response, found in *Tanya*, the philosophical work of Rabbi Shneur Zalman of Liady, the first rebbe of Chabad, is the notion that all of creation is an illusion and that only God exists; once one penetrates beyond the illusion, one realizes that God actually *is* omnipotent but cannot be seen as such within our existence.[7]

Two other important kabbalistic concepts relate to the *tzorekh gavoha*.[8] *Adam Kadmon*, the "primordial man," is a macrocosm of the human being, but actually a way of understanding God. We humans in this world are modeled on the divine body—that is, the *sefirot*—and, at least to some degree, God and man can be understood from each other. More than that, we influence the divine body because of the "mirroring" effect; a mitzvah performed with proper intention will produce a result within the appropriate spot in *Adam Kadmon*, in the *sefirotic* realm.

The second concept is *yihud*, "unification." According to the kabbalists, the universe only "works" properly when the *sefirot* are connected, when benefit (often referred to as *shefa*, "influx") may flow in both directions. This is particularly true for *Malkhut* and *Tiferet*. Think of this as if it were a highly sophisticated plumbing system; only when all the pipes are "unified" and nothing interrupts the flow does the whole system function. But sin intervenes; the *sitra ahra* (other [evil] side) disrupts the system, in part because sin can separate *Malkhut* from the other *sefirot*.

Mitzvot are therefore brought into the service of *yihud* to overcome these negative powers.

The belief that God needs the human act (or thought) is basic to Mainline Kabbalah, and perhaps to the entire mystical enterprise. Rationalists said that the mitzvot were needed *l'tzaref*, "to refine," human beings,[9] and they asked, with Job 35:6–7: "If you sin, what do you do to Him? . . . If you are righteous, what do you give Him?" Kabbalists responded: *l'tzaref* also means "to join"—that the mitzvot were given to join us to God. In other words, the *sefirot* (though not the *Ein Sof*) are affected by human activity. The upper world needs the lower world. Try as the philosophers might to purify the idea of God, they could only succeed in making God less real to the faithful.

Here are two Rabbinic antecedents to this kabbalistic idea that God needs us:

> **Rabbi Shimon ben Yohai says: A parable. A man brought two ships, tied them to anchors and iron weights, stationed them in the middle of the sea, and built a palace upon them. As long as the two ships are tied to each other, the palace stands firm. Once the ships are separated, the palace cannot stand. Thus it is also with Israel: when they do the will of God, He builds His upper chambers in the heaven; when they do not do His will, as it were, He [only] builds His vault upon the earth. Similarly Scripture says: "This is my God, and I will glorify Him" (Exod. 15:2); when I acknowledge Him, He is glorious, but when I do not acknowledge Him, He is, as it were, not glorious. "For I will proclaim the name of God; ascribe greatness unto our God" (Deut. 32:3); when I proclaim His Name, He is great, but when I do not, [He is not great], as it were. Similarly, "So you are My witnesses, declares the Lord, and I am God" (Isa. 43:12); when you are My witnesses, I am God, but when you are not My witnesses, I am, as it were, not God. (*Sifrei*, Ve-zo't ha-berakhah, sec. 346)[10]**

Without a human witness to God's greatness, how much difference does God's greatness make? As Heschel put it, "In this world, God is not God unless we are His witnesses."[11]

> **"And now, let the power of God be increased." (Num. 14:17) [What does this mean?] When Israel does the will of the Holy One, Blessed be He, they add strength to the power of the One Above, as it says, "And now, let the power of God be increased." And when Israel does not do the will of the Holy One, Blessed be He, they, as it were, reduce strength from the power of the One Above, as is written: "the Rock that bore you, you weakened" (Deut. 32:18).[12] (*Midrash Eikhah Rabbah* 1:33)[13]**

Study of Torah is one thing. Performance of its mitzvot is another. But they lead to the same result: by doing them, you add to God's power, and by not doing them, you subtract from it. Many other Rabbinic teachings suggest that when Israel does God's will this has other effects that bring direct reward to Israel.[14] Here, the purpose is independent of any benefit for Israel; it is all about increasing God's influence. Kabbalists would claim this text as proof that, while the *Ein Sof* remains unchanged, the *sefirot* are indeed affected by our actions.[15]

The idea of the *tzorekh gavoha* is assumed from the earliest kabbalistic texts, among them the following:

> **How does one give *hesed* [love] to the Creator? By studying Torah. For whoever learns Torah for its own sake gives *hesed* to his Creator, as it is written: "He rides in the heaven with your help and with His majesty in the skies" (Deut. 33:26). Thus, when a person learns Torah for its own sake, you help Me and I ride in the heavens, "with His majesty in the skies." (*Bahir* 185)[16]**

The primary implication of this teaching is straightforward: if you study God's Torah purely from appreciation that it is God's word, you help God by adding to His majesty. And it is not merely a show of respect;

it is an act of love. Perhaps the belief that "everyone needs love" applies to God as well! Just as one expresses love for someone by assisting with the person's needs, the deepest love of God is expressed by learning Torah with the intention of unifying God's name.

The following text takes two Rabbinic teachings with no discernible mystical connotations and broadly reinterprets them to draw out a mystical meaning as well.

> We learn: "All your deeds shall be *l'shem shamayim* [for the sake of heaven]" (Pirkei Avot 2:17). In other words, to unite the Name, which is *Malkhut*, as is known, with Heaven, which is *Tiferet*, as is known. The sages also taught in the language of the Mishnah: "Everything that the Holy One, Blessed be He, created in His world, He only created for His Glory" (Pirkei Avot 6:11). This means one must worship the Name for the Glory of the Name, to increase the power above and unite the Great Name with its Glory. It is true that the revealed explanation is that He created it for His Glory, as the Zohar wrote: "so that His Divinity would be known,"[17] so there would be creatures who would know and recognize Him. And both of these explanations are true and depend upon each other. (*Shnei Luhot ha-Brit, Toldot Adam, Sha'ar ha-Gadol*, sect. 11)

On the surface (what Shelah calls "the revealed explanation"), the first Pirkei Avot text seems to say that all our motivations should be pure, that our good deeds should be done not to advance our own needs, but for higher needs. But the phrase *l'shem shamayim* is also interpreted literally, to unite the Name, that is, the *sefirah* of *Malkhut*, with *shamayim*, "Heaven," which is code language for the *sefirah* of *Tiferet*. Thus this teaching is read: all deeds should be in order to unite these *sefirot*, to unify God's Name on the supernal level, which is the purpose of the *tzorekh gavoha*. So it is not enough simply to fulfill the mitzvot, even if one does so wholeheartedly and with appropriate joyfulness. They must be fulfilled with the proper, kabbalistic intention, to unify the Name, to unify the *sefirot*. This is not simply about the normal requirement to recite prayers with *kavanah*, appropriate concentration and intention, but about the specific kabbalistic intention.

The second Pirkei Avot text seems to imply that if God had any need of the Creation, it was only to build a world in which there would be human beings who would be aware of Him. The kabbalistic interpretation has it just the opposite: God needs us to unite the Name with its Glory (i.e., to unify *Malkhut* and *Tiferet*). All prayer should be intended for this purpose.

In both texts Shelah acknowledges both the straightforward, "revealed" understanding of the text, called the *peshat*, as well as a mystical explanation; one does not eliminate the other. The sages understood that whatever creative interpretations could be given to a text, *ein mikra yodei midei peshuto*,[18] the text continues to maintain its basic meaning along with whatever else is derived from it.

Thus, for Shelah, prayer is ultimately meant to strengthen God, to serve the *tzorekh gavoha*, the need that goes beyond anything for which a Jew may pray or that he may express within prayer. All this is within the classical Rabbinic framework for prayer and its long-established normative rules, although these rules take on new significance, even when their content remains the same. Prayer must be done in a particular form and order, but also accompanied by the proper intentions and attentiveness. And the stakes are extremely high: "For one who transgresses one mitzvah is as if he transgresses against all of them."[19] If the Godhead will be affected, then one may not slip anywhere, and certainly not when one approaches God in prayer.

Petitionary prayer, such as for healing, is not only acceptable within this view, but encouraged. After all, it is presumed that such healing would also strengthen God. Elsewhere, Shelah affirms that such prayer can indeed save life and help us prevail in many personal battles with negative forces that fill the world.[20] Not all kabbalists accepted this completely; Meir ibn Gabbai (see below) taught that bringing such requests in prayer "is like one who brings profane things into the Temple court and contaminates the holy sanctuary"![21]

Some mystical passages, particularly in the Zohar, are virtually incomprehensible to the uninitiated. Even if one understands something about the *sefirot*, it can be frustrating to read and interpret a text when it speaks in code language. In this next segment, breaking the code leads to an affirmation of the *tzorekh gavoha* and the unity of the *sefirot*.

Even the enemies of Israel play a role in the kabbalistic scheme:

> **"Amalek came" (Exod. 17:8). Rabbi Shimon said: Mystery of wisdom! He came from a decree of severe judgment, and a single war took place above and below. You cannot find a word in Torah that does not contain supernal secrets of wisdom linked to the Holy Name. The Holy One, Blessed be He, said, as it were: When Israel are virtuous below, My power gains strength over all. When they are not virtuous, they, as it were, weaken the power above, and the power of severe judgment is strengthened. (Zohar 2:65b)[22]**

This is part of a longer teaching about the implications of the war waged against the Israelites by Amalek. Why does Amalek begin this war? When the Israelites came out of slavery in Egypt, they complained about God and said to Moses: "Why did you bring us up from Egypt, to kill us and our children and livestock with thirst?" (Exod. 17:3) Instead of being grateful, they brazenly "tried the Lord, saying: Is the Lord present among us or not?" (Exod. 17:7) The fact that Amalek's attack follows immediately in the Torah's account led careful readers to suggest that this war was brought upon them as a punishment for their disrespect. This reading is not original to the Zohar, or the kabbalists in general.[23] Thus, the "decree of severe judgment" comes upon the Israelites. However, the Zohar tells us that it is not just a war within our world, but is one "single war," with effects on the supernal level parallel to those in this world. We have seen this "mirroring" frequently, and the lesson here is that sin on this earthly level stirs up evil effects both here and above.

A notion frequently emphasized in the Zohar that all of the Torah is God's Name, and thus reveals His inner Being, is related to the idea in this text that every word in Torah contains secrets of wisdom "linked to the Holy Name."[24] Presumably the reason this is mentioned here is to emphasize that the story of Amalek in the Torah conveys some information about God, that is, the *sefirot*.

The conclusion of this teaching underscores the importance of devotion to the *tzorekh gavoha*. When Israel's virtue contributes to God's strength, His judgment is properly controlled and measured out. If Israel is not virtuous, judgment gets the upper hand and God's power (of compassion) is weakened. Although it is true that the phrase "as it were"—frequently seen in such texts—hedges all these statements somewhat, God as the *Ein Sof* is never altered, let alone weakened; but God's power as manifested through the *sefirot* still depends on human deeds, most specifically those of Israel.

Every event in Jewish history plays a role in this cosmic drama, even one that might seem to be specifically for our own benefit:

> "And they shall know that I the Lord am their God who brought them out of the land of Egypt that I might abide among them" (Exod. 29:46). The presence of the *Shekhinah* in Israel is also for the *tzorekh gavoha* and not the *tzorekh hedyot* [human need]. . . . Israel has the power to either weaken or strengthen the power above, depending upon their deeds. (Rabbeinu Bahya, commentary on Exod. 20:1)[25]

Why did God bring the Israelite slaves out of Egypt? We would normally assume that He did so to free the slaves themselves. The kabbalistic understanding is that this is a human need and, however pressing it might be, it is not of the level of the divine need. The Exodus itself is ultimately for *God*'s sake; it fulfills a divine need.

Next we see a talmudic reading that speculates about what happened when Moses ascended to meet with God and receive the Torah, followed by a kabbalistic explanation of the higher meaning of this experience.

> When Moses ascended on high, he found that the Holy One, Blessed be He, was binding crowns for the letters [of the Torah]. He said to him: "Moses, is there no *shalom* in your city?" Moses answered: "Does a servant say *shalom* to his master?" God said: "You should help me." Immediately, he said: "Now may the power of my Lord increase, as You have said" (Num. 14:17). (B. Shab. 89a)

> This matter [the *tzorekh gavoha*] is extremely difficult; it cannot be grasped by any intellect. This is because the human intellect cannot imagine that the supernal *tikkun* [repair or healing] is placed in the power of those below and that worship and prayer are for the *tzorekh gavoha*, were it not that the Holy One, Blessed be He, revealed this secret to the lord of the prophets [Moses], until he wondered at this. Thus the sages said, "He was binding crowns." This is the binding together and union of the letters, which is the secret of the powers of the united Name [in which these powers] are bound together. (Ibn Gabbai, introduction to *Avodat ha-Kodesh* [The service of the Holy One])[26]

The Rabbis suggest that since God was preparing to give Moses the Torah He also prepared the crowns that are attached to many letters of the Torah (as can be seen in any Torah scroll). This, of course, presumes the Rabbinic belief that the text of the Torah existed before and was in some sense a blueprint for the Creation![27] It also assumes that language is not just a tool for human communication, but (as we have seen earlier, especially in *Sefer Yetzirah*) includes the basic building blocks of creation.

Moses is silent as he approaches God. One reading of their dialogue is that God says to him: Don't people greet each other properly where you come from? Don't you at least say "*shalom*"? Moses responds by saying: A servant doesn't behave this way to his master; he waits for the master to speak. God responds: You should at least help Me out! This may simply mean that common courtesy (in this very uncommon situation) would suggest that Moses should at least wish God success in completing His work.[28] Thus the Rabbis suggest that this is why Moses responds by speaking of increasing God's power.

But a more explicitly kabbalistic reading of the dialogue understands that when God says "there is no peace in the city," it means that the Torah is being neglected or violated. Moses's response says: Is this truly possible? Even if we neglect the Torah, does that lessen its eternal truth? God's response in effect says that you have been told what God requires of you: to help Him, to help achieve the higher aim.[29]

Meir ibn Gabbai, one of the important sixteenth-century kabbalistic thinkers, wrote with an eye toward the reader grounded somewhat in philosophical thinking. Here he might well be speaking for many of us who find it hard to imagine that human action can help heal God. But he interprets God's work in this talmudic passage—binding crowns—to mean that He was unifying the letters. *Kosher* (*kuf-shin-reish*, from a different root than the word "kosher" as commonly used) means to link, to provide a *kesher*, a "connection," between the letters of the Torah, which also compose God's Name. And what God is revealing to Moses is that he also can unify God's Name, and that this is Moses's ultimate task. It is also the Jewish people's task, performed through learning Torah and fulfilling the mitzvot with the proper intentions.

As we will see in the next text, the kabbalist must be free from any impure motivation for personal gain.

The man who worships without the expectation of receiving a reward is a man whom his Creator has bestowed with the grace of entering the inner [meaning] of the hidden wisdom [i.e., of the Kabbalah], and knows and perceives that by reciting *Barekh aleinu* and *Refa'einu* ["Bless us," "Heal us"] [among the blessings contained in the weekday "Amidah"], the intention is to draw down the blessing and the

shefa within each and every blessing, to a certain *sefirah*, as we know. Behold, this man worships the Holy One, Blessed be He, and His *Shekhinah*, as a son and a servant serving his master with a perfect worship, out of love, without deriving any benefit or reward from that worship ... because the wise man [i.e., the kabbalist] by the quality of his [mystical] intention, when he intends during his prayer, his soul will be elevated by his arousal from one degree to another, from one entity to another, until it arrives and is welcome and appears before its Creator, and cleaves to its source, to the source of life. Then a great influx will be emanated upon her from there, and he will become a vessel, a place and a foundation for [that] influx, and from him it will be distributed to all the world ... until the *Shekhinah* will cleave to him. (Cordovero, *Pardes Rimonim* [The orchard of pomegranates], gate 32, ch. 1, as taught by Abraham Azulai)[30]

For the kabbalist, every single prayer has its particular purpose to accomplish in the supernal realm, as a result of which it draws down some measure of *shefa*, the flow from above that sustains the universe and all good within it. The kabbalist in prayer actually performs the prayer according to its literal meaning, but also intends his energy toward the proper place within the *sefirot*. If you know the true meaning—that is, the kabbalistic meaning—of the prayers, you will complete all the prayers and your intentions will be appropriate to accomplish some portion of this higher need.

Note also the formula of worshiping "the Holy One, Blessed be He, and His *Shekhinah*," code language for the unification of *Tiferet* and *Malkhut*. As shown in chapter 22, this unification is made explicit in connection with many prayers and is found in various prayer books in use today. Although there is talk of "cleaving," that is, *deveikut*, in both directions (the soul cleaving to God and the *Shekhinah* cleaving to the soul), it is important to note that in this text and many others *deveikut* is not a goal in and of itself but is purely for the sake of the *tzorekh gavoha*.

Like the mitzvot, *deveikut* is ultimately used to repair the Divine Name. While benefit comes to this world when the *tzorekh gavoha* is met, this is clearly downplayed in the statement that one prays "without deriving any benefit or reward from that worship."

The idea of becoming a vessel for this divine purpose is not so different from the notion of the tzaddik, the "righteous one" who serves as an intermediary between the supernal realms and our own. (Both are associated with the *sefirah Yesod*, which is the direct link between *Tiferet* and *Malkhut*.) This concept became a major theme in the development of Hasidism (see chapter 25).

Interestingly, this is offered as a commentary on Pirkei Avot 1:3, the teaching of Antigonus of Sokho: "Be not like those who serve the master with the expectation of receiving a reward." He clearly views devotion to the *tzorekh gavoha* as the ultimate fulfillment of this maxim.

Much as we might wish religion to improve us (or, often, to improve others!), personal development here is incidental to the primary purpose, the higher need. As Heschel puts it: "The purpose of man's service is to *give strength to God*, not to attain one's own individual perfection. Man is able to stir the supernal spheres. 'The terrestrial world is connected with the heavenly world, as the heavenly world is connected with the terrestrial one.'[31] In fulfilling the good, the corresponding sphere on high is strengthened; in balking it, the sphere is weakened."[32]

Part 4
Further Developments in Kabbalah

12

Prophetic-Ecstatic Kabbalah
ABRAHAM ABULAFIA

Mainline Kabbalah is focused on God. But as Mainline Kabbalah was developing, another form of Kabbalah came into being that was strictly focused on people—their experiences and longings for God and how to go about achieving them: Prophetic or Ecstatic Kabbalah. It is called "prophetic" because it was designed to enable a person to reach a level of divine knowledge, or prophecy, through some kind of union with God. And it is deemed "ecstatic" because the experiences involved, the highest form of contemplation, are associated with some form of an ecstatic state.

This expression of mysticism is primarily identified with the thirteenth-century Spanish teacher Abraham Abulafia. Although Abulafia was contemporaneous with the theosophical kabbalists and taught his system to at least one of the most renowned among them, his teachings were not widely accepted; his primary impact came much later, through Moshe Cordovero and many of the Hasidic masters. He was strongly influenced by many aspects of Maimonides's thinking, but was also drawn to *Sefer Yetzirah* and the work of Eleazar of Worms. Ultimately he developed his own system and achieved mystical experiences with messianic overtones; at one point he went to Rome to attempt to convert the pope and was only spared from martyrdom by the pope's sudden death.

Abulafia assumed that revelation was not a one-time event and not restricted to Moses or the other biblical prophets. Instead, through specific mystical practices, capable individuals could also achieve such revelation, by seeking to achieve an intense form of *deveikut*, an ecstatic union with God. At this level of enlightenment the mystic would receive information about the secrets of the Torah and God's decrees for the future, the prayers of the angels, and other magical knowledge. In the process of receiving revelation through this experience and attaining a level of prophecy, one would seek to reach the peak of his spiritual potential.

The mystic reached this ecstatic experience of intense *deveikut* through meditation on the letters of the Alef Bet, especially via permutations of the letters of the Divine Name. Thus Abulafia's form of mysticism was sometimes referred to as the "path of Names," in contrast to the "path of *sefirot*." As we will see, this approach is very much a direct outgrowth of many Rabbinic teachings as well as subsequent influences. Although much of the prophetic mystical experience takes place independently of normative Jewish practice, Abulafia is generally faithful to traditional Jewish ritual and ideas.

Chapter 5 addressed the sanctity of the Temple. In the talmudic teaching below we find that within the Temple there was some expectation of a visual experience of God.

> [Deut. 16:16: "Three times a year—on the Feast of Unleavened Bread, on the Feast of Weeks, and on the Feast of Booths—all your males shall appear (*yei-ra'eh*) before the Lord your God in the place that He will choose."] Yohanan ben Dahavai said in the name of Rabbi Yehudah: A man who is blind in one eye is exempt from appearing [at the Temple on the pilgrimage festivals, as it is said: *yir'eh* (He will see), *yei-ra'eh* (He will be seen)]. [Both words are represented with the same letters. Thus the text lends itself to the following interpretation:] As He comes to see, so He comes to be seen; just as [He comes] to see with both eyes, so also [He is] to be seen with both eyes. (B. Hag. 2a)

Many understood the service of the *Kohen Gadol* to include a vision of

God;[1] here and elsewhere it is suggested that ordinary Jews who came to the Temple on the festivals could have such an experience.[2] And though the Rabbis generally did not expect *giluy Shekhinah* (a visible representation of God) in their time—they only used this term in the Passover Haggadah![3]—many did believe it would happen in the future as it had happened in the past. This also recalls the *pardes* text in chapter 3, which appears to contain some elements of Prophetic Kabbalah in the ecstatic, unitive experience of Ben Azzai.

Some overlap does exist between *Merkavah* mysticism and Prophetic Kabbalah, and there is good reason to agree with Heschel's statement that "the *Merkavah* mystics, following perhaps late prophetic traditions about the mysteries of the divine throne, were striving to behold the celestial sphere in which the secrets of creation and man's destiny are contained."[4] Even before the Temple was destroyed we have seen that the maintenance of its purity—which ensured access to the Divine—was a primary concern for many Jews. And afterward, when it seemed that the Presence of God was no longer available, the *Merkavah* mystic sought to re-access that Presence and visit the supernal Temple, corresponding to what had been the worldly Temple.

There are also some very important differences between Prophetic Kabbalah and the older *Merkavah* mysticism. Prophetic Kabbalah, for example, is primarily centered on attaining an ecstatic awareness within the mystic and—unlike the *Merkavah* mysticism—not particularly interested in knowledge of the divine realm for its own sake. But it also clearly seeks to accomplish much larger goals beyond the experience.[5] Furthermore, the striving for *deveikut* is absent in *Merkavah* mysticism, which is much more attuned to specific, practical goals and information; thus, it is more akin to what we originally referred to as Affective Kabbalah.

The following is an excerpt quoted in the first kabbalistic work to appear in Eastern Europe (sixteenth century). Unlike the Mainline Kabbalah texts, it is a highly personal account of what happens to the mystic, focused on what happens to him, not what it does for God.

A great secret [concerning a teaching in *Midrash Bereshit Rabbah* 27:1]: "Great is the power of the prophets, who make the form resemble its Former." We have already explained what seems to be the meaning of this secret, but I then found a passage from one of the earlier authors on this subject, and my heart urges me to record it, for it offers an explanation of the foregoing. The following is the text of that account.

The deeply learned Rabbi Nathan, of blessed memory, said to me: "The complete secret of prophecy to a prophet consists in that suddenly he sees the form of his self standing before him, and he forgets his own self and ignores it . . . and that form speaks with him and tells him the future. And according to this our sages said: "Great is the power of the prophets who make the form [appearing to them] resemble its Former." And the learned sage, Rabbi Abraham ibn Ezra, of blessed memory, said:[6] "The one who hears [at the time of prophecy] is a human being, and the one who speaks is a human being." And another learned man wrote the following: "It occurred to me, by the power of combination [of letters of the holy Names of God] and by solitary meditation, that I encountered that light which accompanied me, as I have discussed in the book *Sha'arei Tzedek* [written by a student of Abulafia].[7] But to see my own form standing before me: this I was not granted, and this I cannot bring about." Yet another learned man writes the following: "And I, the young one, know and acknowledge with full certainty that I am not a prophet nor the son of a prophet, and I have not the holy spirit and I do not make use of the heavenly voice; these things have not been vouchsafed to me, and I have not taken off my garment or washed my feet. Nevertheless, I call heaven and earth to witness—as the heavens are my witness and my Guarantor is on high!—that one day I was sitting and writing down a kabbalistic secret, when suddenly I saw the form of my self standing before me, and my own self disappeared from me, and I was forced and compelled to cease writing." Likewise, while we were composing this book, and adding the vowel points to the Four-Letter Name, strange objects appeared before our eyes, like the image of red fire at sunset, until we were confused and stopped. And this happened to us several times while we were writing. (Moses of Kiev, *Shushan ha-Sodot*, 171–72)[8]

On the surface, the midrashic passage quoted here is somewhat cryptic. One way to read it is that the great power of the prophets is their creativity, their ability to explain God's revealed word and thus bring down to earth the divine message in such a way as to inspire the (human) form to be like the One who forms them. Ibn Ezra's comment (which might simply be taken as a statement that human beings are the vehicle for prophecy) is interpreted to mean that after the receipt of prophecy, the one who hears it is still a person, but a very different person. Thus, the mystical meaning given to the midrashic text is that prophecy causes the prophet to create a form of himself that resembles God, or at least resembles God much more closely. Here, the goal of mystical experience is that after one reaches prophecy, one sees a clear and precise vision of one's most ideal, developed self. You see yourself as you are today, and as you can be in the future; hopefully, the vision will even show you the way to make the transition. What we are seeing here, the creation of a soul, is almost as impressive as the mystics we saw earlier who believed in the creation of a living being, that is, a golem.

Now a sampling of the teachings of Abulafia himself, on how to bring about this mystical experience.

If you are wise and love God with all your heart, reflect on the root from which you were hewn. Know that you have been taken from the Throne of Glory and been endowed with the light of reason and created in God's image, and brought into existence by the grace of His Being, and your coming here has not been purposeless. Return therefore, for the Holy One of Israel has redeemed you and His holy Name is your glory. Hearken therefore, my son, to these words of mine. Bind them upon your neck, write them upon the tablets of your heart. They will be a jewel of grace upon your head and a necklace around your throat. Trust in God, not in man, for cursed is he who trusts in man.

Strive day and night to meditate on the Torah of the Lord, the Torah of Moses, the man of God, the divine wisdom. Read the prophetic books with understanding. Sing the words of the Writings. Study the sayings of the sages of blessed memory with a clear and alert mind. Gaze with divine intelligence into the works of the kabbalists. Here you will discover that which you seek and you will see that they all cry out in protest against the absence of wisdom, against unworthy deeds, and against limited understanding. For not a single word contains neither wisdom nor understanding nor knowledge nor word nor deeds, in the Torah, the Prophets, the Writings, and all the words of the Rabbis.

After you have done this, set your heart to know the glorious and tremendous Name of God, praised be He. Engrave it upon your heart never to be erased. For in this connection the Rabbis say that the sacred Names are not to be erased. Since they point to a picture of God, how then can that which depicts be erased since He who is depicted can never be erased? Never utter the Names without concentration but sanctify them, know them, and reflect that they are the angels of all being and the angels of God sent to you in order to raise you higher and higher and elevate you over all the nations upon earth. . . .

Now the time has come to elevate you in the stages of love so that you become beloved on high and delightful here on earth. First, begin by combining the letters of the Four-Letter Name. Gaze at all its combinations. Elevate it. Turn it over like a wheel which goes round and round, backwards and forwards like a scroll. Do not leave it aside except when you observe that it is becoming too much for you because of the confused movements in your imagination. Leave it for a while and you will be able to return to it later. You can then make your request of it and when you attain to wisdom do not forsake it. For the initial letters and the final letters, the numerical values, the *notarikons* [abbreviations], the combination of letters and their permutations, their accents and the forms they assume, the knowledge of their names and the grasping of their ideas, the changing of many words into one and one into many, all these belong to the authentic tradition of the prophets. By means of these, God will answer when you call upon Him, for you belong to His family. And now, my son, the secret of the Lord is with those who fear Him and to them will He make His covenant known. He will make known His covenant to the man who fears Heaven and whose covenant is perfect. (Abulafia, from manuscript)[9]

What do we learn from this description? First, this particular form of mystical experience comes with some substantial prerequisites. One must "love God with all your heart," meditate on the Torah "day and night," along with the rest of Scripture and the Rabbinic tradition, and appreciate the wisdom that is contained in all their words. One must also appreciate the sanctity of the Names of God and their purpose, which is "to raise you higher and higher." And, critically, one must "reflect on the root from which you are hewn." For Abulafia, knowledge of God, which goes along with self-knowledge, precedes an experience of union.[10]

Having fulfilled these prerequisites, one is ready for the meditative experience of what Abulafia called *hokhmat ha-tzeiruf*, combination of and meditation on the letters of the Alef Bet (and especially those of the Four-Letter Name) in such a way as to detach the self from material form and join with God. Normal Mysticism expressed its goal as purifying individuals: *l'tzaref et ha-beriyot*.[11] But the root *tz-r-f* can also have the meaning of "combining," and Abulafia makes this experience, *tzeiruf ha-otiyot*, the mystical practice of letter combination, his primary goal. After completely accepting the sanctity of the words of the Torah, one can attain a higher status through proper meditation on the permutation of its letters.

Meditating on the letters is intended to move the mystic into an autohypnotic trance, particularly when accompanied by specific postures, breathing exercises, tunes, visualization of colors, and specific written and mental meditations. These meditations, or mantras, "are not simple, and while one goal is to block out sensory distractions, an additional goal is stimulation and excitation of the mental process,"[12] perhaps to cause a sensory overload and thereby induce a mystical trance. This is also found in *Merkavah* mysticism, but there we see much more concern about the dangers of the ascent; the farther you go up, the farther and harder you can fall. Abulafia does not seem to be too worried about this danger.

Abulafia likens this process of *tzeiruf ha-otiyot* to playing a stringed instrument.

> **The strings touched with the right hand or the left hand vibrate, and the experience is sweet to the ears, and from the ears the sound travels to the heart and from the heart to the spleen [i.e., source of emotion]. The joy is renewed through the pleasure of the changing melodies, and it is impossible to renew except through the process of combinations of sounds. The combination of letters proceeds similarly. One touches the first string, that is, analogically, the first letter, and the right hand passes to the others, to the second, third, fourth, or fifth strings, and from the fifth it proceeds to the others. In this process of permutations new melodies emerge and vibrate to the ears, and then touch the heart. This is how the technique of letter combinations operates. . . . And the secrets which are disclosed in the vibrations rejoice the heart, for the heart then knows its God and experiences additional delight. (Abulafia, from manuscript)[13]**

This is certainly not a "normal," or normative, religious experience! It does not draw on magical powers or meet a divine need. Instead, by connecting with a holy process, it "touches the heart" and unifies the mystic with God. While it may be considered a form of *deveikut*, its purpose here is to create for the mystic an ecstatic experience, one that through union allows him to tap into God's wisdom and experience prophecy. Additionally, this text expresses profoundly the divine quality that may be inherent in the human inventive process, suggesting that artistic imagination draws on a meditative creativity similar to that of Abulafia's teachings.

One aspect of Maimonides's teaching that influenced Abulafia is the idea of the Active Intellect or Agent Intellect, a notion developed originally by Aristotle that understands human intellect as having two parts, passive and active. The passive intellect apprehends the forms of things, but the active intellect makes sense out of them, turning potential into actual knowledge, in the same way that light turns potential into actual color.

Many medieval philosophers regarded this Agent Intellect as coming from outside a person and having a divine aspect. Thus, if you could be unified in some way with this Agent Intellect, you could attain a state of prophecy. Maimonides held that the true reality of prophecy is "an overflow from God . . . through the intermediation of the Active Intellect."[14] Maimonides had hoped to restore prophecy as a step toward bringing the Messiah. He taught that there were different levels of human perfection, the highest of which was intellectual perfection, the part of a person closest to God.[15] Furthermore, the sages had taught: *Hakham adif mi-navi* (the sage is preferred to the prophet)[16]—that there was an intellectual level valued even above prophecy. In the Middle Ages many believed that at least some form of prophecy was once again available.[17]

Abulafia took what seemed to him to be the next reasonable step: *deveikut* and prophecy could be used to create a series of techniques to attain an even higher level of prophetic experience, which would achieve messianic proportions. He identifies the Agent Intellect with the angel Metatron, who would provide certain Divine Names to the mystic. This angel is equated with the supernal Torah, the source of all wisdom. Accordingly, in the next text, Abulafia provides a description of the perfect mystic.

Just as his Master [the Agent Intellect] who is detached from all matter is called the Knowledge, the Knower and the Known, all at the same time, since all the three are one in Him, so will he, the exalted man, the master of the exalted Name, be called intellect, while he is actually knowing; then he is also "the known" like his Master, and then there is no difference between them, except that his Master has His supreme rank by His own right and not derived from other creatures, while he is elevated to his rank by the mediation of the creatures. (Abulafia, *Commentary on Sefer ha-Yashar* [Book of the upright])[18]

This highly intellectualized mysticism virtually elevates the mystic to the level of God! Being a "master of the exalted Name," that is, being able to manipulate the various Names of God, is the key to achieving this level. As Abulafia writes elsewhere, "It is already known to every prophet from the prophets of Israel that it is impossible for any person in the world to reach the level of prophecy except if he has received the tradition concerning the knowledge of the Name [of God]."[19]

The statement that there is "no difference" between the Master (God) and the master of the Name (the mystic) indicates not only that the mystic taps into divine knowledge, but that there is in fact, as Moshe Idel notes, a state of mystical union between God and the mystic, "the total fusion of the human intellect with a comprehensive entity—the divine Active Intellect."[20] In this perfect actuality, "He and he become one entity, inseparable during this act."[21] It should be noted that many scholars of Jewish mysticism, most notably Gershom Scholem, were of the opinion that virtually no sense of mystical union existed in Jewish mystical experience.[22] Abulafia clearly thought otherwise.

Here is a more detailed set of directions about how to arrive at and manage this ecstatic experience.

Be prepared to meet your God, O Israelite! Make yourself ready to direct your heart to God alone. Cleanse the body and choose a special place where none will hear your voice. Sit in one place . . . and do not reveal your secret to any man. If you can, do it by day in your house, even if just a little, but it is best if you complete it during the night. When you prepare yourself to speak to the Creator and you wish Him to reveal His might to you, be careful to detach all your thoughts from the vanities of this world.

Cover yourself with your tallit, put tefillin on your head and arm, that you may be filled with awe of the *Shekhinah* which is near you. . . . Cleanse your clothes, and if possible, let all your garments be white, for this is most helpful in leading the heart to the fear and love of God. If it be night, kindle many lights, until all is bright.

Then take ink, pen, and a tablet, and remember that you are about to serve God in joy and with gladness of heart. Now begin to combine a few or many letters, to permute and combine them rapidly until your heart is warm. Be mindful of their movements and of what emerges in the process. And when you feel that your heart is warm and when you see that by combining letters you can grasp new things, which by tradition or by your own reason you would not be able to know, and when you are thus prepared to receive the influx of divine power which flows into you, then turn all your true thought to envision God and His exalted angels in your heart as if they were human beings sitting or standing near you; feel yourself like an envoy whom the king and his ministers are sending on a mission, and he is waiting to hear something about his mission, be it from the king himself or from his servants.

Having imagined this very vividly, turn your whole mind to understand with your thoughts the many things conjured up in you through the letters imagined. Ponder on them as a whole and in all their detail, like one to whom a parable or a dream is being related, or who meditates on a deep problem in a scientific book, and try thus to interpret what you will hear, that it may as far as possible accord with your reason. . . .

And all this will happen to you after you have flung away tablet and quill, or after they have dropped from you because of the intensity of your thought. Beware: the stronger the intellectual influx within you, the weaker will become your outer and inner parts. Your whole body will be seized with strong trembling, so you will think that surely you are about to die, because your soul, overjoyed with its knowledge, will leave your body. And be ready at this moment consciously to choose death, and then you will know you have come far enough to receive the influx. And then, wishing to honor the glorious Name by serving it with the life of body and soul, veil your face and be afraid to look at God.... Then return to your bodily needs, rise and eat and drink a little, or refresh yourself with a fragrant odor, and restore your spirit to its place until another time, and rejoice at your lot and know that God loves you! (Abulafia, *Hayyei ha-Olam ha-Ba* [The life of the world to come])[23]

This description of an Abulafian mystical experience begins, as one might expect, with important prerequisites. Unlike many Jewish rituals, this is to be performed alone; Abulafia may have been the first kabbalist to emphasize this as a condition for mystical experience. One must eliminate all mundane thoughts and make sure that both body and clothing are completely clean (something most of us would probably take for granted centuries later!); one wears white clothing and dons tallit and tefillin so as to maximize the appropriate sense of awe. It is best performed at night, in a room filled with candles. Although Abulafia does not make it explicit here, the mystic must also, as with other forms of Jewish mysticism, be morally perfected and fully observant, even though his observance of the commandments may have no direct bearing on the experience he is about to have.[24] Finally, prepare the place and the writing implements, and remember that this is to be a joyful experience!

Then one begins the process of the permutation of the Name. While

Abulafia does not go into detail here, a typical technique might use the Four-Letter Name or one of its sacred variations, beginning with writing the Name and various permutations, followed by recitation of the letters, and finally contemplation of them.[25] All this would lead the mystic into an altered state, where he would perceive that the angels were next to him, and whose intensity will make irrelevant any further writing. The mystic's body will seem weak to the point of death,[26] but his awareness will be maximally heightened![27]

Nonetheless, the mystic—even though he should be ready to die within this experience—must return from it. He is liberated from temporal connections but freed to serve God and fulfill his responsibilities to the community on a higher level. Abulafia himself lived an extremely active life; in addition to his many writings, he traveled extensively, taught many disciples, and preached to both Jews and Christians. But he would have preferred to be alone with God.[28]

> **The masters of the Kabbalah of the *sefirot* have thought that they would unify the Name of God and avoid any belief in the Trinity; but [instead] they have caused His Decadization ['*Issruhu*]. Just as the gentiles say that He is three and the three are one, so also some of the kabbalistic masters believe and say that the Godhead is ten *sefirot* and the ten are one. Therefore they have multiplied God at His maximum, and they [have] compounded Him in the most extreme manner, since there is no multiple greater than ten. (Abulafia, *V'zot Li-Yehudah* [This (blessing) for Judah], Deut. 33:7])[29]**

Abulafia is clear to distinguish himself from the Mainline Kabbalists, using the same criticisms we would expect to hear from those whose mysticism is much more of the "Normal" variety. He is certain that his Kabbalah is the true wisdom. Abulafia did believe in "*sefirot*," but his understanding of them is very different; he sees them as ten "intellects" within the Active Intellect. When the mystic becomes one with these, he also unifies all the divine aspects.[30] In effect, these *sefirot* are both divine and human qualities; since human beings share these qualities with God, the mystic has the possibility of attaining mystical union. Once again, the lower world mirrors the supernal realm.

> This is the mystery of how to pronounce the glorious Name. Make yourself right. Meditate in a special place, where your voice cannot be heard by others. Cleanse your heart and soul of all other thoughts in the world. Imagine that at this time, your soul is separating itself from your body, and that you are leaving the physical world behind, so that you enter the future world, the source of all life distributed to the living. This [the future world] is the intellect, which is the source of all wisdom, understanding, and knowledge, emanating from the King of Kings, the Holy One, Blessed be He. . . . Your mind must then come to join His mind, which gives you the power to think. Your mind must divest itself of all thoughts other than His thought. This becomes like a partner, joining you to Him through His glorious, awesome Name.
>
> You must therefore know precisely how to pronounce the Name. . . . When you begin, pronounce the *Alef* with any vowel, it is expressing the mystery of unity. You must therefore draw it out in one breath and no more. Do not interrupt this breath in any manner whatsoever until you have completed the pronunciation of the *Alef*. Draw out this breath as long as you extend a single breath. At the same time, chant the *Alef*, or whatever other letter you are pronouncing, while depicting the form of the vowel point.
>
> The first vowel is the *holem* [the sound of "o"], [a dot] above the letter. When you begin to pronounce it, direct your face toward the east, not looking up or down. You should be sitting, wearing clean, pure white robes over all your clothing, or else wearing your tallit over your head and crowned with your tefillin. You must face east, since it is from that direction that light emanates to the world.

[Chanting permutations of the Divine Name
would begin with these sounds:

OYO OYA OYEI OYEE OYU (representing *Alef*, with the vowel
   holem, followed by *Yud* with the different vowels)
AYO AYA AYEI AYEE AYU (representing *Alef*, with the vowel
   kamatz, followed by *Yud* with the different vowels)
EIYO EIYA EIYEI EIYEE EIYU (representing *Alef*, with the vowel
   tzeireh, followed by *Yud* with the different vowels)]

With each of the twenty-five letter pairs, you must move your head
properly. When you pronounce the *holem* [long "o" sound], begin
facing directly east. Purify your thoughts, and as you exhale, raise
your head, little by little, until when you finish, your head is facing
upward. After you finish, prostrate yourself on the ground. Do not
interrupt between the breath associated with the *Alef* and the breath
associated with the other letter in the pair. You may, however, take
a single breath, and it may be long or short. Between each pair of
letters, you may take two breaths without making a sound, but not
more than two. If you wish to take less than two breaths, you may
do so. After you finish each row of letters, you may take five breaths,
but no more. If you wish to take less, you may do so. If you change
anything or make any mistake in the order in any row, go back to
the beginning of the row. Continue until you pronounce it correctly.

Just as you face upward when pronouncing the *holem*, face downward when you pronounce the *hirik* [ee sound]. In this manner, you
draw down the supernal power and bind it to yourself. When you pronounce the *shuruk* [long "u" sound], do not move your head upward
or downward. Instead, move it straight forward [neither lowering
nor raising it]. When you pronounce the *tzeireh* [long "a" sound],
move your head from left to right. When you pronounce the *kametz*
["ah"], move it from right to left.

In any case, if you see any image before you, prostrate yourself before it immediately. If you hear a voice, loud or soft, and wish to understand what it is saying, immediately respond and say: "Speak, my Lord, for Your servant is listening" (1 Sam. 3:9). Do not speak at all, but incline your ear to hear what is being said to you. If you feel great terror and cannot bear it, prostrate yourself immediately, even in the middle of pronouncing a letter. If you do not see or hear anything, do not use this technique again all that week. . . .

If you feel that your mind is unstable, that your knowledge of Kabbalah is insufficient, or that your thoughts are bound to the vanities of the time, do not dare to pronounce the Name, lest you sin all the more. (Abulafia, *Or ha-Sekhel* [The light of the intellect])[31]

Once again, we are given specific preparations for the mystical experience. One separates oneself from the mundane and the physical world as much as possible, and prepares to connect to the Active Intellect, that is, the Mind of God, through the link provided by the Sacred Name. And this Name is to be pronounced, or rather chanted, as part of a meditation complete with breathing directions, head movements—often to be matched with different vowels—and prostrations.[32] All of this would likely focus the mind and body to synchronize, send the mystic into "overload," and create an altered consciousness so as to make him receptive to images, sounds, and new wisdom.[33]

With God's Name available virtually anywhere and at any time as a conduit to the higher realms, it can be said that according to Abulafia, the Divine is indeed within everything. Moshe Idel refers to his thought as a "limited pantheism," described as "the presence of the separate (i.e., the spiritual) everywhere."[34] It should not be surprising that Abulafia does not place special significance on the Land of Israel in relation to his mystical system.

For several centuries, very few people studied or practiced Abulafia's brand of Kabbalah, until Cordovero integrated it with what he calls here the "pleasant," that is, the Mainline Kabbalah of the Zohar:

There are four categories of [the study of] Torah: (1) the simple narrative level, the material enclothing of the Torah; (2) the study of the law and midrashic lore, in their literal sense; (3) the study of the "pleasant Kabbalah" such as the secrets explicated by the Zohar . . . for all of the midrashim and *mishnayot*, as well as all the laws and commandments, contain inner secrets and pleasant secrets; and (4) the spirituality of the letters, their essence and combination, one within the other. (Cordovero, *Pardes Rimonim, Sha'ar ha-Otiyot* [Gate of letters], Gate 27, ch. 1)[35]

Cordovero certainly did not take the Mainline Kabbalah lightly; he wrote a vast commentary on the Zohar! But here, and in general, he places the Prophetic Kabbalah on an even higher level.[36] Through Cordovero and others, Abulafian Kabbalah made its way into the practice of the early Hasidic masters and continues to affect the development of Jewish mysticism. Variations on this form of meditation have become popular among non-Hasidic Jews as well, and we can expect further developments in this field as Abulafian Kabbalah becomes better known within the Jewish community.[37]

13

The Role of the Torah

The sages of past centuries, and Orthodox Jews today, read the Torah as the literal word of God, along with interpretations known and yet to be uncovered. But kabbalists understood it to convey even more, endowing the Torah's laws and stories with symbolic meaning, as we have already seen regarding the Zohar. For these mystics, every action was charged with ultimate significance, and conversations and events within the Torah were understood to reflect processes within the *sefirot*.

Mysticism always contains the potential for a rebellion against established law. After all, if one has a "direct line" to God and can "tap in" to His will, why does one need the law as handed down? (Of course it is always possible that even a "direct line" may be corrupted, as with the "telephone" game where a whispered message is significantly altered along the chain of communication; see chapter 21 for some examples of how this antinomian tendency influenced the messianic impulse).

With rare exceptions, Jewish mystics generally have been loyal to established law while understanding its meaning in a radically different way. They have, however, added various customs and practices and, most especially, reinterpreted the meaning of existing practices. This presumes, as the mystics believe, that the Torah contains a potentially infinite number of meanings, which await our discovery through study and mystical experience. As David Ariel has put it, "The Kabbalists studied Torah, or decoded Torah, because it was a window to divinity. They were not concerned with the plain meaning of the text but with the meta-text of the Torah."[1]

The first text in this chapter, a lengthy (and greatly abridged) episode from the Zohar, is an excellent illustration of this belief as well as many other ideas underlying much of Jewish mysticism, and thus merits extended attention. It is referred to as *Sava d'Mishpatim*, the old man who expounds on many of the verses from *parashat* Mishpatim (Exodus 21–24).

One night, Rabbi Hiyya and Rabbi Yosi met at the Tower of Tyre. They lodged there, delighting in each other. Rabbi Yosi said: "How happy I am to see the face of *Shekhinah*! For just now, the whole way here, I was pestered by an old man, a donkey driver, who kept asking me riddles the whole way.

"What is a serpent that flies in the air and wanders alone, while an ant lies comfortably between its teeth? Beginning in union, it ends in separation.

"What is an eagle that nests in a tree that never was—its young plundered, though not by created creatures? Ascending, they descend; descending, they ascend. Two who are one, and one who is three.

"Who is a beautiful maiden without eyes, her body concealed and revealed? She emerges in the morning and is concealed by day, adorning herself with adornments that are not.

"All this he asked on the way, and I was annoyed. Now I can relax! If we had been together, we would have engaged in words of Torah, instead of other words of chaos."

Rabbi Hiyya said: "That old donkey driver, do you know anything about him?"

He answered, "I know that his words have no substance. For if he knew anything, he would have opened with Torah, and the way would not have been empty!"

Rabbi Hiyya said: "That donkey driver, is he here? For sometimes in those empty ones, you may discover bells of gold!"

He said to him, "Here he is, getting fodder ready for his donkey."

They called him, and he came over to them. He said, "Now two are three, and three are like one!"

Rabbi Yosi said: "Didn't I tell you that all his words are empty and inane?"

Rabbi Yosi's initial comment is based on numerous teachings in the Rabbinic tradition suggesting that one who welcomes the wise, or one's friend, is considered to be welcoming the *Shekhinah*.[2] But despite his pleasure, Rabbi Yosi is irritated at having had to travel with someone who seems to be an ignoramus, speaking in "silly" riddles instead of discussing elevated matters that might also evoke the presence of the *Shekhinah*. We will not here discuss much about the first two riddles except to note that they refer to stages in the process of reincarnation, a subject very important to many kabbalists (see chapter 19). Rabbi Hiyya is more hesitant than Rabbi Yosi to assume much about the donkey driver, since he may possess "bells of gold," that is, concealed wisdom. (The High Priest, Aaron, wore bells of gold on his robe, and bells also serve as a mark of revelation in Rabbinic texts.[3])

The last part of the second riddle is solved as the donkey driver joins the two sages; two become three and the three join together as one. It is as if the donkey driver knew that this conversation would take place.

He sat before them and said: "Rabbis, I have become a donkey driver only a short time ago. Before, I wasn't one. But I have a son, and I put him in school; I want him to engage in Torah. When I find one of the Rabbis traveling on the road, I guide his donkey from behind. Today I thought that I would hear new words of Torah. But I haven't heard anything!"

Rabbi Yosi said, "Of all the words I heard you say, there was one that really amazed me. Either you said it out of folly, or they are empty words."

The Old Man said, "And which one is that?"

He said, "The one about the beautiful maiden."

The Old Man opened and said, "'God is with me; I have no fear. What can any human do to me? God is with me, helping me.... It is good to take refuge in God.' (Ps. 118:6–8)

"How fine, lovely, precious and sublime are words of Torah! But should I say them in the presence of those from whose mouths, until now, I have not heard a single word? But I should speak, because there is no shame at all in saying words of Torah in the presence of anyone!"

We learn that the donkey driver has recently been "reincarnated" into this task; perhaps this information, along with Rabbi Hiyya's caution, brings Rabbi Yosi to ask about the one riddle he thought might have some importance. But the old man is somewhat reticent to reveal the meaning of this, given that he knows nothing of his company or whether they are prepared for esoteric wisdom.[4]

It is of interest that, as we frequently see regarding the behavior of the sages, the old man does not simply speak; he "opens" his discourse. This suggests the opening of a shade to let in the light, very much in the spirit of the explanation that will follow.

The Old Man covered himself.... He opened and said, "'Moses went inside the cloud and ascended the mountain' (Exod. 24:18). What is this cloud? The one of which it is written, 'I have set My bow in the cloud' (Gen. 9:13). We have learned that the rainbow removed her garments and gave them to Moses. Wearing that garment, Moses went up the mountain; from within it, he saw what he saw, delighting in all, until here."

The comrades came and fell down before him and, weeping, they said, "If we have come into the world just to hear these words from your mouth, it is enough for us!"

... The Old Man said: "Companions, not for this alone did I begin to speak, for an old man like me doesn't rattle or call with just a single word. Human beings are so confused in their minds! They do not see the path of truth in Torah. Torah calls out to them every day, cooing, yet they do not want to turn their heads. Even though I said that a word of Torah emerges from her sheath, is seen for a moment, then quickly hides away—that is certainly so, but when she reveals herself from her sheath and quickly hides, she does so only for those who know her and recognize her."

Recall the text from chapter 3 where Rabbi Eleazar ben Arakh shows his teacher what he has learned about hidden wisdom; in the parallel passage to that text from the Babylonian Talmud, when the student begins to teach, the master not only dismounts from his donkey, but also wraps himself up in a cloak.[5] When the old man covers himself at the outset of his explanation, this may be an allusion to the earlier text, suggesting that this was a practice prior to revealing such secrets.

In good Rabbinic fashion, the old man associates different verses from the Torah with a common note. Here the cloud into which Moses enters is linked with the cloud in which the rainbow was placed after the Flood. In Ezek. 1:28, the divine Glory is compared to "the appearance of the bow in the cloud on a rainy day." Thus some commentators see the rainbow as representing the *Shekhinah*. We have noted that *sefirot* are associated with different colors, and thus the rainbow of *Shekhinah* is understood as a pathway to the *sefirot* above. Similarly, in this view, Moses ascends into the cloud to experience the delights of the higher levels. Other commentators understand the rainbow as a representative of *Yesod* (i.e., a muted phallic symbol),[6] or *Tiferet* descending to *Yesod*, wrapped within the cloud of *Shekhinah*.[7]

Moses serves as the facilitator for the now-familiar union of *Tiferet* and *Shekhinah*. His garments also help protect him from the power inherent in the higher levels. It may be helpful to note that the Zohar treats Moses as the husband of the *Shekhinah*;[8] the emphasis on "delighting" provides a further erotic tinge to the subject. (This is a recurring theme within this text;[9] see chapter 14 for the role of the erotic in Jewish mysticism.)

Rabbi Yosi's and Rabbi Hiyya's responses are similar to comments found in earlier Rabbinic texts and clearly indicate that they recognize the wisdom previously concealed by the donkey driver. But the donkey driver makes it clear that what he has said (which is considerably more than what is included here) is just the beginning. He is also saddened because so few people turn toward the wisdom of the Torah. It beckons them, offering them great delights, but they are unaware and unfocused. If they would "know her and recognize her," if they would apply their energies and focus on the Torah, she would reveal herself further.

> "This may be compared to a beloved maiden, beautiful in form and appearance, concealed secretly in her palace. She has a single lover, unknown to anyone, except to her, in concealment. Out of his love for her, this lover passes by her gate constantly, lifting his eyes to every side. Knowing that her lover is constantly circling her gate, what does she do? She opens a little window in her secret palace, reveals her face to her lover, then swiftly withdraws, concealing herself. None of those near the lover sees or notices, only the lover, and his inner being and heart and soul follow her. He knows that out of love for him she revealed herself for a moment, to arouse him.
>
> "So it is with a word of Torah: she reveals herself only to her lover. Torah knows that he who is wise of heart circles her gate every day. What does she do? She reveals her face to him from the palace and beckons him with a hint, then swiftly withdraws to her hiding place. None of those there knows or notices; he alone does, and his inner being and heart and soul follow her. Thus Torah reveals and conceals herself, approaching her lover lovingly to arouse love with him."

Now the old man provides an answer to the third riddle. The maiden is probably "without eyes" because no one (presumably excepting her lover) has seen her. The idea of Torah as a hidden princess within a palace is found in Rabbinic literature,[10] but also fits well within medieval Spain; students may well find it reminiscent of the Rapunzel story. Instead of a prince, the hero of this parable is the mystic who pays attention and understands when the Torah gives him a glimpse of her hidden mysteries. Of course in this story he is the one who is seduced!

> "Come and see! This is the way of Torah: At first, when she begins to reveal herself to a human, she beckons him momentarily with a hint. If he perceives, good; if not, she sends for him, calling him 'simple': 'Tell that simple one to come closer, so I can talk with him!' As it is written: 'Whoever is simple, let him turn here, he who lacks understanding' (Prov. 9:4). As he approaches, she begins to speak with him from behind a curtain she has drawn, words suitable for him, until he reflects little by little. This is *derasha*. Then she converses with him from behind a delicate sheet, words of riddle, and this is *haggadah*.
>
> "Once he has grown accustomed to her, she reveals herself to him face to face and tells him all her hidden secrets, all the hidden ways, concealed in her heart since primordial days. Then he is a complete man, husband of Torah, master of the house, for all her secrets she has revealed to him, concealing nothing.
>
> "She says to him, 'Did you see the hinting word with which I beckoned you at first? These are the secrets! This is what it is!'
>
> "Then he sees that one should not add to these words or diminish them. Then [the] *peshat* of the verse, just like it is! One should not add or delete even a single letter. So human beings must be alert, pursuing Torah to become her lover."

We see here the expanding meaning of Torah; the student is taught *derasha*, homiletical and imaginative interpretation. At the next level, he is taught *haggadah*, here meaning allegorical interpretation. But eventually he learns all that was concealed "since primordial days," before Creation, and becomes complete, knowing all of the *sod*, the mysteries of the Torah that were previously unknown to him. She takes off all her adornments (thus addressing that portion of the riddle dealing with "adornments that are not"), and he experiences revelation without any obstacle. He thus becomes a *ba'al Torah*, a "husband of Torah." Normally *ba'al Torah* would be idiomatically translated as "master of Torah," a scholar, but here the word *ba'al*, "husband," is understood literally. And what does it mean to have this unfettered access? It means not only knowledge, but power, as the Zohar tells us elsewhere: "For whoever engages in Torah has no fear of mishaps of the world; he is protected above and protected below. Furthermore, he binds all demons of the world and sends them down to the depths of the great abyss."[11]

Peshat is the simple meaning of the text, but the verb can also mean "to strip." While one may not add to or subtract from the words of the Torah (Deut. 13:1, "You shall not add to it and you shall not diminish it"), the *peshat* is just the beginning, from which one "strips" layers of meaning, ultimately coming to love the inner meaning of the Torah. While the *peshat* as simple meaning of the text is never completely lost, the text seen through the eyes of the lover gains new, even infinite levels of revelation. And this is part of the mystic's experience of closeness with God, perhaps an infinite closeness; he now knows exactly why nothing should be "stripped" from the Torah, for every detail, every allusion to higher realms, gives him a better glimpse of God.[12]

> He was silent for a moment. The comrades were amazed; they did not know if it was day or night, if they were really there or not....
>
> "Enough, comrades! From here on, you will know that the Evil Side has no power over you. I, Yeiva Sava, have stood before you to arouse these words."
>
> They rose like one awaking from sleep and prostrated themselves before him, unable to speak. After a while they wept. Rabbi Hiyya opened and said: "'Let me be a seal upon your heart, like the seal upon your hand' (Songs 8:6).... Love and sparks of flame of the heart

will follow you! May it be God's Will that our image be engraved in your heart as your image is engraved in ours!"

He kissed them and blessed them, and they went.

When they rejoined Rabbi Shimon and told him all that happened, he was delighted and amazed. He said, "How fortunate you are to have attained all this! Here you were with a heavenly lion, a mighty warrior compared with whom many warriors are nothing, and you did not recognize him right away! I wonder how you escaped being punished by him! The Holy One, Blessed be He, must have wanted to save you!" (Zohar, *Sava d'Mishpatim* 2:94b–95a, 99, 105b, 114a)[13]

Omitted from this account are many more teachings from the old man, which, if given orally, might have taken hours. But Rabbi Yosi and Rabbi Hiyya are captivated. We are told that they did not know if they were really there or not; one wonders where else they might have thought they were. Perhaps they imagined themselves to be in the heavenly academy envisioned by the Rabbis of old.[14] Where else could they have received such wisdom? And indeed he concludes by telling them that the power of his teaching will protect them from all evil. He also reveals his name, Yeiva Sava (*Sava*, "elder"). Yeiva Sava was a relatively minor figure in the Talmud, who lived in the third century. The Zohar itself is attributed to a second-century sage, Shimon bar Yohai; here, as with many of the *Heikhalot* texts, the Zohar introduces another historical figure and places kabbalistic wisdom in his mouth.[15]

When the Torah is viewed in this way, study of Torah is also a mystical experience, insight into the divine nature. But the reverse is also true; mystical experiences generate interpretations of the Torah that then become mystical texts. Although the kabbalists dealt with some highly theoretical issues, they believed that their mysticism was primarily experiential. This is not to say that the story of our text actually happened, only that it may have been the result of a mystical experience, which gives us a fuller understanding of the text.

The verse Rabbi Hiyya cites is used to express the love between *Knesset Yisrael* (the People of Israel) and *ha-Kadosh Barukh Hu* (the Holy One, Blessed be He), *Shekhinah* and *Tiferet*. It is with this image (and a brief Torah teaching, omitted here) that Rabbi Hiyya blesses Yeiva Sava, who in turn blesses them and departs. Finally, we see that Rabbi Shimon, on receiving their report, reacts primarily with surprise that they even survived the encounter, after failing initially to recognize that they were in the presence of "a supernal lion"!

We see in this account many important aspects and principles of Jewish mysticism:

> From the appearance of the donkey driver and his subsequent revelation as "a supernal lion," we are reminded that what is apparent and revealed is not necessarily what is real.
>
> An important part of the task of the mystic is to penetrate through the veil of reality and perceive what is concealed.[16]
>
> Mystical interpretation of the Torah [*sod*] is the true interpretation, providing access to God, actual *deveikut*.
>
> The mystical understanding of Torah includes symbolic language and contains multiple levels of meaning.[17]
>
> The gap between humankind and God, like the garments of the maiden, is an illusion.
>
> Mystical experience is transformational, a vehicle through which one may reach higher consciousness, and it is accessible to the one who masters the appropriate techniques.

In the following text, the Zohar replies directly to advocates of the philosophical approach to Jewish life, who believe that the Torah is a book much like other books, and certainly not to be compared to a lover.

Rabbi Shimon said: "Woe to the person who says Torah presents a mere story and ordinary words! If so, we could compose a Torah right now with ordinary words, and better than all of them, to present

matters of the world! Even rulers of the world possess words more sublime. If so, let us follow them and make a Torah out of them. Ah, but all the words of Torah are sublime words, sublime secrets!

"Come and see: The world above and the world below are perfectly balanced; Israel below, the angels above. Of the angels it is written: 'He makes his angels spirits' (Ps. 104:4).[18] This relates to the celestial realm. But when they descend, they put on garments of this world. If they did not put on a garment befitting this world, they could not endure in this world, and the world could not endure them. If this is so with the angels, how much more so with Torah, who created them and all the worlds, and for whose sake they all exist. In descending to this world, if she did not put on the garments of this world, the world could not endure.

"So this story of Torah is the garment of Torah. Woe to the person who thinks that the garment is the real Torah and not something else! He will have no portion in the world to come. That is why David said: 'Open my eyes, so I can see wonders out of your Torah' (Ps. 119:18): that is, what is under the garment of Torah.

"Come and see: There is a garment visible to all. When those fools see someone in a good-looking garment, they look no further. But the essence of the garment is the body; the essence of the body is the soul. So it is with Torah. She has a body: the commandments of Torah, called "the embodiment of Torah." This body is clothed in garments, the stories of this world. Fools of the world look only at that garment, the story of Torah; those who know more do not look at the garment, but rather at the body under that garment. The wise ones, servants of the King on high, those who stood at Mount Sinai, look only at the soul, root of all, real Torah. In the time to come, they are destined to look at the soul of the soul of Torah.

"Come and see: So it is above. There is garment, body, soul, and soul of soul. The heavens and their hosts are the garment. The Community of Israel [*Knesset Yisrael*] is the body who receives the soul, beauty [*Tiferet*] of Israel. So She is the body of the soul. The soul we have mentioned is *Tiferet* of Israel, real Torah. The soul of the soul is the Holy Ancient One. All is connected, this one to that one.

"Woe to the wicked who say Torah is merely a story! They look at this garment and no further. Happy are the righteous who look at Torah properly! Just as wine must be contained in a jar, so Torah must be contained in this garment. So concerning Torah, look only at what is under the garment. All these words and all these stories are garments." (Zohar 3:152a)[19]

To the mystic, the Torah is not merely composed of stories, ordinary words. All its words are "sublime secrets," garments for the true wisdom. Angels—like those who came to Abraham in Genesis 18—appear as human beings, putting on "the garments of this world." Similarly, the Torah puts on the garments of its stories and words, but just as a wise person will not assume that the fine garments of a wealthy person will tell you much about the person's character, the mystic sees through these garments to the true meaning, to the soul of the Torah, that is, all that the stories and laws embody. The discussion about removing the garment should be understood in the same way as in the previous text.

The Rabbinic tradition teaches that the souls of *all* Jews, including all Jews to be born in the future, were present at Mount Sinai.[20] But here the Zohar suggests that only the "wise ones," that is, the mystics, were present. In his commentary Daniel Matt writes: "Perhaps only mystics are aware that they were present at Sinai."[21] In other words: All Jews were there, but not all remember the experience, only those who cultivate the memory through their devotion to mystical truths. They "look only at the soul, root of all, real Torah"; they see beyond the surface and penetrate to the deepest level of meaning.[22]

As earlier noted, *Knesset Yisrael* is code language for *Malkhut*, or *Shekhinah*, who receives into herself *Tiferet*. And *Tiferet* is associated with the Written Torah. But there is also a soul beyond *Tiferet*, the "Holy

Ancient One"; that is code for the *Ein Sof*, the source of everything. It is the *Ein Sof* that created the Torah as a blueprint for Creation, as a way of conveying the supernal world to us.

Knowledge of Torah, of course, goes hand in hand with knowledge of God, as emphasized in this eighteenth-century Hasidic teaching:

> **What is the meaning of "Know Him in all your ways" (Prov. 3:6)? When the Holy One, Blessed be He, gave the Torah, the entire world was filled with the Torah, for it says: "As I live, says the Lord, and as the Lord's Presence fills the whole world" (Num. 14:21);[23] thus, the Torah and the Holy One, Blessed be He, are one. Now there is nothing in which the Torah is not within it. This is the meaning of "Know Him in all your ways." And anyone who says that the Torah is one thing, and the things of this world are another, is a heretic. (Pinhas of Koretz, *Midrash Pinhas*, 21a)[24]**

God, who fills the world, fills the world with Torah; the Torah relates to everything. Thus the Torah and God are both found together, everywhere. By learning Torah, or fulfilling its commandments and its lessons, one achieves *deveikut*, a deep intimacy with God. Rabbi Pinhas is fixed on this understanding of Torah as containing all things and being unified with God's Presence—to such a degree that anyone who denies it, who suggests a separation between the Torah and worldly matters, is decreed to be a *kofer*, a heretic, who denies an essential element of Jewish faith. Furthermore, if "there is nothing in which the Torah is not within it," for practical purposes, there can be an infinite number of meanings given to the Torah.[25]

From the idea that the Torah contains infinite meaning, it is a relatively small step to the idea that the Torah is composed of names of God, or actually is in its entirety one Name of God. As Isaiah Tishby notes, "This idea gives the Torah a quality of divinity, like the *sefirot*, which are also conceived as a fabric woven of Divine Names; and it also opens the door to free-ranging mystical interpretations of Scripture."[26]

Rabbinic Judaism understood one of the essential divisions among the commandments to be between *mishpatim* and *hukkim*.[27] *Mishpatim*, "judgments," are directives readily understood as essential to the framework of society. *Hukkim*, "decrees," are the laws not readily understood, perhaps—at least seemingly—having no rational basis. Why does the Torah not spell out the reasons why such laws should be observed? Some theorized that doing so might encourage rationalizing nonadherence to the command; one could decide that the purpose of the mitzvah could be better served by some other action, and this might undermine the fabric of Jewish life entirely. Of course in the medieval period Jews faced different pressures than they had earlier; there were alternative erudite religious expressions available, so both philosophers and kabbalists felt a need to explain why all the mitzvot remained compelling. But when philosophers tried to defend observance of *hukkim* through explanations of their purposes, rather than teaching their cosmic effects, the kabbalists complained that this led people to justify *not* observing them at all![28] As Daniel Matt notes, "The Kabbalists felt that they had thereby subordinated the divine command to human reason."[29] Reason could also lead people to dispense with the commandments if their purpose could be fulfilled through some other means.

The kabbalists did, in fact, believe that there were reasons for the *hukkim* to be observed, but that only Kabbalah provided such an understanding. These mitzvot would benefit God in some way (see chapter 11 on the *tzorekh gavoha*), and their performance would affect the *sefirotic* realm. Either way, the precise reason is only revealed to the mystics. The next text (by Nahmanides in the generation before the writing of the Zohar) is an expression of this approach.

These forbidden relationships are included within the category of the *hukkim*, which are "decrees of the King."[30] Such a decree is a matter that arises in the mind of the King, who is wise in the management of the kingdom. He is the One who knows the need and benefit of that

order which He commands, but He does not reveal it to the people, except to the wisest of His advisors. (Nahmanides, commentary on Lev. 18:6 [a prohibition of incestuous behavior: "None of you shall come near anyone of his own flesh to uncover nakedness:[31] I am the Lord"])[32]

Incest may seem like a logical prohibition to us, but there may not be a clear ethical reason why consenting adults should not be able to engage in it. Therefore, the sages classified it as one of the *hukkim*. And Nahmanides's teaching here applies to all the *hukkim*: God knows why, and only the wisest human beings also know. Those people, of course, are the kabbalists! They understand the cosmic effects of the fulfillment or violation of specific mitzvot.

What might it mean for us if "the garments of the maiden," the gap between God and us, turned out to be an illusion? We would find access to divine wisdom and, perhaps, share in God's power. And while the mystic definitely should prefer wisdom to power, both remain incentives for bridging the gap.

14

Sexuality in Jewish Mysticism

"God loves you!" That doesn't sound like something many Jews would hear in synagogue. But it would be perfectly consistent with Jewish tradition, not only from the standpoint of Normal Mysticism (where God's love for Israel is mentioned frequently in the liturgy), but also as a powerful metaphor for the mystic's longing for intimacy with his Beloved.

Erotic themes play an important role in Jewish mystical experiences and texts. But these themes did not replace normal sexual life, which was expected of most mystics. As traditional Jews, most understood and, to the best of our knowledge, abided by the teaching that "whoever does not engage in propagation is considered by Scripture to be shedding blood and diminishing the likeness [of God]."[1] The Zohar also taught that one who does not procreate causes the *Shekhinah* to depart,[2] while a married man is constantly accompanied by the *Shekhinah*.[3]

While we don't know what happened in their bedrooms, we should not assume that the use of sexual metaphors in the mystical life was, as Moshe Idel suggests, "a compensation for the frustration of 'real' erotic experiences. Abraham Abulafia, Isaac of Akko, [and] . . . other kabbalists . . . were seemingly married or, at least, [were] persons who viewed sexual relations as religiously licit."[4] (There were a few important exceptions, most notably Rabbi Nahman of Bratslav.[5]) While the mystics shared the general Rabbinic concern about the power of the sexual drive, it may be precisely because most of them enjoyed an active sexual life that they understood the accuracy of the sexual metaphors.

Jewish mystics never separated love from sex and its procreative potential. The mystics are always aware that, as Byron Sherwin notes, "the organ of generation bears the sign of the covenant. Through this organ flow the seeds for the perpetuation of the Jewish people and of the human race."[6] For this reason and others that we will examine, the sexual act has great significance for the mystic.

As we have read, *deveikut*, "cleaving," is a core term for the mystical relationship with God. This is the same term the Bible uses when it tells us that "a man leaves his father and mother and cleaves to his wife, so that they become one flesh" (Gen. 2:24). So it is not uncommon for *deveikut* and the erotic to be understood in similar terms.

In the commentaries on Song of Songs, the biblical book that deals most directly with sexual love, the sages enthusiastically interpreted the book as a metaphor for the love relationship between God and the Jewish people; they even called the book the "Holy of Holies" among the biblical books (see chapter 4). The fact that many reject the Rabbis' metaphorical reading does not change the role it played within the tradition. For those who do read it as an exaltation of physical love, its presence in Scripture certainly serves to emphasize that the sexual drive is mandated within Jewish life.[7] For the sages and the mystics, it served as a frequently repeated message: physical love is a way to understand spiritual love. The way we encounter a beloved sexually may say much about how we encounter the Divine.

The Temple—at least in the Rabbinic imagination—was a location for some erotic themes (see chapter 5). When the Israelites performed the commandments properly, the cherubim were believed to turn toward each other, expressing the love between God and Israel "like the love of male and female." Just as man and woman naturally bond, so God and Israel should naturally bond. The Temple itself, as the meeting point for the "lovers" God and Israel, is even compared to the nuptial bed.[8]

For the kabbalists, everything that exists is thus a consequence of and intrinsically related to the higher union of God and Israel among the *sefirot*. Thus anything to do with physical love has this extra spark of overwhelming importance. When one's sexuality is attached to "the circle of life," and even to realms beyond our understanding, one has a sense of being able to "find our place on the path unwinding in the circle,"⁹ to find our role in God's plan, as well as our own. Finally, the flip side of this affirmation of marital sexuality's importance is that all other sexual activity can do immense cosmic harm. This would be true not only of adultery, but also of homosexual and masturbatory acts.

What does the Torah tell us about the relationship of man and woman? The Creation story is commonly understood to say that Adam is created first, and Eve is then formed from his rib. But the Rabbis in this text suggest something very different.

> **"You form me behind and before"** (Ps. 139:5). **Rabbi Jeremiah ben Elazar said: When the Holy One, Blessed be He, created the first man, he created him a hermaphrodite, as it is said: "Male and female He created them [and called them Adam]"** (Gen. 5:2). **Rabbi Samuel bar Nahman said: When the Holy One, Blessed be He, created the first man, He created him double-faced [*du-partzufim*], then He split him and gave him two backs, one on this being and one on the other. [Others] objected to him: But it is written, "He took one of his ribs [*mi-tzal'otav*]"** (Gen. 2:21)! **He replied: That means, one of his two sides, just as it says: "And for the other side [*tzela*] of the Tabernacle"** (Exod. 26:20). (*Midrash Bereshit Rabbah* 8:1)

Rabbi Jeremiah begins with a verse in Psalms, interpreting it to mean that the first human is formed "behind and before," that is, dual sided, with both male and female sexual organs; as per Gen. 5:2, they are "Adam," one human being. Rabbi Samuel adds another textual basis for this, showing that the word *tzela* in Gen. 2:21 actually means "side." Thus the original human being was two sided, dual sexed. From this we should understand that sexual union is a natural state . . . if, of course, one finds one's "other half"! So the union of male and female is actually a reunion, which has implications for how the mystics understood the significance of sex.

We turn to a thirteenth-century kabbalistic text on sexuality, *Iggeret ha-Kodesh* (*The Holy Letter*). The author is unknown, although the text was frequently misattributed to the thirteenth-century Torah scholar Nahmanides. It deals not only with the sanctity of marital relations, but also their reflection of a union on the supernal level.

> **Know that the male is the mystery of wisdom and the female is the mystery of understanding. And the pure sex act is the mystery of knowledge. Such is the mystery of man and woman in the esoteric tradition. If so, it follows that proper sexual union can be a means of spiritual elevation when it is properly practiced, and the mystery greater than this is the secret of the heavenly bodies when they unite in the manner of man and woman. . . .**
>
> **On all these matters of which we have spoken [i.e., the divine powers, the *sefirot*], they are the mystery of the arrangement of the order of the universe, and its structure in the likeness of males and females [who are] in the secret of the giver [of the influx] and the receiver.[10] . . . The union of man with his wife, when it is proper, is the mystery of the foundation of the world and its civilization. (*Iggeret ha-Kodesh*, chap. 2)[11]**

By now, some of the references to the *sefirot* may be clearer. "Wisdom" refers to *Hokhmah*, and "understanding" to *Binah*, a masculine-feminine set of *sefirot*. There is mystery in how each one operates and mystery in how the male and female unite. It is not clear from this text whether we infer the divine mystery from the human one or the other way around. What is certain is that they are deeply bonded, to the point that sex performed with pure intention brings about the presence of the *Shekhinah*.[12]

When done properly—and, as we will see, *only* when done properly—

sex brings about not only the union of man and wife, but the *re*union of the original couple referred to above *and* the supernal union that sustains all human life. In this view, sex is central to understanding the universe. But it is sanctified sex that brings about all the most important results, as the next set of excerpts makes clear, . . . but it must be sex that is sanctified in every way.

> **Abraham concentrated his thought at the time of union, and his thoughts cleaved to the upper thoughts. Therefore he merited having a son worthy of what was promised to him by God. . . .**
>
> **In the instance in which a man has no intention of concentration for the sake of heaven, that seed drawn from him is a fetid drop, in which God has no portion, no share and is called "perverting his way" (Gen. 38:9). . . .**
>
> **One who has an improper thought at the time of intercourse, the filthy thought defiles the drop and from this issues forth an evil, wicked and filthy foundation. (*Iggeret ha-Kodesh*, excerpts)[13]**

In this view, the "best" sex is when one's thoughts are holy thoughts, linked to the *sefirot*. If a man does this, perhaps he will be rewarded with a holy son.[14] Since seed must be devoted to a holy purpose, the mystical literature reacts in an extreme way against masturbation.[15] But even permitted intercourse can be problematic if one's thoughts are not devoted to the higher levels. Clearly, unbridled sexual desire is not part of the program of the *Iggeret ha-Kodesh*.

From marital intimacy we turn to intimacy between God and Israel in the Zohar's representation of Shavuot, the festival commemorating the giving of the Torah at Mount Sinai:

> **Rabbi Shimon was sitting engaged in Torah on the night when the Bride is joined with Her Husband. For we have learned: All those Companions initiated into the bridal palace need—on that night when the Bride is destined the next day to be under the canopy with Her**

Husband—to be with Her all night, delighting with Her in Her adornments in which She is arrayed, engaging in Torah, from Torah to Prophets, from Prophets to Writings, midrashic renderings of verses and mysteries of wisdom: these are Her adornments and finery.

She enters, escorted by Her maidens, standing above their heads. Adorned by them, She rejoices with them the whole night. The next day She enters the canopy only with them, and they are called "members of the canopy." As soon as She enters the canopy, the Holy One, Blessed be He, inquires about them, blesses them, and crowns them with bridal crowns. Happy is their share! Rabbi Shimon and all the Companions were singing the song of Torah, innovating words of Torah, each one of them; Rabbi Shimon and all the other Companions rejoiced. (Zohar 1:8a)[16]

This night is no mere "revelation," not just a moment when the Jews meet God. It is the meeting of the Bride and Her Husband,[17] *Shekhinah* and *Tiferet*, the Oral Torah and the Written Torah, uniting to reenact symbolically this extraordinary moment on the cosmic level through Jews physically studying Torah, stimulating the divine union of these *sefirot*. The mystics, "Companions," must be occupied with Torah all night (including, as we see, all three segments of the Bible as well as Rabbinic texts) as "members of the canopy," the bridesmaids and groomsmen for the pair. The continuation of this text notes that they are called "masters of the covenant with the bride"; this refers to the covenant of circumcision, which to the kabbalists implies control over their sexual urge and sexual fidelity. Hence they are able to ascend to a higher level and can participate in the supernal union.[18] The fact that she is "adorned" also alludes to the mystics' need to be "adorned" with knowledge of Torah.[19]

The night described here led to the popular ritual for the evening of Shavuot known as *Tikkun Leil Shavuot*, where Jews study Torah throughout the night and celebrate the moment of revelation (reenacted in the day's Torah reading) at services held at the earliest possible time in the morning. We have already made mention of the term *tikkun*, which refers here to a ritual that performs a cosmic "repair" and also "adorns" the Bride, *Shekhinah*. At this time, "She enters," that is, *Shekhinah* enters to be with the mystics as they study Torah. While there is no historical evidence that *Tikkun Leil Shavuot* was a significant practice among Jews in the time of the Zohar, it was developed and greatly elaborated among the Lurianic kabbalists beginning in the sixteenth century.[20]

This practice underscores the great significance of the Torah in the *sefirotic* realm. But the Torah also has a place in the discussion of the erotic in our tradition, even today. As Zalman Schachter-Shalomi has written: "Go to any synagogue and witness the Torah service. Worshipers remove the Torah from the ark, and the Torah wears a great big crown, and they carry the Torah all around, and everybody touches and embraces her like a queen and kisses her, kisses the hem of her garment, as it were. Then they delicately undress her, place her gently on the table, roll her open, and read from her. Clearly, Torah is feminine."[21]

Among the many interesting passages in the Zohar that illustrate the ultimate purpose of sexuality, here is one that deals with the behavior of the mystic on the road and at home.

> As long as one lingers on the way, he must guard his conduct, so that supernal coupling will not separate from him, leaving him defective, lacking male and female. In town he must, when his female is with him; how much more so here [on the road], for supernal coupling is linked with him! Further, this supernal coupling protects him on the way, not parting from him until he returns home. Upon entering his house he should delight the lady of his house, for she engendered that supernal coupling. As soon as he reaches her he should delight her anew, for two reasons. First, because the joy of this coupling is joy of mitzvah, and joy of mitzvah is joy of *Shekhinah*. Further, he increases peace below, as is written: "You will know that your tent is at peace, attend to your abode and not sin" (Job 5:24). Is it a sin if

one does not attend to his wife? Certainly so, for he diminishes the splendor of supernal coupling coupled with him, engendered by the lady of his house. Second, if his wife conceives, supernal coupling pours into it a holy soul, for this covenant is called Covenant of the Holy One, Blessed be He. So one should focus on this joy as on the joy of Sabbath, coupling of the wise. (Zohar 1:49b–50a)[22]

While a man is away, the *Shekhinah* is with him, making him a whole person, as long as he preserves his sexual purity. And what happens when he returns? He must give his wife pleasure—but not for their own pleasure. First, when he gives pleasure to his wife, he gives pleasure to the *Shekhinah*. True, it does "increase peace below," according to the verse quoted from Job. But if the husband does not "attend to his wife," it is wrong because it deprives the *Shekhinah* of Her own necessary union (with *Tiferet*). And secondly, proper coupling at this time creates a reaction on the supernal level, and "supernal coupling pours into it a holy soul," meaning that when *Shekhinah* and *Tiferet* mate, they produce a holy soul that is then deposited in the fetus created by the mystic and his wife.

On the surface, the Zohar seems to make very little of sexual desire or marital intimacy for their own sake. There's nothing that says this couple might *feel* like having sexual intercourse after the husband was on a long journey. Rather, they should mate upon his return for these two primary purposes: to bring joy to *Shekhinah* and hopefully to conceive a child. The text also refers to the long-standing Rabbinic tradition of sexual intercourse on Shabbat, particularly by the sages.[23]

But, for the kabbalists, the same purposes for sex hold true when a couple are to mate on Sabbath evening (as well as after her monthly immersion in the *mikveh*). If he doesn't couple with her in all of these circumstances, it's a sin . . . not because he doesn't show proper affection to his wife, but because he dishonors the *Shekhinah* and prevents Her union with *Tiferet*!

The text does of course make reference to the "joy of coupling" and "delighting" his wife; the supernal intentions that accompany this do not alter the fact that indeed a joyful coupling takes place between them. And we should also note that the "higher purpose" of the union is much more an issue for the man than for his wife. The pressure to "perform" sexually is increased because the stakes are much higher for the male, if he is indeed cognizant of the supernal effects he seeks to bring about.

As earlier noted, the Zohar almost certainly was produced in the thirteenth century when the Christians were reconquering Spain. This passage may also be seen as a comment on the Jewish approach to healthy and mandated sexuality, as opposed to the monastic abstinence of the Christian religious leadership, which purported to be pious but actually failed to achieve what the Zohar sees as key religious purposes.[24]

Finally, shortly after this text, just as the mystics are about to conclude the discussion, Rabbi Shimon is struck with another insight (see chapter 10): "Whoever desires to penetrate the wisdom of holy unification should contemplate the flame ascending from a glowing ember, or a burning candle." Perhaps Rabbi Shimon's insight directly results from addressing the erotic implications of *deveikut*.

An eighteenth-century Hasidic text teaches that prayer and *deveikut* have a direct connection with sexuality:

> **Prayer is coupling with the *Shekhinah*. Just as at the beginning of coupling there is movement, so one must initially sway in prayer. And afterward, one can remain immobile and be attached to the *Shekhinah* with great *deveikut*. As a result of his swaying, man is able to attain a powerful stage of arousal. For he will ask himself: Why do I cause myself to sway? Surely it is because the *Shekhinah* stands before me. This will cause him to arrive at great *hitlahavut* [rapture]. (*Tzava'at ha-Rivash*, 6b)[25]**

What is the true significance of "shuckling," swaying during prayer? The Hasidic master says that what one does on earth is a parallel to what one seeks with the Beloved on high, a true cleaving. As undeniably erotic as this text is, two caveats must be added. One is that it was not teaching that "shuckling" serves a sublimated sexual impulse. The other is that in Hasidism—unlike the Zohar—the God-man relationship is much more frequently expressed in father-son terms than in such erotic terms.[26] Nonetheless, this text and the next two stand out in their frank juxtaposition of prayer and copulation.

> "From my flesh, I shall see God" (Job 19:26). [This means that] just as no child can be born from physical copulation unless it is performed with a vitalized organ and with desire and joy, so it is with spiritual copulation, that is, through the study of Torah and prayer. When this is done with a vitalized organ and with joy and delight, then it gives birth. (Ba'al Shem Tov, *Keter Shem Tov*, #16)[27]

> "From my flesh, I shall see God": [*Yesod* corresponds to] the sexual organ, which is the seat of one's greatest physical pleasure. This pleasure comes about when man and woman unite, and it thus results from unification. From the physical, we perceive spiritual joy. (Ba'al Shem Tov, as quoted in *Toldot Yaakov Yosef*, 1:57, Lekh-Lekha, *Mitzvat Milah*)

The verse from Job, in its original context, simply says: while I am still alive, I want to behold God. However, beginning in the late Middle Ages, the mystics gave it another meaning, consistent with the concept of *Adam Kadmon* (see chapter 11): people can better know God by knowing themselves).[28] As *Shnei Luhot ha-Brit* says: "From the image and likeness of a human being, the existence of God can be known and is revealed."[29] And a key aspect of the human being is bisexuality . . . that is, two sexes regularly seeking unity.

What do we know about God from the sexual act? The Ba'al Shem Tov answers that the spiritual meeting with God has the same qualities as "good sex": it is arousing, gives joy, and produces appropriate results. The message of the mystics is that sexuality is one of God's greatest physical gifts; hence in both of these texts and more broadly, according to Byron Sherwin, "for the Jewish mystics, the procreative act is a paradigm of the ultimate religious experience."[30] As Moshe Cordovero puts it, "No other commandment exists that would have the relation between man and woman resemble the coupling from on high in all ways as does this one."[31] In other words, nothing quite evokes the sacred like sexuality... sanctified and sanctioned sexuality, to be sure.

But along with sanctified sexuality, we see its opposite, found most especially in the myths surrounding Lilith (see chapter 7). Her name appears once in the Bible, in Isa. 34:14, but its meaning there is unclear. In Kabbalah, she is the dark side (or *sitra ahra*) of the *Shekhinah*; in early legend, she was Adam's first wife (and later, Eve's rival). The earliest talmudic mention portrays Lilith as a demon who might seize a man sleeping in a house alone, although this probably also alludes to any illicit desire as well as an actual demon creature.[32] Merging with this earlier legend is the first full story of Lilith as Adam's wife,[33] which can be found in the late midrashic work *Alpha Beta d'Ben Sira*.[34] In this legend, Lilith is the demonic foil of *Shekhinah* and becomes a figure standing for the power of unlawful sex; she is identified with all the powers of the realm of impurity. A later illustration of this can be found in the sixteenth-century Algerian work *Tzafnat Paneiah*, where Delilah is understood to be identical with Lilith.[35]

Sexuality outside the boundaries of law was a particularly sensitive issue for the mystics. As we have noted, mysticism in general—because it involves a more direct connection with God—suggests a lessening of the need for law, but this presents a special problem when it comes to powerful sexual temptations. (Indeed Jewish leaders in the seventeenth and eighteenth centuries were especially concerned about sexual activity within two heretical sects, the Sabbateans and the Frankists.) Most mystics were careful not to cross this line, and this reticence may well have contributed to the strength of the myths around Lilith.

The Zohar has much to say about the activity of Lilith, expanding her role considerably:

Come and see. From the crevice of the great deep, above, there came a certain female, the spirit of all spirits, and we have already explained her name was Lilith. At the very beginning, she existed with Adam. When Adam was created and his body had been completed, a thousand spirits from the left side gathered together around the body, each one wanting to enter it, but they could not, and in the end the Holy One, Blessed be He, rebuked them. Adam therefore was lying down, a body without a spirit, and he had a green pallor, and all these spirits were hovering around him. At that moment a cloud descended and drove away all these spirits. Concerning this moment it is written: "And God said, Let the earth bring forth a living soul." (Gen. 1:24)

We have already explained that the female became pregnant by the male in the soul of Adam and produced the spirit that was comprised of two sides, as was proper, so it could be breathed into Adam. This is the meaning of "and He breathed into his nostrils the breath [or soul] of life and Adam became a living soul" (Gen. 2:7)—a really living soul....

When Adam arose his wife was fastened to his side, and the holy soul within him spread to this side and to that, and nourished both sides, because it was comprised of both. Subsequently, the Holy One, Blessed be He, split Adam, and prepared his female....

When Lilith saw this she fled, and she is now in the cities of the sea, still intent on injuring mankind. When the Holy One, Blessed be He, destroys wicked Rome, and it becomes an eternal desolation, He will bring up Lilith and settle her in the ruins.... This is the meaning of "Lilith shall repose there, and find herself a resting place" (Isa. 34:14). (Zohar 3:19a)[36]

The "crevice of the great deep" is the place from which evil emanates and Lilith develops. The word used for "crevice" (*nukba*) is essentially the same as the word for "female." This and the entire text express the deep ambivalence about the feminine and its power over the male . . . written from the male viewpoint, of course.

The female and male, as usual, represent *Malkhut* and *Tiferet*, and also "the life below" and "Israel." The idea of the original "dual-faced" creation noted above is seen again here, but in the *sefirot* and not only in the original human being; we are also taught that the *tzela*, the "bone" referred to in Genesis, is the same word as in the building of the Tabernacle, where it can *only* mean "side." Further, this "soul" is the result of a supernal mating between male and female within the *sefirot*. There is also a nice pun included here in the original; when God breathes into the creature, He does so *b'apav*, "in his nostrils." However, *b'apav* can also mean "into his faces," thus referring to the dual nature of that first person.

Under these circumstances—that is, in the face of legitimate sexuality—Lilith cannot fully use her power and so goes away, returning only to fulfill the biblical verse and rest among the ruins of the destroyed city of the wicked. However, this is not the whole story. The text of the Zohar goes on to discuss "remedies" against Lilith—a prayer to recite, covering the heads of the husband and wife together, sprinkling water around the bed—so as not to give her a chance to take advantage of even the slightest opportunity.

Why is Lilith allowed to exist? One theory, expressed in our next text, suggests that she provides a test for fools who succumb to temptation.

The secret of secrets: From the strength of the fierce noon of Isaac, from the wine lees, a naked shoot came forth, comprising together male and female, red like a lily, and they spread out on several sides, down several paths. The male is called Samael, and his female is always included with him. Just as on the side of holiness, so on "the other side" there are male and female, included one with the other. The female of Samael is called "snake," "a wife of harlotry," "the end

of all flesh," "the end of days." Two evil spirits are attached to one another. The male spirit is fine, the female spirit spreads out down several ways and paths, and is attached to the male spirit.

She dresses herself in finery like an abominable harlot and stands at the corners of streets and highways in order to attract men. When a fool approaches her, she embraces him and kisses him, and mixes her wine lees with snake poison for him. Once he has drunk, he turns aside after her. When she sees that he has turned aside after her from the way of truth, she takes off all the finery that she had put on for the sake of this fool.

The finery she uses to seduce mankind: her hair is long, red like a lily; her face is white and pink . . . her tongue is sharp like a sword; her words smooth as oil; her lips beautiful, red as a lily, sweetened with all the sweetnesses in the world; she is dressed in purple, and attired in thirty-nine items of finery.

This fool turns aside after her, and drinks from the cup of wine, and commits harlotry with her, completely enamored of her. What does she do? She leaves him asleep on the bed and ascends to the realms above, accuses him, obtains authority, and descends. The fool wakes up, thinking to sport with her as before, but she takes off her finery, and turns into a fierce warrior, facing him in a garment of flaming fire, a vision of dread, terrifying both body and soul, full of horrific eyes, a sharpened sword in his hand with drops of poison suspended [and dripping] from it. He kills the fool, and throws him into *Gehinnom*. (Zohar 1:148, *Sitrei Torah*)[37]

Isaac, as previously noted, is associated with the *sefirah* of *Gevurah* (Power) or *Din* (Judgment); hence, the severe heat attached to him here. Sometimes, judgment leaves some "dregs" in the realms of holiness. Out of those dregs come Samael, a male demon (frequently also referred to as Satan), and "his female" (Lilith), for whom the text reserves various slurs; in any case, they are working as a team.[38] She works as a harlot, but her sole purpose is to cause man to sin so that she can obtain authority to kill him. The "sharpened sword" is taken from a talmudic description of the Angel of Death;[39] when she takes off all her "finery," she exposes herself as that angel, now empowered (and revealed to be a powerful male) to punish the "fool" for his sin.

The mystical tradition teaches that the most highly developed individuals should be able to comprehend the Divine, but not merely by way of spiritual development; the physical and its pleasures, if properly appreciated, can help us better understand and approach God. As the early kabbalist Isaac of Acre put it: "A man who does not desire a woman is like a donkey, or even less than one. In other words, from the physical, one may apprehend the worship of God."[40]

Ours is an age that emphasizes individuality. But both physically and spiritually we lose something in asserting our separateness at all cost. In the mystical view, sexual union attempts to reestablish the relationship with that which is beyond our selves, and perhaps—as in the best of loving relationships—we can do it without sacrificing the self.

15

Sin, *Teshuvah,* and the *Yetzer ha-Ra*

TIKKUN

It is commonly believed by Jews that the notion of "original sin"—the idea that the sin of Adam and Eve is passed down to the entire human race—was Christian, and certainly un-Jewish. But it is not so simply dismissed, particularly in the thought of the mystics.

Rabbinic Judaism generally understood humans to be caught between two impulses: the "good impulse," *yetzer ha-tov,* and the "evil impulse," *yetzer ha-ra.* When we let the *yetzer ha-ra* have its way, that is when sin enters. But as inevitable as the presence of the *yetzer ha-ra* is, it is not altogether undesirable, because it is also part of the drive to survive and thrive as human beings; midrash tells us: "Were it not for the *yetzer ha-ra,* a man would not build a house, take a wife, procreate, or engage in business."[1] This truth is reflected in the talmudic dictum that "the greater the man, the greater the *yetzer.*"[2]

But Judaism, perhaps influenced by Christian sources, also contains ideas that suggest a form of "original sin." Such ideas postulate a solution along with the statement of the problem; the Talmud says that "when the serpent came upon Eve,[3] he injected into her a *zohama* [here meaning some kind of moral impurity or sensual passion]. When the Israelites stood at Mount Sinai, their *zohama* departed; but the idolaters who did not stand at Mount Sinai, their *zohama* did not depart."[4] In other words, the Torah contains the antidote, the means to train individuals to control their *yetzer ha-ra.* But the basic concept of inherent sin, *yetzer ha-ra,* is present.

We find a similar message in a Rabbinic comment on Gen. 3:21, "And the Lord God made for Adam and his wife garments of skin ['*or*, spelled *ayin-vav-reish*], and clothed them."[5] We are told that Rabbi Meir (second century CE) possessed a text of the Torah that referred not to garments of skin, but garments of light (*'or*, spelled *alef-vav-reish*). According to this text, it is possible to understand the original garments as having been wholly spiritual; after the sin of Adam and Eve, they became physical garments. The Zohar reads it in precisely this fashion: "At first they wore garments of light, and he [Adam] was waited upon by the highest beings. . . . Now that they sinned, [they wore] garments of skin, soothing the skin, not the soul."[6] The Bible is not especially optimistic about human nature;[7] an example of an extreme view, but one generally justified in the books of the Tanakh, is Gen. 6:5: "The Lord saw how great was man's wickedness on earth, and how every plan devised by his mind was nothing but evil all the time."

The trespass of Adam and Eve also expresses many of the tensions between male and female, which, in Kabbalah, had grave consequences. As Heschel put it, "The creature became detached from the Creator, the fruit from the tree, the tree of knowledge from the tree of life, the male from the female, our universe from the world of unity, even the *Shekhinah* . . . from the upper *sefirot*. Owing to that separation the world was thrown into disorder, the power of strict judgment increased, the power of love diminished and the forces of evil released."[8] In other words, sin has negative consequences in the higher realms. Fortunately, *teshuvah*, "repentance," has positive consequences that can repair the damage done by sin. Like other virtues, *teshuvah* improves the workings within the *sefirot*, countering the negative effects of sin.

The Zohar has much to say about the roots and purposes of sin:

> When the Holy One, Blessed be He, came to create the world and to reveal the deep from within the hidden, and disclose light out of darkness, they were all intermingled. Therefore, light emerged from

darkness, and from the hidden came forth the deep, one issuing from the other. Similarly, evil comes forth from good; from mercy comes judgment. And all are intertwined, the good impulse and the evil impulse. (Zohar 3:80b)[9]

Determining just what is sinful is a big challenge, to put it mildly. Will dropping a bomb and killing innocent civilians save more lives in the long run? Will withholding help from someone who is needy lead her to "hit bottom" and finally resolve to make the changes she must make? It is not always so clear what is "sinful." The text above suggests that our struggle with the concept of sin goes right back to Creation, even preceding the first human sin.[10] (See chapter 17 for more on the intertwining of good and evil within the *sefirot*.)

The Zohar locates the origin of sin in the Garden of Eden . . . but not in the way we might suspect:

> "The Lord God banished him from the Garden of Eden . . . He drove out *et* Adam" (Gen. 3:23-24). Rabbi Elazar said: We do not know who divorced whom: if the Holy One, Blessed be He, divorced Adam or not. But the word is transposed: "He drove out *et*." *Et*, precisely! And who drove out *et*? Adam—Adam drove out *et*! Therefore it is written: "The Lord God banished him from the Garden of Eden." Why did He banish him? Because Adam drove out *et*, as we have said. (Zohar 1:53b)[11]

The Zohar deals with three questions of concern about the original biblical verse and Rabbi Elazar's rephrasing of it: (1) The two verses seem to be saying the same thing: God expelled the human being from the Garden of Eden. Why the apparent repetition? (2) The Hebrew word *et*, normally used to indicate that the following word is the direct object of the sentence, has no meaning in and of itself and is often interpreted as providing an amplified meaning to the verse.[12] Might there be such a meaning here? (3) "Divorced" is one translation of the Hebrew *garash*; it can also mean "drive out." Numerous midrashic texts interpret this to mean that Adam was driven out because of some indecency.[13] Here, as always, sin interferes with man's relationship with God. But how exactly should we understand this situation?

The Zohar provides a new meaning to the word *et*, based on the fact that it is composed of *alef* and *tav*, the first and last letters of the Alef Bet.[14] *Et* is seen as a name of the *Shekhinah*, which encompasses all divine language. So the verse can be reinterpreted as follows: "He drove out *et*, the *Shekhinah*. [Who did it?] Adam." Adam's sin was in divorcing the *Shekhinah*. More precisely, he divorces Her from Her proper mate, *Tiferet*, by worshiping Her alone. This sin is considered a great secret in the Zohar; here we have only a vague allusion to it.[15] However, it is also based on a midrashic text suggesting that "as soon as Adam sinned, the *Shekhinah* withdrew to the first heaven,"[16] that is, withdrew from accessibility to human beings. The Zohar thus addresses all three questions. The second verse does not repeat the fact that God expelled Adam; it says that Adam drove away the *Shekhinah*. The word *et* is provided with a meaning; it represents the *Shekhinah* Herself. And the divorce is understood to be the separation of the *Shekhinah* from the other *sefirot*.

Sin, in general, disrupts the *sefirotic* system and in effect "divorces" the *Shekhinah* from the rest of the *sefirot*, thereby making it impossible for the *Shekhinah* to receive the influx from above that then sustains the rest of the world. Thus sin does not affect just the individual, it affects the entire cosmos. If there is an "original sin," this is it; in driving away the *Shekhinah*, Adam has dissolved the supernal union, leaving Her in exile. Fittingly, his punishment is to be exiled from the Garden of Eden. This is the state of humankind and God together: as we continue to look for our home, God also looks for a home where His "parts," the *sefirot*, can be properly reunited. This theme of exile plays a prominent role in Kabbalah, and in the Zohar in particular, where the wanderings of the mystical sages are always in the background.[17]

The Zohar's reading of the Garden of Eden story finds the source of sin within human impulses, in the *yetzer ha-ra*:

"Now the serpent was the shrewdest of all the wild beasts." (Gen. 3:1) Of the serpent, Rabbi Yitzhak said: This is the *yetzer ha-ra* [evil impulse]. Rabbi Yehudah said: This was an actual serpent. When they came before Rabbi Shimon, he said to them: They are indeed one and the same thing, for this was Samael, who makes his appearance riding on a serpent. The form of the serpent is Satan, and they are one and the same thing. . . .

"Now the serpent was the shrewdest." This is *the yetzer ha-ra*, the Angel of Death. Being the Angel of Death, he inflicted death upon the whole world. This is the mystery of the words, "I have decided to put an end to all flesh" [literally, "the end of all flesh has come before Me"] (Gen. 6:13): the one who ends all flesh, who takes the soul from all flesh. (Zohar 1:35b)[18]

Was the snake really a snake, or something else in disguise? The Talmud provides a suggestion: "Resh Lakish said: Satan, the *yetzer ha-ra*, and the Angel of Death are one and the same."[19] Additionally, a midrash suggests that Samael "took his band and descended and saw all the creatures. . . . He determined that the most cunningly evil was the serpent, as it says: 'Now the serpent was the shrewdest' (Gen. 3:1). The serpent looked like a camel, and Samael mounted and rode him."[20] So the earlier traditions provide support for the idea that the different manifestations are "all one," all created by God.

If God created all, and the *yetzer ha-ra* is also one of God's creations, how can it defy God by pushing people toward sin?

Everything the Holy One, Blessed be He, has made, both above and below, is for the sake of revealing His glory,[21] and everything is for the sake of His service. But did you ever see a servant who accuses his Master, opposing everything that his Master wishes? The will of the Holy One, Blessed be He, is that man serve Him at every moment, walking in the path of truth, so He can merit many benefits. Since this is His will, how can an evil servant come and oppose, by his Master's will, luring people to an evil path, distancing them from the good path, and causing them to disobey the will of their Lord?

But indeed, it is doing the will of its Master. This may be compared to a king who had an only son, whom he loved greatly. Because of his love for him, he commanded his son never to approach an evil woman, for whoever approached her would be unworthy of entering the king's palace. The son consented that he would lovingly do his father's will.

Outside of the palace lived a harlot of great beauty and charm. One day, the king said, "I want to see my son's devotion to me." He sent for the harlot and said to her, "Go and seduce my son," to see his son's devotion to him. What did the harlot do? She went after his son and began embracing him, kissing him, seducing him with all kinds of enticements. If the son is worthy and obeys his father's command, he will rebuke her; he pays no heed to her and thrusts her away from him. Then the father rejoices in his son and brings him into the palace, giving him gifts and presents and great honor. Who caused all this honor for the son? You must admit: that harlot!

And that harlot: does she deserve praise for this or not? Surely, she does in every way. First, because she carried out the king's command; second, because she brought upon the son all this honor, all this goodness, all this love of the king toward him. Therefore it is written, "And behold, it was very good" (Gen. 1:31). "Behold, it was good"—this is the Angel of Life; "very good"—the Angel of Death. It is certainly very good for one who fulfills the will of his Master!

Come and see: if not for this accuser, the righteous would not inherit those supernal treasures reserved for them in the world to come. Happy are those who have encountered this accuser, and happy are those who have not encountered him. Happy are those who did encounter this accuser and escaped his clutches, for through him they inherit all that goodness, all that bliss, all those delights of the world to come, of which it is written, "No eye has seen [them], O God, but You" (Isa. 64:3). Happy are those who did not encounter him, for through him they would have inherited *Gehinnom*, and been banished from the land of the living, those wicked people who do not heed their Lord and are drawn after him. Therefore, the righteous should be grateful to him, for because of him they inherit all the goodness, bliss, and delight in the world to come.

What is the benefit for this accuser when the wicked obey him? Even though he has no direct benefit, he fulfills the will of his Master. Furthermore, he grows more powerful because of this. Since he is evil, he grows stronger when evil is done, like a wicked person whose wickedness does not intensify until he kills a man. Once he has killed people, he grows stronger, becomes more powerful and has pleasure. So too the accuser grows stronger after he entices people, accuses them, and kills them. Then he is pleased, grows stronger, and becomes more powerful.

Just as the side of life grows stronger when men are good and walk on the straight path, similarly, this accuser is strengthened and becomes more powerful when the wicked obey him and are dominated by him, may the Merciful One save us. Happy are those who are worthy to defeat and overturn him. (Zohar 2:163a–b)[22]

The *yetzer ha-ra* is the "servant who accuses his Master," and yet it actually does the Master's will. In the parable, the son represents the soul. God wants to know: how devoted are our souls, how much do we love God?

Next the Zohar quotes a midrashic piece interpreting the verse from Genesis as referring to the Angel of Life and Angel of Death.[23] This is based on a Hebrew pun: the word *me'od*, "very," sounds and looks like the word *mot*, death. In the midrashic text, the Angel of Death is "very" good, because he slays those who fail to perform good deeds. Here in the Zohar, the Angel of Death provides temptation, which—if a person conquers it—will earn him great reward, the "land of the living," that is, paradise. Of course, one might fail such a test, which is why the Zohar says that those who have not been so tested are also happy!

It is interesting to consider this description of evil empowering evil, such that it becomes addictive and even enjoyable. But beware, because sin makes everything worse and makes it progressively more difficult to reunite *Malkhut* with all the other *sefirot*. In the conclusion, we are reminded that God's power is increased by the performance of good deeds.

The next text is based on a talmudic teaching relating that every Friday afternoon two angels, one good and one evil, accompany a man as he goes to his house prior to Shabbat.[24] If the house is appropriately prepared for Shabbat, the good angel celebrates and says: "May it be so again for another Shabbat." Then the evil angel, against his will, must say: "Amen." Conversely, if the house is not prepared, the evil angel says: "May it be so again for another Shabbat," and the good angel must say: "Amen." (This is the source of the common Friday evening hymn *Shalom Aleikhem*, composed as a greeting to the two angels.)

> **Rabbi Shimon opened: "When a man's ways please God, He causes even his enemies to be at peace with him" (Prov. 16:7).** Come and see how carefully one should align his paths toward the Holy One, Blessed be He, in order to fulfill the commands of Torah! For they have established that a person has two angelic messengers from above to couple with him, one on the right and one on the left, coupling with him, appearing wherever he does anything, called *yetzer tov* and *yetzer ra*.
>
> If one comes to purify himself and engage in commands of Torah, that *yetzer tov* coupled with him overpowers the *yetzer ra*, who then makes peace with him, turning into his servant. But when a person relapses, setting out to defile himself, that *yetzer ra* overpowers and overwhelms the *yetzer tov*, as we have established. Indeed, when that person comes to purify himself, how strongly he is empowered as the *yetzer tov* prevails. [In so doing,] "he causes even his enemies to be at peace with him," for the *yetzer ra* is overturned by the *yetzer tov*. Therefore Solomon said, "Better to be lightly esteemed and have a

servant" (Prov. 12:9). What is the meaning of "and have a servant"? The *yetzer ra*. So when a person follows the commands of Torah, "He [i.e., God] causes even his enemies to be at peace with him," i.e., the *yetzer ra*.

Come and see: since Jacob trusted in the Holy One, Blessed be He, and all his ways were for His sake, "He causes even his enemies to be at peace with him"; [this is] Samael, the power and strength of Esau, who made peace with Jacob. Since he made peace with him and confirmed those blessings, Esau made peace with him, and until Jacob was at peace with that official appointed over him [i.e., over Esau], Esau did not make peace with him. So everywhere, power below depends on power above. (Zohar 1:144b)[25]

In this text, the two angels are more directly identified with *yetzer ha-tov* and *yetzer ha-ra*, the good and evil impulses. Additionally, they are clearly "from above," that is, from the *sefirot*, specifically from *Hesed* and *Gevurah* (or *Din*), the sources of love and judgment. Here, as David Blumenthal puts it, the *yetzer ha-ra* "is that dimension of God's being that establishes and enforces limits, that judges, and that can, indeed, seize control of God's providential action."[26] It may seem strange to consider an impulse for evil as divine, but this is accepted in Rabbinic Judaism, and the source of this evil in the divine realm is spelled out in the Zohar. However, if one "comes to purify himself and engage in commands of Torah," he will control the other impulse and put it at his service, as suggested at this chapter's opening.

In the concluding section, the evil angel Samael is seen as the power aligned with Jacob's brother, Esau, who according to the Zohar and some earlier Rabbinic traditions is Jacob's (anonymous) opponent in the famous wrestling match of Gen. 32:25–33. Since the angel is unable to prevail, he makes peace with Jacob, and his partner, Esau, made peace with Jacob as well. Once again, we see that a success on the supernal level brings about success in the lower realms, and vice versa.

But how should a person respond who fails to prevail over the evil impulse? In other words, when human beings sin, what must we do to repent and restore ourselves? In Rabbinic Judaism, the process of repentance involves acknowledgment of a sin, confession to God, regret over the sin, restitution when necessary, and a resolution to change. In the kabbalistic scheme, of course, more is involved; this is the topic of our next texts.

While we have briefly noted the concept of *tikkun* and will refer to it in the next text, it is important not to confuse it with the contemporary usage of the term *tikkun olam*—any form of social action that brings about improvement in the world. The idea of *tikkun olam* (originally *tikkun ha-olam*[27]) stems from Rabbinic literature, where it is used as a halakhic term, as a *takkanah*. This is "a legislative fiat intended for the public good,"[28] in the general sense of "the improvement of society" and preventing some form of injustice,[29] as well as with reference to ordinary repairs. Occasionally, it has a slightly different sense, as in the "Aleinu" prayer, where part of the Jewish mission is *l'taken olam b'malkhut Shaddai*, "to repair the world in the Kingdom of the Almighty," signifying the sense of preparing the world for a future where God's will is carried out in every way. This is not taken to mean that all people will subscribe to the Jewish faith, only that idolatry will ultimately be uprooted. Only rarely is the term used in a spiritual or penitential sense.

For the kabbalists, the *olam*, the world that is to be repaired, is not this world so much as the world of the *sefirot*, the supernal realm. In our text, *tikkun* means to repair damage done in the divine world, not in this world. It presumes that such damage has taken place and is pervasive, but that we can help repair it. Furthermore, God needs us to do this, particularly through our mindful participation in prayer and observance of holy days and their rituals, while we strenuously avoid sin. All these presumptions are essential to Mainline Kabbalah. In the Zohar, as Gilbert Rosenthal indicates, "*tikkun ha-olam*, repair of this world by rabbinic sages and judges, has been displaced or superseded by mystical *tikkun olamot*, otherworldly repair of worlds."[30] We will see in the next chapter that this concept is developed and emphasized further by the kabbalists of Safed. How does repentance function within the *sefirotic* realms?

> **Rabbi Yehudah opened: "When a man opens a pit, or digs a pit and does not cover it, and an ox or an ass falls into it, the one responsible for the pit must make restitution" (Exod. 21:33–34). If so, how much more responsible is the one who harms the world through his sins! And yet, surprisingly, even though he harms the world, he can repent, as it is written: "When a man or woman commits any wrong . . . he shall confess the wrong he has done. He shall make restitution" (Num. 5:6–7). This is truly of benefit to them, because he has made repentance. He has actually made her, as it were, for he has restored that which he had damaged in the world above. How? Through repentance, as it is written, "When a man or woman commits any wrong . . . he shall confess the wrong he has done. He shall make restitution [i.e., repentance]." Repentance repairs everything, repairs the world above, repairs the world below, repairs the person himself, repairs the whole world.**

We begin with a biblical teaching: the owner of a pit who is careless bears responsibility for harm caused by his negligence, even though he had no desire to harm anyone and planned no evil act. Given that one is responsible for negligence, what does that say about the one who sins on purpose? We can assume that his responsibility is much more serious and that his liability—whether before man or God—is much more severe. But perhaps through repentance he can reduce or eliminate this liability. Hence the second verse, which speaks of "restitution" (*heshiv*), which is also understood to mean *teshuvah* (repentance).

What does it mean, "to make repentance"? Here it is understood as not simply performing acts of repentance, but as having created a realm for repentance. Just as sin damages the *Shekhinah* by interrupting Her connection with the higher levels and cutting off Her support from them, *teshuvah* repairs the damage and restores the flow of influence, thus re-creating, that is, "making" the *Shekhinah*. While *teshuvah* is meant to repair the soul of the sinner, the problem is that the soul, like everything else, depends on the *Shekhinah*'s support. So *teshuvah* is not simply about repairing the individual penitent's character, but about repairing the entire cosmos.

"When you are in distress because all these things have befallen you and, in the end, return to the Lord your God and obey Him. For the Lord your God is a compassionate God." (Deut. 4:30-31) "When you are in distress": from this we learn that repentance is best before *Din* (Judgment) dwells in the world. For once *Din* is indwelling, its power grows stronger, and then who can remove it from the world or drive it away? Once it is present, it does not depart until its task is completed. But after it has been completed, and a man repents, he restores all the worlds. This is indicated by "all these things have befallen you, and in the end." And it is also written, "Return to the Lord your God. . . . For the Lord your God is a compassionate God."

> What is the significance here of "and in the end"? It is meant to include the Assembly of Israel, which is in exile and shares their sorrow, never forsaking them [i.e., Israel]. Therefore, even when the Holy One, Blessed be He, brings judgment upon the world, He wants Israel to return in repentance so that He might benefit them both in this world and the next; and nothing can stand in the way of repentance.
>
> Come and see. Even the Assembly of Israel is called "repentance." And if you would say that upper repentance is nowhere to be found, nevertheless this is called "repentance," when [the penitent] brings mercy [*Rahamim*] back toward her, and she returns as head of all those multitudes and nourishes them. And repentance is at her highest when the soul surrenders itself to her, and she takes it when it is in a state of penitence. Then all is restored above and below; he is restored together with the whole world. One wicked man in the world causes damage to countless others. Woe to the wicked; woe to his neighbor! (Zohar 3:122)[31]

Another verse concerning repentance is cited and interpreted. The phrase "in your distress because all these things have befallen you" is understood to refer to the process of judgment, distressing because of the punishment one earns for the sin. However, if one repents immediately afterward, this may "head off" the judgment and the consequences. (Elsewhere the Zohar teaches that repentance overcomes everything; even a divine oath to punish is only made on the contingency that the person to be disciplined does not repent!)[32] But once that process begins, and the negative force of judgment grows stronger, repentance may have a more difficult time taking hold. Even after the process has been completed (when "all these things have befallen you," meaning that judgment and punishment have taken place), proper *teshuvah* is still important, because its effects within the supernal realms are still necessary.

The "Assembly of Israel" (*Knesset Yisrael*) is code language for the *Shekhinah*. The *Shekhinah* is also at the "end" of the *sefirotic* chain; she is referred to as the "end of days" because, of the seven lower *sefirot* she is the "end," the last, and these seven *sefirot* are also taken to represent the seven days of Creation. The message below the surface of this text is as follows: The *Shekhinah* is damaged and exiled by the force of sin, but repentance heals Her and restores Her to Her place. Repentance, even after judgment, thus leads to a supernal *tikkun*, a repair of the damage above as well as within the individual.

While *teshuvah* is associated with the *Shekhinah*, its roots come from *Binah*; thus, we have reference to an "upper repentance." Sometimes it may seem that this "upper repentance" is cut off from the lower realms and cannot be linked with the *Shekhinah*. Nonetheless, "this," the *Shekhinah*, is called "repentance" if one's penitence is sufficient to restore the link with Mercy (another name for *Tiferet*). She then "returns as head of all that company and nourishes them," meaning that whatever angels and other supernal beings are within that realm receive support and influence from Her. (See chapter 19 for more about the role of angels in Jewish mystical texts.)

What brings repentance its "highest" impact? When the person performing repentance offers up his own life, returning his soul to the *Shekhinah*, the source of all souls, this is understood as the most complete and decisive repentance, which restores everything "above and below." Conversely, "one wicked person," that is, a sinner who fails to repent, causes damage to many others, including the innocent. In short, the mystical view of repentance has much more serious implications—cosmic effects, to be sure—than just those affecting the character of the individual.

The sixteenth-century kabbalist Elijah de Vidas vividly describes his understanding of the effects of sin and repentance within the *sefirot*:

> We have already explained[33] that one who sins causes the withdrawal of the supernal mother from Her children, or the removal of the lower mother from the lower worlds. The greater the flaw, the greater the resulting withdrawal. The word *teshuvah* refers to the intention to restore previous levels and repair them to their original status. This can be compared to the removal of water flowing from a fountain, in order to nourish various gardens, orchards, fields, and vineyards; along comes some fool who diverts the [channel of] water toward the trash, or to some empty place where it will serve no purpose. The owner of the fountain will be angry at him, first because he caused this watering of his fine gardens to be stopped, and secondly because he spoiled and broke the [original] channel.
>
> The consequences of actual sin are much more grave than in this case. For if one spoils the channels of the divine *shefa* [flow] from coming to their appropriate places, by diverting them he has angered the King, the Lord of Hosts; he takes holiness and diverts it to impurity; he causes a place that should be dry and barren [of support] and waters and saturates it. . . . *Teshuvah* repairs the broken channels, restores the *shefa* to its proper place, everywhere according to the flaw within him. (De Vidas, *Reishit Hokhmah, Sha'ar ha-Teshuvah*, ch. 2, sect. 2)

De Vidas offers a wonderful analogy of an irrigating fountain and then reminds us that the fountain of *shefa* provided to human beings is of infinitely greater importance. Just as one must not nourish weeds, one must not provide support for the evil powers in the universe "that should be dry and barren," but only the powers that maintain God's blessings. The stakes are high—all the more reason why *teshuvah* must take a central place in the mystical life.

The last teaching on repentance comes from Rabbi Abraham Joshua Heschel, the more remarkable for having been written on the eve of the Holocaust.

> **The most unnoticed of all miracles is the miracle of repentance. It is not the same thing as rebirth; it is transformation, creation. In the dimension of time there is no going back. But the power of repentance causes time to be created backward and allows re-creation of the past to take place. . . . God brings about this creation for the sake of humanity when a human being repents for the sake of God. (Heschel, "The Meaning of Repentance" [published in Berlin, eve of Yom Kippur, 1936])[34]**

Heschel's mystical approach is dealt with in more detail in chapter 27. He offers a less overtly kabbalistic but clearly mystical interpretation. The object of repentance is not merely self-improvement, but putting one's life in the context of God, akin to the *tzorekh gavoha* we have already examined. Repentance is a miracle; it is infinitely greater than personal change, and the act from below causes a response from above, in much the same way that the workings of the *sefirot* have been described.

As always, when dealing with the problem of sin, we are left with questions and challenges. Does repentance have some impact beyond personal improvement? Do we as modern Jews believe in the *yetzer ha-ra* and, if so, how can we manage it?

16
Lurianic Kabbalah

Following the persecutions, forced conversions, and then exile of the Jews of Spain in 1492, an extraordinary Jewish community developed in the city of Safed, in the Galilee. Although this community was in the Land of Israel, its members thought of themselves and all Jews as essentially remaining in a state of exile. For them, exile was not geographical but cosmic.

The community of Safed was unlike any other in Jewish history; as Solomon Schechter put it, it was "essentially spiritual in its character, made and developed by men living lives purified by suffering, and hallowed by constant struggle after purification and holiness."[1] There was a great deal of ascetic behavior (see chapter 18), with emphasis placed on repentance and ethical purification. But there was also great joy in the practice of religious acts, especially on Shabbat and festivals, just as in normative Rabbinic Judaism but with the addition of new interpretations and rituals.

Throughout most of the sixteenth century, this community attracted a very impressive array of kabbalistic thinkers, whose scholarship abounded in virtually every aspect of Jewish life. Among them were Moses Cordovero, Elijah de Vidas, Eliezer Azikri, and above all Isaac Luria (1534-72), whose ideas formed the basis for a whole new kabbalistic school of thought (although, as we will see, some of his ideas have roots in earlier Jewish tradition).

Luria, who was born in Jerusalem and lived for a while in Cairo, only lived in Safed for the three years prior to his death and never wrote down any of his teachings. These were shared with a small circle of students, most notably Hayyim Vital (1543–1620), who put much of his master's thought into writing (although these were only widely circulated after Vital's death).[2]

Lurianic Kabbalah has been described by Lawrence Kushner as "Kabbalah on steroids."[3] To begin to understand it, we need to consider several concepts:

1. *Tzimtzum*, which means "contraction." As Louis Jacobs explains it: "The Zoharic answer to the problem of how the finite universe emerged from the Infinite is that God caused the ten *sefirot* to emanate from Him. Lurianic Kabbalah gives a very different answer. This is that God 'withdrew from Himself into Himself' to leave room for the finite universe."[4] God contracts within Himself; this is an essential part of creation, giving human beings space within which to operate freely. Put differently: In the beginning was the *Ein Sof*, which was infinite and thus infinitely large, literally, "without end." "Everything was filled with the limitless light of the presence of God," writes Kushner. "There was only one logical problem: There was no room for creation." Luria's idea was that God withdrew Himself, "not unlike what any good parent or teacher must routinely do: get out of the way so that the child or student can have room in which to learn and grow."[5]

This contraction may be essential for Creation, but it does have a drawback: it allows space for evil. When God contracts His essence, this leaves an empty space (*tehiru*) in which all things can come into being. Within this space there remains a trace of the Divine, referred to as *reshimu*, which has been compared to the aroma of an empty perfume container or the milk left on the glass of a bottle after it is emptied. But it also makes room for death, for imperfection, and for whatever choices a human being might make, for evil as well as for good. In addition to "contraction" *Tzimtzum* can mean "concentration"—that when God withdraws from one realm, His Presence is more "concentrated" where it remains.

Is *tzimtzum* a metaphor, or is God's withdrawal a physical (or metaphysical) reality?[6] Even if it is "only" a metaphor, it powerfully expresses the tension between nearness to and distance from God. We will shortly see an illustration of how some kabbalists insisted on this point.

2. *Shevirat ha-kelim* literally means "the breaking of the vessels." However, it expresses the idea of a cosmic flaw within the original creation, truly a crisis within the Divine. Luria's view of the process of creation was that after the original *tzimtzum*, the light of *Ein Sof* emerged into the empty space, eventually producing the ten *sefirot* that were intended to serve as vessels (*kelim*) to contain this primordial light.[7] Unfortunately, the light proved too strong to be contained by the seven lower *sefirot*, and they were shattered. Sparks of this light scattered throughout the universe, becoming trapped within shards (*kelippot*) of the broken vessels, and ultimately sustaining them. These shards both form the material world and serve to house the evil from the "other side" (*sitra ahra*), which is nourished by the light trapped within the shells.

This understanding of creation has one disturbing by-product: God is understood to be the creator of evil as well as good. The notion of a fundamentally "broken" world, which many today accept (particularly since there is something we humans can do about it), implies that, as Shaul Magid puts it, "creation was, in a sense, a failure."[8]

3. *Tikkun* has been described by Joseph Dan as "the most powerful idea ever presented in Jewish thought,"[9] because of its cosmic, even messianic content, affecting every area of Jewish life. In Lurianic Kabbalah it means "repair" or "restoration" of these flaws. God is at work strengthening and reconnecting the *sefirot*, but only human beings can complete the task, most of which takes place through observance of

mitzvot and doing righteous deeds—performed with full consciousness of their kabbalistic significance—and through contemplative means. Zalman Schachter-Shalomi describes the symbolic process in striking fashion: "What happens is like making a stained-glass window, after those big sheets of glass, blue and red and all colors, are shattered; we put it together, and the lead that joins the pieces is our significance, as it were."[10]

Jews have a special assignment in this mission. Significant parts of the *tikkun* can only be performed by individual Jews as they fulfill the Torah's commands and perform additional holy deeds. The ultimate redemption, the coming of Messiah, can only happen when the *tikkun* is complete.[11] Thus, as Lawrence Fine puts it, "Safed appropriated a basic kabbalistic idea concerning the efficacious quality of human action and made it the cornerstone of the religious life by heightening the stakes, so to speak. It is one thing to be concerned about one's own personal spiritual condition, quite another to be responsible for the fate of one's people and even God."[12] It is true that "ordinary" Mainline Kabbalah had already given great power to the individual Jew, but Lurianic Kabbalah certainly added to the urgency of personal action, and all the mitzvot are subordinated to this ultimate goal.[13]

In addition to the statutory prayers—which, of course, were not simply recited, but directed primarily to the *sefirotic* realm—mystical practice in Safed included complex meditative exercises known as *yihudim*, "unifications," devotional practices that would unify the *sefirot* and thus ultimately hasten the redemption. These *yihudim*, usually performed after midnight and at the grave of a righteous man or alone at home, required lengthy and challenging training before one was considered ready to use them; additionally, one had to be thoroughly committed to the kabbalistic ethical and penitential practices, discussed more fully in chapter 18.[14] *Yihudim* took on enormous importance in Safed as the most effective means to unify the supernal realms. Thus, God needs human beings; our actions have taken on decisive significance. Although this was certainly true from the beginnings of Mainline Kabbalah, the emphasis on *tikkun* here heightens the significance of human action considerably.[15]

In addition to developing these three primary concepts—*tzimtzum*, *shevirat ha-kelim*, and *tikkun*—Lurianic Kabbalah introduced an incredibly complex view of the forms within the supernal system, most of which is beyond the scope of this book.[16] But one concept should be noted here, which is a further development of something discussed in chapter 11, *Adam Kadmon*, the "macro-being." In Lurianic teaching, the residue of the *Ein Sof* remains in the vacuum and forms the body of *Adam Kadmon*.[17] The first man was a miniature form of *Adam Kadmon*, not yet a fully physical being, containing portions from all the various *sefirot*, which would have enabled him to redeem the sparks from the material world and accomplish the *tikkun* properly. Unfortunately, the sin of this individual made it impossible for him to carry out this plan. Therefore, *tikkun* must be performed by each individual, through the extraordinarily elaborate guidelines in Lurianic thought. This will serve to restore *Adam Kadmon* to its original place.[18] Additionally, the "limbs" of *Adam Kadmon* form roots, which form individual souls; if your soul's root comes from the same root as another individual's soul, you might be uniquely able to assist with that person's particular task, or *tikkun*.

It is important to see how the kabbalists understood all this in the context of actual Jewish practice. Lawrence Fine explains that "Lurianism was no mere theoretical system, a set of intellectual abstractions. It was a lived and living phenomenon, the actual 'world' of a historically observable community. The ultimate goal of this community was a *pragmatic* one requiring mystical action—nothing less than the return of all existence to its original spiritual condition, a state synonymous with the manifestation of the messianic age."[19]

Lurianic Kabbalah had an enormous impact in the Jewish world, influencing the majority of rabbis for several centuries and playing an important role in the development of both the Sabbatean movement (see chapter 21) and Hasidic thought (below and especially in chapters 23 through 26).[20] But it is also important to note that it is an outgrowth of earlier Kabbalah and that the key concepts were present before Luria came on the scene. The spread of Lurianic Kabbalah also benefited from the invention and development of printing; books (particularly the Zohar) that had been expensive and generally shared with a handful of individuals became available to a much larger audience, and mystical ideas were circulated to the vast majority of Jewish communities.[21]

The first text, from thirteenth-century Provence, is an example of how the idea of *tzimtzum* was used before it became an important part of Lurianic Kabbalah.

> **How did He produce and create this world? Like a man who gathers in and contracts [*metzamtzem*] his breath [alternate reading: contracts Himself], so that the smaller might contain the larger, so He contracted His light into a hand's breadth, according to His own measure, and the world was left in darkness, and in that darkness He cut boulders and hewed rocks. (Anonymous commentary from a manuscript)[22]**

This teaching comes from an early kabbalistic circle connected to a book called *Sefer ha-Iyyun* (Book of contemplation).[23] Before the *Ein Sof* created *Keter*, It withdraws itself into a tiny space, leaving behind darkness (similar to the above-mentioned notion of the *tehiru*, "an empty space") and room for all that is to be formed. Why "a hand's breadth"? Perhaps because in the *mishkan*, the Tabernacle of the Israelites in the wilderness, God tells Moses: "There I will meet with you, and I will impart to you—from above the cover, from between the two cherubim that are on top of the Ark of the Pact—all that I will command you concerning the Israelite people" (Exod. 25:22.) God spoke to Moses from above the cover of the Ark, which according to the Talmud was the thickness of one hand's breadth![24]

The next two texts come from Luria's teachings as mediated through his student Hayyim Vital.

Know that before emanations began or any creatures were created, there was a supernal light filling all being. It was simply everywhere. There was no empty space. You might think of it as thin air or ether. Yet from this simple light of *Ein Sof*, all being issues. It has neither beginning nor end. Everything was this one, simple equally distributed light. And this light is called *Ein Sof*.

There arose in His simple will the desire to create worlds and produce the emanations, in order to bring about God's perfect works and Names and attributes, and this thought was the reason for the creation of everything. . . .

Whereupon the *Ein Sof* contracted Itself, leaving only a point within the center of the actual light. But the light was [also] withdrawn toward the edges that surrounded the central space. What now remained was an empty ether, void of everything, extending from the point in the center [to the edges], like so:

This *tzimtzum* was distributed equally around that empty central point in such a way that this emptiness was completely circular. There were neither corners nor angles. The *Ein Sof* contracted Itself so that It was a perfect circle. This is because the light of the *Ein Sof* needed to be perfectly circular, equidistant in all directions.

As we know from geometry, there is no form more perfect than a circle . . . . In that way all would be equally close to and joined with *Ein Sof* surrounding them all equally. . . .

And thus, after the *tzimtzum* mentioned above, there then remained an empty space, an ether void in the middle of the light of *Ein Sof*. Now, at last, there was a place able to receive the emanations . . . which could draw down the light of *Ein Sof*, a single, straight line of light. (Vital, *Eitz Hayyim, Sha'ar Egolim v'Yosher*, 27)[25]

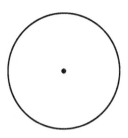

How exactly does the *Ein Sof* perform *tzimtzum*? First, the *Ein Sof* is by definition infinite, so Its light fills all space (and thus cannot be said to be closer to one point than another), until It decides to create something different that would recognize Its reality. Second, It has to withdraw and leave an empty space for everything that is created. As Louis Jacobs puts it, "Where there is God there cannot be any creatures since these would be overpowered by His majesty and swallowed up, as it were, into His being."[26] Third, the *Ein Sof* is perfect; therefore, all that It does follows a perfect form, which is why Vital goes to great pains to emphasize this form.[27] Note also that certain terms such as "before" and "after," or "above" and "below," are not meant to be taken literally; all this activity presumably takes place outside of what we understand to be time and space.

> When the supernal emanator wished to create this material universe, It contracted (*tzimtzem*) Its presence.... At first *Ein Sof* filled everything; it is known that even an inanimate stone is illuminated by It; otherwise the stone could not exist at all; it would disintegrate. The illumination of *Ein Sof* clothes Itself in garment upon garment....
>
> At the beginning of creation, when *Ein Sof* withdrew Its presence all around in every direction, It left a vacuum in the middle, surrounded on all sides by the light of *Ein Sof*, empty precisely in the middle.... The light withdrew like water in a pond displaced by a stone. When a stone is dropped in a pond, the water at that spot does not disappear; it merges with the rest....

So the withdrawn light converged beyond, and in the middle remained a vacuum. Then all the opacity and density of judgment within the light of *Ein Sof*—like a drop in the ocean—was extracted. Descending into the vacuum, it transformed into a *Golem* . . . surrounded in every direction by the light of *Ein Sof*. Out of this mass emanated the four worlds: emanation, creation, formation, and actualization. For in Its simple will to realize Its intention, the emanator reilluminated the *Golem* with a ray of the light withdrawn at first—not all of the light, because if it had all returned, the original state would have been restored, which was not the intention. . . .

To fashion pottery, the potter first takes an unformed mass of clay and then puts his hand inside the mass to shape it, as it is written: "Like clay in the hands of the potter" (Jer. 18:6). So the supernal emanator put Its hand into the amorphous mass, that is, a ray of light returned from above. . . . As this light began to enter the mass, vessels were formed. From the purest light, *Keter*; next, *Hokhmah*; then *Binah*; and so on through all ten *sefirot* . . . . Since *Keter* was the purest and cleanest of all the vessels, it could bear the light within it, and it was not broken at all. But *Hokhmah* and *Binah*, though more translucent than those below, were not like *Keter*. Not having its power, their backs broke, and they fell from their position. . . . As the light descended further, six points appeared, six fragments of what had been one point of light. Thus the vessels shattered. . . . Their spiritual essence, the light, ascended back to the mother's womb, while the shattered vessels fell to the world of creation. . . .

When the light emanated once again—repaired, arrayed anew—it extended only to the end of the world of emanation. "Emanation" denotes this extension of the light of *Ein Sof* during the time of regeneration. Emanation consists of five visages. These visages are reconfigurations of the points of light, capable now of receiving the light, so that no shattering occur[s], as at first. . . . Below these visages the light of *Ein Sof* appears only through a screen. As when you sit in the shade: though the sun does not shine on you directly, it illuminates the shaded area. In a similar manner, the light of *Ein Sof* illuminates the world of creation through a screen, indirectly. (Vital, *Likkutim Hadashim*, 17–23)[28]

Vital provides some additional details here, and much material that requires explanation. As he wrote in the passage from *Eitz Hayyim*, prior to *tzimtzum* the *Ein Sof* illuminates and influences everything. *Tzimtzum* removes the light of the *Ein Sof* into a circle, equidistant at each point from the vacuum in the center.

Why does "judgment" enter into this discussion, and why does it move from the *Ein Sof* into the vacuum? This quality is not simply Judgment, *Din*; it also means creating distinctions, boundaries. Without boundaries, no object or creature could function as distinct from anything else. This has obvious good results; we human beings get to be individuals and not just cells within some broader body. It also creates problems, when we fail to realize that we *are* part of something larger than ourselves, that we are connected to every other being, everything else created by the will of the *Ein Sof*. Nonetheless, for us to exist, this quality of boundedness must "descend into the vacuum" and become a meaningful force of its own.

This quality then mysteriously forms into a mass, here referred to as a *Golem*. By this is meant what we have previously referred to as *Adam Kadmon*, the primordial macro-being, the original "matter" from which all forms are created, including the "four worlds" (see chapter 19).[29] It only receives a "ray" of light from the *Ein Sof*, enough to give it light but not sufficient to return it to its original state. But by virtue of its descent into the material world, it is naturally subject to deterioration and even to evil. This provides an example of how Lurianic Kabbalah deals with the problem of evil, the issue to which the next chapter is devoted.

Now God, like a potter, shapes the *sefirot*, that is, He sends them enough light to give them shape and light. Tragically, *shevirat ha-kelim*, "the breaking of the vessels," takes place; *Hokhmah* and *Binah* are injured, the lower *sefirot* ruptured. The "six points" are the middle *sefirot*, with *Tiferet* in the center. The vessels fall to the second of the four worlds, the world of creation, from which the light will have to be raised and redeemed through the process of *tikkun*, and it then returns to "the mother's womb," that is, *Binah*, the (highest) feminine *sefirah*, giving birth to all below.

When the *tikkun* takes place and the light comes forward once again, it extends to the "end of the world of emanation," that is, through the ten *sefirot*, here reorganized as five "visages," or *partzufim* (a term previously used with reference to the theory of the original human being, which was understood to be two sided, or *du-partzufim*). While Lurianic Kabbalah often uses other terms for these five visages,[30] here we will simply note that they correspond to *Keter*, *Hokhmah*, *Binah*, the middle complex of six *sefirot* with *Tiferet* in the center, and *Malkhut*. Now, however, the divine light pours into these *sefirot* indirectly, as if through a filter, moving through the four worlds (emanation, creation, and so forth) so that each level can tolerate, use, and benefit from what it receives.

We will now see how certain Hasidic figures, particularly Dov Ber, the Maggid of Mezeritch (d. 1772) and the Ba'al Shem Tov's successor as leader of the Hasidic movement, applied this concept of *tzimtzum*.[31] Solomon of Lutzk, the author of this next text and its continuation, was a student of the Maggid.

The first thing one has to know is that God fills all worlds, that no place is empty of Him, and that He is in all worlds, etc. That this is so can be observed from experience. For in all things there inheres the vital energy of the Creator, blessed be He. It is obvious that things have taste or smell or appearance or love; that is, there are things which are loved, or feared, or are beautiful, and so on with regard to the other attributes. Now if one strips away the material aspect of things to consider solely the spiritual aspect in itself—the taste or the smell, etc.—it becomes quite obvious that this is not something

tangible or apprehended by the senses but by man's vital force, by his soul. It follows that it is a spiritual thing, the energy of the Creator which resides in this material thing just as the soul resides in the body. And so it is in connection with all things and all forms of motion. As the author of *Hovot ha-Levavot* (*The Duties of the Heart*) wrote: "All your movements depend on the Creator's will."[32] In all things there are sparks of spiritual energy which come from the Creator, blessed be He, who is the Bundle of Life, the Light of Life, the Fountain of Life, and the Life of Life, and from Him, blessed be He, is derived the vitality of all, from the highest of the high down to the lowest below. This is the meaning of "He concentrated [*tzimtzem*] His *Shekhinah*," i.e., "He resides among creatures below." Every spark is taken from its own world. For example, when something is loved, that love is taken from the world of love. That is, it is obvious there is a source and root from which love is taken for everything that has love.

In order to make this slightly more comprehensible, we should notice that the idea of the root of love is nothing else than the divine energy concentrated, as it were, so that it is experienced in the category of love. For it is obvious there are other forms of energy and spirit which are not experienced in the category of love but in other categories: fear, beauty, etc. All these, as above, are pure energy and spirit, but each is experienced in a different way from the others, since it has been concentrated into a different concentration, i.e., a different experience. But in their inner essence they are all the same, as above, all pure energy and spirit, since they are all derived from a single root in which there is no multiplicity at all. (Solomon of Lutzk, second introduction to *Maggid Devarav l'Ya'akov*, 9–11)

In Kabbalah ideas come from heaven (or the highest *sefirot*). Put more simply, everything here is mirrored in the higher realms. So if you strip away the physical form of something, what remains is the spiritual "idea" mirrored in the nonphysical realm, even if that idea is something we consider to be physical from our own perspective (taste, smell, etc.) This comes from the divine energy that permeates everything, that "fills all worlds." Tapping into such "ideas" brings us to a greater appreciation of and a closer relationship with God. And those sparks of divine energy sustain all life. The soul experiences this vitality; that is why we are drawn to physical things, which are only "material." Here *tzimtzum* is not only the withdrawal of Divinity, but its concentration into the spark where that vitality is most keenly felt.

This view is typical of many Hasidic thinkers, in that it takes the position of panentheism (God is found in everything and everything is contained in God) originally discussed in chapter 9.[33] In this understanding, if we look beyond appearances, we will come to know that that energy maintains all life and to recognize that what is apparent is not necessarily real, that separate entities are interconnected by the divine energy that supports them. (Note: Panentheism is not the same as pantheism—the notion that God actually *is* everything—although some Hasidic teachings did veer toward this idea.)[34]

> This is why the *Tikkunei Zohar* says: "And through it all supernal forms are seen,"[35] namely, apprehension is through the divine *tzimtzum*, as above. The feminine form is used [i.e., "it" is actually *bah*, "through her"] for it [*tzimtzum*] is in the category of the female in relation to what is even higher, the Root of Roots. And he who understands will understand. That is why they [the *sefirot*] are called *olamot* [worlds], because the Creator's energy is hidden [*mit'alem*] and concentrated into one particular form of experience. They are also called measures [*middot*] because they are experienced in a measured way, i.e., in this way and not in another. But in reality each one of them includes all the others. For emanation began in the Root of Roots because of His lovingkindness, in order to benefit His creatures. He needed, therefore, to concentrate of Himself, as it were, no more than a thin line and spark into each quality. But this is from

the energy and splendor of the Creator Himself, blessed be He, as it is written: "And breathed into his nostrils [the breath of life]" (Gen. 2:7). Whoever blows out his breath, blows it out from his very self.

It was theoretically possible for it to continue ad infinitum, as in the verse, "a great voice that did not cease" (Deut. 5:19),[36] but this would not have brought about the purpose intended so that, for His splendor to be revealed, it was necessary that it be measured. Yet these matters are extremely profound, and the most elaborate exposition is required if we are to see how the principle operates in each world. "For one higher than the high watches, and there are those higher than they" (Eccles. 5:7). (Solomon of Lutzk, *Maggid Devarav l'Ya'akov*, 9-11 continued)[37]

The *sefirot* require God's *tzimtzum* to exist. God hides himself (*mit'alem*) so that the worlds (*olamot*) can function.[38] Instead of a constant flow of God's infinite energy, it is limited and conducted into the *sefirot*. "It was necessary that it be measured," that is, that it be directed into a limited space, so that life could come into being and experience and benefit from the divine flow.

The Maggid of Mezeritch himself offered an interpretation of *tzimtzum* that no follower could fail to understand:

"Draw me, we will run after you" (Songs 1:4). A parable: A father sees his son playing childish games with his companions. The father goes up to them and allows the child to see him. When the child sees his father he leaves his games and runs to his father, shouting: "Father!" When the father sees the child is running to him, he walks away, and then the child calls out even louder, "Father! Father!" and runs quickly toward him until he reaches his side. Now when the father first allowed his child to see him, it was so that the child would leave his childish games and run to him. The father is greatly pleased that his child is clever enough for nothing to matter so much to him as his father's love. But when the father notices that the child has left his childish games behind him, he pretends to ignore the child so that the child should have an even greater distaste for the childish games and yearn all the more to be near to his father. When that happens, the father's joy is even greater and great feelings of compassion stem from it, in addition to the joy the child has. It follows that the great joy the father experienced and the resulting joy of the child would not have been possible were it not for the father's *tzimtzum* when he pretended to walk away.... When we attach ourselves to things down below and to temporal pleasures, we are as nothing to Him. But when we have the strongest distaste for worldly pleasures, when we compare them to our love for Him, we cause, as it were, great joy to God, blessed be He. (Dov Ber, the Maggid of Mezeritch, *Maggid Devarav l'Ya'akov*, 18a)[39]

What is the meaning of the verse from the Song of Songs? As we already know, the Rabbis understand the biblical book to be about the relationship between God and humans. In this view, God constricts Himself not merely to produce the world, but to build a stronger relationship with us, His children—to get us to run after Him and to run away from transitory desires. This is a significant twist in the idea of *tzimtzum*, offering a clearly psychological interpretation.[40]

The first leader of Chabad Hasidism, Shneur Zalman of Lyady (1745–1813), offers an additional understanding of *tzimtzum*:

It is possible to understand the error of some, scholars in their own eyes, may God forgive them, who erred and misinterpreted in their study of the writings of the Ari [i.e., Luria], of blessed memory, and understood the doctrine of *tzimtzum*, which is mentioned therein literally: that the Holy One, blessed be He, removed Himself and His essence, God forbid, from this world, and only guides from above with individual providence.... Now, aside from the fact that it is altogether impossible to interpret the doctrine of *tzimtzum* literally, for then it is a phenomenon of corporeality, concerning the Holy One who is set apart from such things many myriads of separations ad infinitum, they also did not speak wisely.... The Holy One, blessed be He, however, contracted the light and life-force in order that it should be able to spread forth from the "breath of His mouth." (Shneur Zalman of Lyady, *Tanya, Sha'ar ha-Yichud v'ha-Emunah* [Gate of unity and faith], ch. 7, 313–19)[41]

Tanya, a systematic treatment of Hasidic philosophy originally published in 1797, has become especially important reading for Chabad Hasidim. (See chapter 26 for more about *Tanya* and Chabad.) Shneur Zalman's primary message here is that one cannot speak of God *actually* withdrawing from the world, because God is not a physical being who could withdraw from His creation.[42] It is only the "light and life-force" that are contracted so that they can be directed properly.

In our last text, contemporary theologian Arthur Green has sought to integrate the lessons of kabbalistic (particularly Hasidic) teachers into a non-Orthodox approach.

In seeing ourselves as living in need of partnership with another for true fulfillment [a man without a wife is called "half a body" by the Zohar], we represent, in human form, the search of the eternal One. This is yet another way in which we are "God's image," though here the likeness is shared with other living creatures as well. To say it differently, the testimony that God is One requires the presence of an other.

But how can there be such an other if life is naught but an infinite coloring of varied manifestations of the One? The God who is all can have no other. Here the divine light has to hide itself that it might be revealed. It withdraws itself from being in order that it might be seen, in order to allow for us to exist as "other," so that we might see and bear witness to it. This paradox of divine self-withdrawal is what the Jewish sages call *tzimtzum* .... In order to be God's "other," we have to be all that the eternal One is not: transitory, corporeal, mortal. God, as it were, seeks out an opposite—and a partner—in us. (Green, *Seek My Face, Speak My Name*, 65–66)

Green's formulation of *tzimtzum* as a requirement for partnership and even the existence of an "other" is a much-simplified version of an eighteenth-century teaching from Menahem Nahum of Chernobyl.[43]

The complexities of Lurianic Kabbalah often made it inaccessible, even for many learned Jews. Yet Lurianic Kabbalah created an additional vocabulary that helped to strengthen Jewish faith in the face of continued crises. This powerful faith in the repair of the vessels, the Lurianic conviction of the coming of a long-desired redemption, created both opportunities and challenges for the next generations.

We next turn to one of the most critical issues of all, for kabbalists and nonkabbalists alike: the problem of evil. How do kabbalists, and particularly the generation of Safed, explain the sufferings they witnessed?

17

The Problem of Evil in Kabbalah

The problem of theodicy (vindicating God in spite of the existence of physical and moral evil) remains the greatest challenge to religious thinkers. Byron Sherwin outlines the issues and how Kabbalah provides some answers.

In Western philosophy and theology, discussion of theodicy, the problem of evil, often relates to the attempt to reconcile three premises: (1) God is good, benevolent, (2) God is omnipotent, all powerful, (3) Evil is real.

These premises assume that if evil is real, God, being benevolent, would not want evil to occur, and, that God being omnipotent, could prevent evil from happening. . . .

For some, evil does not represent the human perversion of a world perfectly created by God. Rather, evil is viewed as having been created by God. Evil is considered an element endemic to creation: "Is it not from the mouth of the Most High that good and evil come?" (Lam. 3:38) "I form light and darkness, I make good and evil; I the Lord do all these things." (Isa. 45:7)

These texts form the foundation of a theodicy that maintains that evil exists because it serves the good, that to expect God to produce the good without the evil upon which it depends is to demand a logical and ontological impossibility. Without evil, good would be unrecognizable and unattainable. Free moral choice between good and evil would become unrealizable.

This view maintains that a polarity of opposites characterizes everything in creation. Only God remains beyond all dichotomies. Everything else, particularly good and evil, exists as a member of a pair of opposites. The existence of one necessarily implicates the existence of the other. The *Sefer Yetzirah*, for example, states (6:2): "God has set each thing to correspond with another; the good against the evil, and the evil against the good...." From this perspective, the existence of evil flows not from the essential nature of God, but from the nature of creation and from the nature of the creative process. In the sixteenth century, the Lurianic kabbalists further developed this approach. Similarly, some modern theologians refer to the evil element, the random and irrational factor built into the fabric of creation....

Lurianic Kabbalah describes destruction, evil and imperfection as necessary aspects of the process of creation.[1] In this view, God cannot create without destroying, not because He is essentially imperfect, but because it is an essential feature of the creative process to include destruction, and because creation, by its very nature, must be imperfect; creation must embody dichotomies such as good and evil. Further, that creation embodies evil as well as good also derives from the empirical observation that evil is a component of created existence. In the Lurianic view, though God [*Ein Sof*] is perfect in essence, God must nevertheless will to relinquish absolute perfection in order to act as a creator.

The Lurianic doctrine of *tzimtzum* [divine contraction] has God withdraw into Himself, thereby corrupting His essential perfection, as the initial step in the process of creation. Furthermore, the Lurianic concept of "the breaking of the vessels" teaches that there is an initial flaw in creation, and that this cosmic flaw reaches back to the creative process itself. Through the process of *tikkun* [restoration], the human creature can repair the flaws which form part of the initial fabric of creation.

A feature of this view is that human actions can amplify through sin and can reduce through righteousness the flaws that are built into creation. From this position, a conceptual jump can be made from the affirmation of a perfect God who compromises His perfection, in order to become a creative God, to the claim that the elements of good and evil embedded in creation reflect parallel components in the nature of the Creator.

While the Lurianic mystics envisaged the continuous purging of the implicitly evil element in the Godhead as a central scene in the divine drama, the earlier kabbalistic text, *Sefer ha-Bahir*, explicitly states [162], "there is in God an attribute that is called evil."

... In a talmudic text, God is described as having made a flawed creation, as having unjustifiably punished one of His creatures—the moon—and as having "sinned."[2] Even more remarkable is this text's assertion that human beings may act to atone for God's "sin."

In this view, evil is an ontologically necessary component of existence, and perhaps even a theologically necessary feature of the divine. Rather than concluding that the necessary existence of evil leads inescapably to nihilism and despair, and rather than perceiving the human condition as one of random victimization, this position asserts to the contrary that the human person may become an active protagonist in the ongoing battle to contain and to control the evil element within the self and within the world. This approach aims at reducing the power of evil in the self, in the world, and even within God, by means of redemptive deeds. This approach perceives evil to be a fact of life, a feature of existence to be reckoned with, rather than a problem to be solved. (Sherwin, *Toward a Jewish Theology*, 63, 69-71)

The three premises Sherwin mentions at the outset do not easily fit together. In some times and places, it has been suggested that evil is an illusion or is simply the absence of the good. But in our time, where we have known Auschwitz and been unable to prevent other cases of genocide, few can muster a case that evil is somehow not "real." And as for the premise of God's goodness, even fewer religious thinkers would be willing to dispense with this. That leaves in question the proposition of God as all powerful.

Less mystically oriented thinkers (most famously in modern times Rabbi Harold Kushner, in his best-selling *When Bad Things Happen to Good People*) have addressed this issue by embracing a "limited God." However, as Sherwin shows, the mystical tradition, particularly within Lurianic Kabbalah, gives us another way to approach this premise, by accepting the presence of evil as a necessary element within creation. Heschel (see chapter 27) also has written on the confusion of good and evil as an element that "goes back to the very process of creation."[3] This was recognized by the sages noted in the following text:

> "And God saw all that He had made, and found it very good" (Gen. 1:31). Rabbi Tanhuma opened: "He brings everything to pass precisely at its time" (Eccles. 3:11). Rabbi Tanhuma said: The world was created when it was due, and it was not fit to be created earlier. Rabbi Abbahu said: From here, we learn that the Holy One, blessed be He, went on creating worlds and destroying them until He created these [heaven and earth] and then He said: "These please Me; those did not please me." Rabbi Pinhas said: The reason for Rabbi Abbahu's statement is "And God saw all He had made, and found it very good," [meaning:] "These please Me; those did not please Me." (*Midrash Bereshit Rabbah* 9:2)

Why does the end of the Creation story tell us that God found it *very good* when we have already been told that the elements of Creation were good? Rabbi Tanhuma uses the verse from Ecclesiastes to understand that it was *very good* only because it was created at a particular time. Rabbi Abbahu goes much further, suggesting that the world is *very good* compared to something else . . . to previous worlds God had created! Those worlds, containing whatever evils they might have in spite of being created by God, make *this* world look very good indeed.

Implicit in Rabbi Abbahu's teaching are two important points. One is the possibility that this world is not the main goal of existence and that others yet to be brought about will supersede it. The other, our main concern here, is the assumption that God's creation is not necessarily perfect and that it may contain elements of imperfection and even evil. And this of course precedes the creation of the first human, let alone his sin. Thus the roots of the idea that evil is built into the framework of creation can be found in Jewish tradition much earlier than Kabbalah.[4] The Zohar also picks up on the theme of previous worlds that did not endure, and this may have been an inspiration for the Lurianic concept of *shevirat ha-kelim*.[5]

We have already seen the idea that the *yetzer ha-ra* serves a divine purpose. But the notion that God creates evil might seem somewhat more radical, if it had not been explicitly mentioned in the Bible: "I form light and create darkness, I make peace and create evil; I the Lord do all these things" (Isa. 45:7). This may be explained in a manner similar to the Zoharic parable of the harlot in chapter 15.

This school of thought in Kabbalah sees evil—though dependent on other forces—as the instrument through which good may be achieved, in that people are provided with the choice to do good. As Isaiah Tishby writes, "Whenever man opts for evil, God brings the power of evil into play against him . . . consequently the evil inclination that seduces and leads man astray, the accusing angel, and the angels of destruction, who chastise and kill, are all the creatures of God, and they all act on His instructions."[6]

However, early in the development of Kabbalah, much of this was already expressed in the *Bahir*, as we will now see.

A king had a beautiful daughter and others desired her. The king knew about it, but could not fight those who wanted to bring his

daughter to evil ways. He came to his house and warned her: "My daughter, do not pay attention to the words of these enemies and they will not be able to overcome you. Do not leave the house, but do all your work at home. Do not sit idle, even for a single moment. Then they will not be able to see you and harm you."

They have one attribute which causes them to leave aside every good way and choose every evil way. When they see a person directing himself along a good way, they hate him. What is it? It is the Satan. This teaches us that the Holy One, Blessed be He, has an attribute whose name is Evil. It is to the north of the Holy One, Blessed be He, as it is written: "From the north will come forth evil upon all the inhabitants of the earth" (Jer. 1:14). Any evil that comes to all the inhabitants of the earth comes from the north.

What is this attribute? It is the form of a hand and a foot. It has many messengers, and the name of them all is Evil Evil [*ra ra*]. Some of them are great, some are small, but they all bring guilt to the world. This is because chaos [*tohu*] is toward the north. Chaos is nothing other than Evil. It confounds [*taha*] the world and causes people to sin. Every *yetzer ha-ra* that exists in man comes from there. And why is it placed to the left? This is because it does not have any authority any place in the world except in the north. (*Bahir* 162–63)[7]

As Scholem noted, the idea that God has a "quality" called evil is preceded in Jewish tradition by the notion of *middat ha-din*, "the quality of judgment," which is understood to be a force that testifies before God against human beings.[8] Sometimes the ministering angels, or even Satan himself, fulfill this function. Here, however, as Scholem wrote, "evil is one of the powers or forces by means of which God acts and manifests himself."[9] In other words, evil is actually one of the *sefirot*.

The daughter in the parable is told to "do all her work at home": that is, internally, concentrating on the virtues and a life of holiness. The king,

God, cannot eliminate this evil aspect, but if one does not "sit idle," if one works against it, it can be managed and controlled.

Why is evil associated with the north? In the Judean kingdom, Jerusalem was protected by valleys, except from the north; thus, this was the logical direction from which they would expect an attack.[10] If one faces east—toward Jerusalem for most Jews—north is on the left, which in Kabbalah is the wrong side, the side corresponding to *Gevurah*, or *Din* (Power, or Judgment). This is the side from which evil might potentially enter. The reference to "a hand and a foot" is obscure but might refer to two of the *sefirot* on the left side that potentially would be sources for evil.

Following is the first of two texts from the Zohar, suggesting the presence of evil forces parallel to the good inherent within the *sefirot*.

> Rabbi Yitzhak said: "The seven good cows" are levels, higher than the others, "and seven lean and ugly cows" (Gen. 41:26-27) are other levels below; these on the side of holiness, and those on the side of defilement.
>
> "Seven ears of grain." Rabbi Yehudah said: These first ones were good, because they were from the right side, of which it is written, "it was good" (Gen. 1:4). And the evil ones were below them. The seven [healthy] ears were from the side of purity, and the seven others were from the side of impurity. And all the levels stand one above the other, one facing the other, and all [of them] Pharaoh saw in his dream.
>
> Rabbi Yeisa said: Did He reveal all these to that evil man, Pharaoh? Rabbi Yehudah answered: He saw what corresponded to them, for there are numerous levels, one facing the other, one above the other. . . . Whatever man is shown in his dream depends on his own character. This determines what he sees and how his soul ascends to gain knowledge, each man according to his level, as befits him. So Pharaoh saw what befitted him, and no more. (Zohar 1:194a)[11]

Of course this interpretation of Pharaoh's dream was never expressed by Joseph! The seven good cows here represent the seven lower *sefirot* from *Hesed* through *Malkhut*, higher than the realms of holiness found in our normal existence. The seven bad cows represent a parallel set of forces within the "other side" (*sitra ahra*), and these are *also* arrayed like the *sefirot* on the "good" side. The second part of Pharaoh's dream portrays seven ears of grain; here, the good ears are on the "right" side, the side of holiness. In the scheme of the *sefirot*, *Hesed* is seen as the right side and *Gevurah*, or *Din*, "Judgment" is the left side, symbolizing evil. So the good ears are above the bad ones, just as the holy and pure "outrank" sin and impurity, but they still "face one another," that is, they exist in corresponding realms.

The text asks whether the Pharaoh, by nature an oppressor and therefore considered wicked, could possibly perceive the holy realms? The answer is that by seeing the levels on the evil side he was able to get some sense of how the holy side might look. But this was all he was entitled to see.

Dreams are of special interest not only in Kabbalah but also in the Rabbinic tradition. The Rabbis believed that dreams were not simply the internal productions of the brain, but also represented an ascent of the soul to the supernal realms. As one of the talmudic sages taught, "A person dreams corresponding to who he is."[12] In other words: the greater the person's level, the more profound his dreams will be and the more intense his vision of Divinity.

The Zohar does not flinch at the notion of God as the source of all evil:

Rabbi Eleazar was sitting before his father [Rabbi Shimon bar Yohai]. He said to him: If there is a defender in the world, it is found in the Matronita [the Queen, i.e., *Malkhut*]. And if there is a prosecutor in the world, it is found in the Matronita. Why? He answered: This may be compared to a King who had a son from his Matronita. As long as the son does the will of the King, the King made his dwelling with the Matronita. But whenever the son did not do the will of the King, the King separated his dwelling from the Matronita. So it is with the Holy One, blessed be He, and the Assembly of Israel [*Knesset Yisrael*]: As long as Israel does the will of the Holy One, blessed be He, the Holy One dwells with the Assembly of Israel. But whenever Israel does not do the will of the Holy One, blessed be He, He does not put His dwelling with the Assembly of Israel. Why not? Israel is the firstborn son of the Holy One, blessed be He, as it is written: "Israel is My firstborn son" (Exod. 4:22). . . . As long as [the People of] Israel are remote from the King's palace, it is as if the Matronita is remote along with them. Why? Because the Matronita did not enforce the rules and strike the son, to guide him on the upright path. For the King never strikes his son but leaves everything in the hands of the Matronita, to govern the palace, discipline her son and guide him on the path of truth toward the King. (Zohar 3:74a)[13]

To properly understand this text, one must remember the codes: "Holy One, blessed be He" and *Knesset Yisrael* are code language for *Tiferet* and *Malkhut*. Given that, the Zohar's message seems to be relatively simple. Do the will of the King, God; keep Him happy, and there will be no evil. Only sin sent into the *sefirotic* realm causes evil. Taken one step further, however, this suggests that just as God's positive energy is supported by good and holy deeds, there is a negative energy within God, fed by evil deeds. Thus, God also has the capability to do things that are evil! This view of God as potentially evil and abusive of His creation is not for the faint of heart.[14]

Alternatively, one can read this text as portraying God as simply distant from His creation, having delegated the "discipline" to the Matronita,[15] *Shekhinah*, or *Malkhut*. If She disciplines the "child" (Israel, or humankind), they are properly guided and their life (all life, for that matter) works out well. If She does not—if they do not follow the rules—catastrophe will result, for God will not connect with His world as He should (*Tiferet* uniting with *Malkhut*).

Cordovero offers a striking metaphor for the intermingling of good and evil:

Where did the evil powers and impurities come from; where were they before their creation? This seems to be a penetrating and difficult question which could confuse the wise, but we have received from our teachers a fine answer to it. This is like wheat which had been cleansed from every impure element so that it is clean and pure; still, when a man eats it and the food is digested in his stomach, a great deal of dirt and excrement will remain there. Now shall we say that when he ate the food, he ate filth and excrement? Of course not. Before it was eaten, that food was truly as pure as could be, completely separated from any excrement or filth. But after it was eaten, the best part is separated from the food, and the excrement remains, even though it did not previously exist. (Cordovero, *Pardes Rimonim*, *Sha'ar ha-Temurot*, ch. 1, 416)[16]

Cordovero believed that the divine world is purely spiritual and cannot be the source of evil. But when things move downward from the divine realm, the descent and distance allow for the development of evil; "some dirt and excrement naturally are to be expected when some good process is going on."[17] Even God is powerless to prevent this development, though it runs counter to His plan.

So if God cannot prevent evil, what is to be done about it? Cordovero gives an answer in the following text, from his brief masterpiece of kabbalistic ethics in a segment dealing with repentance.

Know that Cain himself was evil and derived from the serpent, yet it was said to him: "If you do right, there is uplift" (Gen. 4:7). Do not think that because you derive from evil, there is no hope for you. This is false. "If you do right," and root yourself firmly in repentance, "there is uplift": you will enter that place according to the secret of the good rooted there. For every supernal bitterness has a sweet root, and he could have entered by way of that root to become good. Thus man may turn his evil deeds into good, and his deliberate transgressions are turned into merits.[18] For those [evil] deeds which he committed were prosecutors from the Left Side, but when one returns in complete repentance, he causes those deeds to enter and be rooted above. And all those prosecutors are not nullified, but they transform themselves into good and are rooted in holiness, just as Cain was told he could be good.

Know that if Cain had repented and repaired [his sin], then [even] the sin of Adam—through which Cain was conceived—would have been accounted to him for merit, according to the mystical meaning of "the son brings merit to the father."[19] But Cain did not want to repent, and therefore the entire Left Side draws its sustenance from there. But all its branches will eventually become sweet and be perfect once again. This is for the reason we have given, that man roots himself in the secret of evil and renders it sweet and restores it to good. Therefore, man purifies the evil impulse and brings it into the good so it becomes rooted in holiness above. This is the high level of repentance by which a person should conduct himself; he must ponder on it each day, and repent in some fashion each day, so that all his days will be spent in repentance. (Cordovero, *Tomer Devorah*, ch. 4)[20]

First, why does Cordovero say that Cain was "derived from the serpent"? Because there is a midrashic tradition[21] reflected in the Zohar[22] that says so. "Rabbi Eleazar said: When the serpent injected his impurity into Eve, she absorbed it, so when she copulated with Adam she bore two sons: one from the impure side and one from the side of Adam, Cain resembling both the higher image and the lower. So their paths diverged from one another. Cain was certainly son of the impure spirit and, deriving from the side of the Angel of Death, he killed his brother. Being from his side, from him emerged all evil haunts, goblins, spirits, and demons. Rabbi Yosi said: Cain [*Kayin*] was the nest [*kina*] of evil lairs that materialized from the side of impurity." As noted in chapter 15, the notion of original sin is not absent from Jewish sources!

We have learned that repentance is located in the *sefirah* of *Binah*, a level of the *sefirot* sufficiently high to be free from any evil. Earlier Kabbalah offers rich interpretation of this identification.[23] For instance, the word *Binah*, *beit-Yud-nun-Heh* is an anagram (and thus understood to be code language) for *Ben-Yah*, son of *Yah* (God).[24] It produces the complex around *Tiferet* as well as *Malkhut*, both the masculine and feminine creatures. Furthermore, the word *teshuvah* (repentance) is reread by separating out the last letter, thus becoming *tashuv Heh*, "return the *Heh*" to its place within the Four-Letter Name. There are of course two *Heh* letters in the Name; one is identified with *Binah* and the other with *Malkhut*. Sin removes the second *Heh* from the Name, that is, it interferes with the connection between humans and God. If one repents of a sin, the *Heh* and the connection are restored. However, a higher form of *teshuvah* is not directly connected with a specific sin but a returning to God through a high level of love and awe channeled into Torah study and subsequently into *deveikut*. This *teshuvah* reaches up to the higher *Heh*, connected to *Binah*; thus the connection is much deeper and richer. The idea of daily repentance and examination of one's deeds is an idea already found in the Zohar.[25]

The root of the soul is in *Hokhmah*, as Cordovero states in chapter 3 of *Tomer Devorah*; *Hokhmah* is totally good and compassionate, "a sweet root" above. Had Cain sought this route and repaired the sin of Adam, he would have not merely nullified the sin but changed it into merit. Although he did not do so, nevertheless "all its branches will eventually become sweet" when impurity is eliminated, when the *yetzer ha-ra* is reprogrammed, so to speak, and transformed to good.

In summary, Cordovero understands evil as a part of the creative process that can always and eventually will be transformed into good.[26] Thus, however real evil is, it is temporary. As Joseph Dan explains, "Its appearance as earthly evil is but a stage in the history of a divine particle, which does not affect its inherent, potential goodness. Spiritual power cannot be lost, even the spiritual power used to commit the worst crimes, like murder; it waits until it can return to the root of everything in *Binah* and then will be transformed into goodness equivalent in its degree to its former degree in the realm of evil."[27]

When the Israelites came out of Egypt, along with them there traveled what the Torah refers to as an *erev rav*, a "mixed multitude" (Exod. 12:38), probably slaves from other groups than the Hebrews. The Rabbinic tradition occasionally saw this "riffraff" as a negative influence on the Israelites, responsible for witchcraft,[28] degeneracy, and complaining among the Israelites,[29] and even the construction of the Golden Calf.[30] The mystical tradition adds to this the notion seen in this text, that they are the locus for the original evil of the serpent but will eventually be eliminated from the world.[31]

> "The son of David [Messiah] will not come until all the souls will be born."[32] At that time renewal will come to the world. Then the mixed multitude [*erev rav*] will be erased [*mit'avrin*] from the world. Then it will be said to Israel and Moses that all will have their proper soul mates, and both Adam and Eve will be naked [*arumim*]; they will not be ashamed since licentiousness [*ervah*] will be erased from the world. *Ervah* is the *erev rav* who brought exile into the world: precisely the *erev rav*! It is said about the *erev rav*: "the serpent was the shrewdest of all the wild beasts the Lord God had made" (Gen. 3:1). He was shrewd for evil purposes more than "all the wild beasts," who are the idolatrous nations of the world. The *erev rav* are the children of the serpent in the garden who enticed Eve; they are surely the filth which the serpent placed inside Eve. Cain, who came from this filth, killed his brother Abel. (Zohar 1:28b [*Tikkunei ha-Zohar*])[33]

The mixed multitude may have had the benefit of being at Sinai, but they are still a demonic influence on Israel. Here, evil comes from the serpent. The Torah may be an antidote against its poison, but only for the Jews themselves, not these outsiders, who not only carry the poison but can spread it. Obviously the serpent is a creation of God, but here it is more malevolent than the *yetzer ha-ra* as previously portrayed. This is also an example here of the strong particularism common in Kabbalah, where the power to affect the higher realms is limited to Jews.

Jewish thinkers in general recoil from the idea of an independent reality of evil, which would suggest a second power coequal with God. But how do we reconcile God's goodness with evil as we experience it? The important early Hasidic work *Tzava'at ha-Rivash* (Testament of the Ba'al Shem Tov) offers an interesting approach to the problem.

> It is reasonable to wonder why the Torah specifies, "And behold, it was very good" (Gen. 1:31). However, we also read, "See, I set before you life and good, death and evil" (Deut. 30:15). Where did the evil come from?
>
> We cannot read this as if evil were actually real; rather, the evil is also good, except that it is on a lower level than the completely good. And this is hinted at when the Zohar (1:49b) speaks of "from above and from below."
>
> In this way, when one does good, then the evil is also transformed into good. However, when committing sins, the evil is made manifest. This is like the case of a household broom, designed to sweep the house. It is fairly good, even on its low level. But when it is used to strike a child who is misbehaving, then the broom is transformed into something completely evil. (*Tzava'at ha-Rivash, sect.* 130)[34]

The answer of this Hasidic work to the existence of evil is that evil is a lower level of good and serves a good purpose.[35] Again, this answer is similar to the text of the Zohar in chapter 15, in the parable of the harlot who serves the king. When the Zohar speaks of "above and below," it is referring to the *sefirot* of *Hesed* and *Gevurah* above—the sources of good and evil—and to our world below where evil (due to the power of sin) becomes evil as such, even though it serves a good purpose on a higher level. The broom provides an excellent example of this. It has positive functions, and when it is used for these functions it remains good. If used for evil functions, it draws on its latent evil and becomes evil.

In short, the mystic sees evil as real while still affirming that God's creation is a blessing, albeit with destructive potential. The idea that God is everything would also serve notice that evil too has its source in God; indeed, it is not independent of Him. Lurianic Kabbalah, while acknowledging evil, offered a way for Jews to respond to it. As Jonathan Sacks has put it, "Lurianic Kabbalah was a vision of cosmic catastrophe, but it was a healing vision. Somewhere among the debris . . . are fragments of divine light, and our task is to rescue them and restore them to their place in an ordered universe, a structure of fragile but recoverable harmony. The only way to fight evil the morning after the storm is to do good, countering hate with a no less determined love."[36]

18
Mystical Experiences, Ascetic Practices

The Safed community was a center for mystical aspirations, but one of its most prominent members, Joseph Karo, had an ongoing mystical experience even before arriving. Karo (1488–1575) was born in Spain and went with his family to Turkey after the 1492 expulsion, arriving in Safed only in 1536. One of the most impressive halakhists in Jewish history, he wrote a commentary on Maimonides's code (*Mishneh Torah*) as well as his own monumental commentary, *Beit Yosef* (on the fourteenth-century code *Arba'ah Turim* [Four pillars]); he then produced his own shorter code, the *Shulhan Arukh* (Prepared table), still considered one of the standard codes of Rabbinic practice.[1]

In addition to his wide-ranging halakhic works, Karo also kept a diary of his mystical revelations, later published as *Maggid Mesharim* (Preacher of righteousness). By virtue of his study and piety, and propelled by mystical intentions, Karo (and others who claimed to witness it) understood his experience to involve receiving the presence of a *maggid*, a spiritual force who gave him further instruction and direction in his mystical endeavors. Although his description of the *maggid* was the most extensive of such a phenomenon recorded by mystics, by no means was Karo unique in experiencing such an occurrence.

The text below and its continuation were written by Solomon Alkabetz (1505–76), Karo's fellow mystic and the author of the well-known Sabbath hymn "Lekhah Dodi" (see chapter 22), in a letter to a mystical circle in

Salonika; the "saint" of course is Karo himself. The letter describes an experience that took place on Shavuot, in the 1530s in the Turkish city of Nikopolis where Karo lived.[2] Shavuot celebrates and in some ways is designed to reenact the revelation at Sinai, but for the kabbalists this is the ultimate moment for the "marriage" of *Tiferet* and *Malkhut*.

> Know that the saint and I, his and your humble servant, belonging to our company, agreed to stay up all night in order to banish sleep from our eyes on Shavuot. We succeeded, thank God, so that, as you will hear, we ceased not from study for even a moment. [Alkabetz then lists all the segments of Scripture that they studied.] All this we did in dread and awe, with quite unbelievable melody and tunefulness. We studied the whole of the Order *Zera'im* in the Mishnah and then we studied in the way of truth.
>
> No sooner had we studied two tractates of the Mishnah than our Creator smote us so that we heard a voice speaking out of the mouth of the saint, may his light shine. It was a loud voice with letters clearly enunciated. All the companions heard the voice but were unable to understand what was said. It was an exceedingly pleasant voice, becoming increasingly strong. We all fell upon our faces and none of us had any spirit left in him because of our great dread and awe. The voice began to address us saying: "Friends, choicest of the choice, peace to you, beloved companions. Happy are you and happy those that bore you. Happy are you in this world and happy in the next that you resolved to adorn Me on this night. For these many years had My head been fallen with none to comfort Me. I was cast down to the ground to embrace the dunghills but now you have restored the crown to its former place. Be strong, My beloved ones. Be courageous, My friends. Rejoice and exult, for you belong among the chosen few. You have the merit of belonging to the king's palace. The sound of your Torah and the breath of your mouth have ascended to the Holy One, blessed be He, breaking through many firmaments

and many atmospheres until it rose upward. The angels were silent, the seraphim still, *hayyot* stood without speech and all the host of heaven heard, together with the Holy One, blessed be He, the sound of your voice. Behold, I am the Mishnah, the mother who chastises her children, and I have come to converse with you. Had you been ten in number you would have ascended even higher, but you have reached a great height nevertheless. Happy are those who bore you, My friends, in that by denying yourselves sleep you have ascended so far on high. Through you I have become elevated this night and through the companions in the great city, a mother-city in Israel. You are not like those who sleep on beds of ivory in sleep which is a sixtieth of death, who stretch themselves out upon their couches. But you cleave to your Creator and He rejoices in you. Therefore, My sons, be strong and rejoice in My love, rejoice in My Torah, rejoice in the fear of Me. If you could only imagine My Torah, rejoice in the fear of Me. If you could only imagine one millionth of the anguish which I endure, no joy would ever enter your hearts and no mirth your mouths, for it is because of you that I am cast to the ground. (Alkabetz, in Joseph Karo's *Maggid Mesharim,* introduction)[3]

The letter is addressed to a society in another "mother-city in Israel," probably Salonika. The opening ritual involved reading texts of particular significance for the festival of Shavuot, including the segment from Exodus 19 and 20 on the experience at Sinai and the segment from Exodus 24 involving a mystical experience, found in chapter 2.

It is extremely significant that studying a substantial portion of the Mishnah is part of the liturgy described. As the basic text of the Oral Torah, the Mishnah is identified with the tenth *sefirah, Shekhinah,* or *Malkhut.* It would be natural for the kabbalists to include Mishnah study following study of the Written Torah, identified with *Tiferet,* since the whole point of the exercise is to represent on earth the union of *Malkhut* and *Tiferet* that is to take place in the supernal realms. What is remarkable is that such a mystical experience is strongly attached to a text representing the Rabbinic tradition and *halakhah* in general. Furthermore, the word "Mishnah" is an anagram for the word *Neshamah*, "soul"; this may have suggested the idea that the study of Mishnah would provide an ascent for the soul studying it as well as for a departed soul in whose honor the Mishnah is being studied.[4] Finally, the "way of truth" is a clear reference to kabbalistic wisdom, likely including at least some portion of the Zohar.

During this session, the *maggid*, or "preacher," comes to the group involved in this trancelike experience—through the body of Karo. Significantly, it is during the Mishnah study that this divine visitor arrives, since the voice identifies itself as the Mishnah during this experience. The voice of the *maggid* is initially incomprehensible, but the group is clearly awestruck by it.[5] Then the *maggid* addresses the group as *mehadrin min ha-mehadrin*, the "choicest of the choice," that is, the elite among the devout kabbalists. It tells of its dreadful history, having been thrown to the "dunghills." This mirrors the history of the Land of Israel, particularly in the years of Karo's life.

Shekhinah, or *Malkhut*, the gateway to the upper *sefirot*, is also referred to as *Knesset Yisrael*, the Assembly of Israel, because in the earthly realms Israel also serves as a bridge to higher spiritual levels. But when Israel is in exile, the *Shekhinah* too is in exile and thus vulnerable to all sorts of negative forces.

Scholem explained this *maggid* as "elements of the mystic's unconscious, crystallizing and coming to life and behaving in an autonomous fashion as if they were agents with an identity of their own."[6] Some have described this *maggid* in terms similar to the stereotypical guilt-inducing "Jewish mother," who is constantly exhorting her son, Karo, to devote himself thoroughly to his studies and thus to raise her from her shameful situation.[7] None of this, of course, completely explains quite how the *maggid* was able to guide Karo.

Here is how the mystics reacted to the initial experience:

[The *maggid* said:] "Happy are you. Return to your studies, not interrupting them for one moment. Go up to the Land of Israel, for not all times are opportune. There is no hindrance to salvation, be it much or little. Let not your eyes have pity on your worldly goods for you eat of the goodness of the higher land.... Make haste, therefore, to go up to the land, for I sustain you here and will sustain you there....

All these things did we hear with our own ears and much more of a like nature, all matters of wisdom and great promise. We all broke into tears at the great joy we had experienced and when we heard of the anguish of the *Shekhinah* because of our sins. We also heard the pain of the *Shekhinah*; Her voice was like that of an invalid in Her entreaties. We took courage so that our mouths did not cease from study in joy and dread until daybreak. In the morning we immersed ourselves, as we had done on the previous two days. There we met the sages who had not been present on that night and we rebuked them. We told them of all the good the Lord had wrought on our behalf so that their heart died within them. They smote their own faces and wept aloud. We persisted in our criticism of them since it was because of their absence that we failed to receive further revelations, as we said above. So we said: "Let us join one another the coming night and we shall be ten in number." It was agreed. Now although we did not sleep at all, not even one moment, on the first night, and although we were unable to sleep even during the day, since the saint, may his light shine, expounded the Torah in the afternoon and we all listened, yet we girded our loins to repeat the program of the first night on the second. In the great rejoicing that we were ten in number, they did not wait until the time for the Mishnah reading nor did they wait until midnight [on the previous night it happened exactly at midnight] but no sooner did we begin to read the portions preceding "Hear, O Israel" in Deuteronomy than the voice of our beloved knocked at the door. It began to speak: "Hearken unto me, O my beloved ones, choice ones. Awake and sing you who dwell in the dust, according to the mystery of the supernal dust, the two letters *Heh*" etc. And he spoke many words of wisdom. Afterward he said: "Happy are you, My beloved ones. Happy are you in that you have elevated Me. I have become most elevated now that you are ten in number, the quorum for all sacred matters. Happy are you and happy those who gave you birth. Fear not the reproach of men and have no dread of their insults for you have elevated the Community of Israel and know that you are the chosen few (so did He continue, as above). To Me you cleave and the glory is above your head and there extends over you a thread of mercy. If permission had been granted for the eye to see, you would see the fire surrounding this house. Be strong, therefore. Do not allow the knot to be untied. Elevate Me by reciting in a loud voice "Hear, O Israel" and "Blessed be the name" as on the Day of Atonement."

Thus did he speak many things for about half an hour and we then returned to our studies. At midnight the voice returned, speaking for over an hour, repeating the praises of our studies. The voice said: "See! Did any people ever hear the voice speaking as you did? 'Ask your father and he will inform you; your elders, and they will tell you' (Deut. 32:7), whether during these many hundreds of years they have heard or seen such a thing and yet you have been worthy of it. Therefore, let your eyes be upon your ways from now onward. Let each help his neighbor and say unto his brother be strong. Let the weak say, I am mighty, and let each be great in his own eyes since you belong to the king's palace and have had the merit of entering the vestibule. Endeavor now to enter the great hall and do not leave the vestibule. For whoever leaves to go outside, his blood be upon his head. Awake, My sons, and see that I speak to you. Awake, My beloved ones. Be firm and valiant in battle. Be strong and rejoice and a thread of mercy will be extended over you daily. Observe how intoxicated you are with worldly desires. Awake, O drunken ones, for the day comes when a man must cast away his gods of silver, worldly desires, and his gods of gold, lust for wealth. Go up to the Land of Israel for so you are able to do if it were not that you are trapped in the mud of worldly desires and vanities. Whoever leaves your company and turns away his blood be upon his head. See! How worthy you have been, that of which no others have been worthy" (and so he continued at length in this vein).

[Alkabetz continues:] Now, my sons, hearken unto me. Incline your ears and your hearts to me. Who can be so foolish as to hear these things without resolving to return to the Lord with all his heart and with all his soul and with all his might? I call heaven and earth to be my witnesses that all I have recorded here and in the tract I composed is not even one hundredth of what actually transpired. And even with regard to the tract, you will sometimes note an asterisk after some words, to denote that here a mystery was revealed I could not allow myself to record in writing. (Alkabetz, in Joseph Karo's *Maggid Mesharim*, introduction, continuation)

The initial experience of the *maggid*'s presence and directives was naturally deemed insufficient; it was decided that the presence of other sages might hasten Her return, particularly if ten were present. Ten, of course, signifies the presence of a minyan, the quorum for prayer, but also corresponds to the number of *sefirot*. The sages themselves are linked to the higher levels, and so this adds to the possibility of the *maggid*'s reappearance.[8] So, much deprived of sleep, the sages continue to study and meet again on the second night of Shavuot.

The *maggid* comes again, beginning by referring to these sages as beloved, "choice," and dwelling "in the dust, according to the mystery of the supernal dust, the two letters *Heh*." This is a reference to the two letters *Heh* in the Four-Letter Name. *Heh* is the fifth letter of the Alef Bet, and two of them combine to equal ten, the number of *sefirot* that compose the "supernal dust." Thus the sages, living humble lives "in the dust" on earth, actually dwell in the supernal realms. But the *maggid* cautions that one must not leave "to go outside," emphasizing a theme we saw in early Rabbinic mystical texts: the higher you go, the farther you can fall and the greater the danger in the endeavor.

Noteworthy among the *maggid*'s directives is the call to go to live in the Land of Israel, which Alkabetz and Karo obeyed. Karo, born in Spain and descended from those who faced terrible choices during the Inquisition, also had a strong fixation on martyrdom; for example, note the language the *maggid* uses elsewhere telling Karo how his evil inclination is to be "burned out" with "the fire of the Torah."[9]

In the concluding paragraph Alkabetz refers to another tract, which may have been a separate composition, describing additional experiences with the *maggid*. Since other Jewish mystics have claimed to be visited by a *maggid* of some kind over the succeeding centuries, we can assume that some of the same forces that lay behind Karo's experience continued to exist.[10]

In the next text Hayyim Vital visits his teacher Luria, who gives him extensive directions for mystical practice.

> These are the things that my master of blessed memory told me relating to me and the root of my soul. . . .
>
> One day I visited him, a whole month having passed during which I had performed none of the *yihudim* [unifications] he had prescribed for me. He recognized this in my face, and said: "'If you leave me for a day, I shall leave you for two.'[11] You cause great harm by failing to perform the unifications, for You caused the souls who wished to cleave to you to become separated from you." I gave him the excuse that I [had] only wanted to study the Torah during that time, especially since those souls did not come to me as openly as was appropriate. He replied that despite all this I must not fail to perform these unifications daily. It is more important than the study of the Torah, since it unites the upper worlds and so serves the dual purpose of Torah study and unification. He warned me that when I perform unifications my intention should not be only to attract the soul, but to repair it on high.

When I went with him to Tiberias to Rabbi Akiva's tomb, he also told me that Rabbi Akiva said to him that I should mention Rabbi Akiva's name ten times consecutively before each of the three daily prayers. As a result he will become impregnated in me and will help me very much. He told me there was no need for me to say "Rabbi Akiva," only "Akiva."

He also told me that until the festival of Sukkot in the year 5334 (=1573), I shall need help, and he will assist me whenever I perform unifications. But after that time I will not need any help, since the two-and-a-half years that I sinned when I refrained from studying Torah will be completed. Previously, even if he did help me, it was haphazard, since it was impossible for it to be regular. However, from that time on, it will be regular, praise God.

He also commanded me not to refrain from performing the unifications he had transmitted to me. If I go to prostrate myself on the graves of the righteous, I should do so either on the eve of the New Moon or on the fifteenth day of the month, for then it is more effective than at any other time. I should not go on the Sabbath, festivals, or the New Moon, for at these times their souls ascend to heaven and cannot be communed with at the grave. Once he sent me to the graves of the righteous on *hol ha-mo'ed* [the intermediate days of festivals] to pray there, but I did not prostrate myself. (Vital, *Sefer ha-Hezyonot*, [Book of visions], 4:134, 149-50)[12]

The master referred to is Luria, who is able to "read" his disciple's face and discern significant truths about him.[13] Luria identifies himself with the Torah. Just as one will forget the Torah without regular study, so Vital risks losing all he has learned by failing to perform the master's instructions. Indeed, Vital requires additional assistance from his master because of a period where he had failed to devote himself to Torah study.

So what are the unifications Luria prescribed? They were private meditative exercises that required rigorous training and involved complex

combinations of the various Divine Names.[14] In such mystical meditation, one unifies various Names, which creates a corresponding unity on
the supernal level. These unifications may also have involved a process
Luria believed in called *ibbur*, a temporary joining of the soul of a dead
person to a living individual (hence, such unifications were frequently
performed at the grave of a particular sage or mystic). The root of the
word is the same as that for a woman who is pregnant, conveying the
sense that the soul, like the growing fetus, is added for a limited period. If
the added soul was that of a truly great person, it would be able to assist
the living soul to achieve a higher level for itself.[15] Here we see Luria
directing his disciple to "take on" the soul of Rabbi Akiva, doubtless
because of Akiva's mystical wisdom (seen in the *pardes* story in chapter 3).[16] We are also informed that there are certain favorable times for
accomplishing *ibbur*, as well as times when it is impossible. Chapter 19
further examines this notion, together with the idea of *gilgul*, permanent
reincarnation. How does a *maggid*, or any holy spirit, convey its message?

> **And here is the secret of prophecy and the Holy Spirit. It is assuredly
> a voice sent from above to speak with this prophet, or with this man
> endowed with the Holy Spirit. But this same supernal spiritual voice
> cannot by itself materialize and enter the ears of this prophet, unless
> it first clothes itself in the physical voice which emerges from this
> man's mouth when, at a given moment, he studies Torah or prays and
> the like. And then it [i.e., the supernal voice] clothes itself in it [i.e.,
> the physical voice], joining it, and it comes to the ear of this prophet
> who [then] hears it. And without the man's own present physical voice
> it cannot achieve existence. (Vital, *Sha'ar Ruah ha-Kodesh*, 10a)[17]**

In a moment of trance (or at least a heightened state of awareness), the
maggid takes over the physical voice of the mystic and speaks through him.
Vital writes elsewhere of the body being a garment for the higher soul;[18]
going a step further, here we see the body being taken over temporarily
by yet another soul in order to convey prophetic wisdom to the mystic.[19]

The members of the mystical circles in Safed committed themselves to particular practices (*hanhagot*) that were seen as spiritual and ethical ways to go beyond conventional observance. Many such practices were only intended for a spiritual elite. If one wanted to accomplish the high goals of these circles, one had to be able to live up to these standards and be unusually free from sin and even normal physical desires.[20] Hence we see quite a number of unusual ascetic practices and occasionally even severe mortifications.[21] These practitioners saw the material world as fundamentally flawed; by separating from it as much as possible, they hoped to "clear the air" in the supernal realm, making it possible to bring the *Shekhinah* back from exile to Her proper home and keep Her together with her mate, *Tiferet*. Some of these mystics in Safed were also refugees from the Iberian Peninsula and thus particularly sensitive to the issue of the *Shekhinah*'s exile; some may well have lived previously as hidden Jews.[22]

Here are excerpts from a set of *hanhagot* given to Karo (and his circle) by his *maggid* as part of a broader injunction.

> **Be careful never to speak an unnecessary word, whether during day or night.**
>
> **Take care to avoid any kind of talk that leads to frivolity, and if you overhear such talk, never laugh. This extends to the complete avoidance of mockery.**
>
> **Never lose your temper over mere material things.**
>
> **Do not eat meat at all for forty days, except for a little on Shabbat. Do not eat horseradish.**
>
> **Drink no wine during these days except one drink at the end of the meal.**
>
> **Be gentle in speech to all people.**
>
> **Never be proud. "Be exceedingly humble in spirit."[23]**
>
> **Sleep in your own bed. When you have to have marital relations in order to fulfill the precept to be fruitful and multiply, rise up from**

her bed a half an hour after you have completed the act and return to your own bed.

Be careful to avoid taking pleasure during eating, drinking, and marital relations. Act as if demons were forcing you to eat that food or indulge in that act. You should much prefer that it be possible for you to exist without food and drink, or to fulfill the duty of procreation without intercourse.

Always have your transgressions in mind and be anxious because of them.

Never eat for dessert more than one measure, and no more than twenty of melons, grapes, and raisins. Except on Sabbaths and festivals do not eat of more than one type of fruit. At the beginning of the meal, cut three measures of bread and during that meal eat no more. Never drink your fill of water.

Train yourself to keep your eyes downcast so you will never chance to gaze at a woman forbidden to you.

Have the Mishnah in mind during the meal, and study a chapter of the Mishnah before "Birkat ha-Mazon" (Grace after meals).

Do not allow your mind to wander from Me even for the slightest moment, and limit your enjoyment. When you are eating and desire additional food or drink, desist from it. If you do this at each meal, it will be as if you offered a sacrifice; your table will be an actual altar upon which you slaughter the evil inclination. (Karo, *Maggid Mesharim*, 1)[24]

What are some of the frequent themes in this list? Limiting any kind of pleasure is the most prominent directive. This is in accordance with the talmudic directive, "Sanctify yourself through what is permitted to you,"[25] that is, by denying oneself things that are permitted. Although a countertendency exists within the Rabbinic tradition suggesting that one who takes on the unnecessary stringency of Nazirite vows (Numbers 6) sins against his own soul by depriving himself of permitted pleasure,[26] among the mystics of Safed that countertendency is overwhelmed by the almost total abhorrence of any material pleasure. But for those who take seriously the idea that the *Shekhinah* is in exile, and hence that Jews are in an ongoing state of mourning, it really is difficult to accept mundane enjoyment.

Control of one's speech, often a significant issue in Jewish ethical works, is a major theme here as well, taken to stringent extremes. We do see some emphasis on ethical behavior in all these collections of *hanhagot*.[27] Control of one's thoughts and self-denigration are also key practices, to promote an attitude of great humility and maintain constant repentance. Finally, Torah study and *deveikut* (though this term is not used as such here) are ongoing imperatives among these associates. In contrast to most of the texts we saw in chapter 10, *deveikut* in most of these Safed texts is an extremely private activity, requiring a fair amount of solitude in addition to all the activities that involve the other members of one's mystical society. For the reasons mentioned earlier in this chapter, the Mishnah again receives special attention.

The advice to "act as if demons were forcing you" is taken from the Talmud; there, however, it is given as a way to avoid thinking of a woman other than one's wife. Here, any pleasure whatsoever is considered improper. Foreign as this may seem today, it is fundamental to the view of the Safed mystics.[28]

The last text here offers a parable with an arresting view of mystical experience.

One day, a princess emerged from a bathhouse. One of the idle men standing there saw her and sighed deeply, and said: "Who might give her over to me, that I might have my will with her?" The princess overheard and said to him: "It will come to pass in the graveyard, but not here." When he heard these words, he rejoiced, for he took her to mean that he should go to the graveyard and wait for her there, and that when she would come to him, he could do with her as he wished. This was not her intention; rather, she meant to say that there all were equal: great and small, young and old, despised and honored. But here it could not be, for she is a princess and one of the masses could not possibly approach her.

So that man rose and went to the graveyard, and sat there, constantly thinking of joining with her, always thinking of her form. Because of his great desire only for her, he removed his thoughts from everything [else] sensual, concentrating only on her form and beauty. Day and night he sat there in the graveyard; there he ate and drank, and there he slept, saying to himself: "If she does not come today, she will come tomorrow." He did this for many days, and because of his separation from the objects of sensation, and the exclusive attachment of his thought to one object and his complete concentration and total longing, his soul was separated from sensual things and became attached only to the intelligibles [i.e., that which can only be perceived by the mind], until it became separated from all sensual things, including the woman herself, and he communed with God.

After a short time, he cast off all sensual things and desired only the Divine Intellect, and he became a perfect servant and a holy man of God, until his prayer was heard and his blessing was beneficial to all passersby, so that all the merchants and horsemen and foot-soldiers who passed by came to him to receive his blessing, until his fame spread far about. . . . A man who does not desire a woman is like a donkey, or even less than one. In other words, from the physical, one may apprehend the worship of God. (Isaac of Acre [twelfth to thirteenth century], quoted in *Reishit Hokhmah, Sha'ar ha-Ahavah* [Gate of love], ch. 4)[29]

Through concentrating on this physical desire, one transcends the actual form (the body of the princess in the parable) and can attach one-self to the higher realms, eventually attaining a state of separation from the physical, leading to the highest goal, achieving *deveikut*.

As with the lists of *hanhagot* we saw above, the separation from the physical is an important means to the most critical goals. The texts in this chapter also differ from the texts about *deveikut* in chapter 10 (which precede and follow the period when mystics were active in Safed) where the emphasis on asceticism is minimal. With this perspective, we now turn to uncover some secrets of the higher realms in the next chapter.

Part 5

Additional Issues in Kabbalah

19

Four Worlds, Four Levels of Soul
DEATH AND TRANSMIGRATION

The *sefirot* themselves suggest levels of Divinity, stages between our own existence and a higher reality. But some kabbalists, seeking to know still more about God, advanced another model (superimposed on the model of the *sefirot*, not meant to replace it) that taught the existence of four worlds, four separate dimensions. These levels, proposed after the main parts of the Zohar appeared, are called: *Atzilut* (emanation), *Beri'ah* (creation), *Yetzirah* (formation), and *Asiyah* (making). Three of these terms come from Isa. 43:7: "I have created him [*berativ*] for My glory; I have formed him [*yetzartiv*]; yea, I have made him [*asitiv*]."

The assumption of the kabbalists is that all reality and all realms are interconnected, although there are different models of just how they link. In some versions, each of the four worlds also contains a set of ten *sefirot*, with the last *sefirah* of one world being the first of the next (lower) world. Another theory has the four worlds in between the "actual" ten *sefirot* and our own world. Yet another has those ten *sefirot* as the *sefirot* of the highest of the four worlds, *Olam ha-Atzilut*, and our world of matter (and where evil all too frequently prevails) as the lowest, *Olam ha-Asiyah*. In some models, *Adam Kadmon* stands above all four worlds, as the ultimate prototype from which everything else emanates.

The idea of four worlds also addresses the issue of how God, a spiritual and infinite being, can create the material, finite universe. Jewish theologian Byron Sherwin suggests a comparison of *Ein Sof* to concentrated orange juice, which is then diluted with water. No matter how much water we add, part of the mixture is orange juice. In the same way, God's infinite reality is diluted into materiality—and thus is not all powerful—but part of it is still present in that material universe, albeit in a deteriorated, even damaged state.

Moving in the opposite direction, humankind can ascend through the higher realms in the four worlds by performing holy deeds.[1] The different levels of spirituality represented by the four worlds may help us to understand how we might feel God's influence to be present at some times but absent at others. Human deeds may evoke God's Presence and draw down its influence, although it will be diluted. As Sherwin points out, this model can also be used to explain the presence of evil, since this diluted sanctity is vulnerable to sin and an overemphasis on materiality.

Contemporary discussion of Kabbalah is often centered on these four worlds and their various qualities and occasionally explores the possibility of ascending through the four worlds during the morning prayers.[2] Before we examine a sample of such discussion, we will look at some texts that describe these four worlds. In the first text, each world is distinct, with separate functions and levels of holiness.

> Blessed is He who clothes the king and the Matronita with the ten *sefirot* of *Beri'ah* [creation] . . . for on Shabbat and festivals He dons the garments of royalty, which are the ten *sefirot* of *Beri'ah*, and on weekdays He dons the ten groups of angels, who serve the ten *sefirot* of *Beri'ah*. For the king is within the ten *sefirot* of *Atzilut* [emanation]; He and His essence are one there, He and His life are one there. This is not the case with the ten *sefirot* of *Beri'ah*, for they and their life are not one; they and their essence are not one. And the Cause of all illumines the ten *sefirot* of *Atzilut* and the ten *sefirot* of *Beri'ah*, and He illumines the ten groups of angels and the ten spheres in the firmament, and He does not change anywhere. (Introduction to *Tikkunei ha-Zohar*, 3b)[3]

The world of emanation is the highest realm; "He and His essence are one there," meaning that the *sefirot* in this world are unified with God's essence there, but separated elsewhere. The realm of creation is second, followed by the realms of the angels, and finally, in *Asiyah*, the world of "making," the material spheres below.

> The upper mother nests in the Throne, among the three upper *sefirot*; the central pillar, which comprises six *sefirot*, nests in Metatron; the lower mother nests in the Wheel. . . . For from the Throne came the *neshamot*, and from the *Hayyah* [Creature] the *ruhot*, and from the Wheel the *nefashot*, and they are in *Beri'ah*, *Yetzirah*, and *Asiyah*. On Shabbat and festivals there descend upon them *neshamot, ruhot*, and *nefashot* by way of emanation, and they are the holy spirit from the ten *sefirot*. (*Tikkunei ha-Zohar, tikkun* 6, 23a)[4]

This is a somewhat different model of the four worlds, which intersects with another significant concept in Kabbalah, the existence of different levels of soul. In this text, after the world of emanation we have the world of creation, associated with the divine Throne and *Binah* (hence the reference to the upper three *sefirot*, of which *Binah* is the third). The world of formation is associated with the angel Metatron, often regarded as the highest of all the angels, as well as the "Creature" that (along with the Throne and the Wheel) appears in Ezekiel 1. This level is related to *Tiferet*, the "central pillar" that also is at the center of the middle complex of six *sefirot* above *Malkhut* (the "lower mother" that gives birth to all existence in the realm of human experiences). The world of action is here related to the Wheel and to *Malkhut*, as well as to all sorts of lower beings.

Three levels of individual soul are given here: (1) *nefesh*, the lowest, representing the sheer physical being; (2) *ruah*, the emotional being; (3) *neshamah*, the spiritual being. Accordingly, *nefesh* is said to originate in the lowest world (of action), *ruah* in the world of formation, and *neshamah* in the higher world of creation. We will return to these shortly.

Next we examine, in pieces, a lengthy text from *Shnei Luhot ha-Brit* that explains the "four worlds" in more detail.

> Although the ten utterances are the secret of the emanation of the *sefirot*, nevertheless the root of the building of the world depends on two *partzufim* [faces], *Tiferet* and *Malkhut*. "For God made six days" (Exod. 20:11): These are the six supernal days, the six extremities, *Tiferet*, which contains six *sefirot* that are its pride. "From my flesh, I see God" (Job 19:26). It is like the body, which has its two arms and two legs and the organ of generation, which bestows [*shefa*] to the *sefirah Malkhut*. "God in His holy chamber" (Ps. 11:4), i.e., the chamber of God which receives the influx, and later empties it out below, bringing into existence the worlds *Beri'ah*, *Yetzirah*, and *Asiyah* ....[5]
>
> ... the kabbalists gave *Hokhmah* and *Binah* the names Father and Mother, and *Tiferet* and *Malkhut*, Son and Daughter. "From my flesh, I see God." The existence of the Son comes from Father and Mother. Before the Son was revealed, he existed as part of the Father in great concealment, that is, as the seed sent from the brain, through the spinal cord, and later most discernible as the embryo within the mother. Afterward, when he emerges from his mother's womb, he is revealed to all.

The "ten utterances" refer to God's commands of Creation in Genesis 1, as noted in chapter 6. *Tiferet* and *Malkhut* are corresponding "faces," male and female; we have seen that the whole cosmos depends on their proper interaction. The Creation of six days is seen as an allusion to the complex of *sefirot* surrounding *Tiferet*; Job 19:26 reminds us that the human body is a likeness of this divine structure, with these six *sefirot* passing on the flow of beneficence to *Malkhut* below. And this segment speaks of the *sefirot* within the world of emanation, leading below to the other three worlds, which presumably contain their own similar structures.

Hokhmah and *Binah* bestow the flow from above on *Tiferet* and *Malkhut*; this celestial family, both sets of masculine and feminine *sefirot*, become Father and Mother, Son and Daughter. We are reminded that these personal terms provide an understanding, however metaphorical, of the essence and functioning of the higher levels. Seed is planted in great concealment, and the potential within the seed exists "as part of the Father" before it is implanted within the Mother, only to be "revealed to all" when the child is born. (It was long believed that a father's seed, i.e., the sperm, originated in the brain.)

However, there is an even greater degree of concealment than this one, in the will, the thought to arouse the coupling. We may say that the potential [existence] of the Son was inherent in this will, in great concealment. Later, it was drawn from the brain, through the Father's power, and bestowed upon the Mother. Similarly the two *partzufim* first existed in the secret of the will, the thought, in the secret of *Keter*, which is called "will." As explained in [Cordovero's] *Pardes Rimonim*, *Sha'ar ha-Tzahtzahot* [Gate of brightness], *Keter* is absolutely concealed and *Hokhmah* is the beginning of revelation, in comparison to the deep concealment. This beginning of revelation is revealed by *Binah*. Then *Binah* is *Ben Yah*, *Tiferet* in its place. And its place of reception is *Malkhut*, along with him. For the emanation of the six extremities into their place occurred by means of bestower and receiver, *Hokhmah* and *Binah*. In the same way, when the extension of the six extremities above produce the worlds *Beri'ah*, *Yetzirah*, and *Asiyah*, *Tiferet* bestows and *Malkhut* receives this bestowal and actualizes it. Son and Daughter are comparable to Father and Mother, except Father and Mother are responsible for revealing the emanation of the six extremities and the effect [of what is ordained by the *sefirot*] is revealed by Son and Daughter.

With this introduction, you can understand how the Four-Letter Name of God includes all of the divine emanation. But another fundamental still needs explanation. The kabbalists, especially in *Sefer ha-Pardes*,[6] have already discussed at length the linkage of the worlds. For the upper and the lower cleave together. The upper bestows upon the lower, and the lower is a shadow of the upper. What is in one is in the other, even if the one below is material and the one above spiritual. It is always the case that one is parallel to the other. The entire *ma'aseh Bereshit* speaks of the lower worlds but alludes to the higher worlds. For He, praised be He, brought all the worlds into existence, and all the worlds depend on His great light. Although the light is revealed in a much more refined way in a certain world than in another, this is due to the process of extension. However, everything is from His great light. I will give you an example. The light of the sun casts its light on the moon. Afterward, the moon shines in the atmosphere of the world. From there, the light proceeds from the atmosphere of the world into a single room. The light progressively becomes coarsened because of the process of extension, but it is all one light. So it is with the extension of the worlds, *Atzilut, Beri'ah, Yetzirah,* and *Asiyah.*

The greatest concealment, the highest of the *sefirot*, is *Keter*, which is sometimes referred to as "will," that is, the will of the *Ein Sof.* Thus, it is at this highest level that the idea arises of the system involving the "coupling" (here referring to *Hokhmah* and *Binah*, "the Father's power . . . bestowed upon the Mother"), creating the potential for the Son (*Tiferet*). The word *Binah* itself is an acronym for *Ben Yah*, literally "son of *Yah*" but here referring to the *Yud-Heh* of the Four-Letter Name, which represent *Hokhmah* and *Binah*. Thus the statement that "*Binah* is *Ben Yah, Tiferet* in its place" conveys the message that *Binah* gives birth to the Son, *Tiferet*—here referring to the entire complex of six *sefirot* around *Tiferet*—which is conceived through the joint contributions of *Hokhmah* and *Binah*. "Its place of reception is *Malkhut*," that is, *Tiferet* is received by and mates with *Malkhut*, thus producing the lower worlds.

The continuation of the text reviews what we have already seen, that the supernal world and our own function as mirror images, even though the divine light may be coarser in our world.

The secret of the world of *Atzilut* is that it is like a flame attached to a coal. It is not something separate from it. For the [source of the] flame is in the coal, and in hovering over the coal, the flame is revealed and it is tightly bound to it. Similarly, [the world of] *Atzilut* consists of rays of light from the coal, which were concealed in perfect unity [within it]. The light of emanation consists of supernal lights beyond comprehension. These lights were revealed in the secret of the verses, "And God said: let there be light! And there was light. . . . And the spirit of God hovered" (Gen. 1:3, 1:2). The secret alluded to by the hovering is the arising of the will to contract His light so that it could emanate. This involves no change in either the emanator or the emanation, according to the secret meaning of "And there was light," which our sages of blessed memory interpreted to mean that there was light already. Only, [the light] was completely concealed in its root and supernal source, as was said above. That is the secret of His divinity. For the *Ein Sof* is a soul to the soul of the *sefirot*. They are the souls of everything that would later be brought into existence. And the Cause of Causes is a soul to them, according to the secret of emanated divine essence.

Afterward, the world of *Atzilut* was extended by means of *Malkhut*, through the contraction of its light, and the world [of *Beri'ah*] came into existence. The world of *Atzilut* is a soul to the world of *Beri'ah*, just as *Ein Sof* is a soul to the world of *Atzilut*. Afterward, the world of *Beri'ah* was extended through the contraction of its light and the world of *Yetzirah* came into existence. The world of *Beri'ah* is a soul to the world of *Yetzirah*. Afterward, the world of *Yetzirah* was extended through the contraction of its light and the world of *Asiyah* came into existence. All this occurs through the power of the Cause of Causes, *Ein Sof*, which is the power of the world of *Atzilut*. And the power of the world of *Beri'ah* depends on the power of *Atzilut*, whose power depends on *Ein Sof*. This world of *Beri'ah* is the power of the world of *Yetzirah*. So *Yetzirah* is in the power of *Beri'ah*, which is in the power of *Atzilut*, which is in the power of *Ein Sof*. This world of *Yetzirah* is the power of the world of *Asiyah*, only the light has become concealed and coarsened, according to the nature of the receivers.

In chapter 10 we read a text from the Zohar dealing with the mystical significance of a flame. The world of emanation (and its relationship to its source and what flows from it) is treated similarly to what was taught about the *sefirot*. The original light is hidden and mysterious, only taking on reality in the lower worlds when it finds some "coarse substance" to connect to. The light, the original power of *Ein Sof*, still has its effect, but is diluted further as the power transfers to each lower level.

> Thus the world of emanation can be compared to a flame in a coal. The flame is revealed through the will, which hovers above and is tightly bound to the coal. The world of *Beri'ah* is like one who lights a torch from a flame. The light of the torch does not remain connected in perfect unity to the light of the flame from which the torch was lit. Nevertheless, its level is great. The torch contains a great light in which the light of the flame inheres. The world of *Yetzirah* is comparable to lighting a candle from a flame, and this candle illuminates a dark room.
>
> "And there was light." All the stages of the extension of the worlds are parallel. Only, one is secret, the next more revealed, and the next even more revealed. So it is explained in the Zohar[7] and brought in *Pardes Rimonim, Sha'ar Mahut v'Hanhagah*, chapter 11: "There are four elements in all the worlds." But they are material in the world of *Asiyah*, while at a higher level, in the world of *Yetzirah*, they are spiritual. In other words, Michael is water, Gabriel is fire, Uriel is air, and Raphael is earth. Above, in the world of *Beri'ah*, they are more spiritual, the four *hayyot* [creatures] which bear the Throne [of Glory]. Later, above, they become the four legs of the Throne. Ultimately, in the world of *Atzilut*, they are most spiritual. *Hesed* is water. *Gevurah* is fire. *Tiferet* is air. *Malkhut* is supernal earth. Each

level contains the roots for the level below. Thus everything that exists in the lower worlds alludes to the upper worlds, and from the revealed we reach the concealed. (Isaiah Horowitz, *Shnei Luhot ha-Brit, Toldot Adam, House of Y-H-V-H*, sect. 22–24)[8]

While less tightly connected to the original source, the *Ein Sof*, each level still remains at a high level; however, the lower the level, the more that is revealed. The four worlds are composed of the four elements, but in a more spiritual form at the higher levels; for example, in the world of *Yetzirah*, four archangels represent these elements; in the world of *Beri'ah*, they become four creatures bearing God's throne, creatures like those of Ezekiel's vision. Finally, in the world of *Atzilut*, the elements function as the *sefirot* themselves. As we have seen many times, the lower and upper levels mirror each other; "from the revealed we reach the concealed," that is, we perceive the higher levels from what is shown to us below.

Some modern sources attempt to reinterpret this scheme, using the *sefirot* as representing various psychological aspects of an individual, while the four worlds represent the various dimensions of individual growth, from physical to emotional, mental, and spiritual.[9]

The notion of four worlds is not prominent in all models of Kabbalah, particularly those preceding Safed, but it may have an added attraction for some today because it bears a vague resemblance to the four paths of enlightenment in Theravada Buddhism.[10]

Now we return to the various levels of soul, as described in a lengthy excerpt from the Zohar.

> The human soul is called by three names: *nefesh, ruah, neshamah*. All are comprised within one another, while their power appears in three places. *Nefesh* appears in the grave while the body decomposes in the dust, and she flits about in this world to mingle with the living and to perceive their suffering. When they are in need, she pleads for mercy.

Ruah enters the earthly garden, where she is formed into an image of the body of this world, in a certain garment she dons there. She revels there in pleasures and delights of the radiance of the garden. On Shabbat, New Moons, and festivals, she ascends above, delighting there, and [afterward] returns to her place. On this it is written: "The *ruah* will return to God who gave it" (Eccles. 12:7). Will return: precisely—at these times we have mentioned.

Neshamah ascends immediately to her place, to the place from which she came. Through her the lamp is kindled, shining above. This one never descends below; through this is encompassed the one who is encompassed from all sides, above and below. Until this ascends to be linked with her place, *ruah* is not crowned in the earthly garden and *nefesh* does not rest in her place. As soon as this ascends, all of them attain tranquility. (Zohar 2:141b–142a)

This presents the idea of three levels of the human soul, all with roots in biblical usage and Jewish philosophy. Originally they were identified with the animal, vegetative, and rational qualities.[11] (We will later view a Hasidic text that posits a separation between the Jewish soul and the non-Jewish soul.) Here in the Zohar, *nefesh* (which means simply "soul") again is the lowest and during life denotes the essential physical being. *Ruah* ("breath" or "spirit") appears to have a higher emotional and some limited spiritual quality. Last is *neshamah* (also meaning "breath" or "soul"), which can be said to have a consistent spiritual quality (it "never descends below").[12] While all three levels are intertwined ("comprised within one another"), existing within each individual, it is suggested that we can cultivate the "higher" level of soul.

Elsewhere in the Zohar it is suggested that the *neshamah* develops beginning at age thirteen and may not be fully developed until age twenty.[13] When the physical body dies, the *nefesh* initially remains by the corpse, eventually to wander and intercede for those in need. When the body dies, *ruah* enters a Garden of Eden on this earth, taking on a "garment" that seems to be some approximation of the physical body itself.[14] For the duration of holy days, she is able to rise to the corresponding supernal Garden of Eden. The verse from Ecclesiastes takes on a special meaning in the Zohar's reading; the *ruah* will occasionally return to *Elohim* (the Name of God used here), which is associated with the *Shekhinah*, who dwells in that supernal Garden of Eden.

What happens to the highest level of soul after physical death? *Neshamah* returns "to the place from which she came," that is, to her root in the supernal Garden of Eden where the *Shekhinah* is already seen to dwell. *Neshamah*, as it were, lights the lamp of the *Shekhinah*, stimulating Her so that She might ascend and mate with Her partner, *Tiferet*. As the Zohar puts it elsewhere: "without arousal from below, there is no arousal above."[15]

> When inhabitants of the world are in need, when in their suffering they go to the cemetery, this *nefesh* arouses and she goes flying and arouses *ruah*, and that *ruah* arouses the Patriarchs, and ascends and arouses *neshamah*. Then the Holy One, blessed be He, has compassion on the world, as we have established. Although these matters of the soul have been aroused in other aspects, they are all evenly balanced; this is clarity of the matter, and all is one.
>
> When *neshamah* is hindered from ascending to her place, *ruah* goes and stands by the entrance of the Garden of Eden. But the entrance is not opened for her, and she goes roaming about, unnoticed by anyone. *Nefesh* goes roaming through the world, sees the body breeding worms and enduring the punishment of the grave, and she mourns over it, as they have established, for it is written: "Surely his flesh feels pain for him and his soul mourns for him" (Job 14:22). All suffer punishment until *neshamah* is bound in her place above;[16] then all are bound in their places. For all these form a single bond, corresponding to the pattern above in the mystery of *nefesh*, *ruah*, and *neshamah*. All is one, one bond.

Nefesh has no light of her own at all. This is the one who shares in the mystery of a certain body, delighting and nourishing it with all that it needs, as it is written: "She provides food for her house and a portion for her maidens" (Prov. 31:15). "Her house" is that body, which she nourishes; "her maidens" are those limbs of the body, all of them. *Ruah* is the one who rides on this *nefesh*, controlling her, illumining her with all that she needs, and *nefesh* is a throne for this *ruah*. *Neshamah* is the one who generates this *ruah*, controlling him, illumining him with the light of life; and that *ruah* depends upon this *neshamah*, and is illumined by her radiant light. That *nefesh* depends upon this *ruah*, and is illumined and nourished by him, and all is one bond.

Until this supernal *neshamah* ascends into the flow of [the] Ancient of Ancients, Concealed of all Concealed, and is filled by it, since it is ceaseless, this *ruah* does not enter the Garden of Eden, which is *nefesh*—eternally, *ruah* rests only in the Garden of Eden, and *neshamah* above—and this *nefesh* does not settle in her place within the body below. Similarly, all below separates thus in a human, although they all form one bond. *Neshamah* ascends above into the flow of the well; *ruah* enters the Garden of Eden, corresponding to the supernal pattern; *nefesh* settles in the grave. (Zohar 2:141b–142a, continued)[17]

When you most intensely need to pray for something, the Zohar says, you go to the cemetery, presumably to ask the "soul" to intercede for you on a higher level.[18] Each level of soul stimulates the next: *nefesh*, dwelling at the grave, goes into action, moving off to the Garden of Eden[19] and causing *ruah* to ascend to this supernal garden, to move *neshamah* into action. However, as we have read, sin interferes with this process; *neshamah* may not be able to go up sufficiently, *ruah* is not allowed into the garden, *nefesh* wanders ineffectually. Only when *neshamah* is "bound in her place," that is, secure in its supernal dwelling, can all levels of the soul succeed in this task.

In this model, the three levels of soul correspond to three *sefirot*.[20]

Nefesh, which "has no light of her own," corresponds to the *Shekhinah*, which must accept and reflect the light from the higher *sefirot*. *Ruah* corresponds to the *Shekhinah*'s mate and primary source of light, the complex around *Tiferet*. *Neshamah* is *Binah*, the "mother" of all the lower *sefirot*. Additionally, *Binah* ascends to the "Ancient of Ancients," *Keter*; without the emanation she receives from *Keter*, she cannot assist the lower souls (*sefirot*) to accomplish their tasks. The three levels of soul are fundamentally united and separate within us: united while we are alive, separated afterward. Ultimately the soul is profoundly linked to its divine source.

Next, in a text from Vital, we turn to a model that posits two additional levels of soul beyond *neshamah*. This model was first seen in a Rabbinic teaching (also cited below) and expanded in the years following the Zohar; it became a popular kabbalistic approach after its inclusion in the teaching of Isaac Luria.

> **The soul is called by five names: *nefesh, ruah, neshamah, yehidah, hayyah*. *Nefesh* is the blood, as it says: "For the blood is the *nefesh*" (Deut. 12:23). *Ruah* [is called this] because it ascends and descends, as it says: "Who knows the *ruah* of man, if it ascends [and the *ruah* of the beast, if it descends]" (Eccles. 3:21). *Neshamah* is the breath; as people say, his breathing is good. *Hayyah* [is called this] because all the limbs are mortal, whereas this lives on in the body. *Yehidah* [unique, from *ehad*], because all the limbs are in pairs, but this is unique within the body. (*Midrash Bereshit Rabbah* 14:9)**

> **We begin with what the Rabbis wrote, that there are five names to the soul. From the bottom up, their order is: *nefesh, ruah, neshamah, hayyah, yehidah*. Without doubt, these names were not attributed by Scripture or by chance. But know that the person himself is the spiritual force within the body, while the body is just the garment for the person; it is not the person himself. This is why it is written: "Do**

not anoint [with the sacred oil] any person's body" (Exod. 30:32), as noted in the Zohar 1:20b.[21]

It is known that man connects all four worlds of ABY'A [*Atzilut, Beri'ah, Yetzirah, Asiyah*]. Therefore, there must be within him portions of all four worlds, and each portion is called by one of the five names NRNH'Y [*Nefesh, Ruah, Neshamah, Hayyah,* and *Yehidah*], as will be explained. He does not acquire all of them at one time, but only according to his merits. At first he obtains the lowest of them, *nefesh*. Afterward, if he merits further, he will also acquire the [level of] *ruah*. This is explained in several places in the Zohar . . . [including] 2:94b[22]: "When a person is born, he is given a *nefesh*." (Vital, *Sha'ar ha-Gilgulim* [Gate of reincarnations], 2)

The midrash is loosely based on Gen. 2:8, which contains three of these words for soul (*neshamah, nefesh,* and *hayyah*); the other two are added. But this teaching does not refer to separate souls, only to aspects of the one soul that we acknowledge as part of the soul's unique nature.[23] Nonetheless, this midrashic text serves as a root for the broader teaching about five levels of soul. (Note that in these two texts the levels *Hayyah* and *Yehidah* are switched; in this kabbalistic model, *Yehidah* is the highest "soul level." This may be due to the parallel between *Yehidah* and the unique—*yahid*—quality of *Keter*.[24]) These five levels are not explained by Vital; we are only told that they are not "by chance." They are intended as a much higher force than the body—which is only a garment for the soul—and therefore one should not anoint the body, which is spiritually inferior to even the lowest level of soul.

What does it mean that man "connects" the four worlds? It implies that his soul exists on all these levels. If he performs holy deeds, he elevates his soul and connects it to a higher level; sin, of course, lowers it. And one's deeds have an effect across the cosmos, across all these worlds. One begins with the lowest level, *nefesh*, and works up to a higher soul level, and to a higher world; presumably the higher one's world, the broader one's view and the less one is centered on his own personal soul. In any case the two highest levels are available only to a very few highly developed individuals. Simcha Paull Raphael notes that "those who have awakened these dimensions of their being are able to perceive the infinite grandeur of the divine realms, to enter the everflowing celestial stream—described by the Zohar (2:209a) as the 'bundle of life,' *tzror ha-hayyim*, where all souls are housed."[25]

This notion of expanded consciousness and understanding in Lurianic Kabbalah, and especially in Hasidism,[26] came to be called *mohin d'gadlut*.[27] *Moah* is the brain; *gadlut* comes from *gadol*, "great"; thus the term refers to expanded consciousness, the ability to see more and more from God's view. It is often contrasted with *mohin d'katnut* (*katan* means "small"), lesser, more constricted consciousness.

The continuation of this text includes some of the complicated language found in later parts of the Zohar and in Lurianic Kabbalah; this terminology may be found in contemporary discussions as well.

> Know that every *nefesh* comes only from the world of *Asiyah*, every *ruah* is from the world of *Yetzirah*, and every *neshamah* is from the world of *Beri'ah*. However, most people do not have all five parts— *nefesh, ruah, neshamah*, etc.—but only the *nefesh* from *Asiyah*. But even this *nefesh* has many levels, and this is because *Asiyah* itself also divides into five *partzufim* [lit., faces]. They are called: *Arikh Anpin* [the long face], *Abba* [father], *Imma* [mother], *Ze'ir Anpin* [the short face], and *Nukva d'Ze'ir Anpin* [the feminine (consort) of *Ze'ir Anpin*]. Before a person can merit to attain *ruah* in the world of *Yetzirah*, he must be complete in all five faces of *nefesh* in *Asiyah*.
>
> Even though, as is known, there are those whose *nefesh* is from *Malkhut* in *Asiyah*, and others who are from *Yesod* of *Asiyah*, still, each person must rectify the whole spectrum of *Asiyah*. Only after this can a person receive his *ruah* from *Yetzirah*, since *Yetzirah* is greater than all of *Asiyah*. Similarly, to attain *neshamah* from *Beri'ah*, one needs

to rectify every part of his *ruah* in all of *Yetzirah*, after which he can then receive his *neshamah* from *Beri'ah*. It is not enough for him to rectify only the particular place where his soul-root is grounded. He must rectify all the aspects of each level, until . . . he can attain his *ruah* of *Yetzirah*. It is this way with all the worlds. The upshot of this [rectification] is that one must be involved with Torah and mitzvot which correspond to all of *Asiyah*, not only those corresponding to the specific place to which his *nefesh* is attached. Similarly, if one sins and blemishes a particular spot in *Asiyah*, even though it is not the place to which his *nefesh* is attached, he still must rectify it. (Vital, *Sha'ar ha-Gilgulim*, continued)

Arikh Anpin essentially corresponds to *Keter*. *Abba* and *Imma* are *Hokhmah* and *Binah*, the divine "parents" of the lower *sefirot*. *Ze'ir Anpin* corresponds to the *Tiferet* complex, and his consort, the *Nukva* (as in the Hebrew *nekevah*, "feminine"), who has no name of her own—just as she casts no light of her own but only reflects the light from above—is of course *Malkhut*. Thus the ten *sefirot* are described as a family with five members. In this view, each world contains the ten *sefirot* (and the five *partzufim* listed above). One must be "complete" in every aspect of one soul level before ascending to the next; life constantly presents us with challenges to improve our soul level as well as to rectify whatever defects we acquire on the way.[28] These family members were all mentioned above, but note that Isaiah Horowitz (earlier in this chapter) did not use these additional terms. Although he was well aware of such writings and expressions associated with Lurianic teachings, he used them sparingly.

One way to accomplish such an improvement is through transmigration, the return of the soul in another life. Transmigration is different from reincarnation. Reincarnation suggests a rebirth as an animal or even an inanimate object; this was accepted by some of the early kabbalists (and by Cordovero). Transmigration involves overlaying another entity with all its qualities on top of the original.

> It has been taught: When a man's soul departs, all his relatives and friends in that world [i.e., the afterlife] accompany his soul and show it its place of delight and its place of punishment. If he was virtuous, he sees its place and ascends to dwell and delight in the supernal bliss of that world. But if he was not virtuous, that soul remains in this world until the body is buried in the earth. Once it has been buried, numerous officers of justice seize [the soul] and take it to *Dumah*, and bring it into the abodes of *Gehinnom*.
>
> Rabbi Yehudah said: All seven days, the soul goes from his house to his grave, and from his grave to his house, and mourns for the body, as it is written: "His flesh is in pain for him, and his soul mourns over him." (Job 14:22). It goes and sits in his house. It sees them [i.e., the family] all grieving, and mourns. (Zohar 2:218b–219a)[29]

This is a typical kabbalistic view of the afterlife, in that the virtuous are rewarded and the wicked are punished.[30] The wicked soul is carried off to *Dumah*, which here likely refers to an angel in charge of the dead souls,[31] casting them into *Gehinnom*, the closest Jewish term for "hell."[32] (*Gehinnom* originally referred to *gei Hinnom*, "the valley of *Hinnom*," where the Canaanites practiced child sacrifice.) Rabbi Yehudah expresses the view that the body goes through punishment during the initial week, while the soul grieves for the pain of the body, mourning together with the family while they observe shivah, the week of mourning.[33]

The Zohar addresses another question: Are the dead *really* dead? What are they doing?

> "A man who consults the dead" (Deut. 18:1). "The dead" means here the wicked in the world, among those nations who are idolaters, who are always thought of as "dead." But as for Israel, who are truly righteous, Solomon said with respect to them, "I praised the dead

that have already died" (Eccles. 4:2)—in the past, "that have already died"; but not now when they are alive. Furthermore, when the other nations visit their dead, they do so with sorcery in order to arouse evil spirits. But when Israel visit their dead, they come in great repentance before the Holy One, Blessed be He; they come with a broken heart and fasting into His presence, and all so that those holy souls might plead for mercy for them before the Holy One, Blessed be He. And the Holy One, Blessed be He, has pity on the world because of them. Consequently, we have learned: Even though a righteous man has departed from this world, he is not removed from, or vanished from, all the worlds, since he exists in all those worlds more than in his lifetime. During his lifetime he exists only in this world, but thereafter he exists in three worlds, and is welcome there, as it is written, "The maidens love you" (Songs 1:3). Do not read *alamot* [maidens], but *olamot* [worlds]. Happy is their portion! (Zohar 3:71b)[34]

The Zohar begins by contrasting the idolaters, who devote themselves to pleasures of this life but are in effect already "dead" by virtue of their being disconnected from the source of eternal life, with those who gave up matters of this world in favor of Torah learning and practice of the mitzvot but who continue to "live" even after physical death. Worse still, the idolaters visit their dead through approaching the *sitra ahra* and using its demonic power. Israel, by contrast, is moved by death to repentance and good deeds, bringing about a favorable turn on the supernal level.

Furthermore, the righteous individual is granted access to additional worlds after bodily death. The three worlds correspond to the three souls: the *nefesh* remains in the lower world to advocate for the righteous still here, and, as we have seen, *ruah* goes to the earthly Garden of Eden and *neshamah* to the supernal Garden of Eden. The text concludes with a rereading of the verse from Song of Songs; the midrashic literature frequently reinterprets the word *alamot* in this way, but generally with reference to two worlds (this world and the world to come). The idea that the tzaddik, the "righteous man," is present in worlds beyond our own both during and after this life plays a prominent role in Hasidic thought as well.[35]

Except in the later strata of the Zohar, *gilgul* rarely appears in kabbalistic teaching before the sixteenth century,[36] but it then quickly achieved wide acceptance and later was absorbed into Hasidic thought.[37] If the soul was pure because its behavior in life had been pure, it would naturally reunite with the Divine. Since most of us are not so pure, we cannot do that. But through *gilgul*, we get another chance; if our repentance in life did not sufficiently atone for our sins, the soul will be born into another life. And in that second life our sufferings atone for our earlier sins, and we ultimately get to return to our Source. Thus one could view *gilgul* as a punishment for previous sins, but it probably should more appropriately be appreciated as a second chance (and, at least in theory, with further chances if necessary) to earn one's eternal reward.[38] Generally it was understood that there were families of souls united with common backgrounds or roots, so that (as with modern transplants) the host body would not reject the implanted soul!

Vital outlines the difference between *gilgul* and *ibbur*, the joining of a soul to an existing body and soul:

> **Gilgul is when, as the newborn emerges from its mother's womb, the soul enters that body, and it suffers all the sorrow and sufferings of that body from the moment it came into the world until its death, and it cannot leave until the day of death. But *ibbur* is when the soul exists in this world after a person has been born and grown up; then, another soul enters him and that person is like a pregnant woman [*ubarrah*] who carries an infant in her womb, and thus it is called *ibbur*. (Vital, *Sefer ha-Gilgulim*, ch. 5, 4b)[39]**

Originally *gilgul* and *ibbur* were the same, but the latter term changed after the writing of the Zohar and came to mean what Vital calls it here, where a person comes to take on an additional soul.[40] As noted, the term *ibbur* suggests the metaphor of pregnancy, the possession of an additional soul for a limited period of time. *Gilgul* means that a soul returns to live again for an entire lifetime. In this view, *ibbur* is much more beneficial and easier than *gilgul*; if you are given the soul of a saint, it will make it much easier for you to do saintly acts! One can also see the connection with the concept of *tikkun*, repairing the souls of both the living and the dead.[41]

Luria, Vital's teacher, taught that one could learn to "read" the soul level of another person—whether the individual was in fact reincarnated—and it became widely believed that Luria himself was able to do so. On the whole, belief in *gilgul* grew substantially among the Jews through the next two centuries.

The mystic may seek to transform profoundly awful deeds into mitzvot, so as to assist with the redemption and *tikkun* associated with a particular soul, as in the following example from the sixteenth-century Safed kabbalist Eleazar Azikri:

> **It once happened in Castile that gentiles had designated an ox for sport, it being their custom to beat and afflict an animal. During the night preceding the event a Jew had a dream in which he saw his father, who told him, "Know, my son, that because of my many iniquities I transmigrated into an ox following my death, and it is the very ox designated for affliction and hard blows tomorrow in the people's sport. And so, my son, redeem me and save me that I may flee through a certain place before they kill me by tearing me to pieces alive. Redeem me from their hands: give no thought to the cost involved, and slaughter the ox in a proper manner and feed it to poor students of Torah. I have been informed of this from above and have been permitted to inform you. In this way my soul shall ascend, returning from transmigration into an animal to transmigration into a human being and enabling me to serve the Lord, with God's help." (Azikri, *Sefer Haredim ha-Shalem*, ch. 33, 142)[42]**

This story begins with a particularly un-Jewish activity, causing pain to an animal, but through this case of transmigration, potentially nonkosher meat is made kosher, cruelty is transformed into generosity (feeding hungry Torah students), and the suffering soul is elevated to a higher existence. To come back to life as an animal says something about the kind of life you lived as a human.[43] Conversely, the animal that hosts this soul can be treated with human sensitivity, thus providing it with an appropriate *tikkun*. Once again, we see evidence of the mystical belief: the apparent is not the real. Everyone and everything might actually be something or someone else.

Related to *ibbur* is the phenomenon of the dybbuk, a malevolent spirit that invades a body for ill purpose. The word is from the same root as *deveikut*; it "attaches" to another person. Vital here describes an exorcism that might be described as "curative magic."

> **And by applying this *yihud* we are able to restore his soul somewhat so that he [the spirit] may depart from the person's body. And following is the procedure, as personally tested by myself. For I would grasp that man's arm and put my hand on the pulse, ... since this is where the vestment of the soul is located, and therein it clads itself. And I concentrate upon that soul, clad in the pulse, that he might depart from there by the power of the *yihud*. And while clinging to his hand at the pulse, I recite a particular verse, normally and backward, and concentrate upon the following Divine Names that issue from the text.... In many cases the exorcists said: "Appoint a wicked man over him, and let Satan stand at his right side" (Ps. 109:6), and some additional verses and textual combinations. (Vital, *Sha'ar Ruah ha-Kodesh*, excerpts)[44]**

The phenomenon of a dybbuk has been described by Idel as "inverse Maggidism."[45] A dybbuk comes about when a person, because of particularly grave sins, is not allowed another chance at life; the person's soul wanders, but seeks a haven within the body of a living individual.

Such an individual may have secretly transgressed and thus created a space for the wandering soul to invade it.[46] Exorcisms like this took place occasionally among European Jewry during the seventeenth through nineteenth centuries, though people reported similar experiences long before. Such "possession" experiences may give us reason to wonder about the mystical enterprise, but before coming to any conclusions we need to examine further the ideas and types of experiences that may issue from the spiritual realms into which we have journeyed.

We have seen that the mystical impulse speculates about different rungs of reality and levels of the individual soul, including the levels in which it may find itself after bodily life ends. At the extreme, it may extend into what was described in chapter 1 as Affective Kabbalah, the attempt of the mystic to create a new reality. This leads us to our next two chapters, on magic and messianism, respectively.

20

Magic

Most Jews believe that magic has nothing to do with Judaism. But many Jewish practices are rooted in magical beliefs. For instance, a number of customs related to the Jewish wedding ceremony were based on the belief that they would protect the parties from harm: the bride is disguised from demons by the veil; the bride walks around the groom seven times, creating a "magic circle" around him; and the groom breaks a glass at the conclusion of the ceremony, with the intention of scaring away demons at this moment when the bride's status is changing and she is potentially vulnerable.[1] The fact that all these practices have been reinterpreted and are usually explained in more rational terms does not change how they entered Jewish life. Such practices helped give people a feeling of control over their lives, particularly when they felt most vulnerable.

In Affective Kabbalah (see chapter 1) the goal of the kabbalistic ritual is not to fulfill God's need, but strictly to respond to human needs. It is sometimes referred to as "white" magic because its goal is to accomplish something positive rather than to cause harm. Where the mystic differs from the magician is in his commitment to a religious truth even higher than whatever material goal he seeks to accomplish. Nonetheless, some mystics were willing to use magic to reach these goals.

The Bible seems to be intolerant of sorcery (see Exod. 22:17 and Deut. 18:10-12), but magic does exist within the tradition, beyond the marriage practices already mentioned.[2] Many Jewish rituals, especially during moments of transition where people felt vulnerable to evil forces, started out as magical practices, and their meaning transformed over time. We have already read that many early sages were considered knowledgeable about the Divine Names, and prominent rabbis of later eras, such as Yehudah he-Hasid and Eliezer of Worms among the Hasidei Ashkenaz, and Luria and others in Safed, were certainly aware of and frequently practiced magic. Mystics too occasionally entered a realm in which they would attempt to alter reality to protect themselves and others from such evil forces.

We have read, for example, particularly in dealing with the *sitra ahra* (the "other [evil] side"), that the mystical view accepts the reality of the demonic. However, just as modern science has found ways to deal with threats formerly associated with the demonic, mystical knowledge of the supernal realms gives the mystic power to deal with the demonic.

A few examples of different types of magic include:[3] (1) curative—healing (as with the exorcism of a dybbuk); (2) preventive—warding off harm; (3) creative—being able to bring about something new (as with the golem); and (4) predictive—finding out the future.

Even in the Bible itself, we see examples of prophets performing wonders of various kinds, as with this passage:

> **In those days [King] Hezekiah fell dangerously ill. The prophet Isaiah son of Amoz came and said to him: "Thus said the Lord: Set your affairs in order, for you are going to die; you will not get well." Thereupon Hezekiah turned his face to the wall and prayed to the Lord. He said, "Please, O Lord, remember how I have walked before You sincerely and wholeheartedly, and have done what is pleasing to You." And Hezekiah wept profusely.**
>
> **Before Isaiah had gone out of the middle court, the word of the Lord came to him: "Go back and say to Hezekiah, the ruler of My people: Thus said the Lord, the God of your father David: I have heard your prayer, I have seen your tears. I am going to heal you; on the third**

day you shall go up to the House of the Lord. And I will add fifteen years to your life. I will also rescue you and this city from the hands of the king of Assyria. I will protect this city for My sake and for the sake of my servant David." Then Isaiah said, "Get a cake of figs." And they got one, and they applied it to the rash, and he recovered. Hezekiah asked Isaiah, "What is the sign that the Lord will heal me and that I shall go up to the House of the Lord on the third day?" Isaiah replied, "This is the sign for you from the Lord that the Lord will do the thing that He has promised: Shall the shadow advance ten steps or recede ten steps?" Hezekiah said, "It is easy for the shadow to lengthen ten steps, but not for the shadow to recede ten steps." So the prophet Isaiah called to the Lord, and He made the shadow which had descended on the dial of Ahaz recede ten steps. (2 Kings 20:1-11)

Isaiah is a prophet and a moral authority, but also a healer and a wonder-worker, whose forecast is confirmed by the miraculous backtracking of the sundial. We see him performing deeds that are curative, as in healing Hezekiah, and preventive, as in rescuing Hezekiah and his city from the Assyrians (in both cases he is able to prevail over the natural order). Even to the historian who authored the book of Kings, the prophet is without doubt capable of miracles; indeed this is what gives him his authority.[4] Similarly, the significance of other prophets such as Moses, Elijah, and Elisha is attached to their ability to perform such extraordinary deeds.

Are miracles a sufficient basis for prophetic status? Maimonides certainly did not think so; he said: "For how could the Creator seek help from that which He has created?"[5] Maimonides, writes Menachem Kellner, "thinks more highly of a Creator who creates a cosmos that functions well without tinkering than of one who must constantly 'pull strings and push buttons' to make it work."[6] But Maimonides is responding to the fact that a great many people believed that one who had the status of prophet *could* accomplish such miracles.

The talmudic Rabbis are often portrayed as wonder-workers, and this ability was often seen as a "normal" part of a holy man's job description.

> **Rabbah and Rabbi Zera joined together in a Purim feast. They became intoxicated with wine, and Rabbah arose and cut Rabbi Zera's throat. The next day he prayed on his behalf and revived him. Next year Rabbah said: "Let the master come and we will have the Purim feast together." Rabbi Zera replied: "A miracle does not happen on every occasion." (B. Meg. 7b)**

It may well be that the Rabbinic pair here is not Rabbah and Rabbi Zera, but the Rabbis in the talmudic story about the golem's creation, Rava and Rabbi Zeira.[7] If indeed this is so, then Rava was believed to possess curative as well as creative powers (notwithstanding the fact that he is extremely dangerous when under the influence), resurrecting or at least healing his comrade. We saw this "creative" magic, aimed at generating a new entity, in *Sefer Yetzirah* as well as the golem stories.

Certain ritual objects were believed to have the power to shield those who possessed them from harm. The names of God, and in particular the Four-Letter Name, warded off any force from the *sitra ahra*; earlier sages believed that "the Name of God creates and destroys worlds."[8]

> **Just as the Name is [found] on the angel, so also the tefillin [are found] on the hand and likewise on the head: "And with the shadow of My hands I have covered you" (Isa. 51:16). He safeguards the righteous, so that the prophet sees, so that he may know who was upon me, and who safeguards me by means of the shadow of his hand. This is just as it is now, on the night of Hoshanah Rabbah: whoever has a shadow will live, but whoever has no shadow, and his head is small, without a neck, he will die within the same year, since He then decides in relation to [the amount of] water [of that year]. And the prophet sees the glory that has been created in order that he will see in accordance with the divine will. (Eliezer of Worms, *Sodei Razzaya, Hilkhot Nevuah* [Laws of prophecy])[9]**

Here the tefillin, containing the sacred Name, serve not only as a reminder of the mitzvot and a way to spiritually bind the wearer to God, but also as a safeguard, virtually by the "hands" of God and their corresponding shadow. This was "preventive" magic, warding off harm to the individual. Sukkot included many rituals and prayers for rain, and Hoshanah Rabbah, the final day of Sukkot, was also considered by many to be the last day on which one's "decree" for the year ahead could be changed; the decree was "written" in the "Book of Life" on Rosh Hashanah and "sealed" on Yom Kippur, but it could be revoked up until Hoshanah Rabbah. So this too was a major transition day, and some of the Hasidei Ashkenaz believed that one's shadow on that day would foretell his fate. This was "predictive" magic, anticipating the future and sometimes following up with some form of preventive action against it.

Related to the use of the Divine Name for magical purposes is the whole phenomenon of the *ba'al shem* (literally, "master of the Name") practitioners, of whom Rabbi Israel, who became known as the Ba'al Shem Tov (see chapter 23), is the best known. The earliest known use of this term is in the writings of Rav Hai Ga'on (939–1038); we learn there that not only did such *ba'alei shem* (pl. of *ba'al shem*) exist, but that belief in them was quite common both in Israel and many diaspora lands.[10] Thus it should be no surprise that we see a related belief in the efficacy of the Name among the Hasidei Ashkenaz. Some texts mention Rabbi Samuel, the father of Rabbi Yehudah he-Hasid, as an active *ba'al shem* whose skills were also called upon by non-Jews; many stories suggest that his famous son was also considered a *ba'al shem*, and Rabbi Eliezer of Worms as well.[11] A highly regarded *ba'al shem* could provide a variety of amulets, primarily but not exclusively for preventive purposes, and many books included various such charms collected from numerous sources.[12]

The next example provides a more intense version of the magical usage of God's Name:

Another kind of knowledge . . . is practical Kabbalah, the [knowledge of] God's holy Names which can be permutated into a number of different forms, such as the Name of forty-two, and the Name of seventy-two. Similarly, Rabbi Shimon bar Yohai of blessed memory explained about the Name of seventy-two: "Through this Name is a link to the ancestors through many paths: for judgment, mercy, aid, lovingkindness, awe, [guidance in] Torah, life, death, good or evil. Happy are the righteous who know the ways of Torah and know how to walk [the path of] the Torah of the Holy King."[13] And even though the truth is that it is not proper for every individual to make use of these Holy Names—for who is worthy to use the scepter of the King, other than one who is close to the King—still, we know without any doubt that one who knows how to use [them] and is worthy to do so can bring about wondrous things, as I have witnessed and have heard from one who did so. (De Vidas, *Reishit Hokhmah, Sha'ar ha-Ahavah* [Gate of love], ch. 7, sect. 39-40, 1:472-73)[14]

When De Vidas says he has witnessed such things and heard from one who did them, he is probably referring to Isaac Luria himself. The "Name of seventy-two" permutated the letters of Exod. 14:19-21; these verses tell of the splitting of the Red Sea as the Israelites leave Egypt, and De Vidas goes on to cite the tradition that this was the Name through which Moses accomplished this miracle.[15] In Safed it was widely believed that the Name contained such power.[16] It should be noted that the real taboo did not involve the use of magic—as long as it was white magic—but rather the possible misuse of God's Name.[17]

The *ba'al shem* was able to perform deeds or prepare amulets based on the power of God's Name. Thus in the eighteenth century, when the phenomenon of the *ba'al shem* was widely known and accepted, the Ba'al Shem Tov was known as one who had exceptional powers. (Luria seems not to have been referred to as a *ba'al shem*, but such a description would hardly be surprising.)

Numerous types of miracles were widely accepted among the majority of Jews for centuries. From the tenth century on, for example, many stories tell how a holy man managed *kefitzat ha-derekh*, the miraculous shortening of a journey (although once trains come into being, no further such stories occur).[18] Right into the early Hasidic period, holy men, and particularly kabbalists, are associated with the capacity for magic.

Kabbalists between the twelfth and fifteenth centuries developed a wide-ranging interpretation of a Judaism infused with magical practices, which were often regarded as the highest level of wisdom. In their circles knowledge of Kabbalah might simply be a way to recognize the symmetry between this world and the supernal realms, a stage below the more direct usage of magic. Most kabbalist thinkers, particularly in Italy, treated knowledge of magic as theoretical wisdom and did not go so far as to attempt to put it into practice.[19] The Spanish kabbalists, however, had little interest in theory or philosophy, but felt much more pressure to use such magic. As Idel notes, "If the mission of Israel in the exile was to undo the evil of the world and cause a change in the nature of non-Jewish religions, then magic was the most important instrument to achieve such a grandiose task."[20]

Another form of mystical magic involved what is commonly called "automatic writing," as explained by a kabbalist contemporary with many of the Safed mystics:

> You shall now hear the wonders of the living God about this subject, the secret of the celestial writing, without a hand, without a foot, without ink.... It is the same secret by which the Tablets of the Covenant were written, with the finger of God. You shall then know the secret of the celestial finger and the celestial hand.... Gabriel is the one who writes, and Michael the angel is the scribe. These two angels have the power, derived from their station, to write, if you invoke them, and they write without ink.... Many in Israel have fathomed it, and so do Joseph and me, we have learned it with great effort and

toil. [Here is omitted a detailed section concerning the writing of the Holy Names of twelve and seventy-two letters.]

I have sworn in the name of the living God of Hosts that immediately an angel will descend downward, in order to write, without a hand, without a foot, without a pen. This is what you should say after reciting those holy names: "May there be the will of God," and every time you read the names say the following: I hereby invoke you by the explicit names I have mentioned, that you should immediately show your power and your writing in the lower world, in this paper or this book or this wall or this air, right now, at this time, [show] it and subjugate it by the secret of the celestial ink, whatever it is that I wish, in abbreviated words and the letters and the vocalization marks above, and you should announce it, the meaning of the words, what each word means. I am invoking you with all the power of the letters which I have mentioned, so that immediately, at this time, you should write and engrave and imprint in fire these letters in paper and that the divine fire will not burn the paper, and that the writing will be visible to every eye . . . so that all will know and recognize that this is a divine phenomenon, when they see that there is no ink in it.

. . . I invoke you with the full power of "one God whose name is one" (Zech. 14:9, as quoted in the prayer "Aleinu") and with the full power of the sanctity which is hidden in the secret of every point [i.e., vowel marks], and the full power of the secret of his fire and its color, and in the power and secret of the point, and in the power and secret of the hidden thought, and in the full power of the two halves of a ball, and the full power of "one God whose name is one" which is connected to the supreme point, that immediately your power and your fire will come down and will immediately write this thing which I demand on this paper which I have placed in a certain place, a true thing, or on the wall if it is white. You shall then mention the wall or the air or the place you wish them to write and imprint the writing. You shall then use four kinds of *ketoret* [holy incense] . . . three times with a smoking paper, and in order to give it the needed strength the paper should be treated by smoke before that, and after it is smoked you should enter a room clean of any impurity, and you should recite the names which I have instructed you, forward and in reverse. (Scholem, "The Maggid of Rabbi Joseph Taitazek," in Dan, *Heart and the Fountain*)

From a Jewish standpoint, the original sacred writing appears on the tablets given by God to Moses, "inscribed with the finger of God" (Exod. 31:18). The kind of writing described here, involving the assistance of angels, is said to be linked to this same phenomenon. Through the use of holy Names and with the supernal powers derived from specific letters and even vowels, the mystic claims to be able to write like God, without pen and ink. Like the materialization of a golem, this is to be a form of "creative" magic. We do not know who the author's associate "Joseph" was, although it has been speculated that it might be Rabbi Joseph Della Reyna, of whom we will learn more later.

Among the many powers mentioned are "the two halves of a ball," which may refer to the unification of the *sefirot* and to a verse about God's unity that is "connected to the supreme point," to *Keter*, where there can be no differentiations. Appropriate scents are present, perhaps to overload the senses and aid in the "leap" to the paranormal state in which the mystic is able to move to the supernal realm.

After you have recited it seventy times with the invocation every time, immediately the secret of Gabriel and Michael will descend, their whole stature and their power, and they will write what you ask them to or what you will wish to know, whether it is true or not. I am swearing in the name of God, Praised be He, that it will happen exactly as I am telling you. And then, when you envision this celestial writing, you shall know that there is a God in Israel, you and everyone else who observes this" and the spirit of God is upon you" (Isa. 59:21).

The secret of this supernal writing is the secret of the descent of the power of God in His glory, and the people of the world call it "a written question." . . . With this power you can achieve the ability to write whatever you wish, be it a great deal or just a little. You shall understand the secret of the writing Name, guided by an angel, whenever you wish it, and everything written in this way you should believe to be true as if it were done by God Himself. . . . With this secret there is nothing which you cannot achieve, like actual prophecy itself. . . . Do not hesitate to try it alone or in any way you wish, only the room should be clean and pure of any impure thing, and this you should observe.

This practice should be done with full observance, without any neglect. The woman of the house should be clean of any impurity. It should begin by two days of complete fasting, and on the third day it should be performed. The person doing it should not drink any wine and he should eat on that day only after performing the practice. Before that he should eat three eggs, to give him the power for the Names. It should be performed in the morning and also after midnight. . . . He should use it only in sanctity and purity, and after he has separated himself from a woman for three days and nights; the practice should be performed on the fourth day.

You should preserve this writing, not showing it to scholars and ordinary people, for if he reveals how it was written he will frighten anyone who sees it. This is the secret of the supernal writing, which should be revealed only to those who worship God and revere His Name and to the righteous, only they deserve to know it, and not the evildoers and the sinners of this evil generation, a sinful generation which is completely guilty. (Scholem, "The Maggid of Rabbi Joseph Taitazek," continued)[21]

Magic means that I perform according to the right formula, I produce specific results for me, for us, from higher powers. That is what Taitazek claims here. Seventy recitations of the formula will bring the two angels, who will write what you wish and address your "written question." This is a form of "predictive" magic, providing information helping its practitioners to face the future. Similarly, some mystics would ask a question at night, and whatever dream they would have that night would be interpreted as an answer. This is a natural extension of *Heikhalot* mysticism, where the mystic would learn future history in the divine throne room.[22] The secret of the "writing Name" refers to the idea that if you know this mystical Name of God, this knowledge guides your hand, from above, as you write down this secret information that otherwise is only available in the supernal realms.[23] However, just as there was a high bar for participation in the *Heikhalot* trips, there are strict qualifications for using this technique. Additionally, one is never to show the technique to those not qualified to use it.

Not only sacred Names of God but even sacred books may be able to provide certain powers just by virtue of their presence:

> **Even one who does not understand or even know how to read the language of the Zohar [should read it], for it has the marvelous power to purify and illuminate the soul. (Palaggi, *Torah v'Hayyim*)[24]**

Many sages—including this prominent nineteenth-century Turkish rabbi, in a guide to proper actions—believed in the magical power of the Zohar. You may be surprised to know that at least one prominent organization today makes this same assertion and sells expensive sets of the Zohar—in its Aramaic original—to many who cannot read it. They can turn to this source and others like it to justify their claims.[25]

For some Jews these clearly "magical" aspects actually do possess power, and the following parable addresses those who might dismiss all such rituals and ideals as foolishness.

> **The thirteenth-century Rabbi Isaac of Acre was once observed performing a shamanic rite by an intellectual not of the Jewish persuasion. At the conclusion of the ceremony, the guest approached the rabbi and asked how so wise a sage as he could dabble in such superstitious nonsense. Patiently, the rabbi told the following parable:**

There once lived a man who had never before seen another human being, having grown up in the wilderness far from any human habitation. One day, while venturing about, he happened upon a village. Curious, he approached one of the homes and peered in through the window. To his utter shock, he observed a man and a woman struggling desperately with one another, panting, sweating, and moaning as they grappled. He then burst into the house, pulled the two apart, and asked them what they thought they were doing! They explained to him that they had been engaged in a sacred ritual that joined Creator with Creation, Sky with Earth, Spirit with Matter, and oftentimes even resulted in the formation of another human being! The stranger reacted strongly to such a suggestion, that such a base and vile act could be in any way considered sacred, let alone powerful enough to create another being. So he left in a huff and returned to the wilds. "So you see," Rabbi Isaac explained, "how one cannot comprehend the sanctity or worthiness of a ritual, when one is witnessing it from outside the context of the tradition that conceived that ritual."[26] (Winkler, *Magic of the Ordinary*, 103)[27]

A tale of Jewish magic that also serves as a bridge to the subject of messianism treated in the next chapter is about Joseph Della Reina, a historical figure in the period prior to the expulsion of Jews from Spain. He was associated with a group of Spanish kabbalists, known as the *Sefer ha-Meshiv* circle, who were extremely involved with this kind of "practical" Kabbalah.[28] The story exists in many versions.[29]

The legend claims that Della Reina, with the help of his disciples, used his knowledge to try to force the coming of the Messiah. They engage in a series of extensive fasts and other purifications, leading to visitations with increasingly powerful angels who instruct them in the use of holy Divine Names, and as a result they were able to take Samael, Lilith, and all their demonic hosts captive. The demons beg for food and water, but their captors refuse as they have been instructed and take them to Mount

Seir. As they approach, Della Reina takes a pinch of frankincense to sniff, and Samael begs him for at least a sniff to revive himself. Della Reina, not realizing that the incense is holy and must not be offered to an evil force, gives him a few particles, whereupon Samael and his camp break their bonds, killing and driving insane some of the disciples.

As in many tragedies, we know that the hero of this story, no matter how pious or deserving, must be brought to ruin.[30] In the story, magic "works," but it is never enough. Affective Kabbalah cannot hope to bring about more than small successes; evil cannot be permanently defeated, and the Messiah's coming cannot be forced.

Many kabbalists believed in the power of magic to help them accomplish spiritual goals, acquire sacred information, or ward off demons or other harm. However, that power generally was believed to have limits. The next chapter will focus on those mystics who sought to test those limits to the maximum.

21

Messianism

We have read about the notion of "personal redemption," either through knowledge of hidden truths (chapter 3), repair of certain defects (chapter 18), or even through transmigration (chapter 19). But what about a true Messiah, someone who brings redemption for the Jewish people and more?

The actual doctrine of the coming of a Messiah (*mashiah*, "anointed one"), though it became an accepted article of faith during the Rabbinic era, was not firmly rooted in Judaism in the biblical period.[1] It does, however, appear frequently in one form or another in that society, as it did in many contemporaneous societies. Like other nations throughout history, when the Jews believe they can no longer achieve redemption in real time, they have hoped for something more wondrous that would transcend normal politics. For this, individuals have to be willing to invest themselves in radical change. Of course, as yet messianic movements have never succeeded, but they have played a significant role in Jewish history and have intersected significantly with Jewish mystical movements.

Eliezer Schweid lists four salient qualities that seem to define post-biblical Jewish messianic phenomena:[2]

1. A deeply critical view of the present human condition, particularly as relates to the oppression of the Jews.

2. Belief that the present, tragic situation cannot last much longer, because God has not abandoned His world and His people and will not allow this to continue indefinitely, even if the suffering is a necessary precursor to redemption.

3. While most people cannot understand why the reign of evil continues, certain inspired individuals can read the signs of the future in the present through mystical wisdom; this helps people manage until current difficulties are overcome.

4. The idea is prevalent that eventually the Messiah, a man descended from King David, will appear and "take over" Israel, and perhaps the entire world, bringing about a redemption characterized by justice (including vengeance), the return of the exiles, the reestablishment of the kingdom and the temple sacrifices, and much more.[3] He will not come to uproot the Torah, but to reestablish it.

Another important notion is the risk that is always associated with being the Messiah or following one; if he is not "real," if he cannot ascend politically, other forces will crush him and his followers. Though he is a focus for divine power, he is not a wonder-worker as such.

These beliefs about the Messiah overlap to some degree with presumptions of Jewish mystics that we have seen. So it should be no surprise that mystical circles were involved in various messianic movements throughout Jewish history.

Even the early sages were thinking about what it would mean to live in messianic times and how we might behave differently.

"It is a time to work for the Lord, for they have violated Your teaching" (Ps. 119:126). Rabbi Nathan says: [This means] they have violated Your teaching because it is a time to work for the Lord.

Rava said: The first clause explains the second. Why is it "a time to work for the Lord"? Because "they have violated Your teaching." And the second clause explains the first. Why have they "violated

Your teaching"? Because "It is a time to work for the Lord." (M. Ber. 9:5; B. Ber. 63a)

In certain circumstances the Rabbis agreed that the law should be temporarily suspended. We violate the law, but only because it is "a time to work for the Lord," a unique moment that requires us to do so; for example, the Jews in the Land of Israel during the second century BCE who were under attack could not observe Shabbat (because their enemies did not). Because of others who do evil and break God's rules, we must also break the rules, at least temporarily, in order to work for the Lord and maintain the life of His people.[4] The kabbalists also broke their own rules when necessary. Although in many eras they were extremely reticent to share their teachings publicly or to write them down in books, some believed that in a time when the teachings were in danger of being forgotten or misused, it was acceptable to do so. So rabbis throughout Jewish history often adopted the principle of a temporary violation of the law, in order to preserve the law.

Because messianic times might, by definition, be considered "a time to work for the Lord," the messianic impulse contains within it a certain degree of antinomianism, or at least the potential to lessen the authority of the law. But this only works out well if the messianic time actually comes; if it does not, it is no simple matter to restore the authority of the law.

What are the signs that might tell us the Messiah is coming? One school of thought says: things have to get better; people have to earn the Messiah.[5] The other approach says: things will get worse first;[6] when life becomes terrible, that is when you most need the Messiah.[7] Similarly, another talmudic teaching suggests that the Messiah will not come until people despair of his coming![8]

What role might the mystic play in such times? Could he be a forerunner for the Messiah . . . or even *be* him? Our next two texts address these questions.

Tootruseah, the Lord, the God of Israel, desires and awaits [the mystic] inasmuch as he awaits the redemption and the time of salvation preserved for Israel after the destruction of the second, [the] last Temple.

When will he descend, he who descends to the *Merkavah*? When will he see the pride of the heights? When will he hear the ultimate salvation? When will he see what no eye has seen? When will he [again] ascend and proclaim [this] to the seed of Abraham, his beloved? (*Heikhalot* text)[9]

In this view, the mystic himself becomes the Messiah who will announce God's message to Israel. When he is able to complete his mission, to ascend to the throne room, "see what no eye has seen," and return to proclaim it to his people, then redemption will take place. And God Himself longs for this mission to succeed. Ultimately, salvation depends on the people, that is, the mystics.

The prophet is necessarily called *mashiah* because he is anointed with the supernal oil called "the oil of anointing" . . . with which he utilizes the Names. Actually the *mashiah* must possess two qualities: one, that he first be anointed by God with wondrous prophecy, and two, that he continue to be consecrated by God and people who will hail him as their great king of all times, "and he will rule from sea to sea" (Zech. 9:10). And this is all due to the great intensity of his *deveikut* with the divine intellect and his reception of the power in a strong manner as it was with Moses, Joshua, David, and Solomon. And the issue of *mashiah* will be known by everyone, and this is why there is no more need to announce the issue here, because he is destined to reveal himself shortly in our days. (Abulafia, *Maftei'ah ha-Tokhehot*)[10]

Abulafia makes a strong connection between prophecy and messianism, and, as a student of Maimonides, may have been influenced by his view that prophecy would return before the coming of the Messiah.[11] So the prophet himself functions as a *mashiah*. For Abulafia, the true mystic attains prophecy. It is the mystic who will be accepted as the "great king of all times," after having attained *deveikut*. Abulafia thought of himself as a Messiah and (as noted in chapter 12) hoped to convert the pope to Judaism, thus bringing about the defeat of Christianity, which in turn might hasten the final redemption. And, according to Abulafia, the Messiah "is therefore dormant in every person, and this capacity should be actualized."[12] If a person can become a prophet, he can and should also become the Messiah. But this becomes a much more personal redemption through *deveikut*, and much less a political redemption.

How would the role of the Messiah change if, as in Mainline Kabbalah, his power is wielded within the *sefirot*?

> "He [Judah] binds to the vine his donkey, to a choice vine his ass's foal" (Gen. 49:11). He is King Messiah, who is destined to rule over all forces of the nations, the forces appointed to rule over other, idolatrous nations, the potency through which they are empowered. King Messiah is destined to overpower them, for this vine rules over all those lower crowns through which the idolatrous nations have dominion. This one triumphs above; Israel [the choice vine] conquers and destroys other forces below. King Messiah will overpower them all, as it is written: "poor and riding on an ass, on a donkey" (Zech. 9:9). Donkey and ass are the two crowns through which the idolatrous nations rule from the left side, the side of impurity.

> Why does it say "poor"? Is King Messiah to be called "poor"? But Rabbi Shimon said thus: [It is] because he has nothing of his own, and we call him King Messiah, the holy moon above, who has no light except from the sun. This King Messiah will have dominion, uniting with his site. Then, "see, your King is coming to you" [the preceding phrase in Zech. 9:9], unnamed. If below, he is "poor," for he is in the aspect of the moon. If above, he is "poor" [in the sense of the] speculum which does not shine, "bread of poverty." But even so, "riding on an ass, on a donkey," power of all the idolatrous nations,

to be subjugated beneath him, and the Holy One, Blessed be He, will be empowered in His realm. (Zohar 1:238a)[13]

Judah is the subject of the opening verse, which comes from Jacob's deathbed blessings to his sons. But Judah also is the ancestor of King David, who is traditionally regarded as the ancestor of the Messiah to come. Thus, long before the Kabbalah, the Rabbis associated this verse with the Messiah.[14] In our text Israel, the "choice vine" (Jer. 2:21), will, through the Messiah, control the nations, riding on their symbols, the "ass" and "donkey." It should not be a surprise to see the words "King" and "Messiah" used together; the Jewish Messiah is not only a redeemer but also a king who brings political salvation. As Klausner points out, no Jewish Messiah would have said what is attributed to Jesus in John 18:36: "My kingdom is not of this world."[15]

Who really is the Messiah? The Zohar links him with the moon, which receives all its light from the sun. The moon is code language for the *Shekhinah*, or *Malkhut*, which receives all its light from the higher *sefirot*. Messiah is thus said to unite with "his site," that is, the *Shekhinah*. The King is unnamed here because it refers to both the *Shekhinah* above—the "speculum which does not shine," being able only to reflect light from others—and the Messiah below. Ultimately, this suggests that when permanent harmony exists in the *sefirot* above, the Messiah will rule over all the nations and Israel will be elevated to its rightful place. Spiritual success will lead to political success. Indeed, earlier Kabbalah rarely worried about political success in this world; the focus was exclusively on the higher realms.

We do not know who wrote the following "*genizah* pages," the source of our next text, found by Isaiah Tishby, one of the leading twentieth-century scholars of Jewish mysticism. But they and other literature of this period give clear evidence both that Jews in the Iberian Peninsula underwent acute persecutions at the end of the fifteenth century and that many strongly believed that these were a precursor to the coming of the Messiah, who would avenge the sufferings brought on God's people.

> **"From the time that the regular burnt offering is taken away, and the abomination that makes desolate is set up, there shall be 1,290 days" (Dan. 12:11). This is the news of our redemption in this age: from the day the king of Portugal launched the attack in the palace of Os Estaos against us and our children,[16] when the regular burnt offering and the Torah were taken away from the people of Israel, the abomination of idolatry will last for 1,290 days and Zion and Sinai are to be desolate and also betrayed.**
>
> **"Ask it of me, and I will make the nations your domain, and the ends of the earth your possession" (Ps. 2:8). In this verse there is a hint that the first redemption destined . . . to come, with God's help, will be at the ends of the earth, namely Portugal. God, praised be He, will take us out of there. (*"Genizah* pages" on events from 1497-98)[17]**

The first segment reads the verse from Daniel as a description of events in Portugal during the forced conversions of 1497 to 1498, and a prediction that Christian communities would be destroyed a few years later as divine retaliation. The second passage reads the Psalmist's reference to the "ends of the earth" as alluding to Portugal, which of course was virtually the end of the known world until the discovery of the Western Hemisphere. Thus Portugal would be given into the hands of the Jews.

Messianic speculation was rampant in the wake of the expulsion; even the philosopher Isaac Abarbanel, who was in no way a kabbalist, wrote extensively on the subject and believed that the redemption would occur in his own lifetime. It should not surprise us, then, to see the next text, written in 1606, in which a Lurianic disciple dreams messianic dreams. We have already seen the emphasis of Lurianic Kabbalah on *tikkun*,[18] which would be completed through a redemptive act performed by God or the Messiah, or recognition of such act by the Jewish people or the rabbis, when the Messiah arrives.

12th of Kislev, Tuesday night . . . week of Va-yishlah in which the battle between Jacob and Samael is found, as well as the matter of the chieftains of Esau. . . . The portion from the Prophets is the vision of Obadiah. I saw in my dream a large, high mountain . . . hewed and cut squarely from each of its four sides, like the walls of one square fortification. I ascended on the eastern wall, along the southeastern corner, and asked: Which city is this? I was told: This is Nineveh. Then they told me: This is the evil Rome. . . .

I then saw that from the inside, on the eastern wall, there was a lance stuck in the wall, a very long one, and it was protruding toward the houses of the city, and it was situated halfway up the wall. There was a sword, upside-down, its edge down, stuck in the lance, its handle high above at the top of the wall, for the length of the sword was that of half the height of the wall. They told me: This sword is stuck in this lance since the day the world was created until now, and no person has ever touched it. I looked at it and saw that it was a strong brass, unique, which can cut all sorts of iron as if it was dry straw. It had four edges on its four sides. At the point of the sword, there was something like the mouth of a snake, and they said that anyone struck by this sword will not recover.

I thought to myself: It is such a long time from the creation of the world until now; maybe the sword has become rusty. I looked at it and saw it was completely new. I took it in my hand. The emperor of Rome was told: That sword which no man has ever touched, is now in the hand of a certain Jew. The emperor then ordered to look for me and to kill me. When I was still on top of the wall, I threw the sword from my hand into the city and its tip stuck in the ground in one of the city's courtyards. I then escaped and hid in a cave in Rome where poor people lived, and I hid there until Saturday afternoon. Then I came out, and the emperor's servants found me and brought me to him.

He then ordered: "Remove everyone from here," and he and I remained alone. I said: "Why did you want to kill me? All of you go astray in your religion, like blind people, for the only true Torah is the Torah of Moses and no others are true." He said to me: "I knew all this; therefore, I sent for you, because I knew that there is no one as wise and knowledgeable as you are in the true wisdom. I want you to tell me secrets of the Torah and some of the Names of the Lord your God, praised be He, because I already realize the truth. Therefore do not be afraid that I sought you, for I truly love you." I then related to him some of this wisdom, and woke up. (Vital, *Sefer ha-Hezyonot*)[19]

The Torah reading for the week in which Vital's dream takes place tells of the struggle between Jacob and the angel in Genesis 32, before his reunion with his brother, Esau; the Zohar (1:146a) identifies the angel as Samael. The list of Esau's chieftains was also understood to refer to evil powers, as Esau was associated with both Edom and with Rome and Christianity, and thus with the side of evil. The prophetic reading for that week deals with a prophecy concerning Edom! And so, in his dream, Vital sees himself climbing the walls of Rome. It is almost as if he dreamed that he would do what another messianic figure, a crypto-Jew named Solomon Molkho, had attempted in 1532,[20] or perhaps what Abulafia had tried to do three centuries earlier, to go to the head of the church and convert him, thus bringing about a redemptive triumph for the Jews.

A magic sword comes into his possession. Endangered, he flings it down from the wall into the city, and he hides in a cave among the poor. This is significant because the Talmud says that the Messiah will be found among the beggars of Rome.[21] Eventually he is brought before the emperor (probably the pope himself), whose first words to him echo the words of Joseph in Egypt when he reveals himself to his brothers (Gen. 45:1); the emperor cannot yet reveal his secret desire publicly. Vital brazenly tells the emperor that Judaism is the only true religion and, amazingly, the emperor agrees, telling Vital the same thing a Pharaoh once said to Joseph: There is no one as wise as you! (see Gen. 41:39). Further, the emperor seeks kabbalistic wisdom from Vital, who grants him some.

The fact that Luria and Vital lived in the Land of Israel does not change the fact that they experienced Jewish life as exilic; if the *Shekhinah* is exiled, it makes no difference where individual Jews settle. Nor is it surprising to find that it is Samael, the personification of evil and the demonic forces, who must be defeated on the path to the Messiah, and also that other religions must be proven false. This was widely believed prior to Luria's arrival; Cordovero, for instance, taught that "by perfection of the [kabbalistic] worship, the humiliation of the gentile will occur and their rule will be overthrown, and [it] is understood according to what is known that this world includes two supermundane systems, one holy and one profane."[22] There were also existing traditions that the Messiah would come from Galilee (the Jewish rejection of Jesus notwithstanding),[23] which may also have heightened the sense of mission among the most intensely devoted within Safed. Finally, a story about the birth of Luria himself suggests that the prophet Elijah appeared at his circumcision, from which the child appeared to be healed miraculously by the time he was taken home.[24] This represents a theme frequently seen with messianic figures, as if the child was not quite a normal physical being.

It is not certain to what degree this focus on the Messiah in the sixteenth century was a reaction to the pain dealt to the Jews at the end of the fifteenth. Nor is it certain how much more intense the messianic element in Safed is than it was within the teachings of Abulafia or the Zohar; additionally in Safed, the role of the Jewish mystical elite in bringing the Messiah is much more critical than his "arrival" at God's bidding. It is, however, clear that new energy fed the messianic impulse, leading to a reinterpretation of the Messiah's role during this period; people now believed that the time for his arrival had come.[25] We turn now to the crisis of faith that came in the following century.

Sabbetai Tzvi (1626–76) was a charismatic but unstable young man with an unusual name (Sabbetai, meaning both "Sabbath" and "Saturn") who wandered about, particularly in Turkey, and proclaimed himself to be the Messiah.[26] Only when Nathan of Gaza joined forces with him in 1665 did people begin to pay him serious attention. Within months, Jewish communities all over the world were caught up in a frenzy, where Tzvi's claim was believed and Nathan accepted as his prophet. Few during this period openly opposed faith in Zvi as the Messiah, and very few with particular effect. Nathan developed a theology using symbols and terms from Lurianic Kabbalah and justifying many of his Messiah's bizarre acts, some of which were outright violations of Jewish practice.[27] When Sabbetai Tzvi was taken into custody by the sultan and ultimately forced to convert to Islam, this too was justified as a "descent into the *kelippot*" and thousands of adherents followed him into Islam,[28] forming a sect that the Jews then called the *Donmeh* (loosely translated as "turncoats").[29] The effect on the rest of the Jewish world was deeply disturbing, to say the least.

It is important to note that although this followed a major crisis for Eastern European Jewry (the 1648 Cossack massacres), little evidence exists that Sabbateanism was a direct result of this crisis. If there was any external influence, it may have been the many crypto-Jews who over an extended period attempted to reenter Jewish life, albeit with ideas absorbed from their outward life as Christians.

Nathan of Gaza may have written the next selection (in about 1665) under the influence of a vision, and not simply as an attempt to give additional credence to his Messiah by attributing the text to an earlier, imaginary authority; Nathan himself was widely accepted as a prophet.

And I, Abraham, after having been shut up for forty years grieving over the power of the great dragon that lies in the midst of his rivers, [wondering,] "How long until the end of these awful things?" (Dan. 12:6), when the voice of my beloved knocked: "Behold, a son shall be born to Mordecai Tzvi in the year 5386 [1626] and he will be called Sabbetai Tzvi. He will subdue the great dragon, and take away the strength of the piercing serpent and the strength of the crooked

serpent, and he will be the true messiah. He will go forth to the war without hands [i.e., weapons]. . . . His kingdom will be forevermore and there is no redeemer for Israel besides him. Stand on your feet and hear the power of this man, though he be poor and lean. He is my beloved, the apple of my eye and my very heart . . . and he shall sit on my throne, for 'the hand is the throne of God' (Exod. 17:6)."

. . . And a deep sleep fell on me, and lo, a horror of great darkness in all the land of Egypt. And there came a ferret and a chameleon and brought forth a great light, the light of the hiding of his power. And behold, there was a man, his size was one square cubit, his beard a cubit long and his penis a cubit and a span. He held a hammer in his hand and tore up a great mountain of ten times sixscore thousand. And the man went up the mountain, and there was a pit down to the bottom of the mountain, and he fell in. And he [the man resembling polished brass] said to me: "Do not grieve, for you shall see the power of this man." But I could no longer restrain my grief, and I fell into a deep sleep and saw no more vision for a month until the awesome man came again and said to me: "My son, how great is your strength, since I reveal to you things unknown even to the angels. And now, write the vision and conceal it in an earthen vessel, so it may continue many days. Know that the man of whom I have spoken shall strive hard to know the faith of heaven, and Habakkuk prophesied concerning him, 'the just shall live by his faith' (2:4), because for a long season Israel will serve without the true God, but he shall restore the crown to its pristine glory. His contemporaries shall rise against him with reproaches and blasphemies; they are the 'mixed multitude' (Exod. 12:38), the sons of Lilith, the 'membrane above the liver,' the leaders and rabbis of the generation. He will do wondrous and awesome things, and he will give himself up to martyrdom to perform the will of his Creator." (Nathan of Gaza, attributed to a Rabbi Abraham of Germany in the thirteenth century)[30]

This view presents a wide array of powerful evil forces, which presumably can only be defeated through the use of even more powerful (i.e., kabbalistic) forces and with information "unknown even to the angels." The liver and the "membrane above the liver" are kabbalistic references to Samael and Lilith.[31] It is noteworthy that the "leaders and rabbis" who would "rise against him" (i.e., against Sabbetai Tzvi) are referred to in such vituperative language.

Messianism is an important issue in the Hasidic world today, though there is a range of opinion on the subject among the Hasidic masters. But any discussion of it should begin with a letter by Rabbi Israel, the Ba'al Shem Tov, describing a vision in which he encounters the Messiah, written about 1751.

> I went higher, step by step, until I entered the palace of the Messiah in which the Messiah studies the Torah together with all the *tannaim* and the saints and also the seven shepherds. There I witnessed great rejoicing and could not fathom the reason for it, so I thought that, God forbid, the rejoicing was over my own departure from this world. But I was afterward informed that I was not yet to die since they took great delight on high when, through their Torah, I performed unifications here below. To this day I am unaware of the reason for that rejoicing.
>
> I asked the Messiah: "When will the Master [i.e., the Messiah] come?" And he replied, "You will know of it in this way: it will be when your teaching becomes famous and revealed to the world ... and when what I have taught you and you have comprehended will spread so that others,[32] too, will be capable of performing *yihudim* [unifications] and having soul ascents as you do. Then will all the *kelippot* be consumed and it will be a time of grace and salvation." I was astonished to hear this and greatly distressed that it would take such a long time, for when will such a thing be possible? Yet my mind was set at rest in that I learned there three special charms [*seggulot*][33] and three holy Names and these are easy to grasp and to

expound, so I thought to myself, it is possible by this means for all my colleagues to attain to the stages and categories to which I have attained, that is to say, they too will be able to engage in ascents of the soul and learn to comprehend as I have done. But no permission was given to me to reveal this secret for the rest of my life. (From a letter of Rabbi Israel, the Ba'al Shem Tov, to his brother-in-law)[34]

Most of the Ba'al Shem Tov's teachings were publicized or published by his followers; this is one of the very few things he is considered to have written personally. He gave the letter to one of his primary disciples, Jacob Joseph of Polonnoye, to deliver to his brother-in-law, Abraham Gershon of Kutow, then in Palestine. Ironically, because Jacob Joseph's trip was aborted, the intended recipient never saw the letter. It was published in 1771, over ten years after the Ba'al Shem Tov's death.

The vision in this letter, a response to a perceived threat against the Jewish people, bears a significant resemblance to the *Heikhalot* visits to the highest realms. The Ba'al Shem Tov makes no messianic claim for himself; he claims only to have visited and conversed with the Messiah and to have learned that the spread of his own teaching will stimulate the final redemption.[35]

Magic plays a significant role for him, as should be expected of someone who acquired the title of *ba'al Shem*, one who is able to use the power of the Names to benefit those in need. However, he himself is not permitted to spread the magical knowledge he has acquired, through which he would have been able to advance the final redemption. His own role is prophetic and certainly preparatory to the Messiah, but no more.

There is no plan, no process, no goal—let alone a specific year—as to when the Jewish situation will be improved. Some scholars, including Gershom Scholem, understood this to mean an indefinite postponement of the Messiah's arrival. It is probably true that even several generations after the disaster with Sabbetai Tzvi people would not want to take a chance on any more imminent redeemer. Scholem and others referred to this as a "neutralization" of messianism.[36] Thus, as Jonathan Garb puts it, messianism in Hasidism "is geared towards internal perfection rather than historical change."[37]

> A teaching of the Ba'al Shem Tov: Every Jew must rectify and enhance the aspect of the full stature[38] of the Messiah that is related to his own individual soul. As is known, the name Adam [*a-d-m*] is the acronym of Adam, David, Messiah. This is so because Adam's full stature extended from one end of the world to the other. All Jewish souls are encompassed within the full stature of Adam, the first man. Afterward, because of the sin, his full stature was diminished. Similarly, the Messiah will possess the full stature of all Jewish souls, encompassing six hundred thousand souls as it was before Adam's sin. Therefore every individual Jew must endeavor to enhance the aspect of the Messiah that is related to his soul, so that the entire stature is rectified and established. Then there will be an unending and general unity [of souls]. May it happen speedily and in our days. (Menahem Nahum of Chernobyl, *Me'or Einayim* [The light of the eyes], *parashat* Pinhas, 91b)[39]

This text is an excellent example of the potential tension within messianism in Hasidism. The coming of the Messiah depends on each one of us, presumably on all of us. Perhaps you or I will be the one who will complete the task of rectifying the stature of Adam and bring about the "unending and general unity." Thus, there is not necessarily an imminent redemption, but there could be if we fulfilled our responsibilities! In this view, Adam before the sin in the Garden of Eden could be reconstituted in order to transform him into the Messiah.

The notion of Adam extending from one end of the world to the other is talmudic.[40] The theme of Adam being an acronym for Adam, David (the ancestor of the redeemer), and Messiah originates in the thirteenth century with Moses de Leon and appears frequently in Horowitz's *Shnei Luhot ha-Brit*; the Ba'al Shem Tov and his students may well have borrowed it from this work.[41] The number six hundred thousand represented the number of adult male Jews believed to be present at Sinai, and thus frequently served as a symbol for the entire Jewish people.[42]

The messianic impulse remained strong among various Hasidic groups (see chapter 26). Although the details are still debated, it was widely believed that Rabbi Jacob Isaac Horowitz, the Seer of Lublin (also discussed in chapter 25) and one of the most notable wonder-workers among the Hasidic masters, led an attempt to force the coming of the Messiah, along the lines of Joseph Della Reina.[43] And we will now see a teaching from Rabbi Nahman of Bratslav (1772–1811, the great-grandson of the Ba'al Shem Tov), indicating his feeling that he himself might be the Messiah.

> "There are seventy nations, divided between the domains of Esau and Ishmael [i.e., Christendom and Islam]. Each of these domains is composed of thirty-five kingdoms, and they will be conquered in the future by the two messiahs, Messiah ben Joseph and Messiah ben David. And there is one tzaddik in whom these two messiahs are combined." He said several other things there, more than have been printed. At that point the table broke, because so many people were pressing around him. He became harsh and said: "Are there gentiles sitting around my table? Are these then messianic times, that gentiles should approach the tzaddikim, as in 'All the nations shall flow unto him' (Isa. 2:2)?" (Nahman of Bratslav, *Hayyei Moharan*, 1:6)[44]

In Jewish tradition there were two conceptions of the Messiah.[45] First would come Messiah ben Joseph, sometimes seen as a suffering figure, sometimes as a warrior; he would come to announce the imminent arrival of the real Messiah, the Messiah ben David, and prepare Israel, perhaps leading them to Jerusalem. Among previous kabbalists, both Luria and his disciple Vital had been believed to be incarnations of Messiah ben Joseph, although (in a time-honored theological maneuver) the generations were deemed unworthy of Luria and Vital actually revealing themselves. Even the founder of modern political Zionism, Theodor Herzl, was eulogized by pre-state chief rabbi, Abraham Isaac Kook (see chapter 27), as "Messiah ben Joseph." In this text, the "one tzaddik" is likely Nahman himself. It is also likely that the omitted part is his announcement that he himself is indeed the Messiah ben Joseph, and he hopes that now the people will be worthy. Nahman, who fought depression and physical illness, saw himself as "the suffering tzaddik whose pains contain within them the hope for redemption."[46]

Ironically, although Nahman died quite young and without a great deal of success, Bratslav Hasidism has never replaced him and continues to maintain itself. We will look further at some of his teachings in chapter 24.

Finally, the rebirth of a Jewish state has led to speculation that we might be experiencing the beginning of the redemption:

> **The true redemption, which is to be manifested in the complete resettlement in the land and the revival of Israel in it, is thus seen to be a continuation of renewed settlement in the land, accompanied by the ingathering of the captive exiles within its boundaries.... Hence, when this state of ours is in full control, both internally and externally, then the fulfillment of this mitzvah of the inheritance can be truly revealed—the mitzvah which is the basis and essence of all mitzvot that, by means of our role, can accomplish the act of redemption. (Tzvi Yehudah Kook)[47]**

Christian evangelical doctrine about the Apocalypse—which would be preceded by the entire Jewish people returning to Israel—is no secret to many in the United States. You may be surprised to find that contemporary "nationalist Orthodoxy" bears a resemblance to such doctrine. Kook (1891-1982), the son of Rabbi Abraham Isaac Kook and a prominent leader of the "settlement movement," taught that building Jewish settlements on the land given to the Jews by God would hasten the coming of the Messiah. As Menachem Kellner notes on this text, "Rabbi Kook is perfectly clear: Jewish rule over the whole land of Israel, its complete resettlement by Jews, and the Ingathering of the Exiles not only make the messianic redemption possible, but guarantee it. They are necessary and sufficient conditions for the coming of the Messiah and must be accomplished before he can come. They are *pre-requisites* of the messianic advent, not signs that it has occurred."[48]

Now, unlike among many Orthodox thinkers prior to the founding of the Jewish state, there is no passive "waiting" for the Messiah; the involvement of the faithful is a requirement. Once again, the notion of "intrinsic sanctity" plays an important role in contemporary Israel, shared by many Jews, some of whom are much more overtly mystical in their approach to the land. The notion of "full control" would also suggest the absence of non-Jews or at least of their rights as citizens of a modern state.

The pendulum of Jewish thought, which had swung away from mystical messianism for close to two hundred years, has returned through both Hasidic and Zionist influences. The Jewish people, constantly facing various threats and crises, are periodically prone to support movements that evoke this radical solution.

22

Prayer and Ritual in the Mystical Life

Some Jews perform rituals and recite prayers out of a sense of solidarity with other Jews, or just a feeling of obligation. But many do so hoping to create an intense sense of nearness to God.

Most Jewish prayer is conducted according to an established liturgy, although it has historically been open to new additions and variations. Prayer, along with specific symbolic actions, is also a component of ritual activity; thus, it is natural to treat these two subjects together. We will see how the mystics added new practices and also reinterpreted existing practices in the light of their own approach. This is particularly true of the Mainline Kabbalists who dominated Jewish thought for centuries, for whom ritual and prayer were intended primarily to bring about activity within the *sefirot*. Others, most especially within Hasidism—to be examined in subsequent chapters—sought to attain intense *deveikut* and ecstatic experience, while still focusing on meeting God's needs, completing and perfecting His creation.

The nineteenth-century rabbi Samson Raphael Hirsch once noted: "The catechism of the Jew consists of his calendar."[1] In other words, the liturgy of the weekday, the Sabbath, and festivals reflected the most basic beliefs that Judaism passed on from generation to generation. It is with this in mind that we should consider the importance of how the mystical impulse transformed both the text of the liturgy and its meaning.

Who is like the Lord our God; who is like our Master; who is like our King, who is like our Creator? None is so holy as our God, for there is none like Him and there is no Rock like our God. Rabbi Ishmael said: Rabbi Akiva heard all these hymns and everything related to this matter when he descended to the *Merkavah*; he comprehended and learned them before His Glory, for the ministering angels of the Holy One, Blessed be He, chanted them before Him and blessed His glorious Name, and would exult for each blessing and praise. (*Heikhalot* text)[2]

Rabbi Akiva's journey is for the purpose of hearing the angelic hymns and passing them on—perhaps together with their power?—to his fellow sages.[3] However, what matters here is the text of this song. Some readers will recognize the Hebrew of the initial lines (slightly changed here): *mee kEloheinu, mee kAdoneinu, mee k'Malkeinu*. This is an early version of what later became "Ein Keloheinu" (There is none like our God), a popular hymn included near the end of the Shabbat and festival morning services. The repetitive rhythmic chant would be intended to induce a trance or at least a change of state, moving the mystic along his path to the *Merkavah*.

Other prayers originated or made a significant appearance in the *Heikhalot* literature. An early version of the "Aleinu" prayer, concluding each of the daily services, also appears in one of the *Heikhalot* texts,[4] introduced as the prayer that Rabbi Akiva offered when witnessing the angels before God's throne. The story of the ten martyrs from Rabbinic legend was given much broader treatment in these texts and ultimately became part of the Yom Kippur *Musaf* service. And the daily "Kedushah" is critically important to the *Heikhalot* literature, although the *Heikhalot* mystics may simply have been expanding the meaning and significance of the existing ritual.[5] They believed that Israel's recitation of the "Kedushah" actually completed the corresponding prayers of the angels! The "Kedushah" as we have it is a base for and somewhat less intense version of the *Heikhalot* prayers and visions we read about in chapters 4 and 5, more a part of Normal Mysticism. The Zohar also added on its own interpretation.[6]

We begin by exploring various interpretations of the meaning behind the recitation of "Shema Yisrael," the most basic statement of Jewish faith.

> **Rabbi Joshua ben Korha said: Why does the paragraph with "Shema Yisrael" precede that of "V'hayah Im Shamoa"? So that one might first acknowledge God's sovereignty, and afterward accept the obligation of the commandments. (M. Ber. 2:2)**

In the second century CE, the time of the Mishnah, this order of recitation of the paragraphs in the "Shema" was already established. So why does the section of Deuteronomy 6 (including "Shema Yisrael" and "Ve-ahavta," "You shall love the Lord your God . . .") precede the segment read from Deuteronomy 11 ("If you will obey the commandments . . .")? The answer given here is straightforward and thematic: one first acknowledges God's authority to command, and then the implications of such authority.

Of the various forms of mysticism, this is consistent primarily with Normal Mysticism. Prayer with proper *kavanah*, "intention," is intended to evoke God's Presence; combined with Torah study as it is here, it also presents to us a message from God.

> **When Rabbi Akiva was taken out for execution, it was the time to recite the "Shema." While the executioners ripped his flesh with iron combs, he was accepting God's kingship [i.e., reciting "Shema"]. His disciples said to him: Even to this point? He said to them: All my life I have been troubled by the verse, "You shall love the Lord your God with all your soul," [meaning] even if God takes your soul [even if you die for loving God]. I said: When will I have the opportunity to fulfill this? Now that I have the opportunity, shall I not fulfill it? He**

prolonged the word *ehad* [one] until he died while saying it. A heavenly voice went forth and proclaimed: Happy are you, Akiva, that your soul departed with the word *ehad*. (B. Ber. 61b)

The problem is how he established that he loved God with all his heart and all his soul by prolonging the word *ehad* until he died while saying it. It is because a human being's love for God consists in the fact that, from his own perspective, a human being is worth nothing. He comes from God and returns; everything returns to God. Besides God, there is nothing; there is only the Lord and the Lord is one.... Because God is one and there is nothing besides God, everything returns to God.... Now, Rabbi Akiva prolonged the word *ehad* until his soul departed, since insofar as God is one, the soul returns to God.... This is the explanation of the love of God. The Torah teaches: "Hear O Israel! The Lord our God, the Lord is one. You shall love the Lord your God." For since God is one, no existing being in the world is separated from God; all things that exist depend upon and cleave to God, since He is the basis for all. It is for this reason that love applies to God. Indeed, love of God is more fitting than love of anything else. For in every kind of love between two human lovers, though they may cleave to one another, nevertheless, each retains his or her individuality. However, in the love of a human for God, a human being can completely return his spirit and soul to God to the extent that he loses his individual existence and completely cleaves to God, as it is written, "to love the Lord your God . . . and to cleave to Him" (Deut. 11:22). This is complete love . . . when someone surrenders one's life to God, for by so doing, one completely cleaves to God. (Judah Loew of Prague, *Netivot Olam* [Eternal Paths] 2:39)[7]

Rabbi Akiva, the leader among the mystics on the journey to the *pardes* discussed in chapter 3, was tortured to death by the Romans for teaching Torah after they had forbidden it. Nonetheless he expresses his gratitude for being able to show his love for God "with all his soul," even at the cost of his life. His recitation of the "Shema" is not the "Normal" mystical experience described in the Mishnah previously. Judah Loew emphasizes the mystical aspect of this recitation of "Shema" in a somewhat different way. For him, Rabbi Akiva is not merely entering an experience of union with God, but also acknowledging the universal nature of such experience in death. "God is one" means that everything is one within God, everything is unified within God. Furthermore, love of God is the greatest love, the one in which a person willingly surrenders himself completely. This understanding of the meaning of reciting the "Shema," in which the individual declares his willingness to yield his very self to God, is markedly different from what we saw in the Mishnah; it is akin to what we understand as *deveikut*.

In the Zohar, as we might expect, recitation of the "Shema" is the time to concentrate on "the mystery of unification."[8] This next excerpt, from *Sh'nei Luhot ha-Brit*, takes this goal even further.

> **Ein Sof watches over them [the *sefirot*] from the beginning of their emanation. Ein Sof bestows the influx in them and illuminates them with its light. The influx of this light causes them to bond in a true and powerful union. This influx is never lacking. They [the *sefirot*] are all nourished from the best of the influx.... From this perfection, they provide bread, law, and food to the rest of the worlds: the worlds of Creation, Formation, and Making. The sustaining of the connection among [the four] worlds and the elements, until the hub of our world, depends upon the influx. Were it to be withheld for even an instant, all the material worlds would vanish into oblivion. However, the spiritual elements would return to their source....**
>
> **This is the correct intention a person should have in mind when reciting "Shema." In so doing, a person unites all the worlds from below to above, until the First Cause. For all of these [four worlds] are connected and united, each effect with its cause, level after level,**

until the First Cause. By means of God's great and holy influx, they are connected from the first point to the point of the hub, the center of the world.... The correct intention in reciting "Shema" is that we unite all the *sefirot* with one another, and all of them with the One who caused them to come forward. Thereby, we make God King over all creatures, great and small. For God, by means of His great and holy influx, bestowed by His emanations, is the cause of their existence....

It is also found in the words of Shimon bar Yohai [in the Zohar], that in the union of the recitation of "Shema," one should cause the downward increasing of the flow of the influx. The meaning here is that because of Adam's initial sin and also because of our sins, the conditions of the earth deteriorated, and the influx which had been bestowed on all the worlds at the time of emanation became diminished. It is no longer at the same degree of power and strength as it was before the sin of Adam. Consequently, we must now increase the flow, through the union in the recitation of "Shema," so that the emanation will bestow the same great light upon the worlds, as it did before the sin, and the worlds will be strengthened as before.

Each of the *sefirot* has its own treasury. For example, *Keter* is the treasury for absolute, pure compassion. *Hokhmah* is the treasury of wisdom, *Binah* of repentance, *Hesed* of lovingkindness, *Gevurah* of wealth, *Tiferet* of Torah. And so it is for all the *sefirot*. The influx is released, depending upon the need for human action at a particular time. There might be a need for pardon, forgiveness, and atonement; then it becomes necessary to draw down the influx from the supernal pure whiteness which is *Keter*, which whitens the sins of Israel.... By means of *Binah* in union with the Supernal Father, *Hokhmah*, the influx is released to *Malkhut*. *Binah* and *Malkhut* are thereby united by the six *sefirot* between them. There are a multitude of examples of this, all of which are initiated in response to human action....

The ultimate purpose of one who worships God is to do everything for God's Name, to cause pleasure to the Creator ... for through the increase of the flow down of the influx above, that is caused by the arousal of the worshiper, the influx descends below and everything is at peace. (Isaiah Horowitz, *Shnei Luhot ha-Brit*, excerpts from *Sha'ar ha-Gadol* [The great gate], sect. 48-67)[9]

This is an example of Affective Kabbalah and how the mystics influenced by it interpreted the standard recitation of "Shema Yisrael." The presumption, as with Mainline Kabbalah (note that reference is made to the Zohar and the "increasing of the influx"), is that the flow of sustenance from above continually maintains the universe, in much the same way that oxygen makes our own lives possible. If all the oxygen were suddenly sucked out of a room, everyone within it would die; similarly, without the "influx" of divine light, the material world would disappear.

To recite "Shema" is to affirm that the "First Cause"—either *Ein Sof* or *Keter*—brings about all these worlds, and to reunite them with their Creator. Sin clogs up the *sefirotic* system; proper fulfillment of the mitzvot (such as the recitation of "Shema") and other acts of piety and repentance that reunite *Tiferet* and *Shekhinah* serve to repair the "plumbing" of the system, as it were, and, if not to restore it to pristine condition, at least to improve accessibility to the influx. But this text also suggests that access to certain *sefirot* will draw down qualities or benefits. If you know what you need, in your meditation, you can draw it down from the appropriate spot in the supernal realm. There remains a significant emphasis on the *tzorekh gavoha*, the divine need. But by meeting God's need, you can also achieve your own.

Next, we turn to one of several examples of how the Zohar reinterprets the meaning of the "Amidah."

When they reach *emet v'yatziv* ["true and firm," the beginning of the blessing immediately before the "Amidah"], the bride is fully adorned with all her attendants; when they reach *ga'al Yisrael* ["who has redeemed Israel," the conclusion of this blessing], all must stand erect. For when they come to *emet v'yatziv*, her attendants lift her, and she lifts herself to the supernal King; when they reach *ga'al Yisrael*, the holy supernal King appears in His levels to receive her, and we must stand in awe and trembling before the supernal King, just as when He stretches forth His right hand toward her, and puts His left hand under her head, and then the two embrace, kissing, as one.

This occurs during the first three blessings; one must concentrate his will and focus his intention on all these rectifications and the order of the prayer. His mouth, his heart, and his will must be as one. Now that the supernal King and the Matronita are joined with joy and kisses, whoever has a request should offer it now, in this auspicious hour. After one has made his request of the King and the Matronita, he directs his will and his heart to the last three blessings so as to arouse the hidden delight, since through these three blessings She is blessed with another cleaving. (Zohar 2:200b)[10]

Every "Amidah" begins with the same three blessings and ends with the same three blessings; on weekdays, there are an additional thirteen petitions in the middle, while on Sabbath and festivals there is but one blessing in the middle, in honor of the holy day itself. The mystic is to approach and then recite the opening segment of the "Amidah" with the unification of *Shekhinah* and *Tiferet* (the "King") in mind; if this is done properly, it initiates a period during which both the statutory petitions and any others offered are most likely to be fulfilled.[11] One then completes the "Amidah" with the intention of renewing the "embrace" within the *sefirot*.

Now we turn to other rituals, prayers, and meditations developed in the service of the mystical impulse. (See chapter 7 for the place of "Shir ha-Kavod," also known as "An'im Zemirot," a product of the Hasidei Ashkenaz.)

Many recite the following declaration of intent before donning the tallit: For the sake of the unification of the Holy One, Blessed is He,

and His Presence, in fear and love to unify the Name—*yud-kei* with *vav-kei*—in perfect unity, in the name of all Israel. (*Siddur Kol Ya'akov* [commonly known as the "Art Scroll" siddur], 4)

Many who use this siddur, one of the most popular in English-speaking Orthodox congregations, might not be aware of this kabbalistic reflection, which occasionally appears as an introductory meditation prior to blessings over the performance of various commandments. The mystics commonly used this formulation, which stressed that the purpose of the mitzvah was the *zivugga kadisha*, the holy (and primary) unification of *Kudsha B'rikh Hu* (*Tiferet*) and *Shekhintei* (*Shekhinah*). This formulation, seen in many Orthodox prayer books today, is, as noted in *Siddur Kol Ya'akov*, "a prayer that the Kabbalistic spiritual qualities of the commandment be realized."[12] The individual mystic may find some additional meaning below the surface of this unification, perhaps in the feeling associated with connecting to "the circle of life"; not only does the mystic assist God, but he experiences a certain harmony by finding his proper place in doing so. Beginning in the sixteenth century we see many examples of kabbalistic notes within the prayer book and other rituals, including how one observes the Passover seder.[13]

Here is copied the pattern of the Ari's plate from *Eitz Hayim*, and this is the meaning of it: . . . one takes three *shmurah matzot*, and sets one, representing the *Kohen*, above, and beneath it another, representing *Levi*, and below this one another, representing *Yisrael*, which correspond to the three intelligences, the *Abba Ila'ah* [upper father; i.e., *Keter, Hokhmah*, and *Binah*]. Afterward one takes the *maror, karpas*, and *haroset*, the three kinds of dishes, and the shank bone of the roasted lamb, and the roasted egg, setting these five items above the *matzot* as follows: the shank bone, representing *Hesed*, goes on your right, and the egg, representing *Gevurah*, goes on your left. *Maror*, which alludes to *Tiferet*, goes in the center between the shank bone and the egg, because *Tiferet* maintains the balance between *Hesed* and *Gevurah*. Afterward the *haroset* goes on the right, directly below the shank bone, because the *haroset* alludes to *Netzah*. And after that the *karpas*, alluding to *Hod*, goes on your left, directly below the egg. Then one takes some *hazeret* [lettuce] and sets it directly below the *maror*, in the center, for this corresponds to *Yesod*. And this [*hazeret*] is used for the sandwich. And the plate itself, which includes all of them, is *Malkhut*. Thus there are the ten *sefirot* of wisdom. And one should not alter this arrangement, and happy is the one whose intention is according to the above. (Ashkenazi, *Be'er Hetev* on the *Shulhan Arukh*; O.H. 473:4, note 8, quoting Luria)

Most seder plates today have six items on them, as organized by Luria and recommended here by the eighteenth-century Polish commentator Ashkenazi, in order to represent the ten *sefirot* through the six items, the three slices of matzah, and the plate itself.[14]

The most famous poem of that era's mystics, written in the sixteenth century, has become the centerpiece of the *Kabbalat Shabbat* service (which also was invented as a new ritual in Safed).[15]

לְכָה דוֹדִי לִקְרַאת כַּלָּה, פְּנֵי שַׁבָּת נְקַבְּלָה.

Lekhah dodi, likrat kallah, p'nei Shabbat n'kablah!
Go forth my love to meet the bride.
Shabbat's reception has arrived!

(1) "Keep" and "Remember" were uttered as one
By our Creator, beyond comparison.
God is One and His Name is One,
Reflected in glory, in fame, and in praise....[16]

(8) Break out of your confines to the left and the right[17]
Revere the Lord in whom we delight.[18]

Messiah ["son of *Peretz*"] is coming to gladden our sight,
Bringing joy and rejoicing in fullness of days.[19]

(9) Come in peace, soul mate, sweet Bride so adored,[20]
Greeted with joy, in song and accord,[21]
Amid God's people, the faithful restored,[22]
Come, O Bride; come, O Bride.
—*Excerpts from "Lekhah Dodi," Alkabetz*[23]

An entire book has been written on the kabbalistic ideas contained within "Lekhah Dodi";[24] included here are only a few excerpts and comments. This hymn quickly became the centerpiece of the *Kabbalat Shabbat* service developed by the Safed mystics, which became normative practice throughout the Jewish world. Even in the talmudic period, however, Shabbat was greeted as a bride or queen;[25] it probably seemed appropriate to include such a greeting at the moment of transition from ordinary time to holy time, from weekday to Shabbat, between the six psalms recited to represent the six days of the week (95–99 and 29) and the special psalm for Shabbat, Psalm 92.[26]

The author, Solomon Alkabetz (the brother-in-law of Moses Cordovero), included his name as an acrostic using the opening letters of the song's first eight stanzas. But he included a great deal more. Looking at the Hebrew letters in the refrain, you will find twenty-six letters, fifteen in the first segment and eleven in the second. This is a precise parallel to the numerical value of the two halves of the Four-Letter Name: the value of the first two letters is fifteen and of the second two, eleven. The actual verse on which the refrain is based ("Come my beloved, let us go into the field"; Songs 7:12) is about the love of an earthly bride and groom, but, as we know, there is a corresponding union on a higher level, which is celebrated as we begin the Shabbat. Moreover, *dodi*, "my beloved," can be seen as code language for God. If you reverse its letters, you have *Yud-Daled-Vav-Daled*. *Daled* and *Heh* are both abbreviations for God's Name and can be seen as interchangeable. Thus, *dodi* is a version of the

Four-Letter Name of God,[27] which is also the Name applied in Kabbalah to *Tiferet*, a masculine principle in the *sefirot*.

The first stanza recalls the two versions of the Ten Commandments in Exodus 20 and Deuteronomy 5, and in particular how they differ in relation to Shabbat. Exodus says "Remember" the Sabbath day; Deuteronomy says "Keep," "Guard," the Sabbath day. The Rabbis reconciled the difference between the two verses by suggesting that God stated them simultaneously, "as the mouth cannot say, nor the ear hear."[28] Thus it was natural to include a reference to this idea among the many scriptural and Rabbinic references in "Lekhah Dodi." Incidentally, having these two versions of the mitzvah is one of the prominent reasons given for the custom of lighting two candles prior to the beginning of Shabbat, and some kabbalists understood this to be a reference to this double union, on earth and above.[29]

However, we see that "guard" in Exodus precedes "remember" in Deuteronomy. Why did Alkabetz reverse the order from that of Scripture? It might seem that he did it simply because it conveniently allowed the *shin* of *shamor* to serve as the first letter of the stanza, conveniently leading into the acrostic of his first name, Shlomo. However, he also achieves a more significant purpose. One of the earliest kabbalistic texts, the *Bahir*,[30] gives a different reason for the two versions of the Sabbath commandment. It says: "*Zakhor* [remember] refers to *zakhar* [the male]. *Shamor* refers to the bride." *Zakhor*, the masculine, is thus associated with the central *sefirah* of *Tiferet* and with the Sabbath day. *Shamor*, the feminine, is associated with the *sefirah* of *Malkhut* and with the evening of Shabbat.[31] Which comes first? Of course, the Jewish day begins with night, so *shamor* must come before *zakhor*.[32]

In the eighth stanza, why does Alkabetz quote the verse referring to the right and the left, and what do right and left represent? In the representation of the *sefirot*, *Hesed* is on the right, and *Gevurah* the left. These also correspond to the Patriarchs Abraham and Isaac, respectively. Abraham is the father of Ishmael and so is associated with the realm of Islam. Isaac is the father of Esau and thus in Rabbinic thought connected to the realm of Christianity. Neither alone can reach the upper *sefirot*; *Tiferet*, corresponding to Jacob, which is the middle ground, the mediating *sefirah*, can do so.[33] It is as if there is a ceiling over the sides of the divine building, which are occupied by the non-Jews, while Israel has the "express elevator" to the top of the structure.

There was a talmudic teaching that God offered the Torah to all the nations before he revealed it to Israel.[34] As Alkabetz was surely aware, the Zohar (3:192a) adapted this theme and applied it to the children of Esau and Ishmael. This suggests that the claims to prophecy of Islam and Christianity must be rejected;[35] practically and philosophically Christianity and Islam are seen by Mainline Kabbalah as unable to reach the higher *sefirot*, the level privileged to the Jewish people.

Furthermore, in Islam the Sabbath is on Friday; in Christianity the Sabbath is on Sunday. Thus they are to the right and left of the Jewish Shabbat. This then is a prayer that the holiness of Shabbat will extend right and left to the rest of the week, just as the holiness of Jerusalem and the Land of Israel will be radiated right and left throughout the world, and ultimately that the holiness of Judaism itself will be spread to the world.[36]

Alkabetz's encoded message thus reads as follows: When the Messiah (*ben Peretz*) comes, Christians and Muslims alike will acknowledge the truth of Judaism and ascend to the higher level of the Torah. What was once made desolate will be returned to its previous glory and its appropriate position in the world. And this is still connected to the supernal unification. There too right and left will overcome the breach (presumably created by the sin in the Garden of Eden) and live in balance together. Peretz is ten generations before King David, suggesting to the kabbalist that the ultimate redemption flows through all the ten *sefirot*. Thus this stanza refers to four dimensions: the People of Israel, the sacred space of Jerusalem and Israel, the holy time of Shabbat, and the supernal union flowing through the ten *sefirot* to *Malkhut*.[37]

To what is Alkabetz referring in the last line of this stanza? According to his own commentary,[38] it is *Ha-Kadosh Barukh Hu*, or *Tiferet*, in which "we shall rejoice and delight." This fits with the use of the Four-Letter Name in the second line of the stanza. It can also refer to the Shabbat itself, "the day which God has made, let us rejoice and delight in it" (Ps. 118:24). It can refer to Jerusalem, the source of earthly joy, and it can also refer to the day when all will accept God's Kingship, "the day on which God will be One and His Name One" (Zech. 14:9). Perhaps Alkabetz intends it to refer to all these four dimensions that are emphasized throughout "Lekhah Dodi."

In the final stanza, the bride comes and the ceremony may begin. Following the practice of earlier Rabbis, the phrase *Bo'ee kallah* ("Come, O bride") is repeated. But here it bears special significance for this event is two rituals; it is both coronation and nuptial ceremony.[39] The wedding on the supernal levels is conducted with the help of the *sefirah Yesod*, for *shalom* is code language for *Yesod*. *Yesod*, the sixth *sefirah* below *Binah*, facilitates the union of *Tiferet* and *Malkhut*, the seventh of the lower seven *sefirot*.[40] *Malkhut* also arises to crown her husband. They are granted additional powers on this day, much as the Jew is crowned with the *neshamah yeteirah*, an "additional soul" level for Shabbat.

"Lekhah Dodi" celebrates four different interwoven themes: Israel and Jerusalem as holiness in space, Shabbat as holiness in time, the Jewish people as holiness set among humanity, and the holiness of God made manifest in the *sefirot*. Through them all we will rejoice in a messianic time that also restores the time before Adam's sin.

On Sukkot, it is a long-standing custom—known as *Ushpizin*, "guests"—to invite one of seven ancestors to the sukkah each evening.

> Be seated, be seated, exalted guests; be seated, be seated, holy guests; be seated, be seated, guests of faithfulness; be seated in the shade of the Holy One, Blessed be He....

[Each day:] I invite to my meal the exalted guests:

[On the first day:] May it please you, Abraham, my exalted guest, that all the other exalted guests dwell here with me and with you: Isaac, Jacob, Moses, Aaron, Joseph, and David.

[On the second day:] May it please you, Isaac. . . .

[On the third day:] May it please you, Jacob. . . .

[On the fourth day:] May it please you, Moses. . . .

[On the fifth day:] May it please you, Aaron. . . .

[On the sixth day:] May it please you, Joseph. . . .

[On the seventh day:] May it please you, David. . . . *(Ushpizin* ritual for Sukkot)[41]

The custom of inviting the "seven shepherds" to one's sukkah originates in the Zohar, so that "when a man dwells in this dwelling, the shade of faith, the *Shekhinah* spreads her wings over him from above,[42] and Abraham and five other righteous ones make their dwelling with him. Rabbi Abba said: Abraham, five righteous ones, and King David make their dwelling with him.[43] There is just one problem with this version of the ritual: the chronological order of the seven shepherds is wrong! Why is Joseph, who should be fourth, before Moses, moved to sixth? The answer is that, as noted back in chapter 9, Joseph—who resisted sexual temptation—is associated with *Yesod.* He is thus moved to the next-to-last *sefirah,* the sixth of the seven lower *sefirot,* to correspond with his proper place in the *sefirotic* realm. Not every version of *Ushpizin* is so arranged, but this was the order followed by Luria and is the one followed in the Sephardic liturgy, also maintained by Hasidim. Other practices on Sukkot are given kabbalistic interpretations as well.[44]

The institution of *Tikkun leil Shavuot,* a Torah study session on the first night of Shavuot that initiates the celebration of God giving the Torah at Mount Sinai, may go back to the *Heikhalot* mystics,[45] and it very likely existed in some form during the time of the Zohar.[46]

May it be your will, Lord our God and God of our fathers, that our learning of what we will study tonight will bring You satisfaction, and that it will bring us satisfaction and strength so that we might continue setting the crown on the head of *Ze'ir*, and [we will] make twenty-four adornments for the *Shekhinah*, corresponding to the twenty-four books [of the Bible], which correspond to the twenty-four permutations of Your great Name. (From the prayer before study at the *Tikkun leil Shavuot*)[47]

In the sixteenth century, the *Tikkun leil Shavuot* becomes extremely prominent; Alkabetz testifies to its existence in Joseph Karo's Balkan community even before Karo came to Safed and likely Alkabetz practiced it himself in his native Salonika.[48] This particular text is based on the practice of Isaiah Horowitz,[49] and the purpose of the study session is clearly not merely to dovetail with Sinai, but to replicate it in some sense through the coronation of God and thereby to facilitate the union of *Ze'ir* (*Tiferet*) and the *Shekhinah*.

A lengthy list could be made of Sabbath and festival rituals that have been created or influenced by kabbalistic thought.[50] We will conclude with one text about Shabbat that has found its way into some contemporary prayer books.

The mystery of Sabbath: she is Sabbath as she unifies with the mysterious One, causing that One to settle upon her. Prayer for the entrance of Sabbath, for the precious Holy Throne is united in mystery of One, arrayed for the supernal Holy King to rest upon Her. When Sabbath enters, she unites, and separates from the *sitra ahra*. All evil forces of judgment are removed from her. She dwells in union with the holy light, adorned with many crowns for the Holy King. All powers of wrath and masters of judgment flee; no other power reigns in all the worlds. Her face shines with supernal radiance as she is crowned from below by the holy people, all of whom are adorned with new souls. Then, beginning prayer, blessing Her with joy and beaming faces, saying: *Barkhu et YHVH ha-Mevorakh*—"*et YHVH*," precisely, to open by addressing Her with blessing. (Zohar 2:135a–b)[51]

Every holiday has a special function in the supernal realm. In the Zohar segment prior to this one, six special days are mentioned, to parallel the six *sefirot* above the *Shekhinah*. The "mystery of Sabbath," her special function, is that she is the seventh *sefirah*, the *Shekhinah* herself. As we saw in "Lekhah Dodi," Shabbat is the time of the unification, the marriage of *Tiferet* and the *Shekhinah*. So what should take place at the critical point of transition from weekday to Shabbat? First, in this unity, the *Shekhinah* is no longer susceptible to the *sitra ahra*, the demonic powers that may attack her during the week, and so no force of judgment can prevail. Additionally, as noted above, on Shabbat Jews are blessed with a *neshamah yeteirah*, an "extra soul." This Rabbinic notion[52] is understood by the kabbalists to suggest that Israel is able to ascend higher in the *sefirotic* realm, accompanying the *Shekhinah* to her partner.

These and many other sections of the siddur indicate the enormous effect the mystical impulse has had on Jewish prayer and ritual, even when communities and congregations do not pay great attention to its power or seek to develop a more intense relationship with God. Of all varieties of Jews in existence today, it is the Hasidic world that most clearly maintains a central role for the mystical impulse. It is to the development of that world and its views that we now turn.

Part 6

Hasidism

23

The Ba'al Shem Tov and His Teachings

Why did Hasidism, a new mystical movement, come into being and flourish as it did among the Jews of Eastern Europe? Whereas early scholarship focused largely on historical factors, viewing Jewish mysticism in general and Hasidism specifically as a response to hardship and despair, more recent scholarship locates the roots of Hasidism in early expressions of Jewish mysticism.

Early scholars (and in fact most researchers through the mid-twentieth century) saw Hasidism's development as a response to historical factors that included the Cossack massacres of hundreds of thousands of Jews in the Ukraine (1648-49), the phenomenon and conversion to Islam of Sabbetai Tzvi (1666), a wave of blood libels through Poland in the early eighteenth century, and the social patterns of Jewish life in Eastern Europe, where the road to leadership (through scholarship or wealth) was open to only a very few and most Jews remained impoverished.

Also until the last century many scholars viewed Hasidism as a rejection of modernity, even though the beginnings of the Enlightenment in Western Europe happened decades after the first stirrings of Hasidic life in the 1730s and 1740s; Moses Mendelssohn (1729-86, in Dessau and Berlin), the engineer of modern Judaism's beginnings in Western Europe, was only a child at this time.

Although the above-mentioned events may have had a modest role in the development of Hasidism, more recent scholarship no longer accepts that Hasidism was a turn away from the world and toward mystical explanations and experience in the face of Jewish suffering and disappointment, nor necessarily to Sabbateanism,[1] but rather sees it as an outgrowth of Hasidic-like circles that existed well before the beginnings of an actual movement,[2] including the Hasidei Ashkenaz discussed in chapter 7. Their kabbalistic teachings were part and parcel of the mainstream of eighteenth-century Jewish thought.

In fact the first center of Hasidism, in the city of Miedzyboz, developed not at a moment of historical despair but at a time when the city and its Jews were doing rather well economically.[3] And Hasidism continues today in the United States, Israel, and other Western countries under much more favorable economic circumstances than existed in eighteenth- and nineteenth-century Eastern Europe. Furthermore, at least in the immediate geographical area of the Ba'al Shem Tov, no major economic crisis faced the Jewish community, nor were Jews in the eighteenth century much affected by persecutions like those of the seventeenth century. Taken together, these realities undermined the thesis that Hasidism developed and thrived only as a reaction to one crisis or another.

What we know is that Hasidism coalesced around a set of ideas taught to a circle of disciples who within a generation brought those ideas to large numbers of Jews in Eastern Europe. Hasidic writers trace these ideas back (or at least attribute them) to one individual, and contemporary scholars conclude that it is impossible to separate completely the teachings of the master from those of his disciples, or even the disciples' students.[4]

The initial Hasidic master and teacher was Israel, a charismatic *ba'al shem*, a healer and wonder-worker who became known simply as the Ba'al Shem Tov (or "Besht"; about 1700–1760). He had no prominent pedigree and no famous teacher,[5] but it was his disciples who transformed the landscape of Eastern European Jewry and built the great revivalist movement of Hasidism. Little is known about his early years, but he is believed to have been orphaned quite young; his education was unconventional, and he only revealed his powers as a *ba'al shem* and influential teacher at age thirty-six. It is clear that the role of wonder-worker—one that characterized a number of other major Hasidic masters—was a significant factor in the Ba'al Shem Tov's public life, giving him the status necessary to reach and affect the masses. Although the Ba'al Shem Tov may have been well acquainted with the intricacies of the Talmud, he was much more concerned that his students "seek communion with the sages as well as comprehension of their ideas."[6]

All the Hasidic groups share four common characteristics: (1) the heritage of the teachings of the Ba'al Shem Tov; (2) the central role of the tzaddik; (3) a belief that there is nothing devoid of God; and (4) a strong emphasis on *deveikut*.[7]

Virtually all Hasidic groups identify with the spiritual legacy of the Ba'al Shem Tov, even though there was no true Hasidic "court" around him and much of the movement's momentum came after his lifetime.[8] Abraham Joshua Heschel writes that in a period when "the mere fulfillment of [religious] regulations" was seen as most essential to living as a Jew, "along came the *Besht* and taught that Jewish life is an occasion for exaltation. Observance of the Law is the basis, but exaltation through observance is the goal."[9]

The following is a text from *Keter Shem Tov*, an early collection of teachings attributed to the Ba'al Shem Tov and stories about him.

> **I heard a certain Hasid tell what happened when Rabbi Dov Ber of blessed memory heard of the fame of the holy rabbi, the Ba'al Shem Tov, how all the people flock to him and how he achieves awesome and tremendous things by the power of his prayers.[10] Now Rabbi Dov Ber was a most acute scholar, thoroughly familiar with the whole of the Talmud and all the Codes, and he possessed ten measures of wisdom in the Kabbalah. Astonished at the reports he had heard concerning the high rank of the Ba'al Shem Tov, he decided he would**

journey to meet him in order to put him to the test. Since Rabbi Dov Ber was very industrious in his studies, after two or three days of his journey, during which time he was unable to concentrate on his studies with the same devotion as in his own home, he was sorry for having decided to go.

When he eventually arrived to the Ba'al Shem Tov, he thought he would hear some words of Torah from him, but instead the Ba'al Shem Tov told him a tale of how he had undertaken a journey of many days during which he had no bread to give to his gentile coach driver and how a poor gentile came along with a sack of loaves so he was able to buy bread with which to feed his driver. He told him other tales of this sort. When he came the next day, the Ba'al Shem Tov told him of how on that journey he had no fodder to give to his horses, etc. Now all these tales he related contained great and marvelous wisdom if one could only understand it, but since Rabbi Dov Ber failed to appreciate this, he returned to his inn, saying to his servant: "I wish to return home right away, but since it is so dark we shall stay on here until the moon shines brightly and then we shall be on our way."

At midnight, just as Rabbi Dov Ber was getting ready to depart, the Ba'al Shem Tov sent his servant to summon him and he heeded the summons. The Ba'al Shem Tov asked him: "Are you a scholar?" He answered in the affirmative. "So I have heard, that you are a scholar. And do you know the wisdom of the Kabbalah?" "Yes, I do," replied Rabbi Dov Ber. The Ba'al Shem Tov then instructed his servant to bring a copy of the [Lurianic] book *Eitz Hayim* and the Ba'al Shem Tov showed Rabbi Dov Ber a passage in this book. Rabbi Dov Ber looked at the passage and then expounded it to the Ba'al Shem Tov. But the Ba'al Shem Tov said: "You have not the slightest degree of understanding of this passage." So he looked at it again, and then said to the Ba'al Shem Tov, "The correct interpretation of this passage is as I have stated it, but if your honor knows of another meaning, let him tell it to me and I shall judge which is more correct."

Then the Ba'al Shem Tov said: "Arise!" and he rose to his feet. Now this particular text contained many names of angels, and no sooner did the Ba'al Shem Tov begin to recite the text than the whole house was filled with light, and fire burned around it, and they actually saw the angels mentioned in the text. He said to Rabbi Dov Ber: "It is true that the meaning of the text was as you stated it to be, but your study of it had no soul in it." On the spot Rabbi Dov Ber ordered his servant to journey home while he himself remained in the home of the Ba'al Shem Tov, from whom he learned great and deep topics of wisdom. The Hasid heard all this from the holy mouth of Rabbi Dov Ber, may his memory be for a blessing. (*Keter Shem Tov*, no. 424)[11]

Though this particular text is the stuff of legend (like a great many stories about the Ba'al Shem Tov), it contains some extremely important points. First, becoming a Hasid, a follower of the Ba'al Shem Tov, generally involves some kind of conversion experience, akin to what many Christians today describe as being "born again." Prior to his conversion Dov Ber is portrayed as being the kind of rabbi of whom early Hasidim were the most critical (see the below text on Noah): devoted to his studies, devout, but aloof from the Jewish masses.[12] Second, God is present in all things; behind the commonplace there is "great and marvelous wisdom." Indeed, as Louis Jacobs points out, the "etc.," which is part of the original text, is a common device in Hasidic (and occasionally other mystical) texts, suggesting meanings beyond what is being stated explicitly, hidden mysteries that are available to one who has the awareness to look for them. Third, apparently many Jews of the time, including many made most anxious by the development of Hasidism, seemed to understand that this phenomenon must contain at least some truth. Others who, like Dov Ber, were initially hostile (e.g., Jacob Joseph of Polonnoye, who also recorded many of the master's teachings) were similarly brought into the circle of the Ba'al Shem Tov. This happened not through superior knowledge—indeed all other evidence indicates that, strictly speaking, Dov Ber is much the greater scholar—but through the soul with which the Ba'al Shem infuses it, even the way he sings it. This also alludes to something else that readers likely understand very well by now—that one can possess much information about Kabbalah and still not enjoy a mystical experience. Like many individuals seeking greater intensity, commitment, and enthusiasm within (or beyond) their religion, the true mystic does not just want to know the names of the angels but to experience their presence.

This episode also signals the downgrading of Lurianic practices among the Hasidic masters. While the Ba'al Shem Tov is well aware of Lurianic teachings and occasionally will cite them[13]—and, as this text shows, is reputed to be capable of using them for practical ends—their knowledge and practice is not seen as essential for most Hasidim, who need not generate such wonders. As we will see, some of the Lurianic ideas were simplified and reinterpreted, suggesting a hint of the influence of Judah Loew of Prague, who managed to express kabbalistic ideas without much overt kabbalistic jargon. This text also suggests some devaluation of the intense cultivation of talmudic study; the Ba'al Shem Tov saw prayer with *kavanah* and *deveikut* as more important than knowledge of Torah. While Hasidism generally did not directly deprecate Torah study, it did not restore it to the level it had occupied until the mid-nineteenth century. As Heschel put it, Hasidism "taught that scholarship for its own sake could be an idol."[14]

This story has additional importance in light of the fact that Dov Ber, later known as the Maggid of Mezeritch, becomes the successor to the Ba'al Shem Tov, the acknowledged leader among his followers, and was primarily responsible for the development of Hasidism as a movement that would be led by his many disciples.

The second characteristic of all Hasidic groups is *the importance of the tzaddik*. Literally "the righteous one," the tzaddik is a charismatic leader who links his followers to the supernal realm.[15] While the idea of such a leader also existed in Safed in the Lurianic period, it takes on additional significance in the Hasidic setting. In this period, most rabbinic scholars played a very limited public role; traveling preachers might have exhorted the people to repent their sins, but they generally had little lasting impact. This relative vacuum left the Hasidic master much room to operate, and in some ways he became a forerunner of the modern congregational rabbi. (However, one should be cautious about viewing Hasidism as a major force for social change.)[16]

Most prominently, the tzaddik has both unlimited authority—as noted, the Ba'al Shem Tov was said to have received his from heaven through an ancient prophet—and even more so unlimited responsibility for his followers. His roles are diverse; in addition to being involved in the public affairs of the Jewish community, sometimes he functions as priest and healer, sometimes as royalty to his loyal followers, sometimes as performer of rituals akin to the Kabbalah of Abulafia that grant him prophetic wisdom,[17] and sometimes as mystic who (as noted in chapter 12) is provided a direct line to the ultimate wisdom; this enables him to provide the deepest interpretation of the Torah, without in any way undermining the existing norms of Torah study. While the tzaddik is presumably able to perform wondrous acts (and a significant part of his authority stems from the stories that detail this ability), he is also a teacher of Torah and arrives at new understandings of its text, which show that he is much more than just a charismatic figure. It is not coincidental that, as noted in chapter 9, the term "tzaddik" is associated with the *sefirah Yesod*, linking the lower and higher realms and providing a means for Hasidim to draw closer to God.[18]

The tzaddik saw his role very differently than did other rabbis of that time and place, as illustrated in this teaching attributed to the Ba'al Shem Tov:

> **"There were ten generations from Adam to Noah, to indicate how forgiving God was." (M. Avot 5:2) All the ten generations caused Him anger, but they were not punished until the generation of Noah.**

God would still have forgiven them, but Noah stirred up wrath. He brought the flood upon them.

[God told Noah:] You did not go out to save your people, to purify them and teach them how to serve their Creator, but only locked yourself in your house [which Abraham did not do]; therefore, you shall be locked up in the ark, where you will suffer. You were not a shepherd to your people, sometimes going without sleep in an effort to reach them, to help them and raise them; therefore you shall now be a shepherd to the animals and, in the work of caring for them, sleep shall vanish from your eyes. (Jacob Joseph of Polonnoye, *Ben Porat Yosef* 18c; *Toldot Ya'akov Yosef* 17b)[19]

This interpretation of the biblical text may seem far-fetched, and we must remember that the Torah is not being read as literal truth, but as a way of expressing all sorts of social and contemporary matters, often in the form of a parable. At the beginning of the story of Noah, we are told that "Noah was a righteous man in his generation" (Gen. 6:9). The question dealt with by the Rabbis is whether Noah is only righteous by the standard of his generation, a time of evil, or is righteous by *any* reasonable standard? While many commentaries regard Noah as only comparatively righteous, this teaching takes a particularly harsh view of Noah, faulting him for failing to reach out to those around him and not attempting to lift them out of their debased state. It is aimed especially at the rabbinic leaders contemporaneous with the Ba'al Shem Tov, who were generally removed from the people, studying in seclusion (like the Maggid of Mezeritch prior to his conversion) and lacking consideration for and even feeling contempt for the average Jew.

The true tzaddik must restore the unity between the leader and his people, in order to create a true bond between the people and God. The possibility exists that instead of raising them up he will be lowered to their level, but this is the chance he must take. As Samuel Dresner describes it, "To be in the world but a little above it, is the goal. Not to escape the evil thought or the evil man, but to take issue with them both, and turn them to the Lord."[20]

The Ba'al Shem Tov tempered some of Jacob Joseph's more ascetic inclinations and instead taught him less severe practices,[21] thus "converting" him from the old style of piety to his own. Jacob Joseph collected and (in the 1780s, well after the death of the Ba'al Shem Tov) published many of the Ba'al Shem Tov's teachings. This text is typical of these teachings in that the Ba'al Shem Tov emphasizes novel interpretations of Scripture and not talmudic acumen. Shaul Magid notes that Jacob Joseph "is *reintroducing* the Bible as the primary template for Jewish spirituality and, in doing so, is reinserting the Bible into a traditional Jewish world that was dominated by the study of Talmud and codes."[22]

Not only was the tzaddik accessible to the common people, but both tzaddik and the people were perceived as incomplete without the other:

The tzaddikim are the first two letters of the Divine Name. The common people are the last two letters. (Jacob Joseph of Polonnoye, *Tzafnat Paneiah*, 48d)[23]

Without a proper relationship between the tzaddik and the people, God's Name cannot be unified or the flaws in the cosmos rectified. It should also be understood that while the tzaddik must descend to the level of the people to unite with them, the Hasid also accepts the authority of the tzaddik. Regardless of whether the tzaddik lives nearby or far away, he is the Hasid's link to the higher realms. (While many moderns might look askance at this idea, it has actually expanded into non-Hasidic Orthodox Jewry in more recent times.[24]) One source of this close connection between tzaddik and the individual Hasid is an idea from medieval Kabbalah that on the supernal level the souls of different individuals may have an affinity for each other. Hence a particular tzaddik might have a special ability to assist those individuals with whom he shared the same soul "root."

The third common characteristic of Hasidic groups is *a view of divine reality as the unity of all things*; ultimately, all that exists is God.[25] Grasping this concept is a primary goal of mystical awareness. The early Hasidic teachers are fond of quoting the Zoharic dictum: *Leit atar panuy minei*: "There is nothing devoid of Him."[26] Thus, the idea of God's Oneness, as expressed in the "Shema," takes on a new understanding.

> "Hear O Israel, the Lord our God, the Lord is One" (Deut. 6:4).
>
> The term *ehad* [one] in the reading of the "Shema," which proclaims the unity of God, causes us to say there is nothing in the whole world other than the Holy One, who fills the whole earth with His glory. The principle intention [behind recitation of "Shema"] is that we should consider ourselves null and void, and understand there is nothing to us but the soul within us, which is part of God above. Hence there is nothing in the whole world except the One God.
>
> Our principal thought when reciting the word *ehad* should be that the whole earth is full of His glory and there is nothing devoid of Him. (Pinhas of Koretz, *Likkutei Amarim*, 14d)[27]

Hasidic teaching frequently emphasizes that "the whole earth is filled with His glory" (after Isa. 6:3, as noted in chapter 2) and that God is present and directly accessible everywhere. Pinhas of Koretz (d. 1790), a contemporary and friend of the Ba'al Shem Tov—perhaps better described as an admirer than a disciple[28]—takes this theme to a most forceful conclusion (to be sure, one that not all the Hasidic masters would agree with). To recite the "Shema" is to emphasize that the entire material world is an illusion, including human beings. "God is One" ultimately means that God is everything. And as the next text illustrates, He can be found everywhere, even in the most elementary activities. This is one reason why Hasidic teaching pleased the ordinary Jews, who found the stories and parables of their teachers especially appealing.

The realization that God is everywhere also led to an emphasis on joy within faith, since God's Presence would be infinitely more meaningful and joyful than the presence of a human king . . . and more accessible too. If God is so accessible, there is no need for the enormously complex meditations and *yihudim* associated with Lurianic prayer, and little if any need for self-mortification. All the tzaddik has to do is draw down the divine power and make it more available to his followers.[29]

In doing so, the tzaddik is able to perceive much more than the rest of us:

> **Do not see anything in the world as it appears, but raise your eyes to the heights, meaning the aspect of your contemplation and study, to see only the divinity clothed in all things of the world. For there is nothing besides Him, and there must be hidden holy sparks at all levels of being, granting them [those levels of being] vitality. (Zev Wolf of Zhitomer, *Or ha-Meir*, Pekudei, 85)[30]**

The notion of the "hidden holy sparks" was born in Lurianic Kabbalah, but here it is much more personal, referring to sparks that only one particular individual can claim insofar as they relate to his personal mission (whether he is aware of such a mission or not). This idea serves to unify everything within God and override any sense of the material world. Many early Hasidic masters went through a period of personal "exile," wandering from place to place, partly in sympathy with the *Shekhinah* in exile, but also seeking opportunities to uncover and elevate these fallen sparks. Once again, we find that the apparent is not the real; ordinary places and things do indeed contain holiness. If there is nothing devoid of God, not only do all things take on importance but, in a certain aspect, all things are the same:

> **"I have set [*shiviti*] God always before me" (Ps. 16:8). *Shiviti* is associated with the concept of *hishtavut*, equanimity in all things, so that whatever should happen to a person, he would consider it just the same, regardless of whether people praise him or insult him. Thus with regard to food, whether it be delicacies or anything else, everything should be the same in his eyes, since the *yetzer ha-ra* [evil impulse] will**

be entirely removed from within him. And he will say about anything that happens: "Was it not sent from the Blessed God? In His eyes, it is fitting." And all of his intentions will be for the sake of heaven. But from your own perspective, [whatever happens will make] no difference. And this is a very high level. (*Tzava'at ha-Rivash*, no. 2)[31]

Tzava'at ha-Rivash literally means "The Testament of the Ba'al Shem Tov," but the Ba'al Shem Tov himself did not write it; it probably comprises teachings heard from Dov Ber of Mezeritch, edited by his students. And it is not exactly a "testament" in the sense of a last will, but more a book of *hanhagot*, recommended practices for followers, like those mentioned in chapter 18.

Hishtavut (related to the root word *shaveh*, "equal") is an important ideal in Hasidism, drawn from earlier ethical teachings. It means that one is not affected by the opinions of the world, whether by praise or criticism, reward or punishment, or indeed by any matters that normally provide ego-satisfaction or physical gratification. While the earliest Hasidic masters did not heavily emphasize the need for humility, except for the tzaddik himself, the concept of *hishtavut* fits directly into the Hasidic program.

This popular verse, Ps. 16:8 (noted in chapter 2), is here understood to mean: because I put God before me, whatever else happens to me is all the same. If a person continually practices this principle of *hishtavut*, the evil impulse will have no power over him and nothing will shake him from his focus on God. Ultimately, this idea also depends on the concept of *deveikut*. And so we turn to the fourth common characteristic among Hasidic groups, which is the emphasis on seeking *deveikut*.

It is a great achievement to keep in mind always that you are close to the Creator and that He surrounds you on all sides, as it is written, "Happy is the man who, when he thinks not of God, it is to him as a sin" (Ps. 32:2). This means that the instant you stop thinking about your *deveikut* to God, you incur a sin.

Our *deveikut* to God should be such that we need not make a special mental effort each time to be aware of a feeling of nearness to Him. We should perceive the Creator intellectually as the Place of the world, and man as a microcosm. Thus we fulfill the verse, "I have set the Lord always before me" (Ps. 16:8). (*Keter Shem Tov*, no. 169, 42)[32]

The verse in Psalm 32 is generally translated much differently; for *Ashrei adam lo yahshov Adonai lo avon*, the NJPS translation is "Happy the man whom the Lord does not hold guilty." (*Yahshov* can mean "to consider," or simply "to think.") The Ba'al Shem Tov repunctuates and reinterprets the verse as "Happy is the man who, when he does not think about God, he considers it a sin." In other words, a person should constantly be meditating on God, that is, should be in a state of *deveikut*, so much so that when he lapses from this state he considers it a flaw, at least for himself. Indeed, it should be so normal a state for him that he requires no special effort to sustain it, and it should be strong enough to help him hold on to it in circumstances that might normally distract him from this sense of nearness to God. Thus, the Ba'al Shem Tov's reinterpretation of Ps. 32:2 virtually makes *deveikut*—rather than Torah study—into the "default" relationship with God. (While Torah study can also be a means to developing, maintaining, or deepening one's *deveikut*, this does not mean that the priorities have not changed, or that the study of Torah occasionally might not be an obstacle to *deveikut*.)

"The Place," *Ha-Makom*, is one of God's names, and the idea of God as "the Place of the world" is found in Rabbinic text.[33] Here we see an extension of what was expressed in the earlier text from Zev Wolf of Zhitomer: the physical world is within God, but God is not limited to the physical world. As noted in chapter 9, this notion is generally referred to as panentheism—distinct from the idea of pantheism, where God is held to be identical with nature and the cosmos. Drawing on previous mystics, particularly Cordovero, the Hasidic masters frequently emphasize that God "fills all worlds." Thus God is extremely near to human beings—who, after all, are considered microcosms of the divine body in Kabbalah—and *deveikut* is therefore a much more natural state than one might think. It requires no ascetic practices;[34] one can simply take one's stray thoughts and physical desires and use them to elevate the material dimensions of life, so that the soul better cleaves to the Divine.[35] This emphasis on God's "presence" rather than God's authority (although the Hasidic masters certainly do not deny God's authority) may help to explain the attraction of Hasidism today as well as in its early flourishing.[36]

In Hasidic thought the verse from Psalm 16 is a frequent expression of the goal of *deveikut*. However, as the Hasidic masters often remind us, there is also the idea that each person is *helek Eloha mi-ma'al*, "a part of God from above" (Job 31:2). Accepting this, it is easier to accept as well some form of union or reunion with God.

The significant influence of Isaiah Horowitz is apparent from the emphasis on the importance of *deveikut* as a spiritual practice and making it a natural part of one's relationship with God: one should compare this teaching of the Ba'al Shem Tov (and many other Hasidic teachings on *deveikut*) with the text from Horowitz's *Shnei Luhot ha-Brit* noted in chapter 10.

It is not clear that the Ba'al Shem Tov intended *deveikut* as normative practice beyond an elite; generally it is the tzaddik whose strong *deveikut* enables others to achieve some *deveikut*, albeit at a lower level. It is the tzaddik who serves as the bridge between people and God, and he is obliged to fulfill this responsibility.

In chapter 10, a teaching of the Ba'al Shem Tov says: "When you have *deveikut* with God . . . . you are alive in essence." God *is* life; if you are connected to God, you are, as it were, alive "in essence." But if you are not connected to God, you just happen to be alive. *Deveikut* might be said to "recharge" a person with the essence of life.

"But you who cleave to the Lord your God are alive every one of you this day" (Deut. 4:4). This means that *deveikut* is the cause of true

life. When you have *deveikut* with God, the life of life, you are alive in essence. When you interrupt your *deveikut*, you are alive only by accident. Just as heat is of the essence of fire, but is only accidental to water, so that the heat does not endure when the water is removed from the flame [so it is with *deveikut*].

Regarding *deveikut*, the sages remarked on the verse "and to cleave to Him" (Deut. 11:22): "How can one cleave to Him? Is not God "a devouring fire" (Deut. 4:24)? But it means to cleave to His attributes."[37] This means cleaving to Him through the Torah. The Ba'al Shem Tov also said: Surely when you are occupied with prayer and Torah, which is wholly composed of God's Name, you ought to be in a state of strong *deveikut*, and when performing your mundane activities the rest of the day, you should still have some *deveikut*, fulfilling the mitzvah: "I have set God always before me" (Ps. 16:8).

To what may this be compared? To a candle or a burning coal. As long as there is still a living spark in it, the flame can be revived. If not even a spark is left, however, the fire must be produced anew. (*Keter Shem Tov*, 1:84, 11b)[38]

We read the Rabbinic interpretations of *deveikut* in chapter 10, but here they are interpreted as cleaving to God through prayer and Torah. The notion of the whole Torah as one name of God goes back to Nahmanides, in the thirteenth century.[39] In this view, the deeper, secret meaning of the Torah is that it is a way to connect with God Himself. Thus in both prayer and Torah study, one essentially meditates on God's Name, thus fulfilling the verse from Psalm 16 once again. And one requires a stronger form of *deveikut* during those activities, so that one can maintain some level of it at other times. Conversely, if one allows the "spark" to be extinguished during mundane activities, it is harder to reignite it during prayer and Torah study.

The earliest Hasidic masters emphasized maintaining *deveikut* within the mundane and thereby elevating the mundane to a higher level, often expressed as *avodah b'gashmiut*, the worship of God through physical acts, understood as an extension of the idea of God's Presence in all places. Although some Hasidic leaders advocated the rejection of material concerns,[40] other masters sought to infuse material reality with a maximum of holiness. For instance, instead of fasting, the Hasid is directed to meditate on the holy sparks within the food he eats and on the ultimate source of the holiness that provides him with energy. One does not abstain from permitted marital sex, but brings to it a heightened awareness of the act's holiness, acknowledging the beauty and pleasure it gives the Creator. Thus, worship is not confined to "spiritual" matters; matter is made spiritual.

The tzaddik is able to take the *yesh*, the physical, revealed world, and make it serve the *ayin*, the spiritual, concealed world:

> **"The acts of the righteous [tzaddikim] are greater than the making of Heaven and earth."[41] This means that the act of Creation involved the emergence of something [*yesh*] out of nothing [*ayin*], whereas the tzaddikim involve turning something into nothing. For in whatever they do, even if it is something physical like eating, they raise up the holy sparks within that food, and so in all they do, they convert something into [the divine] nothing. (Rabbi Dov Ber of Mezeritch, *Maggid Devarav l'Ya'akov*, 24, no. 12)[42]**

The talmudic text cited in the above refers to Torah sages in general, suggesting that through their deeds they take the Creation to its ultimate purpose. But here the Maggid refers to the Hasidic tzaddik and his concentration on *bittul ha-yesh*, the nullification of the self, turning the self to *ayin*, seemingly to "nothingness," but actually to the infinite God who cannot be understood. Thus he is able to "convert something into nothing." Although this emphasis is not new and actually appears in one of the major codes of Jewish law[43]—suggesting that this either was or should have been widespread—it is frequently noted in early Hasidic thought.

Finally, here is an early Hasidic text (from a book compiled by

Menahem Mendel of Vitebsk, a disciple of Dov Ber of Mezeritch) showing just how intense *deveikut* could be in the Hasidic view: virtual mystical union!

> *Deveikut* means that there should be nothing separating [one from God]; then one can have *deveikut*. The Ba'al Shem Tov provides an analogy: just as it is impossible to glue two pieces of silver except by scraping clean the two places where the glue is to adhere, so too, between God and the person there can be no "rust" or anything separating. (*P'ri ha-Aretz*, Ki Tissa, 13b)[44]

We have examined some fundamentals of early Hasidism and those aspects that remain common denominators of Hasidic thought today. The charismatic personality of the Ba'al Shem Tov led to the development of a movement that emphasized powerful leaders, often with great magnetism in their own right, as well as a new emphasis on ecstatic prayer. These are themes that we will encounter again in the next chapter.

24

The Role of Prayer and the Ba'al Shem Tov's Successors

Hasidism is often associated with ecstatic experiences in prayer, and a concept vital to the Hasidic view of prayer is *hitlahavut*, from the root *l-h-v*, meaning "flame." *Hitlahavut* is thus "being aflame,"[1] in a state of rapture or ecstasy; it conveys the sense that prayer ought to take one beyond Normal Mysticism, into an enthusiastic, passionate yearning for God's Presence. Such an experience is unlikely to happen with regularity; however, once one has had such a rapturous moment, it becomes a "base line" for one's spiritual life, contributing to the ongoing striving for the less intense feeling of *deveikut*. Thus, as Heschel declared, "Jewish life is an occasion for exaltation. Observance of the Law is the basis, but exaltation through observance is the goal."[2]

Zussia was a disciple of the holy Dov Ber, the Maggid of Mezeritch. But he was a most remarkable pupil, this Zussia! In all the years he spent at Mezeritch, he never heard a single exposition of the word of God from the lips of his famous teacher. The holy Dov Ber would open the book and begin to read: "And the Lord has spoken," and that was enough for dear Zussia. He was seized by such ecstasy as soon as he heard those four words that he was unable to listen further. This happened each time. Whenever he heard the words, "The Lord has spoken," he was carried away in rapture. He would begin to shout at the top of his voice: "The Lord has spoken! The Lord has spoken!" and would not

stop, so that his famous fellow disciples were obliged to put him out into the courtyard to have some peace and quiet. Zussia offered no resistance. He had no idea at all what was going on. His whole body shook. In the courtyard he would continue his shouting: "The Lord has spoken! The Lord has spoken!" and throw himself about like an epileptic. It was always a long time before he quieted down. When he was finally able to return, the master's exposition would already be over long since. Thus it was that Zussia never heard a single exposition by the holy Dov Ber. We call this sort of ecstasy *hitlahavut*. (Dov Ber of Mezeritch, a story of Zussia, disciple of the Maggid)[3]

Before beginning to pray, one should reflect that he is prepared to die while praying, as a result of his concentration. There are actually some whose concentration in prayer is so intense that, were nature left to itself, they would die after only five or six words in the presence of the blessed God. Once he thinks of this, he will say to himself: "Why should I have any hidden motive or pride while praying," since he is prepared to die after only a few words. In reality, it is [through] the blessed God's great mercy that He gives him strength to complete his prayer and remain alive. (*Keter Shem Tov*, no. 168)[4]

The second text addresses a serious challenge to meaningful prayer: when I pray, how do I avoid thinking of myself, and just think of God? The simple answer is to focus on self-nullification, which is potentially permanent! If one takes it seriously, this kind of prayer is an intense and even dangerous business. When one truly "burns" with fervor in prayer, it is possible to "burn up" and "extinguish" oneself.

One of the most consistent advocates for *hitlahavut* and one of the most famous Hasidic masters was Levi Yitzhak of Berditchev (1740–1809), a disciple of Dov Ber of Mezeritch. Levi Yitzhak's love for his fellow Jews was legendary. His fervent devotion was matched by the passion of his challenges to God, and many stories are told of defiant prayers he hurled at the Almighty, pleading for mercy for his people. He came to Hasidism as a young married man with an embarrassed, prominent father-in-law who regarded his son-in-law's growing attachment to Hasidism as foolishness. The frustrated father-in-law said to him: "I forgive you everything, if you will just tell me what you've learned with the Maggid that is so special." Levi Yitzhak responded simply: "There is a God in Heaven who created the world." His father-in-law exclaimed: "Who doesn't know that?" He called in the maid and asked her, "Do you know who created the world?" Surprised at being asked such a question, she said: "God in Heaven!" But Levi Yitzhak said: "Yes, anyone can say this, but only one who has learned from the mouth of the Great Maggid can know it."[5]

As a young rabbi, Levi Yitzhak was run out of rabbinic positions three times. Only when he settled in Berditchev, in the northern Ukraine, did things begin to go well, and he made his community into a major center of Hasidism. He served as a tzaddik for his Hasidim (and helped to shape the role of the tzaddik) and spread Hasidic teachings through his writing, including his *Kedushat Levi* (published beginning in 1798).

> A person should [always] pray with great *hitlahavut*. However, at present, due to our many transgressions, we have such weakened consciousness, we are not able to begin and immediately pray with great *hitlahavut*, but only reach such vitality halfway through our service. However, when the righteous Messiah comes—may it be soon!—then all will know the Lord, as it is written: "The earth will be filled with the knowledge of the Lord as the waters cover the sea" (Isa. 11:9). Then we will immediately be able to begin [prayer] with *hitlahavut* and great fire. (*Kedushat Levi*, Levi Yitzhak of Berditchev, 290a)[6]

For Levi Yitzhak, the goal is constant *hitlahavut*. His distress is not because we cannot attain it . . . but because we cannot attain it immediately! When all is set right in the Messianic Age, we will have *hitlahavut* as soon as we desire. While Levi Yitzhak is a strong believer in Torah study and the performance of all the mitzvot, the distinction that makes the difference is *hitlahavut* in prayer, which is consistent with the Ba'al Shem Tov's teachings. This led to a much greater respect for the prayer of the ordinary Jew, which could also be performed with *hitlahavut*.[7] Indeed, for Levi Yitzhak, it seems that the key to the fulfillment of every mitzvah is the enthusiasm behind it.

In *hitlahavut* one may "lose" one's self . . . which fits with other Hasidic ideas about prayer, most especially *bittul ha-yesh* (self-nullification) and the management of stray thoughts during one's devotion. This is the theme of the next text, in which we will compare Joseph Karo's standard code, the *Shulhan Arukh*, with the Hasidic approach to prayer.

> One who prays must direct his heart to the meaning of the words he brings forth from his lips, as if the *Shekhinah* were before him. He must remove all troubling thoughts, leaving only his pure intention in prayer. He should consider it as if he were speaking before a king of flesh and blood, for whom he would order his words carefully and with much intentionality, so that he would not stumble. All the more should he do so before the king of all kings, the Holy One, Blessed be He, who plumbs all thoughts. This is what the pious [Hasidim] and men of accomplishment would do, sitting in solitude and directing their prayers until they would be stripped of corporeality, and strengthen[ing] their intellect until they come near the level of prophecy. And if some other thought would come to them during prayer, they would be silent until this thought would be nullified, thinking of matters which would subdue the heart and redirect it toward the Heavenly Father, and not of matters which divert them. (*Shulhan Arukh*, O. H. 98:1)

> "If I am not for myself, who will be for me? But if I am for myself, what am I?" (Pirkei Avot 1:14) When in prayer, you must be stripped of corporeality and not feel your self-existence in this world. This is

what Hillel meant in saying: "If I am not for myself, who will be for me"; if I arrive at the state where I no longer know or feel myself, not knowing if I am in this world or not, then I no longer fear stray thoughts. For what stray thought can occur to me!

But "if I am for myself," if I consider myself as having separate existence in this world, then, on the contrary, I am regarded as nothing, so "what am I," what is my service worth before the blessed God? For then, stray thoughts disturb me, and I am as nothing in this world. The essential purpose of one's creation in this world is divine service, but I cannot do this [properly] because I am disturbed by stray thoughts. (*Tzava'at ha-Rivash*, no. 62)[8]

Even the *Shulhan Arukh* sets a high standard for prayer, though it may be argued that this is a standard only for exceptional individuals (the pious and the accomplished), particularly since it even speaks of arriving at prophecy. While the Hasidic text is rooted in the *Shulhan Arukh*, borrowing much of its language, it goes even further, suggesting that this standard of self-nullification is the only way to avoid any distraction in prayer. If one is bothered by stray thoughts, it is because one is "for himself," too caught up in the physical concerns of his existence.

There are those who serve the blessed God with their human intellect, and others whose gaze is fixed as if on *Ayin* [nothingness], and this is impossible without divine help. . . . He who is granted this supreme degree, with divine help, to contemplate the *Ayin*, loses the reality of his intellect and he is as if stricken dumb . . . but when he returns from such a contemplation to the essence of [his] intellect, he finds it full of the divine splendor [*shefa*]. (*Kedushat Levi*, Pekudei, 176)[9]

Levi Yitzhak here refers to normal prayer, and to a level beyond normal prayer, possible through God's grace, in which the person surrenders his intellect (similar to the previous text above, in which he surrenders any sense of his corporeal self).[10] As we read in chapter 8, *Ayin* is the opposite of *Yesh*, the material, visible world. Levi Yitzhak says elsewhere, "*Ayin* is the way in which all things are maintained beyond nature, and *Yesh* is the way that nature is . . . since the imperceptible is implied in *Ayin* and the perceptible is implied in *Yesh*."[11] All things live in polarity, resolved within God who alone is One.

What is new here is that when a person returns from this intense contemplation of the *Ayin*, of what is normally hidden from our perceptions, he comes back with a large dose of God's *shefa*, the overflow of grace that both sustains and gives glory to the universe. In other words, mystical experience is ultimately not merely a form of intense engagement with God; it is life changing. When one has *mohin d'gadlut*, a form of higher consciousness that transcends our normal physical and mental boundaries, we bring back something else from the experience, which leads us to new realizations in the future.

The Ba'al Shem Tov generally advocated a "balanced" practice in prayer, but if prayer did not have at least a minimum of *kavanah*, it was considered totally ineffective. We will see evidence of both positions in the following texts. Hasidism covers a range of positions on this and other issues; as will be explained in chapter 25, many Hasidic masters took quite different roads, while still maintaining fidelity to the path of the Ba'al Shem Tov as they understood it.

Once the Ba'al Shem Tov and his disciples were on a journey. In a forest along the way, they chanced upon an abandoned synagogue and decided to pray the *Minha* [afternoon] service there. The disciples opened the door and invited their master to be the first to enter. Just as he was about to step inside, the holy Ba'al Shem Tov stopped and would not cross the threshold. The Hasidim were perplexed but reluctant to question their master. But after a while, when the sun began to set and it would soon be too late for *Minha*, they summoned up the courage to ask why he would not enter. The Ba'al Shem Tov replied, "I can't go in because it is so crowded; there is no room for us." The Hasidim were astounded, because the synagogue was empty. Taking note of their confusion, he explained: "A prayer, when uttered sincerely and wholeheartedly, always sprouts wings and soars upward to the Throne of Glory of the Creator Himself. But I sense that the people who once prayed here had no *kavanah*. Their prayers had no wings and collapsed and fell upon another, so that the building is now densely packed with dead, wingless prayers—and there is no room for us." (A story of the Ba'al Shem Tov)[12]

One may be assured that the abandoned synagogue (in this likely apocryphal story) was a non-Hasidic synagogue where the formal rules of prayer were stringently observed. Perhaps the absence of *kavanah* is the very reason why the synagogue has been abandoned; in a sense, it has been ruined through its misuse.

How, then, does one achieve *kavanah*, concentration in prayer? As noted, the Ba'al Shem Tov rejected the path of self-mortification and instead sought to accept and then elevate one's thoughts. One of his associates, Rabbi Nahman of Horodenka (who was born about 1680 and apparently outlived the Ba'al Shem Tov), testified that despite immersions in extreme cold and heat, "I was unable to free myself of straying thoughts until I had been converted to the wisdom of the Besht."[13]

I heard a teaching in the name of my teacher [the Ba'al Shem Tov] on the talmudic directive: "Rabbi Zeira said: 'Whoever says "*Shema, Shema*," is silenced.' Rav Pappa said to Abaye: 'Perhaps [he repeated himself because] he did not have *kavanah* at first.' Abaye answered: 'Who treats one's relationship with Heaven as a casual friendship? If he didn't have proper *kavanah* at first, he deserves to be jabbed with the blacksmith's poker until he does!'"[14]

And my teacher challenged this, saying: "But the question still remains! Perhaps the person actually did not have proper *kavanah* at first, and now wants to fulfill his responsibility and pray with proper *kavanah*! Furthermore, why did Rabbi Zeira choose the *Shema* in explaining this law, rather than some other verse?" The Ba'al Shem Tov answered by examining the meaning of accepting the responsibility of the Kingship of Heaven [*kabbalat ol malkhut shamayim*]. One is obligated to believe that the whole earth is filled with His blessed glory, and no place is devoid of His Presence ... even with all one's thoughts! His blessed reality is within them, and every thought has in it the entire divine being.

So if an unseemly or strange thought comes to a person during prayer, [he should understand that] it came so that he can rectify and elevate it. If he does not believe this to be so, it indicates that his acceptance of the responsibility of the Kingship of Heaven is not complete, for he denies God's Presence [within the thought]. This is how we can understand the teaching of the Talmud about "*Shema, Shema.*" (Jacob Joseph of Polonnoye, *Ben Porat Yosef*, 38d–39a)[15]

The talmudic passage has a straightforward explanation. "Shema" is not to be repeated, for this would suggest more than one divine power. When it is proposed to Abaye (late third to early fourth century CE, Babylonia) that one might be repeating it only because he failed to say it with the required *kavanah* initially, Abaye responds sarcastically that no one should have the chutzpah to recite "Shema" without preparing his thoughts properly.

Noting that the question was not really addressed, the Ba'al Shem Tov explains that the real problem is that if one were to repeat "Shema" for this reason, it would be because of a failure to recognize the greater need of the moment: to take the stray thought that interfered with one's *kavanah* and raise that thought to a higher level. We have already seen that Hasidism teaches that "there is no place devoid of God"; this is true even of such stray thoughts. Even our sinful thoughts can be redirected and elevated. Similarly Levi Yitzhak of Berditchev taught that a lower form of "love" could be purified by joining it to God.[16]

This may also remind readers of an idea previously observed (see particularly chapter 16), that even the *yetzer ha-ra*, the "evil impulse," serves God. Our next text presents a further example of this.

> **From the Ba'al Shem Tov: Once there was a king who ruled strictly, and sent one of his servants to test his subject provinces by pretending he was a servant in rebellion against his master. Several of the subject provinces took up combat against him [the servant] and prevailed over him, while others went along with him. But in one state, there were wise men who sensed that this was all at the request of the king. The moral is clear: there are some who combat the evil impulse . . . resisting him until they conquer their impulse through severe combat and self-mortifications. And there are others who feel that he is carrying out the will of the Creator. (*Keter Shem Tov*, no. 115)[17]**

If the *yetzer ha-ra* is indeed "the will of the creator," then we should not try to eradicate it or triumph over it, but work *with* it.[18] Otherwise, all one's rigorous efforts are simply obstacles to God's will. The physical world is not only not to be rejected, it is to be celebrated as a means to appreciate the higher realms.

An important theme in Hasidic thought is how spiritual thought (as opposed to simply intellectual thought) elevates the mundane to the Divine. We have seen this in Mainline Kabbalah and will consider examples here.

> **Consider that just as you contemplate material things, you contemplate the *Shekhinah*'s presence beside you. This is called *avodah b'katnut* [service through lesser consciousness]. In this state you may occasionally comprehend that there are many spherical heavens encircling you, while you stand on a point of this small planet earth; the whole world is as nothing compared to the Creator, who is the *Ein Sof* who performed the *tzimtzum* and made space within Himself to create the worlds. Even if you understand this intellectually, you are unable to ascend to the upper worlds. This is the meaning of**

"From afar the Lord appeared unto me" (Jer. 31:2), that we see God only from a distance.

But through worshiping God with *gadlut* [greater consciousness], you strengthen yourself with great force and ascend in your thought, penetrating all the heavens at once, rising beyond the angels and the *ofanim* and the seraphim and the Thrones. This is perfect worship. (*Tzava'at ha-Rivash*, no. 137)[19]

Katnut, lesser consciousness, is here understood as just an intellectual contemplation, a feeling of being just an insignificant part of the cosmos. But through a full giving over of one's spirit, one arrives at a more powerful form of *deveikut* that crashes through all obstacles; all it takes to go from the mundane to the Divine is one's thought or, more precisely, one's spiritual commitment to a certain directed thought. Such thought pushes one beyond the physical senses and even the visible heavens (the mention of "the angels and the *ofanim* and the seraphim and the Thrones" is an allusion to the Four Worlds discussed previously). This principle was expressed elsewhere by Jacob Joseph of Polonnoye: "Man must believe that God's glory fills the earth, that there is no place devoid of Him, and all human thoughts contain His being, and each thought presents a divine entity."[20]

Paradox is frequently a significant factor in Hasidic texts, often effectively engaging the rebbe's followers. This is particularly true of the following tale told of another Hasidic master, Rabbi Israel of Ruzhin (1796–1850).

In the name of Hasidic leader R. Israel of Ruzhin, the story is told of a certain young man who was living at his father-in-law's house in a town dominated by the opponents of Hasidism. He had promised his father-in-law on a handshake [with the validity of an oath] that he would not travel to visit the Maggid of Mezeritch, but his desire to go could not be restrained; he broke his promise and traveled to

Mezeritch on more than one occasion. His father-in-law consulted the town's rabbi and was told that, according to the *halakhah*, his daughter must be divorced from her husband. Once the couple were divorced, the young man was thrown out of his father-in-law's house and remained penniless. He lived in the *beit midrash* [study house] until he fell ill and died. The rebbe of Ruzhin concluded the story with the following insight. "When the Messiah comes, this young man will take his case to a court of law presided over by the Messiah himself. He will summon his father-in-law and charge him with having caused his death but the father-in-law will defend himself on the grounds that he had simply followed the ruling of the town's rabbi. The town's rabbi will be summoned next and he will point to the *halakhic* basis for his ruling. The Messiah will then wish to know why the young man had broken his promise to his father-in-law, and the young man will plead: I was very eager to visit the rebbe! The Messiah will pronounce as follows. To the father-in-law he will say: You followed the ruling of the town's rabbi and you have acted justly. To the rabbi he will say: You ruled according to the *halakhah* and you have acted justly. But I, the Messiah, will say: I have come to those who have acted unjustly!" (Hasidic story)[21]

This text refers to the opponents of Hasidism in its early generations, generally known as *Mitnagdim*: "opponents," precisely. The *Mitnagdim* did not oppose Hasidism because they were opposed to mysticism; on the contrary, they themselves generally accepted the kabbalistic theology. However, they accepted the idea that kabbalistic knowledge should be limited to a small elite, due to their pessimistic view of the average Jew's capacities. To some extent this may be a result of the influence of the Hasidei Ashkenaz, who centuries earlier emphasized the power of the *yetzer ha-ra* and the need for vigilance against it. Hasidic masters were much more optimistic about the ability of their followers to aspire to and achieve a higher spiritual life.[22]

God's rules are supposed to be set out in the *halakhah*. But when the *halakhah* leads to injustice, the Messiah—or his stand-in, the tzaddik—must protest, even by holding God responsible. Levi Yitzhak especially was known as one who stood up to God in such situations. It is understood that everyone else must do their part, but that is not enough; as Samuel Dresner summarizes, "the people must repent, the leader must purify himself, but God also must take pity."[23]

The use of parables plays an important role for many Hasidic masters, most effectively among them Rabbi Nahman of Bratslav (1772–1811). (His longer stories, told near the end of his life, are also deserving of significant study.) Nahman was the great-grandson of the Ba'al Shem Tov, but he sought his own unique path. His approach emphasized a much more powerful reliance on faith and is often contrasted with the more complex mysticism of other early Hasidic masters.[24] Often in dispute with other Hasidic leaders and maintaining what seems to have been a small but extremely loyal following, he eventually settled in Bratslav in 1802, then leaving for Uman the year before he died. Though he died quite young and without enormous success, Bratslaver Hasidism has continued without ever replacing him with another rebbe. They are thus occasionally referred to as the "dead Hasidim"; thousands still make pilgrimages to his grave in Uman in the Ukraine, particularly for Rosh Hashanah. Perhaps they feel less need for another leader because the exceptional intensity and beauty of his writing provides as much access as they need.[25]

The evil impulse is like a prankster running through a crowd showing his tightly closed hand. No one knows what he is holding. He goes up to each one and asks, "What do you suppose I have in my hand?" Each one imagines the closed hand contains just what he desires most. They all hurry and run after the prankster. Then, when he has tricked them all into following him, he opens his hand; it is completely empty.

The same is true of the evil impulse. He fools the world, tricking it into following him. All men think his hand contains what they desire. But in the end, he opens his hand; there is nothing in it and no desire is ever fulfilled. So it is with all worldly pleasures, which are like sunbeams in a dark room. They may actually seem solid, but one who tries to grasp a sunbeam finds nothing in his hand. The same is true of all worldly desires. (Nathan of Nemirov, *Sihot ha-Ran*, no. 6)[26]

What really *is* the evil impulse within us? For Rabbi Nahman, it is the vain struggle for whatever worldly pleasure we desire, which we may believe will magically bring us happiness and fulfillment. Paradoxically, if we follow it, we wind up with nothing, or at least nothing of any substance. Rabbi Nahman thus indirectly advocates turning away from the matters of this world, in favor of the *bittul ha-yesh*, the self-nullification advocated by other Hasidic thinkers.

This is another example of diversity within Hasidism. Whereas Nahman is unusually inclined to asceticism, with an extra dose of concern about sexual desire (see below in this chapter for a striking example), most Hasidic masters, even those who emphasized self-nullification, did not accept the need for fasting more than the law required, let alone refraining from permitted sexuality. As we have read, they preferred to seek *avodah b'gashmiut*, service to God through elevation of the physical and its desires, sometimes (as above) referred to as "stray thoughts."

Once there was a prince who had lost his mind and thought he was a turkey. He would sit naked under a table and eat the crumbs and bones off the floor. All the doctors lost hope of curing him from this malady, and the king was very sad.

Finally, a person came and said that he would cure him. This wise man removed his clothing and joined the king's son under the table. "Who are you and what are you doing here?" asked the son. "Who are *you* and what are *you* doing here?" said the wise man. "I am a turkey," said the son. "I am also a turkey," said the wise man. So they both sat there together for some time until they grew accustomed to each other.

Then the wise man signaled, and shirts were given to him. The wise man said, "Do you think that a turkey cannot wear a shirt? One can wear a shirt and still be a turkey." So they both put on a shirt.

After a while, he signaled and some pants were given to him. He told the son, "Do you think that if you wore pants, you would not be a turkey anymore? One could wear pants and still be a turkey." Soon they both put on the pants, and so on.

Then he signaled and human food was given to him, and he said to the king's son: "Do you think that if one eats human food, one cannot remain a turkey? We can eat and still be turkeys."

Then he said: "One can be a turkey and eat while sitting at a table." He finally cured the king's son completely.

The moral here is self-explanatory. Should one say that one who wants to become close to God cannot do so for he is like a turkey, in the sense that he is human and materialistic? That is not so; step by step one can come closer and closer to serving God until he succeeds. (Nahman of Bratslav, *Sippurim Nifla'im* [Wondrous stories])[27]

This text's final paragraph may have been added by the editor; the moral of the story is not quite so "self-explanatory"! A counselor might well explain the story by saying that if you want to help someone, you have to gain rapport with them and see the world from their viewpoint. This also relates to the role of the tzaddik; in order to repair the souls of his followers, he must descend to their level. And the mystic might also explain this story with reference to the idea of "descent for the sake of ascent" (see chapter 19, and also chapter 21 on the Sabbatean phenomenon), going into the lowest levels of existence in order to raise up the holy sparks. Sin is an extraordinarily powerful force, a barrier to *deveikut*, and the tzaddik has to take radical measures to help his followers overcome it. Here Nahman differs significantly from most of the early Hasidic masters, who saw the gulf between God and humankind as an illusion.

Nahman saw no salvation in reason or science; he frequently disparaged the developing field of medicine and strongly urged reliance on faith alone.[28] This factor, among others, led him to an intense longing for messianic redemption.

Nathan of Nemirov was Nahman's leading disciple and transmitter of his teachings.

> **Copulation is difficult for the true tzaddik. Not only does he have no desire for it at all, but he experiences real suffering in the act, suffering which is like that which the infant undergoes when he is circumcised. This very same suffering, to an even greater degree, is felt by the tzaddik during intercourse. The infant has no awareness, so his suffering is not so great. But the tzaddik, because he is aware of the pain, suffers more greatly than does the infant. (Nathan of Nemirov, _Shivhei ha-Ran_, no. 17)[29]**

The true tzaddik in this text, of course, is Nahman himself. Some may jump to the conclusion that Nahman was a closeted homosexual; this is far from clear, and Nahman seemed to want to eliminate _all_ sexual desire.[30] As his biographer, Arthur Green, notes, Nahman pays a high price for his mastery of his sexual activity, and the theme of sexual guilt and the dangers of sex consistently recur in his teaching.[31]

Finally, we see how Dov Ber reinterprets the Lurianic idea of the "breaking of the vessels":

> **A king commanded his servants to raise up a very large mountain, removing it from its place—an impossible task! So his servants decided among themselves to dig and break up [sh-v-r] the mountain into tiny pieces, so that each person would be able to carry a small portion appropriate to his own particular strength. And in this way they carried out the king's command.**

Similarly in this way, God, the King of the universe, commands us to raise up the holy sparks. . . . And it was for this very purpose that the *shevirah* [breaking of the vessels] came about, so that each person might then be able to raise up the fallen sparks, each one according to his own spiritual level. (Dov Ber of Mezeritch, *Or Torah*, on Ps. 126:1, 47a)[32]

In this parable, the "breaking up" of the mountain turns out to be the "breaking up" of the vessels. But in Lurianic Kabbalah, the *shevirat ha-kelim* was a catastrophe; in Hasidism, it is a means to a greater end through which every person will raise up the holy sparks and assist in the repair of the universe. The impossible task of Lurianic *tikkun* is thus "chunked down" into more manageable goals for each individual.

The emphasis on intensity in prayer and the role of the tzaddik continued after the deaths of the Ba'al Shem Tov and Dov Ber, the Maggid of Mezeritch. The ordinary Jew understood from early Hasidic teaching that even though he was not highly learned, God nevertheless depended on him for the positive functioning of His creation.

How would Hasidism develop after the initial generation of leadership? And as it became an established movement, how would it maintain and promote the mystical impulse? This is the question to be addressed next.

25

The Growth of Hasidism
and Its Search for Truth

The initial Hasidic masters were the students of Dov Ber, the Maggid of Mezeritch. But as they established leadership in various towns throughout Eastern Europe, no centralized leadership emerged after the death of Dov Ber. Instead, most of these leaders established their own dynasties in their communities, with the leadership now passing to their children rather than to other charismatic disciples. Furthermore, as Hasidism became more accepted as part of the established Jewish community, many of these Hasidic "courts" became more affluent, and the tzaddik often lived much more lavishly than his predecessors. Additionally, by this time Hasidic masters had become extremely astute at placing their followers in various offices and institutions within the Jewish communities in their region, thus expanding their own powers. Finally, different trends developed among the various Hasidic groups. Some emphasized the role of the individual charismatic teacher, the tzaddik; others stressed more the specific teachings of the tzaddik or of the founding generations of Hasidism.

We have touched on how the tzaddik exhibited different aspects of leadership in promoting the goals of mystical activity within the framework of Hasidic life.[1] The tzaddik absorbed much of the role of *ba'al shem* as healer and source of blessing. He used symbols of royalty, as befits one believed to have great cosmic power. (Menahem Mendel Schneerson, the seventh Chabad leader, was hailed not only as Messiah but as

Ha-Melekh Ha-Mashiah, "King Messiah"; see chapter 26). Tzaddikim used terms suggesting their own high capacity for revelation, falling just short of prophecy, as they discussed prophetic dreams and the "holy spirit." When they taught of the *sefirot*, they often tended to "psychologize" them, focusing on their qualities so that the average listener could actually imagine these qualities within his own character.[2] And of course they fulfilled the traditional role of rabbi, as scholars who learned and taught Torah and as symbolic exemplars of the Jewish tradition as a whole. Perhaps these features of Hasidic leadership could (and often do) inform leadership in the broader society, an issue that deserves further study. Maintaining personal balance while carrying out the symbolic aspects of leadership often proved enormously challenging for the Hasidic masters, as will be seen more than once among the thinkers addressed in this chapter.

Rather than examining the broad sweep of Hasidic thought, we will here survey the thought of several Hasidic masters in a particularly interesting school of tzaddikim that stretched from the late eighteenth century through the mid-nineteenth century. The first of these is Jacob Isaac Horowitz (1745-1815), also known as the *Hozeh*, the Seer of Lublin. A disciple of Dov Ber and a student of other prominent Hasidic masters, he was believed to have clairvoyant powers even as a youth; and his leadership established Hasidism as a major force in central Poland. His court was renowned for being particularly joyous, as expressed in a story about Naftali Tzvi of Ropshitz, the assistant to the Seer. He was once asked why the Seer and his followers didn't bring the Messiah. He answered: "I'll tell you the truth; it was so good [being with the Seer] that we forgot to bring him."[3] But the Seer was especially emphatic about the need for the tzaddik to produce results—supernaturally, if necessary—to meet the needs of his followers.

"If there is no bread, there is no Torah." (Pirkei Avot 3:17) It is incumbent upon the tzaddik to be occupied with Torah, precisely in order

to draw down bread [sustenance]. For it is known that the light and holiness of the Blessed God is garbed in the letters of the Torah . . . he must be able to draw down from above [to meet] the needs of people on earth, provide ample sustenance before anything else . . . his first goal should be [to see] that they have their needs, before [causing] the world to return in repentance. (Jacob Isaac Horowitz, *Zikaron Zot*, 71)[4]

While the Seer accepted the role of tzaddik, he believed it to be primarily for the benefit of the community and its material needs. Why does the tzaddik study Torah, perform the commandments, or otherwise seek communion with God? Not for his own sake, certainly, nor even—at least not initially—for the spiritual well-being of the people, but first of all for the people's physical needs. The Seer, who was raised in security and stability, came to realize that this was a prerequisite for his own spiritual development and would probably be so for most of his followers.[5] Paradoxically, as Byron Sherwin notes, "the most spiritual person, performing the most spiritual acts, must produce the most concrete and material results."[6] Perhaps this is why (as noted briefly in chapter 21) the Seer felt compelled to strive for the coming of the Messiah, the ultimate concrete result.

Horowitz was far from alone among the early Hasidim in understanding his prayer as having effects in the material world; for instance, Rabbi Jacob Joseph of Polonnoye wrote: "The quintessence of the intention [of the prayer] is that the person who prays should direct his intention to cause the descent of the spirituality from the supernal degrees to the letters that he pronounces, so that these letters will be able to ascend to the supernal degree, in order to perform his request."[7] If the tzaddik really has any role in the higher worlds, he has to be able to draw down from them something substantial. The Seer clearly believed he provided this, even to the most worldly of his supporters.

Anyone blessed with the clairvoyant powers the Seer was understood to possess might well misuse those powers. The Seer confirms in the following text that he will only use those powers for purposes God sees as appropriate.

> I do not pray for anything unless I see in advance whether it is the divine will to pray for it. (Jacob Isaac Horowitz, *Zikhron Devarim*, 149)[8]

Even at this point not all the Hasidic masters were comfortable with such emphasis on wonder-working. Another early Hasidic master, Barukh of Medzibozh, upon being told that another tzaddik was performing miracles, reacted by saying: "How utterly useless they are! When Elijah performed miracles, we are told that the people exclaimed, 'The Lord, He is God' (1 Kings 18:19). But nowadays, the people grow enthusiastic over the reputed miracle-worker and forget entirely to say, 'The Lord, He is God.'"[9] As we will see, others also rebelled against the Seer in this matter.

> I love the evil person who knows he is evil more than the tzaddik who says he's righteous. Why? Because the evil person who knows he is evil speaks the truth. But the tzaddik who says he's righteous lies. As it is written: "There is no one in the world who does not sin" (1 Kings 8:46). Hence the righteous man who claims he's righteous is false, and God hates falsehood and deception. (Jacob Isaac Horowitz, *Nifla'ot ha-Rebbe*, 27b)[10]

The tzaddik must always struggle to be extremely humble and not be trapped by the adoration of his followers, while still accepting the responsibilities of the relationship. The possibility of egotism and even a small degree of fraud is always a threat to him. His wonder-working abilities were only the means to bringing his people to a greater awareness of God.

In chapter 18 we read earlier sets of *hanhagot*, recommended practices of the mystics and their circles. Here is a short excerpt from what is apparently a list of practices that the Seer had written for his personal usage, based on his own inner turmoil.

I have made up my mind not to think any longer of what people think of me. If the thought happens to enter my mind, I must remember that it makes no difference.

I must be careful never to think about money.

I must never want anything from this world, only for the Lord, blessed be He, alone.

I must remember never to forget God.

And to be very careful not to reveal that which resembles prophecy and, if it becomes necessary, to do it with great circumspection with the help of God. (Jacob Isaac Horowitz, *Divrei Emet, Hanhagot*, 7-8)[11]

We see in the Seer's words a significant emphasis on maintaining *hishtavut*, equanimity as well as humility in all matters. Part of this involves great reticence in using his powers publicly, refraining from anything resembling a "flaunting" of his powers. The goal "never to think about money" is of some interest in view of the tendency of many tzaddikim to concentrate on collecting donations and maintaining a lavish court, even though at least some of these tzaddikim took little or no personal benefit from this wealth. Finally, it was very important for the Seer "never to forget God," to maintain his *deveikut* constantly. He once said that "if a man forgets to cleave to God for 1 second of the 3,600 seconds in an hour, it would be better if he remained like a body without a soul, and be called dead."[12]

One of the Seer's close associates and a teacher for many of his students was also named Jacob Isaac; perhaps to differentiate him from the Seer, he became known as Yehudi ha-Kadosh, "the Holy Jew" (1765–1814). As the Seer's students began to attach themselves to the Yehudi, the latter established his own court in Przysucha, seeking to provide his own disciples with a higher degree of self-consciousness, thus providing a means to understand their own impulses, deepen their personal integrity, and acquire greater spiritual depth.[13] Although he remained a great admirer of the Seer, the Yehudi was opposed to what he regarded as the overemphasis on the tzaddik's abilities. The Seer was deeply troubled over the departure of his disciple, but was also quoted as saying: "The truth is that the path of the Yehudi is higher than ours, but what can we do; ours was created by Rabbi Elimelekh [of Lyzhansk, a disciple of Dov Ber of Mezeritch]."[14]

> What mastery is there in being a wonder-worker? Any man of a certain achievement [in God's service] has in his power to turn heaven and earth topsy-turvy, but to be a Jew—that is really hard! (Jacob Isaac, the Yehudi, *Siah Sarfei Kodesh* 4:17, no. 67)[15]

It is known that early Hasidim, particularly among the Seer's followers, often held many superstitious beliefs, but the Yehudi believed that for a tzaddik to allow this was simply vulgar. The key question for the Yehudi was whether a tzaddik could make his Hasid into a better Jew, which requires serious effort, including the Torah study that would refine a person. Thus the Yehudi sought to rebalance Hasidic life and strengthen the priority of Torah learning. Harry Rabinowicz notes that "with all his strength, the Yehudi fought against superficiality, stressing sincerity and total involvement in prayer, study, and every human relationship."[16] True, a tzaddik could accomplish great things in the world, but to be a Jew, to change oneself . . . that is an even greater task![17] The tzaddik's role is to give wings to his students, not to make them subservient to him. (Other tzaddikim sometimes took a position between that of the Seer and the Yehudi, that is, believing that wonder-working was reserved for only the greatest Hasidic masters, excluding themselves.)

The Yehudi and his disciples (as well as some of the earlier rebbes, including the Seer) deviated from tradition in one respect: they were not particular about observing the proper times for prayer, but might wait until they felt adequately prepared and properly mindful. The deeper issue was not whether one followed the rules of prayer or anything else, but whether one could make the tradition one's own, without using the rules as a substitute for active religious experience. For the Yehudi, the need to "change oneself" on a regular basis took precedence over the rules designating the temporal boundaries of prayer; he taught that "all the rules a person makes for himself to worship God are not rules, and this rule is not a rule either."[18]

Although prayer was certainly ecstatic for the Yehudi (though not to be done so boisterously as to attract attention), he restored much greater emphasis on traditional Torah study, believing that "learning Talmud and Tosafot purifies the mind" and prepares one for prayer.[19] The school of the Yehudi is less focused on Kabbalah in general, and certainly not on Affective Kabbalah; thus, we see much less focus on messianism and much more on the life of the individual. Even the ideas of "nullifying the self" or "seeing the world as a lie," which play a prominent role in early Chabad thought (see chapter 26), are far too extreme for the Yehudi. Unlike Chabad, succession in the school of the Yehudi generally was not hereditary, although some of the leaders' children did become secondary leaders.[20]

The Yehudi believed that too many Hasidic leaders were focused not only on the material well-being of their followers (like the Seer), but also on their own:

> There are three levels in the service of God. The first is one who is occupied with mitzvot and good deeds the entire day and yet believes he has still accomplished nothing; he is at the highest level. The second who has so far done nothing worthwhile, but he knows that he has not yet corrected anything in this world; this too is good, for there is hope that he will take it upon himself to do *teshuvah*. But one who is a tzaddik and knows he is a tzaddik, deceives himself all his days, and his devotion to the Torah and the mitzvot go for nought. (Jacob Isaac, the Yehudi, *Tiferet ha-Yehudi*, 45, no. 101)[21]

A tzaddik without proper humility is no tzaddik at all and cannot experience true awe (*yirah*). Worse yet, he deceives himself and others around him, despite the fact that overcoming self-deception was considered one of the most basic priorities for every Hasid, with truth the highest priority. For every Hasid, and most particularly for the tzaddik, one has to reach the point where everything is seen as much as possible through God's perspective.

> "Justice, justice, you shall pursue" (Deut. 16:20). The Yehudi said to me concerning this verse: this is the essence. . . . a man is given life in order to correct what he needs to correct, right up until his life is completed. This is why it says "justice" [twice]; even if one has corrected his actions, he must go for additional "justice," further correct his deeds in greater holiness. (Jacob Isaac of Przysucha, *Nifla'ot ha-Yehudi*, 38)[22]

This school of tzaddikim is committed to constant self-improvement and rigorous analysis of one's actions, motives, and weaknesses. It is a process that continues throughout life and is never fully completed; for one to believe that it could be finished would be a gross act of hubris. (Perhaps this is why the Yehudi was much more ascetically inclined than most Hasidic masters.) The Yehudi was also quoted as saying that if a person serves God in the same way today as yesterday he has in fact been diminished, "for a person is always in the aspect of becoming, and not standing."[23]

After the Yehudi's death, most of his students accepted the leadership of Simha Bunim (1765–1827). Unlike most Hasidic masters, he had traveled widely, successfully engaged in the pharmacy business, learned German, Latin, Polish, Yiddish, and Hebrew, and even lived in Western Europe, apparently adopting Western dress during this period. When he initially turned to Hasidism, he became a follower of the Seer of Lublin, but eventually turned to the Yehudi and went with him to Przysucha. Adding to the importance of Simha Bunim's ascension to leadership was the deaths of two major Hasidic masters in the same year: the Seer of Lublin was injured in a fall that led to his death the next summer and another major Hasidic master, Israel Hapstein, known as the Kozhnitzer Maggid, died about the same time.

Simha Bunim deemphasized the more ecstatic side of Hasidism, seeing the intellectual path of Torah learning as a more reliable guide to one's spiritual growth. (To some degree, this also lowered the intense reliance on the tzaddik.) The ideas of *deveikut* and *hitlahavut* were less compelling for him. But like the Yehudi he strongly believed that a particular path existed for each individual (within the bounds of tradition, to be sure), as is illustrated in the next text. For Simha Bunim, the world is no illusion, but a path through which human beings may carry out God's will, each in one's own unique fashion.

> "I clothed myself in righteousness and it fit me" (Job 29:14).[24] Also with regard to commandments, divine service, and perfection, a person should clothe himself in something designated for him. That is the meaning of "and it fit me." (Simha Bunim, *Kol Simha*, Mase'ei, 103)[25]

Simha Bunim emphasizes here the critical need for authenticity, doing what fits you as an individual. While he may not have heard the phrase "Know thyself" in any of the languages he knew, he certainly expressed the need to know one's own limitations and temptations as well as one's strengths. Sometimes, one must make the tradition fit oneself; he taught that "if keeping Shabbat is just a remembrance, something one remembers that he saw his father do, he may be called Shabbat-observant, but he is not doing God's will, for he is not thinking about that at all."[26]

> "A person should have two pieces of paper, one in each pocket, to be used as necessary. On one of them [should be written] "The world was created for my sake" (B. San. 37a), and on the other, "I am dust and ashes" (Gen. 18:27). (Simha Bunim in *Siah Sarfei Kodesh*, 1:50, no. 233)[27]

Simha Bunim and others within Przysucha and its school were not ascetically inclined.[28] One tzaddik may need to afflict himself to control his impulses, whereas another is perfectly fine maintaining a much more normal life. The latter is a much more worldly view, a view of a person at home with himself, understanding his urges,[29] and balanced in all things. That would also be a fair description of Simha Bunim.

> It is well known that God created the world with the Torah. The Holy One, Blessed be He, looked into the Torah and organized all existence. It follows that the Torah is the norm[30] of all existence, and the norm of Torah is that the world should function according to nature. Therefore, all miracles and wonders which are above nature are an exception to the norm of Torah, and [by performing them] it is as if a person has transgressed. (Simha Bunim, *Kol Simha*, Mase'ei, 103)[31]

We have already encountered the notion, long a standard among the mystics and beyond, that the Torah preceded the Creation. Many mystics would certainly dispute the conclusion Simha Bunim draws from this idea—that although the tzaddik may have the power to bring about miracles, doing so would violate God's design and therefore God's will as expressed in the Torah.[32] Indeed, one could hardly imagine a position more opposite to that of the Seer of Lublin.

After the death of Simha Bunim, most of his followers turned to Menahem Mendel Morgenstern (1787–1859), who after his move to the town of Kotzk became known simply as the Kotzker Rebbe. Beginning as a disciple of the Seer of Lublin, he then followed the Yehudi and Simha Bunim. The Kotzker was an original thinker with a blazing need for total sincerity in religious life, to the point of scorning all convention. Like Simha Bunim, he understood that the fervor and even the joy that Hasidism had emphasized in its early generations could also be mere ritual. Feelings, even love, could blind a person to the most important truths. Even Torah study had its dangers; Heschel emphasizes that "the hazard lurked that a man might be filled with himself, with conceit, with self-satisfaction. Such feelings were nothing less than idol worship and kept him far from the Truth he sought."[33]

"And the anger of the Lord was kindled *b'Moshe*" (Exod. 4:14). [The *b'* in *b'Moshe* is usually translated "against," but literally means "in," within Moshe.]

At first Moses refused to go to Pharaoh. But when the anger of the Holy One, Blessed be He, at Israel's sufferings in Egypt, began to be kindled in Moses himself, he went to redeem them. And so it should be so far as every tzaddik is concerned. Whatever he does on behalf of the community of Israel, he should do because the anger of the Holy One, Blessed be He, burns within him. (Kotzker Rebbe, *Amud ha-Emet*, Shemot, 17-18)[34]

The Kotzker Rebbe was always a passionate and often an angry man. While most Hasidic masters were known for their compassion, the Kotzker felt that anger was also divine when directed against what was unacceptable (and he saw much within the world and even within himself as unacceptable). Contemporary Jewish leaders might at least occasionally take a page from the Kotzker's indignation, knowing that it is often easier to accept things among our people and in our community to which we should not consent.[35]

There is a dark side to this kind of passion for truth and unwillingness to compromise, which makes it difficult for one to cope with life and leadership. Nonetheless the Kotzker believed no compromise was possible when it came to putting God above the individual. The Kotzker did warn against mere outward displays of piety and stressed that it would be far better not to appear pious at all;[36] one who worries about what others think of him is not really serving God.

Like Simha Bunim and the Yehudi, as well as some of the earlier Hasidic masters, the Kotzker wrote no works of his own; his teachings survive only through collections provided by his students and others. It is possible that this was a conscious choice—to place his emphasis on the individual relationship between the tzaddik and his follower. As Heschel put it, "the most important aspect of Hasidism is that it lives in personalities; without the charismatic person there is no teaching of Hasidism."[37] Many of the Kotzker's most famous teachings were sharp "one-liners." Here are three well-known examples:

> If I am I because I am I, and you are you because you are you, then I am I and you are you. But if I am I because you are you, and you are you because I am I, then I am not I, and you are not you.[38]

> It is possible to bring the dead back to life. Still better is to bring the living back to life.[39]

> "They shall make for Me a sanctuary, and I shall dwell among them" (Exod. 25:8). This teaches that each person must make a sanctuary inside himself, so the Divine Presence can dwell there. (Kotzker Rebbe, various sources)[40]

For the Kotzker, imitation is a terrible sin; each person must define himself and find his own way, not just seek to distinguish himself from other people. The role of the tzaddik is to teach people to find their own personal direction rather than to follow his own (or, still worse, to follow public opinion). Those who follow someone else's path are not really living their own life; perhaps this is why he speaks of bringing the "living back to life" (the Kotzker, as we have already seen, was not impressed with the value of performing wonders, or indeed anything to do with Affective Kabbalah). Of course, the direction has to include a way to serve God, making a place within oneself to make God's Presence real. Serving God effectively often requires clearing away obstacles. Some are created by the ego. Others are created by unnecessary philosophical speculation about God, and the Kotzker was a firm believer in the intrinsic sanctity of the Jewish people and the depth of the Jewish faith-commitment to rise above the level of any philosophical inquiry. The Kotzker (in contrast to the Seer) also believed that one of the obstacles was the pursuit of wealth; Heschel notes that "as long as it was voluntary, poverty was a preferable goal to strive for."[41]

Finally, we will look at a parable that the Kotzker likely invented out of his own experience of leadership:

There was once a Jew who had a snuffbox made of goat horn. He lost the snuffbox and went around bemoaning his loss. "Woe is me. Not only do we live in the darkness of exile, but such a fate had to befall me, to lose my wonderful snuffbox." The holy goat came to him. This holy goat wanders the earth and has horns which reach the heavens and kiss the stars. The goat, seeing the Jew crying, bent down and said to him: "Cut off a piece of my horn and make yourself a new snuffbox."

The Jew cut off a piece of horn, made a new box, and put his snuff into it. Consoled, he went to the *beit midrash* [study house] and offered the worshipers more snuff. Jews took some snuff and were full of awe. Such snuff! A taste of paradise! Such a thing has never before existed! And the box is beautiful. Where did you get the snuffbox?

The Jew told the story of the snuffbox and the holy goat. The whole crowd dashed out of the *beit midrash* in search of the holy goat. The goat, as was its custom, wandered around the world with its long horns touching the skies and kissing the sun, the moon, and the stars. The crowd caught it and bound it with ropes. The holy goat was good-natured and let everyone take a piece of horn. Everyone took a piece and made a snuffbox. Among the Jews there was joy and gladness. But the holy goat wanders the world without horns. (Kotzker Rebbe, various sources)[42]

As we have seen, the role of the tzaddik has its dangers. For the Kotzker himself, these were less moral issues—the possibility of being seduced into the lower level of his followers—than psychic issues. In fact, drained by the demands of leadership, he increasingly separated himself until collapsing in the fall of 1838 and spending the next nine months in bed. While not totally secluded from his followers, he was to some degree isolated from them for the remaining twenty years of his life.

In the fall of 1839 Mordecai Joseph Leiner, seeing that the Kotzker

Rebbe was no longer functioning as he had previously, left Kotzk to found his own school in Izbica, Poland. Unlike the Kotzker, Simha Bunim, and the Yehudi, Leiner published many of his teachings. His *Mei ha-Shiloah* ("the waters of Shiloah," Isa. 8:6, referring to the tunnel of water understood to have sustained Jerusalem) had two parts, the first of which was printed in Vienna in 1860, six years after Leiner's death. Most Hasidic books were published in Poland or Russia; this was probably printed in Vienna because it was considered so heretical that no Jewish printer in the more traditional Eastern European areas would touch it. The second part was not printed until 1922, by which time Leiner's dynasty was thoroughly accepted within the framework of the Hasidic world. Outside of Hasidic circles, very few Jews knew much about his writing until the 1960s, when the entertainer and teacher Shlomo Carlebach quoted them frequently.

Leiner combined traditional Hasidic practice with radical philosophy. He taught that every event is in the hands of heaven, under God's control, thus challenging the basic notion of human free choice. Since every event is determined by God, so are human sins; thus Leiner offers a defense for many of the sins recorded in the Bible.[43] Even in matters of the most blatant transgressions, reality is never quite how it appears!

He also raised a question that further challenged the primacy of Torah: if the tzaddik receives revelation directly from God, can this overrule existing human law, at least for him personally?

> **"The Lord said to Moses, Speak to the *Kohanim* [priests], the sons of Aaron, and say to them: None shall defile himself for any [dead] person among his kin" (Lev. 21:1).**
>
> **None of the deeds performed in the world are by chance, but come through God's providential action. Know that the will of God is to do what is good for His creatures. Man might be resentful when he perceives some act of God's judgment; in more limited judgment it seems that the world behaves randomly, but man should know**

that everything is in the hands of heaven and it is well possible to be bitter over this.

Here God warns the *Kohanim*, who perform God's service. None shall defile himself for someone, i.e., they should have no bitterness over God's judgments, for this is a defilement of the soul. Bitterness comes into the world as a result of such judgments, the deprivations and losses found in the world. . . . Therefore, God commanded to tell the *Kohanim* . . . to have no such bitterness over these judgments, for they are always God's intentions and they are [intended] for good. Even though they function as if they were judgments or punishments, they are ultimately [intended] for good. (Leiner, *Mei ha-Shiloah*, Emor, 1:122)

Leiner gives a drastic rereading to the ritual impurity that the *Kohanim* are supposed to avoid. The deeper impurity is the bitterness brought on by suffering and "judgments," that is, the losses life brings. But if you serve God—and that is the mission of the *Kohanim*—then you must see such things differently and not fall prey to despair. While all events may be in the hands of heaven, how we understand them is of high importance.

"[Jacob] blessed Joseph, saying: The God in whose ways my fathers Abraham and Isaac walked, the God who has been my shepherd from my birth to this day" (Gen. 48:15).

Jacob humbles himself before his ancestors Abraham and Isaac, saying that they possessed a high degree of wisdom [*hokhmah*] and understanding [*binah*], so they were able to extend [their knowledge of] the will of God from their own resources. Even if the blessed God opened a very small opening for them, they widened and extended it through their own wisdom, in order to carry out the will of God. Thus they were also able to understand matters about which God had granted them no explicit illumination. [When the Torah says they] "walked," it means they were able to go forward on their own.

But as for me, "the God who has been my shepherd from my birth to this day" implies that in even the smallest action I might take, I need God to enlighten my eyes so as to know His will. I need illumination to know whether it still conforms to His will, or whether He wants me to change it. . . . In this respect, Jacob was the greatest of the Patriarchs, for it is an exceptionally exalted situation for God to direct a person continually. (*Mei ha-Shiloah*, Va-yehi, 1:59)[44]

In Jewish tradition, while Jacob is honored as one of the Patriarchs, few would consider him to be *more* righteous than Abraham and Isaac.[45] Leiner's radical understanding here is that Jacob is honored with continual direction from God. While the Patriarchs were believed to be graced with knowledge of the commandments, they were yet to be given to the Jewish people, through Moses; Jacob, blessed with ongoing divine revelation, would not have needed such knowledge. Thus Leiner arrives at the startling conclusion that certain people (in particular, a tzaddik!) might be exempt from the normal rules of the Torah!

"On a sign from the Lord they made camp and on a sign from the Lord they broke camp; they observed the Lord's mandate at the Lord's bidding through Moses" (Num. 9:23).

The removal of the cloud and God's dwelling was only observed by Moses. Similarly, in every generation, the tzaddik of the generation sees the will of God, as it is written: "The lips of the tzaddik know [God's] will" (Prov. 10:32).[46] The holy Yehudi saw that God's will in his generation was to delay the time of prayer . . . so it would not be [overly] fixed, lifeless. (*Mei ha-Shiloah*, Beha'alotekha, 2:93)[47]

While it is natural among the Hasidic masters to assume that the tzaddik has greater knowledge of God's will than his followers, not all the tzaddikim will go so far as to say that this entitles them to act contrary to the norms understood to be established by the Torah. Yet here Leiner is able to claim precedent from the Yehudi for his radical reliance on revelation. The Yehudi himself would never have claimed any precedent, but would only have given reasons for making exceptions regarding the time of prayer, rather than claiming that he had divine "permission" to do so. We also see here an example of how the radical position of one tzaddik might be pulled back to the communal norm by a later tzaddik, while still affirming that the previous tzaddik was right; meanwhile, the later tzaddik could hold a very different, perhaps even more radical view. Thus it is possible for God to hold more than one position on a given issue!

After the death of the Kotzker Rebbe in 1859, his immediate successor, Isaac Meir Alter of Ger (1799–1866, also known as Hiddushei ha-Rim, "novellae of Rabbi I. M.," the title of his book), moved away somewhat from the Kotzker's more radical views. Isaac Meir (who at the time lived in Warsaw but moved to the town of Ger, Poland, in 1860) was one of the century's most noted Torah scholars; while he offered a different approach from the Kotzker, Simha Bunim, and the Yehudi, he maintained a reverence for those teachers. He both revitalized kabbalistic terminology and underscored the importance of advanced Torah study. Rabinowicz summarizes: "Rabbi Simha Bunim of Przysucha's credo was 'Love of God,' that of Rabbi Menahem Mendel Morgenstern of Kotzk was 'Fear of God,' and the motto of Rabbi Isaac Meir of Ger was 'Study the Torah.'"[48]

Despite great personal tragedy (Isaac Meir outlived all thirteen of his children) and reluctance to accept leadership, he eventually took over the guidance of the Kotzker's remaining followers. His Gerer dynasty was later led by his grandson, Judah Leib Alter (1847–1905), the Sefat Emet (meaning, "words of truth," from his final discourse ending with these words from Prov. 12:19),[49] who was also known for combining talmudic expertise with Hasidic leadership, with little overt emphasis on the intricacies of kabbalistic terminology. This dynasty has continued to the present day.

Meanwhile, the dynasty begun by Mordecai Joseph Leiner continued under his successors (and spun off a few other important leaders).

Mordecai Joseph's son, Jacob Leiner (1818–78), while moderating some of his father's positions, explained and expanded on much of the ideology within *Mei ha-Shiloah*. He was succeeded by his son, Gershon Heinokh Leiner (1839–91), an extremely original thinker and charismatic leader. Although most of the followers of this school perished in the Holocaust, it too remains alive today. Like other groups of Hasidim, these two branches offered a richness of Jewish insights while dealing with the political upheavals of the nineteenth century.

I conclude with an interesting observation from Samuel Dresner, one of the leading scholars of Hasidism: "Hasidism has been described as a revival movement, and revival movements do not as a rule endure. Not so Hasidism. Emerging in eighteenth-century Eastern Europe, it has continued down to our very day even in the most unexpected of places, despite repeated warnings as to its decay and imminent collapse. Fuel was somehow found to stoke the fires from time to time, so that the waves that broke upon the Hasidim could not extinguish the light. Neither the challenge of modern science and thought of the nineteenth century, nor the Communist suppression of the twentieth—not even the Nazi onslaught with its unparalleled destruction of their communities, their leaders, and their followers—sealed their doom."[50]

26
Chabad Hasidism

Many Jews today only know Hasidism through its most visible adherents, those of Chabad. Why does this group call itself "Chabad"? What does it teach and why does it have a more public face than other Hasidic groups today?

Chabad is an acronym for three *sefirot*, *Hokhmah*, *Binah*, and *Da'at*, "awareness." (*Da'at* is inserted below *Hokhmah* and *Binah* in some versions of Kabbalah where *Keter* is a transition stage or understood as the same as *Ein Sof*.)[1] But according to Chabad thought, these are not only *sefirotic* realms, but have specific definitions.

> *Hokhmah* is wisdom in its potential stage. In the *sefirotic* realm it is the divine thought of creation before the details have, as it were, become actualized in thought. In man's psychic life *Hokhmah* is the intuitive flash by which an idea emerges in the mind. Once the idea has come into being it becomes actualized through deep reflection—*Binah*—on its implications. When, as a result, the mind becomes powerfully attached to the idea it has grasped, when the idea becomes part of the person engaged in contemplation, this higher awareness, *Da'at*, is attained. (Jacobs, *Seeker of Unity*, 64)[2]

The first Chabad rebbe, Shneur Zalman of Lyady, was a great prodigy, outstripping most of his teachers at an early age. After the Ba'al Shem Tov died when Shneur Zalman was fifteen, his uncle began to share with him the Ba'al Shem Tov's teachings. By age twenty, Shneur Zalman was torn between two approaches to Judaism; he decided he needed to go one way or the other, either to Vilna (representing the opponents of Hasidism, particularly Elijah, the Vilna Ga'on, and his undiluted focus on the study of Torah) or to Mezeritch (the home of the Maggid, Dov Ber, the successor to the Ba'al Shem Tov). As the story has it, he started heading toward Vilna and then said: "Study I know something about already; what I don't know is how to serve God in prayer."[3] He thus decided to go to Mezeritch and became a follower of the Maggid, even becoming a *hevruta* (study partner) of the Maggid's son.

Shneur Zalman's first major written work was a halakhic tome, the *Shulhan Arukh ha-Rav*. The work was not finished for many years and only published in full in 1814, after his death; however, the first segment was completed when he was just twenty-seven years old, in 1772, the year the Maggid died. A few years later Shneur Zalman became an acknowledged Hasidic leader in Lithuania and Belarus.

His most famous book is his philosophical work, *Tanya* [It was taught], published in 1797. It attempts to outline a course for spiritual growth and understanding for the individual who is not a tzaddik, but who wishes to attain an intense closeness with God. To those not familiar with the vocabulary of Kabbalah, or even of traditional Judaism, it is extremely difficult to follow.[4] But within the world of Chabad and through its teachers it has had an enormous impact.

In the tiny segment of Chabad literature we will review below, we will examine four subjects: (1) the idea of God as including all existence; (2) the nature of the soul; (3) how one serves God; and (4) the particular Chabad approach to the needs of the hour, including the coming of the Messiah.[5]

For Shneur Zalman, *deveikut* with God to the point of awareness of God within oneself is critical:

> When a person cleaves to God, it is very delightful for God, and very sweet for God, so much so that He will swallow it into His heart; ... a

person becomes one substance with God in whom he was swallowed, without being separate [from God] to be considered as a distinct entity at all. This is the meaning [of] "and you shall cleave to God"—i.e., literally. (Shneur Zalman, *Commentary on the Siddur*, 51)[6]

Not only is this an example of mystical union, but also of reunion, because at a certain point the mystic realizes that he was never really separate from God. As the intellect apprehends God, the individual understands that he is indeed always connected with God. Rami Shapiro suggests the image of a fresh sponge immersed in a tub of water, where the water fills the sponge completely and there is no place where the water is not.[7] That is what it means to be "swallowed" by God. In this text, in contrast to much of Hasidic teaching, it is the intellect, not emotion, that brings one to this understanding. The activity that leads the person to that apprehension is the process of *deveikut*. This is a logical conclusion from the idea that God fills all worlds; God also fills the person, who ultimately has no more individual identity than the waves that come out of the ocean. That independent being is illusory.

Even though it appears to us that the worlds exist, this is a total lie. (Shneur Zalman, *Torah Or*, Ki Tissa', 172)[8]

According to Shneur Zalman, not only is our own individual existence an illusion; so is everything else in what we apprehend as the physical world. One important point derived from this is that what we understand to be *tzimtzum*, God's contraction to make space for individuals and for free choice, is just our understanding, but not real. Seeing ourselves as individuals is just our own misapprehension; from God's standpoint, nothing exists outside God, and therefore there can be no *tzimtzum* at all. This view is referred to as "acosmism"; everything is God, but we apprehend things as separate entities. Even the ego and its activity are understood to be a manifestation of God. Shneur Zalman notes elsewhere that "the essential thing is to train one's mind and thought

continually, so it will always be fixed in his heart and mind, that everything one sees . . . is the outer garments of the King,"[9] that is, a physical
demonstration of God's Presence.

> Just as a man rejoices when he is left an inheritance of a large amount
> of money for which he has not toiled, how infinitely more should we
> rejoice over the heritage our fathers have left us, namely, the doctrine
> of the true unity of God, that even on this earth down below "there
> is nothing else beside Him" (Deut. 4:35), and this is the meaning of
> His dwelling down below. (Shneur Zalman, *Tanya*, 1:33)[10]

A plain reading of the verse quoted yields a very different idea: "It
has been clearly demonstrated to you that the Lord alone is God; there
is none beside Him." The point is that only one God exists and no other.
But Shneur Zalman takes the words *ein od milvado*, normally understood
to mean "none beside Him," to mean "there is nothing else beside Him,"
thus providing a textual basis for his radical acosmism.[11] One becomes
aware of God's Presence in all things through absorption in the Torah
and observance of the commandments and their deeper meaning.[12]
Shneur Zalman may have absorbed this idea initially in a major study
he undertook in his youth of Horowitz's *Shnei Luhot ha-Brit*,[13] where it
plays a significant role. Sometimes this idea is shaded in vague language,
but it is an assumption underlying much of Chabad teaching.

> Vital wrote in *Sha'ar ha-Kedushah* . . . that in every Jew, whether
> righteous or wicked, there are two souls, as it is written, "The souls
> [*neshamot*] which I have made" (Isa. 57:16), [alluding to] two souls.
> There is one soul which originates in the *kelippah* and the *sitra ahra*,
> and which is clothed in the blood of a human being, giving life to the
> body, as is written, "For the life of the flesh is in the blood" (Lev. 17:11).
> From it stem all the evil characteristics deriving from the four evil ele-
> ments contained in it, which are: anger and pride, which emanate from
> the element of fire, the nature of which is to rise upward; the appetite

for pleasures, from the element of water, for water makes all kinds of enjoyment grow; frivolity and scoffing, boasting and idle talk, from the element of air; and sloth and melancholy, from the element of earth.

From this soul also stem the good characteristics which are to be found in the innate nature of all Israel, such as mercy and benevolence. For in the case of Israel, this soul of the *kelippah* is derived from *kelippat nogah*, which also contains good, as it originates in the mystery of the Tree of Knowledge of Good and Evil. [*Nogah* means radiance;[14] however, the term *kelippat nogah* here refers to the individual's misguided sense of himself as separate.] The souls of the nations of the world, however, emanate from the other, unclean *kelippot* which contain no good whatever, as is written in [Vital's] *Eitz Hayim* 49, ch. 3, that all the good that the nations do, is done from selfish motives. So the Talmud comments on "The kindness of the nations is sin" [*v'hesed le'umim hatat*] (Prov. 14:34):[15] All the charity and kindness done by the nations of the world is only for their own self-glorification, and so on.[16]

The second soul of a Jew is "a portion of God above" (Job 31:2)…. So, allegorically speaking, have the souls of Jews risen in the [divine] thought, as it is written: "My firstborn son is Israel" (Exod. 4:22), and "You are children to the Lord your God" (Deut. 14:1). That is to say, just as a child is derived from his father's brain [i.e., seed], so, as it were, the soul of each Israelite is derived from the blessed God's thought and wisdom. (Shneur Zalman, *Tanya*, 1:1–2)

Shneur Zalman teaches that there are two souls, an animal and a divine soul, which live in constant tension but are interdependent. The animal soul—like the *yetzer ha-ra*, the "evil impulse"—is not entirely evil (and not entirely physical), but is still rooted in evil, feeding the illusion of one's independent existence. It does not perceive itself as part of God, but still serves as a "garment" for the existence of the divine soul. The divine soul, the true reality, provides vitality to the whole person and seeks to transform its animal counterpart. The ongoing struggle for the Hasid is to cause his divine soul, the Godly "portion," to prevail over his animal soul, to be part of God, and to recognize that he is not separate from God. (The child "derived from his father's brain" refers to the medieval belief that sperm originated in the brain.)

It is a given for Shneur Zalman (and, as we have seen, for many other Jewish mystics)[17] that this divine soul is only present within Jews. While we can understand why such opinions would have been held, such presumptions are jarring to the modern reader.[18] Ultimately they are an extension of the belief in the intrinsic sanctity of the Jewish people, which need not mean that Jews are understood to have unique cosmic powers or status. But often they are so understood among kabbalists, and such ideas still exist among some Jews today.[19] Although many non-Jews have shown an affinity for "kabbalistic" teachings, Kabbalah remains a field clearly interrelated with Jewish beliefs and practices.

One of the assertions of Chabad Hasidism is that they are the authentic inheritors of the Ba'al Shem Tov's legacy.[20] They have crafted much of their own version of their early history with this claim in mind, and other Hasidic history (written by Chabad or other Hasidim) has often been edited with similar goals. Most prominently, one of the important compilations about the Ba'al Shem Tov, *Shivhei ha-Besht*, was initially published in White Russia in 1814; this was over a half-century after the Ba'al Shem Tov's death, but only a very short time after Shneur Zalman's. Thorough research has indicated that this book was compiled and printed by a Chabad follower[21] in such a way as to promote some specific goals that were very important within Chabad.

When the time came to find a successor for Shneur Zalman as the leader of Chabad, there were two possibilities: Shneur Zalman's oldest son, Dov Ber, and Aaron Ha-Levi Horowitz, considered by many to be Shneur Zalman's leading student and a polished speaker and teacher.[22] Close friends in their youth, the two men grew apart in Shneur Zalman's later years, partly over ideological issues, but perhaps with an awareness that one would eventually have to prevail over the other. Many Chabad leaders did not believe that Dov Ber "fit" the ideal of a Hasidic leader; others felt that he was adequate, but not someone they would personally follow, as he tended to rehash much of his father's teaching. Still others felt that no one could truly replace Shneur Zalman. To make matters worse, Shneur Zalman himself had not publicly expressed an opinion on the matter of succession and left no will.

Dov Ber was forced to campaign and put forward a platform for leadership of Chabad; he claimed that his teachings were a reiteration of what he had learned from his father, although Aaron could likewise claim to understand Shneur Zalman's program correctly. To Dov Ber's benefit, he was able to publish his father's books as well as many of his own, while Aaron—who preferred oral teaching, in line with early Hasidic practice—failed to use the printed word to support his own teachings.[23]

The portrayal of the Ba'al Shem Tov in *Shivhei ha-Besht* bore a distinct similarity to Dov Ber, unlike previous texts that contained the Ba'al Shem Tov's teachings and stories of his life. As Moshe Rosman notes, "both men [Dov Ber and the Ba'al Shem Tov] began their leadership careers in small villages, far from the mass of Chasidim and in difficult economic circumstances. Both met with initial skepticism from potential followers. Both concentrated more on forming individual relationships with people and helping them solve their problems than on delivering public sermons or developing Talmudic virtuosity. Both traveled to their followers, rather than holding court for a limited elite. Both limited ascetic behavior among their followers and stressed genuine joy as a mode of divine service."[24]

While some of the grand claims about the Ba'al Shem Tov were factually correct, several are disputed; furthermore, the emphasis on all these parallels in *Shivhei ha-Besht* is notable. A number of "new" stories in the book also support Dov Ber's disapproval of using ecstatic techniques in prayer unless one already had a connection with God, always treating the Ba'al Shem Tov's ecstatic behavior "as involuntary rather than calculated and conscious."[25] Aaron, on the other hand, fully accepted ecstatic techniques as a means to achieve a connection with God.

Prior to this time, Hasidic leadership had not generally been passed from father to son. But in *Shivhei ha-Besht* the role of Eliezer, the father of the Ba'al Shem Tov, is given major expansion. The Ba'al Shem Tov, previously understood to have learned from biblical and prophetic figures, is here seen as the son of a righteous father and the student of another figure, a Rabbi Adam Ba'al Shem, whose writings are preserved through the student. Thus Dov Ber is understood to be like this portrayal of the Ba'al Shem Tov and, Rosman writes, "could be seen not as attempting to initiate a new succession principle but as continuing in the same path as the founder of the movement."[26] This image of the Ba'al Shem Tov does not fit that of previous sources, but certainly strengthened Dov Ber's claim to leadership.

In any event, Dov Ber did become the primary leader of his father's Hasidim, and his teachings, particularly on prayer, helped shape Chabad practice.

> **Every person, according to his intelligence, his knowledge, his heart, and according to the extent of his training from his youth in the service of the heart, will recognize his stage and the place he has attained, and will discern in his soul all the detailed errors into which he has fallen. If there are people whose souls are perfect and whose hearts are truly focused on God, let them take good care to know themselves at all times, so they do not deceive themselves. For it appears that the main confusion, resulting in a diminution of the light of the Torah and the service of the heart, even for those who seek and desire God's nearness, is none other than self-delusion. The cause is weak effort in seeking God to the full extent with a whole heart. People want to draw near to God from a distance, but their heart is not really in it. . . .**
>
> **The important thing is to pay the fullest attention to the proper understanding of the truth concerning the subject of the words of**

the living God. To this goal, one should devote his soul and heart all the days of his life of vanity. Why should he allow vanity and falsehood to enter the soul, so he distances himself and does not draw near [to God], God forbid? As the Yiddish saying goes, *mi soll sich nit narren* ["One should not fool oneself"]. It is well known and widely admitted that the main intermingling of good and evil is found in one who fools himself.

However, all this applies to those who seek the Lord, who search for and desire in truth the nearness of God. But this is not to be found among the majority of our followers. It is therefore necessary to rebuke openly, out of hidden and open love, to reveal and inform each one [about] his defects. Even if his soul weeps in secret and he is truly aggrieved, pride and self-love cover everything, to the point that he sees no fault at all in himself, and in his own eyes all the ways of every man are pure. For this there is no hope. (Dov Ber, *Tract on Ecstasy*, 162–63)[27]

Shneur Zalman had firmly established a very slow, meditative pattern of worship for his followers, focused on the disciplined arousal of one's awareness of his responsibilities before God. The mystic must be certain that his service to God is uncontaminated. His feelings may run deep, but true service is self-nullification; therefore, whatever ecstatic feelings he may have may simply be an obstacle. True self-nullification, Naftali Loewenthal writes, "is an emotionless state, in which there is no self-awareness."[28]

For Aaron, total self-nullification was an impossible standard. Dov Ber recognized that it was too high for most people, and that a person might forbid himself any form of ecstasy, "until eventually he is prepared to think of any external matter, or he slumbers and falls asleep."[29] Here he criticizes those who try to achieve a level that is beyond their capacity, while still insisting on self-nullification as the ideal service.

Dov Ber's *Tract on Ecstasy* was printed more than a decade after his death; the intense technique discussed within it was likely only available to a few handpicked students.[30] However, it remained the "correct" path of contemplation and was the subject of much emphasis by the fifth Chabad rebbe in the late nineteenth and early twentieth centuries.[31]

We now skip ahead to the sixth rebbe, Yosef Yitzhak Schneerson, who faced the challenge of maintaining a Hasidic community within Communist Russia and then escaped in March 1940. He came to the United States and established Chabad headquarters in the Brooklyn, New York, neighborhood of Crown Heights.

> **Our teacher, the Besht, his soul is in Eden, is the aspect and gradation of Moses, the first of the leaders of Israel in the course of all the generations until the luminous time of the disclosure of our righteous Messiah, verily, soon. ... The dispersion of Moses in each and every generation, each generation until the coming of our righteous Messiah, is the dispersion of the power of our teacher, the Besht, his soul is in Eden, and the disclosure in each generation is the revelation of the supernal light more strongly, and this is in accord with the manner of the order of the elevations, from elevation after elevation, of the holy soul of our teacher, the Besht, his soul is in Eden, for when he was in this world, there was a disclosure of the aspects of _nefesh_, _ruah_, and _neshamah_, and after his departure from this world, in the secret of "Greater are the righteous [in death than in life]," and the revelations in the disciples of his disciples and in the last generations are revelations that are revealed through the gradations of _hayyah_ and _yehidah_ of the soul of our teacher, the Besht, his soul is in Eden. (Yosef Yitzhak Schneerson, letter dated October 28, 1943)[32]**

We have already learned about the five levels of soul, and that the two highest levels are attained by very few individuals. According to Yosef Yitzhak Schneerson, the Ba'al Shem Tov had such an exalted soul, so much so that he was like Moses in his own time. (He writes elsewhere that Shneur Zalman similarly was "the Moses of Chabad.")[33] Here, in contrast to the views of nonmystics and even some of the mystics, Moses is not forever above every possible achievement of other human beings; rather, the soul of Moses continues to be dispersed "in each and every generation."

If there is such a soul in every generation, who is that soul in the time when Yosef Yitzhak Schneerson is writing? It can be none other than the rebbe himself, who is "the 'totality' of his [i.e., Moses's] being (*der gantser Moshe*), indeed, the 'very same' person (*der zelber Moshe*), albeit reincarnated in a different body."[34] Furthermore, in Rabbinic tradition Moses has also been viewed in messianic terms, as the one who was the first redeemer and will be (or will be the model for) the final redeemer.[35]

While messianism was somewhat muted in early Hasidism as well as early Chabad, Shneur Zalman occasionally speaks of his generation as that of the "footsteps of the Messiah." A number of the early Hasidic masters also believed that the redemption was not far off.[36] Here, of course, the message takes on a good deal more urgency.[37] Even before 1943 Yosef Yitzhak Schneerson speaks of "immediate redemption," although he ceased to use this phrase after the war.[38]

After the death of Yosef Yitzhak Schneerson, the leadership of Chabad passed to his son-in-law, Menahem Mendel Schneerson, who became the seventh rebbe of Chabad and expanded the movement considerably, establishing outposts to reach out to Jews around the world. Why did this become so important to Chabad, when other Hasidic groups (and most ultra-Orthodox Jews, for that matter) remained primarily focused on maintaining their own communities? In chapter 21, we read the letter of the Ba'al Shem Tov to his brother-in-law, in which he described his vision of and discussion with the Messiah. The Messiah told him that he would come "when your teaching becomes famous and revealed to the world." Thus Schneerson taught that it was imperative to spread Chabad's teachings (seen as the logical development of the Ba'al Shem Tov's teachings) as widely as possible, to make it possible to speed the coming of the Messiah.[39] Below we see two brief examples. The timing of this follows on the very un-messianic suffering of the Jewish people during the Holocaust years. How much of the intensity of Chabad's messianism can be attributed to this cannot be said for sure.

> Thus it is clear that whoever believes in the Besht, and in the words that the Besht heard from the King Messiah, is obligated to believe also that now there are the wellsprings of the Besht, and there is now the matter of the dissemination of the wellsprings; hence he should believe that he may arrive on any day, verily will the Messiah come. . . . And consequently, this is clear proof that the holy task of disseminating the wellsprings of the Besht and the leaders after him, so that they shall also spread outward, is incumbent upon each of us, for the coming of the Messiah in actuality here below is dependent on this. (From a talk by Menahem Mendel Schneerson, January 12, 1957, the seventh yahrzeit of Yosef Yitzhak Schneerson)[40]

> On behalf of the matter of "Your wellsprings will spread outward" (Prov. 5:16), our rabbis and leaders would dispatch emissaries to different places in order to disseminate the wellsprings of the teaching of Hasidism, as it was in each and every generation. And in the last generations—since the Messiah must come immediately, and his arrival is dependent on the spreading of the wellsprings outward—this is with an increased distance and magnitude. (From a talk by Menahem Mendel Schneerson, October 11, 1958)[41]

The use of the word "wellsprings" (*ma'ayanot*) is shorthand for the verse cited from Proverbs, clearly focusing on the Ba'al Shem Tov's message and the need for outreach in order to bring the Messiah. And that need, even in 1958, is clearly expressed as "immediate." While it is true that Schneerson was more educated and sophisticated than most Hasidic masters (and likely understood well the possibilities for expansion in the United States and beyond), these texts clearly show that Chabad justified its outreach to more assimilated Jews because it was necessary for the messianic goal. Such outreach had its risks; two major followers of Chabad, Zalman Schachter (later Schachter-Shalomi) and Shlomo Carlebach eventually went their own ways, leaving the fold and concentrating on different programs of outreach.

One other important motivation for this approach was what was understood to be the spiritual decline of the generations. This was expressed even by the fifth rebbe, Sholom Dov Ber Schneerson, who insisted that his followers study the mystical meaning of the Torah: "The first generations did not need this because they were perfectly righteous and learned Torah for its own sake. . . . But in the last generations . . . the hearts diminished . . . it is a mitzvah to disclose, and generation after generation, the matter of unveiling the inner nature of Torah becomes more and more urgent."[42] This sense affected other twentieth-century Jewish mystics, as we will see in chapter 27.

> The single difference for us is that, in the past, someone could think that when he came to the rebbe, he could tell him things he wanted to tell, and hide things he wanted to hide from the rebbe, but now it is clear to all that the rebbe also knows the things that are concealed within us, for in the past the rebbe was garbed in a physical body, which is not so now, since he is above the limitations of the physical body, wholly in a state of spirituality. Moreover, inasmuch as "the righteous man who dies is found in all of the worlds more than when he is alive" (Zohar 3:71b) . . . it is certain that the rebbe governs the world in its entirety . . . as it was until now, and on the contrary, "with greater rank and greater strength" (Gen. 49:3). And just as until now every one of us maintained that the rebbe would lead us to greet our righteous Messiah, so it must be maintained now as well. (From a talk by Menahem Mendel Schneerson, February 25, 1950, concerning his father-in-law's death four weeks earlier)[43]

The sixth rebbe may no longer be physically present, but as far as his (future) successor is concerned, he can do more now that he is no longer limited to a corporeal body! Thus, even though eventually a new leader will step forward, the old leader is still present, and perhaps will even return. Elliot Wolfson explains that "the physical demise of the sixth rebbe is merely a test of faith, the concealment, which is part and parcel of the 'birth pangs' that precede the coming of the savior."[44] He remains the leader and the vehicle through whom people can receive the teachings of Hasidism and thus through whom they can most closely cleave to God. Indeed the idea that death is really only arrival at a higher plane of existence was a principle within early Chabad teachings.[45] If Menahem Mendel Schneerson believed this about his father-in-law, it should not surprise us to see that many, if not most Chabad followers today believe it about Menahem Mendel himself.[46]

The occasion of this next discourse was extremely important for Menahem Mendel Schneerson; it was his inaugural address as the newly recognized leader of Chabad Hasidism.

> **In the language of the Rabbis of blessed memory, all things sevenfold are cherished, though not everything cherished is sevenfold.[47] It is clear from this that the essence of the gradation is that it is the seventh, and since it is the seventh it is cherished by us.... And thus my saintly teacher and father-in-law, *Admor* [*Adoneinu, Moreinu V'Rabbeinu*; "our master, our teacher, our rabbi"] [when he first came to America], explained that also in the matter of the privileging of the sevenfold the advantage of the first is discerned ... and he explained the level of the first, who was Abraham our father, on account of his worship, which was the worship of self-sacrifice.... So great was the level of his worship and self-sacrifice that the reason Moses merited that the Torah be given through him was that the sevenfold is privileged, and he was the seventh in relation to the first.... And this is the esteem of the seventh, that it draws down the *Shekhinah* and, more than this, it draws down the essence of the *Shekhinah* and, more than this, it draws down to the lower beings. And this is what is demanded from each of**

us in the seventh generation . . . for we find ourselves in the footsteps of the Messiah, at the end of the footsteps, and the work is to complete the drawing down of the *Shekhinah*, and not only the *Shekhinah* but the essence of the *Shekhinah* and specifically in the lower beings. . . . This is the very preciousness of the seventh generation, for several powers were given and revealed on our account. And by means of the service in this manner, the essence of the *Shekhinah* will be drawn below into this corporeal and material world, and it will be on a higher level than before the transgression. (Discourse by Menahem Mendel Schneerson on January 17, 1951, the first *yahrzeit* of Yosef Yitzhak Schneerson, commenting on a teaching of Yosef Yitzhak Schneerson that was released on January 28, 1950, the day of his death)[48]

The Rabbinic teaching to which Schneerson refers at the outset says that seven righteous men drew the *Shekhinah* down into the physical world: Abraham, Isaac, Jacob, Levi, Kehat, Amram, and Moses. Referring to his predecessor rather than to himself directly, he draws a correspondence from this teaching to the seven leaders of Chabad. Since Moses is the seventh of the righteous listed in this group, there is a correspondence from Menahem Mendel (as the seventh rebbe) to Moses. While each of the seven rebbes embodies the spirit of Moses, the humblest of men and the seventh of those responsible for the critical task of making God's Presence felt on earth, the seventh rebbe, continuing the work of his father-in-law, would have to complete a special task.[49]

And my saintly teacher and father-in-law, *Admor*, "who bore our sickness, and who endured our suffering" (Isa. 53:4), "but he was wounded because of our sins, crushed because of our iniquities" (Isa. 53:5), just as he saw our torment, he should come swiftly in our days to redeem his flock from the spiritual exile and from the physical exile together . . . and, moreover, he should conjoin and bind us to the substance and essence of the Infinite, blessed be He. And this is the inner intent of the descent and concatenation of the worlds, and the matter of the transgression and its rectification, and the matter of the death of the righteous, for by this means the glory of the blessed Holy One ascends. When he leads us out of exile "with an exalted hand" (Exod. 14:8), "and all of Israel will have light in their dwellings" (Exod. 10:23), and "then Moses and the Israelites will sing [this song to the Lord]" (Exod. 15:1), "The Lord will reign forever and ever" (Exod. 15:18), and they conclude "And the Lord shall be king . . . the Lord shall be one and His name shall be one" (Zech. 14:9). All this comes about on account of the death of the righteous, which is harder than the destruction of the Temple, and since we have been through all these things, now the matter depends only on us, the seventh generation. And we should merit to see the rebbe here below, in a body . . . and he should redeem us. (Later in the same discourse by Menahem Mendel Schneerson, January 17, 1951)[50]

It is striking that in speaking of his predecessor, Menahem Mendel refers to the same texts that Christians have traditionally understood as referring to their own Messiah, the texts from Isaiah 53 about God's "suffering servant." And his death, like that of Jesus as the Christians understand it, is meant to lead to the redemption, through his physical return. Menahem Mendel Schneerson never claimed to be the Messiah, but given that he sees himself as having the responsibility for completing the tasks of his father-in-law, it is fair to say that he understood his own role as messianic in nature. The next text gives further evidence of this.

The complete and true redemption must be immediately and without delay through the agency of our righteous Messiah, the emissary [of whom it was said] "the one you will send as your agent" (Exod. 4:13), my saintly teacher and father-in-law, *Admor*, the leader of our generation, and this is extended to the one who has filled his place after him, for he has filled the place of his father [the fifth rebbe], *Admor*, as it has been said several times in relation to the seven branches of the candelabrum and the seven guests [of *Ushpizin*]. (From a talk by

Menahem Mendel Schneerson to Chabad emissaries, November 2, 1991)[51]

Here Yosef Yitzhak Schneerson, the sixth rebbe, corresponds to the sixth of another set of seven: the seven lower *sefirot*. We have already seen in chapter 22 how the *Ushpizin* relate to these seven *sefirot*. For Menahem Mendel, it can be no coincidence that the sixth of these seven *sefirot* is understood to link to the biblical Joseph, neatly corresponding to his predecessor. The perfect unity of *Yesod* and *Malkhut* is also messianic in nature. Thus he himself—Menahem Mendel—must play a role in completing the work of his father-in-law, the task of bringing the Messiah, "immediately and without delay."

> **The rational soul [which is the matter of the divine image] in the Jew is not comparable to the rational soul in the gentile . . . for the rational soul of the Jew is in a manner different from the rational soul in the human species . . . for Israel is called "sons of God," as they have a divine soul, and thus their rational soul is also in another manner than the rational soul in the human species. And the principle difference between them is that the intellect of the divine soul is humble . . . it can attain nullification, which is not so in the intellect of the world [the rational soul] that effectuates being . . . and it can lead to arrogance . . . when it acquires an intellectual matter. (From a talk by Menahem Mendel Schneerson, June 11, 1977)[52]**

The seventh rebbe played a very active role in reaching out to important non-Jewish leaders in the United States and elsewhere, because he strongly believed in teaching non-Jews the *sheva mitzvot b'nei Noah*, the seven Noahide laws that Judaism regards as obligatory for all human beings.[53] But fundamentally, even in his later years, he accepted the position staked out in *Tanya* by Shneur Zalman (see above) distinguishing the Jewish soul from the non-Jewish soul. Only the former received the Torah and can attain a certain level.[54]

Today, Chabad Hasidism continues, despite the death of the seventh rebbe in 1994 and the fact that no rebbe has replaced him. Some of their followers include in their prayers explicit declarations that the seventh rebbe was the Messiah, while others are more cautious about such statements.[55] Aside from a few critics of the messianic doctrine, Chabad is accepted as a part of the Jewish community as they promote their many programs. As Pinchas Giller notes, "their network of religious schools, synagogues, college chaplaincy,[56] drug rehabilitation centers, meat processing and distribution and the myriad ways that Chabad puts itself out there. . . . This is perhaps the way it has always been with messianic movements in Judaism; they rise, fail, and the remnants are reabsorbed into Judaism and become part of its normal structure."[57]

Why does Hasidism remain such a powerful model today? Probably because some other models lack its intensity and mystical faith. Furthermore, it has been philosophically coherent (though in different models), and it treats Jewish practice and Jewish survival with great seriousness. Therefore, we have good reason to assume that it will survive for many more centuries to come.

Part 7
Mysticism, Action, and Reaction

27

Three Twentieth-Century Mystics

Although many twentieth-century Jewish mystics deserve study (including Menahem Mendel Schneerson; see chapter 26),[1] this chapter focuses on just a few themes in the teachings of three important figures: Abraham Isaac Kook, Kalonymous Kalman Shapira, and Abraham Joshua Heschel. Kook and Heschel were passionately engaged in some of the most critical issues of their times, and Shapira lived at the center of the Holocaust, arguably the most critical challenge to Jewish survival and Jewish faith of all time. I include excerpts from their writings to show that, in spite of the tenor of the times (dealt with in more detail in chapter 28), Jewish mysticism continued and developed in new directions.

Abraham Isaac Kook (1865–1935) was not only a prolific author but also the chief rabbi of Palestine (i.e., prior to the founding of the State of Israel) and probably the most important rabbi to actively support the Zionist movement. Ideologically he occupied an unusual position among the Orthodox in the Land of Israel in three respects. First, Kook was not only tolerant of the secular Zionists in Israel, he believed they were truly divine instruments, part of the "beginning of the redemption." Kook believed, like some of the Hasidic masters, that no thought was without value; even atheism served a holy purpose.[2] Second, he was appreciative of and very knowledgeable about many modern non-Jewish thinkers and movements; as we will see, his universalistic vision plays an important role in his thought.[3]

(Both of these positions would be surprising to someone encountering Kook, whose appearance and general behavior were Orthodox in the extreme.) Third, he incorporated earlier themes of Jewish mysticism in his own approach.

> Greater than [the study of philosophy] is the mystical quest, which by its nature penetrates to the depth of all thought, all feelings, all tendencies, all aspirations, and all worlds, from beginning to end. It recognizes the inner unity of all existence, the physical and the spiritual, the great and the small, and for this reason there is, from its perspective, no largeness or smallness. Everything is important; everything is invested with marked value.... Because of this advantage, mystical vision, in being able to embrace within itself all thoughts and all sparks of the spiritual, is alone fit to chart for us the way to go. Therefore, the mystical dimension alone is the soul of faith, the soul of the Torah. From its substance derives all that is revealed, all that is circumscribed, all that can be conceived by logic, and all that can be carried out in actions. The far-reaching unity of the mystical dimension embraces all creatures, all conditions of thought and feeling, all forms of poetry and exposition, all expressions of life, all aspirations and hopes, all objectives and ideals, from the lowest depths to the loftiest heights. (Kook, *Orot ha-Kodesh* [Lights of holiness], 1:9–10)[4]

This text bears a marked similarity to Hasidic teachings that emphasize the unity of all things. Only the mystical approach, a direct experience of God's Presence, can help one to recognize this; philosophy is insufficient. Kook, however, believed that since God is to be found in all things, the more we know of and understand His creation, the more ways we have to better understand and approach God.[5]

Under normal circumstances, like other Jewish mystics, Kook would be reluctant to discuss mystical matters. But he sees the challenges of his era as sufficient reason to override that reluctance.

I invoke the verse "There is a time to act for the Lord" (Ps. 119:126) in order to publicly discuss the secrets of Creation [*ma'asei Bereshit*], in the light of what my spirit has absorbed from the spirit of God that envelops those who fear Him and enter into His secret. (Kook, *Iggerot ha-Reiyah* [Letters of Rav Kook], 2:11, no. 347)[6]

For Kook, the special conditions of his time include the national situation, the development of the growing Jewish community in Israel, but also the very personal revelation he believes he has received, "what my spirit has absorbed," his own contact with the "spirit of God." Elsewhere, for those who feel such a contact, Kook speaks of the study of Kabbalah as both spiritual self-fulfillment and national fulfillment for the Jewish people (and consequently also providing a broader, more cosmic result). Like some mystics before him, he "believed that the dissemination of Kabbalah in our generation was the means for delivering Judaism from secularization."[7]

In Kook's writing, individual redemption is intertwined with that of the Jewish people. In the modern State of Israel, this combination creates the potential for volatility among the "religious Zionist" camp;[8] indeed, the school of thought initiated by Kook's son, Rabbi Tzvi Yehudah Kook, promoted the nationalistic elements much more strongly, while the father's vision "was both mystical and national, both internal and historical."[9] For Abraham Isaac Kook and many of his followers, the return to the Land of Israel suggested the likelihood of a parallel return of prophecy.

Indeed, Kook believed that the mystical approach was not only right, but essential:

It is not the purpose of the highest level of mystical knowledge to be disseminated in the world in a quantitative manner, that many become knowledgeable of it. This is impossible. If the many become familiar with its outer expression, they will remain totally ignorant of its inner content, and this will prove more detrimental than beneficial. But this knowledge must reach those who possess the precious virtue of contemplating lofty subjects.

Those individuals, by their lofty state of spirituality, elevate the world from its lowliness by the mere fact of their existence, and not by any perceptible exertion. The secrets of the inner world they do not reveal, and they cannot reveal. But whatever the mighty illumination, with all its force, affects substantively through the diffusion of its sparks even on what is openly known, on the glance of every eye, on every utterance and gesture, on the nature of the will, on the thrust of life, exerts an impact and lends firmness; it strengthens and hallows everything. (Kook, *Orot ha-Kodesh* 1:86)[10]

Kook's approach is consistent with many earlier Jewish mystics, in that it is elitist and restricted but necessary in order to "elevate the world from its lowliness." Somewhat later in this section, he adds that the type of person described in this text "should realize that in perfecting his own nature he is perfecting and redeeming not only himself but also the community at large and even the world."[11]

Kook writes elsewhere of his own mystical experiences in ways that evoke the *Heikhalot* experiences, stripped of the many obstacles noted in chapter 4: "It [Kook's soul] shall soar. . . . It shall fly rapidly and roam through the inner recesses of chambers and sanctuaries, it shall sing, it shall rejoice silently, it shall visit the holy sanctuary."[12]

While Kook was certainly a believer in the sanctity and the special role of the Jewish people and, for that matter, in the intrinsic sanctity of the Land of Israel, a universalistic theme also pervades his teachings, recognizing a higher unity and promoting love for every person, as an extension of the highest love, the love of the God who creates every person.[13] In this, Kook is strongly different from the Hasidic masters who generally were, at best, uninterested in secular learning, secular Jews, or non-Jews.[14] For Kook, God is in all things, animate and inanimate; holiness is found everywhere.

As there are holy sparks in the food we eat, so are they in all human activities, and similarly so in everything we hear and read. At times worldly pursuits from the most remote order of being become associated with the profound principles of the Torah, and everything serves a divine purpose, in the perspective of the holy. . . . The holy sparks embedded in the food we eat rise together with the holy sparks that ascend from all movements, all speech, all actions and acquisitions. To the extent that there is good and uprightness in all expressions of life is there an ascent of the holy sparks in food and drink and in all things that yield keenly felt pleasures. (Kook, *Middot ha-Rayah* [Moral principles])[15]

This is clearly influenced by the Hasidic perspective; while other Jewish mystics, particularly in the Lurianic school, saw the physical world as contaminated, Kook sees the Divine within every part of it. *Tikkun* for Rav Kook is definitely about repairing the person, as well as something more. Similarly, his mysticism is different from Mainline Kabbalah and its emphasis on affecting the higher realms.

The Hasidic master Kalonymous Kalman Shapira (1889–1943) is also known as the Piasetzner Rebbe.[16] (Piasetzne was just outside of Warsaw.) Prior to World War II, he was well known as an outstanding educator and a widely respected leader within the Hasidic world in a time of great challenge. Shapira was deeply concerned with the revitalization of Hasidic life and sought to develop a core of students who would carry out this task. After the Nazi invasion of Poland and the death of much of his family, he lived inside the Warsaw Ghetto and continued to teach and preach under the oppressive conditions prevailing. He buried his sermons within the ghetto shortly before being transported; they were discovered after the war and published under the title *Eish Kodesh* (*Sacred Fire*). Here are two excerpts from this work, expressing how he responded to the catastrophe that decimated Polish Jewry and ultimately included his own murder.

"Jacob lived in Egypt seventeen years." (Gen. 47:28)

Rashi, quoting the midrash,[17] asks: "Why is this segment 'closed'?" That is, why does the Torah text as written continue directly from the previous narrative [without the space that usually precedes a new segment]? Rashi explains: "Because as soon as our father Jacob died, the eyes and hearts of the Jewish people were blocked. Another explanation is: Jacob wanted to reveal the end of the exile to his sons, but it was blocked from him."

How shall we understand "Jacob wanted to reveal the end of the exile to his children, but it was blocked from him"? Does it mean that the desire of our patriarch Jacob in this matter was thwarted?

The holy Zohar (1:227b) on the verse "Jacob blessed Joseph and said" (Gen. 48:15) asks the following: What blessing did Joseph receive, when Jacob actually blessed only Joseph's sons? Why then does the verse say "Jacob blessed Joseph"? The Zohar answers as follows: Joseph was blessed because the blessings of a person's sons are his own blessings. Consequently, the blessing of Joseph's children is a blessing for Joseph.[18]

With this, we can understand the talmudic teaching: "God said: Ishmael, my son, bless Me. Rabbi Ishmael ben Elisha blessed God, saying: May it be Your will that Your mercy overcome Your anger and Your mercy prevail over your other attributes, so You deal with Your children compassionately and be more gracious to them than the law demands. He nodded His head to me."[19]

When the Holy One said to Rabbi Ishmael "Bless Me!" Rabbi Ishmael blessed the Jewish people that God should treat them mercifully. From what we have discussed above, we can easily understand this talmudic story, because "the child's blessings are the blessings of his parents." And similarly, the blessings of the Jewish people are the blessings of God. Conversely, when our father Jacob died, the Jewish people descended into the depths of suffering, to the point where even the Torah was damaged and wounded. This, then, is our greatest and ultimate hope: that if our suffering has such an effect and causes damage at such supernal levels, then surely God will save us.

"Our father Jacob wanted to reveal the end of the exile to his children, but it was blocked from him." This circumstance in itself heralds the end of the exile. If this chapter of the Torah text is "blocked off" because our father Jacob was blocked and prevented from revealing the end, which suggests that knowledge of the end was denied him, then the damage was indeed cosmic. Similarly, whenever we see that the troubles have grown so great that the Torah itself and the study halls of the synagogues and the yeshivas are all closed and locked, we can take heart. For it is clear from these circumstances that the damage is cosmic and reaches the small and the great, and so we can surely trust to God that the end is close. (Shapira, *Sacred Fire*, 28-29, Va-yehi)

This teaching was given on December 23, 1939, within two months after the death of Shapira's son, mother, daughter-in-law, and sister-in-law, all of whom died during, or as a result of, the Nazi invasion of Poland. While the creativity and depth of the teachings here and throughout *Eish Kodesh* are extraordinary, the very fact that Shapira continued to teach under such circumstances is astonishing. As his biographer, Nehemia Polen, notes: "Beyond anything Rabbi Shapira said to his Hasidim, the very fact that he did not allow himself to be crushed by the events of the war was surely the greatest teaching of all."[20]

The first part of this teaching quotes the relevant texts that Shapira uses to make his point: Rashi's comments on the biblical text, the Zohar's amplification of another aspect of the text, and the talmudic story.

First, in a Torah scroll, there is normally a break from one weekly reading to the next, but not at the beginning of this portion; Rashi quotes two explanations about what this "blockage" represents. For Shapira, the "blockage" also alludes to the blockage of Jewish life and well-being created by the Nazi onslaught. The biblical verse leaves us with an obvious question: if it says Jacob blessed Joseph, why does the text only tell of Jacob's blessings for Joseph's children? The answer in the Zohar is that if the children are blessed, the father is as well. The converse is assumed; if the children are cursed and oppressed, so is the father. The Jews are God's children, and their current suffering is also understood to be God's suffering.

Following this is the talmudic story that we originally encountered in chapter 5. The sufferings of the Jews cause "even the Torah" (and certainly the *sefirot*) to be damaged. Because God Himself is affected, inevitably a reaction against such evil will take place and "God will save us." When the damage is so great, we can and must believe that God will not allow such cosmic damage for very long.

In 1939 it is not yet clear how much evil will triumph. Shapira understands the cataclysm in classical kabbalistic terms. It is not going to end, as some believed, simply because God would intervene on the side of His people. It must end because God cannot allow such damage to Himself. (The idea of using Kabbalah for the sake of power is either impossible or impermissible for Shapira.) As the war continued, Shapira increasingly acknowledged the unprecedented extent of the Nazi war against the Jews and that the suffering far exceeded anything in Jewish history.[21]

"A vision [*hazon*] shown Isaiah son of Amoz, concerning Judah and Jerusalem, in the days of Uzziah, Ahaz, and Hezekiah, kings of Judah" (Isa. 1:1, the beginning of the haftarah for this Shabbat).

Why is this Shabbat named for the haftarah? We learn in the midrash: "There are ten expressions of prophecy, but which is the harshest of all? Rabbi Eliezer said: A vision is the harshest, as it is written, 'A cruel vision was told me' (Isa. 21:1)."[22] Of prophecy in general, we know nothing. But a simple explanation, reflecting our situation, may be as follows. We have previously spoken about how apparent it has become that hearing and speaking of pain and suffering is a very far cry from actually experiencing it. Hearing and speaking of it is vastly different from having to witness it, let alone undergoing

it, God forbid. When in Scripture and in the writings of our blessed sages we studied descriptions of the agony endured at the destruction of the Temple, we thought we had some notion of pain. At times we even cried while learning their teachings. But now, it is plain that hearing about sufferings is vastly different from seeing them, let alone enduring them, God forbid. They cannot be compared even minimally. Therefore, of the various levels of suffering revealed to the prophets—whether through a verbal prophecy, the divine voice heard from heaven, or other types of prophecy—the harshest level of all was when prophets were shown a vision. The harshest of all prophecies was when they had to watch a realistic simulation of the pain and suffering. This is the meaning of "a cruel vision was told me."

This was what Ulla and other sages of the Talmud meant when they spoke of the birth pangs of the Messiah. Ulla said: "Let the Messiah come; I will not see it."[23] Even though they knew of the suffering that will accompany the birth pangs of the Messiah, they did not want actually to witness the Jewish people enduring such agony. According to what we have said above, their intention was not simply to spare themselves the discomfort of having to witness such pain. They were responding to other sages who had so much to say about the agony that precedes the birth of the Messiah. They were expanding upon the words of those other sages, saying: "As much as we know, and as much as we imagine we are describing the suffering in words, we are still far, far short of the truth. Knowing of pain and speaking of suffering are nothing like having to watch it. So, even though I know about them, I still do not want to see them. Let the Messiah come; I will not see it."

This is the meaning of God's words to Moses: "I have truly seen the suffering of My people in Egypt . . . because I know his pain" (Exod. 3:7). At the simplest level, it might be asked: Why does God say, "I know," after already having said, "I have seen"? A father may know that his son will benefit greatly from surgery and yet be unable to stand and watch the operation being performed upon him. As we said above, knowing about pain cannot be compared to actually watching it. And so, even though the surgery is for the son's good, the father is unable to watch, for while it is happening, the father's knowledge is void; he cannot bear in mind the benefits of the operation because he is aware only of his son's pain. Like all the other exiles and sufferings, the exile in Egypt was for the benefit of the Jewish people. This is what God meant when He said, "I have truly seen the suffering of My people," meaning: "Because I have seen and watched, I know only their pain. I cannot bear in mind the benefits that will come of it. I know only the pain they feel." Therefore, God continued, "Now go. I am sending you to Pharaoh. Bring My people, the Israelites, out of Egypt."

Shabbat Hazon, the vision of Isaiah, is the harshest prophecy of all, because it is cruel to have to witness pain. Therefore, we read this haftarah in the week in which Tisha b'Av occurs, and the Shabbat is called by the name of the haftarah, Shabbat Hazon, Shabbat of vision. In heaven, they are already seeing the pain of the Jewish people, as God says: "I know his pain," and only his pain, not the benefit that will come of it. With this we can bring about the salvation, at the level of "Open Your eyes, and see" (Dan. 9:18). The haftarah begins with a vision, harsher than all other levels of prophecy, but it ends with salvation: "Zion will be redeemed with justice, and her captives with charity" (Isa. 1:27). (Shapira, *Eish Kodesh*, 337-39, for Shabbat Hazon, July 18, 1942 [Shabbat Hazon is the Shabbat before the Ninth of Av, a day of mourning for tragedies that befell the Jewish people])

What is the importance of calling the Shabbat before Tisha b'Av "Shabbat Hazon," referring to Isaiah's vision of destruction? Shapira recognizes that whatever we said or thought about the torments of past generations was nothing compared to seeing it, to experiencing it in the present. We who are living through the Nazi terrors, who must see our loved ones dying or in anguish . . . we *know* these sufferings in a way that the prophet vividly saw them. And when you know them so directly, they are not about theology, cannot be explained as serving God's needs. And the sages of the Talmud, though they believed that much suffering would likely accompany the coming of the Messiah, nevertheless did not want to see such suffering, even in a good cause. (Similarly, some readers may be reminded of the "justification" a few have offered for the Holocaust in saying that without the sacrifice of the six million, the State of Israel could not have come into being.) Even a father who sees his son undergoing a necessary operation cannot bear to watch it; all the more so when the pain one sees is inflicted without cause.

For the prophets, and for the Piesetzner Rebbe as well, in the words of Walter Kaufmann, "their piety is a cry in the night, born of suffering so intense that they cannot contain it and must shriek, speak, accuse, and argue with God—not about him—for there is no other human being who would understand, and the prose of dialogue could not be faithful to the poetry of anguish. . . . Jewish piety has been a ceaseless cry in the night, rarely unaware of 'all the oppressions that are practiced under the sun,' a faith in spite of, not a heathenish, complacent faith because."[24]

This haftarah is almost totally a vision of the Jewish people's suffering, but it ends on a note of hope. Perhaps Shapira read it as a parallel to the years of suffering, which he hoped would soon come to an end.

This was the final teaching recorded in *Eish Kodesh*; the following spring Shapira himself was deported to the labor camp of Trawniki, near Lublin, where he is believed to have been murdered together with other workers in November 1943. Obviously we cannot know what Shapira's response to the totality of the Holocaust might have been after the war. One can reasonably speculate that it would have been expressed in terms consistent with his mystical view of the damage to the cosmos (i.e., the *sefirot*), and with some degree of hope for the future. Indeed, many of the decimated Hasidic groups reorganized and rebuilt after the war and continue to grow today.

Born in Warsaw in 1907, Abraham Joshua Heschel was descended from a line of Hasidic rebbes and bore the name of one of the most noted Hasidic masters, Avraham Yehoshua Heschel, the Apter Rebbe. He was believed to be destined for high leadership in the Hasidic world, but in his teens chose to leave the Hasidic community and eventually became a professor. Escaping from Europe weeks before the beginning of World War II and the Holocaust that consumed most of his family, he went to the Hebrew Union College in Cincinnati and later to the Jewish Theological Seminary in New York, where he taught and wrote until his death in 1972.

Heschel lived with a foot in two worlds: the academic, rationalist, Western society (see chapter 28) on the one hand, and the mystically oriented Hasidic world that had nurtured him on the other.[25] As his daughter, Susannah Heschel, writes: "While my father always encouraged Jews to become more engaged in Jewish study, observance, and prayer, he also warned against attempting to imitate previous generations—that, he said, would be 'spiritual plagiarism,' a loss of integrity and a destruction of Judaism's authenticity."[26]

Inspired by the Hebrew prophets and the mystical tradition, Heschel became involved in various interfaith endeavors—most prominently in discussions with Catholic leadership that helped to reshape the Vatican's teachings toward Jews and Judaism, as well as in the civil rights and anti-Vietnam War movements. In his numerous books, articles, and speeches, he articulated a mystical orientation that resonated for many Jews and non-Jews, while always insisting on the uniqueness of Jewish thought. He left behind the formal role of tzaddik, but was referred to by one of his students as "the tzaddik of his generation."[27] Most of his teachings are compatible with Mainline Kabbalah and certainly demonstrate an awareness of the range of Jewish mystical experience.[28] Even when he describes mystical experience in the third person or in nonmystical terms, many readers will sense that he is sharing his experience with them.[29]

What characterizes man is not only his ability to develop words and symbols, but also his being compelled to draw a distinction between the utterable and the unutterable, to be stunned by that which is but cannot be put into words.

It is the sense of the sublime that we have to regard as the root of man's creative activities in art, thought and noble living. Just as no flora has ever fully displayed the hidden vitality of the earth, so has no work of art ever brought to expression the depth of the unutterable, in the sight of which the souls of saints, poets and philosophers live. The attempt to convey what we see and cannot say is the everlasting theme of mankind's unfinished symphony, a venture in which adequacy is never achieved. Only those who live on borrowed words believe in their gift of expression. A sensitive person knows that the intrinsic, the most essential, is never expressed. Most—and often the best—of what goes on in us is our own secret; we have to wrestle with it ourselves. The stirring in our hearts when watching the star-studded sky is something no language can declare. What smites us with unquenchable amazement is not that which we grasp and are able to convey but that which lies within our reach but beyond our grasp; not the quantitative aspect of nature but something qualitative; not what is beyond our range in time and space but the true meaning, source and end of being, in other words, the ineffable. (Heschel, *Man Is Not Alone*, 4–5)

Many mystics note that the experience of intimacy with God is ineffable; that is, it cannot be expressed in words.[30] Some see this as a disadvantage, a flaw; Heschel sees it as a sign of the legitimacy of such experience, for the higher reality cannot be conveyed in human terms. Yet one who wishes to approach it must overcome the desire to reduce it to common words; as Heschel puts it elsewhere: "Man is driven to commune with that which is beyond the mystery. The ineffable in him seeks a way to that which is beyond the ineffable."[31] The normal senses are insufficient for such purposes: "There is a higher form of seeing. . . . The grandeur of nature is only the beginning. Beyond the grandeur is God."[32]

For Heschel, awe and amazement are essential prerequisites for the path to relationship with God. But how does the normal life of the Jew, the regulated system of daily prayers and blessings, fit with such high goals?

> At first sight prayer appears to be a communication of ideas or feelings through spoken words. Every one of us bears a vast accumulation of unuttered sorrows, scruples, hopes, and yearnings, frozen in the muteness of his nature. In prayer the ice breaks, our feelings begin to move our mind, striving for an outlet. It is not an expression of things accidentally stored up in our minds but an emanation of what is most personal in us, an act of self-expression.
>
> Yet, in a sense, prayer starts where expression fails.[33] The words that reach our lips are often but waves of an overflowing stream touching the shore. We often seek and miss, struggle and fail to adjust our unique feelings to the patterns of texts. The soul, then, intimates its persistent striving, the riddle of its unhappiness, the strain of living twixt hope and fear. Where is the tree that can utter fully the silent passion of the soil? Words can only open the door, and we can only weep on the threshold of our incommunicable thirst after the incomprehensible. A certain passage in the morning prayer was interpreted by the Kotzker rabbi to mean that God loves what is left over at the bottom of the heart and cannot be expressed in words. It is the ineffable feeling which reaches God rather than the expressed feeling. (Heschel, *Moral Grandeur and Spiritual Audacity*, 349–50)

The fixed liturgy, the words of the prayer book, are not the goal; they are the stimulus to the soundless expression of the soul, which is real prayer. Indeed, it is too easy to simply focus on the words and forget that the goal is beyond words.[34] Ultimately, as Heschel wrote, "to pray is to take notice of the wonder, to regain a sense of the mystery that animates all beings."[35] Prayer for Heschel is not the recitation, but the "spiritual ecstasy"[36] that leads to devotion. And it is not solely about the experience of the one who prays; "There is something which is far greater than my desire to pray, namely, God's desire that I pray."[37] "To pray is to dream in league with God, to envision His holy visions."[38] Surely that is a description of mystical experience.

For Heschel, the prophets were the greatest examples of those who were most closely attuned to God's perspective.

> The prophets had no theory or "idea" of God. What they had was an *understanding* . . . . To the prophets, God was overwhelmingly real and shatteringly present. They never spoke of Him as from a distance. They lived as witnesses, struck by the words of God, rather than as explorers engaged in an effort to ascertain the nature of God; their utterances were the unloading of a burden rather than glimpses obtained in the fog of groping. (Heschel, *Prophets*, 221)

> What is the essence of being a prophet? A prophet is a person who holds God and men in one thought at one time, at all times. Our tragedy begins with the segregation of God, with the bifurcation of the secular and sacred. We worry more about the purity of dogma than about the integrity of love. We think of God in the past tense and refuse to realize that God is always present and never, never past; that God may be more intimately present in slums than in mansions, with those who are smarting under the abuse of the callous. (Heschel, *Insecurity of Freedom*, 93)

The mystical view and ethics constantly intersect in Heschel's writings; here, he expresses a view about societal inequalities in kabbalistic terms. For Heschel, the prophets are inspired by a powerful sense of God's Presence, which cannot be explained through philosophical examination of their experiences or through definitions. As he puts it elsewhere, "religion begins with God's question and man's answer."[39] The prophet is a witness to God's message and His very reality. And the prophet links

God with human beings and their sufferings and cruelties. He conveys the message that God has an "ultimate concern with good and evil" and cares for every human being, in and beyond this life.[40] The term "segregation of God" is likely his translation of *galut ha-Shekhinah*, "the exile of the *Shekhinah*," a profound way of expressing the prophetic sense of God's absence in the face of injustice.[41]

> **To some people explanations and opinions are a token of wonder's departure, like a curfew after which they may not come abroad. In the kabbalists, the drive and the fire and the light are never put out.**
>
> **... To the kabbalists God is as real as life, and as nobody would be satisfied with mere knowing or reading about life, so they are not content to suppose or to prove logically that there is a God; they want to feel and to enjoy Him; not only to obey, but to approach Him. They want to taste the whole wheat of spirit before it is ground by the millstones of reason. They would rather be overwhelmed by the symbols of the inconceivable than wield the definitions of the superficial. ...**
>
> **The kabbalist is not content with being confined to what he is. His desire is not only to *know* more than what ordinary reason has to offer but to *be* more than what he is; not only to comprehend the Beyond but to concur with it. He aims at the elevation and expansion of existence. Such expansion goes hand in hand with the exaltation of all being. (Heschel, "Mystical Element in Judaism," 602–3)**

The mystical drive is not satisfied with explanations, definitions, and dogma about God. Heschel suggests that "we do not think Him, we are stirred by Him."[42] One does not understand God, but must experience God's Presence. Though the experience may be overwhelming, it is still something to "enjoy," to "taste,"[43] to feel, just as God "feels" for human beings.

> **Jewish mystics are inspired by a bold and dangerously paradoxical idea that not only is God necessary to man but man is also necessary**

to God, to the unfolding of His plans in this world. Thoughts of this kind are indicated and even expressed in various rabbinic sources. "When Israel performs the will of the Omnipresent, they add strength to the heavenly power; as it is said, To God we render strength. When, however, Israel does not perform the will of the Omnipresent, they weaken—if it is possible to say so—the great power of Him who is above; as it is written: You weakened the Rock that begot you" (Deut. 32:18). (Heschel, "Mystical Element in Judaism," 604)[44]

In chapter 11 we read about the idea of the *tzorekh gavoha*, the divine need, and cited biblical passages in support of this notion, similar to the passages that Heschel quotes here. (But Heschel rarely uses overtly kabbalistic language.)[45] Here we see another approach to it, based on the idea that human beings have an element of the Divine. The idea of man as *helek Eloha mi-ma'al*, "a portion of God from above" (Job 31:2), was important to many Hasidic figures and some who influenced them, such as Judah Loew of Prague and Isaiah Horowitz. If human beings are indeed part of God, that kinship makes more possible human approach to God and makes more plausible the possibility that God needs us to fulfill His purposes. While there are limits as to how much of God can be comprehended, there are no limits in approaching God.

The mitzvot, for Heschel, are "mysterious sacramental acts" through which we attest to God's reality,[46] much like the midrashic teaching: "'So you are My witnesses, declares the Lord, and I am God' (Isa. 43:12): if you are My witnesses, then I am God, but if you are not My witnesses, then I am, as it were, not God."[47] Heschel, however, places strong emphasis not only on the ritual mitzvot but also on the ethical duties of Judaism as serving this divine need. This fits together with his appreciation of the demands of the prophets. As he writes elsewhere: "The goal of all efforts is to bring about the restitution of the unity of God and world. The restoration of that unity is a constant process and its accomplishment will be the essence of messianic redemption."[48]

Since no one can comprehend the full significance of an action, let alone what God desires or why He desires it, Heschel urges modern Jews to presuppose God's Presence, overcome their natural skepticism, and engage with the life and community of Torah.

> **A Jew is asked to take *a leap of action* rather than *a leap of thought*: to surpass his needs, to do more than he understands in order to understand more than he does. In carrying out the word of the Torah he is ushered into the presence of spiritual meaning. Through the ecstasy of deeds he learns to be certain of the presence of God.**
>
> **. . . In exposing our lives to God we discover the Divine within ourselves and its accord with the Divine beyond ourselves. If at the moment of doing a mitzvah once perceived to be thus sublime, thus Divine, you are in it with all your heart and with all your soul, there is no great distance between you and God. (Heschel, *Man's Quest for God*, 106)**

Through holy deeds, one may perceive God . . . even within the self. Heschel cautions against simply doing the deed without *kavanah*, without awareness or reflection, calling this "religious behaviorism."[49] Ultimately "God is, then, wholly other from what we know in human experience, but God can be discovered if we are sensitive enough to the clues in nature, the Bible, and in sacred deeds and worship and if those lead us to the insight of the reality of God behind all those phenomena and His importance for our lives."[50] God's Presence is available to everyone, even without the tzaddik; indeed, "every reader should be inspired to become a tzaddik."[51] Elsewhere, Heschel contrasted the idea of a leap of action to the Danish theologian Soren Kierkegaard's "leap of faith," similarly arguing that action precedes faith and thought.[52]

Each of these three individuals dealt with urgent political events, but addressed them from within their own mystical impulse. Their lives and teachings suggest that mysticism need not be a force that moves one away from the currents of human affairs.

With such mystical giants in the past century; why was I never taught about mysticism at any phase of my Jewish education? That is the question we must face at the end of our analysis.

28

Concealment and Distortion
of Jewish Mysticism

If Jewish mysticism was so important and influential in Jewish life for so long, why is it so rarely a part of Jewish education today? The roots of mysticism's absence today reach back to the nineteenth-century school of scholarship about Judaism known as "Wissenschaft des Judentums" ("Judaic studies" or "the Science of Judaism"), which was based on critical investigation of Jewish literature and culture using advanced methods to analyze the origins of Jewish traditions. Using scholarly methods to analyze Jewish ideas, the goal was to make Judaica its own field of study in higher learning, rather than a weak (older) sister to Christianity. While Wissenschaft scholars made critical contributions to understanding Jewish life, they too suffered from a few biases, one of which was to see Jewish mysticism as an irrational importation from foreign sources.[1] A prime example can be found in the work of the premier and powerfully influential Jewish historian, Heinrich Graetz (1817–91).

> **The secret science of the Kabbalah, which hitherto had assumed a modest deportment and been of a harmless character, began to foment discord in Ben Adret's time [i.e., Rabbi Solomon ben Adret, Spain, 1235–1310], ensnare the intelligence and lead astray the weak. What it lacked in intrinsic truth and power of conviction, it endeavored to supply by presumptiousness. (Graetz, *History of the Jews*, 4:1)**

Graetz's objectivity as a historian departs when he deals with thirteenth-century Kabbalah. The entire mystical trend is seen as an aberration, injurious to Jews and Judaism. The rationalist philosophers are the "true" Jews; the kabbalists and mystics are either frauds or grossly mistaken.

The question about Moses de Leon (1250–1305) is only whether he was a selfish or pious impostor. His intention was certainly to deceive and lead astray.... Of careless prodigality, Moses de Leon expended everything that he had without reflecting what would remain for the morrow; he made use of the Kabbalah which had come into fashion to procure for himself a rich source of revenue.... He commenced the composition of books under feigned but honored names. If he put the doctrines of the Kabbalah, worn threadbare, to be sure, into the mouth of an older, highly venerated authority, some imposing name from the dazzling past—taking care, of course, to make the coloring and the method of presentation archaic—would not such a composition be eagerly swallowed?... And thus there came into the world a book, the Zohar, which for many centuries was held by Jews as a heavenly revelation.... But seldom has so notorious a forgery so thoroughly succeeded.

The Zohar with its appendages in no wise develops a Kabbalistic system... but plays with the Kabbalistic forms as with counters—with the *Ein Sof*, with the number of the *sefirot*, with points and strokes, with vowels, accents, with the Names of God and the transposition of their letters, as well as with the Biblical verses and aggadic sayings—casts them about in eternal repetition, and in this manner produces sheer absurdities. Occasionally it gives a faint suggestion of an idea, but in a trice it evaporates in feverish fancies, or dissolves in childish silliness.

Through its constant use of coarse expressions, often verging on the sensual, in contradistinction to the chaste, pure spirit pervading Jewish literature, the Zohar sowed the seeds of unclean desires, and later on produced a sect that laid aside all regard for decency. Finally, the Zohar blunted the sense for the simple and the true, and created a visionary world, in which the souls of those who zealously occupied themselves with it were lulled into a sort of half-sleep, and lost the faculty of distinguishing between right and wrong. Its quibbling interpretations of Holy Writ, adopted by the Kabbalists and others infected with this mannerism, perverted the verses and words of the Holy Book, and made the Bible the wrestling-ground of the most curious, insane notions. (Graetz, *History of the Jews*, 4:11-12, 14, 22-23)

Graetz dismisses De Leon, the presumed author of the Zohar, as a deceiver. (As noted in chapter 8, more recent scholarship suggests that others were also involved in its composition.) Graetz is clearly aware of the Zohar's symbolic language, but treats its methodology as "absurd" and "silly." Furthermore, it is clear that Graetz, living in the Victorian era, is deeply discomfited by the erotic elements in the Zohar. Rarely has so significant a historian allowed himself to express his own bias so directly!

With the exception of a few scholars (most prominently Solomon Schechter, who wrote numerous essays on various aspects of Jewish mysticism), these prejudices dominated Jewish scholarship until the work of Gershom Scholem (1897–1982). While Scholem was not a mystic and did not have positive feelings about the mystical enterprise, particularly Hasidism, he was untroubled by the mystical challenge to philosophy, because he saw the two approaches as complementary rather than exclusive. Scholem did not shy away from criticizing other scholars; speaking directly of Graetz and other "detractors" of the Zohar, he wrote that "charges of this kind simply misconstrue both the morality and the tendency of the Zohar, and are hardly relevant even to the literary form of presentation; but above all they completely ignore the problem presented by the resurrection of mythology in the heart of mystical Judaism, of which the Zohar is the classical representative."[2] Scholem indeed regarded much of mystical Judaism as "mythical," but nonetheless saw its power as a valid expression, often just under the surface of the more rational (read: respectable) Judaism of the day, and perhaps even as a primary and necessary source for the regeneration of Judaism.

But while Scholem's scholarship overturned many of the earlier assumptions about Jewish mysticism, it did not immediately alter the general sense that it did not have a place in contemporary (again, read: respectable) Jewish life. Twentieth-century rabbinical schools did not emphasize the mystical impulse as a part of Judaism; indeed Heschel was often treated as an outsider at the Jewish Theological Seminary of America, in some measure because of his identification with a mystical approach.[3] When its dominant faculty member, talmudist Saul Lieberman, introduced Scholem before a lecture at the seminary, he said: "You know what I think about mysticism. Mysticism is nonsense. But the *history* of nonsense: that is scholarship!"[4] Such contempt for mysticism, even among devoutly observant scholars, can be attributed to many of the same impulses that motivated Graetz and others from the Wissenschaft school.

Many of Scholem's assumptions have been revised by later scholarship, most notably that of Moshe Idel. While most of these issues are beyond this book's scope, let me mention just two. We have already read about the role historical events may have played in the growth of mystical movements; Scholem, for example, maintained that Lurianic Kabbalah was a response to the suffering related to the expulsion from Spain in 1492. Idel and others have shown that many ideas in Lurianic Kabbalah existed well before it coalesced in Safed, and thus (as later was true regarding the founding of Hasidism) it should be seen as having developed more organically. Additionally, Scholem generally assumed the impossibility of a modern approach to kabbalistic belief and practice, ignoring evidence to the contrary that is well documented beyond Idel's work by younger scholars such as Jonathan Garb and Jody Myers (see below).[5] This has important implications for the future of Jewish mystical development.

Now let us examine what Graetz tells us about the mystical movement of his own time.

There arose in Poland a new Essenism, with forms similar to those of the ancient cult, with ablutions and baths, white garments, miraculous cures, and prophetic visions. Like the old movement, it originated in ultra-piety, but soon turned against its own parent, and perhaps hides within itself germs of a peculiar kind. . . . It seems remarkable that, at the time when Mendelssohn declared rational thought to be the essence of Judaism, and founded, as it were, a widely-extended order of enlightened men, another banner was unfurled, the adherents of which announced the grossest super-stition to be the fundamental principle of Judaism, and formed an order of wonder-seeking confederates. . . . The origin of the new Hasidim, who had already become numerous, and who sprang up very rapidly, is not so clear as the movement started by Mendelssohn. The new sect, a daughter of darkness, was born in gloom, and even today proceeds stealthily on its mysterious way.

In Poland, in Ba'al Shem's time, with the terrible mental strain created by the Kabbalah in connection with the Sabbatian fraud, the feverish expectation of imminent Messianic redemption, everything was possible and everything credible. In that land the fancy of both Jews and Christians moved among extraordinary and supernatural phenomena as in its natural element. Israel [the Ba'al Shem Tov] steadfastly and firmly believed in the visions seen when he was under mental and physical excitement; he believed in the power of his prayers. In his delusion he blasphemously declared that prayer is a kind of marriage union [*zivvug*] of man with the Godhead [*Shekhinah*], upon which he must enter whilst in a state of excitement.

Israel need not have been a trickster to obtain followers. Mysti-cism and madness are contagious. He particularly attracted men who desired to lead a free and merry life, at the same time hoping to

reach a lofty aim, and to live assured of the nearness of God in seren-
ity and calmness, and to advance the Messianic future. They did not
need to pore over talmudical folios in order to attain to higher piety.

The Deity reveals Himself especially in the acts of the tzaddik;
even his most trifling deeds are to be considered important. The
way he wears his clothes, ties his shoes, smokes his pipe, whether he
delivers profound addresses or indulges in silly jokes—everything
bears a close relation to the Deity, and is of as much moment as
the fulfillment of a religious duty. Even when drawing inspiration
from the bottle, he is swaying the upper and nether worlds. All these
absurd fancies owed their origin to the superstitious doctrines of
the Kabbalah. (Graetz, *History of the Jews*, 5:374-75, 377, 378-79, 382)

Graetz saves his fiercest criticism for Hasidism. Granting the sincerity
of the Ba'al Shem Tov, he proceeds to denigrate everything else about
his approach. It is "a daughter of darkness," based on "the grossest of
superstition." Most obviously Graetz comes to his criticism with the pre-
conception that "mysticism and madness are contagious." No reputable
contemporary scholar, even if only familiar with the mystics covered in
chapter 27, would make such a claim. In fact, Graetz himself was not
conversant in Hasidic sources; Samuel Dresner notes that "there is no
evidence that Graetz had anything but the meagerest familiarity with
Hasidic literature. In spite of all this, his conscience was clear and he felt
quite justified in publishing his opinions. So powerful was the prejudice
of the time."[6] Nor was this bias at all unusual among the Wissenschaft
scholars[7] or, to a lesser extent, their successors.[8]

After the Holocaust and the decimation of many Hasidic communities,
it was widely believed that Hasidism could not survive in the modern
world, as the next two texts illustrate.

Beginning with the Talmudic era, there crept into Jewish thought
a persistently mystical and life-denying element. But mysticism
never really achieved a dominant position among Jews except for

relatively brief periods when, under the stress of persecution, Jewish life became constricted. Then there were those who were eager to escape into the unreal and shadowy world of Cabala. . . . They were men disenchanted with life who sought to construct a bridge between "this vale of tears" and God.

. . . In the twilight years of the Renaissance, while the Christian world was richly developing its sciences, its arts and the humanities, the Jews, yielding to the hammer blows of their enemies, were growing culturally weaker. Superstition, excessive piety and delirious cabalistic dreams proved excellent modes of escape from the unhappy reality of Jewish life. The legends about the 16th century Cabala masters of Safed in Palestine—Moses Cordovero, Joseph della Reina, Alkabetz, Hayim Vital, and Isaac Luria, better known as "The Ari"—wove their web of morbid enchantment around Jewish daily thinking and feeling. In addition to harassment from death, hunger, epidemics and persecution, the average Jew now had to endure the terror of a shadowy world haunted by unspeakable demons, specters, ghosts and *dybbukim* [transmigrating souls]. . . .

Although Hasidism, as a movement, is practically extinct at the present time, isolated circles of Hasidim are still to be found, even in New York, Boston, Philadelphia and Chicago. (Nathan Ausubel, introduction to "Cabalists, Mystics, and Wonder-Workers," in *Treasury of Jewish Folklore* [1948], 175-78)

Ausubel's ideas about Jewish mysticism and its negative qualities ("life-denying," "unreal," "delirious," "morbid") sound like they are a direct inheritance from Graetz. Perhaps Ausubel felt the same need to sanitize Judaism for Americans, and American Jews, after the war, as Graetz did for his readers a century earlier. In the end, though, his presumption that the Hasidic world was "practically extinct" has been proven wrong.

The following was written at some point after World War II by the brother of Jiri Langer, who grew up in an assimilated Czech Jewish family and became immersed in Hasidism, ultimately authoring a well-known book on its teachings. Langer died in Palestine in 1943. His brother Frantisek, a physician and author, wrote a foreword that appeared in the first English edition of Jiri Langer's *Nine Gates to the Chassidic Mysteries* in 1961, but the exact date of its writing is unknown.

It may be that among the Jews in Israel or New York there are a few handfuls of the old Hasidic believers still adhering to the customs which they have brought from their old homes. But these are merely so many reminiscences of the past. The mystical reality of the Hasidim cannot last under the blue sky of Israel or amidst the bustle of the streets of Brooklyn. It could only exist in that utter isolation from the world and time which it enjoyed in Galicia, in that poverty in which all were equal, in that freedom in which they were subjected to nought save the will of God, and in that spiritual grandeur which came to dwell in their villages through the wisdom and miracles of their saintly rabbis. And thus it was that my brother Jiri depicted it for the last time in his sweet and smiling book, thereby erecting for the Hasidim an eternal monument to preserve their memory for all time. (Frantisek Langer, foreword to Jiri Langer, *Nine Gates*, xxxi)

Frantisek Langer presumably speaks for many assimilated Jews who have some nostalgic feelings for Hasidic life and teachings, but who believe it could not possibly prosper in the modern world and see it as inevitably attached to the "poverty" of Eastern European Jewry. Of course it is in both Israel and Brooklyn that the Hasidim particularly thrive today.

In the mid-twentieth century, a few scholars encouraged a broader appreciation of Hasidism. Two examples follow.

The great Hasidim were the repair men of the Holy of Holies. In Hebrew *tevot* means both boxes and *words*. It was through the word that they entered the Holy of Holies. In the Hasidic movement the spirit was alive in the word. It was a voice, not a mere idea. It emanated in words that had the power to repair, to revive, to create. Judaism today is in need of repair. The spirit is stifled, the word is emaciated; we do not know how to find access to the "Upper Chamber." (Dresner, *Zaddik*, 7)

Allowing for the exceptions, the Hasidim were, and still are, highly gifted practitioners of the art of religion, pursuing, with the exercise of the full creative imagination and with a heartwarming naiveté masking a mature sophistication, their aim of bringing God down to man and encouraging man to rise on the rungs of the ancient ladder linking heaven and earth. Hasidic panentheism, with its stress that all is in God, that He is "closer than breathing and nearer than hands and feet," is a powerful antidote to reductionism in religion. Hasidism speaks clearly to affirm that for religion to be relevant it must be seen as *sui generis*, an ultimate end, not a means to another end, be that end family harmony, the avoidance of juvenile delinquency, the promotion of ethical conduct, the furtherance of world peace, or the survival of the Jewish people—all of them supremely worthy ends, but for the truly religious, by-products of the ultimate end, part of that totality we haltingly call the worship of God. Dean Inge has remarked with justice that the breakdown of authoritarian religion frequently results among people deeply committed to a religious outlook in an approach that stresses religious experience, which goes a long way toward explaining the lure of mysticism—religion in its most intense form, as this has been defined—for a generation bored with religious formalism and disillusioned with behavioristic patterns and passive obedience as substitutes for spontaneity and a fresh response to the call of the divine. (Jacobs, "Relevance and Irrelevance," 2:22-23)

Dresner, a student of Heschel, a scholar of Hasidism, and a prominent Conservative pulpit rabbi, saw firsthand the "need of repair" in American Jewish life. Jacobs too was a scholar of Hasidism and a prominent British pulpit rabbi; he criticizes "reductionism" in religion, that is, the practice of taking all the complexities of faith and simplifying them to the point of distortion. For him, Hasidism is a reminder of the ultimate purpose of all religion as well as the need to provide spontaneity and renew Jewish life within a community bogged down in established patterns. This is similar to Heschel's discussion of prayer in *Man's Quest for God*.

Does it take a special kind of atmosphere for Jewish mysticism to thrive? Perhaps all it requires is an environment where Jewish tradition is taken seriously as a way to bring meaning to our lives; ultimately, in such surroundings, the mystical impulse is so deeply rooted that it is destined to affect a substantial number of the souls within it.

> Saadia Gaon, who lived in the tenth century, claimed that Jews are a people only by virtue of Judaism. On the other hand, the twelfth-century poet Judah Halevi reminds us that "if there were no Jews, there would be no Judaism."
>
> For centuries, the view expressed by Saadia was the dominant one. The preservation and the continuity of Jewish faith took precedence. Since Jewish faith was assumed to be the raison d'être for the existence of the Jewish people, the primacy of the religion of the Jews over the Jewish people was affirmed both in theological teachings and in communal actions. But with the Holocaust this changed. The priority became the physical survival of the Jewish people. It is now becoming increasingly clear, however, that Jewish religious faith provides the basis for the meaning of Jewish survival; that spiritual meaning is the premise on which physical survival is based. Jewish survival for the sake of survival is logically a tautology and sociologically a self-defeating strategy. Preoccupation with Jewish survival has deflected attention from the fundamental question: Survival for what? (Sherwin, *Sparks Amidst the Ashes*, 7)

Jewish life still faces external threats, but in the overwhelmingly open society in which most Jews live today, the option of assimilation into other cultures, and even other religions, exists in a way that most premoderns could never have imagined. Jews who affirm that they and every other religion and culture should have the *right* to survive are often unable to give a compelling answer as to *why* the Jewish religion should survive. The answers that seemed obvious to scholars throughout the nineteenth and well into the twentieth century no longer seem to work for many Jews. As we have read, in previous eras it was widely believed that having rational reasons for performing the mitzvot often led to people rationalizing *not* performing them; it was only when people felt that doing them had some cosmic significance that they felt compelled to maintain them.

Perhaps Jewish mysticism simply provides answers to the questions Jews ask.

How and why did the kabbalists succeed—where the philosophers had failed—in decisively shaping the religious consciousness of the Jewish people? The actual triumph of kabbalism in the sixteenth century is a fact beyond dispute. It is only the interpretation of this fact which is at issue. Rationalist historians, such as Graetz and others, have offered an engagingly simple explanation; persecution and suffering had dimmed the light of reason and paved the way for an eruption of mystical obscurantism. It is hardly necessary to expend many words over an "explanation" whose bias is so obvious. The real answer to the question should be positive, not negative in character. Kabbalism triumphed because it provided a valid answer to the great problems of the time. To a generation for which the facts of exile and the precariousness of existence in it had become a most pressing and cruel problem, kabbalism could give an answer unparalleled in breadth and in depth of vision. The kabbalistic answer illuminated the significance of exile and redemption and accounted for the

unique historical situation of Israel within the wider, in fact cosmic, context of creation itself. (Scholem, *Sabbetai Sevi*, 20)

What were the "great problems of the time" that Kabbalah answered? Scholem believed that these problems had to do with the dissonance between Jewish chosenness and Jewish suffering.[9] But there are other questions Jews were also asking, and ask now, as we will see below. Scholem himself was not immune to a certain prejudice concerning some of the elements he studied, and he did not believe that scholars could accurately assess mystical thought except by remaining apart from the mystics.[10] However, he and other scholars of Jewish mysticism did sense the possibility of finding serious answers to the religious questions they themselves were facing in the middle of the twentieth century.[11]

If Scholem is correct, then the only question remaining is whether Kabbalah can continue to provide satisfying answers to modern Jews. At least a fair number of leading Jewish thinkers believe it can.

Three sources of Kabbalah—the teachings of Jewish Kabbalists, metaphysical religious literature, and academic scholarship—were drawn upon during the late 1960s during the religious transformation that accompanied the American political turmoil of the time. A sizable number of young people voiced dissatisfaction with their parents' religious lives and with conventional modes of practicing established religions. They accused religious leaders and institutions of being unresponsive to social ills, overly focused on buildings and institutional preservation, and spiritually vacuous. Some looked for new approaches or revived neglected elements from within their inherited religious traditions. Many religious rebels deliberately looked outside their heritage. They experimented with a variety of newly available religious options such as Buddhism, Hinduism, nature-centered and Native American religions, New Age, and all types of meditation and mysticism. College-aged Jews were disproportionately represented among this cohort.

In response, a few rabbis and educators devised strategies for drawing alienated and unlearned Jews back to Judaism. A number of American Orthodox rabbis recognized that Kabbalah contained many of the features that the young found attractive in "foreign" religions. Rabbis Zalman Schachter (later Schachter-Shalomi, [1924–2014]) and Shlomo Carlebach (1924–1994), Chabad emissaries assigned to American college campuses, were the first of these to include kabbalistic teachings and ecstatic practices in their "outreach" work.[12] In 1969 Rabbi Philip Gruberger (later Philip Berg, b. 1929), a student of the late rabbis Levi Krakovsky and Yehuda Brandwein, founded the Research Centre of Kabbalah to publish the kabbalistic writings of others and his own New Age version of their lessons; this eventually led to the creation of the Kabbalah Learning Center chain. Rabbi Aryeh Kaplan (1934–1983) began in 1978 to add translations of kabbalistic texts and essays on Kabbalah to his extensive writings directed toward potential or actual "returnees to Judaism" (*ba'alei teshuva*). By this time, courses in Jewish Studies were entering American college curricula, and academic works on Jewish mysticism became more available and increasingly utilized for spiritual, artistic, and literary ends. (Myers, "Kabbalah at the Turn of the 21st Century," 179)

Myers has written extensively on contemporary interest in Kabbalah, especially in America. She traces some of this interest back to the developments of the 1960s and the questioning of authority that accompanied them. To reach this generation, the conveyors of Kabbalah in some cases reduced the authority that lay behind Kabbalah and in others soft-pedaled or postponed the confrontation with authority until such time as "returnees" could more willingly accept it.

From antiquity throughout the medieval period, mysticism was an integral part of Jewish thought. The Bible pulsates with mystical imagery, from Moses' radiant encounters with God in the *ohel mo'ed* to Ezekiel's wheel within a wheel. Rabbinic tradition continued

this daring dance of imagery, and the Talmud speaks of a mystical *Sefer Yetzirah* that the Talmudic sages would read and tells us of the great halakhic master, Rabbi Akiva, who would routinely travel to the highest spheres of heaven (there to commune with angels and to delight in visions of God). Great medieval commentators were also often mystics (one thinks of the Ramban [Nahmanides], Solomon ibn Gabirol, and Rabbi Abraham ben Maimon, son of the Rambam).

As we entered modernity, many western Jews insisted that their future and their freedom required shedding what they perceived as parochial orientalism. They fashioned a Judaism that was decorous and strictly rational (according to 19th Century European standards), denigrating Kabbalah as backward, superstitious, and marginal.

Now, a few hundred years later, we have reaped a bountiful benefit from their openness to modernity. . . . Jews have participated in modernization with gusto, and have contributed well beyond our numbers. But we have also paid a high price for the chill secularism and the straight-jacket of an arrogant rationalism. . . . Our scientific materialism has produced miracles of technology, medicine, and physical comfort . . . [but the] . . . inadequacy of scientific materialism to account generously for those aspects of our lives that matter most . . . have caused a new generation to look once more to ancient fountains of insight, not to deny the value of reason and science, but to supplement those ways of knowing with other, more intuitive ways of perceiving, connecting, signifying. Ours is an age hungry for meaning, for a sense of belonging, for holiness. In that search, we have returned to the very Kabbalah our predecessors scorned. "The stone that the builders rejected has become the head cornerstone" (Ps. 118:22). (Artson, "From the Periphery," 28)

Bradley Shavit Artson, the dean of the (Conservative) Ziegler School of Rabbinic Studies in Los Angeles, summarizes many points made here and throughout this volume. Mysticism historically played a central role in Judaism; for reasons external to Judaism itself we have turned away from it. But Artson says that we need it and cannot turn away from it indefinitely. In the same article, he notes, a society that rejects the infinite value of human life, and with it our ability to connect with God, will, in the name of its "rationalist" bias, produce other evils as well.

Among a variety of reasons for the recurring interest in Jewish mysticism, Jody Myers has listed the following:[13]

1. Kabbalah can be a source for constructing a less authoritarian theology and view of the cosmos.[14]
2. Kabbalah can be a source for a nonliteral approach to Scripture.
3. Kabbalah can be a source for alternative understandings of religious practice and forms of worship.
4. Kabbalah may be a way to dovetail religion and science, to the degree it provides meaningful information about existence or even serves as "an accurate guide to the operations of the universe."[15]
5. Kabbalah can be a source for *tikkun*; that is, it can be a way of looking at the world with hope.
6. Kabbalah can provide answers to the problem of evil that make sense to moderns.

While some of this interest is well founded, one wonders how much of it will be supported by authentic substance. Jonathan Garb reported a few years ago that "an advertisement for a new coffee house in Jerusalem recently promised 'Kabbalah, Hasidism, Zionism, Judaism, and Fun.'"[16] This may be the contemporary equivalent of what Rabbi Moshe Isserles complained about in chapter 8: "Many ordinary people . . . not even knowing how to explain the weekly Torah portion or a Torah passage with the commentary of Rashi, run to learn Kabbalah."[17] Nonetheless, the mystical impulse remains firmly grounded in Jewish history and in the experience of many Jews today.

Based on the following two texts, I add a seventh factor to the above six: the mystical tradition adds an energy that helps many Jews feel a powerful connection with God.

> There was a man who lived in the mountains. He knew nothing about those who lived in the city. He sowed wheat and ate the kernels raw. One day he entered the city, and was offered good bread. He said, "What is this for?" They said, "Bread to eat!" He ate, and it tasted very good. He said, "What is it made of?" They said, "Wheat." Later they brought him cakes kneaded in oil. He tasted them and said, "What are these made of?" They said, "Wheat." Later they brought him royal pastry kneaded with honey and oil. He said, "And what are these made of?" They said, "Wheat." He said, "I am the king of all of these, for I eat the essence of all of these!"
>
> Because of that view, he knew nothing of the delights of the world; they were lost to him. So it is with one who grasps the principle and does not know all those delectable delights deriving, diverging, from that principle. (Zohar 2:176a–b)[18]

As we saw in chapter 13, there are different levels of interpretation of the Torah. The kernels of wheat may be understood as the *peshat*, the simple meaning of the text; the bread, cake, and royal pastry go through midrash, *remez* (allegory), and finally *sod*, the mystical meaning of the Torah. The story can also be seen as a general critique of the rational-philosophical approach to Jewish life, suggesting that those who fail to see or experience its mystical meaning miss out on the energy that sustains and enlivens it. This can be true both for those who reject and those who accept a traditional reading of the Torah as given directly from God.

Melila Hellner-Eshed suggests that, on the one hand, "truth is not found solely in pure essence or in a pure source, but rather in the delights that one can develop from such a source. . . . The Zohar does not create a simple world, a kernel of wheat. Rather, it is characterized by complexity, refinement, sophistication, and depth—the secret of its great charm."[19]

On the other hand, she asserts, "we find also the apparent wish to return to the primal source. . . . The ability to hold fast to the kernel of wheat that is the *peshat*" is key to the approach of the mystic; "the words of the Zohar are indeed new and at times exceedingly daring, but they are always connected, in one way or another, to antiquity and to the archaic source—to the antiquity of the holy text, the tradition, the depths of the soul, or the divine itself."[20]

> To the Kabbalists God is as real as life, and as nobody would be satisfied with mere knowing or reading about life, so they are not content to suppose or to prove logically that there is a God; they want to feel and to enjoy Him; not only to obey, but to approach Him. They want to taste the whole wheat of spirit before it is ground by the millstones of reason. (Heschel, "Mystical Element in Judaism," 602)

Within this brief text lies the last and perhaps most important factor in the revival of Jewish mysticism: There will always be Jews who seek a more direct experience of God, in spite of those who claim it cannot be had; Heschel's student Edward Kaplan wrote that through Heschel's teaching he found "an entrance to Jewishness that aspired to a concrete experience of the divine."[21] And some of these searching Jews will sense that this is not merely their own seeking of God, but it is God who is seeking them.

Suggestions for Further Reading

JEWISH MYSTICISM IN GENERAL

Byron Sherwin, *Kabbalah: An Introduction to Jewish Mysticism*
Pinchas Giller, *Kabbalah: A Guide for the Perplexed*
David Ariel, *Kabbalah: The Mystic Quest in Judaism*
Joseph Dan, ed., *The Heart and the Fountain: An Anthology of Jewish Mystical Experiences*
Louis Jacobs, *Jewish Mystical Testimonies*
Daniel Matt, *The Essential Kabbalah: The Heart of Jewish Mysticism*
Moshe Hallamish, *An Introduction to the Kabbalah*
Rachel Elior, *Jewish Mysticism: The Infinite Expression of Freedom*
Gershom Scholem, *Major Trends in Jewish Mysticism*
Elliot Wolfson, *Through a Speculum That Shines*

EARLY JEWISH MYSTICISM

Peter Schafer, *The Origins of Jewish Mysticism*
Joseph Dan, *The Ancient Jewish Mysticism*
Rachel Elior, *The Three Temples: On the Emergence of Jewish Mysticism*
Arthur Green, *Keter: The Crown of God in Early Jewish Mysticism*
(on Hasidei Ashkenaz) Ivan Marcus, *Piety and Society*

EARLY KABBALAH AND THE ZOHAR

Joseph Dan, ed., and Ronald C. Kiener, trans., *The Early Kabbalah*
Arthur Green, *A Guide to the Zohar*
Isaiah Tishby, *The Wisdom of the Zohar*.
Daniel Matt, *Zohar: The Book of Enlightenment*

Daniel Matt, trans. and commentary, *The Zohar: The Pritzker Edition* (nine volumes as of this writing)

Melila Hellner-Eshed, *A River Flows from Eden: The Language of Mystical Experience in the Zohar*

ECSTATIC/PROPHETIC KABBALAH

Moshe Idel, *Studies in Ecstatic Kabbalah*

LURIANIC KABBALAH AND RELATED THEMES

Lawrence Fine, *Safed Spirituality*

Lawrence Fine, *Physician of the Soul, Healer of the Cosmos: Isaac Luria and His Kabbalistic Fellowship*

Gershom Scholem, *Sabbatai Sevi: The Mystical Messiah*

HASIDISM

General

Louis Jacobs, *Hasidic Thought*

Louis Jacobs, *Hasidic Prayer*

Samuel Dresner, *The Zaddik: The Doctrine of the Zaddik according to the Writings of Rabbi Yaakov Yosef of Polnoy*

Maurice Lamm, *The Religious Thought of Hasidism: Text and Commentary*

Rachel Elior, *The Mystical Origins of Hasidism*

Early Hasidism

Moshe Rosman, *Founder of Hasidism: A Quest for the Historical Ba'al Shem Tov*

Immanuel Etkes, *The Besht: Magician, Mystic, and Leader*

Significant Hasidic Figures and Their Teachings:

Arthur Green, *Tormented Master: A Life of Rabbi Nahman of Bratslav*

Arthur Green, *The Language of Truth: The Torah Commentary of the Sefat Emet, Rabbi Yehudah Leib Alter of Ger*

Samuel Dresner: *The World of a Hasidic Master: Levi Yitzhak of Berditchev*

Michael Rosen, *The Quest for Authenticity: The Thought of Reb Simhah Bunim*

Elliot R. Wolfson, *Open Secret: Postmessianic Messianism and the Mystical Revision of Menahem Mendel Schneerson*

Zalman Schachter-Shalomi, *Wrapped in a Holy Flame: Teachings and Tales of the Hasidic Masters*

TWENTIETH-CENTURY FIGURES AND MODERN THOUGHT

Abraham Joshua Heschel, *God in Search of Man* and *Heavenly Torah: As Refracted through the Generations*, among his many works

Abraham Isaac Kook, *Abraham Isaac Kook: The Lights of Penitence, The Moral Principles, Lights of Holiness, Essays, Letters, and Poems*, translated and with an introduction by Ben Zion Bokser

Nehemia Polen, *The Holy Fire: The Teachings of Rabbi Kalonymus Kalman Shapira, the Rebbe of the Warsaw Ghetto*

OTHER ACADEMIC WRITING ON JEWISH MYSTICISM

I have noted above two books by Gershom Scholem (*Major Trends in Jewish Mysticism* and *Sabbatai Sevi: The Mystical Messiah*); his other writings are also classics in the field.

Of great importance is the work of Moshe Idel, in particular *Kabbalah: New Perspectives*.

See also various works of Elliot Wolfson, Joseph Dan, and Jonathan Garb.

Much more continues to be produced by young Israeli scholars, most of it not yet translated into English.

Notes

1. WHAT IS JEWISH MYSTICISM?

1. Quoting Bernard McGinn from "Selective Affinities," cited in Elior, *Mystical Origins of Hasidism*, 113–14, from Elior and Schafer, eds., *Creation and Re-creation in Jewish Thought*, 85–102. See also discussion in Schafer, *Origins of Jewish Mysticism*, 1–9, and Tirosh-Samuelson, "Jewish Mysticism," 399. Alternatively, Robert Eisen defines it as "an attempt to have a direct and intimate relationship with the divine. Now the division between mysticism and normal religion is not necessarily a sharp one. After all, ordinary religious people strive to have a close relationship with the divine. The point is that mystics are much more focused on this type of experience and attempt to achieve it in an unusually intense form." "Revival of Jewish Mysticism," 28.

2. Rachel Elior describes this point of view, which informs the mystical texts analyzed in this book, as including "the overwhelming awareness of the presence of the living God and the immediate access to the omnipresence of the divine." *Mystical Origins of Hasidism*, 113.

3. Citations from Zohar 2:15b, *Midrash ha-Ne'elam*.

4. As Elliot Wolfson has put it, "mystical experience, like experience more generally, is contextual. . . . [T]he mystic's religious tradition provides an interpretative framework that is a constitutive factor of the mystical experience itself." Wolfson, *Through a Speculum*, 52–53. See notes there for further discussion and reference. Also note Scholem, *Major Trends*, 5–6: "there is no such thing as mysticism in the abstract. . . . [T]here is only the mysticism of a particular religious system, Christian, Islamic, Jewish mysticism and so on." This view contrasts with those who "defined mysticism primarily in terms of an individual experience that occurs suddenly and passively . . . as a phenomenon that transcends specific religious traditions." Swartz, "Mystical Texts," 395.

5. "Indeed, literary evidence attests that the religious experience described in

the different currents of Jewish mysticism from Late Antiquity through the Middle Ages is overwhelmingly visual." Wolfson, *Through a Speculum*, 4.

6. "Mysticism developed in Judaism without any consciousness on the part of its creators as to its meaning and nature. Hebrew, like Arabic, does not have a word equivalent even partially to the Latin-Christian term of 'mysticism.' Any identification of a certain Jewish religious phenomenon as 'mystical' is a modern scholarly decision, which relies on the modern scholar's understanding of the term; there is no intrinsic demand in the texts themselves for such a usage." Dan, "Language of the Mystics," 7.

7. See Sherwin, *Kabbalah*, 13–27, and particularly 26n1, for a lengthy explanation of where this model varies from previous and current scholarship. I have used slightly different terminology.

8. Wolpe, *Floating Takes Faith*, 39.

9. Buxbaum, *Jewish Spiritual Practices*, 52.

10. "'Theosophy' is a term employed by scholars to refer to symbolic systems that are understood by their authors to represent concealed aspects of the divine world." Lachter, "Introduction: Reading Mysteries," 5.

11. "Mystical Element in Judaism," 621.

12. See Janowitz, "God's Body," 192.

13. See, e.g., Green, "The *Zaddiq* as *Axis Mundi*"; Sherwin, *Kabbalah*, 119–20.

2. MYSTICISM IN THE BIBLE

1. Noted in Plaut, *Haftarah Commentary*, 168.

2. See comments of Michael Fishbane in *Etz Hayim*, 451–52.

3. Compare with Isa. 40:5, "And the glory of the Lord shall be revealed," as translated by Freehof, *Book of Isaiah*, 205. NJPS gives: "The Presence of the Lord shall appear." See also below, Ezekiel 1 and Exodus 33.

4. A brief summary of these attempts can be found in Shatz, "Biblical and Rabbinic Background," 18–26.

5. See M. Meg. 4:10; B. Meg. 31a.

6. "Ex. 25:18–22; 37:7–9; I Kings 6:23–28; I Chron. 3:10–14 each mention only two cherubim, but this passage combines the totals. The combination is justified because the former texts mention two cherubim in relation to the Ark and the latter mention two cherubim as features of the Holy of Holies in the Temple. Ezekiel's total could be based upon his observation of the Ark in the Temple or his reading of earlier texts." Comments of Marvin Sweeney in Berlin and Brettler, *Jewish Study Bible*, 1046. Schafer, *Origins of Jewish Mysticism*, is more skeptical of this identification, because the *hayyot* are not bound to the Temple.

7. "The four creatures symbolize earthly and cosmic wholeness: unity amid multiplicity, like the four countenances themselves. The many faces

further indicate divine omnipresence. Similarly, the many eyes on the wheeled disks (v. 18) suggest divine omniscience and providence." Michael Fishbane, *Etz Hayim*, 1322.

8. Sarna, *JPS Torah Commentary: Exodus*, 153.

9. Suggested in Schafer, *Origins of Jewish Mysticism*, 105.

10. This is all the more striking when read as a counternarrative to the vision of Moses in Exodus 33, discussed below. "Ezekiel is the new Moses, who has seen more of God than Moses and any of his predecessors." Schafer, *Origins of Jewish Mysticism*, 47.

11. Plaut, *Haftarah Commentary*, 735. See also Wolfson, *Through a Speculum*, 22.

12. On this issue, see Schafer, *Origins of Jewish Mysticism*, 50–51.

13. "Here too nothing is said of the feet, only what is beneath them, viz., the likeness of a pavement of sapphire, which, as various ancient and medieval Jewish interpreters and some more recent biblical scholars have noted, may be an elliptical reference to the Ark." Wolfson, "Images of God's Feet," 145.

14. Sarna, *JPS Torah Commentary: Exodus*, 153.

15. Comments of Jeffrey Tigay in Berlin and Brettler, *Jewish Study Bible*, 163; see also comments of Sweeney, *Jewish Study Bible*, 1048.

16. See Onkelos on the passage, and the comments of Rav, B. Ber. 17a. It is interesting that those present here take part in a meal, which Hecker suggests is a sealing of the covenant with God. *Mystical Bodies, Mystical Meals*, 24–25.

17. Maimonides, *Guide of the Perplexed* 1:4.

18. Tigay in Berlin and Brettler, *Jewish Study Bible*, 163.

19. Potok in *Etz Hayim*, 328, correcting Sarna, *JPS Torah Commentary: Exodus*, 15.

20. Tigay in Berlin and Brettler, *Jewish Study Bible*, 110. "Fire, because of its nonmaterial, formless, mysterious, and luminous characteristics, is frequently used in descriptions of the external manifestation of the Divine Presence." Sarna, *JPS Torah Commentary: Exodus*, 14; see references n. 9.

21. Sarna, *JPS Torah Commentary: Exodus*, 214.

22. Sarna, *JPS Torah Commentary: Exodus*, 215, continuing: "No human being can ever penetrate the ultimate mystery of God's Being. Only a glimpse of the divine reality is possible, even for Moses."

23. Wolfson, *Through a Speculum*, 26: "There is no absolute rejection of the claim that God has a visible form. . . . Nevertheless, Ex. 33:20 and 23 do state that Moses could not have a vision of the divine form in its frontal aspect, implying, therefore, that he, like other mortal humans, could not see the likeness of God in its fullest manifestation." Further, see discussion in Heschel, *Heavenly Torah*, particularly 303–6.

24. As noted (without citation) in Schafer, *Origins of Jewish Mysticism*, 80n104. Of interest also is the discussion of sources on the passage in Liebes, *Jewish Myth and Jewish Messianism*, 24–25.
25. B. Yev. 49b; similarly, *Midrash Vayikra Rabbah* 1:14.
26. Nahmanides's commentary on Exod. 33:18. See also Nahmanides on Gen. 18:1 for a further treatment of these issues.
27. See also B. Sanh. 22a.
28. Citations from Scholem, *Major Trends*, 7–8. See Schafer's critique in *Origins of Jewish Mysticism*, leading him to this conclusion (22): "Scholem's description of the origins of the earliest manifestation of Jewish mysticism is a tangle of contradictions. . . . He was transfixed by his own definition of the origins of mysticism."

3. MYSTICISM IN THE TALMUD

1. Compare the version in T. Hag. 2:1; see Schafer, *Origins of Jewish Mysticism*, 182, who does not make much of the differences.
2. "Ideas and motifs borrowed from the cosmogonic teachings of the Persians, Greeks and Gnostic sects infiltrated into the circles that came in contact with them. All these were sufficient to make the study of the 'Work of Creation' an esoteric doctrine." Urbach, *The Sages*, 184. "At all events it appears that the restrictions imposed upon occupying oneself with the 'Work of Creation' could not stand up to the pressure of questions, whether from within or without. The journeys of the sages to Egypt, Syria, and Asia Minor, as well as the proliferation of sects in *Eretz-Israel*, intensified the need to know what answer to give." Urbach, *The Sages*, 191.
3. See Blumenthal, *Understanding Jewish Mysticism*, 1:9, 12.
4. Urbach's comment is perhaps an overstatement, but generally true: "Their eyes and their hearts were turned Heavenward, yet one type was not to be found among them—not even among those who occupied themselves with the 'Work of the Chariot' and the 'Work of Creation'—namely the mystic who seeks to liberate himself from his ego, and in doing so is preoccupied with himself alone. They saw their mission in work here in the world below." *The Sages*, 18.
5. "But the story of creation in the book of Genesis, with its obscurities and discrepancies, presented them with problems and difficulties. There were still current among the people legends that resembled the remnants of the mythical epics that are to be found in the Scriptures themselves. Ideas and motifs borrowed from the cosmogonic teachings of the Persians, Greeks and Gnostic sects infiltrated into the circles that came in contact with them. All these were sufficient to make the study of the 'Work of Creation' an esoteric doctrine, which can be transmitted only to individuals." Urbach,

The Sages, 184. "The Gnostics were members of various sects in the early centuries of the Common Era who believed there were two gods, an evil deity who was responsible for the creation of the world, and a transcendent deity, the source of the human soul." Fine, "Kabbalistic Texts," 308n. On the broader question of Gnostic influence within Jewish mysticism—a complex issue beyond the scope of this book—see Deutsch, *Gnostic Imagination,* who notes with approval (12) Scholem's acceptance of the idea that even the most Gnostic-like forms of Jewish mysticism "can be fully explained as developing from within, on Jewish foundations." *On the Kabbalah and Its Symbolism,* 98.

6. *Heavenly Torah,* 281.
7. *Otzar ha-Midrashim, Atzilut* 4.
8. B. BB 89b. On the possible overlap between this Mishnah and *Heikhalot Zutarti* (*Synopse,* 335), see Schafer, *Origins of Jewish Mysticism,* 284–85.
9. Urbach, *The Sages,* 193n8, indicates that "this is also demonstrated by the difference in style."
10. "Quite literally, in expounding Ezek. 1, one 'looks' at what is 'above,' namely at God's throne in the heaven above the created world, and this is deemed a dangerous enterprise, because such unrestrained curiosity could damage God's glory." Schafer, *Origins of Jewish Mysticism,* 185.
11. Parallel passages in B. Hag. 14b, T. Hag. 2:1.
12. Abelson points out that moving from the donkey is an act of humility; the mystic "must be cleansed of every vestige of pride" before he can receive this information. *Jewish Mysticism,* 33.
13. See Schafer, *Origins of Jewish Mysticism,* 188–89.
14. *Avot d'Rabbi Natan* 14; *Midrash Kohelet Rabbah* 7:7.
15. On this term, see Jacobs, *Jewish Mystical Testimonies,* 21–22.
16. See Scholem, *Jewish Gnosticism,* 16; Liebes, *Studies in the Zohar,* 176n101.
17. However, the Talmud (B. Hag. 13a,14a) interprets Isa. 3:3 to say that "the mysteries of the Torah can be transmitted only to one with five attributes: *the captain of fifty, the man of rank, the counselor, the cunning charmer, and the skillful enchanter.*" That is, one had to be fifty years old (or perhaps a master of the *Humashim!*), a person of status, a counselor, and knowledgeable in magic and incantations. See also the discussion in Hallamish, *Introduction to the Kabbalah,* 45–46.
18. See, e.g., Verman, *History and Varieties of Jewish Meditation,* 20.
19. Cordovero himself suggested the age of twenty to reach at least half the age of "understanding" suggested in M. Avot 5:25. See *Or Ne'erav,* part 3, ch. 1; Robinson translation, *Moshe Cordovero's Introduction to Kabbalah,* 56.
20. *Mishneh Torah, Hilkhot Yesodei ha-Torah,* 4:13.
21. See Goshen-Gottstein, *The Sinner and the Amnesiac,* 53.

22. Parallels and variants in T. Hag. 2:3–4 and Y. Hag. 2:1. See discussion of this text in Schafer, *Origins of Jewish Mysticism*, 196–202.

23. Jacobs, *Jewish Mystical Testimonies*, 22.

24. Idel, "Mysticism," 650–51. This would be all the more true of the expanded form of the narrative in *Heikhalot Zutarti*, which expresses the dangers in more detail. The dangers involved with acquiring the secrets of "practical Kabbalah" were considerably greater, even with a qualified master; e.g., the story of the Ba'al Shem Tov and his student Rabbi Nahum, as related in Buxbaum, *Light and Fire*, 38–39, and sources in n. 29.

25. Sherwin, *Kabbalah*, 42, and see remarks there. "Despite or perhaps because of the biblical prohibition against viewing God's face, rabbinic literature abounds with discussions concerning the possibility of seeing the divine face." Deutsch, *Gnostic Imagination*, 102, provides numerous samples. Ben Azzai "turns into a prototype of the mythic mystic who encounters the holy and timelessly unites within himself heavenly and earthly holiness." Elior, *Jewish Mysticism*, 80. Similarly Schafer, *Origins of Jewish Mysticism*, 199. Compare this with the death of the three sages in the *Idra Rabba* of the Zohar (3:144a) and comments of Liebes in *Studies in the Zohar*, 52, 55.

26. See, e.g., the passage from *Midrash Hallel* quoted in Idel, "Mysticism," 644. Hallamish (*Introduction to the Kabbalah*, 70) believes that "it is not plausible that the text [of the verse] is meant to extol this venerated sage."

27. Note the two texts from *Heikhalot Zutarti* cited in Arbel, *Beholders of Divine Secrets*, 36.

28. B. Yev. 63b.

29. This is briefly and inconclusively discussed in B. Sot. 4b.

30. Sweeney, "Pardes Revisited Once Again," 53.

31. Schafer, *Origins of Jewish Mysticism*, 208–9. Alternatively, Maimonides saw Ben Zoma as weak in absorbing the details of the *ma'aseh Merkavah*, the philosophical metaphysics that might ensure individual redemption. See *Guide of the Perplexed* 3:51; Sherwin, *Kabbalah*, 44.

32. B. Hag. 15a.

33. Liebes, *Jewish Myth and Jewish Messianism*, 174n67.

34. B. Kid. 39b.

35. An interesting resource on this subject is Goshen-Gottstein's *The Sinner and the Amnesiac*; I have adapted the phrase "constructed image" from his comment on Elisha ben Abuyah and Eleazar ben Arakh (7).

36. Sherwin, *Kabbalah*, 43. Thus, "the mystical experience is replete with physical, psychological, and spiritual dangers. It is certainly not for everyone but for the very, very few. And even among these, few achieve the goal, while most fall short. This seems to be the Talmud's way of saying that it is

better for most men to have a Normal mystical experience . . . [that] poses no dangers and is readily accessible to everyone."

37. As per the story of Rabbi Hiyya in Zohar 2:14a–15a, *Midrash ha-Ne'elam*, noted in Tishby, *Wisdom of the Zohar*, 1:130–31. It may be that Rabbi Hiyya's willingness to weep for his inability to cross over the barrier is the factor that grants him the right to do so. In general, at least prior to the Zohar, the dominant opinion supported the maintenance of esoteric matters for a small elite, as per Hai Ga'on: "Secrets of the Torah are given only to the resourceful sage who knows how to keep secrets, to the silent one of understanding. They are whispered to him and given to him as general principles; he runs with them and from heaven is shown in the great secret recesses of his heart, as the Midrash states: 'One who understands the whisper.' 'One who understands' means that he can derive the implications of what he is told." *Otzar ha-Geonim, Otzar ha-Teshuvot* on B. Hag. 4:11–12, as cited in Idel, *Language, Torah, and Hermeneutics*, 176n125. See also the teaching of Todros Abulafia and similar tensions in various ages cited in Hallamish, *Introduction to the Kabbalah*, 21–23.

38. Idel, "Mysticism," 651.

39. See Deutsch, *Gnostic Imagination*, 13–14.

40. See Dan, "Religious Experience of the *Merkavah*," 289.

4. SONG OF SONGS AND *MA'ASEH MERKAVAH*

1. M. Yad. 3:5.

2. B. Ket. 62b. On the development of this into an esoteric understanding by the mystics, see, e.g., Ginsburg, *Sabbath in the Classical Kabbalah*, 108–21.

3. Dan, *Ancient Jewish Mysticism*, 70.

4. Dennis, *Encyclopedia of Jewish Myth*, 240; see also Dan, *Ancient Jewish Mysticism*, 67–77; Sherwin, *Kabbalah*, 141.

5. Dan, *Ancient Jewish Mysticism*, 73–74. See also Schafer, *Origins of Jewish Mysticism*, 307, and Martin Samuel Cohen, *Shi'ur Qomah*, 66.

6. See Jackson, "Origins and Development of *Shi'ur Qomah*." It is nearly impossible to identify definitively the earliest sources for *Shi'ur Komah*; Scholem's tentative suggestions of apocalyptic writings (e.g., Slavonic Enoch) and the Qumran writings are possibilities at best. See discussion in Deutsch, *Gnostic Imagination*, 82–86. There is evidence that earlier texts gave outsize dimensions to angels: "That God was conceived to be of such vast proportions may well have been a later development, fully manifest in the (late) *Shi'ur Komah* traditions. . . . Could it be that, once the vast size of the angels was adopted by the Christians (and, worse, these angels became divine figures), the Jewish tradition came to insist that only God himself has gigantic dimensions, and no longer the angels—because the

latter could become, all too easily, powerful competitors of the one and only God?" Schafer, *Origins of Jewish Mysticism*, 315.

7. Based on Blumenthal, *Understanding Jewish Mysticism*, 53. See also Swartz, "Ancient Jewish Mysticism."

8. A precise definition of Gnosticism is elusive. Scholem noted that the danger-filled trip of the *Merkavah* mystic is a "Jewish variation on a Gnostic theme" and that the use of seals, magical names, etc., is common ground between Gnostic and *Merkavah* texts as well. However, it is not at all clear that all such practices are necessarily either Gnostic or Jewish. Deutsch, *Gnostic Imagination*, 20-21, 26-29, 37, 45 (with P. S. Alexander's proposal of methodological models for comparing Gnosticism and *Merkavah* mysticism), and 54-55 (surveying the parallels).

9. On the relationship between the *Heikhalot* circles and the Rabbinic Judaism of the day, see Wolfson, *Through a Speculum*, 75-79. Dan also notes that "most scholars, beginning with Scholem, did not realize the deep division between talmudic-midrashic Judaism and the basic concepts of *Heikhalot* mysticism; rather, they tended to view the *Heikhalot* mystical attitude as the esoteric stratum of mysticism inherent- and integrated-with talmudic Judaism. I believe this to be erroneous." "Language of the Mystics," 17n23.

10. As noted in Martin Samuel Cohen, *Shi'ur Qomah*, 182n1: "The *Merkavah* is never actually described as a chariot; presumably the term is a reflex of the ancient Near Eastern motif of the divine chariot-throne." "The term *Merkavah*, literally meaning 'chariot,' does not appear in the Masoretic text of the Hebrew Bible when describing the throne of God. However, the term is used in I Chron. 28:18 to designate the structure formed by the cherubs that frame the Ark of the Covenant in Solomon's temple. In Ben Sira 49:8 the throne of Ezekiel's vision is called the *Merkavah*." Swartz, "Mystical Texts," 394.

11. See Wolfson, *Through a Speculum*, 79-80; Schafer, *Origins of Jewish Mysticism*, 245; Green, *Keter*, 16-17; Idel, *Ascensions on High*, 30; Sherwin, *Kabbalah*, 141-42.

12. See Blumenthal, *Understanding Jewish Mysticism*, 56-57, 60-61, 67-68, 70-71, 72; Dan, *Ancient Jewish Mysticism*, 100-107.

13. Scholem, *Kabbalah*, 6; noted in Wolfson, *Through a Speculum*, 110, and see discussion in Schafer, *Origins of Jewish Mysticism*, 3n4; Swartz, "Mystical Texts," 404; and comments of Dan, *Ancient Jewish Mysticism*, 79-81.

14. The numbers given at the end of each segment correspond to the sections of the various manuscripts given in Schafer, *Synopse*, as noted and translated (with changes here based on my own translations and those of Schafer in *Origins of Jewish Mysticism*, 268-75) from the edition of Wertheimer, *Batei Midrashot*, 1:90-114, in Blumenthal, *Understanding Jewish Mysticism*, 54-72.

15. There is a superficial connection with the Narrative of the Ten Martyrs that appears in sections 107-21. Perhaps it is only such a time of need that can justify this blatant desire for power in the higher realm. See also discussion in Dan, *Ancient Jewish Mysticism*, 176-78.

16. B. Ber. 7a, and see virtual repetition in *Synopse*, 151; T. Hal. 1:10.

17. Schafer, *Origins of Jewish Mysticism*, 79n101.

18. "On the one hand, the rabbis felt a close intimacy with God, which enabled them to deal in meticulous detail with the mysteries of His attributes. On the other hand, they feared for the King's honor. It is to this end that angels were created, since it is easier to speak of them than of God; angels help to keep the suitable distance, and this is also their role in *Heikhalot* literature." Liebes, *Jewish Myth and Jewish Messianism*, 33.

19. There were a fair number of midrashic teachings that interpreted the experience at Sinai similarly, but "with the important exception that the *Merkavah* and its attendant environment had descended to the people at Sinai." Chernus, *Mysticism in Rabbinic Judaism*, 11; he also theorizes that the Merkavah mystics may have used this tactic to gain legitimacy for their teachings "to claim that one was actually repeating the experience of the Israelites at Sinai . . . [that] would create a chain of tradition going back to the very inception of the covenantal relationship" (13), and that the Rabbis may have countered this tactic by underscoring the uniqueness of what the Israelites saw at Sinai.

20. Similarly, one is allowed to ascend to the Merkavah if he "has read the Torah, Prophets and Writings, *Mishnayot, Midrash, Halakhot* and *Haggadot*, and learns the interpretation of the *Halakhot*, prohibition and permission, who abides by every prohibition that is written in the Torah and observes all the warnings of the laws, statutes and instructions which were said to Moses at Sinai." Section 234, as quoted in Schafer, *Origins of Jewish Mysticism*, 39. "All these texts go to great lengths to stress their strict conformity, even in the most minute detail, to *halakhic* Judaism and its prescriptions." Scholem, *Jewish Gnosticism*, 10.

21. Josh. 2:19; Ezek. 33:4.

22. E.g., this excerpt from *Sefer ha-Razim* quoted in Verman, *History and Varieties of Jewish Meditation*, 162: "The seventh firmament, all of it is sevenfold light, and from its light all the heavens shine. . . . There is no calculation or limit to the great light within it, and the fullness of the light illumines all the earth. The angels are fixed in pillars of light, and their light is as the light of the brilliant star [i.e., Venus] and cannot be extinguished, for their eyes are like flashes of lightning, and they stand upon the margins of (the divine light), and glorify in awe the One who sits upon the Throne of Glory." That is the highest level, and it is all light.

23. B. Hag. 12a; *Midrash Bereshit Rabbah* 3:6.
24. "Ritual purity, which is not the same as good hygiene or spiritual virtue, was considered in ancient Judaism to be required of anyone who wanted to approach the presence of God in the Temple.... It was believed that in order to be with divine beings such as angels, it was necessary to attain a state of ritual purity beyond anything required by Jewish law." Swartz, "Book of the Great Name," 342.
25. See Gen. 30:20.
26. Blumenthal suggests: "I adjure you, Surya, angel of the presence, to protect me from the power of _____," changing the name with each oath.
27. Dan, *Ancient Jewish Mysticism*, 106-7.

5. THE TEMPLE

1. "The Western Wall was understood as one of the places where the *Shekhinah*, God's incarnate presence in the world, was always present. For this reason, the Western Wall was the object of messianic expectations, as it would certainly be the cornerstone of the Temple to be built in the Messianic period." Giller, *Reading the Zohar*, 12.
2. Martin Samuel Cohen, *Our Haven and Our Strength*, 431.
3. Perhaps, as suggested in B. Shab. 30a and by the twelfth- to thirteenth-century commentator David Kimchi, the psalm was recited when the Ark of the Covenant was brought within.
4. See Sarna, *Songs of the Heart*, 127-28, 133-34.
5. Translation with reference to those of Green, *Keter*, 62, and Sherwin, *Kabbalah*, 108-9.
6. As noted in Green, *Keter*, 63. There is also a Cairo Geniza document that clearly regards *Akatriel-Yah* as a name of God; see Dennis, *Encyclopedia of Jewish Myth*, 6.
7. *Synopse*, 151.
8. "It emerges clearly from various parallels to this tradition in *Heikhalot* writings that 'entry into the *Pardes*' and '*lifnai velifnim*' are one and the same thing: entry into the sphere of sanctity, representing the source of life, after the destruction of the Temple. Indeed, both Rabbi Ishmael and Rabbi Akiva were third-generation *tannaim*, active in the second century CE, when the Temple was no longer standing." Elior, *Three Temples*, 244-45. See also Scholem, *Jewish Gnosticism*, 51-54.
9. Wolfson, *Through a Speculum*, 19. Further discussion of this can be found in Elior, "Early Forms of Jewish Mysticism," 758-59, including the lengthy closing note 27.
10. See also parallel in B. Yoma 39b.
11. Other traditions suggest that God was seen at Sinai, e.g., *Pesikta d'Rav*

Kahana 12:22, noted in Chernus, *Mysticism in Rabbinic Judaism*, 23. For other midrashic texts on the special role of the earthly Temple, see, e.g., *Midrash Shemot Rabbah* 33:4, *Midrash Tanhuma*, Va-yak'hel 7, *Midrash Tanhuma*, Pekudei 1–3, and *Midrash Tehillim* 30:1.

12. *Three Temples*, 3.

13. See Tishby, *Wisdom of the Zohar*, 1:273: "the worlds, with all the beings they contain, and especially man, are constructed on the pattern of the *sefirot*, 'according to the form that is above.' The *sefirot* are the divine master-copy of non-divine existence, both in general and in particular. 'He made the lower world on the pattern of the upper world, and they complement each other, forming one whole, in a single unity.' (Zohar 1:38a) 'He made this world to match the world above, and whatever exists above has its counterpart below.'" (Zohar 2:20a, *Midrash ha-Ne'elam*; see Tishby, *Wisdom of the Zohar*, 2:569)

14. See Schafer, *Origins of Jewish Mysticism*, 270: "The allusion to the Temple serves as a hint that the mystic's ascent to the seventh heaven is nothing less than an ascent to the heavenly Temple."

15. Many scholars believe that the original temple calendar year was the 364-day year, as noted in Himmelfarb, "Merkavah Mysticism Since Scholem," 25.

16. See Elior, *Three Temples*, 30.

17. Elior, *Three Temples*, 41.

18. As translated in Elior, *Three Temples*, 67. See also Idel, *Kabbalah and Eros*, 31, with no important differences for our purposes.

19. Elior, *Three Temples*, 68, noting B. Yoma 21b. See also Idel's comments, *Kabbalah and Eros*, 31–33.

20. See Idel, *Kabbalah and Eros*, 59.

21. Noted in Heschel, *Heavenly Torah*, 100; see 101–3 on the tension between the existence of the cherubim and the prohibition against images.

22. See Elior, *Three Temples*, 9–11, 26–27, 38–39; Schafer, *Origins of Jewish Mysticism*, 112: "Emerging from the lower ranks of the priesthood, the Maccabean family hardly had any more entitlement to the office of high priest than the 'usurpers' that they had so bitterly opposed." Also Horsley, "Popular Messianic Movements," 92–93: "Since the Hasmoneans were not a Zadokite family, Jonathan and Simon could not legitimately assume the high priesthood. Yet instead of reviving royal expectations and titles, the Hasmonean leaders assumed the high priestly office—thereby attesting the strength and centrality of the latter and the apparent dormancy of the former in Maccabean times."

23. Elior, *Three Temples*, 38. Schafer notes that a similar conclusion has been suggested from other sources, such as "The Book of the Watchers"

(1 En. 1-36): "The remaining Watchers in heaven are the true priests: the true Temple service has been moved from earth to heaven because of the defilement of Jerusalem Temple." *Origins of Jewish Mysticism*, 66; see also his comments on "The Testament of Levi" as a Jewish critique of the Jerusalem Temple, 69.

24. "Scholem noted the potential significance for the study of Jewish mysticism of such poetic texts, mentioning both the *Hodayot*, the Thanksgiving Psalms, and the "Angelic Liturgy," as the *Songs of the Sabbath Sacrifice* was then known, in *Jewish Gnosticism*; in his additions to the second edition of *Jewish Gnosticism*, he comments that the publication of fragments of the Angelic Liturgy had borne out their significance for the *Heikhalot* literature." Himmelfarb, "Merkavah Mysticism since Scholem," 21-22, citing Scholem, *Jewish Gnosticism*, 2-4.

25. *The Complete Dead Sea Scrolls in English*, 228, 514.

26. On the theories about the identity of the "Wicked Priest," see Elior, *Three Temples*, 38n30.

27. See in particular Himmelfarb, "Merkavah Mysticism since Scholem."

28. Elior, *Three Temples*, 40.

29. See the Apocryphal Psalm included in Vermes, *Complete Dead Sea Scrolls*, 313; Elior, *Three Temples*, 50-51.

30. As translated in Elior, *Three Temples*, 104, 116.

31. Frequently in the Qumran literature, "the everlasting communion of angels and humans, guaranteeing a perpetual flow of divine knowledge, is . . . envisaged in priestly terms." "The angels who offer the celestial sacrifices are modeled on the priests (or more precisely on the high priests) in the earthly sanctuary." Finally, these sectarians most likely "regard themselves as standing together with the angels and intermingling with them *in heaven*." Schafer, *Origins of Jewish Mysticism*, 128, 140, 151.

32. Some of the terms in the Qumran literature also are quite similar to those of the *Heikhalot* literature referring to the knowledge acquired by the *Merkavah* mystic, as noted by Schafer, *Origins of Jewish Mysticism*, 127-28. He concludes later that we are dealing with a communal mysticism, "which puts itself in a hypnotic state and, being led through the celestial Temple, experiences the divine throne." *Origins of Jewish Mysticism*, 143.

33. As Elior has put it elsewhere in a discussion of *Heikhalot* literature, "The most plausible explanation for the emergence of this new approach to hitherto forbidden realms is apparently a visionary eruption that, drawing on a sanctified ancient ritual tradition, refused to accept a cruel, arbitrary reality in which the cultic center of a thousand years, the focus of centuries of religious worship from the days of David's and Solomon's First Temple followed by the Second Temple, no longer existed after the year 70. Denying

the historical fact of the destruction of the Temple and the annihilation of the priestly service, this eruption created a new spiritual world that rested on a mystical-ritual fulcrum, a surrogate for the no longer extant Temple." "Early Forms of Jewish Mysticism," 754–55. I am much less certain about the denial of the historical fact of the destruction than Elior, but in full agreement on how much *Heikhalot* mysticism served as a surrogate for the Temple.

34. See discussion in Elior, "Early Forms of Jewish Mysticism," 766–71, and below in chapter 22.

35. *Heavenly Torah*, 78; translation from *Torah min ha-Shamayim b'Aspaklarya shel ha-Dorot*, 1:37.

36. The precise quote, from B. Shab. 22b: "It is a testimony to one and all that the Shekhinah rests upon Israel."

37. *Midrash Tanhuma*, Pekudei 2.

38. As Matt notes (see below), the Hebrew verb *b-s-m* conveys two senses, that of being sweetened and also being firmly established.

39. This interpretation "is based on a midrashic rendering of *Shir ha-Shirim*, Song of Songs, as *shir she-ameru oto ha-sharim ha-shorerim*, 'a song uttered by the chanting singers.'" Matt, *Zohar: The Pritzker Edition*, 5:310.

40. Largely as translated by Matt, *Zohar: The Pritzker Edition*, 5:310.

6. *MA'ASEH BERESHIT, SEFER YETZIRAH, AND SEFER HA-BAHIR*

1. *M. Avot* 5:1.

2. Sherwin, *In Partnership with God*, 181–85. On Judah Loew, see below, chapter 10.

3. Blumenthal, *Understanding Jewish Mysticism*, 1:13; Matt, *Essential Kabbalah*, 187. On divine truth through language, see Dan, "Language of the Mystics," particularly 11–12 and 23.

4. Elior, "Early Forms of Jewish Mysticism," 785.

5. See Dan, *Ancient Jewish Mysticism*, 199; Swartz, brief discussion and references in "Mystical Texts," 418. Dan suggests that the book seems to be a "scientific" text of the kind most likely to have appeared in the eighth or ninth century.

6. I have referred to the translations of Hayman, *Sefer Yesira*; Matt, *Essential Kabbalah*, 76 (and notes, 186–88); Blumenthal, *Understanding Jewish Mysticism*, 1:15–17; Aryeh Kaplan, *Sefer Yetzirah*, 5–56; Bokser, *Jewish Mystical Tradition*, 65–67; sections of Dan, *Ancient Jewish Mysticism*, e.g., 203; also brief comments of Sherwin, *Kabbalah*, 58. See also Idel, *Golem*, 10–12, on the significance of chapter 2 of *Sefer Yetzirah*.

7. "Language of the Mystics," 12. He also notes that this belief was shared by most Christians.

8. Blumenthal, *Understanding Jewish Mysticism*, 1:15.

9. "This is meant to suggest the theoretical aspect. That is to say, the hidden side of God truly is infinite, yet another, apprehensible aspect is within the reach of our intellect due to its very limitation or, more precisely, it appears to us in limit and measure. It acts to a restricted extent within the confines of a limited reality." Hallamish, *Introduction to the Kabbalah*, 126. *Sefer* can also be translated as "text": "representative of facts, axioms, principles. It is etched in stone, it is absolute, it is irrevocable, it is the Laws of Nature, it is the parts of us that are set, programmed, formatted: it is the laws of physics and mathematics. Text is pre-planned, pre-destined, thought out and implemented in conclusion and perfection." Winkler, *Magic of the Ordinary*, 25–26.

10. Dan, *Ancient Jewish Mysticism*, 202.

11. Hayman, *Sefer Yesira*, 66, translates it as "basis," a parallel to *yesod*; this is possible, but I am not convinced.

12. The seven doubles are *beit, gimel, dalet, kaf, peh, reish,* and *tav*. It is questionable as to whether *reish* should be included in this group, but there are a few places in the Torah where it has a *dagesh*, so kabbalists (though not grammarians) do group it with the others.

13. Or "covenant of the Unique One," as suggested by Blumenthal.

14. Blumenthal, *Understanding Jewish Mysticism*, 1:16.

15. Dan, *Ancient Jewish Mysticism*, 204.

16. Dan, *Ancient Jewish Mysticism*, 210–11.

17. Dan, *Ancient Jewish Mysticism*, 205.

18. *Midrash Bereshit Rabbah* 4:2.

19. The seraphim come from the vision of Isaiah 6. Blumenthal notes the Rabbinic belief that both prophets saw all the heavenly beings; *Understanding Jewish Mysticism*, 1:18.

20. See Dan, *Ancient Jewish Mysticism*, 208.

21. Or possibly the "six edges [of the universe]" as per Hayman, *Sefer Yesira*, 89.

22. On the implications of this, see Dan, *Ancient Jewish Mysticism*, 209. He does not believe these six extremities represent the six *sefirot* and holds that this last segment may be a late attempt to rectify their absence from the text. For a different view, see Blumenthal, *Understanding Jewish Mysticism*, 1:19.

23. As Blumenthal (*Understanding Jewish Mysticism*, 1:43) notes, this piece is not in all manuscripts; Hayman, *Sefer Yesira*, 181–82, includes none of the ones that use it. It does seem a logical text with which to illustrate this point, even if it may be a later addition.

24. Ronit Meroz has suggested that parts of the *Bahir* date back to tenth-century Babylonia; see her article, "Middle Eastern Origins." Others date it even as early as the eighth or ninth century, as noted in Tirosh-Samuelson, "Jewish Mysticism," 406.

25. I have consulted translations in Aryeh Kaplan, *Bahir*, and Bokser, *Jewish Mystical Tradition*.
26. As made explicit in the translation in Bokser, *Jewish Mystical Tradition*, 85.
27. Hallamish, *Introduction to the Kabbalah*, 208; emphasis in the original.
28. E.g., B. Shab. 89b.
29. Hallamish, *Introduction to the Kabbalah*, 291.
30. Hallamish, *Introduction to the Kabbalah*, 296–98.

7. HASIDEI ASHKENAZ

1. His father, Rabbi Samuel ben Kalonymus, also left behind teachings that were included in *Sefer Hasidim*, but otherwise very little of Samuel's writing has survived.
2. "Pietists in *Sefer Hasidim* are described as struggling to live among a nonpietist Jewish majority and Christians, both of whom pose a threat to the pietists' way of life. To minimize outside influence on them, the authors generally advise pietists to avoid contact with the others unless they, the pietists, can do so from a position of relative strength." Marcus, "Devotional Ideals of Ashkenazic Pietism," 358. It was likely that these pietists were widely ridiculed by other Jews because of their stringencies and their rejection of the rest of the community; see the comments of Simhoni quoted in Marcus, *Piety and Society*, 5. To a significant degree *Sefer Hasidim* is also "an indictment of lawless communal leaders as well as of rabbis who pervert justice and of the rich who exploit the poor." *Piety and Society*, 7.
3. See Laenen, *Jewish Mysticism*, 111.
4. Sherwin, *Kabbalah*, 172; see Marcus, *Piety and Society*, 11.
5. See Marcus, *Piety and Society*, 32.
6. See Scholem, *Major Trends*, 96–97.
7. See Dan, "Gershom Scholem's Reconstruction," 168.
8. Marcus, *Piety and Society*, 16; see also Giller, *Kabbalah*, 19.
9. "Most German Pietists rejected the view that the Glory is a created light extrinsic to God; rather, they wavered between the view that the Glory is emanated from God and thus attached to the deity and the view that the Glory is an image within the mind of the prophets or mystics and not an entity outside the mind. They distinguished between the Upper Glory—an amorphous light called the Presence (*Shekhinah*) or Great Splendor—and the Lower Glory, which was an aspect that assumes different forms within the prophetic or mystical imagination." Tirosh-Samuelson, "Jewish Mysticism," 405.
10. Marcus, "Devotional Ideals of Ashkenazic Pietism," 363, and see Marcus, "Prayer Gestures in German Hasidism," 55–56. On the technical term *kavod ha-nir'eh* among Hasidei Ashkenaz, see Scholem, *Major Trends*, 112–13.

11. B. Ber. 17a.

12. Largely as translated in Jacobs, *Jewish Mystical Testimonies*, 49-53, and including some of his commentary. See there for his comments on the source of his text.

13. NJPS: "I am ever mindful of the Lord's presence."

14. Similarly Eleazar writes: "The soul is filled with the love of God and is wrapped up in bonds of love, happiness and joy. One who loves God is not like a servant who serves his master unwillingly. Rather, even if he is prevented from doing so, his heart burns with the love to serve God, and he delights to fulfill completely the will of his creator." *Piety and Society*, 36, translation of Marcus from *Sefer ha-Rokeiah, Hilkhot Hasidut*, 5. There is also significant erotic content to the discussion about the knowledge of the *Merkavah* among Hasidei Ashkenaz; see Tirosh-Samuelson, "Jewish Mysticism," 405-6.

15. Green, *Keter*, 107. Much of what follows is based on his commentary, 109-20. The translation is that of Israel Zangwill as found in Green, *Keter*, 108-9.

16. *Mekhilta ba-Hodesh* 5, *Shirta* 4.

17. From Eleazar's *Commentary on Ezekiel's Chariot*, as noted in Wolfson, "Images of God's Feet," 157. "It is the human body that serves as the image of some aspect of the divine. Moreover, we know that speculations on Song of Songs 5:10-16, the physical description of the male lover, lie at the heart of this tradition and generated an enormous literature in Jewish mysticism." Marcus, "Prayer Gestures in German Hasidism," 46, citing also Lieberman's *Mishnat Shir ha-Shirim* in Scholem's *Jewish Gnosticism*, 118-26. Interestingly, Marcus later (58) cites a passage from Eleazar's *Sha'arei ha-Sod* where the author denies that any of these gross anthropomorphisms apply to the Creator, claiming they are only figurative language.

18. See discussion in Green, *Keter*, 112n9.

19. E.g., B. Shab. 88b.

20. See sources in Schwartz, *Tree of Souls*, 259.

21. "The poet thinks that the upper *Kavod* desires the one who prays and expresses this yearning by adorning its head with the speaker's prayers ("He beautifies Himself with me"), as it were. The line continues with the hope that the upper *Kavod* will reciprocally become the poet's crown. After expressing this hope about mutual bonding or union, the author will return to prophetic images emphasizing the head." Marcus, commentary on *Shir ha-Kavod* in Lawrence A. Hoffman, *My People's Prayer Book*, 10:189.

22. E.g., *Midrash Be-midbar Rabbah* 12:8.

23. Marcus, commentary on *Shir ha-Kavod* in Lawrence A. Hoffman, *My People's Prayer Book*, 10:189.

24. Interestingly, the expression is included in *Shi'ur Komah* as well. Martin Samuel Cohen, *Shi'ur Qomah*, 208n33.

25. On this see Green, *Keter*, 116–17, and his comments in n. 17; Martin Samuel Cohen, *Shi'ur Qomah*, 173.

26. Green, *Keter*, 118n20.

27. Translated by Joseph Dan in *Studies in Jewish Mysticism*, 89; the original source is MS Jerusalem, Jewish National and University Liberty, 80 3 296, fol. 7r.

28. This idea may be rooted in the Talmud; B. Er. 13a suggests that omitting a letter of the Torah or adding one "may cause the destruction of the entire universe." The point of our text, however, concerns the cosmic importance of the words of the siddur, not the Torah.

29. Also, much attention is given to techniques to prevent distractions of any kind. See Marcus, "Prayer Gestures in German Hasidism," 48, followed by a lengthy discussion of where to look during prayer.

30. MS Paris BN 772, fol. 159b, as noted and translated by Wolfson, "Metatron and *Shi'ur Qomah*," 87–88.

31. For Eleazar of Worms, "magic is religion and the highest form of religion is magic. The reason for this development of thought is the apotheosis of language as a divine and creative power and the corresponding anthropological definition that the ability to use this divine language is the essence of humanity itself." Grozinger, "Between Magic and Religion," 43. Thus, one ought to be able to use the divine power to create life if one manages the level of purity associated with the ascetic life of the Hasidei Ashkenaz (even though this was not quite so severe for Eleazar as it was for Yehudah he-Hasid).

32. B. Kid. 71a briefly mentions not only the Four-Letter Name, but also special names of twelve and forty-two letters entrusted only to an elite. On the use of this Name among the Hasidei Ashkenaz, see Idel, *Enchanted Chains*, 109–14.

33. See Kramer, *God and Man*, 219–26.

34. "The *lilits* proper possessed two outstanding characteristics in medieval folklore which gave them distinct personality: they attacked new-born children and their mothers, and they seduced men in their sleep. As a result of the legend of Adam's relations with Lilit, although this function was by no means exclusively theirs, the *lilits* were most frequently singled out as the demons who embrace sleeping men and cause them to have the nocturnal emissions which are the seed of a hybrid progeny." Trachtenberg, *Jewish Magic and Superstition*, 36, and see talmudic references, nn. 32–33.

35. See, e.g., brief excerpt and discussion in Giller, *Kabbalah*, 88–89.

36. There were other small mystical circles during this period, notably the *Iyyun* circle and the Unique Cherub circle. Because they had more limited long-term impact, we have omitted consideration of them. Those interested may consult Mark Verman, *Books of Contemplation*, and Joseph Dan, *"Unique Cherub" Circle*, on these two groups.

8. THE *EIN SOF*

1. *Torat ha-Olah* 4:3 (72b). I am grateful to Dr. Morris Feierstein, who originally provided me the precise reference in the Prague edition located at hebrewbooks.org. Similarly, Isserles's notes on *Shulhan Arukh, Yoreh De'ah* 246:4: "One may not dally in *Pardes* until he has first filled himself with meat and wine, by which I mean knowledge of what is permitted and what is forbidden and the laws of the mitzvot." See other citations in Hallamish, *Introduction to the Kabbalah*, 330n73.

2. Sherwin, *Kabbalah*, 25. Similarly, "detaching kabbalistic practice from traditional Judaism would be like performing an operation with instruments that are not sterile." Giller, *Kabbalah*, 8. See Horowitz, *Shnei Luhot ha-Brit, Masekhet Shavuot, Ner Mitzvah*, sect. 27: "After he fills his belly with Scripture, Mishnah, and Talmud, let him occupy himself, in fear and awe, in holiness and purity, with the wisdom of the Kabbalah, in the Zohar and the *Tikkunim* and their commentators. . . . And whoever has not seen this wisdom, has seen no lights in his lifetime."

3. *God in Search of Man*, 43.

4. Or as Scholem put it: "*Ein Sof* is the absolute perfection in which there are no distinctions and no differentiations." *Kabbalah*, 89.

5. See Dan, "Gershom Scholem's Reconstruction," 163.

6. *Guide of the Perplexed* 1:50; p. 139.

7. See Matt, "*Ayin*: The Concept of Nothingness," esp. 65–72. See also Sherwin, *Kabbalah*, 56–57. Further, note Ben-Shlomo, "Gershom Scholem on Pantheism," 58, on the explanation of *Ayin* and *Yesh* in the writings of Azriel of Gerona.

8. "Perhaps the best available metaphor for the conception of God as the Holy Nothingness is that God is the ocean and we are the waves. In some sense each wave has its moment in which it is distinguishable as a somewhat separate entity. Nevertheless, no wave is entirely distinct from the ocean which is its substantial ground. The waves are surface manifestations of the ocean. Our knowledge of the ocean is largely dependent on the way it manifests itself in the waves." Rubenstein, *Morality and Eros*, 185–86.

9. Thirteenth century, as quoted in Meir ibn Gabbai's *Derekh Emunah*, 2–3, cited in Dan, *Early Kabbalah*, 91, 93–94; Matt, *Essential Kabbalah*, 29.

10. This early fourteenth-century anonymous work is cited in Scholem, *Major Trends*, 353n8.

11. The verse is frequently translated as "beside Me," but "with Me" is the literal meaning of the words, and the kabbalist offers an interpretation suggesting the separation of the "Me," the *Ein Sof*, and other manifestations of God, expressed through the *sefirot*.

12. This follows the translation in Tishby, *Wisdom of the Zohar*, 1:258; see also Ariel, *Mystic Quest*, 61. *Tikkunei ha-Zohar* is a later composition that was attached to the primary body of the Zohar. See Scholem, *Kabbalah*, 218–19.

13. See, e.g., Hallamish, *Introduction to the Kabbalah*, 124, and nn. 16–18.

14. This follows the translation in Tishby, *Wisdom of the Zohar*, 1:259. *Ra'aya Meheimna* is another work added onto the text of the Zohar; see Scholem, *Kabbalah*, 218.

15. As Gershom Scholem put it: "In this sense the fundamental differentiation between the *'Ein Sof* and the first *sefira* is connected to the problematics of pantheism. This differentiation is the focus of the problem, and Cordovero especially was fully aware that the transition from *'Ein Sof* to the First *sefira*, the *Urakt*, is a step whose significance is infinitely greater than the sum of all the steps taken thereafter. Beginning with this act everything is in effect prescribed, for the pure turning of God to create constitutes the act of creation, even if to us it seems to have many stages and infinite processes. Within the Godhead all these are one and the same act." From "Ten Unhistorical Aphorisms," 212, quoted in Ben-Shlomo, "Gershom Scholem on Pantheism," 63, who adds: "According to Cordovero, the world of emanation—the *sefirot*—is comprehended within the divine Will, which is itself included in the *Ein Sof*. Even in this highest state, where the *sefirot* are united within their source, 'they are nevertheless not truly identical with the substance of *Ein Sof*, which apprehends them while remaining unapprehended by them.'" The kabbalists frequently wrestle with this problem.

16. "The generation in which Rabbi Shimon is present is completely worthy and devoted, completely sin-fearing. *Shekhinah* dwells among them. This is not so in other generations. So words are expressed openly and not concealed. In other generations this is not so; secret words from above cannot be revealed, and those who know are afraid." Zohar 3:79a.

17. Most recently Wolfson has suggested an overlap between the Zohar and a contemporaneous text, *Sha'arei ha-Zaken* [The Gates of the elder], in "Anonymous Chapters." The book of the Zohar "remained a snowballing collection of random homilies collected by aficionados for the first hundred years or so of its development. The studies of Wolfson, Boaz Huss, Yehuda Liebes, Ronit Meroz, Daniel Abrams, and Avraham Elqayam have all served to blur the identity of the Zohar as a single composition by a single author, or even a single book. The single authorship of the Zohar was a guiding principle of the academic study of Kabbalah until the aforementioned scholars argued for the possibility of multiple authors and levels of composition." Giller, "Kabbalah and Contemporary Judaism," 234. For a cogent argument for earlier contributions to the Zohar, see Meroz, "Middle Eastern Origins."

18. Largely following Tishby, *Wisdom of the Zohar*, 1:257; see also Matt, *Zohar: The Pritzker Edition*, 6:383–84.
19. As noted in Matt, *Zohar: Book of Enlightenment*, 266.
20. Tishby, *Wisdom of the Zohar*, 1:257n4.
21. This book should not be confused with the earlier book of the same title, quoted in chapter 4.
22. Similarly, Menahem Nahum of Chernobyl, eighteenth-century Hasidic master: "There is nothing besides the presence of God; being itself is derived from God and the presence of the Creator remains in each created thing." *Me'or Einayim* on *parashat* Noah; see Green, *Menahem Nahum of Chernobyl*, 100.
23. See translation in Jacobs, *Jewish Theology*, 52.
24. This eighteenth-century teaching is attributed to Yehiel Mikhel of Zlotchov, who based it on a sermon of Dov Ber, the Maggid of Mezeritch. See translation in Lawrence Kushner, *Way into Jewish Mystical Tradition*, 19.
25. A similar tendency can be seen in the nineteenth-century Hasidic master Rabbi Judah Leib Alter of Ger; *Sefat Emet*, Be-midbar, 5631: "The whole idea for someone who strives to understand Torah is to annihilate one's own thoughts and opinions in order to comprehend what the Torah is saying and what God wants. *Midrash* (*Be-midbar Rabbah* 19:26) likens Torah to a wilderness, which is to say that it must be ownerless like a wilderness. . . . The word *midbar*, wilderness, means to guide or to rule over. And the experience of being in the wilderness means to submit to its rule. This is to say that one must annihilate one's selfhood so that the only active power is the divine life force within him." See also translation in Green, *Language of Truth*, 219–20.
26. See translations in Shapira, *Conscious Community: A Guide to Inner Work*, 51–52; Lawrence Kushner, *Way into Jewish Mystical Tradition*, 13.
27. As in *I'm God, You're Not*, 152–53.

9. THE *SEFIROT*

1. See discussion in Hallamish, *Introduction to the Kabbalah*, 164–65.
2. "To the prophets, the gulf that separates man from God is transcended by His pathos. For all the impenetrability of His being, He is concerned with the world and relates Himself to it." Heschel, *Prophets*, 228.
3. See Matt, *Zohar: The Pritzker Edition*, 8:230.
4. Thus Heschel could say: "All of human history as seen by the Bible is the history of *God in search of man*. In spite of man's failure, over and over, God does not abandon His hope to find righteous men." *Prophets*, 438.
5. *Otam*, as written in this text, is without a *vav*. Thus the translation would be that "you yourselves shall make them." On the previous midrashic derivation of this change, see Tishby, *Wisdom of the Zohar*, 3:1169n50.

6. Fine, "Purifying the Body," 119, also noting that "the upper triad of *sefirot* (*Keter*, *Hokhmah*, and *Binah*) corresponds to the divine 'head,' or the several dimensions of God's intellect." See also Fine et al., *Jewish Mysticism and the Spiritual Life*, xvi. On some of the details in these diagrams of the *sefirot*, see Idel, *Enchanted Chains*, 50.

7. Zohar 2:144a. See also Fine, *Safed Spirituality*, 7.

8. "Man's soul emanates from an upper region where it has a spiritual father and a spiritual mother, just as the body has a father and mother in this world. The souls that abide in our bodies are a weak reflection of our upper souls, the seat of which is in heaven." Heschel, "Mystical Element in Judaism," 605. "In particular, human deeds, especially the deeds of Jews, affect the well-being of the *sefirotic* realm. This is because humans, created in the divine image, mirror God. When Jews perform the commandments properly, they empower the deity, and when they commit sins, they diminish divine power." Tirosh-Samuelson, "Jewish Mysticism," 408-9. "As well as being a map of the workings of the Divine, and the structure of the Universe, the *sefirot* are mirrored in the human soul. Hence, human beings resemble the *sefirot* isomorphically, and each *sefirah* can be mapped on the human body." Giller, *Kabbalah*, 45. "Our own bodies reflect and thereby symbolize the constituent elements of the life of God." Fine, "Kabbalistic Texts," 326.

9. We omit here consideration of the *sefirah Da'at* that is seen in certain kabbalistic systems. Note also that the *sefirot* are referred to by many names and "codes"; these generally will be dealt with as they appear in specific kabbalistic texts.

10. See Matt, "*Ayin*: The Concept of Nothingness," 76-77.

11. In *Hokhmah* and *Binah*, "the building and creation of the cosmos as well as that which divides things begins. They are parallel emanations from *Keter*, representing the active and the receptive principle." Heschel, "Mystical Element in Judaism," 607.

12. This idea is most vividly expressed in the Rabbinic period in *Midrash Bereshit Rabbah* 12:15: "*Adonai Elohim*: this may be compared to a king who had some thin glasses. The king said: If I pour hot water into them, they will burst; if cold, they will contract [and crack]. What did the king do? He mixed hot and cold water and poured it into them, and so they remained. Thus said the Holy One, Blessed be He: If I create the world only with the quality of mercy, its sins will be great; if only with the quality of justice, the world cannot exist. So I will create it with the quality of justice *and* with the quality of mercy, and may it stand." This and similar references can be found in Liebes, *Jewish Myth and Jewish Messianism*, 27-32. See also comments in Eitan Fishbane, "*Zohar*," 54, and Fine, "Kabbalistic Texts," 322.

13. The primordial Torah also has a place in the *sefirotic* realm and is understood as originating in *Hokhmah*.

14. "The *sefirah Yesod* represents the qualities of transmission, fertilization, and masculine sexuality and eroticism. It is the dynamic, erotic quality in divinity of appropriately timed gathering, storing, and discharging, as well as disclosure and concealment, and is thus symbolized by the male sexual organ." Hellner-Eshed, *River Flows from Eden*, 33–34.

15. "The *Shekhinah* is called figuratively the *Matrona* that is separated from the King and it signifies that God is, so to speak, involved in the tragic state of this world. In the light of this doctrine the suffering of Israel assumed new meaning. Not only Israel but the whole universe, even the *Shekhinah*, 'lies in dust' (Zohar 2:9b) and is in exile. Man's task is to bring about the restitution of the original state of the universe." Heschel, "Mystical Element in Judaism," 610. "The exile of the Jewish people represented a separation of the masculine and feminine principles of the Divinity, and the Redemption of the Jewish people would constitute the reunion of those principles." Sharot, *Messianism, Mysticism, and Magic*, 33.

16. "This unification, it should be stressed, is really a reunification, a return to what had been the normal situation before its disruption by the destruction of the sanctuary and the exile of the people, and it shall in no way be viewed as a culmination of the cosmic process of creation." Liebes, *Studies in the Zohar*, 2–3.

17. Bloom, *Gershom Scholem*, 8.

18. See Idel, "Land of Israel," 172–73.

19. See Idel, "Land of Israel," 174, quoting Zohar 2:23a. "By the act of circumcision, one becomes righteous and attains intimacy with *Yesod*'s partner, *Shekhinah*, the land." Matt, *Zohar: The Pritzker Edition*, 4:78n30. On Schafer's theory that the feminine image of the *Shekhinah* is influenced by the Christian cult of the Virgin Mary, see the discussion in Tirosh-Samuelson, "Gender in Jewish Mysticism," 196–99, 208–9; and Idel, *Kabbalah and Eros*, 46–49.

20. Attributed to Prof. Fritz Rothschild.

21. Translation and commentary based on Tishby, *Wisdom of the Zohar*, 1:259–62; Matt, *Essential Kabbalah*, 50–51, 171–73; Jacobs, *Jewish Ethics, Philosophy and Mysticism*, 115–20; and Ariel, *Mystic Quest*, 85.

22. Note also that the Zohar speaks of such matters as given to Adam but no one else, not even higher beings; the holy angel Hadraniel tells him: "Adam, Adam, treasure away the precious glory of your Lord, for permission has not been granted to supernal beings to know it, only to you!" Zohar 1:55b; Matt, *Zohar: The Pritzker Edition*, 1:312.

23. The "garments" referred to here are an allusion to three of the four worlds

of emanation. "The *sefirot* of each world constitute a garment for the preceding world, as well as a body that is clothed in the *sefirot* of the following world." Matt, *Essential Kabbalah*, 172. However, we have deferred discussion of the four worlds until chapter 19.

24. B. Ber. 61a, end.

25. Spelled out in full in the Hebrew, as we shall soon see.

26. "The emanation of the first three *sefirot, Keter, Hokhmah* and *Binah*, is referred to by the term 'the intellect' (*ha-muskal*), since in these first three *sefirot* the divine idea unfolds concerning the origins of creation. The second triad in this system—*Hesed, Din* and *Tiferet*—is often referred to as 'the psychic' (*ha-murgash*), while the last triad of *Netzah, Hod* and *Yesod*, from which the conditions for life emerge, is called 'the natural' (*ha-mutba*)." Laenen, *Jewish Mysticism*, 50.

27. As noted in Tishby, *Wisdom of the Zohar*, 1:260n29.

28. Matt, *Essential Kabbalah*, 172, translates *libba*, the Aramaic form of *lev*, as "heartmind," noting that "in Hebrew, the heart is the seat of the intellect as well as the emotions." While this formulation is completely accurate, I have omitted such language.

29. Jacobs, *Jewish Ethics, Philosophy and Mysticism*, 118.

30. Based on Idel, *Kabbalah*, 136–53, and the briefer summary in Sherwin, *Kabbalah*, 58–60. Giller, *Kabbalah*, 56–57, deals only with the first two of these.

31. The *sefirot* "are viewed as character traits of the divine personality. God's hiddenness now has a psychological dimension that links the soul of the creator to human beings who were created in the divine image." Tirosh-Samuelson, "Jewish Mysticism," 406.

32. "The *sefirot* are reflected and apprehensible in all realms of reality via concrete symbols. The symbolic aspects of the *sefirot* are unlimited, in both the spiritual and the material realms. However, the symbols are not allegorical representations, which have no existence in the divine realm they symbolize; on the contrary, their real existence is within the system of divine powers, and the things that serve as means of symbolization are images of the concealed supernal reality." Tishby, *Wisdom of the Zohar*, 1:47–48. It should be said that there are those who treat the *sefirot* as metaphorical, e.g., Lawrence Kushner, *I'm God, You're Not*, 153: "*Sefirot* are a metaphor for trying to comprehend how the One could possibly make this world of so many apparently discrete and discordant parts. The *sefirot* themselves are alternatively described as dimensions of the divine and the human psyche, the steps in the emanative process of creation, or because everything is made of God, the *sefirot* are also an image of the infrastructure of reality itself." While this partakes of views 3 and 4, it does not quite grant the *sefirot* "reality." Close to this is the position of Dan: "Is it true that the *Shekhinah*

marries the masculine part of the divine realm? Of course not. These are nothing but symbols, which, when taken as if they were human, earthly terms that have a literal meaning, do not convey anything. This picture of a divine wedding is a kabbalistic symbol that has no literal significance; only the mystic, who has had a glimpse of the mystical truth beyond human knowledge and sensory awareness, can have some inkling of the reality behind the symbols." *Jewish Mysticism and Jewish Ethics*, 90–91.

33. See Tishby, *Wisdom of the Zohar*, 1:342–43; Matt, *Zohar: The Pritzker Edition*, 7:53–54.

34. See Tishby, *Wisdom of the Zohar*, 1:309; Matt, *Zohar: The Pritzker Edition*, 1:107–9; and extensive analysis on the theme of *botzina d'kardenuta* in Giller, *Reading the Zohar*, 70–87.

35. Matt, *Zohar: The Pritzker Edition*, 1:108a. See Scholem, *Kabbalah*, 149.

36. Matt, *Essential Kabbalah*, 38.

37. Cordovero also deals with the visualization of colors as a device in meditative prayer in *Pardes Rimonim*, gate 32, ch. 2; this passage is translated and briefly discussed in Idel, "Kabbalistic Prayer and Colors," 23.

38. For more details on this phenomenon, see Idel, *Kabbalah*, 103–11, and *Enchanted Chains*, 228–32.

39. Tishby, *Wisdom of the Zohar*, 2:642–43.

40. On Michael and Gabriel, see also Zohar 2:231a; Tishby, *Wisdom of the Zohar*, 2:648.

41. NJPS: "He makes the winds His messengers."

42. Tishby, *Wisdom of the Zohar*, 2:635–36.

43. "The Book *Bahir* and the *Zohar* are mystical midrashim. In every external methodological way, they are midrashim, in the full sense of the term. They differ from the classical midrashim in one most meaningful way: their conclusions are not truth expressed by language, but truth expressed by linguistic symbols, intrinsically supported by the mystical meta-linguistic experience of the author." Dan, "Language of the Mystics," 21.

44. NJPS: "The one no less than the other was God's doing."

45. *Midrash ha-Ne'elam* is the earliest part of the Zohar, a separate composition that was integrated into the Zohar's text. See Giller, *Reading the Zohar*, 5–6.

46. *Shnei Luhot ha-Brit, Toldot Adam, Sha'ar ha-Gadol*, sect. 20.

47. 1:77b.

48. See translation of Schochet, 86–87. Also see sect. 99 for another example of "knowing" as joining.

49. See the similar teaching of Horowitz in *Shnei Luhot ha-Brit, Asarah Ma'amarot, Ma'amar Shlishi and Revi'i*, sect. 65.

50. Tishby, *Wisdom of the Zohar*, 2:648–49; Matt, *Zohar: The Pritzker Edition*, 4:421–23.

51. See the many references culled by Matt, *Zohar: The Pritzker Edition*, 4:421n189; note also the use of *ish ha-Elohim* in Zohar 1:236b.
52. B. Ber. 7a.
53. This probably refers to the broader "complex" of the six *sefirot* around *Tiferet*, if the first two angels are associated with *Hokhmah* and *Binah* and the last with *Malkhut*.
54. See, e.g., *Midrash Vayikra Rabbah* 11:7 and *Bereshit Rabbah* 3:6, among those noted in Matt, *Zohar: The Pritzker Edition*, 4:422n191.
55. Also in the midrashic text, *Pesikta d'Rav Kahana* 12:20.
56. Tishby, *Wisdom of the Zohar*, 2:649n117, says it refers to Jacob alone. The two lights have just been mentioned, and I consider that a more likely explanation here.
57. Blumenthal, *Understanding Jewish Mysticism*, 1:125.

10. *DEVEIKUT*
1. Sherwin, *Mystical Theology and Social Dissent*, 128; see Maimonides, *Guide of the Perplexed*, 3:51–54. Interestingly, Maimonides's own son (and many of those following immediately upon Maimonides himself) opted for a much stronger version of *deveikut*, virtual union. See Idel, *Studies in Ecstatic Kabbalah*, 4–5, for the texts.
2. Based on Matt, *Zohar: The Pritzker Edition*, 1:282–86; see also Tishby, *Wisdom of the Zohar*, 1:319–22.
3. A contextual translation of *amei ha-aretz*.
4. Maimonides cites this approvingly in *Mishneh Torah, Hilkhot De'ot* 6:2.
5. Similarly *Midrash Tanhuma*, B'reishit (Warsaw) 7, beginning: "The Holy One, Blessed be He, is called Just and Upright [*tzadik v'yashar*]. Therefore He has created man in His image, only so man might be just and upright like God Himself."
6. Weinstein translation, 291, but with significant modifications.
7. *Sifrei* (Numbers) 115, as noted in Matt, *Zohar: The Pritzker Edition*, 1:283.
8. See *Seder Eliyahu Rabbah* 5:7.
9. See above remarks on *Knesset Yisrael*.
10. "The Zohar's chief concern with the mysteries of the divine world is as an object of mystical contemplation, not as a guide for ecstatic mystical experience. The author of the Zohar does not speak in the language of an elite, but rather expresses the emotions and fears of ordinary people. Unlike the philosophers, who challenged the simple faith of the people, mystics of the type represented by the Zohar's author saw and presented their views of the Godhead as fully in keeping with traditional beliefs about the God of creation and revelation." Tishby, "Gershom Scholem's Contribution," 46.
11. Matt, *Zohar: The Pritzker Edition*, 1:284.
12. B. Ber. 61b, telling of Rabbi Akiva's martyrdom at the hands of the Romans.

13. Translated in Sherwin, *Kabbalah,* 99-100; also see *Mystical Theology and Social Dissent,* 135.

14. Sherwin, *Kabbalah,* 89-90, including *Netivot Olam* 2:29.

15. B. Shab. 118b.

16. Translated in Sherwin, *Mystical Theology and Social Dissent,* 134.

17. See Sherwin, *Mystical Theology and Social Dissent,* 133.

18. See Fine, "Kabbalistic Texts," 350.

19. See, e.g., *Sha'ar ha-Kedushah,* ch. 4: 21. De Vidas also emphasizes that ascetic practices are not necessary: "And he need not mortify his flesh or torment himself by fasting, for *devekut* depends on nothing but ardent desire [for God]." *Sha'ar ha-Ahavah,* end of ch. 4. For a concise analysis of *deveikut* in the thought of sixteenth-century Safed, see Etkes, *Besht,* 120-21.

20. Also, in some texts *deveikut* protects one from the dangers of the world. See, e.g., the text from Isaac of Acre in *Me'irat Einayim,* cited in Idel, *Enchanted Chains,* 101-2.

21. For all texts from *Toldot Adam,* see Krassen's translation in *Isaiah Horowitz: The Generations of Adam.*

22. See, e.g., *Sefer ha-Mitzvot,* positive mitzvot, no. 8.

23. On Gen. 2:17.

24. This "quote" is actually a combination of *Sifrei* (Ekev) 13 and the idea contained in the text of B. Sot. 14a above.

25. On the idea of constant *deveikut* as a fulfillment of this particular verse, note also the Hasidic Rabbi Moshe Teitelbaum (1759-1841): "You should fulfill 'I have placed the Lord before me always,' so that you do not turn your mind from God consciousness for even one minute." Quoted from *Hanhagot Tzadikim,* 48:19, in Buxbaum, *Jewish Spiritual Practices,* 10. For a look at this verse from the point of view of "Normal Mysticism," see Moshe Isserles on *Shulhan Arukh,* O. H. 1:1.

26. See Lamm, *Religious Thought of Hasidism,* 150-51, and variant translation in Krassen, *Uniter of Heaven and Earth,* 58.

27. See the introduction to Nahmanides's commentary on the Torah.

28. Again, note the influence of Shelah; see Krassen, *Isaiah Horowitz,* 40, and see 88 for another example of this key verse in Hasidic thought.

29. Similarly, *Noam Elimelekh* on Lekh Lekha, 7a, cited in Verman, *History and Varieties of Jewish Mysticism,* 37: "It is stated, 'One who is standing in the Diaspora and wishes to pray should direct his heart towards the land of Israel; one who is standing in the land of Israel should face Jerusalem.' (B. Ber. 30a) Accordingly, all Jewish prayers pass through the same gate. Therefore, if a person wants his prayers to be heard he should imagine that he is praying in the land of Israel and that the Temple is standing and the altar and inner chamber are operational and behold he is presently living in

the land of Israel. By means of this [visualization] he will achieve illumination and complete *devekut* in order to pray with utmost concentration with fear and love, as if he were standing in the Holy of Holies."

30. I have noted the translation and commentary in Lamm, *Religious Thought of Hasidism*, 170–71.

31. In Harold Kushner, *Etz Hayim*, 1007.

11. TZOREKH GAVOHA

1. Moses is praised because "with every mitzvah he tried to unite *Ha-Kadosh Barukh Hu (Tiferet)* with the *Shekhinah* in all assemblies, above and below." Zohar 2:119a (*Ra'aya Meheimna*).

2. There are several references in the Babylonian Talmud to *tzorekh gavoha*—Shab. 116b and 121b, MK 9a, Men. 64a—but the "divine need" referred to in these examples differs from the kabbalistic understanding of divine need, meaning instead "for the need of the cult or Temple." To the best of my knowledge, the earliest direct kabbalistic use of the phrase is found in Nahmanides's commentary to Exod. 29:46.

3. Krassen, *Isaiah Horowitz*, 14.

4. "The notion of divine omnipotence seems either unknown or irrelevant to biblical and to rabbinic theology." Sherwin, *Toward a Jewish Theology*, 71.

5. *Pesikta Rabbati* 28:3, and see discussion of this issue in Heschel, *Heavenly Torah*, 114–21.

6. Sherwin, *Toward a Jewish Theology*, 71.

7. See second section, *Sha-ar ha-Yihud v'ha-Emunah*.

8. Based on Faierstein, "God's Need for the Commandments," 47–48.

9. See *Midrash Tanhuma*, Shemini 8; Matt, "Mystic and the *Mizwot*," 393.

10. I have consulted the translation of Hammer, 358–59.

11. *Moral Grandeur*, 163. Similarly, "Happy is the one who grows up in Torah and labors in Torah, and gives *nahat ruah* to his Creator, for His will is done." (B. Ber. 17a)

12. NJPS translates as "neglected."

13. See also *Shnei Luhot ha-Brit, Toldot Adam, Sha'ar ha-Gadol*, sect. 14.

14. E.g., *Aggadat Bereshit* 15 and 39: "The nations of the world also want to come under the wings of the *Shekhinah* when Israel does the will of the Holy One, Blessed be He." "Happy are Israel; when they do the will of the Holy One, Blessed be He, He raises them like the ministering angels."

15. See Faierstein, "God's Need for the Commandments," 53–54.

16. See also *Shnei Luhot ha-Brit, Toldot Adam, Sha'ar ha-Gadol*, sect. 17.

17. While Krassen cites this as *Tikkunei Zohar*, introduction 2, I have not found this exact quote there.

18. E.g., B. Shab. 63a.

19. *Shnei Luhot ha-Brit, Asarah Ma'amarot, Ma'amar Shlishi U'revi'i*, sect. 70.
20. *Shnei Luhot ha-Brit, Asarah Ma'amarot, Ma'amar Shlishi U'revi'i, Ki Tetze, Torah Or*, sect. 7.
21. See Faierstein, "God's Need for the Commandments," 55.
22. See translation and commentary in Matt, *Zohar: The Pritzker Edition*, 4:356–57.
23. On Amalek as punishment for the Israelites' insolence, see in particular *Midrash Tanhuma*, Yitro 4 (Buber), and the end of *Midrash Shemot Rabbah* 26:2.
24. On this idea, see references in Matt, *Zohar: The Pritzker Edition*, 4:320n429, of which the best review of the idea is Tishby, *Wisdom of the Zohar*, 3:1085–86.
25. This fourteenth-century text is also cited by Shelah; *Shnei Luhot ha-Brit, Toldot Adam, Sha'ar ha-Gadol*, sect. 23.
26. Both texts also cited by Shelah; *Shnei Luhot ha-Brit, Toldot Adam, Sha'ar ha-Gadol*, sect. 13.
27. See *Midrash Bereshit Rabbah* 1:1 and 1:4. "Not only language, but the text existed before the creation: The Torah came into being long before anything else, cosmos or Man, ever existed. Language and text had their independent, autonomous existence within the divine world before any kind of human communication could be conceived.... Language is not an attempt to describe existing things; rather, existing things are the unfolding of powers which lie within language." Dan, "Language of the Mystics," 8.
28. As per Rashi's commentary on the passage.
29. *Avodat ha-Kodesh* (5) also notes that when Moses says *yigdal na koah Adonai*, God responds, *salahti kidvarekha*; it is the strengthening of God that brings about pardon and *tikkun* at both the lower and the supernal levels.
30. This is the expanded version cited in Abraham Azulai's *Masekhet Avot* 3a; translated in Idel, "On the Theologization of Kabbalah," 132; see also Idel, *Hasidism*, 100–101, and *Enchanted Chains*, 184. Comparing it to the original text as I have it (483a), I am not sure that this version should not be attributed to Azulai himself, even though he clearly lifts a great deal directly from Cordovero. However, it is well placed, as the analysis will indicate. I have varied slightly from Idel's translation.
31. Zohar 1:70b. Or as Matt translates, "For the upper world depends upon the lower, and the lower upon the upper." *Zohar: The Pritzker Edition*, 1:413. Heschel generally follows the Soncino translation.
32. Heschel, "Mystical Element in Judaism," 616.

12. PROPHETIC-ECSTATIC KABBALAH

1. See Kadushin, *Rabbinic Mind*, 233–34, quoting Y. Yoma 5:3, 42c, and B. Ber. 7a, a text noted in chapter 5; also 245–49, about the controversy between the Pharisees and Sadducees on this topic.

2. See Kadushin, *Rabbinic Mind*, 239–41, citing David Zvi Hoffmann, ed., *Mekhilta d'Rabbi Shimon*, 159. In my judgment, Kadushin does not resolve the issue of the connection between *giluy Shekhinah* in sacrificial worship and some link between them in the *Tefillah* "which can only be reminiscent of an experience of *giluy shekhinah*" (*Worship and Ethics*, 165) in view of his position that "there is no *giluy shekhinah* when the *Tefillah* is recited." (166) In connection with the idea of *giluy Shekhinah* in the Temple, Wolfson (*Through a Speculum*, 64n51) quotes a most interesting kabbalistic text from Joseph of Hamadan in *Sefer Tashak*: "Therefore the Holy One, Blessed be He, said to Moses our master, peace be upon him, 'Tell the Israelite people to bring me (gifts)' (Exod. 25:2); they should make a body and soul for God and I will take bodily form in it." See also Zohar 3:67a.

3. Kadushin, *Rabbinic Mind*, 237–38.

4. Heschel, "Mystical Element in Judaism," 612.

5. "It is the human being that is in central position instead of God. In this current the focus is on the attainment of an ecstatic awareness of the individual mystic, without the latter being concerned about the restoration of the internal harmony of the divine world." Laenen, *Jewish Mysticism*, 120. Accordingly, the *Merkavah* prayers that have survived, such as "Ein Keloheinu" or "Ha-Aderet v'ha-Emunah," are often quite simple: "In these hymns of praise to God, the focus is not on their theological or literary content but on their ability, through rhythmic recitation, to induce a certain frame of mind." Sherwin, *Kabbalah*, 143.

6. In his commentary on Dan. 10:21.

7. Scholem, *On the Mystical Shape*, 312n7. On the whole issue of solitude as a preparation for mystical experience, see Hallamish, *Introduction to the Kabbalah*, 49–53.

8. As translated in Scholem, *On the Mystical Shape*, 253–54, and Sherwin, *Kabbalah*, 150–51. Scholem dates this particular text included in *Shushan ha-Sodot* to the late thirteenth or early fourteenth century.

9. According to the translation of Jacobs, *Jewish Mystical Testimonies*, 59–61.

10. "Knowledge of God is treated as the highest perfection of man, and it is explicitly connected, according to several medieval philosophers, with man's union with the active intellect." Idel, *Studies in Ecstatic Kabbalah*, 19.

11. E.g., *Midrash Bereshit Rabbah* 44:1.

12. Sherwin, *Kabbalah*, 153. Note also Idel, *Language, Torah, and Hermeneutics*, xi, and see further 11–14, 23–27. Wolfson also notes Abulafia's firm conviction of both the power of the Hebrew language and the role of the Jews: "Just as Hebrew is the 'natural language,' that is, the language of creation and thus the basis for all other languages, which, by contrast, are deemed to be 'conventional,' so the Jewish people represent the ethnicity that embodies

the human ideal most fully. This standing is connected more specifically to their possession of the divine name." "Abraham ben Samuel Abulafia," 76.

13. Translated and published by Scholem, *Ha-Kabbalah shel Sefer ha-Temunah v'shel Avraham Abulafia*, ed. J. Ben-Shlomo, 208; cited in Sherwin, *Kabbalah*, 160.

14. *Guide of the Perplexed* 2:36.

15. *Guide of the Perplexed* 3:51.

16. E.g., B. BB 12a.

17. See Heschel's essay in *Prophetic Inspiration after the Prophets*, especially 13–41.

18. *Commentary on Sefer ha-Yashar*, MS Rome-Angelica 38, fol. 31b–32a, cited in Idel, "Abulafia's Secrets of the Guide," 295.

19. From MS Munich-BS 40, fol. 226b, translated in Wolfson, *Abraham Abulafia—Kabbalist and Prophet*, 69. For a similar example from Abulafia's *Shomer Mitzvah*, see Idel, *Enchanted Chains*, 94–95.

20. Idel, *Enchanted Chains*, 7. See also his *Absorbing Perfections*, 338–39.

21. From Abulafia's *Sitrei Torah*, cited in Idel, *Studies in Ecstatic Kabbalah*, 5–6; quoted more fully in Idel, "Universalization and Integration," 30: "[They] will be united with it after many hard, strong, and mighty exercises, until the particular and personal prophetic [faculty] will become universal, permanent and everlasting similar to the essence of its cause, and he and He become one entity." See also in *Studies in Ecstatic Kabbalah*: (1) 13 and the quote from *Or ha-Sekhel*: "the grasping [of the soul], the human intellect which is emanated from the separated active intellect, causes the union of the soul to her God; this union is the cause of the soul's eternal life, similar to the life of her God." (2) 15 and the quote from Abulafia's commentary to the *Book of the Testimony*: "He is I and I am He, and it is forbidden to disclose this issue in a more explicit fashion." See also Idel's discussion of the text in *Kabbalah*, 62, and the related text from Isaac of Akko dealing with the "divine intellect" on 67.

22. E.g., *Major Trends*, 122–23. See also Scholem, *Messianic Idea in Judaism*, 203–4: "Whereas in Catholic mysticism 'Communion' was not the last step on the mystical way . . . in Kabbalism it is the last grade of ascent to God. It is not union, because union with God is denied to man even in that mystical upsurge of the soul, according to kabbalistic theology. But it comes as near to union as a mystical interpretation of Judaism would allow." This is further discussed in Idel, *Studies in Ecstatic Kabbalah*, 21n11; the entire first chapter is titled, "Abraham Abulafia and *Unio Mystica*." Also see Idel, *Enchanted Chains*, 6–11.

23. Scholem, *Major Trends*, 136–37; Sherwin, *Kabbalah*, 158–59; Jacobs, *Jewish Mystical Testimonies*, 62–63; Aryeh Kaplan, *Meditation and Kabbalah*, 93–106, which also includes a detailed derivation of this Name and an extended exercise, which unfortunately is too lengthy for inclusion here.

24. "These commandments may be, indeed, indispensable, even after the mystic returns from the World-to-Come to this world. But they seem to be neutralized in the moments of spiritual elation." Idel, *Language, Torah, and Hermeneutics*, xiii.

25. See, e.g., the excerpt from *Otzar Eden ha-Ganuz* cited in Aryeh Kaplan, *Meditation and Kabbalah*, 84–86.

26. Compare another excerpt from the same book: "And when he begins to practice letter-combination . . . he will feel fear and trembling, and the hairs of his head will stand up and his limbs will tremble." Idel, *Studies in Ecstatic Kabbalah*, 110, and see also 114, where some of the texts of Prophetic Kabbalah warn of the danger that one might wind up like Ben Azzai of the *Pardes* episode.

27. On a different ecstatic text, Idel writes: "It is as though the human body prepares itself by the techniques to be appropriated by different divine aspects, even as it weakens. God takes possession of the body to the extent that the body opens itself to the divine presence, by resorting to gradually more divine forms of letter combinations." *Enchanted Chains*, 101.

28. "This activity, fraught with messianic overtones, was considered by Abulafia to be a necessary evil, obviously inferior to the experience of being with God. Thus, his public activity was considered an escapist interruption to the unitive experience." Idel, *Studies in Ecstatic Kabbalah*, 19–20.

29. See Idel, "On the Theologization of Kabbalah," 141; *Studies in Ecstatic Kabbalah*, 55–56n8.

30. "The divine unity is expressed within and through the ten *sefirot*, which he identifies as the ten separate intellects. . . . [T]he human intellect plays an active role in unifying God through the ten separate intellects. That is, by becoming one with the Active Intellect through conjunction, the individual unifies the divine overflow of all ten intellects within the Active Intellect, which in a manner of speaking represents the unification of God." Wolfson, "Mystical Rationalization," 353.

31. See Aryeh Kaplan, *Meditation and Kabbalah*, 88–92.

32. "In its goals, the ecstatic Kabbalah of Abraham Abulafia recalled (and audaciously extended) the Maimonidean doctrine of prophecy whereby the human and divine intellects temporarily merge. In its techniques, Abulafia's Kabbalah has been called a Judaized Yoga, replete as it is with breathing exercises, postures, and highly developed forms of recitation and meditation." Ginsburg, *Sabbath in the Classical Kabbalah*, 13. On another of the ecstatic techniques and its results, see the example in Idel, *Studies in Ecstatic Kabbalah*, 15–16.

33. "According to the late thirteenth-century ecstatic kabbalist R. Nathan ben Sa'adyah, after combining the letters he was able to produce so many

innovations on intellectual issues that even ten copyists could not commit them to writing." Idel, *Enchanted Chains*, 224.

34. Idel, *Studies in Ecstatic Kabbalah*, 13 and note 77. Note also that Scholem "demonstrated that the mythic and the pantheistic, which at times seem contradictory, can appear together. For example, he showed that the mythic imagery of the *Shi'ur Komah*, the early mystical work which describes the Godhead in the form of a supernal man of colossal dimensions, could be given a pantheistic interpretation, by which 'reality in its entirety constitutes this mystical figure of the Godhead.'" Ben-Shlomo, "Gershom Scholem on Pantheism," 61, quoting Scholem from *Pirkei Yesod be-Havanat ha-Kabbalah v'Semaleha* (Jerusalem: Mossad Bialik, 1976), 172.

35. See Idel, *Studies in Ecstatic Kabbalah*, 139–40.

36. See Idel, *Studies in Ecstatic Kabbalah*, 168n191. For another example of Cordovero's use of Abulafian meditation in *Pardes Rimonim*, see Idel, *Enchanted Chains*, 97.

37. For a contemporary example, see Jay Michaelson's website http://www .learnkabbalah.com/basic_meditation_techniques/ (accessed on March 31, 2015). See also Huss, "Formation of Jewish Mysticism," on what he calls the "contemporary canonization of Abulafian meditation."

13. THE ROLE OF THE TORAH

1. Ariel, *Mystic Quest*, 120.

2. Additionally, "the state of the relations among the companions also relates to their status as symbols of the *sefirot*, for hatred among them represents division among the *sefirot* and a flaw in the supernal world, while love among them is a condition for the disclosure of the secrets of the Torah." Liebes, *Studies in the Zohar*, 37, and note discussion on 38–40; see also among the *hanhagot* of the Safed mystics, discussed below in chapter 18.

3. On these issues, see Matt, *Zohar: The Pritzker Edition*, 5:3.

4. I.e., the passage from B. BB 89b noted in chapter 3 concerning Rabban Yohanan ben Zakkai's ambivalence: "Woe to me if I say it, woe to me if I do not say it." Noted in Liebes, *Studies in the Zohar*, 175n95, and see his comments in the text, 30 and 41.

5. B. Hag. 14b.

6. The link between *keshet* and the male organ is made more explicitly in B. Sanh. 92a. On the rainbow as *Yesod*, see Zohar 1:18a–b, and Matt, *Zohar: The Pritzker Edition*, 1:139n245; also Cordovero, *Tikkunei Zohar im Perush Or Yakar* 2:222 as cited by Wolfson, "Engenderment of Messianic Politics," 237n116.

7. On the role of the rainbow, see Matt, *Zohar: The Pritzker Edition*, 5:32,

as well as the sources cited there, including particularly Idel, *Kabbalah*, 227–29, and Wolfson, *Through a Speculum*, 337–38n40.

8. This is implied in Zohar 3:187b, as well as 3:300a; see discussion in Idel, *Kabbalah*, 383n114.

9. As Liebes put it, "Eros dwells at the peak of *Sava d'Mishpatim*." Quoted in Giller, *Reading the Zohar*, 67.

10. E.g., *Midrash Devarim Rabbah* 8:7.

11. Zohar 1:242a–b; see Matt, *Zohar: The Pritzker Edition*, 3:481. This statement is somewhat more far reaching than its predecessors in the Rabbinic tradition cited by Matt, e.g., B. Ber. 5a and BB 7b–8a; *Midrash Tanhuma*, B'reishit 1 (Warsaw). On the power of the disclosure of Torah, see Liebes, *Studies in the Zohar*, 55–57, and also 69 on the meaning of this "face-to-face" disclosure.

12. See Hallamish, *Introduction to the Kabbalah*, 218.

13. Translation and commentary based on Matt, *Zohar: The Pritzker Edition*, 5:1–139, which contains a wealth of material beyond the limitations of this work. Among the many discussions of the parable, see particularly Tishby, *Wisdom of the Zohar*, 3:1084–85; Talmage, "Apples of Gold," 317–18; Idel, *Kabbalah*, 227–30.

14. E.g., B. Pes. 53b and BM 85a.

15. "R. Yeiva is a hidden tzaddik, disguising his true nature and eking out an existence at the margins of society. The romantic motif of the spiritual possibilities of the socially marginal is characteristic of the Zohar and flowered in Shabbateanism and eighteenth-century Polish Hasidism." Giller, *Reading the Zohar*, 42.

16. M. Avot 4:27: "Do not look at the jar, but rather at what is inside."

17. On the mystic's reticence in describing his experience, see Mendes-Flohr, *Gershom Scholem*, 12. See also the segment from Meir ibn Gabbai, *Avodat ha-Kodesh*, cited in Scholem, *Messianic Idea in Judaism*, 300: "For the differences and contradictions do not originate out of different realms, but out of the one place in which no difference and no contradiction is possible. The implicit meaning of this secret is that it lets every scholar insist on his own opinion and cite proofs for it from the Torah, for only in this manner and in no other way is the unity [of the various aspects of the one stream of revelation] achieved. Therefore it is incumbent upon us to hear the different opinions, and this is the sense of 'these and those are the words of the living God.'"

18. The verse is generally translated: "He makes the winds His messengers." But the key words have two meanings; *ruah* can be "spirit" or "wind," and a *mal'akh* may be "an angel" or "a messenger." Furthermore, either word can be subject or object. The author of the Zohar reads them in order.

19. See Matt, *Essential Kabbalah*, 135–37; Matt, *Zohar: The Book of Enlightenment*,

43-45, 204-7; Matt, *Zohar: The Pritzker Edition*, 8:518-21; Jacobs, *Jewish Ethics, Philosophy and Mysticism*, 121-24; Fine, "Kabbalistic Texts," 337.

20. E.g., *Midrash Shemot Rabbah* 28:4.

21. *Zohar: The Book of Enlightenment*, 206. In a second commentary he says: "To be a mystic is to remember the primordial revelation." *Essential Kabbalah*, 209.

22. "The Torah has a double significance: literal and symbolic. Besides their plain, literal meaning, which is important, valid, and never to be overlooked, the verses of the Torah possess an esoteric significance, 'comprehensible only to the wise who are familiar with the ways of the Torah.'" Heschel, "Mystical Element in Judaism," 614; the citation is from Zohar 2:95a.

23. Slightly misquoted in the original text.

24. Noted and translated in Idel, *Enchanted Chains*, 152, from the Warsaw 1876 edition, 23b.

25. Isaac the Blind (~1160-1235) said: "Although your mitzvah seems finite at first, it expands to infinity. While all perishable things are finite, the human being can never fully comprehend Your mitzvah." Commentary on *Sefer Yetzirah* 1:6, cited in Matt, "Mystic and the *Mizwot*," 377-78. This notion continued to develop as the Jewish mystical tradition expanded; see also Tishby, "Gershom Scholem's Contribution," 53-54.

26. Tishby, "Gershom Scholem's Contribution," 52.

27. *Sifra* on Lev. 18:4.

28. For an excellent example, see Moshe de Leon, *Sefer ha-Rimmon*, cited in Scholem, *Major Trends*, 397-98n154.

29. Matt, "Mystic and the *Mizwot*," 376. See also Dan, "Gershom Scholem's Reconstruction," 169-70.

30. This phrase is used to describe a law not otherwise justified; see B. BB 159a and Yoma 10a.

31. "In the Torah, *to uncover the nakedness* is a euphemism for sexual intercourse. It may also serve to imply that, in a society where people dressed modestly, seeing a person undressed would inevitably lead to sexual contact." Harold Kushner, *Etz Hayim*, 689.

32. See Matt, "Mystic and the *Mizwot*," 380.

14. SEXUALITY IN JEWISH MYSTICISM

1. Rabbi Elazar ben Azariah in T. Yev. 8:5. See also Urbach, *The Sages*, 217, 227.

2. Zohar 1:264b. See also Tishby, *Wisdom of the Zohar*, 3:1362, for related texts.

3. Zohar 1:228b.

4. Moshe Idel, "Sexual Metaphors," 199. See also Fine, *Safed Spirituality*, 15.

5. See Green, *Tormented Master*, 37-40, 167-70; Liebes, *Jewish Myth and Jewish Messianism*, 126-28, 134-46.

6. Sherwin, "Human Body," 102.
7. Even for those who did not include it regularly, Song of Songs also had an indirect presence in the Shabbat liturgy, through the many references to it in "Yedid Nefesh" and "Lekhah Dodi" (the latter to be discussed in chapter 22).
8. Commenting on the royal bed of Song of Songs 3:7: "*His* [Solomon's, in the Rabbinic interpretation] *bed*: this is the Temple. And why is the Temple compared to the bed? Just as this bed serves fruitfulness and multiplication, so too the Temple; everything that was in it was fruitful and multiplied." *Midrash Tanhuma*, Naso 16 (Buber). According to a Gnostic treatise, this idea of the Holy of Holies as bedroom is ancient: "The mysteries of truth are revealed, though in type and image; the bridal chamber, however, remains hidden. It is the holy in the holy. The veil at first concealed how God controlled the creation, but when the veil is rent and the things inside are revealed, this house will be left desolate." Gospel of Philip, quoted in Idel, "Sexual Metaphors," 203. See also Sherwin, "Human Body," 103.
9. From "The Lion King," music and lyrics by Elton John and Tim Rice, copyright 1994.
10. The giver and receiver are *mashpia u'mekabbel*, terms for masculine and feminine beings.
11. See Seymour J. Cohen, *Holy Letter*, 80, 90–92, and see his introduction on the various manuscripts and the authorship of the work.
12. "The human mystical intention that has to accompany the sexual union can cause the supernal light—and the *Shekhinah* as well—to descend on man during sexual intercourse." Idel, "Sexual Metaphors," 205; see also Seymour J. Cohen, *Holy Letter*, 142, 146. "The sexual act which draws down the *Shekhinah* fulfills not only a human but a divine need." Sherwin, "Human Body," 102.
13. Seymour J. Cohen, *Holy Letter*, 180, 94, 162.
14. See related comments in Idel, "Sexual Metaphors," 207–8.
15. See also Zohar 1:219b: "One who fornicates with his hands, emitting and wasting seed fruitlessly. For we have learned: Whoever emits his seed fruitlessly is called evil and does not see the face of *Shekhinah*." Matt, *Zohar: The Pritzker Edition*, 3:327.
16. See Matt, *Zohar: The Pritzker Edition*, 1:51–52.
17. On the betrothal of God and the Jewish people at Sinai, see B. Ta'an. 26b; Israel is later described as "*bat zug l'ha-Kadosh Barukh Hu*"; Cordovero, *Tomer Devorah*, ch. 1, sect. 4.
18. Matt, *Zohar: The Pritzker Edition*, 1:53n382, describes them as "those who have mastered the sexual urge, leading holy sexual lives. Since they embody the quality of *Yesod*, the divine phallus, their virtue is proclaimed by *Yesod*."

Note also Meir ibn Gabbai's statement: "When man and woman truly unite, all is one body, and the cosmos rejoices for it becomes one complete corpus." *Avodat ha-Kodesh*, sec. 4, ch. 13, 122b, cited in Sherwin, "Human Body," 101.

19. "Just as a bride is adorned with twenty-four ornaments, and lacking one of them, she is considered worthless, so a disciple must be fluent in twenty-four books [of Tanakh]; lacking one of them, he is worthless." *Midrash Shir ha-Shirim Rabbah* on 4:11.

20. On the underlying ideas and development of *Tikkun leil Shavuot*, see Liebes, *Studies in the Zohar*, 74–82.

21. Schachter-Shalomi, *Wrapped in a Holy Flame*, 162, on Theodore Reik's comments about the feminine in Judaism. Note that the Zohar in 3:55a also treats tefillin as a representation similar to that assigned here to the Torah; see Tishby, *Wisdom of the Zohar*, 3:1163; Matt, *Zohar: The Pritzker Edition*, 7:349.

22. Matt, *Zohar: The Pritzker Edition*, 1:275–76.

23. B. Ket. 62b.

24. For a different view of marital sexuality in the Zohar, see Giller, *Kabbalah*, 112–17.

25. *Tzava'at ha-Rivash*, 6b; a translation with minor variations and commentary (not germane to our purposes) can be found in Schochet, *Tzava'at HaRivash*, 54–55; also Jacobs, *Hasidic Prayer*, 60.

26. Jacobs, *Their Heads in Heaven*, 142 and 148n13.

27. Page 4a; translation in Jacobs, *Hasidic Prayer*, 60.

28. As noted in Jacobs, *Their Heads in Heaven*, 171n32.

29. Introduction to *Toldot Adam*, sect. 3. See also the section of Karo's *Maggid Mesharim* cited in *Shnei Luhot ha-Brit, Sha'ar ha-Gadol*, sect. 64.

30. Sherwin, "Human Body," 101.

31. *Tefillah l'Moshe* (commentary on the siddur), 213a, cited in Mopsik, "Body of Engenderment," 60.

32. B. Shab. 151b. Presumably she "seduces" him, causing a nocturnal emission. On the development of attitudes toward nocturnal emission, see Hundert, *Jews in Poland-Lithuania*, 131–37.

33. See Scholem, *Kabbalah*, 357.

34. See, e.g., Graves and Patai, *Hebrew Myths*, 65–69.

35. See Idel, *Kabbalah and Eros*, 145.

36. See Tishby, *Wisdom of the Zohar*, 2:539–40; Matt, *Zohar: The Pritzker Edition*, 7:119–21.

37. Tishby, *Wisdom of the Zohar*, 2:538–39. *Sitrei Torah* is a commentary on certain verses of Genesis, parallel to the Zohar and printed together with it, including allegorical explanations on the mysteries of the soul.

38. "Samael is like the soul and Lilith like the body. Deeds are wrought by Lilith with the power of Samael." Tishby, *Wisdom of the Zohar*, 2:538n36.

39. B. Av. Zar. 20b.
40. Quoted in *Reishit Hokhmah, Sha'ar ha-Ahavah* (Gate of love), end of chapter 4; see Wineman, *Beyond Appearances,* 65–66.

15. SIN, *TESHUVAH,* AND THE *YETZER HA-RA*

1. *Midrash Bereshit Rabbah* 9:7.
2. B. Suk. 52a.
3. The idea of the serpent's "infection" is stated in 2 Esdras 4:30.
4. B. Shab. 146a and Yev. 103b. Similarly the comment of Rabbi Abraham ben David of Posquieres quoting these texts, noted in Sherwin, *Studies in Jewish Theology,* 241. See also discussion of the seduction and defilement of Eve in Giller, *Enlightened Will Shine,* 35.
5. *Midrash Bereshit Rabbah* 20:12.
6. Zohar 1:36b, and see comments in Matt, *Zohar: The Pritzker Edition,* 1:230.
7. For a short summary, see Heschel, *Insecurity of Freedom,* 129–30.
8. Heschel, "Mystical Element in Judaism," 609. Kabbalah, however, provides us the opportunity to correct the flaw and reconstitute the cosmos; see Krassen, "New Year's," 85.
9. See Soncino's *The Zohar* translation, 5:91; Matt, *Zohar: The Pritzker Edition,* 8:4–5.
10. On the drawing of evil from the holy, see Heschel, *Insecurity of Freedom,* 134.
11. See Matt, *Zohar: The Pritzker Edition,* 1:297–98.
12. E.g., B. Pes. 22b.
13. Most directly *Midrash ha-Gadol* on the verse: "This teaches that he was divorced like a wife divorced from her husband because of some indecency." Noted with other sources in Matt, *Zohar: The Pritzker Edition,* 1:297n1436.
14. But not totally new, as Matt (*Zohar: The Pritzker Edition* 1:298n1437) notes: Rev. 1:8 contains the same idea, "I am *alpha* and *omega.*"
15. But see *Zohar Hadash* 19a, *Midrash ha-Ne'elam,* as noted in Matt, *Zohar: The Pritzker Edition,* 1:298n1438. This note provides much more detail on the potential meanings of the story that are omitted here.
16. *Midrash Bereshit Rabbah* 19:7.
17. On the role of these wanderings, see Wolfson, "Walking as a Sacred Duty," 184 and 188; also Werblowsky, "Safed Revival," 15; Tishby, *Wisdom of the Zohar,* 1:382–87; Hallamish, *Introduction to the Kabbalah,* 178. Finally, most recently, see Greenstein, *Roads to Utopia.*
18. See Matt, *Zohar: The Pritzker Edition,* 1:224–25.
19. B. BB 16a.
20. *Pirkei d'Rabbi Eliezer* 13.
21. Based on M. Avot 6:11.

22. Matt, *Zohar: The Pritzker Edition*, 5:441–42; Tishby, *Wisdom of the Zohar*, 2:805–7.

23. *Midrash Bereshit Rabbah* 9:10.

24. B. Shab. 119b.

25. Matt, *Zohar: The Pritzker Edition*, 2:305–6.

26. Blumenthal, *Banality of Good and Evil*, 192.

27. As noted in Rosenthal, *"Tikkun ha-Olam,"* 214n1.

28. From commentary of Daniel Landes in Lawrence A. Hoffman, *My People's Prayer Book*, 6:145; Landes also notes the slight broadening of this understanding of *tikkun olam* in the medieval period, particularly through Maimonides.

29. E.g., *Mekhilta, Mishpatim* 20 and the frequent usage in M. Git., ch. 4.

30. Rosenthal, *"Tikkun ha-Olam,"* 225.

31. See Tishby, *Wisdom of the Zohar*, 3:1519–21; Matt, *Zohar: The Pritzker Edition*, 8:291–92.

32. Zohar 2:106a; see Matt, *Zohar: The Pritzker Edition*, 5:117.

33. In the initial section of *Reishit Hokhmah, Sha'ar ha-Yirah*, 9:11–14, 10:7.

34. Heschel, *Moral Grandeur*, 69.

16. LURIANIC KABBALAH

1. Schechter, "Safed in the Sixteenth Century," 210.

2. On other students of Luria, see, e.g., Giller, *Reading the Zohar*, 24–26.

3. On its challenge to moderns, see Lawrence Kushner, *I'm God, You're Not*, 165.

4. *Seeker of Unity*, 50.

5. Lawrence Kushner, *I'm God, You're Not*, 166. See also Fine, "Contemplative Practice of *Yihudim*," 65. It should be noted, however, that the concept of *tzimtzum* does appear long before the time of Luria. See Idel, *"Tzimtzum* in Kabbalah and in Research," particularly 60–68, for his treatment of the concept as far back as the thirteenth century in Nahmanides's commentary on *Sefer Yetzirah*, and Giller, "Kabbalah and Contemporary Judaism," 233.

6. Such a reality would mean there was a place where God was not! There are various interpretations of this. To cite one: "R. Nahman [*Likutei Moharan* 64:4] describes the *hallal ha-panui*—the vacated space which God leaves when He creates the world. In the kabbalistic thought of R. Isaac Luria, God withdraws the plenitude of His being to *make space* for a world. In R. Nahman's version, a similar space must exist between human beings if they are to imitate God and create their own worlds." Zornberg, *Murmuring Deep*, xviii–xix.

7. This myth of *shevirat ha-kelim* is actually found as early as the fourteenth century; see Idel, "Anonymous Kabbalistic Commentary," 152–53.

8. Magid, *From Metaphysics to Midrash*, 18. See also Fine, *Safed Spiritual-ity*, 62.

9. Dan, *Jewish Mysticism and Jewish Ethics*, 98.

10. "Worlds of Discourse," 119.

11. The notion of *Adam Kadmon* is somewhat different in Lurianic Kab-balah. "In the earlier Kabbalah *Adam Kadmon* is the name given to the totality of the *sefirot*. In the Lurianic Kabbalah, on the other hand, *Adam Kadmon* is a kind of intermediary between *Ein Sof* and the *sefirot*. The *sefirot* are contained in potentiality in *Adam Kadmon*. They do not emerge into actuality until the stage known as *Olam ha-Atzilut*, the world of emanation." Jacobs, *Seeker of Unity*, 51–52. We will examine the idea of "four worlds," including the "world of emanation," in chapter 19.

12. Fine, *Safed Spirituality*, 9.

13. E.g., "for Luria, the messianic theme of the ingathering of the exiles did not signify primarily the return of the Jewish people to the concrete land of Israel, but the reintegration of the scattered soul sparks of the fractured divine anthropos." Wolfson, "Engenderment of Messianic Politics," 216. "Daily encounters with disaster were repaired by daily encounters with visions and visitors from the other world. Everything had a meaning; every mishap had its source in some misdeed, which could be revealed and repaired by con-templating and penetrating Luria's formidably elaborate construct or, more directly, through magic. This coupling of belief and conduct emerged under the high, blue skies of Safed—in the thin air of loss and lonely anguish, where divine personae enacted a sacred drama." Lenowitz, *Jewish Messiahs*, 129.

14. For a detailed examination of *yihudim* and the qualifications necessary to begin participating in them, see Fine, "Contemplative Practice of *Yihu-dim*." On meditation in Safed somewhat more generally, see Werblowsky, "Safed Revival," 23–29.

15. Joseph Karo (to be discussed in chapter 18) also held that study of Mai-monides's *Mishneh Torah* would serve as a *tikkun* both for the student and the entire world; see his comments in *Kesef Mishneh* on the introduction to the *Mishneh Torah*. Rosenthal, "*Tikkun ha-Olam*," 227–28, notes the frequent stress on the idea of *tikkun* in the works of both Judah Loew of Prague and Isaiah Horowitz.

16. An excellent introduction to these complexities and the Lurianic "myth" as a whole is provided in Magid, *From Metaphysics to Midrash*, 20–32.

17. See Jacobs, "Uplifting of Sparks," 102.

18. E.g., Lurianic practice as listed by Meir Benayahu and included in Fine, *Safed Spirituality*, 68; see also Rosenthal, "*Tikkun ha-Olam*," 226.

19. Fine, *Safed Spirituality*, 64–65. Similarly, see Dan, *Teachings of Hasidism*, 10, and Giller, *Reading the Zohar*, 29–30.

20. "Hasidism in general and Chabad in particular accept the Lurianic Kabbalah as a revelation of divine truth." Jacobs, *Seeker of Unity*, 51.

21. "Lurianic Kabbalah, especially as carried by Luria's most prominent disciple, Chaim Vital, who recorded his teacher's practices and ideas, coincided with the invention of printing. As a result, kabbalistic thought traveled quickly throughout the Jewish world in printed volumes that invited easy access by students." Lawrence A. Hoffman, *My People's Prayer Book*, 7:28.

22. Cited by Scholem, *Kabbalah*, 129, and *Origins of the Kabbalah*, 450n202; Matt, *Essential Kabbalah*, 92, 194.

23. See Verman, *Books of Contemplation*. For another important example of *tzimtzum* in the thirteenth century, see the excerpt from Nahmanides's commentary on *Sefer Yetzirah* cited in Matt, *Essential Kabbalah*, 93, 195. "The elucidation of the origins of such crucial conceptions in Lurianic Kabbalah such as *tzimtzum*, *shevirat ha-kelim*, and *Adam Kadmon* or *tikkun* must be conducted against the background of existing traditions before we turn to other solutions." Idel, "Particularism and Universalism," 335.

24. B. Sanh. 7a.

25. See Lawrence Kushner, *Way into Jewish Mystical Tradition*, 81-84; Jacobs, *Jewish Ethics, Philosophy and Mysticism*, 130-33.

26. Jacobs, *Jewish Ethics, Philosophy and Mysticism*, 131.

27. Similarly Vital, *Sha'ar ha-Hakdamot*, 14: "When [*Ein Sof*] determined to create its world and to issue forth the world of emanated entities [the *sefirot*], to bring to light the fullness of His actions, names and attributes, this being the reason for the creation of the world, . . . *Ein Sof* then withdrew itself from its centermost point, at the center of its light, and this light retreated from the center to the sides, and thus there remained an empty space, a vacuum." Cited in Fine, *Physician of the Soul*, 128.

28. See Matt, *Essential Kabbalah*, 94-95, 195-96; part of this text is also translated in Idel, *Golem*, 146.

29. See Idel, *Golem*, 146.

30. A useful and not overly detailed discussion can be found in Jacobs, "Uplifting of Sparks," 104-5.

31. Interesting also is the treatment of this and other Lurianic concepts in the Kabbalah of Yehuda Ashlag (1885-1954), best known today because of how his teachings have been reworked in the Kabbalah Learning Centre. On *tzimtzum* and *shevirat ha-kelim*, for instance, see Myers, "Marriage and Sexual Behavior," 261-62.

32. Bahya ibn Pakuda, *Duties of the Heart*, *Sha'ar ha-Behinah*, ch. 5, 1:168-69.

33. On various interpretations of *tzimtzum*, see Jacobs, *Jewish Theology*, 34; Green, "Hasidism," 321.

34. See Ben-Shlomo, "Gershom Scholem on Pantheism," 66-67.

35. Actually a rewording of *Tikkunei ha-Zohar* 140a.

36. A creative translation, fitting the needs of this message. *V'lo yasaf* would more likely mean "did not add," i.e., God spoke these words but no more.

37. See translation and commentary in Jacobs, *Hasidic Thought*, 67-70.

38. For other examples of this idea of the *olam*, "world," being derived from what is *he'alem*, "hidden," see Hallamish, "Teachings of R. Menahem Mendel," 273n22.

39. Translated in Jacobs, *Hasidic Thought*, 77-78.

40. And note the similar parables in Wineman, *Hasidic Parable*, 52-53, 68.

41. See also Elior, *Paradoxical Ascent to God*, 82.

42. As Joseph Irgas put it, "if *tzimtzum* were literal, there would be a place where He is not, for in every vacant place only a line as thin as a thread was descending." *Shomer Emunim*, second controversy, 39b, as noted in Elior, *Paradoxical Ascent to God*, 83. "The early Hasidic masters also rejected the literal understanding of *tzimtzum* for two essential reasons. First, such an understanding involves anthropomorphism. . . . Secondly, while they strove to emphasize the presence of God in the universe, the notion of *tzimtzum* stresses God's withdrawal." Hallamish, *Introduction to the Kabbalah*, 201.

43. See Green's *Menahem Nahum of Chernobyl*, 152 (teaching on *parashat* Hayyei Sarah), and 181-82 (on *parashat* Pinhas) for other examples of this master's treatment of *tzimtzum*.

17. THE PROBLEM OF EVIL IN KABBALAH

1. My emphasis added. As with much else in Lurianic Kabbalah, there are roots for these views in the earlier mysticism. See Idel, "Particularism and Universalism," 334-35.

2. B. Hul. 60b; see also *Yalkhut Shimoni*, B'reishit 8, and discussion in Heschel, *Heavenly Torah*, 121-23.

3. Heschel, *Insecurity of Freedom*, 134, and see 135.

4. See also *Pirkei d'Rabbi Eliezer* 3.

5. See Matt, *Zohar: The Pritzker Edition*, 1:171, citing 3:128a and 3:292b from the *Idra Rabba* and *Idra Zuta*, respectively.

6. Tishby, *Wisdom of the Zohar*, 2:448.

7. See Aryeh Kaplan, *Bahir*, 60-61.

8. *Origins of the Kabbalah*, 150.

9. *Origins of the Kabbalah*, 150, and see there also on (1) the function of *tohu*, "chaos," in the philosophical as well as kabbalistic thinkers of the time; see also on this Matt, *Zohar: The Pritzker Edition*, 1:118n75; (2) the etymology of the term "Satan."

10. Berlin and Brettler, *Jewish Study Bible*, 923.

11. See Matt, *Zohar: The Pritzker Edition*, 3:186–87; Tishby, *Wisdom of the Zohar*, 2:484, and commentary therein.

12. Y. Ma'as. Sh. 4:6, 55b, as noted in Matt, *Zohar: The Pritzker Edition*, 3:187n54. See also Zohar 1:183a in Matt, 3:116, and references collected there.

13. Translated and discussed in Idel, *Kabbalah and Eros*, 139; see also Matt, *Zohar: The Pritzker Edition*, 7:500–501.

14. On some of the possible consequences of this, see Blumenthal, *Facing the Abusing God*, particularly 265–67.

15. Matronita is an "Aramaized form of Latin *matron*, 'matron, married woman, noble lady,' often applied in the Zohar to *Shekhinah*, the wife of *Tiferet*." Matt, *Zohar, The Pritzker Edition*, 5:596.

16. Translated in Dan in *Jewish Mysticism: The Modern Period*, 333.

17. Dan, *Jewish Mysticism: The Modern Period*, 343. See also Jacobs, *Seeker of Unity*, 54.

18. Rather than simply being nullified. See B. Yoma 86b.

19. B. Sanh. 104a.

20. Jacobs, *Palm Tree of Devorah*, 88–89; Miller, *Palm Tree of Devorah*, 80–83, 177–78.

21. *Pirkei d'Rabbi Eliezer* 21; see also B. Shab. 145b–146a.

22. 1:54a; see Matt, *Zohar: The Pritzker Edition*, 1:303, and note also 2:167b; Matt, *Zohar: The Pritzker Edition*, 5:472n803.

23. Zohar 3:122–24, *Ra'aya Meheimna*.

24. These are "the two consonants that represents the supernal Father and Mother." Idel, *Ben*, 406.

25. E.g., 1:191b.

26. This does leave one other interesting question. If evil is subservient to good, why is it called "evil" at all? "The answer is that, in practice, evil goes beyond the task assigned to it, and seeks to extend its reign and its power in the world, so that it may seize a larger portion of emanated abundance." Hallamish, *Introduction to the Kabbalah*, 173.

27. Dan, *Jewish Mysticism: The Modern Period*, 343.

28. See Rashi on Exod. 32:4.

29. Rashi on Exod. 32:7, based on *Midrash Shemot Rabbah* 42:10, and on Num. 11:4.

30. See *Midrash Tanhuma*, Ki Tissa' 21.

31. On this general issue, along with the identification of the *erev rav* with elements in the Spanish community contemporary with the Zohar, see Tishby, *Wisdom of the Zohar*, 3:1432–44.

32. B. Yev. 62a and others.

33. See translation (slightly expanded) and comments in Magid, *From Metaphysics to Midrash*, 84–88.

34. See Schochet, *Tzava'at HaRivash*, 123-25; Lawrence Kushner, *Way into Jewish Mystical Tradition*, 126-27.
35. See the interesting comments about the approach of the Ba'al Shem Tov in Zeitlin, *Hasidic Spirituality*, 187.
36. Sacks, *To Heal a Fractured World*, 207.

18. MYSTICAL EXPERIENCES, ASCETIC PRACTICES

1. Karo followed Sephardic practice, but Moses Isserles of Krakow added glosses covering Ashkenazic divergences.
2. Werblowsky, *Joseph Karo*, 108-11.
3. See Jacobs, *Jewish Mystical Testimonies*, 99-103, 116. His translations are based on the first edition of *Maggid Mesharim* (Amsterdam, 1704), to which I did not have access; I have referred to the 1773 Zolkava edition for some of the texts. See also Isaiah Horowitz, *Shnei Luhot ha-Brit, Masekhet Shavuot, Ner Mitzvah*, sect. 5.
4. See, e.g., the ethical will of Naftali ha-Kohen Katz (d. 1719), as noted in Bar-Levav, "Ritualizing Death and Dying," 166.
5. On Karo's experience and the voice of the *maggid,* see Schechter, "Safed in the Sixteenth Century," 214.
6. *Sabbatai Sevi*, 209.
7. See Fine, "Purifying the Body," 125.
8. "When all ten *sefirot* are mirrored on earth then the unification is complete." Jacobs, *Jewish Mystical Testimonies*, 119.
9. *Maggid Mesharim,* 59b; Jacobs, *Jewish Mystical Testimonies*, 116, 122. Karo "carried the shame for the body felt by many other Safed kabbalists to an extreme, primarily through his identification of the ultimate service of God with the utter dissolution of the body." Fine, "Purifying the Body," 127. See also Werblowsky, *Joseph Karo*, 153-56, on Karo's compulsive desire for mortification and ridding himself of sin.
10. See Fine, "*Maggidic* Revelation," 157, and Scholem, *Sabbatai Sevi*, 82-83. Note that at least one important kabbalist, Rabbi Elijah, the Ga'on of Vilna, adamantly refused to accept guidance from a *maggid*. See the citation in Hallamish, *Introduction to the Kabbalah*, 112.
11. Y. Ber. 9:5; see also its usage in Zohar 3:36a.
12. See translations in Jacobs, *Jewish Mystical Testimonies*, 130-31; Faierstein, *Jewish Mystical Autobiographies*, 156, 169-70.
13. On this skill, known as metaposcopy, and other such readings Luria performed on Vital, see Fine, *Physician of the Soul*, 153-64.
14. Details can be found in Fine, "Contemplative Practice of *Yihudim*."
15. "*Ibbur* . . . is temporary and usually takes place only when one is an adult. Its purpose is to allow the *nefesh* of a sage of a previous generation to

enter the body of someone who is spiritually prepared to receive this impregnation in order to accomplish some task or fulfill some commandment that was left uncompleted in the previous lifetime. The choice of host is also determined by a connection or affinity in their respective soul ancestry." Faierstein, *Jewish Mystical Autobiographies*, 26.

16. Of related interest are Luria's thoughts on the idea of creation of "souls and new spirits by the thirty-two paths and three branches," as per *Sefer Yetzirah*. See Idel's comments in *Golem*, 147, and notes therein.

17. See translation in Fine, "*Maggidic* Revelation," 145.

18. *Sha'arei Kedushah* 1:1.

19. And note also the continuation: "This is the secret [explanation] of the verse in 2 Sam. 23:2: 'The spirit of the Lord speaks by me and His word is upon my tongue.' For the spirit and the word that is the first speech [i.e., the supernal speech], already created through study of Torah and performance of a mitzvah as described above, rests at this moment on him upon his tongue. And voice and speech actually issue from his mouth, and truly speak through his mouth. And the man then hears it." *Sha'ar Ruah ha-Kodesh*, 10a-b.

20. Heschel, "Mystical Element in Judaism," 615–16: "A new form of living was the consequence of the kabbalah. Everything was so replete with symbolic significance as to make it the potential heart of the spiritual universe. How carefully must all be approached. A moral rigorism that hardly leaves any room for waste or respite resulted in making the kabbalist more meticulous in studying and fulfilling the precepts of the Torah, in refining his moral conduct, in endowing everyday actions with solemn significance. For man represents God in this world. Even the parts of his body signify divine mysteries."

21. See Fine, "Contemplative Practice of *Yihudim*," 76–77, for some representative examples. See also Werblowsky, "Safed Revival," 12. Asceticism and abstinence are considered essential for the necessary level of repentance.

22. "Having accepted baptism against their will, these penitents sought to atone for their sins by recourse to especially severe acts of self-mortification. There is no doubt that the presence of these individuals contributed to the emotional climate of atonement and penance in this community." Fine, *Safed Spirituality*, 15.

23. M. Avot 4:4.

24. See Fine, *Safed Spirituality*, 55–57; Jacobs, *Jewish Mystical Testimonies*, 104–5. Fine's translations are based on the Vilna, 1865 edition.

25. B. Yev. 20a.

26. E.g., B. Ta'an. 11a, Naz. 19a.

27. See Fine, "New Approaches," 101.

28. For a similar list of *hanhagot* taught by Cordovero, see Fine, *Safed Spirituality*, 34–38.

29. See Idel, *Studies in Ecstatic Kabbalah*, 115–19; Sherwin, *Kabbalah*, 184–85. Note also comments of Eitan Fishbane in *As Light before Dawn*, 251–52.

19. FOUR WORLDS, FOUR LEVELS OF SOUL

1. Sherwin, *Kabbalah*, 89–90.
2. See, e.g., Giller, *Kabbalah*, 137–38. Luria posits a model of the four worlds corresponding to Scripture, Mishnah, Talmud, and Kabbalah. For a discussion of this see Fine, "Study of Torah as a Rite."
3. See Tishby, *Wisdom of the Zohar*, 1:250.
4. See Tishby, *Wisdom of the Zohar*, 2:558.
5. On this overspill and its creation of the four worlds, see Jacobs, "Uplifting of Sparks," 106.
6. Cordovero's *Pardes Rimonim*.
7. This refers to Zohar 2:23b, which refers not to the four "worlds" as such but to the four elements (fire, air, water, earth) linked to the four directions, "and from them the Holy One, blessed be He, prepared a single body, a supernal array." See Matt, *Zohar: The Pritzker Edition*, 4:83. Shelah here proceeds to link the elements with the four worlds.
8. See Krassen, *Isaiah Horowitz*, 79–83.
9. See, e.g., Mark Malachi, "From the Depths of Silence," in Hoffman, *Opening the Inner Gates*, 168–72.
10. "The four paths are brief but decisive stages in realizing or becoming conscious of nirvana. With each successive realization, the practitioner deepens an understanding of the supramundane reality, nirvana. As his comprehension of the changeless deepens, his entanglement with the world of changing phenomena weakens." Aronson, *Love and Sympathy*, 4.
11. Scholem, *Kabbalah*, 155; see also Raphael, *Jewish Views of the Afterlife*, 278.
12. See Giller, *Reading the Zohar*, 36–37.
13. See Zohar 2:98a and the comments of Matt, *Zohar: The Pritzker Edition*, 5:24–25. Note also that segments in the Zohar and particularly in *Midrash ha-Ne'elam* distinguish between the communicative, animal, and intellectual natures of the soul.
14. "According to Kabbalah, before descending to earth each soul is clothed in an ethereal body resembling the physical body she will inhabit on earth. She retains this form while in the physical body until shortly before death, and then regains it afterward." Matt, *Zohar: The Pritzker Edition*, 5:300n305.
15. 1:235a, and see comments in Matt, *Zohar: The Pritzker Edition*, 3:424n597.
16. Matt omits the word "above" from the translation, but the meaning is problematic without it, and the text has the word *l'eila*.
17. Generally translated according to Matt, *Zohar: The Pritzker Edition*, 5:299–302. See also Scholem, *Zohar*, 96–97.

18. This stems from Rabbinic sources; e.g., B. Ta'an. 16a: "Why do they go out to the cemetery [on fast days]? . . . So the dead will ask mercy for us."

19. As Matt notes (*Zohar: The Pritzker Edition*, 5:301n307, and see references there), according to the Zohar, the Garden of Eden is adjacent to the Cave of Machpelah where the Patriarchs are buried, so their souls may also be brought into action on behalf of those in need.

20. See also Giller, *Reading the Zohar*, 37, on another division seen elsewhere in the Zohar.

21. The point of that text being that the body clothes the soul. See Matt, *Zohar: The Pritzker Edition*, 1:156. NJPS translates the verse: "It must not be rubbed on any person's body."

22. Actually part of *Tikkunei ha-Zohar*. See also Zohar 3:25a, comparing the linking of soul levels to the procedure of blowing glass.

23. On this teaching and its place in the evolution of the Pharisees' view of the soul, see Giller, *Kabbalah*, 84–87.

24. Hallamish, *Introduction to the Kabbalah*, 263.

25. Raphael, *Jewish Views of the Afterlife*, 282, 313–14.

26. This ties into an idea we will see further along, particularly in Hasidism: the issue of the animal soul and its relationship to some higher soul level. "The function of the animal body and soul is to serve the rational, contemplative soul, and if a man follows his animal soul, that is to say if his vision remains limited by the horizons of the material world, he is 'an animal in human form.' However, 'man was created for no other reason than to raise everything up from a lower to a higher level, and to subordinate the outward to the inner reality by discovering His divinity, blessed be He, in everything, there being no place where He is not.'" Hallamish, "Teachings of R. Menahem Mendel," 274; citations from *P'ri ha-Aretz* on Be-har and Va-yiggash.

27. I have not found any use of the terms prior to the works of Vital. These terms "are derived from Lurianic Kabbalah, where they serve to designate alternating modes in the ongoing life of the *sefirot* within God. These terms too are now psychologized, and in Hasidism they refer to a person's worship in an ordinary ('lesser') state of mind as opposed to true contemplative prayer and the state of either detachment or rapture it requires." Green, "Teachings of the Hasidic Masters," 379.

28. Many Hasidic masters emphasize the need to repair one's defect and achieve *berur*, a "clarification" of this defect. On this subject, see Faierstein, "Personal Redemption in Hasidism," 219–20. More generally, in Lurianic kabbalah, *berur* refers to the sifting out of the holy sparks in the material world. See Eitan Fishbane, *Sabbath Soul*, 118, for a useful brief explanation.

29. Tishby, *Wisdom of the Zohar*, 2:857; Matt, *The Zohar: Pritzker Edition*, 3:320–21.

30. Similarly Zohar 1:79a, where at the time of death three angelic messengers review the person's life.
31. "*Dumah*, literally 'silence,' is a name for the netherworld in the Bible. See Psalms 94:17: 'Unless God had been my help, my soul would have nearly dwelt in *dumah*.' . . . In rabbinic literature *Dumah* is the angel in charge of the souls of the dead (B. *Ber.* 18b, *Shab.* 152b, *Sanh.* 94a). In the *Zohar* he retains this role but also oversees Hell. See 1:8a–b, 62b, 94a, 102a, 124a (*Midrash ha-Ne'elam*), 130b, 237b." Matt, *Zohar: The Pritzker Edition*, 3:320n106. At least according to some sources, *Dumah* also asks the soul its Hebrew name, which may be forgotten in the shock of death, thus requiring special spiritual preparations. Noted in Raphael, *Jewish Views of the Afterlife*, 293–94.
32. On *Gehinnom* (or *Gehenna*) in the Zohar, see Raphael, *Jewish Views of the Afterlife*, 298–308.
33. Similarly, see Zohar 3:126a–127a; Unterman, *Kabbalistic Tradition*, 240–41. Other texts suggest seven divine judgments and punishments; see Zohar 2:199b,3:127a.
34. Tishby, *Wisdom of the Zohar*, 2:862–63; Matt, *Zohar: The Pritzker Edition*, 7:475–76.
35. See, e.g., Shneur Zalman of Lyady, *Tanya, Iggeret ha-Kodesh*, ch. 27; cited in Lamm, *Religious Thought of Hasidism*, 501–4. Related to this is the phenomenon of the tzaddik who is able to discover another person's incarnation. See Etkes, *Besht*, 51.
36. An exception can be found among the kabbalists of Gerona, in particular Nahmanides; see Scholem, *Origins of the Kabbalah*, 458–59.
37. Why did it become so fixed a part of Jewish thought at this time? Giller suggests that "a great morbidity seems to have accompanied the Jewish experience following the Spanish expulsion. The *gilgul* doctrine, with its premise that the spirits of the dead are never really lost, that they walk among us again in the bodies of little children, became an attractive motif of psychological renewal." *Reading the Zohar*, 68.
38. *Gilgul* is "a dispassionate response to the effects of sin. The soul's fate is based on an empirical system of values for sin and virtue." Giller, *Reading the Zohar*, 37, and see 38–42 in particular on the different understandings of this in Safed.
39. Hallamish, *Introduction to the Kabbalah*, 292; he refers to another edition that was not accessible to me, but appears likely to have the same text as here.
40. See Giller, *Reading the Zohar*, 37–38, 40–41.
41. See Nigal, *Magic, Mysticism, and Hasidism*, 73–74; Jacobs, "Uplifting of Sparks," 121–22. On the issue of resurrection among the kabbalists, see Vital, *Eitz ha-Da'at Tov*, Mishpatim, 20a; Hallamish, *Introduction to the Kabbalah*, 307, and Giller, *Reading the Zohar*, especially 37–58. Another, more

expanded primary discussion of this topic can be found in Vital, *Likkutei ha-Shas*, 12a; see translation in Unterman, *Kabbalistic Tradition*, 145–46. See also Raphael, *Jewish Views of the Afterlife*, 324–26.

42. See Wineman, translation and commentary in *Beyond Appearances*, 86–87.

43. E.g., a story recorded in *Shivhei ha-Besht* and cited in Nigal, *Magic, Mysticism, and Hasidism*, 56–57, where a Torah scholar whose initial transgression was neglect of the ritual washing of hands and eventually violated most of the commandments was transmigrated into the frog, which lives in water. "The Ba'al Shem Tov effected a correction for his soul and caused it to ascend, until the frog died." Nigal also comments (57–58) that "it cannot be ruled out that this contains a barb directed against certain types of Torah scholar whose wisdom is greater than their piety. . . . An additional conclusion to be drawn from the story is that any fit Jew is likely to attain merit for the transmigrated soul with a good deed or even with a good thought." On the theme of transmigration into animal bodies, see Raphael, *Jewish Views of the Afterlife*, 318–19, and Giller, *Kabbalah*, 96.

44. Taken from Nigal, *Magic, Mysticism, and Hasidism*, 118; *Sha'ar Ruah ha-Kodesh*, sect. 14, 89–93.

45. "Jewish Magic," 107. If one can have a positive "possession" experience such as Karo described, it makes sense that there could be "negative" possession.

46. Scholem, *Kabbalah*, 349; see also Nigal, *Magic, Mysticism, and Hasidism*, 108. "Originally, *dybbukim* were considered demons possessing the fragile body of a sick person. . . . With the spread of the doctrine of *gilgul*, *dybbukim* were seen as wicked souls, unable to transmigrate, who would possess selected, weakened, and receptive individuals, often for vengeance." Raphael, *Jewish Views of the Afterlife*, 323.

20. MAGIC

1. Sherwin, *Kabbalah*, 197–98; see Trachtenberg, *Jewish Magic and Superstition*, 174. In the medieval period, "apart from a few scholars in southern Europe, almost nobody doubted the existence of demons. Only a few demons were seen to have distinguishing characteristics; some remained from talmudic times, but demons from the non-Jewish environment were adopted en masse in the Middle Ages." Sharot, *Messianism, Mysticism, and Magic*, 35; see there, 36–37, for other examples of practices meant to deal with demons.

2. Yuval Harari borrows the use of "the principle of family resemblance" from Wittgenstein, to describe the relationship between some of the phenomena in religion and magic. See Harari's "What is a Magical Text?" 110–11.

3. On these various types of "white" magic, see Sherwin, *Kabbalah*, 198.

4. See Sherwin, *Workers of Wonders*, 18; Yehezkel Kaufmann, *Religion of*

Israel, 158, says that this is the uniqueness of Isaiah: "The book of Kings mentions, of all the literary prophets, only Isaiah—and then not as a teacher or exhorter, but as a foreteller and a wonder-healer."

5. *Guide of the Perplexed* 2:6.

6. Kellner, *Maimonides' Confrontation with Mysticism*, 279; the quoted phrase is from Yeshayahu Leibowitz.

7. As suggested in Sherwin, *Kabbalah*, 63.

8. *Pesikta Rabbati*, ch. 21.

9. As corrected from manuscript and translated in Idel, *Enchanted Chains*, 110–11.

10. Nigal, *Magic, Mysticism, and Hasidism*, 3–4.

11. Nigal, *Magic, Mysticism, and Hasidism*, 8–10.

12. See Etkes, *Besht*, 32.

13. Zohar 3:151a.

14. See also partial translation from the abridged *Reishit Hokhmah* in Fine, *Safed Spirituality*, 146.

15. Matt, *Zohar: The Pritzker Edition*, 258n216, cites the many sources on this Name and its powers. See also Trachtenberg, *Jewish Magic and Superstition*, 90. There is a useful discussion of prevailing magical practices in Eastern European Jewish society up to the beginning of the Hasidic path, found in Etkes, *Besht*, 7–45.

16. "The power of Jewish amulets stemmed from the popular belief in Hebrew letters as primordial forms that shaped the world and nurtured its creative energy." Petrovsky-Shtern, "You Will Find It in the Pharmacy," 16, and see references n13.

17. "There is a sense of both despair and daring, . . . despair because of the absence of the classical channels of communications with the divine, and daring because recourse to the only remaining device, the divine name, was felt to be a major religious taboo. It was only the desolate religious plight of the Jews that drove them . . . to appeal to a divinatory quality of the divine name." Idel, *Enchanted Chains*, 79–80; see also 157–60 for examples of Hasidic masters' uses of the Name.

18. See Nigal, *Magic, Mysticism, and Hasidism*, 33–49.

19. Idel, *Enchanted Chains*, 85–86.

20. Idel, *Enchanted Chains*, 87; see also 88–90 on the differences between the two types of magic and the motivations behind each, and 91–93 for examples from Cordovero in which the mystic addresses the *sefirot* in their appropriate colors or magically uses the Divine Names in order to draw down the divine power.

21. As translated by Dan, *Heart and the Fountain*, 177–80.

22. Sherwin, *Kabbalah*, 201.

23. On the magical nature of such use of the Name, see Idel, *Enchanted Chains*, 81-84. "The remarks in *Tikkunei ha-Zohar* regarding the *kulmus* [quill] imply that the author employed the technique of automatic writing in composing that work in particular." Giller, *Reading the Zohar*, 7; see there for details. There are some similarities to the phenomenon of spontaneous utterances, where the influence of a holy place—usually the tomb of a tzaddik—grants an understanding of some aspect of Torah; see Hallamish, *Introduction to the Kabbalah*, 84-86.

24. Published 1846; 78a. Noted in Hallamish, *Introduction to the Kabbalah*, 213.

25. See Myers, *Kabbalah and the Spiritual Quest*, 127-31. This idea also appears in Cordovero; see Krassen, *Uniter of Heaven and Earth*, 83.

26. On the integration of magic and religion, see Grozinger, "Between Magic and Religion," 28-29.

27. Story from *Me'irat Einayim*, Va-yikra' 184. Winkler's retelling and expansion of this text is decidedly creative, but still appropriate for this chapter.

28. A brief note on this connection can be found in Goldish, "Mystical Messianism," 118-19.

29. An excellent version can be found in Dan, *Heart and the Fountain*, 184-94. On the magical aspects of this story, see also Idel, *Enchanted Chains*, 94-98.

30. "Spiritual activism, when all realistic and practical outlets are closed, easily turns into magical activism, and Jewish legend knows of kabbalist masters who decided to force the messianic advent by means of extreme mortifications, special meditations and kabbalistic incantations. These legends, the best known of which is that concerning Rabbi Joseph della Reyna, usually end with the kabbalist adept falling a prey to the daemonic powers which he had meant to vanish." Werblowsky, "Messianism in Jewish History," 47. It is interesting to note that one of the taboos violated by Della Reyna was that of using incense in his magical practice (Idel, *Enchanted Chains*, 96). The irony is that his failure comes through offering some of that incense to Samael, thus raising his sin to the level of idolatry.

21. MESSIANISM

1. Saperstein, *Essential Papers on Messianic Movements*, 8. Exceptions are noted in Sarachek, *Doctrine of the Messiah*, 7-11. "We find in the period of the prophets many words of prophecy which without any doubt refer to the expected redemption, yet contain *no hint* of a personal Messiah." Klausner, *Messianic Idea in Israel*, 8. An excellent example of this is the well-known vision of Isa. 2:2-4, discussed in Klausner, 69-71, and see there, 13-35, on the earliest roots of the idea in Scripture. He also notes (220) that in much of the biblical period, the notion of "an individual Messiah had no great importance."

2. Schweid, "Jewish Messianism," 61. For a view of what a Messiah might think of himself, see Smith, "Messiahs."

3. See Giller, *Reading the Zohar*, 12–13.

4. See Wolfson, *Venturing Beyond*, 239.

5. For instance, "Rabbi Levi said: If Israel would observe the Shabbat appropriately even one day, the son of David would come. Why? Because it is considered equal to all the mitzvot." *Midrash Shemot Rabbah* 25:12.

6. See M. Sot. 9:15.

7. Discussion of some other early Rabbinic sources on messianism can be found in Scholem, *Messianic Idea in Judaism*, particularly 54–56; Sarachek, *Doctrine of the Messiah*, 12–21.

8. B. Sanh. 97a. See discussion of a number of such texts in Klausner, *Messianic Idea in Israel*, 444–46.

9. Schafer, *Synopse*, 218. See translation in Schafer, *Origins of Jewish Mysticism*, 274.

10. Translated in Idel, *Messianic Mystics*, 64; cited from MS Oxford 1605, fol. 46b.

11. As noted in Idel, *Messianic Mystics*, 63.

12. Idel, *Messianic Mystics*, 70; see also 73–74.

13. See Matt, *Zohar: The Pritzker Edition*, 3:448.

14. See, e.g., *Midrash Bereshit Rabbah* 98:9.

15. Klausner, *Messianic Idea in Israel*, 392.

16. The palace of Os Estaos is where forced conversions took place in 1497.

17. Translated in Tishby, "Acute Apocalyptic Messianism," 263–64.

18. It is generally the case that "what appears to be primarily a personal act of *tikkun* partakes in the far larger task of messianic restitution. The redemption of the individual soul is a small but absolutely vital part of the infinitely complex effort to redeem divinity as a whole." Fine, "Contemplative Practice of *Yihudim*," 81.

19. Dan, *Heart and the Fountain*, 203–12; Faierstein, *Jewish Mystical Autobiographies*, 97–99.

20. Molkho, born Diego Pires to a family of crypto-Jews in Portugal in 1500, was eventually burned at the stake by the Roman emperor (not the pope). See Lenowitz, *Jewish Messiahs*, 103–23.

21. B. Sanh. 98a; see Faierstein, *Jewish Mystical Autobiographies*, 317n80.

22. See *Or Yakkar* (Jerusalem, 1962), 4:155, as cited in Elior, "Messianic Expectations and Spiritualization," together with explanation of this issue, 292–93. "The messianic temper of the Safed kabbalists is also evident in their feeling of living at a crucial, in fact eschatological, moment in history. This awareness was already present, although in a very low key, among the early kabbalists. But it was greatly intensified in the sixteenth century.

They were living at a turning point of history, marked by the revelation of the ultimate mysteries of divine wisdom and more especially the Lurianic teachings." Werblowsky, "Safed Revival," 16.

23. See *Yalkut Lekah Tov* on Num. 24:17 (noted in Kasher, *Torah Shleimah* 41:144); Zohar 2:7b.

24. Lenowitz, *Jewish Messiahs*, 129-31, 265-66.

25. "The amazing achievement of the Safed Revival was its explosive (as subsequent developments showed) combination of kabbalistic mysticism and messianism—and a short-term messianism to boot, that is, messianism not on the horizon of a distant future but as an immediate expectation." Werblowsky, "Safed Revival," 11.

26. On his manic-depressive illness, see Scholem, *Sabbatai Sevi*, 125-38. On the possibility that Sabbetai Tzvi was influenced by his name's connection with Saturn, see Idel, "Saturn and Sabbatai Tzevi." "Some of the messiahs were lucky enough to be born with a name that serves their texts as evidence of their destiny, like Reubeni, of Davidic lineage; Yeshua (Jesus) the Savior; Hayim (Vital), both of whose names mean 'life'; Israel (the Besht); or Menachem (Schneerson), the comforter, the name of the Messiah in the Book of Zerubbabel." Lenowitz, *Jewish Messiahs*, 267.

27. On the use of such deeds to rescue the divine sparks, see Jacobs, "Uplifting of Sparks," 114.

28. On why many followed Tzvi even after his apostasy, see Scholem, *Sabbatai Sevi*, 689, also 796-97. On the similarities between early Christianity and Sabbateanism and related issues, see Davies, "From Schweitzer to Scholem," particularly 343-44.

29. "His conversion to Islam was interpreted as if it echoed the conversions of the Jews of Iberia to Catholicism, but in his case it would come to be seen not as forgivable in one facing death but as required for the messiah, who had to reach the lowest depths of baseness in order to gather there the sparks of light that, once raised up, would complete the repair of the cosmic order." Lenowitz, *Jewish Messiahs*, 149. "There still remained holy sparks among the Gentiles, and these awaited their rescue. In order to achieve this final restoration it was necessary for the Messiah to descend into the domain of the *kelippot*, here represented by Islam, to elevate the holy sparks still imprisoned there." Jacobs, "Uplifting of Sparks," 114.

30. Dan, *Heart and the Fountain*, 213-22.

31. See Zohar 3:224b; Tishby, *Wisdom of the Zohar*, 2:792n121-22.

32. It has been suggested that this may only refer to his disciples, and that even in this early stage the Ba'al Shem Tov was leader of a study center in Medzibozh. See Rosman, *Founder of Hasidism*, 168-69.

33. Idel translates this as "remedies" based in part on a parallel to the magical

text *Shimmushei Torah*; see "Jewish Magic," 105. He tentatively dates this book as far back as the third century CE; see his comments in *Absorbing Perfections*, 138–39.

34. Jacobs, *Jewish Mystical Testimonies*, 148–55; Hundert, *Jews in Poland-Lithuania*, 168–71, and Sherwin, *Kabbalah*, 218–19; also partially translated in Kallus, *Pillar of Prayer*, 2–3. See also Etkes, *Besht*, 282–88, on the different versions and authenticity of the letter.

35. For a summary of the scholarly debate on the meaning of this conversation between the Ba'al Shem Tov and the Messiah and its implications for the development of Hasidism, see Etkes, *Besht*, 82–87 and the following note.

36. After the failure of Sabbetai Tzvi, "'auto-messianism,' as Martin Buber has called it, declined steadily. A few more minor convulsions in the wake of the Sabbatean movement and personal messianism ceased to be a real possibility and thus a real danger. The spiritual revival movement in 18th century Polish and Ukrainian Jewry, known as Hasidism, seems to have brought about, at least to some extent, a neutralization of the explosive possibilities of utopian and apocalyptic messianism by teaching a way of redemption through mystical inwardness." Werblowsky, "Safed Revival," 50.

37. Garb, "Rabbi Kook and His Sources," 78. "Through attainment of devekut and comparable spiritual goals, the Hasid can attain a state of mind as if he personally were in the messianic age." Loewenthal, "Neutralisation of Messianism," 59.

38. *Komah sheleimah*. Lamm suggests "gestalt" as a better translation, noting that "the term implies the mystic configuration of the Messiah."

39. See Lamm, *Religious Thought of Hasidism*, 561.

40. B. Hag. 12a.

41. See, e.g., *Masekhet Pesahim*, third drasha for *Shabbat ha-Gadol* on *parashat* Metsora', sect. 31, and others. "This acronym apparently means that Adam's soul has been reincarnated in the body of David, who will return as the Messiah. This nexus between Adam, the primordial ideal man, King David, representing the middle point of history, and the Messiah, betokening the end of history, is quite telling from the point of view of a kabbalistic historiosophy. The letters in the acronym—*alef, dalet, mem*—appear in alphabetical order, thus supporting the historical sequence of the personages they represent." Idel, *Messianic Mystics*, 189–90.

42. Some Hasidic masters viewed the Messiah as having more limited power; see, e.g., the teaching of the "Yehudi" (discussed in chapter 26) in *Nifla'ot ha-Yehudi*, 58a, noted in Lawrence Kushner, *Way into Jewish Mystical Tradition*, 151–52 (citation corrected). This view of a "little" Messiah may have been a necessary stage for at least some of the Hasidic masters following the debacle of Sabbatianism.

43. See Sherwin, *Workers of Wonders*, 104. On the Seer's fall from a window and its interpretation among the Hasidim, see Assaf, *Untold Tales of the Hasidim*, 97–119.

44. See Green, *Tormented Master*, 190.

45. Beginning with B. Suk. 52. "The Messiah son of Joseph is a mere figment of the imagination, an aberration from Biblical Messianism. The Talmud alludes to him only twice, but the later Targumim and Midrashim describe his meteoric appearance and mission with some detail. Both Messiahs will collaborate in the final redemption, as did Moses and Aaron in the Egyptian Exodus." Sarachek, *Doctrine of the Messiah*, 16. See also Klausner, *Messianic Idea in Israel*, 483–501.

46. Green, *Tormented Master*, 190. "Reb Nahman threw himself into the cause of universal redemption. His messianic calendar, from Rosh Hashanah 1804 onward, was cluttered with extraordinary efforts on all fronts: instituting rites of purification; collecting, editing, and disseminating his teachings; the birth of his son Shloyme Ephraim upon whom great messianic hope was now placed." Roskies, "The Master of Prayer," 72. See also Deutsch, "Rabbi Nahman," 200–202.

47. Quoted in Schnall, *Beyond the Green Line*, 19; cited in Kellner, "Messianic Postures in Israel Today," 512. The original source noted in Schnall is "Zionism and Biblical Prophecy," in Tirosh, *Religious Zionism*, 176–77.

48. Kellner, "Messianic Postures in Israel Today," 512.

22. PRAYER AND RITUAL IN THE MYSTICAL LIFE

1. *Judaism Eternal*, 1:3.

2. Based on the various manuscripts in Schafer, *Synopse*, 105–6. Note also the extended variation of "Ein Keloheinu" from the *Sefer Raziel* text in Martin Samuel Cohen, *Shi'ur Qomah: Texts and Recensions*, 85.

3. Schafer, *Origins of Jewish Mysticism*, 255–56. Schafer refers to this kind of experience as "*Unio liturgica*, the liturgical communion of the *Merkavah* mystic, as Israel's emissary, with God." Perhaps it is technically more accurate to describe it as liturgical communion with the angels.

4. See Schafer, *Synopse*, 551.

5. See, e.g., Schafer, *Synopse*, 260–62. "The premise behind the *Kedushah*, and behind the prayers in *Ma'aseh Merkavah* [i.e., the specific work with this title], is that the angels are conducting a liturgy in heaven while the human community praises God on earth." Swartz, "Mystical Texts," 410.

6. Zohar 2:129a–b.

7. See Sherwin, *Kabbalah*, 98–100.

8. Zohar 2:133b–134b. There were other interpretations of the significance of proper recitation of "Shema Yisrael" in Zoharic literature. See, e.g., Zohar

2:43b (*Pikkudin*; noted as 2:53b in Liebes) and discussion of this and other options in Tishby, *Wisdom of the Zohar*, 3:971–73, and Liebes, *Studies in the Zohar*, 140–42. In De Leon's *Sefer ha-Rimmon* (as well as other kabbalistic works), "prayer is understood as an effort to unite the divine forces by means of an impulse generated from below." Wolfson, "Mystical-Theurgical Dimensions of Prayer," 45.

9. Sherwin, *Kabbalah*, 129–32; Krassen, *Isaiah Horowitz*, 338–51.

10. Excerpted in Tishby, *Wisdom of the Zohar*, 3:967; see also Matt, *Zohar: The Pritzker Edition*, 6:143.

11. We see a certain magical construct in attitudes toward prayer running through Safed to Hasidism: "According to the *Besht* and his disciples, mystical prayer consists in concentration in prayer and the pronunciation of the letters of the words of prayer as if these sounds were the palaces or the containers of the divine influx that enters these sounds and permits the mystic to unite with the divine overflow. This understanding of prayer is not a new one; as I have already noted, it is a continuation of the Cordoverian theory regarding Kabbalistic prayer. The basic assumption, according to Cordovero and his sources, is that mystical activity is achieved when the divine spirituality descends into the words of prayer." Idel, "Jewish Magic," 101.

12. *Siddur Kol Ya'akov*, 4. According to Menahem Nahum of Chernobyl, the unification of *Ha-Kadosh Barukh Hu uShekhintei* unifies "the body with the soul and the life force, which is the blessed God Himself, and this brings about unification in all the worlds." *Me'or Einayim* on *parashat* Be-ha'alotekha, 85b.

13. "Evidence of the high status of the kabbalistic myth may be found in its liturgical uses; from the sixteenth century onward, kabbalistic excerpts were extensively included in prayerbooks. These excerpts range from short allusions, such as the formula *l'shem yichud* stated before performing the commandments, all the way to long passages meticulously describing kabbalistic beliefs." Liebes, *Jewish Myth and Jewish Messianism*, 7.

14. Similarly with other Passover rituals: "We were commanded by God to eat the matzah in order to cleave to the Pure Power and to add power to It," i.e., *not* to simply feel what the redeemed slaves felt when *they* ate the matzah. Joseph Alashkar, 1528, cited in Idel, "Universalization and Integration," 40. The very celebration of Passover serves this purpose: "rejoicing brings forth rejoicing, and the joy of Israel causes the Holy One Himself to be glad." Zohar 3:40b, cited in Heschel, "Mystical Element in Judaism," 617.

15. Note also that the singing of "Shalom Aleikhem" and "Eishet Hayil" ("Woman of Valor"), the final segment of Proverbs, at the Shabbat table, are also kabbalistic additions from this era. The latter is sung not in honor of the woman of the home, but for the *Shekhinah*. Idelsohn, *Jewish Liturgy*, 54.

16. Notably Alkabetz adapted terms used in the Bible to refer to Israel, now referring to God. See particularly Deut. 26:19, and also Jer. 13:11 and 33:9.

17. Isa. 54:3. This chapter further conveys the metaphor of marriage between God and Israel.

18. Based on Isa. 29:23, but substituting the Four-Letter Name in place of *Elohim*. The Four-Letter Name is associated with *Tiferet*, which mediates between right and left, *Hesed* and *Gevurah*.

19. The last phrase is based on Isa. 25:9, which refers to the salvation, the deliverance to be brought about by the Messiah.

20. Prov. 12:4 is a direct reference for this phrase *ateret ba'lah*; however, it is noteworthy that the phrase *ateret tiferet* is used several times in Isa. 62:3, Jer. 13:18, Prov. 4:9 and 16:31.

21. Based on Esther 8:15.

22. Referred to in the Torah: Exod. 19:5; Deut. 7:6, 14:2, and 26:18.

23. Translation adapted from Hammer, *Or Hadash*, 21–22, and Joel M. Hoffman in *My People's Prayer Book*, 8:115–16.

24. Kimelman, *Mystical Meaning*; a brief summary is contained in his essay in Hoffman, *My People's Prayer Book*, 8:118, 128–32.

25. "Rabbi Hanina would wrap himself in his cloak and stand at sunset at the outset of Shabbat, proclaiming, 'Come, let us go forth to welcome Queen Shabbat!' Rabbi Yannai put on his Shabbat cloak at the outset of Shabbat, proclaiming, 'Come forth, O bride; come forth O bride!'" B. Shab. 119a.

26. Note also that the song has nine stanzas; if you add the refrain, you have a parallel to the ten *sefirot*. And just as the refrain enlivens the entire composition, *Keter*, the first of the *sefirot*, gives life to all the others. As we shall see, the first two and ninth stanzas focus on Shabbat; the middle six focus on Jerusalem. This also represents the unification of the *sefirot*. And the rebuilding of Jerusalem is connected to the observance of Shabbat; the six days of the week are desanctified time, as a Jerusalem in ruins is in space. For further details see Kimelman, *Mystical Meaning*, 47.

27. As per Cordovero, noted in Kimelman, *Mystical Meaning*, 59.

28. B. Shevu. 20b. It has also been suggested that *zakhor* refers to the positive mitzvot connected with Shabbat and *shamor* to the negative mitzvot, but this is not necessarily inconsistent with the idea of both being spoken at once. Nahmanides (on Exod. 20:8) weaves this together with the conception of *shamor* as feminine, representing only those mitzvot women must observe. See also Rabbenu Bahya on Exod. 16:25 and 20:8. Noted in Kimelman, *Mystical Meaning*, 37–38.

29. See references in Kimelman, *Mystical Meaning*, 41–42. On the notion of *zakhor* and *shamor* as referring to the Sabbaths of this world and the world to come, see Kimelman, 80, and the sections from *Shnei Luhot ha-Brit* noted there.

30. Section 182. On the two Sabbaths in early Kabbalah, see also Nahmanides on Exod. 20:8 and 31:13; Tishby, *Wisdom of the Zohar*, 3:1220–21.

31. Zohar 3:115b: "*Zakhor* and *shamor* are linked as one; *zakhor* in the day, *shamor* in the night." See also Zohar 2:118b (*Ra'aya Meheimna*), similarly. The discussion in *Bahir* is largely repeated by Nahmanides as well, as noted in Tishby, *Wisdom of the Zohar*, 3:1221; other texts from the Zohar are noted in Tishby, 3:1223.

32. Note also the teaching of *Tikkunei ha-Zohar* 21, 45a (cited in Kimelman, *Mystical Meaning*, 40), that this is so that "*ishah maz'ra'at tehilah.*" ("The woman brings forth seed first.")

33. Indeed, as Kimelman points out (122), the words *v'et Adonai* are interpreted as a reference to the union of male and female, *Tiferet* and *Malkhut*. See Zohar 1:15b and comments of Matt, *Zohar: The Pritzker Edition*, 1:113–14.

34. B. Av. Zar. 2b.

35. Wolfson, *Venturing Beyond*, 131–32.

36. Kimelman, *Mystical Meaning*, 83, notes the connection between Shabbat and the spread of the Jewish body politic in the teaching (B. Shab. 118): "He who delights in the Shabbat is given an unbounded heritage." It is noteworthy that this spread comes from the heritage of Jacob (*Tiferet*), who mediates between right and left. We should also note the significance of prayer in the Land of Israel, particularly during the time of the Temple, as in, e.g., Zohar 1:84b: "When Israel dwelled in the Holy Land, everything was harmonious, as it should be, . . . and they performed (their) worship, piercing the firmaments of the world (conceived as curtains), so that worship ascended to its place above. For the Land is exclusively suited to worship by the People of Israel." See notes in Matt, *Zohar: The Pritzker Edition*, 2:39–40. "Supernal harmony as achieved by the union of *Tiferet* and *Malkhut* is, therefore, to be induced by the performance of Jewish ritual in the Land of Israel. Later on, the Safed Kabbalists repeat the lesson: 'Supernal union is achieved by Israel's prayers only in the Land of Israel, but not abroad' (Azulai, *Hesed l'Avraham*, pp. 19b–20a), and holy harmony can be restored only by the complete return of all the tribes of Israel to their peculiar areas in the Land. Without the return of the entire people, the Divine Pleroma fails to reach its supreme and perfect status." Idel, "Land of Israel," 176. This is an interesting parallel to the Christian idea that the redemption can only come after the Jews all return to Israel.

37. Kimelman, *Mystical Meaning*, 82.

38. Cited in Kimelman, *Mystical Meaning*, 130n237, along with Zohar 3:105a.

39. Kimelman, *Mystical Meaning*, 16, cites the passage from Zohar 3:272b, which states this explicitly. Cordovero's interpretation (cited on 15) is similar.

40. This usage is parallel to that of Zohar 1:45a–b, as noted in Tishby, *Wisdom of the Zohar*, 2:613.

41. *Siddur Etz Chayim*, 766–69; compare *Siddur Kol Ya'akov*, 720–23.
42. Since the *Shekhinah* dwelled with the Israelites in the wilderness continually. The sukkah represents God's protective clouds of glory; see B. Suk. 11b.
43. 3:103b; see Tishby, *Wisdom of the Zohar*, 3:1305–8; Matt, *Zohar: The Pritzker Edition*, 8:163; Fine, "Kabbalistic Texts," 330–40.
44. On the *arba minim*, the "four species," see Zohar 1:220a–221a; Tishby, *Wisdom of the Zohar*, 3:1308–14. "When all four species, with the proper number of each species, are taken together the whole *sefirotic* world is symbolically united. The *etrog*, citron, represents *Malkhut*, the tenth *sefirah*. The *lulav*, the palm, is *Yesod*, the ninth *sefirah*. [Naturally enough, since the *lulav* can be understood as phallic; DH] The *aravot*, willow, of which two branches are used, represent the seventh and eighth *sefirot*, *Netzah* and *Hod*. And finally, the *hadasim*, myrtle, of which three branches are used, represent the fourth, fifth, and sixth *sefirot Hesed*, *Din*, and *Tiferet*. The three uppermost *sefirot*, *Keter*, *Hokhmah*, and *Binah* are above human influence and therefore not included." Faierstein, "God's Need for the Commandments," 51.
45. See Liebes, *Studies in the Zohar*, 78–81.
46. Liebes, *Studies in the Zohar*, 160–61; Wolfson, *Through a Speculum*, 365. On the *Tikkun leil Shavuot* in general, see Matt, "Adorning the 'Bride,'" where he translates and comments on the passage in Zohar 1:8a describing such a ritual.
47. *Tikkun Leil Shavuot ha-Mefo'ar*, 9.
48. Matt, "Adorning the 'Bride,'" 75.
49. See *Shnei Luhot ha-Brit, Masekhet Shavuot, Ner Mitzvah*, sect. 5.
50. One example that I have omitted for reasons of space is the Tu b'Shevat seder, although its popularity today has to do less with its original emphasis on *teshuvah* and more with its revision into ecological concerns. See Krassen, "New Year's Day," for a text of this ritual and a thorough discussion of its significance.
51. See Matt, *Zohar: The Pritzker Edition*, 5:251–52.
52. Found in B. Beitz. 16a.

23. THE BA'AL SHEM TOV AND HIS TEACHINGS
1. See Green, "Early Hasidism," 441, and Scholem, *Major Trends*, 329–30. "Both Buber and Scholem were in agreement that Hasidism had to be understood as part of a longer historical process whose crucial turning point was the diffusion of Lurianism and its messianic explosion in Sabbateanism and Frankism. In their understanding, the emergence of Hasidism was historically related to the spiritual situation of the Jews in Poland after the decline of these movements. In other words, they saw Hasidism as a response to a great spiritual crisis." Idel, "Martin Buber and Gershom Scholem," 391. Idel

proposes (393) "that the speculative literature of Hasidism reflects mainly the mystical relationship between the tzaddik and the Divine, whereas the narrative writings reflect the social dimension of Hasidism, namely the relationship of the mystic who returns from his mystical experience to the social sphere in order to contribute to the improvement and welfare of his community." "My basic assumption is that notwithstanding the fact that Lurianism, Sabbateanism, and kabbalistic *musar* literature (ethical and moralistic writings) all displayed a certain affinity of religious atmosphere and genre with Hasidism and were closest to it in both time and space, the alternative sources which were available to the Hasidic masters in the construction of their own spiritual configurations were both more numerous and more diverse. In print, more kabbalistic works were available to them than Sabbatean ones, more pre-Lurianic writings than Lurianic ones; and as for the kabbalistic *musar* literature, its popularity and admittedly immense influence must be placed in a larger context so as to permit a fuller acknowledgement of the parallel influence of purely theological works. These works, available in print, were instrumental in opening up kabbalistic doctrines to a wider public no less than the popular *musar* works." Idel, "Martin Buber and Gershom Scholem," 394. For further discussion of how this issue played out among historians, see Etkes, "Study of Hasidism."

2. See, e.g., Rosman, *Founder of Hasidism*, 13–15; 27, where he notes that there were "*hasidim* before Hasidism"; and 39: "Hasidism, then, was an outgrowth of an already existing religious orientation and not, as many have suggested, a radically new phenomenon that came as history's response to a crisis of Judaism or of Jewish society."

3. Noted in numerous places in Rosman, *Founder of Hasidism*, particularly 66–69; see also 159–70. Dynner, *Men of Silk*, 89–116, documents some of the patronage received in the first generations of Hasidism.

4. For instance, "Nigal and Gries have argued convincingly that all of the material in Jacob Joseph's books was no more than notes he had written down throughout the years. The publishers edited this material with little or no input from the aged author. . . . Hasidic belief and practice, in general, at that time (1780) reflected the teachings of the man whom tradition has regarded as the Besht's successor, the Maggid of Mezeritch." Rosman, *Founder of Hasidism*, 100, 105; see also 139–42.

5. He claimed his "teacher" was Ahiyah ha-Shiloni, mentioned in 1 Kings 11–15 and later connected to Rabbi Shimon bar Yohai, the hero of the Zohar. Etkes, *Besht*, 72–73, noting that the stories relating him to a *ba'al shem* known as Rabbi Adam are "a complete fabrication."

6. Heschel, *Passion for Truth*, 64.

7. See Elior, *Mystical Origins of Hasidism*, 2–3.

8. In the felicitous language of Meshullam Feibush Heller at the beginning of *Yosher Divrei Emet*, "all of them drank from one stream, namely, the divine Rabbi Israel Ba'al Shem Tov."

9. Heschel, from an essay on "Hasidism as a New Approach to Torah" included in *Moral Grandeur*, 34. See also Rosman, *Founder of Hasidism*, 2 and 178-79.

10. On some of the testimonies of his ecstatic prayer (some of it likely apocryphal, but certainly impressive on the whole), see Etkes, *Besht*, 124-28, and 150. On the significance of prayer for the Ba'al Shem Tov, see Heschel, *Moral Grandeur*, 37.

11. See Jacobs, *Hasidic Thought*, 3-5. An alternate version of the story from *Shivhei ha-Besht* can be found in Ben-Amos, "Israel ben Eliezer," 506-8.

12. Incidentally, other versions of this story suggest that Dov Ber, who suffered from poor health, went to visit the Ba'al Shem Tov with the hope of receiving some healing. While the physical healing did not come to pass, "this encounter points to another of the Ba'al Shem Tov's important charismatic gifts: *the power to awaken in others the capacity for direct mystical experience* .... We may consider this another example of Rabbi Israel's function as Teacher, an initiatory power that thoroughly transformed the Maggid's spiritual life and made him the Ba'al Shem Tov's disciple for life." Krassen, "Rabbi Israel Ba'al Shem Tov," xvii.

13. For an excellent annotated example, see Kallus, *Pillar of Prayer*, 198-99.

14. From Heschel's lectures, quoted in Dresner, *Heschel, Hasidism, and Halakha*, 38.

15. "The Hasidic rebbe is a quasi-divine being. His figure is characterized by tales of miracles and cosmic repair; claims of embodying the soul of a previous messiah figure; in some cases, asceticism and, in others, its antithesis." Lenowitz, *Jewish Messiahs*, 199.

16. See Ettinger, "Hasidism and the *Kahal*," 70. There is a good deal of interest in redemption in early Hasidism, but generally not of the sociopolitical variety. E.g., on Hasidic immigration to Israel, see Barnai, "Historiography of the Hasidic Immigration," particularly 379-80.

17. "Recent historical research has shown that this strand of mystical praxis, long intentionally hidden by the self-censorship of the mystics and the reluctance of printers, played a major role in the new growth of Kabbalah in the sixteenth century and had not a little influence on certain aspects of Hasidism. In these sources, most of which are preserved only in manuscript, the prophetic claim is made quite openly." Green, "Typologies of Leadership," 147.

18. See Green, "Typologies of Leadership," 129-31.

19. See Dresner, *Zaddik*, 106.

20. Dresner, *Zaddik*, 182. See also *Kedushat Levi*, Lekh Lekha, 25b, noted in Dresner, *World of a Hasidic Master*, 25, commenting on Gen. 17:4: "As for

Me, this is My covenant with you: You shall be the father of a multitude of nations." "The purpose of the tzaddik's service of God is to raise up the lower levels to the Blessed Creator, as it is written in the Zohar, 'We must appear before the King.' (*Tikkunei Zohar*, no. 40, 80a.) But there is great danger to the tzaddik involved with this descent in order to bring up others, so he must cleave to the *Ein Sof*, Blessed be He. This therefore is what God promises Abraham: 'As for Me, this is My covenant with you,' My covenant will be My bond, that I will be 'with you,' even when you will be 'father of a multitude of nations' (i.e., among the nations)." Also, it was taught in the name of the Besht that "one must descend to *Gehinnom* on behalf of God." Quoted from *Pe'er Yesharim* in Schatz-Uffenheimer, *Hasidism as Mysticism*, 36.

21. From the Besht's letter to Jacob Joseph: "Every single morning when you study, attach yourself to the letters with total devotion to the service of your Creator . . . and then they will soften the verdicts with their root and lift the verdicts from you. And do not deny your flesh, God forbid, to fast more than is required or is necessary." Rosman, *Founder of Hasidism*, 115. This clearly contributed to the growth of Hasidism: "By eschewing asceticism, the Ba'al Shem Tov removed a most daunting obstacle facing the potential Hasid. Without the physical commitment required to carry out fasts and flagellations, the Kabbalistic doctrines and rituals were much more accessible." Rosman, 183.

22. Magid, "Hasidism," 153, and see also 154.

23. Noted in Dresner, *Zaddik*, 140, and see his comments there.

24. See Dan, "Hasidism: The Third Century," 420.

25. "In this mystic deepening of the monotheistic belief, the entire cosmos is understood as a reflection and garment of God as the Divine is clothed in the world of being." Wineman, *Hasidic Parable*, xxiii.

26. *Tikkunim* no. 70, 122b. Interesting is Hillel Zeitlin's comment: "The *Besht*'s God is one that lives, strives, grows, blossoms, suffers and composes, thinks and creates that for which the heart is torn and the soul longs. The *Besht*'s God is in man, even in his lacks and sufferings, his sin and smallness." *Hasidic Spirituality*, 15.

27. Noted in Lamm, *Religious Thought of Hasidism*, 8–9.

28. On the life and teachings of Pinhas, see Heschel, *Circle of the Baal Shem Tov*, 1–43.

29. E.g., *Toldot Ya'akov Yosef*, p. 731, sect. 25 (see Dresner, *Zaddik*, 188); *Keter Shem Tov*, no. 273a, p. 36.

30. See Elior, *Mystical Origins of Hasidism*, 76.

31. See Lamm, *Religious Thought of Hasidism*, 442–43; also translation in Schochet, *Tzava'at HaRivash*, 4–5, and parallel passage with extension in *Keter Shem Tov*, 1:220.

32. See Lamm, *Religious Thought of Hasidism*, 140. Similarly the version quoted from *Divrei Moshe* in Heschel, *Circle of the Baal Shem Tov*, 121-22.

33. *Midrash Bereshit Rabbah* 68:9: "He is the Place of the world, but the world is not His place."

34. Indeed, the Ba'al Shem Tov generally rejected all non-normative ascetic practices; see his letter to Ya'akov Yosef of Polonnoye, cited in Etkes, *Besht*, 180-81. His Hasidim "maintained that true piety by no means consists in chastisement of the body." Solomon Maimon, cited in Rosman, *Founder of Hasidism*, 35. See also the teaching from *Kedushat Levi*, 61, cited in Dresner, *World of a Hasidic Master*, 148-49. It should be noted that "the Besht too practiced self-mortification at an early stage of his career, before he turned to his special method of divine worship." Etkes, *Besht*, 122.

35. On this theme, see Etkes, *Besht*, 144-47.

36. See comments of Green, "Hasidism," 320-21.

37. *Sifrei*, Ekev 13; B. Sot. 14a.

38. Lamm, *Religious Thought of Hasidism*, 150-51.

39. See the introduction to Nahmanides's *Peirush al ha-Torah*.

40. E.g., *Tzava'at ha-Rivash*, no. 5: "Cause your thought to cleave above and do not eat or drink too much, only what health requires.... Always endeavor to separate yourself from the physical." Noted in Krassen, *Uniter of Heaven and Earth*, 55. Krassen also points out a helpful distinction between two types of *deveikut*: "Where *deveikut* refers to a technique that leads to *hishtavut*, the source is that of the fourteenth-century Kabbalist, R. Isaac of Acre. Where *deveikut* means a mystical state, the sources can be any of several popular Kabbalistic-ethical works, especially *Reshit Hokhmah*, *Shnei Luhot ha-Brit*, and *Sefer Haredim*." (56-57)

41. B. Ket. 5a.

42. See Jacobs, *Hasidic Prayer*, 75.

43. See *Arba'ah Turim*, O. H. 98, which claims that earlier practitioners "were concentrating their thought and intending in their prayer so as to arrive at a state of divestment of corporeality, and the strengthening of the intellectual spirit, so that they reached a state close to the level of prophecy." Noted in Idel, "*Adonai Sefatay Tiftah*," 16.

44. See Kallus, *Pillar of Prayer*, 36. Similarly the testimony of the Seer of Lublin that "whenever a new Hasid came to him, he instantly took his soul out of him, cleansed it of all stain and rust, and put it back into him, restored to the state it had been in the hour he was born." Noted in Buber, *Tales of the Hasidim: Early Masters*, 307.

24. THE ROLE OF PRAYER AND THE BA'AL SHEM TOV'S SUCCESSORS

1. Heschel, *Passion for Truth*, 47.

2. Heschel, *Moral Grandeur*, 34.

3. As told in Langer, *Nine Gates*, 119-20, with minor changes.

4. See Jacobs, *Hasidic Prayer*, 93-94.

5. Dresner, *World of a Hasidic Master*, 22.

6. See Dresner, *World of a Hasidic Master*, 102.

7. "The Besht was thus able to shift from the traditional perspective reflected in the Mishnaic dictum 'nor is the commoner a Hasid' (Pirkei Avot 2:5), and to suggest instead that in certain cases the commoner too is a kind of Hasid—if his prayer is pure." Etkes, *Besht*, 109.

8. See Kallus, *Pillar of Prayer*, 107; Schochet, *Tzava'at HaRivash*, 49-50. See also the shorter version in *Tzava'at*, no. 97.

9. See Idel, *Hasidism*, 117, and Scholem, *Major Trends*, 5.

10. As Idel (315n86) points out, this has precedent in the Kabbalah of the thirteenth century. Compare Zeitlin's comment: "The more you reach the Nothing that lies within all being, the divine inwardness, the closer you are to truth, to the Godly, to the essence of creation. You reveal the mask and see before you the King in His glory, the endless light." *Hasidic Spirituality*, 76.

11. *Kedushat Levi*, B'reishit, 1; cited in Elior, "Paradigms of *Yesh* and *Ayin*," 170.

12. I have used here the version in Lamm, *Religious Thought of Hasidism*, 177-78, with modest variations; see also Buxbaum, *Light and Fire*, 256-57, and the sources noted at 397n56.

13. Quoted from *Shivhei ha-Besht* in Etkes, *Besht*, 146.

14. B. Ber. 33b-34a.

15. Karetz ed.; see Kallus, *Pillar of Prayer*, 124.

16. See Dresner, *World of a Hasidic Master*, 152.

17. See Etkes, *Besht*, 139.

18. On the influence of Shelah here, see Krassen, *Uniter of Heaven and Earth*, 48-49.

19. See Lamm, *Religious Thought of Hasidism*, 148-49; Schochet, *Tzava'at HaRivash*, 132-33.

20. Jacob Joseph of Polonnoye, *Ben Porat Yosef*, 39a; correction from the citation in Elior, *Mystical Origins of Hasidism*, 77, who adds: "This approach also reflects the blurring of boundaries between the divine spirit and the human spirit: creative human thought, expressed linguistically, is infinite, and by virtue of its infinity is identical with the infinite creativity of the divine." Similarly, "When a man thinks about the higher worlds, then he is in the higher worlds, for where a man's thoughts range, there he is." *Tzava'at ha-Rivash*, no. 69. "The soul, after all, is characterized uniformly by Hasidic masters as being consubstantial with the divine; this is the ontological basis undergirding the experience of *devekut*—the soul can be conjoined to the One because it is of the same essence." Wolfson, "Immanuel Frommann's Commentary," 199.

21. From R. Solomon Tellingator, *Tiferet Yisrael* (Jerusalem, 1945), 35-38; quoted in Mondshine, "Fluidity of Categories," 316-17.
22. See Nadler, *Faith of the Mithnagdim*, particularly its conclusion, 173-75.
23. Dresner, *Zaddik*, 238. As another brief example of the use of paradox on a different theme is told of Rabbi Naftali of Ropshitz: "one of his young followers received from him instructions for the order of his day, a precise and detailed order of worship, and when the Hasid turned to go, the Rabbi recalled him and said: 'But sometimes you must do the *exact* opposite.'" Quoted in Mondshine, "Fluidity of Categories," 313. (Levin, *Hasidim Mesaprim* 3:28; I have not been able to access the original.)
24. See particularly Weiss, "Mystical Hasidism," and *Studies*, 43-55.
25. "The fact that no master succeeded R. Nahman becomes more understandable when we see his disciples' unique relationship to his text. Becoming absorbed in *Likkutei MoHaRan* through devotional reading and living by its precepts does not only give the disciple access to the teachings of the tzaddik—it gives him/her access to the tzaddik himself." Magid, "Associative Midrash," 16. My presumption is that this is true in a different way of Nahman's other writings as well.
26. See Wineman, *Hasidic Parable*, 33; Kaplan, *Rabbi Nachman's Teachings*, 9-10.
27. Thus according to Greenbaum's *Under the Table*, 285, 289; *Sippurim Nifla'im* is a collection of teachings and stories of Rabbi Nahman, edited by Shmuel Horowitz. (I have not been able to access the original.) I have primarily used the version of the story included in Aryeh Kaplan's *Gems of Rabbi Nachman*, 162-63.
28. See comparison of his faith with the contemplative approaches of the Maggid and Shneur Zalman of Liady, as outlined in Weiss, *Studies*, 43-55.
29. See Green, *Tormented Master*, 39.
30. See Green, *Tormented Master*, 167-70.
31. See Green, *Tormented Master*, 39. Similarly see his disciple Nathan of Nemirov in *Hilkhot Chodesh* 3:9, cited in Eitan Fishbane, *Sabbath Soul*, 135-43, particularly the conclusion, "The righteous merit to break the body entirely."
32. See Wineman, *Hasidic Parable*, 10.

25. THE GROWTH OF HASIDISM AND ITS SEARCH FOR TRUTH
1. On this see Green, "Typologies of Leadership," also cited in chapter 23.
2. See an excellent example in Jacob Isaac Horowitz, *Zot Zikaron*, 68, noted in Dynner, *Men of Silk*, 197-98.
3. Noted at http://heichalhanegina.blogspot.com/2007/07/chozehs-clock .html, accessed 03/12/2015; probably based on the story in Buber, *Tales of the Hasidim: The Early Masters*, 308.
4. See Elior, "Between *Yesh* and *Ayin*," 437.

5. This opinion was anything but unanimous among Hasidic masters. "The Maggid of Kozhenitz maintained that being prosperous was detrimental to the life of piety, while the Seer of Lublin insisted that material well-being enhanced one's ability to live a saintly life." Heschel, *Passion for Truth*, 176.
6. Sherwin, *Workers of Wonders*, 110; see 108–15 on Jacob Isaac Horowitz's thinking and his disciples. Similarly Horowitz in *Zikaron Zot*, 40, noted in Sherwin, 109: "[The tzaddik] must draw Israel near to their Father in Heaven and see to it that if any of them are prevented from doing God's will as it should be done because of lack of necessities as, for example, because of poverty, which makes a person disregard the sense of his Creator, he [the tzaddik] draws down their needs for them." Likewise *Zikaron Zot*, 75, cited at length in Dynner, *Men of Silk*, 29–30.
7. *Ben Porat Yosef*, 17c, noted in Idel, "Jewish Magic," 94. Idel also comments that "the late fifteenth-century Spanish conception of demonic magic, or the much older magical practice of creating a golem, were rejected by eighteenth-century Hasidism, in favor of the Italian type of magic" mediated through Cordovero's teachings (Idel, "Jewish Magic," 104). Frequently, the power of the tzaddik is understood to be that he is able to reverse the power of the letters "by means of his study and prayer, so that he turns *met* (death) to *tam* (flawless) or *nega* (plague) into *oneg* (joy)." From *Shivhei ha-Besht*, as noted in Goetschel, "*Torah Lishmah*," 265.
8. Cited in Idel, *Hasidism*, 211; I have been unable to locate this edition.
9. Noted in Newman, *Hasidic Anthology*, 262.
10. See Sherwin, *Worker of Wonders*, 113.
11. See Jacobs, *Hasidic Thought*, 147–48.
12. Moses M. Walden, *Nifla'ot ha-Rebbe*, 55, no. 130; cited in Buxbaum, *Jewish Spiritual Practices*, 47.
13. "The Polish school moved away from the concept of the tzaddik as miracle worker and intermediary between man and God. The emphasis was instead placed on the tzaddik as spiritual guide and teacher." Faierstein, *All Is in the Hands of Heaven*, 64. Green describes this school as "a puritanical reform movement within Hasidism." *Language of Truth*, xx, and see also xxiv.
14. Cited from Jacob Aryeh of Radzymin, introduction to *Bikkurei Aviv*, 6, in Rosen, *Quest for Authenticity*, 44. "In his book *Noam Elimelekh*, which appeared two years after his death and was widely read among the Hasidim, Elimelekh wrote that God had given the tzaddikim powers to influence the higher spheres and determine the fate of men, both in this world and the next." Sharot, *Messianism, Mysticism, and Magic*, 161.
15. As cited in Mahler, "Hasidism and the Jewish Enlightenment," 469; in neither the excerpt nor the original book and its notes is it clear whether he is citing the Piotrkow 1923 or Lodz 1927 edition. The fourth volume is not

online at hebrewbooks.org as of this writing. See also translation in Rosen, *Quest for Authenticity*, 94; Dynner, *Men of Silk*, 184.

16. Rabinowicz, *Hasidism*, 130.

17. Apropos of this is the teaching of Yitzhak of Vorki on the opening of Deut. 11:26, "See, I [God] have set before you" should be read as "See the I," i.e., look at yourself. "The spiritual pilgrimage commences with an inward gaze, with the individual's encounter with his or her own self." Sherwin, *Sparks Amidst the Ashes*, citing the text from *Siah Sarfei Kodesh* (Lodz, 1931), 2:58b.

18. Barukh ben Avraham of Kosov, *Tiferet ha-Yehudi*, 21b.

19. Barukh ben Avraham of Kosov, *Tiferet ha-Yehudi*, 13b. It has also been suggested that "a powerful motivation (i.e., for the renewed study of Talmud) seems also to have been political expedience. According to firsthand testimony, R. Simha Bunim prevailed upon his disciples to leave off their studies of Zohar and midrash and return to talmudic studies so that they could more successfully compete for rabbinic posts throughout the region. 'Is it not fitting,' he chided them, 'that spiritual descendants of the Besht break into [rabbinical] posts throughout the Ashkenazic lands?'" Dynner, *Men of Silk*, 55, citing *Ramatayim Tzofim*, 195 (Warsaw, 1885). This would be an example of how the community at large drew the Hasidic world away from somewhat radical change and back toward existing values in an important realm.

20. "The Holy Jew's sons reverted to miracle working and only succeeded in attracting a portion of their father's following." Dynner, *Men of Silk*, 28.

21. Rosen, *Quest for Authenticity*, 191.

22. See Rosen, *Quest for Authenticity*, 190.

23. Cited from *Beit Ya'akov*, Shabbat *hol ha-mo'ed* Sukkot, 91b, in Rosen, *Quest for Authenticity*, 35. In short, "The *Yehudi* saw a superficiality within Hasidism as it existed in his day. He demanded the analytical scrutiny of the mind and the purification of the soul. This invitation was open to anyone who could participate. Przysucha was a reaction to the shallowness of a mass movement. It was not just that it had an aversion to the paraphernalia of the court of the tzaddik. It was also the fact that any movement with too large a number of people would inevitably function at a lower common denominator in the service of God." Rosen, *Quest for Authenticity*, 350.

24. NJPS: "and it robed me."

25. Rosen, *Quest for Authenticity*, 139n6.

26. Berger, *Torat Simha*, no. 51, in *Simhat Yisrael*, 36b. See there also *Torat Simha*, no. 48 (cited Rosen, *Quest for Authenticity*, 142) in which he teaches that "if a person wants to keep a stringency only because his father kept it and he wants to do as his father did, he is not allowed to do so." On the overlap between the school of Przysucha and Romanticism, see Rosen, 338–48.

27. Rosen, *Quest for Authenticity*, 184. (In his Hebrew notes, this text is given as no. 232 in *Siah Sarfei Kodesh*.)
28. See in particular Berger, *Torat Simha*, 56b, no. 289; Rosen, *Quest for Authenticity*, 186.
29. Simha Bunim acknowledges the struggle with sexual urges: "When a young man wraps himself in a tallit he thinks and imagines that he (is complete). But isn't his wife also standing with him beneath the tallit?" Rosen, *Quest for Authenticity*, 183, from *Siah Sarfei Kodesh*, 4:38, no. 2.
30. The Hebrew term used here is *seder*, conventionally translated as "order."
31. Rosen, *Quest for Authenticity*, 97.
32. Uncharacteristic is the story told of Simha Bunim, "The Forbidden Way," quoted in Buber, *Tales of the Hasidim: Later Masters*, 256–57.
33. Heschel, *Passion for Truth*, 11.
34. Cited in Jacobs, *Hasidic Thought*, 197–98.
35. "The Kotzker devoted his active life to questioning the spiritual vapidity of his fellow Jews." Heschel, *Passion for Truth*, 153. Similarly, 202: "Almost all of his sayings are either calls for self-examination or the result of self-scrutiny."
36. See *Amud ha-Emet*, Yitro, 24; Jacobs, *Hasidic Thought*, 198.
37. Heschel, *Moral Grandeur*, 35.
38. Cited from various sources in Rosen, *Quest for Authenticity*, 144.
39. Kaplan, *Chasidic Masters*, 176, citing *Emet ve-Emunah*, no. 901, p. 562.
40. Kaplan, *Chasidic Masters*, 181; *Emet ve-Emunah*, no. 157, pp. 111–12.
41. Heschel, *Moral Grandeur*, 177. On this school's denial of the value of worldly life, see, e.g., Mahler, "Hasidism and the Jewish Enlightenment," 470–71. On the Kotzker and sexuality, see Heschel, *Moral Grandeur*, 220–22. It should be noted that the Kotzker did not advocate asceticism for its own sake; for him, "mortification of the flesh was a cheap exercise and did not affect one's inner life." Heschel, 229.
42. I have used the translation from Faierstein, *All Is in the Hands of Heaven*, 13, citing Heschel's book on Kotzk. See also Rosen, *Quest for Authenticity*, 43.
43. In particular, in *Mei ha-Shiloach*, Pinhas, 1:164–65; see Faierstein, *All Is in the Hands of Heaven*, 33–34; Weiss, *Studies*, 229–31.
44. See Weiss, *Studies*, 216.
45. With the exception of some kabbalists; see Sack, *Shomer ha-Pardes*, 65–67. See also Zohar 2:23a.
46. NJPS: "The lips of the righteous know what is pleasing."
47. Noted in part in Rosen, *Quest for Authenticity*, 234.
48. Rabinowicz, *Hasidism*, 210. "A mass movement was created where the individual was sacrificed to the enterprise of producing one truly great Torah scholar. This was a complete retrenchment from the individuality and sense of personal autonomy that R. Bunim espoused as obligatory upon any

human being who desired to come close to God. *It is as if the whole enterprise of Przysucha came to an end with Chiddushei ha-Rim.*" Rosen, *Quest for Authenticity*, 275; emphasis in the original.
49. See Green, *Language of Truth*.
50. Dresner, *Heschel, Hasidism, and Halakha*, 36.

26. CHABAD HASIDISM

1. See Hallamish, *Introduction to the Kabbalah*, 154. "In our language *da'at* is consciousness, awareness, the state in which we have a fully developed image of the object and therefore can say that we *know* it. The *sefirah* of *da'at* within the Godhead refers to that stage when God sees all things throughout eternity as objects, having a full and clear picture of them. In other words, He sees all things *as they are about to be created.*" Zeitlin, *Hasidic Spirituality*, 108.
2. Jacobs, *Seeker of Unity*, 64.
3. Told at a *farbrengen* to Zalman Schachter-Shalomi and noted in Schachter-Shalomi and Miles-Yepez, *Hidden Light*, 34. A more expanded version of this early history can be found there.
4. "In examining the Chabad tradition, one must bear in mind that the books, sermons, documents, and letters were all written in a sociocultural context in which the *halakhic* and kabbalistic associations were taken for granted, so that a passing allusion was sufficient to make its meaning clear." Elior, "HaBaD," 159. While Shneur Zalman did not normally reference or share the most intricate kabbalistic concepts, he was certainly conversant in them, as illustrated by this anecdote: "Rabbi Shneur Zalman had some volumes in his library that were off limits even to his disciples. These books were marked 'Under Rabbenu Gershom's ban in this world and the next,' and even his own son did not dare to read them. When a fire consumed a considerable part of Rabbi Shneur Zalman's library, he asked his son if he could at least mention one item from these books so that his father might remember the rest. But Rabbi Dov Ber replied that he had not dared to read them because of the seal. Rabbi Shneur Zalman rebuked him, saying, 'For *Hasidut* one should risk even the life of the world to come.'" From a story told at a *farbrengen*, recounted by Rabbi Zalman Schachter-Shalomi in *Spiritual Intimacy*, 87.
5. I have adapted this from the slightly different approach of Elior; see "HaBaD," 160.
6. Cited by Idel, "Universalization and Integration," 43, from *Commentary on the Siddur* (Brooklyn, 1980).
7. Shapiro, *Tanya*, 18.
8. Elior, "HaBaD," 161.
9. *Tanya* 1:42.

10. See Jacobs, *Hasidic Thought*, 125–26.

11. Similarly, see Elior, *"HaBaD,"* 160–61.

12. *Tanya* 1:52.

13. See particularly *Toldot Adam, Beit ha-Behirah*, sect. 4. For another example of how this teaching influenced Hasidic teaching, see Krassen, *Uniter of Heaven and Earth*, 86–87.

14. On the term in earlier Kabbalah, see Matt, *Zohar: The Pritzker Edition*, 6:157n144, and Giller, *Reading the Zohar*, 48–50.

15. NJPS translates: "Sin is a reproach to any people."

16. B. BB 10b.

17. That this view was not unique to Shneur Zalman among Chabad thinkers is clear from the eschatological vision of the second rebbe, Dov Ber Schneerson: see *Sha'arei Teshuvah*, 74a (Brooklyn, 1995); trans. in Wolfson, "Status of the (Non) Jewish Other," 246.

18. "The idea that gentiles don't have a *neshamah* [i.e., the higher level of soul discussed by Shneur Zalman; DH] is the dirty little secret of much kabbalistic belief.... Of course, there are gentiles with *neshamot* according to all kabbalists. At the very least, the 'righteous gentiles' (*hasidei umot ha-olam*), who perform heroic acts of loving kindness, have souls according to most kabbalistic systems. Still, many kabbalists believed that at least some gentiles don't have a *neshamah*." Giller, *Kabbalah*, 91, and see further there.

19. Examples can be found in Wolfson, *Venturing Beyond*, 25n40, 124–28; Wolfson provides some of the historical context for such thinking.

20. According to some sources, Shneur Zalman himself claimed to be the "spiritual grandson" of the Ba'al Shem Tov." See the sources noted in Dynner, *Men of Silk*, 310n96.

21. Israel Yoffe; on how he accomplished this, see further Rosman, *Founder of Hasidism*, 206–9 and 276n85.

22. On his teachings, see Jacobs, *Seeker of Unity*.

23. Rosman, *Founder of Hasidism*, 199–201, 206–7. It is also noteworthy how Shneur Zalman himself is portrayed as the legitimate heir of the Ba'al Shem Tov; on this, see Rapoport-Albert, "Hasidism after 1772," particularly 112n123 and 124n184.

24. Rosman, *Founder of Hasidism*, 205.

25. Rosman, *Founder of Hasidism*, 205.

26. Rosman, *Founder of Hasidism*, 209.

27. See Jacobs, *Tract on Ecstasy*, 241; Unterman, *Kabbalistic Tradition*, 277–78.

28. Loewenthal, "Habad Approaches to Contemplative Prayer," 293, noting that Shneur Zalman also took this position, at least later in his life. "The divine *Ayin* can only be encountered when man is himself in a state of *Ayin*." Jacobs, introduction to *Tract on Ecstasy*, 14.

29. From his letter noted as an appendix in Jacobs, *Tract on Ecstasy*, 179.
30. As pointed out originally by Elior; see Loewenthal, "Habad Approaches to Contemplative Prayer," 297.
31. Loewenthal, "Habad Approaches to Contemplative Prayer," 298-300.
32. *Iggerot Kodesh*, no. 2166, 8:19; see Wolfson, *Open Secret*, 8.
33. As noted in Wolfson, *Open Secret*, 8. This idea has reverberated in the teachings of Chabad follower Yitzhak Ginsburgh, with results similar to those noted about Mordecai Joseph Leiner in the previous chapter; see Garb, *Chosen Will Become Herds*, 81.
34. Wolfson, *Open Secret*, 8-9, citing the interpretation of the seventh rebbe in *Torat Menahem* 5712, 3:41.
35. *Midrash Kohelet Rabbah* 1:28; see other references in Wolfson, *Open Secret*, 311n93.
36. See references in Wolfson, "Walking as a Sacred Duty," 195-96.
37. Yosef Yitzhak taught in 1941 that "every Jew should remember that it is not the people of Israel who are dying, God forbid, it is the world giving birth to twins—a new Jewish people and a new land of Israel are being born. . . . The birth pangs have started but will not last long." *Ha-Keriah v'ha-Kedushah* (Jerusalem, 1942), 20, as noted in Elior, "Lubavitch Messianic Resurgence," 385. Thus, Chabad's approach "was radically *transformed* by Rabbi Yosef Yitzhak. He advocated an extreme *apocalyptic perception* of history, orientated towards a transcendental messianic turning point which would inevitably occur in the very near future. . . . Only a belief in the concealed messianic significance of the events could refute the cruelty of their revealed meaning and resolve the tragic plight of a seemingly impotent divine providence in the light of desperate human experience." Elior, 387.
38. See his message in the Chabad magazine *Ha-Keriah v'ha-Kedushah* 1:9 (separate from the book of the same title cited above), as cited by Elior, "Lubavitch Messianic Resurgence," 388-89. See also Loewenthal, "Neutralisation of Messianism," 63-64.
39. It should be noted that "in Chabad Hasidism, the widespread dissemination of Kabbalah as a practical program began under the fifth rebbe (R. Shalom Ber Schneerson), who introduced the study of Kabbalah in the Tomkhei Tmimim Yeshiva that he established in 1897." Garb, *Chosen Will Become Herds*, 33.
40. See Wolfson, *Open Secret*, 36; Schneerson, *Torat Menahem* 5717, 2:40.
41. See Wolfson, *Open Secret*, 37; Schneerson, *Torat Menahem* 5719, 1:187.
42. Schneerson's *Etz ha-Hayyim* (Brooklyn, 1973), 42, as noted in Hallamish, *Introduction to the Kabbalah*, 94-95.
43. See Wolfson, *Open Secret*, 5-6; Schneerson, *Torat Menahem* 5710, 16.
44. Wolfson, *Open Secret*, 6.

45. See Wolfson, *Open Secret*, 6–8.

46. See also comments of Garb, *Chosen Will Become Herds*, 68–69. "In another text, the seventh rebbe described his predecessor as 'the supreme and omnipotent master' and 'the epitome of goodness'—expressions that are usually reserved for God Himself." Garb, 69, citing *Torat Menahem* as noted in Sheli Goldberg's PhD dissertation, "The *Zaddik*'s Soul after His Histalkut," 241. (Correction of Garb's book based on his Hebrew original.)

47. *Midrash Vayikra Rabbah* 29:11.

48. Wolfson, *Open Secret*, 11–12; Schneerson, *Torat Menahem* 5711, 1:194–95, 202.

49. "Just as Moses had the mandate to reveal the Torah in the world—thereby fusing the natural and the supranatural—so, too, Schneerson assumed the duty of completing the work of redemption begun by the sixth rebbe." Wolfson, *Open Secret*, 12. See also Elior, "Lubavitch Messianic Resurgence," 394.

50. Wolfson, *Open Secret*, 18; Schneerson, *Torat Menahem* 5711, 1:202–3.

51. Wolfson, *Open Secret*, 20, citing *Sihot Kodesh* 5752 (Brooklyn, 1992), 1:318, a text I was unable to locate; a similar version of this Yiddish address is found in Schneerson, *Sefer ha-Sihot* 5752, 1:97–113.

52. Wolfson, *Open Secret*, 239, citing Menahem Mendel Schneerson's *Sefer ha-Ma'amarim* 5737 (Brooklyn, 1994), 273–74, and the Yiddish version in *Likkutei Sihot* (Brooklyn, not specified), 15:60–61.

53. See Telushkin, *Rebbe*, 158–62, 443, 503.

54. See also Wolfson, *Open Secret*, 144 and 152–53. Similarly, Schneerson displays a belief in the immutable difference between the Jewish and non-Jewish soul when dealing with the issue of conversion: "it is never the non-Jew who converts, for the one who converts does so because there is a holy spark within him, but for some reason it fell into a place to which it does not belong, and when he converts—after several reasons and attempts— then the holy spark is liberated and it joins the 'torch' and the 'light,' that is, the Torah, the commandments, and the blessed holy One." Wolfson, "Status of the (Non)Jewish Other," 252; Schneerson, *Torat Menahem*, 5718, 2:61–62. The adage "the convert who converts is compared to a newborn infant" (*ger she-nitgayyer k'katan she-nolad damei*; B. Yev. 62a and Bek. 47a, among others) "indicates that the convert is not an 'entirely new reality' (*metziut hadashah l'gamrei*) but rather s/he is like a baby that existed prenatally before entering the world." Wolfson, *Open Secret*, 253, from the rebbe's talk on January 29, 1983, in Schneerson, *Torat Menahem* 5743, 2:925.

55. On this, most recently, see David Berger, "Did the Rebbe Identify Himself as the Messiah"

56. Although most Chabad Hasidim themselves do not attend college, the campus is one of their most successful opportunities to spread the "wellsprings" of Torah and fulfill this step, which they view as essential for the

final redemption. On the Chabad rejection of secular learning, see Shneur Zalman of Lyady, *Tanya* 1:8, 33–34: "he who occupies himself with the sciences (*hokhmot*) of the nations of the world is included among those who waste their time in profane matters, insofar as the sin of neglecting the Torah is concerned, as is explained in the laws concerning Torah study (in *Shulhan Arukh ha-Rav*). Moreover, the impurity of the science of the nations is greater than that of profane speech."

57. Giller, *Kabbalah*, 174–75.

27. THREE TWENTIETH-CENTURY MYSTICS

1. Arthur Green treats Heschel together with Yehudah Leib Alter of Ger (1847–1905, the Sefat Emet, mentioned in chapter 25) and Hillel Zeitlin (1871–1942), another Polish thinker influenced by Hasidism, in "Three Warsaw Mystics." He notes (5) that "each of them is shaped by inner experiences or by a profound inner awareness of the direct presence of God, a presence that shatters the bounds of our ordinary way of seeing reality. God is the only true Being, before whom all other existence pales by comparison, or from whose existence all other being needs to be renewed in each moment. God is not an idea, not an abstraction, but a, indeed *the*, living reality." On Zeitlin, see Zeitlin, *Hasidic Spirituality for a New Era*, edited by Green.

2. As Naor puts it in his notes to *Orot*, 274n363, in Kook's view "those who are true to the Torah perspective must not give credence to the lie that there is such a creature as a *chiloni*, 'a secular Jew.' This is a contradiction in terms. A Jew by his very nature is *elohi*, godly." On the development of Kook's views into a nationalist messianic approach, see Garb, *Chosen Will Become Herds*, 37–51.

3. "The talmudic teaching, 'A person ought not pray save in a place that has windows' (B. Ber. 34b), was interpreted by Kook symbolically, as a call to awareness and receptivity to the world at large." Kaplan and Shatz, introduction to *Rabbi Abraham Isaac Kook*, 3. Nonetheless, Kook often spoke of non-Jewish influences as unfortunate imports; "any thought that did not develop wholly within the camp of Israel could subvert the edifice of Israelite faith and life." *Orot*, 171.

4. See Kook, *Abraham Isaac Kook*, 194–95.

5. Kook, *Orot ha-Kodesh* 2:555; see Kook, *Abraham Isaac Kook*, 220–21.

6. Noted in Garb, *Chosen Will Become Herds*, 23 (reference here corrected). Similarly see Garb, 85, and the passage on prophecy quoted from *Arfilei Tohar* and *Shmonah Kevatzim*.

7. Garb, *Chosen Will Become Herds*, 29. See Kook, *Orot ha-Kodesh* 1:141: "To purify the hearts and to engage the mind in lofty thoughts that originate in the secrets of the Torah became an absolute necessity in the last

generation for the survival of Judaism." Noted in Hallamish, *Introduction to the Kabbalah*, 95.

8. See Garb, *Chosen Will Become Herds*, 43–44; 93–95; and on national mysticism among other groups in Israel today, 47–51.

9. Garb, "Rabbi Kook and His Sources," 78. Garb suggests here that Kook's mystical-national vision is rooted in the eighteenth-century Kabbalah of Moses Hayyim Luzzatto and the circle of the Vilna Ga'on.

10. See Kook, *Abraham Isaac Kook*, 209–10.

11. Kook, *Orot ha-Kodesh* 1:88; see Garb, *Chosen Will Become Herds*, 25–26.

12. Kook, *Hadarav*, 46; cited in Garb, *Chosen Will Become Herds*, 167n88.

13. See Kook, *Orot ha-Kodesh* 2:458–59; Kook, *Abraham Isaac Kook*, 228–29.

14. Kook "consciously distanced himself from those aspects of Eastern European traditionalism he regarded as too narrow, parochial, and rigid in style and outlook." Fine, "Rav Abraham Isaac Kook," 37. On the other hand, it should be noted that Kook's love for all people did not mitigate his hostility to other religions, particularly Christianity; see, e.g., Kook, *Orot*, 122–24.

15. Included in *Musar Avikha*, 72; Kook, *Abraham Isaac Kook*, 158.

16. For a full biography, see Polen, *Holy Fire*.

17. *Midrash Bereshit Rabbah* 96:1.

18. On the meaning of the original Zohar passage, see Matt, *Zohar: The Pritzker Edition*, 3:371n362.

19. B. Ber. 7a.

20. Polen, *Holy Fire*, 14.

21. See particularly his postscripts to the teachings in *Eish Kodesh*, cited in Polen, *Holy Fire*, 34–35.

22. *Midrash Shir ha-Shirim Rabbah* 3:2.

23. B. Sanh. 98b.

24. Walter Kaufmann, *Faith of a Heretic*, 168. (I am indebted to Rabbi Michael Friedland who reminded me of this comment.)

25. "Few were the scholars who, while growing up in a Hasidic ambiance, studied in German universities, were active in that country for a while, but made most of their career in a totally different cultural environment, the United States, while caring so much for the state of Israel. Few underwent so much emotional turmoil, but kept alive the early heritage they cherished, and were capable of expanding it beyond the parochial frameworks in which it was embedded. In fact, it seems that Heschel is the single scholar of Jewish mysticism whose identification with, and commitment to, a living Jewish tradition is so evident." Idel, "Abraham J. Heschel," 83.

26. Heschel, *Abraham Joshua Heschel*, 103. See also *God in Search of Man*, 27: "Two sources of religious thinking are given us: *memory* (tradition) and *personal* insight. We must rely on our memory and we must strive for fresh insight."

27. Dresner, *Heschel, Hasidism, and Halakha*, 25.

28. A more detailed evaluation of his approach to Kabbalah can be found in Idel, "Abraham J. Heschel."

29. E.g., Edward K. Kaplan, review, 191: "I call this event mystical illumination; Heschel calls it intuition or insight."

30. Although Heschel places great emphasis on this idea, similar language can be found in the work of the other two mystics considered in this chapter. Kook says words are inadequate and quotes the teaching from Zohar, *Idra Rabba*, 3:128a: "The world is sustained by the secret." *Iggerot ha-Reiyah*, 1:216. Shapira teaches: "That which each person perceives of God and which cannot be explained or related to someone else comprises the real secret and the mystery." *Sacred Fire*, 119 (alternative translation in Polen, *Holy Fire*, 49); Ki Tetse', September 14, 1940. As Marvin Fox puts it, "the infinite, by its very nature, cannot be confined by definitions or captured in any linguistic formulation." "Rav Kook: Neither Philosopher nor Kabbalist," 80. It should also be noted that both Kook and Heschel were poets; on Kook, see particularly the analysis in Gellman, "Poetry of Spirituality." Heschel's youthful poetry is collected and translated in *Ineffable Name of God*; see also Green, "Three Warsaw Mystics," 38–44.

31. Heschel, *God in Search of Man*, 353. Shapira and Kook make similar points on the mystic's inability to express the experience in words. Shapira discusses it in the context of what makes Hasidism distinct: "The intellectual component is only a part of Hasidism. . . . This is similar to our inability to explain prophecy intellectually, because only a prophet really knows what it is, and it is so obvious to him that he cannot understand why others don't see what he sees. . . . The same thing goes for Hasidism, which is the revelation of a spark of an ember of the capability for prophecy that lies dormant within each and every Jew." *Chovas HaTalmidim*, 256–57.

32. Heschel, *God in Search of Man*, 97.

33. Similarly Heschel, *Man's Quest for God*, 39.

34. "Man may forfeit his sense of the ineffable. To be alive is a commonplace; the sense of radical amazement is gone; the world is familiar, and familiarity does not breed exaltation or even appreciation." Heschel, *Who Is Man?*, 116.

35. Heschel, *Man's Quest for God*, 5. Green notes that this sense of wonder "about God who fills the universe" is a sign of Heschel's affinity for Hasidism. "Abraham Joshua Heschel," 65–66.

36. *Man's Quest for God*, 18.

37. *Man's Quest for God*, 58.

38. *Man's Quest for God*, 19.

39. Heschel, *Man Is Not Alone*, 76.

40. Heschel, "Jewish Theology," in *Moral Grandeur*, 163.

41. Thanks to Byron Sherwin for this insight and others concerning Heschel.

42. Heschel, *God in Search of Man*, 160.

43. On the connection between "taste" and mystical experience, see Hecker, *Mystical Bodies, Mystical Meals*.

44. *Pesikta d'Rav Kahana* 25:1. (Heschel cites a different edition.)

45. "In Heschel's case there seems to be a strong avoidance of Kabbalistic language altogether. But this in itself is an old tradition, cloaking mystic insight in the normative vocabulary of tradition, one that has its roots in the *MaHaRal* of Prague [i.e., Judah Loew; DH], not surprisingly a major influence ... on Heschel." Green, "Three Warsaw Mystics," 5.

46. Green, "Three Warsaw Mystics," 46.

47. *Pesikta d'Rav Kahana* 12:6, noted in Heschel, *Heavenly Torah*, 110.

48. *Man Is Not Alone*, 112.

49. *Man's Quest for God*, 54.

50. Dorff, "Walking with God," 99.

51. Green, "Three Warsaw Mystics," 50. Green notes elsewhere that "Heschel knows the world is in need of great charismatic religious figures." "Abraham Joshua Heschel," 70.

52. *Passion for Truth*, 184–89.

28. CONCEALMENT AND DISTORTION OF JEWISH MYSTICISM

1. "The one area in Judaism that the Wissenschaft rabbis could not abide was Kabbalah. German Jewish scholars were embarrassed by the irrational, supernatural, exotic nature of Jewish mysticism. While they had found ways to rationalize and Westernize the lessons of the Torah and Talmud (or jettison what did not fit, since they did not believe in the divine origin of those literatures), Kabbalah could not be assimilated into their scientific Judaism. The solution was to speculate that this was a foreign accretion that had wormed its way into Judaism from Middle Eastern idolatry." Goldish, "Kabbalah, Academia, and Authenticity," 64.

2. *Major Trends*, 228, and see also Scholem's comments on 1.

3. See Edward K. Kaplan, *Spiritual Radical*, 108–10. Kaplan deals as well with other factors that created distance.

4. Various versions of this anecdote exist, as there are many still living who were present; Edward K. Kaplan prints another version in *Spiritual Radical*, 406n36. No version I have heard changes the substance of Lieberman's comment, and most versions do place the comment within the walls of the seminary.

5. For further details and numerous references on this issue, see Giller, *Kabbalah*, 166–68.

6. Dresner, *Zaddik*, 17.

7. "While Sabbatean manuscripts were being avidly collected by the Jewish librarians of the West, who considered them bizarre testimony of a movement long dead, Hasidic documents, even the most valuable, though readily accessible—Hasidism, after all, was a living, challenging phenomenon—were virtually ignored as worthless. The librarians followed the example of their doyen, Moritz Steinschneider, the master bibliographer who insatiably ransacked every nook and cranny in search of Hebrew manuscripts, but freely admitted that he knew next to nothing about Hasidic literature." Dresner, *Heschel, Hasidism, and Halakha*, 44. Heschel suggested that the Wissenschaft rejection of Hasidism was part and parcel of their sympathy with what they saw as the more liberal, "cultured" Sephardic mode, which they preferred to the Ashkenazic tradition. See his "The Two Great Traditions," particularly 420–21, quoted at length in Dresner, *Heschel, Hasidism, and Halakha*, 47–49.

8. Even Simon Dubnow, a much more sympathetic scholar of Hasidism, fell prey to a related kind of negative analysis; see Rapoport-Albert, introduction to *Hasidism Reappraised*, xix. It was suggested that Hasidism is a response to abnormal conditions, so one can understand why it is abnormal. It was believed that "hardship . . . encouraged the flight into mysticism; peace and quiet generated rationalism. . . . Joseph Weiss, though still a student, ridiculed this simplistic formula and showed easily that it led to misrepresentation of the facts." Katz, "Joseph G. Weiss," 4.

9. "The reason for the hold of Lurianic Kabbalah on Jews everywhere was that it provided a key to the mystery of their suffering at the hands of the Gentile world and made that suffering tolerable. In medieval Europe, the one inescapable fact about Jews was that they were in exile, at the mercy of the whims of their Gentile rulers. In 1492 they had been expelled cruelly from Spain; in 1648–49 there were horrendous massacres in Poland. How could Jews continue to bear the burden of their exile? Lurianic Kabbalah provided the answer in subtle, mystical terms which satisfied." Davies, "From Schweitzer to Scholem," 344–45, and see further there.

10. For example, "a man of genius like Rabbi Nahman of Brazlav impresses us by his extravagant references to the power of the tzaddik, but he does so because in his case one senses an obvious concern for the spiritual aspects of tzaddikism. With many others, however, this spiritual character is only faintly or not at all recognizable, and the greatest and most impressive figure of classical tzaddikism, Israel of Ruzhin, the so-called Rabbi of Sadagora, is, to put it bluntly, nothing but another Jacob Frank [a well-known eighteenth-century apostate] who has achieved the miracle of remaining an orthodox Jew." Scholem, *Major Trends*, 332. Assaf's biography of Israel of Ruzhin (*The Regal Way*) serves as ample refutation of Scholem's ill-treatment. See also

Giller, *Kabbalah*, 167. Perhaps Goldish is right in suggesting that "Scholem would have been astounded to see a new wave of Jewish practice in our day, fueled not by a mystical appropriation of the secular, but by the same kabbalistic books, ideas, and practices from the Middle Ages that he spent his own lifetime studying. He would surely have been even more surprised to see the wave led by academics trained largely through the study of his own writings!" "Kabbalah, Academia, and Authenticity," 65.

11. Scholem's student Isaiah Tishby particularly notes this in commenting on the negative attitude of nineteenth-century scholars vs. those in the twentieth century; see *Paths of Faith and Heresy*, 22, and the comments of Idel, "On the Theologization of Kabbalah," 158–59.

12. On these "renegades," see Giller, *Kabbalah*, 177–78, and concerning other mystics of some interest today, 180–86; on Yehudah Ashlag and roots of the Kabbalah Learning Centre approach, see Garb, *Chosen Will Become Herds*, 29–32. See also Lachter, "Introduction: Reading Mysteries," 13. "[It] may make the academics uncomfortable, but nothing the Centre actually teaches—feel-good Kabbalah Lite, the inclusion of non-Jews, the completely untraditional use of Jewish symbols, the power of Kabbalah to affect the physical world—lacks a solid precedent in traditional Kabbalah, and the other popular Kabbalah teachers know it." Goldish, "Kabbalah, Academia, and Authenticity," 67.

13. "Kabbalah at the Turn," 180–87.

14. On the attempt to build secular approaches to Kabbalah, see further Garb, *Chosen Will Become Herds*, 121. As we have noted, the granting of great responsibility to the individual added to the popularity of Kabbalah in previous ages: "There can be little doubt that the appeal of Kabbalah had something to do with this new sense of opportunity and responsibility with which it endowed religious life. For it suggested that even if the external realities of history—and Israel's situation within that history—cannot be decisively shaped by individual action, the inner, spiritual realities can be." Fine, "Kabbalistic Texts," 329.

15. Myers, "Kabbalah at the Turn," 184.

16. Garb, *Chosen Will Become Herds*, 110.

17. *Torat ha-Olah* 4:3 (72b).

18. See Matt, *Zohar: The Pritzker Edition*, 5:532–33.

19. Hellner-Eshed, *River Flows from Eden*, 47.

20. Hellner-Eshed, *River Flows from Eden*, 48.

21. Edward K. Kaplan, review, 190.

Glossary

Abba: "Father"; corresponds to the *sefirah* of *Hokhmah*.

Abba Ila'ah: "the Higher Father"; used to refer to various configurations of the upper *sefirot*, sometimes within *Hokhmah*, sometimes within the group of *Keter*, *Hokhmah*, and *Binah*.

ABY'A: acronym for the four worlds, *Atzilut*, *Beri'ah*, *Yetzirah*, and *Asiyah*.

acosmism: the idea that everything is God, but we see things as separate entities.

Active Intellect: a term used in philosophy and in the works of Abraham Abulafia referring to that part of the intellect that turns potential knowledge into actual knowledge.

Adam ha-Elyon: "the higher being"; the supernal *anthropos*; see *Adam Kadmon*.

Adam Kadmon: "the primordial man"; a macrocosm of the human being, but actually a way of understanding God, particularly used in Lurianic Kabbalah.

Affective Kabbalah: human-centered mystical activity; involvement in God's inner life so as to address personal or communal needs.

Agent Intellect: a divine aspect through which one achieves higher knowledge; see "Active Intellect."

aggadah: "lore," "tales"; the homiletical and nonlegal sections of Rabbinic literature, generally contrasted with *halakhah*.

"An'im Zemirot": See "Shir ha-Kavod."

anthropomorphism: the attribution of human form, behavior, or qualities to God.

Arikh Anpin: literally, "the long face"; corresponds to the *sefirah* of *Keter*.

Ashkenaz: referring to Germany, or (Ashkenazic) Jews of Central or Eastern European background.

Asiyah: or, *Olam ha-Asiyah*, "the World of Making"; the lowest of the four worlds that comprise the realm of the *sefirot*.

Atzilut: or, *Olam ha-Atzilut*, "the World of Emanation"; the highest of the four worlds that comprise the realm of the *sefirot*.

avodah b'gashmi'ut: literally, "service through the material"; the worship of God through physical acts, understood as an extension of the idea of God's Presence in all places.

Ayin: "Nothingness" or relating to that which is not material. Related to *ein*, Hebrew word of negation. Opposite of *Yesh*.

ba'al shem: One who wrote amulets for healing and protection, generally involving one of God's Names; literally, "Master of the Name." Plural: *ba'alei shem*.

Bahir: mystical book, generally dated in twelfth century; literally, "brightness."

"Barukh She-amar": opening prayer of *Pesukei de-Zimra*; "Blessed is He who spoke (and the world came into being)."

beinoni: an average individual.

Beri'ah: or, *Olam ha-Beri'ah*, "the World of Creation"; the second of the four worlds that comprise the realm of the *sefirot*.

Besht: acronym for Ba'al Shem Tov.

Binah: "Understanding"; the third of the ten *sefirot*, treated as a feminine aspect of God.

Bittul ha-Yesh: "Self-nullification," i.e., the level of extreme humility required for certain kinds of mystical experience.

botzina d'kardenuta: a "spark of impenetrable darkness," referring to the initial concealed impulse of emanation or creation.

brit bein ha-betarim: "the covenant between the pieces"; a covenant between God and Abraham recorded in Genesis 15.

Chabad: Hasidic dynasty begun by Shneur Zalman of Lyady, famous for worldwide outreach to Jews. Acronym for three *sefirot*, *Hokhmah*, *Binah*, and *Da'at*. Often referred to as "Lubavitch," a town in Russia that was the Chabad headquarters.

cherub: a celestial creature displayed on the Ark of the ancient Temple, part human, part animal in form. Plural: cherubim.

Da'at: "Awareness"; one of the upper *sefirot* in some kabbalistic models.

demut: "image" or "likeness," generally referring to some physical likeness of God.

Deus absconditus: Christian terminology for the concealed aspect of God.

Deus revelatus: Christian terminology for the revealed aspect of God.

deveikut: "cleaving" to God, a major theme in Jewish mystical practice.

Din: "Judgment"; often used as term for the fifth *sefirah*. See *Gevurah*.

derash: the potential underlying meaning of a Torah text, given life through homiletical interpretation. One of the four means of interpreting the Torah. Also, *derasha*.

du-partzufim: "two faces," referring to the masculine and feminine elements built into creation; also, to the myth of the initial human being created with both masculine and feminine features.

dybbuk: a transmigrating soul that invades the body of another individual. Plural: dybbukim.

Ecstatic Kabbalah: see Prophetic Kabbalah.

"Ein Keloheinu": "There Is None Like Our God"; hymn in the Sabbath and festival morning services, based on one of the early *Heikhalot* hymns.

Ein Sof: "without end," the "Infinite"; kabbalistic term referring to a transcendent, unchanging God.

El: a name of God, frequently combined with other words to form names of individuals and angels.

Elohim: a Name of God frequently used in the Bible; often understood as conveying the quality of justice or judgment. In Kabbalah, associated with the *sefirah* of *Malkhut*.

emet v'yatziv: "true and firm"; the beginning of the blessing immediately before the "Amidah."

Enoch Metatron: a conflation of the angel Metatron with the biblical character Enoch, whose death is recorded differently from others in the Genesis genealogy.

erev rav: the "mixed multitude" that accompanied the Israelites in the Exodus from Egypt, generally considered a negative influence on the Israelites.

et: used to indicate that the following word is the direct object of the sentence, but has no meaning of its own.

farbrengen: A Hasidic gathering for learning, celebration.

ga'al Yisrael: "who redeemed Israel": the conclusion of the blessing immediately before the morning "Amidah."

galut ha-Shekhinah: "the exile of the *Shekhinah*"; the sense that God is walled off from humankind in times and places of injustice.

gan Eden: the Garden of Eden, or "paradise"; Eden sometimes used as code language for the *sefirah* of *Hokhmah*.

Gehinnom: generally referring to a purgatory-like place after life; derived from *gei Hinnom*, the valley of *Hinnom* outside Jerusalem, where child sacrifice took place in ancient times.

Gemara: the completion of the Babylonian and Palestinian Talmuds, the discussions of the sages about the Mishnah and various other issues, edited ~sixth century; "study" or "learning."

gematria: Numerological system based on the order of the Hebrew alphabet through which each Hebrew word is given a numeric value, often understood to contain mystical significance.

genizah: "storage place"; depository for holy books and writings deemed inappropriate for normal disposal. Often a reference to the Cairo Genizah, the contents of which were first brought to the world through Solomon Schechter.

Gevurah: "Power"; the name of the fifth *sefirah*, balanced with *Hesed*. Sometimes referred to as *Din*.

gilgul: process of reincarnation, the birth of the soul in another body in a subsequent generation.

giluy Shekhinah: "revealing of the *Shekhinah*"; some form of visual experience of God, such as was believed to take place at the Temple in Jerusalem.

Gnostics: various sects beginning second century CE that taught dualist approaches, i.e., two divine forces, and a stark separation between the spiritual and material world. From the Greek word *gnosis*, "knowledge"; Gnostics claimed superior knowledge of the spiritual world.

golem: a being artificially constructed in the form of a human and given life.

haftarah: The assigned prophetic reading following the Torah reading on Shabbat and festival mornings. Plural: *haftarot*.

Haggadah (Passover): The structured "telling" of the Passover and Exodus story, read at the seder on the first two nights of Passover.

halakhah: Jewish law, literally the "path" on which a traditional Jew walks. Similarly, the "halakhic" life.

Ha-Makom: name for God, "the One who is every place"; from *makom*, "place."

hanhagot: religious practices, generally recommended by a mystic or mystical school to adherents, often only for an elite.

Hasid: "pious," "saintly"; generally referring to a pietist belonging to one of the mystical movements. Plural: Hasidim. Also: *Hasidut*, involvement with or study of one of these mystical movements.

Hasidei Ashkenaz: German pietists and mystics of eleventh to thirteenth centuries.

Hasidism: mystical revivalist movement beginning in eighteenth century.

Hasmoneans: family of Jewish leaders beginning in second century BCE, initially commonly known as "Maccabees," military leaders in the revolt against Antiochus IV, and then political leaders in the century of independence following the revolt.

hayyah: one of the highest levels of soul; related to *hayyim*, "life."

hayyot: among the living creatures contained in the chariot of Ezekiel 1; related to *hayyim*, "life."

heh: the fifth letter of the Hebrew alphabet; included twice in the

Four-Letter Name of God. Sometimes used as a code for *Malkhut* or *Binah*, feminine aspects among the *sefirot*.

Heikhalot mysticism: a form of mystical practice involving a spiritual ascent to the *heikhal*, the divine "palace."

Hesed: "Love," the fourth *sefirah*; sometimes referred to as *Gedulah*, "Greatness." Balanced with *sefirah* of *Gevurah*.

Hevra: the society of sages during the early Rabbinic period (up to ~sixth century CE).

hishtavut: "equanimity," a degree of indifference to praise or criticism; from *shaveh*, "equal."

hitbodedut: "self-isolation" in order to be alone with God; in Prophetic Kabbalah, concentration on visual meditation; frequently used in Hasidism to denote private, spontaneous vocal prayer.

hitbonenut: from *binah*, "understanding"; referring to understanding acquired through in-depth study and contemplation.

hitlahavut: "rapture" or "ecstasy" in prayer; from root meaning "flame," thus "being aflame" with desire for God's Presence.

Hokhmah: "Wisdom"; the second of the ten *sefirot*, treated as a masculine aspect of God.

hokhmat ha-tzeruf: the practice of combination of and meditation on the letters of the Alef Bet (and especially those of the Four-Letter Name), taught by Abraham Abulafia.

Hod: the eighth of the ten *sefirot*, "Splendor," connected to the capacity for prophecy.

Hoshanah Rabbah: the last day of Sukkot, often considered to be the final conclusion of the penitential period centered around Rosh Hashanah and Yom Kippur. The climax of the morning service involves seven processions around the sanctuary while reciting "Hoshanah" ("Save us") prayers; hence its status as the day of the "Great Hoshanah."

hukkim: "decrees," laws of the Torah that seem to have no rational basis.

ibbur: a temporary joining of the soul of a dead person to a living individual.

Imma: "Mother"; corresponds to *sefirah* of *Binah*.

ineffable: that which cannot be expressed in words.

Jubilees: early Jewish book, second century BCE.

Kabbalah: a set of esoteric knowledge and secret traditions concerning God and paths of religious experience; literally, "received," often understood as the "tradition" received about such knowledge.

Kabbalat ol malkhut shamayim: The acceptance of the "yoke" of the Kingdom of Heaven, i.e., affirming one's commitment to God's Kingship.

Kabbalat Shabbat: "Welcoming of the Sabbath," a preface to the regular evening service on Friday evenings, composed of six Psalms, the joyous song "Lekhah Dodi," and an additional two Psalms.

Kadosh Barukh Hu: "The Holy One, Blessed be He"; in Kabbalah, code language for the *sefirah Tiferet*; sometimes appears in the Aramaic form (*Kudsha Berikh Hu*).

kavanah: the intention that accompanies an act, usually a prayer.

Kavod: in the Tanakh, God's Presence made manifest in the world. Literally, "glory" or "honor."

"Kedushah": A central prayer included in every repetition of the "Amidah" in traditional liturgy; literally, "holiness."

kefitzat ha-derekh: The miraculous "shortening of a journey" through magical means.

kelippat nogah: Idiom in Hasidic literature referring to the individual's sense of himself as separate from God. See also *kelippot* and *nogah*.

kelippot: "shells," "shards"; in Lurianic Kabbalah, the fragments that contain evil after the shattering of the vessels at creation and require restoration to their proper places. Singular: *kelippah*.

Keter: the highest of the ten *sefirot*; literally, "Crown"; sometimes referred to as "Will," the will that causes all existence.

Knesset Yisrael: "The Assembly of Israel"; in Kabbalah, code language for the *sefirah* of *Malkhut*.

Kohen: "priest"; descendant of Aaron, the brother of Moses; responsible for carrying out the Temple service. Plural: *Kohanim*.

Kohen Gadol: the High Priest in the Jerusalem Temple; performed the sacred service on Yom Kippur and various other occasions.

Lilith: in Jewish folklore and mystical texts, a female demon who attacks newborn children and their mothers, and causes nocturnal emissions.

"Lekhah Dodi": song included in *Kabbalat Shabbat* service, composed by sixteenth-century kabbalist Solomon Alkabetz and initially popularized through the kabbalists of Safed.

l'tzaref: both "to refine" and "to join," used in discussions of the purpose of the mitzvot (they are for refining human character and joining us to God). Also "to combine"; see *hokhmat ha-tzeruf*.

ma'aseh Bereshit: literally, "the work of Creation"; the study of metaphysical questions about life's origins not dealt with in the biblical account of Creation.

ma'aseh Merkavah: "the work of the chariot," i.e., the mystical study and experience of higher realms, most especially concerning the interpretation and meaning of Ezekiel 1.

maggid: "preacher" or a spiritual power that reveals itself to a Jewish mystic, e.g., as happened to Joseph Karo; see *Maggid Mesharim*.

Malkhut: the lowest of the ten *sefirot*, generally a feminine quality; literally, "Kingdom"; also frequently referred to as the *Shekhinah*.

mashiah: "anointed one"; Messiah.

Matronita: "noble lady," applied in the Zohar to the *Shekhinah* or *Malkhut*.

merkavah: "chariot," generally referring to the mysterious chariot of Ezekiel 1. Also used to describe "*Merkavah* mysticism" that began approximately second century CE.

Metatron: an archangel who, in some models, provided certain Divine Names to the mystic.

Mezeritch: Polish town that became the center of Hasidic life under the leadership of Dov Ber, the Maggid.

middat ha-din: "the quality (or force) of judgment"; contrasted with *middat ha-rahamim*, "the quality of mercy."

midrash: "study," "interpretation," homiletical biblical exegesis.

Midrash ha-Ne'elam: "The Hidden Midrash," the earliest part of the Zohar; a separate composition that was integrated into the Zohar's text.

Miedzyboz: Polish town that became the first center of Hasidism in the eighteenth century.

mikveh: ritual bath for immersion, used for conversions, monthly purification by women following the cessation of the menstrual period, and occasionally by men as an expression of heightened desire for purification.

milah: "word"; as part of the expression *brit milah*, refers to the covenant of circumcision.

Minha: the daily afternoon prayer service.

mishkan: the Tabernacle in the wilderness prior to the Israelite entry into the Promised Land; a precursor to the Jerusalem Temple.

Mishnah: "Teaching"; the digest of the Oral Torah compiled by Rabbi Judah the Prince approximately 200 CE, containing six major segments.

mishpatim: "judgments," directives of the Torah readily understood to be essential to the framework of society.

mitnagdim: "opponents," i.e., the opponents of Hasidism within the traditional Jewish communities of Eastern Europe.

mitzvah: "divine command," or an act that carries out such a command. Plural: mitzvot.

mohin d'gadlut: "higher consciousness"; often contrasted with *mohin d'katnut*, "lesser [i.e., normal] consciousness."

Musaf: Additional service included on Shabbat and festival mornings.

nefesh: "soul"; also referring to the lowest, most clearly physical of the soul levels.

neshamah: "soul"; also referring to the third, more spiritualized level of the soul. Also an anagram for Mishnah. Plural: *neshamot*.

neshamah yeteirah: The "additional soul [level]" understood to be bestowed on Jews for the duration of Shabbat.

Netzah: seventh of the ten *sefirot*, "Eternity" or "Victory," connected to the capacity for prophecy.

nogah: "radiance." See also *kelippat nogah*.

Nukva: "Feminine," sometimes referred to as *Nukva d'Ze'ir Anpin*, "the feminine [consort] of *Ze'ir Anpin*"; corresponds to the *sefirah* of *Malkhut*.

ofanim: the "wheels" of the chariot in Ezekiel 1.

panentheism: The doctrine teaching that God is found in everything and everything is contained in God.

pantheism: a doctrine that identifies God with nature or the universe.

pardes: the "orchard" of mystical experience; the word is used in Songs 4:13.

partzufim: "faces"; see *du-partzufim*.

peshat: the straightforward, contextual understanding of the biblical text. Also considered one of the four means of interpreting the Torah.

Pesukei de-Zimra: hymns and psalms composing the preliminary section of the morning service; literally, "Verses of Song."

Prophetic Kabbalah: a method of achieving some form of union with God and accessing divine wisdom.

Qumran: caves near the Dead Sea location of a sect that withdrew from Jerusalem and mainstream Jewish society beginning in the second to first centuries BCE; best known for the caves in which the Dead Sea Scrolls were hidden.

Rahamim: "Mercy"; another term for the *sefirah Tiferet*.

Raya Meheimna: a commentary on the Zohar, generally printed together with it; literally, "The Faithful Shepherd."

remez: literally "hint," "allusion"; also refers to one of the four means of interpreting the Torah, allegory.

ruah: "spirit," generally also "wind" or "breath"; also refers to the second level of "soul" in Kabbalah, sometimes thought of as the emotional being; also used as *ruah ha-kodesh*, "the holy spirit."

Sabbatean: one who believed that Sabbetai Tzvi was the Messiah.

Safed: community in the Galilee that became a major center of sixteenth-century Jewish mystical practice and teaching.

Samael: male demon, sometimes referred to as Satan; counterpart to Lilith.

sappir: deep blue jewel referred to in Tanakh, most notably in Ezekiel 1 and Exodus 24; lapus lazuli; the root is the same as that of the word *sefirah*; also related to *m'sapper*, "tell."

sefirah: one of the ten divine emanations in creation. Plural: *sefirot*.

seggulah: "charm," "remedy." Plural: *seggulot*.

Shabbat Hazon: the Sabbath prior to the fast day of Tisha b'Av, so called because the prophetic reading is the opening chapter of Isaiah, which begins with the word *hazon*, "vision."

Shavuot: festival commemorating the giving of the Torah, seven weeks after the beginning of Passover; literally, "weeks."

shefa: divine flow through the *sefirot* providing support, splendor.

Shekhinah: the "Divine Presence," conveying a sense of God's intimate nearness; in Kabbalah, the tenth and lowest *sefirah*, also understood as having a feminine quality; frequently referred to as *Malkhut*. Also code language for the Oral Torah.

shevirat ha-kelim: Lurianic term from his myth of creation; literally, "the breaking of the vessels," the tragic shattering of the vessels containing the light of creation.

"Shir ha-Kavod": "Song of Glory"; mystical hymn traditionally included in the Shabbat and festival prayers; popularly attributed to Rabbi Yehudah he-Hasid.

shi'ur komah: the concept in *Heikhalot* mysticism that God has a body, measurable but so large as to be incomprehensible. (Also, the title of a *Heikhalot* work that explicates this concept. Also, the title of a sixteenth-century work by Moses Cordovero.)

shiva: "seven"; the seven days of mourning following the death of a near relative.

shiviti: A plaque placed in home or synagogue as a meditative device, based around the Hebrew words from Ps. 16:8, *"shiviti Adonai*, I have set God always before me."

"Shema Yisrael": the initial words of the declaration of faith in God's Oneness, Deut. 6:4: "Hear O Israel, the Lord our God, the Lord is One."

sitra ahra: "the other side"; the demonic side of the cosmos, often understood as the impure side of the *sefirot*. Opposite of *sitra d'kedushah*, the "side of holiness."

Sitrei Torah: "Secrets of the Torah," a section of Torah teachings added onto the Zohar.

sod: "mystery" or "secret"; one of the four homiletical means of biblical interpretation.

Talmud: "Study"; the work containing the teachings of the later teachers of Palestine and Babylonia. There are two Talmuds: the Jerusalem Talmud (sometimes referred to as the "Palestinian" Talmud), edited approximately 400 CE, and the Babylonian Talmud, edited approximately 500 CE. In this work, "B." followed by an abbreviation refers to a book of the Babylonian Talmud and "Y." to a book of the Jerusalem Talmud.

Tanakh: the Hebrew Bible. The word is an acronym for the Bible's three parts: Torah; *Nevi'im*, or Prophets; and *Ketuvim*, or Writings.

tefillah: "prayer"; often refers specifically to the "Amidah."

tefillin: "prayer pieces" worn on the arm and head during morning prayers by traditional Jews; from the word *tefillah*.

tehiru: Aramaic for "empty"; used in Lurianic Kabbalah to refer to the primordial space remaining after the divine force retracts itself.

teshuvah: repentance; literally, "returning" (to God). In Kabbalah, located in *Binah*.

theosophical or theosophy: based on mystical insight into God's nature.

theurgic or theurgy: human involvement in the inner life of God, used for beneficent purposes, i.e., to accomplish goals on a level above our own.

Tiferet: the sixth of the ten *sefirot*; "Beauty"; also code language for the Written Torah; sometimes referred to as *Rahamim*, "Compassion"; occasionally short for *Tiferet Yisrael*, "Beauty of Israel."

tikkun: "repair" of the divine sparks in order to restore the divine order.

tikkun hatzot: the mystical practice of arising at midnight to mourn for the ancient Temple.

Tikkun leil Shavuot: ritual Torah study on the first night of the festival of Shavuot as preparation for the receiving of the Torah (reenacted in the day's Torah reading).

tikkun olam: "repair of the world"; in Talmud and traditional liturgy, "repairing of God's Kingdom," performing deeds that recognize God's Kingdom; in Lurianic Kabbalah, restoration of God's unity through human deeds.

Tikkunei ha-Zohar: an appendix to the Zohar with seventy commentaries on the opening word of the Torah; literally, "Rectifications of the Zohar"; also known as *Tikkunim*.

Tisha b'Av: "the Ninth of Av," a fast day commemorating the destruction of the two Temples in Jerusalem and other tragedies in Jewish history.

tzaddik: a charismatic leader and spiritual master who is able to connect divine grace and the world below; literally, "righteous one." Plural: tzaddikim.

Tzedek: "Righteousness," "Justice"; often identified with ninth *sefirah*, *Yesod*; related to "tzaddik."

tzelem: the "image" of God mentioned in Genesis 1.

tzeruf ha-otiyot: forming or chanting letter combinations as a mystical technique; see *hokhmat ha-tzeruf*.

tzimtzum: the "contraction" of God to provide space for creation, particularly in Lurianic Kabbalah.

tzitzit: "fringes" traditionally placed on the four corners of a garment in fulfillment of Num. 15:38–41.

tzorekh gavoha: the "divine need," contrasted with human needs.

unio mystica: mystical union.

Ushpizin: Ritual of inviting seven biblical guests on the seven nights of Sukkot; *ushpizin* means "guests" in Aramaic.

"*V'ahavta*": "And you shall love (the Lord your God)" (Deut. 6:5), the verse following "Shema Yisrael"; also used to denote the entire paragraph recited following "Shema Yisrael" morning and evening.

vav: the sixth letter of the Hebrew alphabet, included in the Four-Letter Name of God; also used to signify six of the ten *sefirot* centered around *Tiferet*.

"*V'hayah im shamoa*": "If you shall obey (the commandments)" (Deut. 11:13); also used to refer to the entire paragraph (Deut. 11:13–21) recited after "V'ahavta" morning and evening.

Wissenschaft des Judentums: nineteenth-century studies of Judaica; "Judaic studies" or "the Science of Judaism."

yehidah: one of the highest levels of soul; "unique," related to *ehad*, "one."

"*Yedid Nefesh*": mystical hymn composed sixteenth century by Eliezer Azikri of Safed; today, a common preface to the *Kabbalat Shabbat* service.

Yesh: That which is material, temporal; opposite of *Ayin*.

Yesod: the ninth of the ten *sefirot*, "Foundation"; generally associated with the generative organs.

yetzer ha-ra: The "evil impulse," which the Rabbis generally believed to be within every human being.

yetzer ha-tov: The "good impulse," also believed to be within each person.

Yetzirah: or *Olam ha-Yetzirah*, "the World of Formation"; the third of the four worlds that comprise the realm of the *sefirot*.

YHVH: English rendering of *Yud, Heh, Vav, Heh*, the letters of the Four-Letter Name, the most sacred Name of God; often understood as conveying the quality of mercy or compassion. In Kabbalah, frequently associated with the *sefirah* of *Tiferet*.

yihud: "unification," generally within the realm of the *sefirot*; plural, *yihudim*, generally refers to devotional practices that would unify the *sefirot*.

yirah: "reverence"; sometimes translated as "fear" or "awe."

yordei merkavah: Those who "descended" to the chariot, i.e., to the mystical experience of the divine palaces.

yud: the tenth letter of the Hebrew alphabet and the first letter of the Four-Letter Name of God; also used to represent *Hokhmah* among the *sefirot*.

Zadok: one of the biblical High Priests, from whom *Kohanim* at Qumran claimed descent.

Ze'ir Anpin: "the Short Face"; corresponds to the complex of six *sefirot* around *Tiferet*; occasionally simply *Ze'ir*.

zivvuga kadisha: "holy mating," generally referring to the unification of the *sefirot Tiferet* and *Malkhut*.

zohama: some form of moral impurity, often related to sensual passion.

Zohar: massive collection of mystical teaching; central kabbalistic text, likely composed thirteenth century in Spain; literally, "radiance," "brightness."

Zohar Hadash: "The New Zohar," teachings added into the original text of the Zohar.

Bibliography

PRIMARY HEBREW SOURCES INCLUDING TRANSLATIONS.
Aggadat Bereshit. On Davka Judaic Classics Library II CD-ROM.
Alpha Beta d'Ben Sira. See *Otzar ha-Midrashim*.
Alter, Judah Leib of Ger. *Sefat Emet*. 2 vols. Jerusalem, n.d.
Ashkenazi, Judah ben Shimon. *Be'er Hetev*. On Davka Judaic Classics Library
   II CD-ROM.
Avot d'Rabbi Natan. On Davka Judaic Classics Library II CD-ROM.
Azikri, Eleazar. *Sefer Haredim ha-Shalem*. Jerusalem, 1990.
Bahya ben Asher. *Al ha-Torah*. Edited by C. D. Chavel. 3 vols. Jerusalem: Mossad
   ha-Rav Kook, 1994.
———. *Kad ha-Kemah*. Vol. 1. New York, 1960. Found at hebrewbooks.org.
Bahya ibn Pakuda. *Hovot ha-Levavot/Duties of the Heart*. Translated by M. Hyam-
   son. 2 vols. New York: Feldheim, 1978.
Barukh ben Avraham of Kosov. *Tiferet ha-Yehudi*. Warsaw, 1930. Found at
   hebrewbooks.org.
Batei Midrashot. Edited by A. Y. Wertheimer. Jerusalem: Mossad ha-Rav Kook,
   1950.
Berger, Yisrael. *Simhat Yisrael*, including *Torat Simha*. Piotrkov, 1911. Found at
   hebrewbooks.org.
Cohen, Seymour J., trans. *The Holy Letter: A Study in Jewish Sexual Morality (Iggeret
   ha-Kodesh.)* New York: KTAV, 1976.
Cordovero, Moshe. *Elimah Rabbati*. Lvov: Cohen, 1881. Found at hebrewbooks
   .org.
———. *Or Ne'erav*. Jerusalem, 1990. See also Ira Robinson's translation below.
———. *Pardes Rimonim*. Jerusalem: Yerid ha-Sefarim, 2000.
———. *Shi'ur Komah*. Warsaw: Isaac Goldman, 1883. Found at hebrewbooks.org.
———. *Tomer Devorah*. Translated by Louis Jacobs as *The Palm Tree of Deborah*.
   London: Vallentine Mitchell, 1960.

———. *Tomer Devorah*. Translated by Moshe Miller as *The Palm Tree of Devorah*. Southfield MI: Targum, 1993.

De Vidas, Elijah. *Reishit Hokhmah ha-Shalem*. 3 vols. Jerusalem: Or ha-Musar, 1984.

Dov Ber, the Maggid of Mezeritch. *Maggid Devarav l'Ya'akov* [*Likkutei Amarim*]. Lemberg, 1863. Found at hebrewbooks.org; also Jerusalem, 1971, and Schatz-Uffenheimer edition, Jerusalem: Magnes, 1990; pagination according to Schatz-Uffenheimer unless otherwise noted.

———. *Or Torah*. Lublin, 1910. Found at hebrewbooks.org.

Dov Ber of Lubavitch. *Ma'amorei Admor Ho-Emtzoee Kuntreisim* [including *Kuntres ha-Hitpa'alut*]. Brooklyn: Kehot, 1991. See also translation by Jacobs, below.

Elimelekh of Lizensk. *Noam Elimelekh*. Jerusalem: Yerid ha-Sefarim, 2000.

Gikatilla, Joseph. *Sha'arei Orah*. Warsaw: Orgelbrand, 1883. Found at hebrewbooks .org. Translated by Avi Weinstein as *Gates of Light: Sha'are Orah*. San Francisco: HarperSanFrancisco, 1994.

Hayman, A. Peter. *Sefer Yesira: Edition, Translation, and Text-Critical Commentary*. Tubingen: J. C. B. Mohr [Paul Siebeck], 2004.

Heikhalot books, on Davka Judaic Classics Library II CD-Rom, and see below, Schafer, *Synopse*.

Heller, Meshullam Feibush of Zbarazh. *Yosher Divrei Emet ha-Shalem*. Bnei Brak: Tiferet ha-Sefer, 1999.

Horowitz, Isaiah. *Shnei Luhot ha-Brit*. 5 vols. Jerusalem: Sha'arey Ziv, 1993. See also translation by Krassen, below.

Horowitz, Jacob Isaac. *Zikaron Zot*. Warsaw, 1869. Found at hebrewbooks.org.

———. *Zot Zikaron*. Lvov, 1851. Found at hebrewbooks.org.

Ibn Gabbai, Meir. *Avodat ha-Kodesh*. Jerusalem: Y. Beker, 2010.

Isaac of Akko. *Me'irat Einayim*. Jerusalem, n.d. Found at hebrewbooks.org.

Isserles, Moses. *Torat ha-Olah*. Prague: Mordecai Ben Gershom Katz, 1570. Found at hebrewbooks.org.

Jacob Aryeh of Radzymin. *Bikkurei Aviv*. London: Narod, 1947. Found at hebrewbooks .org.

Jacob ben Asher. *Arba'ah Turim*. New York: Saphrograph, n.d.

Jacob Isaac of Przysucha. *Nifla'ot ha-Yehudi*. Jerusalem, 1987. Found at hebrewbooks .org.

Jacob Joseph of Polonnoye. *Ben Porat Yosef*. Lemberg, n.d. and Karetz, 1781. Found at hebrewbooks.org.

———. *Toldot Ya'akov Yosef*. 2 vols. Jerusalem, 1973. Found at hebrewbooks.org.

Jacobs, Louis, trans. *The Palm Tree of Deborah*. London: Vallentine Mitchell, 1960.

———, trans. *Tract on Ecstasy*. London: Vallentine Mitchell, 2006.

Kaplan, Aryeh, trans. *Bahir*. Northvale NJ: Jason Aronson, 1995.

———, trans. *Rabbi Nachman's Teachings*. Edited by Zvi Aryeh Rosenfeld. Unknown, n.d.

Karo, Joseph. *Maggid Mesharim*. Zolkava, 1773. Found at hebrewbooks.org.

Keter Shem Tov. Brooklyn: Kehot, 2001.

Kook, Abraham Isaac. *Abraham Isaac Kook: The Lights of Penitence, The Moral Principles, Lights of Holiness, Essays, Letters, and Poems*. Translated by Ben Zion Bokser. New York: Paulist Press, 1978.

———. *Hadarav: Personal Chapters*. 2nd ed. Edited by Ran Sarid. Ramat Gan: 2002.

_____. *Iggerot ha-Reiyah*. Jerusalem: Mossad ha-Rav Kook, 1984. Found at hebrewbooks.org.

———. *Musar Avikha*, fourth section of collection. Jerusalem: Mossad ha-Rav Kook, 1985.

———. *Orot*. Translated and annotated by Bezalel Naor. Northvale NJ: Jason Aronson, 1993.

———. *Orot ha-Kodesh*. 2 vols. Jerusalem: Ha-Agudah le'Hotza'at Sifrei ha-Riyha Kook, 1938. Found at hebrewbooks.org.

Krassen, Miles, trans. *Isaiah Horowitz: The Generations of Adam*. New York: Paulist Press, 1996.

Leiner, Mordecai Yosef. *Mei ha-Shiloah*. 2 vols. B'nei Brak: Sifrei Kodesh Mishor, 1990.

Levi Yitzhak of Berditchev. *Kedushat Levi ha-Shalem*. Jerusalem: Torat Ha-Netzah, 1993.

Loew, Judah. *Hiddushei Aggadot*. On Davka Judaic Classics Library II CD-Rom.

———. *Netivot Olam*. On Davka Judaic Classics Library II CD-Rom.

Ma'arekhet ha-Elohut. Mantua, 1558. Found at hebrewbooks.org.

Maimonides, Moses. *The Guide of the Perplexed*. Translated by Shlomo Pines. 2 vols. Chicago: University of Chicago Press, 1963

———. *Mishneh Torah*. On Davka Judaic Classics Library II CD-Rom.

———. *Sefer ha-Mitzvot*. Jerusalem: Mossad ha-Rav Kook, 1975.

Matt, Daniel C. *The Zohar: The Pritzker Edition*. 9 vols. to date. Stanford: Stanford University Press, 2004–.

Menahem Mendel of Kotzk. *Amud ha-Emet*. Tel Aviv: Ha-Mefitsim, 1981.

———. *Emet ve-Emunah*. Jerusalem: Otzar ha-Sefarim shel Yeshivat Amshinov, 2003.

Menahem Mendel of Vitebsk. *P'ri ha-Aretz*. Kapost, 1857. Found at hebrewbooks .org.

Menahem Nahum of Chernobyl. *Me'or Einayim*. Slavuta, 1798. Found at hebrewbooks .org.

Midrash Rabbah volumes. On Davka Judaic Classics Library II CD-Rom.

Midrash Tanhuma. On Davka Judaic Classics Library II CD-Rom.

Midrash Tehillim. On Davka Judaic Classics Library II CD-Rom.

Miktzat Ma'asei Torah. See Vermes, *Complete Dead Sea Scrolls in English.*

Miller, Moshe, trans. *The Palm Tree of Devorah.* Southfield MI: Targum, 1993.

Nahmanides, Moses. *Peirush al ha-Torah.* 2 vols. Jerusalem: Mossad ha-Rav Kook, 1966–67.

Nathan of Nemirov. *Shivhei ha-Ran.* Betar Ilit, 2009. Found at hebrewbooks.org.

———. *Sihot ha-Ran.* Betar Ilit, 2010. Found at hebrewbooks.org. See also translation by Kaplan, above.

Otzar ha-Ge'onim. Edited by Binyamin M. Levin. Vol. 4. Jerusalem, 1931. Found at hebrewbooks.org.

Otzar ha-Midrashim. On Davka Judaic Classics Library II CD-Rom.

Palaggi, Hayyim. *Torah v'Hayyim.* Salonika, 1846. Found at hebrewbooks.org.

Pesikta d'Rav Kahana. On Davka Judaic Classics Library II CD-Rom.

Pesikta Rabbati. On Davka Judaic Classics Library II CD-Rom.

Pirkei d'Rabbi Eliezer. On Davka Judaic Classics Library II CD-Rom.

Rabinowitz, Jacob Tzvi. *Beit Ya'akov.* Piatrkov, 1900. Found at hebrewbooks .org.

Robinson, Ira, trans. *Moshe Cordovero's Introduction to Kabbalah: An Annotated Translation of His "Or Ne'erav."* New York: Yeshiva University Press, 1994.

Schneerson, Menahem Mendel. *Iggerot Kodesh.* Vol. 8. Brooklyn: Kehot, 1984. Found at hebrewbooks.org.

———. *Sefer ha-Sihot 5752.* Brooklyn: Kehot, 1993.

———. *Torat Menahem: Hitva'aduyot.* Various vols. Brooklyn: Kehot, various dates and some undated. Found at hebrewbooks.org.

Schochet, Jacob Immanuel, trans. and annot. *Tzava'at HaRivash: The Testament of Rabbi Israel Baal Shem Tov.* Brooklyn: Kehot, 1998.

Seder Eliyahu Rabbah. On Davka Judaic Classics Library II CD-Rom.

Sefer Yetzirah: The Book of Creation. Translated by Aryeh Kaplan. Boston: Weiser Books, 1997; see also translation by Hayman, above.

Shapira, Kalonymus K. *B'nei Mahshavah Tovah.* Translated by Andrea Cohen-Keiner as *Conscious Community: A Guide to Inner Work.* Northvale NJ: Jason Aronson, 1996.

———. *Chovas HaTalmidim: The Students' Obligation,* and *Sheloshah Ma'amarim: Three Discourses.* New York: Feldheim, 2011.

———. *Sacred Fire: Torah from the Years of Fury 1939–1942.* Translated by J. Hershy Worch. Edited by Deborah Miller. Northvale NJ: Jason Aronson, 2000.

Shneur Zalman of Lyady. *Tanya.* Translated by N. Mindel, N. Mangel, Z. Posner, and J. I. Schochet. Bilingual 2nd ed. Brooklyn: Kehot, 1984.

———. *Torah Or.* Brooklyn: Kehot, 2001. Found at hebrewbooks.org.

Shulhan Arukh. Joseph Karo; Moses Isserles. On Davka Judaic Classics Library II CD-Rom.

Siddur Etz Chayim: The Complete Art Scroll Siddur, Nusach Sefarad. Edited and with commentary by Nosson Scherman. Brooklyn: Mesorah, 1985.

Siddur Kol Ya'akov: The Complete Art Scroll Siddur, Nusach Ashkenaz. Edited and with commentary by Nosson Scherman. Brooklyn: Mesorah, 1984.

Sifrei. On Davka Judaic Classics Library II CD-Rom; see also translation of Reuven Hammer, *Sifre: A Tannaitic Commentary on the Book of Deuteronomy.* New Haven: Yale University Press, 1987.

Sperling, Harry, and Maurice Simon, trans. *The Zohar.* 2nd ed. 5 vols. London: Soncino, 1984. See also translation by Matt, above.

Sternharz, Nathan. *Hayyei Moharan.* Lvov, 1874. Found at hebrewbooks.org.

Talmud, Bavli and *Yerushalmi.* On Davka Judaic Classics Library II CD-Rom.

Tanakh, NJPS translation.

Tikkunei ha-Zohar. On Davka Judaic Classics Library II CD-Rom.

Tikkun Leil Shavuot ha-Mefo'ar. Brooklyn: Makhon ha-Pe'er, 2000.

Tosefta. On Davka Judaic Classics Library II CD-Rom.

Tzava'at ha-Rivash. Brooklyn: Kehot, 1999. See also translation by Schochet, above.

Vermes, Geza, trans. *The Complete Dead Sea Scrolls in English.* Rev. ed. London: Penguin, 2004.

Vital, Hayyim. *Eitz ha-Da'at Tov.* Zolkava, 1871. Found at hebrewbooks.org.

———. *Eitz Hayim.* Richmond Hill NY, 1975.

———. *Likkutei ha-Shas.* Livorno, 1790. Found at hebrewbooks.org.

———. *Likkutim Hadashim.* Jerusalem, 1985.

———. *Sefer ha-Gilgulim.* Frankfort, 1684. Found at hebrewbooks.org.

———. *Sefer ha-Hezyonot.* Jerusalem, 1954.

———. *Sha'arei Kedushah.* Jerusalem, 1926. Found at hebrewbooks.org.

———. *Sha'ar ha-Gilgulim.* Jerusalem: n.p., 1863. Found at hebrewbooks.org.

———. *Sha'ar Ruah ha-Kodesh.* Jerusalem, 1961. Found at hebrewbooks.org.

Walden, Aaron. *Kol Simha.* Jerusalem: Nofet Tzufim, 1997.

Walden, Moses M. *Nifla'ot ha-Rebbe.* Bilgoraj, 1911. Found at hebrewbooks.org.

Yalkut Shimoni. On Davka Judaic Classics Library II CD-Rom.

Yehudah he-Hasid. *Sefer Hasidim.* Jerusalem: Mossad ha-Rav Kook, 1991.

OTHER PUBLISHED SOURCES

Abelson, Joshua. *Jewish Mysticism.* London: G. Bell and Sons, 1913.

Arbel, Vita Daphna. *Beholders of Divine Secrets: Mysticism and Myth in the Hekhalot and Merkavah Literature.* Albany: SUNY Press, 2003.

Ariel, David S. *The Mystic Quest: An Introduction to Jewish Mysticism.* Northvale NJ: Jason Aronson, 1988, and revised version: *Kabbalah: The Mystic Quest in Judaism.* Lanham MD: Rowman & Littlefield, 2005.

Aronson, Harvey B. *Love and Sympathy in Theravada Buddhism.* Delhi: Motilal Banarsidass, 1980.

Artson, Bradley Shavit. "From the Periphery to the Center: Kabbalah and Conservative Judaism," *United Synagogue Review* (Spring 2005).

Assaf, David. *The Regal Way: The Life and Times of Rabbi Israel of Ruzhin*. Stanford: Stanford University Press, 2002.

———. *Untold Tales of the Hasidim: Crisis and Discontent in the History of Hasidism*. Waltham: Brandeis University Press, 2010.

Ausubel, Nathan, ed. *A Treasury of Jewish Folklore*. New York: Crown, 1948.

Bar-Levav, Avriel. "Ritualizing Death and Dying: The Ethical Will of Naphtali Ha-Kohen Katz." In Fine, *Judaism in Practice*, 155–67.

Barnai, Jacob. "The Historiography of the Hasidic Immigration to *Erets Yisrael*." In Rapoport-Albert, *Hasidism Reappraised*, 376–88.

Ben-Amos, Dan. "Israel ben Eliezer, the Baal Shem Tov." In Fine, *Judaism in Practice*, 498–512.

Ben-Shlomo, Joseph. "Gershom Scholem on Pantheism in the Kabbala." In Mendes-Flohr, *Gershom Scholem*, 56–72.

Berger, David. "Did the Rebbe Identify Himself as the Messiah—and What Do His Hasidim Believe Today?" Published July 21, 2014. Accessed April 2, 2015. http://www.tabletmag.com/jewish-news-and-politics/179435/berger-rebbe-messiah.

Berlin, Adele, and Marc Zvi Brettler, eds. *The Jewish Study Bible*. New York: Oxford, 2004.

Bloom, Harold, ed. *Gershom Scholem*. New York: Chelsea House, 1987.

Blumenthal, David R. ed. *Approaches to Judaism in Medieval Times*. Chico CA: Scholars Press, 1984–88.

———. *The Banality of Good and Evil: Moral Lessons from the Shoah and Jewish Tradition*. Washington DC: Georgetown University Press, 2009.

———. *Facing the Abusing God: A Theology of Protest*. Louisville: Westminster John Knox, 1993.

———. *Understanding Jewish Mysticism: A Source Reader*. Vol. 1, *The Merkabah Tradition and the Zoharic Tradition*. New York: KTAV, 1978.

Bokser, Ben Zion. *The Jewish Mystical Tradition*. New York: Pilgrim, 1981.

Buber, Martin. *Tales of the Hasidim: Early Masters*. New York: Schocken, 1947.

———. *Tales of the Hasidim: Later Masters*. New York: Schocken, 1948.

Buxbaum, Yitzhak. *Jewish Spiritual Practices*. Northvale NJ: Jason Aronson, 1990.

———. *The Light and Fire of the Baal Shem Tov*. New York: Continuum, 2005.

Chernus, Ira. *Mysticism in Rabbinic Judaism: Studies in the History of Midrash*. Berlin: Walter de Gruyter, 1982.

Cohen, Arthur A., and Paul Mendes-Flohr. *Contemporary Jewish Religious Thought*. New York: Scribner, 1987.

Cohen, Martin Samuel. *Our Haven and Our Strength: The Book of Psalms*. New York: Aviv, 2004.

———. *The Shi'ur Qomah: Liturgy and Theurgy in Pre-Kabbalistic Jewish Mysticism.* Lanham MD: University Press of America, 1983.

———. *The Shi'ur Qomah: Texts and Recensions.* Tubingen: J. C. B. Mohr [Paul Siebeck], 1985.

Dan, Joseph. *The Ancient Jewish Mysticism.* Tel Aviv: MOD Books, 1993.

———, ed. *The Early Kabbalah.* New York: Paulist Press, 1986.

———. "Gershom Scholem's Reconstruction of Early Kabbalah." In Bloom, *Gershom Scholem,* 155–78.

———. "Hasidism: The Third Century." In Rapoport-Albert, *Hasidism Reappraised,* 415–26.

———, ed. *The Heart and the Fountain: An Anthology of Jewish Mystical Experiences.* New York: Oxford University Press, 2002.

———. *Jewish Mysticism and Jewish Ethics.* Seattle: University of Washington Press, 1986.

———. *Jewish Mysticism: The Modern Period.* Northvale NJ: Jason Aronson, 1999.

———. "The Language of the Mystics in Medieval Germany." In Dan and Grozinger, *Mysticism, Magic and Kabbalah,* 6–27.

———. "The Religious Experience of the *Merkavah.*" In Green, *Jewish Spirituality from the Bible through the Middle Ages,* 289–307.

———, ed. *Studies in Jewish Mysticism.* Cambridge: Association for Jewish Studies, 1982.

———. *The Teachings of Hasidism.* West Orange NJ: Behrman House, 1983.

———. *The "Unique Cherub" Circle: A School of Mystics and Esoterics in Medieval Germany.* Tubingen: J. C. B. Mohr [Paul Siebeck], 1999.

———. and Karl Erich Grozinger, eds. *Mysticism, Magic and Kabbalah in Ashkenazi Judaism.* Berlin: Walter de Gruyter, 1995.

Davies, W. D. "From Schweitzer to Scholem: Reflections on Sabbatai Svi." In Saperstein, *Essential Papers,* 335–74.

Dennis, Geoffrey W. *The Encyclopedia of Jewish Myth, Magic and Mysticism.* Woodbury MN: Llewellyn Publications, 2007.

Deutsch, Nathaniel. *The Gnostic Imagination: Gnosticism, Mandaeism and Merkabah Mysticism.* Leiden: Brill, 1995.

———. "Rabbi Nahman of Bratslav: The *Zaddik* as Androgyne." In Magid, *God's Voice from the Void,* 193–215.

Dorff, Elliot N. "Walking with God in Modern Jewish Thought." In *Walking with God* curriculum, edited by Bradley Shavit Artson and Deborah Silver. Los Angeles, n.d.

Dresner, Samuel H. *Heschel, Hasidism, and Halakha.* New York: Fordham University Press, 2002.

———. *The World of a Hasidic Master: Levi Yitzhak of Berditchev.* New York: Shapolsky, 1986.

———. *The Zaddik: The Doctrine of the Zaddik according to the Writings of Rabbi Yaakov Yosef of Polnoy*. Northvale NJ: Jason Aronson, 1994.

Dynner, Glenn, ed. *Holy Dissent: Jewish and Christian Mystics in Eastern Europe*. Detroit: Wayne State University Press, 2011.

———. *Men of Silk: The Hasidic Conquest of Polish Jewish Society*. New York: Oxford University Press, 2006.

Eilberg-Schwartz, Howard, ed. *People of the Body: Jews and Judaism from an Embodied Perspective*. Albany: SUNY Press, 1992.

Eisen, Robert. "The Revival of Jewish Mysticism and Its Implications for the Future of Jewish Faith." In *Creating the Jewish Future*, edited by Michael Brown and Bernard Lightman. Walnut Creek CA: Altamira, 1999.

Elior, Rachel. "Between *Yesh* and *Ayin*: The Doctrine of the *Zaddik* in the Works of Jacob Isaac, the Seer of Lublin." In *Jewish History*, edited by Ada Rapoport-Alpert and Steven J. Zipperstein, 393–456. London: Peter Halban, 1988.

———. "Early Forms of Jewish Mysticism." In *The Cambridge History of Judaism*, edited by Steven T. Katz, 4:749–91. Cambridge: Cambridge University Press, 2006.

———. "*HaBaD*: The Contemplative Ascent to God." In Green, *Jewish Spirituality from the Sixteenth-Century Revival to the Present*, 157–205.

———. *Jewish Mysticism: The Infinite Expression of Freedom*. Oxford: Littman, 2007.

———. "The Lubavitch Messianic Resurgence: The Historical and Mystical Background 1939–1996." In Schafer and Cohen, *Toward the Millenium*, 383–408.

———. "Messianic Expectations and Spiritualization of Religious Life in the Sixteenth Century." In Ruderman, *Essential Papers on Jewish Culture*, 283–98.

———. *The Mystical Origins of Hasidism*. Oxford: Littman, 2006.

———. "The Paradigms of *Yesh* and *Ayin* in Hasidic Thought." In Rapoport-Albert, *Hasidism Reappraised*, 168–79.

———. *The Paradoxical Ascent to God: The Kabbalistic Theosophy of Habad Hasidism*. Albany: SUNY Press, 1993.

———. *The Three Temples: On the Emergence of Jewish Mysticism*. Oxford: Littman, 2004.

_____ and Peter Schafer, eds. *Creation and Re-creation in Jewish Thought*. Tubingen: Mohr, 2005.

Etkes, Immanuel. *The Besht: Magician, Mystic and Leader*. Waltham: Brandeis University Press, 2005.

———. "The Study of Hasidism: Past Trends and New Directions." In Rapoport-Albert, *Hasidism Reappraised*, 447–64.

Ettinger, Shmuel. "Hasidism and the *Kahal* in Eastern Europe." In Rapoport-Albert, *Hasidism Reappraised*, 63–75.

Faierstein, Morris M. *All Is in the Hands of Heaven: The Teachings of Rabbi Mordecai Joseph Leiner of Izbica*. Hoboken NJ: KTAV, 1989.

———."'God's Need for the Commandments' in Medieval Kabbalah." *Conservative Judaism* 36, no.1 (Fall 1982): 45–59.

———, trans. *Jewish Mystical Autobiographies*. New York: Paulist Press, 1999.

———. "Personal Redemption in Hasidism." In Rapoport-Albert, *Hasidism Reappraised*, 214–24.

Fine, Lawrence. "The Contemplative Practice of *Yihudim* in Lurianic Kabbalah." In Green, *Jewish Spirituality from the Sixteenth-Century Revival to the Present*, 64–98.

———, ed. *Essential Papers on Kabbalah*. New York: New York University Press, 1995.

———, ed. *Judaism in Practice from the Middle Ages through the Early Modern Period*. Princeton: Princeton University Press, 2001.

———. "Kabbalistic Texts." In Holtz, *Back to the Sources*, 305–59.

———. "*Maggidic* Revelation in the Teachings of Isaac Luria." In *Mystics, Philosophers, and Politicians: Essays in Jewish Intellectual History in Honor of Alexander Altmann*, edited by Jehuda Reinharz and Daniel Swetschinski, 141–57. Durham NC: Duke University Press, 1982.

———. "New Approaches to the Study of Kabbalistic Life in 16th-Century Safed." In Greenspahn, *Jewish Mysticism and Kabbalah*, 91–111.

———. *Physician of the Soul, Healer of the Cosmos: Isaac Luria and His Kabbalistic Fellowship*. Stanford: Stanford University Press, 2003.

———. "Purifying the Body in the Name of the Soul: The Problem of the Body in Sixteenth-Century Kabbalah." In Eilberg-Schwartz, *People of the Body*, 117–42.

———. "Rav Abraham Isaac Kook and the Jewish Mystical Tradition." In Lawrence J. Kaplan and Shatz, *Rabbi Abraham Isaac Kook*, 23–40.

———. *Safed Spirituality*. Mahwah NJ: Paulist Press, 1984.

———. "The Study of Torah as a Rite of Theurgical Contemplation in Lurianic Kabbalah." In Blumenthal, *Approaches to Judaism in Medieval Times*, 3:29–40.

———, Eitan Fishbane, and Or N. Rose, eds. *Jewish Mysticism and the Spiritual Life: Classical Texts, Contemporary Reflections*. Woodstock VT: Jewish Lights, 2011.

Fishbane, Eitan P. *As Light before Dawn: The Inner World of a Medieval Kabbalist*. Stanford: Stanford University Press, 2009.

———. *The Sabbath Soul: Mystical Reflections on the Transformative Power of Holy Time*. Woodstock VT: Jewish Lights, 2012.

———. "The *Zohar*: Masterpiece of Jewish Mysticism." In Greenspahn, *Jewish Mysticism and Kabbalah*, 49–67.

Fishbane, Michael. Haftarah commentary in *Etz Hayim: Torah and Commentary*. New York: Rabbinical Assembly and Jewish Publication Society, 2001.

Fox, Marvin. "Rav Kook: Neither Philosopher nor Kabbalist." In Lawrence J. Kaplan and Shatz, *Rabbi Abraham Isaac Kook*, 78–87.

Freehof, Solomon. *The Book of Isaiah: A Commentary*. New York: UAHC, 1972.

Garb, Jonathan. *The Chosen Will Become Herds*. New Haven: Yale University Press, 2009.

———. "Rabbi Kook and His Sources: From Kabbalistic Historiosophy to National Mysticism." In *Studies in Modern Religions, Religious Movements and the Babi-Baha'i Faiths*, edited by Moshe Sharon, 77-96. Boston: Brill, 2004.

Gellman, Jerome I. "Poetry of Spirituality." In Lawrence J. Kaplan and Shatz, *Rabbi Abraham Isaac Kook*, 88-119.

Giller, Pinchas. *The Enlightened Will Shine: Symbolization and Theurgy in the Later Strata of the Zohar*. Albany: SUNY Press, 1993.

———. *Kabbalah: A Guide for the Perplexed*. New York: Continuum, 2011.

———. "Kabbalah and Contemporary Judaism." In Greenspahn, *Jewish Mysticism and Kabbalah*, 231-38.

———. *Reading the Zohar: The Sacred Text of the Kabbalah*. New York: Oxford University Press, 2001.

Ginsburg, Elliot K. *The Sabbath in the Classical Kabbalah*. Albany: SUNY Press, 1989.

Goetschel, Roland. "*Torah Lishmah* as a Central Concept in the *Degel Machaneh Efrayim* of Moses Hayyim Ephraim of Sudylkow." In Rapoport-Albert, *Hasidism Reappraised*, 258-67.

Goldish, Matt. "Kabbalah, Academia, and Authenticity," *Tikkun* 20, no. 5 (Sept.-Oct. 2005).

———. "Mystical Messianism: From the Renaissance to the Enlightenment." In Greenspahn, *Jewish Mysticism and Kabbalah*, 115-38.

Goshen-Gottstein, Alon. *The Sinner and the Amnesiac: The Rabbinic Invention of Elisha ben Abuya and Eleazar ben Arach*. Stanford: Stanford University Press, 2000.

Graetz, Heinrich. *History of the Jews*. 6 vols. Abridged translation. Philadelphia: Jewish Publication Society, 1891-98.

Graves, Robert, and Raphael Patai. *The Hebrew Myths*. New York: Doubleday, 1964.

Green, Arthur. "Abraham Joshua Heschel: Recasting Hasidism for Moderns." *Modern Judaism* 29, no. 1 (2009): 62-79.

———. "Early Hasidism: Some Old/New Questions." In Rapoport-Albert, *Hasidism Reappraised*, 441-46.

———. *A Guide to the Zohar*. Stanford: Stanford University Press, 2004.

———. "Hasidism." In Arthur A. Cohen and Mendes-Flohr, *Contemporary Jewish Religious Thought*, 317-23.

———, ed. *Jewish Spirituality from the Bible through the Middle Ages*. New York: Crossroad, 1986.

———, ed. *Jewish Spirituality from the Sixteenth-Century Revival to the Present*. New York: Crossroad, 1987.

———. *Keter: The Crown of God in Early Jewish Mysticism*. Princeton: Princeton University Press, 1997.

———. *The Language of Truth: The Torah Commentary of the Sefat Emet, Rabbi Yehudah Leib Alter of Ger*. Philadelphia: Jewish Publication Society, 1998.

———, trans. *Menahem Nahum of Chernobyl*. New York: Paulist Press, 1982.

———. *Seek My Face, Speak My Name*. Northvale NJ: Jason Aronson, 1992.

———. "Teachings of the Hasidic Masters." In Holtz, *Back to the Sources*, 361–401.

———. "Three Warsaw Mystics." *Jerusalem Studies of Jewish Thought* 13 (1996): 1–58.

———. *Tormented Master: A Life of Rabbi Nahman of Bratslav*. Tuscaloosa: University of Alabama Press, 1979.

———. "Typologies of Leadership and the Hasidic *Zaddiq*." In Green, *Jewish Spirituality from the Sixteenth-Century Revival to the Present*, 127–56.

———. "The *Zaddiq* as Axis Mundi in Later Judaism." In Fine, *Essential Papers on Kabbalah*, 291–314.

Greenbaum, Avraham. *Under the Table and How to Get Up: Jewish Pathways of Spiritual Growth*. Jerusalem: Tsohar, 1991.

Greenspahn, Frederick E., ed. *Jewish Mysticism and Kabbalah: New Insights and Scholarship*. New York: New York University Press, 2011.

Greenstein, David. *Roads to Utopia: The Walking Stories of the Zohar*. Stanford: Stanford University Press, 2014.

Grozinger, Karl Erich. "Between Magic and Religion—Ashkenazi Hasidic Piety." In Dan and Grozinger, *Mysticism, Magic and Kabbalah*, 28–43.

Hallamish, Moshe. *An Introduction to the Kabbalah*. Albany: SUNY Press, 1999.

———. "The Teachings of R. Menahem Mendel of Vitebsk." In Rapoport-Albert, *Hasidism Reappraised*, 268–87.

Hammer, Reuven. *Or Hadash: A Commentary on Siddur Sim Shalom*. New York: Rabbinical Assembly, 2003.

Harari, Yuval. "What Is a Magical Text? Methodological Reflections Aimed at Redefining Early Jewish Magic." In Shaked, *Officina Magica: Essays on the Practice of Magic in Antiquity*, 91–124. Leiden: Brill, 2005.

Hecker, Joel. *Mystical Bodies, Mystical Meals: Eating and Embodiment in Medieval Kabbalah*. Detroit: Wayne State University Press, 2005.

Hellner-Eshed, Melila. *A River Flows from Eden: The Language of Mystical Experience in the Zohar*. Stanford: Stanford University Press, 2009.

Heschel, Abraham Joshua. *Abraham Joshua Heschel: Essential Writings*. Selected with introduction by Susannah Heschel. Maryknoll NY: Orbis, 2011.

———. *The Circle of the Baal Shem Tov: Studies in Hasidism*. Edited by Samuel Dresner. Chicago: University of Chicago Press, 1985.

———. *God in Search of Man*. New York: Schocken, 1966.

———. *Heavenly Torah: As Refracted through the Generations*. Edited and translated by Gordon Tucker. New York: Continuum, 2005; also original, *Torah min ha-Shamayim b'Aspaklarya shel ha-Dorot*. 3 vols. New York: Soncino, 1962, 1965; Jerusalem: Jewish Theological Seminary Press, 1990.

———. *The Ineffable Name of God: Man*. Translated by Morton M. Leifman. New York: Continuum, 2004.

———. *The Insecurity of Freedom: Essays on Human Existence*. New York: Schocken, 1972.

———. *Man Is Not Alone*. Philadelphia: Jewish Publication Society, 1951.

———. *Man's Quest for God*. New York: Charles Scribner's Sons, 1954.

———. *Moral Grandeur and Spiritual Audacity*. New York: Farrar, Straus and Giroux, 1996.

———. "The Mystical Element in Judaism." In *The Jews*, edited by Louis Finkelstein, 2:602-23. Philadelphia: Jewish Publication Society, 1949.

———. *A Passion for Truth*. New York: Farrar, Straus and Giroux, 1973.

———. *Prophetic Inspiration after the Prophets*. Hoboken NJ: KTAV, 1996.

———. *The Prophets*. Philadelphia: Jewish Publication Society, 1962.

———. *Who Is Man?* Stanford: Stanford University Press, 1965.

Himmelfarb, Martha. "Merkavah Mysticism since Scholem: Rachel Elior's *The Three Temples*." In *Wege Mystischer Gotteserfahrung: Judentum, Christentum und Islam/Mystical Approaches to God: Judaism, Christianity and Islam*, edited by Peter Schafer, 19-36. Munich: Oldenbourg Wissenschaftsverlag, 2006.

Hirsch, Samson Raphael. *Judaism Eternal*. Vol. 1. London: Soncino, 1956.

Hoffman, Edward, ed. *Opening the Inner Gates: New Paths in Kabbalah and Psychology*. Boston: Shambhala, 1995.

Hoffman, Lawrence A., ed. *My People's Prayer Book*, various volumes. Woodstock VT: Jewish Lights, 1997-2005.

Holtz, Barry W., ed. *Back to the Sources: Reading the Classic Jewish Texts*. New York: Summit Books, 1984.

Horsley, Richard A. "Popular Messianic Movements around the Time of Jesus." In Saperstein, *Essential Papers*, 83-110.

Hundert, Gershon David, ed. *Essential Papers on Hasidism: Origins to Present*. New York: New York University Press, 1991.

———. *Jews in Poland-Lithuania in the Eighteenth Century: A Genealogy of Modernity*. Berkeley: University of California Press, 2004.

Huss, Boaz. "The Formation of Jewish Mysticism and Its Impact on the Reception of Rabbi Abraham Abulafia in Contemporary Kabbalah." In *Religion and Its Other*, edited by Heike Bock, Jorg Feuchter, and Michi Knecht, 142-62. Frankfurt: Campus, 2008.

———, Marco Pasi, and Kocku von Stuckrad, eds. *Kabbalah and Modernity*. Leiden: Brill, 2010.

Idel, Moshe. "Abraham J. Heschel on Mysticism and Hasidism." *Modern Judaism* 29, no. 1 (Feb. 2009): 80-105.

———. *Absorbing Perfections: Kabbalah and Interpretation*. New Haven: Yale University Press, 2002.

———. "Abulafia's Secrets of the Guide: A Linguistic Turn." In Wolfson, Ivry, and Arkush, *Perspectives on Jewish Thought and Mysticism*, 289–329.

———. "*Adonay Sefatay Tiftah*: Models of Understanding Prayer in Early Hasidism." *Kabbalah: Journal for the Study of Jewish Mystical Texts* 18 (2008): 7–111.

———. "An Anonymous Kabbalistic Commentary on *Shir ha-Yihud*." In Dan and Grozinger, *Mysticism, Magic and Kabbalah*, 139–54.

———. *Ascensions on High in Jewish Mysticism: Pillars, Lines, Ladders*. Budapest: Central European University Press, 2005.

———. *Ben: Sonship and Jewish Mysticism*. New York: Continuum, 2007.

———. *Enchanted Chains: Techniques and Rituals in Jewish Mysticism*. Los Angeles: Cherub, 2005.

———. *Golem: Jewish Magical and Mystical Traditions on the Artificial Anthropoid*. Albany: SUNY Press, 1990.

———. *Hasidism: Between Ecstasy and Magic*. Albany: SUNY Press, 1995.

———. "Jewish Magic from the Renaissance Period to Early Hasidism." In *Religion, Science and Magic: In Concert and in Conflict*, edited by Jacob Neusner, Ernest S. Frerichs, and Paul V. M. Flesher, 82–117. New York: Oxford University Press, 1989.

———. *Kabbalah and Eros*. New Haven: Yale University Press, 2005.

———. *Kabbalah: New Perspectives*. New Haven: Yale University Press, 1988.

———. "Kabbalistic Prayer and Colors." In Blumenthal, *Approaches to Judaism in Medieval Times*, 3:17–27.

———. "The Land of Israel in Medieval Kabbalah." In *The Land of Israel: Jewish Perspectives*, edited by Lawrence A. Hoffman. Notre Dame IN: University of Notre Dame Press, 1986.

———. *Language, Torah, and Hermeneutics in Abraham Abulafia*. Albany: SUNY Press, 1989.

———. "Martin Buber and Gershom Scholem on Hasidism: A Critical Appraisal." In Rapoport-Albert, *Hasidism Reappraised*, 389–403.

———. *Messianic Mystics*. New Haven: Yale University Press, 1998.

———. "Mysticism." In Arthur A. Cohen and Mendes-Flohr. *Contemporary Jewish Religious Thought*, 643–55.

———. "On the Theologization of Kabbalah in Modern Scholarship." In *Religious Apologetics—Philosophical Argumentation*, edited by Yossef Schwartz and Volkhard Krech, 123–74. Tubingen: J. C. B. Mohr [Paul Siebeck], 2004.

———. "Particularism and Universalism in Kabbalah, 1480–1650." In Ruderman, *Essential Papers on Jewish Culture*, 324–44.

———. "Saturn and Sabbatai Tzevi: A New Approach to Sabbateanism." In Schafer and Cohen, *Toward the Millenium*, 173–202.

———. "Sexual Metaphors and Praxis in the Kabbalah." In *The Jewish Family: Metaphor and Memory*, edited by David Kraemer, 197-224. Oxford: Oxford University Press, 1989.

———. *Studies in Ecstatic Kabbalah*. Albany: SUNY Press, 1988.

———. "*Tzimtzum* in Kabbalah and in Research." Hebrew. *Jerusalem Studies in Jewish Thought* 10 (1992): 59-113.

———. "Universalization and Integration: Two Conceptions of Mystical Union in Jewish Mysticism." In *Mystical Union in Judaism, Christianity, and Islam: An Ecumenical Dialogue*, edited by Moshe Idel and Bernard McGinn, 27-57. New York: Continuum, 1996.

Idelsohn, A. Z. *Jewish Liturgy and Its Development*. New York: Holt, 1932.

Jackson, Howard M. "The Origins and Development of *Shi'ur Qomah* Revelation in Jewish Mysticism." *Journal for the Study of Judaism* 31 (2005): 373-415.

Jacobs, Louis. *Hasidic Prayer*. New York: Schocken, 1972.

———. *Hasidic Thought*. New York: Schocken, 1976.

———. *Jewish Ethics, Philosophy and Mysticism*. New York: Behrman House, 1969.

———. *Jewish Mystical Testimonies*. New York: Schocken, 1976.

———. *A Jewish Theology*. New York: Behrman House, 1973.

———. "The Relevance and Irrelevance of Hasidism." In *The Solomon Goldman Lectures: Perspectives in Jewish Learning*, edited by Nathaniel Stampfer, 2:19-27. Chicago: Spertus College of Judaica Press, 1979.

———. *Seeker of Unity: The Life and Works of Aaron of Starosselje*. New York: Basic Books, 1967.

———. *Their Heads in Heaven: Unfamiliar Aspects of Hasidism*. London: Vallentine Mitchell, 2005.

———. "The Uplifting of Sparks in Later Jewish Mysticism." In Green, *Jewish Spirituality from the Sixteenth-Century Revival to the Present*, 99-126.

Janowitz, Naomi. "God's Body: Theological and Ritual Roles of *Shi'ur Komah*." In Eilberg-Schwartz, *People of the Body*, 183-201.

Kadushin, Max. *The Rabbinic Mind*. New York: Blaisdell, 1965.

———. *Worship and Ethics*. New York: Bloch, 1963.

Kallus, Menachem, trans. and annotator. *The Pillar of Prayer*. Louisville: Fons Vitae, 2011.

Kaplan, Aryeh. *The Chasidic Masters and Their Teachings*. Brooklyn: Moznaim, 1984.

———. *Gems of Rabbi Nachman*. Jerusalem: Chaim Kramer, 1980.

———. *Jewish Meditation: A Practical Guide*. New York: Schocken, 1985.

———. *Meditation and Kabbalah*. York Beach ME: Samuel Weiser, 1982.

Kaplan, Edward K. Review of *Man Is Not Alone*, *Shofar* 26:1 (Fall 2007): 190-93.

———. *Spiritual Radical: Abraham Joshua Heschel in America*. New Haven: Yale University Press, 2007.

———, and Samuel H. Dresner. *Abraham Joshua Heschel: Prophetic Witness*. New Haven: Yale University Press, 1998.

Kaplan, Lawrence J., and David Shatz, eds. *Rabbi Abraham Isaac Kook and Jewish Spirituality*. New York: New York University Press, 1995.

Kasher, Menachem M. *Torah Shleimah*. Combined vol. 40–42. Jerusalem: Beit Torah Shleimah, 1992.

Katz, Jacob. "Joseph G. Weiss: A Personal Appraisal." In Rapoport-Albert, *Hasidism Reappraised*, 3–9.

Kaufmann, Walter. *The Faith of a Heretic*. Garden City NY: Doubleday Anchor Books, 1963.

Kaufmann, Yehezkel. *The Religion of Israel: From Its Beginnings to the Babylonian Exile*. New York: Schocken, 1972.

Kellner, Menachem. *Maimonides' Confrontation with Mysticism*. Oxford: Littman, 2006.

———. "Messianic Postures in Israel Today." In Saperstein, *Essential Papers*, 504–18.

Kimelman, Reuven. *The Mystical Meaning of Lekhah Dodi and Kabbalat Shabbat*. Hebrew. Los Angeles: Cherub, 2003.

———. Untitled commentary on "Lekhah Dodi." In Hoffman, *My People's Prayer Book*, 8:118, 128–32.

Klausner, Joseph. *The Messianic Idea in Israel*. New York: Macmillan, 1955.

Kramer, Simon G. *God and Man in the Sefer Hasidim*. New York: Bloch, 1966.

Krassen, Miles. "New Year's Day for Fruit of the Tree." In Fine, *Judaism in Practice*, 81–95.

———. "Rabbi Israel Ba'al Shem Tov: Prophet of a New Paradigm." In Kallus, *Pillar of Prayer*, xiv–xxv.

———. *Uniter of Heaven and Earth: Rabbi Meshullam Feibush Heller of Zbarazh and the Rise of Hasidism in Eastern Galicia*. Albany: SUNY Press, 1998.

Kushner, Harold. Torah commentary *d'rash*. In *Etz Hayim: Torah and Commentary*. New York: Rabbinical Assembly and Jewish Publication Society, 2001.

Kushner, Lawrence. *I'm God You're Not: Observations on Organized Religion and Other Disguises of the Ego*. Woodstock VT: Jewish Lights, 2010.

———. *The Way into Jewish Mystical Tradition*. Woodstock VT: Jewish Lights, 2001.

Lachter, Hartley. "Introduction: Reading Mysteries." In Greenspahn, *Jewish Mysticism and Kabbalah*, 1–29.

Laenen, J. H. *Jewish Mysticism: An Introduction*. Louisville: Westminster John Knox, 2001.

Lamm, Norman. *The Religious Thought of Hasidism: Text and Commentary*. Hoboken NJ: Yeshiva University Press, 1999.

Landes, Daniel. Commentary in Hoffman, *My People's Prayer Book*.

Langer, Jiri. *Nine Gates to the Chassidic Mysteries*. New York: Behrman, 1976.

Lenowitz, Harris. *The Jewish Messiahs: From the Galilee to Crown Heights.* New York: Oxford University Press, 1998.

Liebes, Yehuda. *Studies in Jewish Myth and Jewish Messianism.* Albany: SUNY Press, 1993.

———. *Studies in the Zohar.* Albany: SUNY Press, 1993.

Loewenthal, Naftali. "Habad Approaches to Contemplative Prayer, 1790–1920." In Rapoport-Albert, *Hasidism Reappraised,* 288–300.

———. "The Neutralisation of Messianism and the Apocalypse." *Jerusalem Studies in Jewish Thought* 13 (1996): 59–73.

Magid, Shaul. "Associative Midrash: Reflections on a Hermeneutical Theory in Rabbi Nahman of Bratslav's *Likkutei MoHaRan.*" In Magid, *God's Voice from the Void,* 15–66.

———. *From Metaphysics to Midrash: Myth, History, and the Interpretation of Scripture in Lurianic Kabbala.* Bloomington IN: Indiana University Press, 2008.

———, ed. *God's Voice from the Void: Old and New Studies in Bratslav Hasidism.* Albany: SUNY Press, 2002.

———. "Hasidism: Mystical and Nonmystical Approaches to Interpreting Scripture." In Greenspahn, *Jewish Mysticism and Kabbalah,* 139–58.

Mahler, Raphael. "Hasidism and the Jewish Enlightenment." In Hundert, *Essential Papers on Hasidism,* 401–95.

Malachi, Mark. "From the Depths of Silence: The Application of Sound in Kabbalistic Healing." In Edward Hoffman, *Opening the Inner Gates,* 160–76.

Marcus, Ivan G. Commentary on "Shir ha-Kavod." In *My People's Prayer Book.* Vol. 10, *Shabbat Morning: Shacharit and Musaf,* edited by Lawrence A. Hoffman. Woodstock VT: Jewish Lights, 2007.

———. "The Devotional Ideals of Ashkenazic Pietism." In Green, *Jewish Spirituality: From the Bible through the Middle Ages,* 356–66.

———. *Piety and Society: The Jewish Pietists of Medieval Germany.* Leiden: Brill, 1981.

———. "Prayer Gestures in German Hasidism." In Dan and Grozinger, *Mysticism, Magic and Kabbalah,* 44–59.

Matt, Daniel C. "Adorning the 'Bride' on the Eve of the Feast of Weeks." In Fine, *Judaism in Practice,* 74–80.

———. "*Ayin:* The Concept of Nothingness in Jewish Mysticism." In Fine, *Essential Papers on Kabbalah,* 67–108.

———. *The Essential Kabbalah: The Heart of Jewish Mysticism.* New York: HarperCollins, 1995.

———. "The Mystic and the *Mizwot.*" In Green, *Jewish Spirituality: From the Bible through the Middle Ages,* 367–404.

———. *Zohar: The Book of Enlightenment.* New York: Paulist Press, 1983.

Mendes-Flohr, Paul. *Gershom Scholem: The Man and His Work.* Albany: SUNY Press, 1994.

Meroz, Ronit. "The Middle Eastern Origins of Kabbalah." *Journal for the Study of Sephardic and Mizrahi Jewry* (February 2007): 39–56.

Mondshine, Yehoshua. "The Fluidity of Categories in Hasidism: *Averah Lishmah* in the Teachings of R. Zevi Elimelekh of Dynow." In Rapoport-Albert, *Hasidism Reappraised*, 301–20.

Mopsik, Charles. "The Body of Engenderment in the Hebrew Bible, the Rabbinic Tradition and the Kabbalah." In *Fragments for a History of the Human Body: Part One*, edited by Michel Feher, Ramona Naddaff, and Nadia Tazi, 48–73. Cambridge: Zone Books, 1989.

Myers, Jody. *Kabbalah and the Spiritual Quest: The Kabbalah Centre in America.* Westport CT: Praeger, 2007.

———. "Kabbalah at the Turn of the 21st Century." In Greenspahn, *Jewish Mysticism and Kabbalah*, 175–90.

———. "Marriage and Sexual Behavior in the Teachings of the Kabbalah Centre." In Huss et al., *Kabbalah and Modernity*, 259–81.

Nadler, Allan. *The Faith of the Mithnagdim: Rabbinic Responses to Hasidic Rapture.* Baltimore: Johns Hopkins University Press, 1997.

Newman, Louis I. *The Hasidic Anthology: Tales and Teachings of the Hasidim.* New York: Bloch, 1944.

Nigal, Gedaliah. *Magic, Mysticism, and Hasidism: The Supernatural in Jewish Thought.* Northvale NJ: Jason Aronson, 1994.

Petrovsky-Shtern, Yohanan. "You Will Find It in the Pharmacy." In Dynner, *Holy Dissent*, 13–54.

Plaut, W. Gunther. *The Haftarah Commentary.* New York: UAHC, 1996.

Polen, Nehemia. *The Holy Fire: The Teachings of Rabbi Kalonymus Kalman Shapira, the Rebbe of the Warsaw Ghetto.* Northvale NJ: Jason Aronson, 1999.

Potok, Chaim. Torah commentary *peshat.* In *Etz Hayim: Torah and Commentary.* New York: Rabbinical Assembly and Jewish Publication Society, 2001.

Rabinowicz, Harry M. *Hasidism: The Movement and Its Masters.* Northvale NJ: Jason Aronson, 1988.

Raphael, Simcha Paull. *Jewish Views of the Afterlife.* Northvale NJ: Jason Aronson, 1994.

Rapoport-Albert, Ada. "Hasidism after 1772: Structural Continuity and Change." In Rapoport-Albert, *Hasidism Reappraised*, 76–140.

———, ed. *Hasidism Reappraised.* London: Littman, 1996.

Rosen, Michael. *The Quest for Authenticity: The Thought of Reb Simhah Bunim.* Brooklyn: Urim Publications, 2008.

Rosenthal, Gilbert S. "*Tikkun ha-Olam*: The Metamorphosis of a Concept." *Journal of Religion*, 85, no. 2 (2005): 214–40.

Roskies, David G. "The Master of Prayer: Rabbi Nahman of Bratslav." In Magid, *God's Voice from the Void*, 67–102.

Rosman, Moshe. *Founder of Hasidism: A Quest for the Historical Ba'al Shem Tov.* Berkeley: University of California Press, 1996.

Rubenstein, Richard L. *Morality and Eros.* New York: McGraw-Hill, 1970.

Ruderman, David B., ed. *Essential Papers on Jewish Culture in Renaissance and Baroque Italy.* New York: New York University Press, 1992.

Sack, Bracha. *Shomer ha-Pardes: Ha-Mekubbal Rabbi Shabtai Sheftel Horowitz mi-Prague.* Beer-Sheva: Ben Gurion University of the Negev Press, 2002.

Sacks, Jonathan. *To Heal a Fractured World.* New York: Schocken, 2005.

Saperstein, Marc, ed. *Essential Papers on Messianic Movements and Personalities in Jewish History.* New York: New York University Press, 1992.

Sarachek, Joseph. *The Doctrine of the Messiah in Medieval Jewish Literature.* New York: Hermon, 1932.

Sarna, Nahum M. *The JPS Torah Commentary: Exodus.* Philadelphia: Jewish Publication Society, 1991.

———. *The JPS Torah Commentary: Genesis.* Philadelphia: Jewish Publication Society, 1989.

———. *Songs of the Heart: An Introduction to the Book of Psalms.* New York: Schocken, 1993.

Schachter-Shalomi, Zalman. *Spiritual Intimacy: A Study of Counseling in Hasidism.* Northvale NJ: Jason Aronson, 1991.

———. "Worlds of Discourse." In Jack Bemporad, ed., *The Inner Journey,* 109–29. Sandpoint ID: Morning Light Press, 2007.

———. *Wrapped in a Holy Flame: Teachings and Tales of a Hasidic Master.* San Francisco: Jossey-Bass, 2003.

———, and Netanel Miles-Yepez. *A Hidden Light: Stories and Teachings of Early HaBaD and Bratzlav Hasidism.* Santa Fe: Gaon Books, 2011.

Schafer, Peter. *The Origins of Jewish Mysticism.* Tubingen: J. C. B. Mohr [Paul Siebeck], 2009.

———. *Synopse zur Hekhalot-Literatur.* Tubingen: J. C. B. Mohr [Paul Siebeck], 1981.

_____, and Mark Cohen, eds., *Toward the Millenium: Messianic Expectations from the Bible to Waco.* Leiden: Brill, 1998.

Schatz-Uffenheimer, Rivka. *Hasidism as Mysticism: Quietistic Elements in Eighteenth-Century Hasidic Thought.* Princeton: Princeton University Press, 1993.

Schechter, Solomon. "Safed in the Sixteenth Century." In *Studies in Judaism,* Second Series, 202–85. Philadelphia: Jewish Publication Society, 1908.

Schnall, David J. *Beyond the Green Line: Israeli Settlements West of the Jordan.* New York: Praeger, 1984.

Scholem, Gershom. *Jewish Gnosticism, Merkabah Mysticism, and Talmudic Tradition.* New York: Jewish Theological Seminary, 1960.

———. *Kabbalah*. Jerusalem: Keter, 1974.

———. *Major Trends in Jewish Mysticism*. New York: Schocken, 1946.

———. *The Messianic Idea in Judaism*. New York: Schocken, 1971.

———. *On the Kabbalah and Its Symbolism*. New York: Schocken, 1965.

———. *On the Mystical Shape of the Godhead: Basic Concepts in the Kabbalah*. New York: Schocken, 1991.

———. *Origins of the Kabbalah*. Princeton: Princeton University Press, 1987.

———. *Sabbatai Sevi: The Mystical Messiah*. Princeton: Princeton University Press, 1973.

_____. *Zohar: The Book of Splendor*. New York: Schocken, 1949.

Schwartz, Howard. *Tree of Souls: The Mythology of Judaism*. New York: Oxford University Press, 2004.

Schweid, Eliezer. "Jewish Messianism: Metamorphoses of an Idea." In Saperstein, *Essential Papers*, 53–70.

Shapiro, Rami. *Tanya, the Masterpiece of Hasidic Wisdom: Selections Annotated and Explained*. Woodstock VT: SkyLight Paths, 2010.

Sharot, Stephen. *Messianism, Mysticism, and Magic: A Sociological Analysis of Jewish Religious Movements*. Chapel Hill: University of North Carolina Press, 1982.

Shatz, David. "The Biblical and Rabbinic Background to Medieval Jewish Philosophy." In *The Cambridge Companion to Medieval Jewish Philosophy*, edited by Daniel H. Frank and Oliver Leaman, 16–37. Cambridge: Cambridge University Press, 2003.

Sherwin, Byron L. "The Human Body: A House of God." In *Threescore and Ten: Essays in Honor of Seymour J. Cohen*, edited by Abraham J. Karp, Louis Jacobs, and Chaim Z. Dimitrovsky, 99–108. Hoboken NJ: KTAV, 1991.

———. *In Partnership with God: Contemporary Jewish Law and Ethics*. Syracuse: Syracuse University Press, 1990.

———. *Kabbalah: An Introduction to Jewish Mysticism*. Lanham MD: Rowman & Littlefield, 2006.

———. *Mystical Theology and Social Dissent*. East Brunswick NJ: Associated University Presses, 1982.

———. *Sparks Amidst the Ashes: The Spiritual Legacy of Polish Jewry*. New York: Oxford University Press, 1997.

———. *Studies in Jewish Theology: Reflections in the Mirror of Tradition*. Portland OR: Vallentine Mitchell, 2007.

———. *Toward a Jewish Theology*. Lewiston NY: Edwin Mellon, 1991.

———. *Workers of Wonders*. Lanham MD: Rowman & Littlefield, 2004.

Smith, Morton. "Messiahs: Robbers, Jurists, Prophets, and Magicians." In Saperstein, *Essential Papers*, 73–82.

Swartz, Michael D. "Ancient Jewish Mysticism." In Greenspahn, *Jewish Mysticism and Kabbalah*, 33–48.

———. "The Book of the Great Name." In Fine, *Judaism in Practice*, 341–47.

———. "Mystical Texts." In *The Literature of the Sages: Second Part*, edited by Shmuel Safrai, Zeev Safrai, Joshua Schwartz, and Peter J. Tomson, 393–420. Assen: Royal Van Gorcum, 2006.

Sweeney, Marvin Alan. "*Pardes* Revisited Once Again: A Reassessment of the Rabbinic Legend Concerning the Four Who Entered *Pardes*." *Shofar* 22, no. 4 (2004): 43–56.

Talmage, Frank. "Apples of Gold: The Inner Meaning of Sacred Texts in Medieval Judaism." In Green, *Jewish Spirituality from the Bible through the Middle Ages*, 313–55.

Telushkin, Joseph. *Rebbe: The Life and Teachings of Menachem M. Schneerson, the Most Influential Rabbi in Modern History.* New York: HarperWave, 2014.

Tirosh, Yosef. *Religious Zionism: An Anthology.* Jerusalem: World Zionist Organization, 1975.

Tirosh-Samuelson, Hava. "Gender in Jewish Mysticism." In Greenstein, *Jewish Mysticism and Kabbalah*, 191–230.

———. "Jewish Mysticism." In *The Cambridge Guide to Jewish History, Religion, and Culture*, edited by Judith R. Baskin and Kenneth Seeskin, 399–423. New York: Cambridge University Press, 2010.

Tishby, Isaiah. "Acute Apocalyptic Messianism." In Saperstein, *Essential Papers*, 259–86.

———. "Gershom Scholem's Contribution to the Study of the *Zohar*." In Mendes-Flohr, *Gershom Scholem*, 40–55.

———. *Paths of Faith and Heresy.* Hebrew. Jerusalem: Magnes Press, 1994.

———. *The Wisdom of the Zohar.* 3 vols. Oxford: Oxford University Press, 1989.

Trachtenberg, Joshua. *Jewish Magic and Superstition.* New York: Behrman, 1939.

Unterman, Alan, ed. *The Kabbalistic Tradition: An Anthology of Jewish Mysticism.* New York: Penguin, 2008.

Urbach, Ephraim E. *The Sages: Their Concepts and Beliefs.* Cambridge: Harvard University Press, 1987.

Verman, Mark. *The Books of Contemplation: Medieval Jewish Mystical Sources.* Albany: SUNY Press, 1992.

———. *The History and Varieties of Jewish Meditation.* Northvale NJ: Jason Aronson, 1996.

Weiss, Joseph. "Mystical Hasidism and the Hasidism of Faith: A Typological Analysis." In Magid, *God's Voice from the Void*, 277–85.

———. *Studies in Eastern European Jewish Mysticism.* Oxford: Oxford University Press, 1985.

Werblowsky, R. J. Zwi. *Joseph Karo: Lawyer and Mystic.* Philadelphia: Jewish Publication Society, 1977.

———. "Messianism in Jewish History." In Saperstein, *Essential Papers*, 35–52.

———. "The Safed Revival and Its Aftermath." In Green, *Jewish Spirituality from the Sixteenth-Century Revival to the Present*, 7–33.

Wineman, Aryeh. *Beyond Appearances: Stories from the Kabbalistic Ethical Writings*. Philadelphia: Jewish Publication Society, 1988.

———. *The Hasidic Parable*. Philadelphia: Jewish Publication Society, 2001.

Winkler, Gershon. *Magic of the Ordinary: Recovering the Shamanic in Judaism*. Berkeley: North Atlantic Books, 2003.

———. *The Soul of the Matter*. New York: Judaica Press, 1982.

Wolfson, Elliot R. *Abraham Abulafia—Kabbalist and Prophet: Hermeneutics, Theosophy, and Theurgy*. Los Angeles: Cherub, 2000.

———. "Abraham ben Samuel Abulafia and the Prophetic Kabbalah." In Greenstein, *Jewish Mysticism and Kabbalah*, 68–90.

———. "The Anonymous Chapters of the Elderly Master of Secrets: New Evidence for the Early Activity of the *Zoharic* Circle." *Kabbalah: Journal for the Study of Jewish Mystical Texts* 19 (2009): 143–278.

———. "The Engenderment of Messianic Politics: Symbolic Significance of Sabbatai Sevi's Coronation." In Schafer and Cohen, *Toward the Millenium*, 203–58.

———. "Images of God's Feet: Some Observations on the Divine Body in Judaism." In Eilberg-Schwartz, *People of the Body*, 143–81.

———. "Immanuel Frommann's Commentary on Luke and the Christianizing of Kabbalah: Some Sabbatean and Hasidic Affinities." In Dynner, *Holy Dissent*, 171–222.

———. "Metatron and *Shi'ur Qomah* in the Writings of *Haside Ashkenaz*." In Dan and Grozinger, *Mysticism, Magic and Kabbalah*, 60–92.

———. "Mystical Rationalization of the Commandments in the Prophetic Kabbalah of Abraham Abulafia." In Wolfson, Ivry, and Arkush, *Perspectives on Jewish Thought and Mysticism*, 331–80.

———. "Mystical-Theurgical Dimensions of Prayer in *Sefer ha-Rimmon*." In Blumenthal, *Approaches to Judaism in Medieval Times*, 3:41–79.

———. *Open Secret: Postmessianic Messianism and the Mystical Revision of Menahem Mendel Schneerson*. New York: Columbia University Press, 2009.

———. "The Status of the (Non)Jewish Other in the Apocalyptic Messianism of Menahem Mendel Schneerson." In Huss et al., *Kabbalah and Modernity*, 221–57.

———. *Through a Speculum That Shines*. Princeton: Princeton University Press, 1994.

———. *Venturing Beyond: Law and Morality in Kabbalistic Mysticism*. Oxford: Oxford University Press, 2006.

———. "Walking as a Sacred Duty: Theological Transformation of Social Reality in Early Hasidism." In Rapoport-Albert, *Hasidism Reappraised*, 180–207.

———, Alfred L. Ivry, and Allan Arkush, eds. *Perspectives on Jewish Thought and Mysticism*. Amsterdam: Harwood Academic, 1998.

Wolpe, David. *Floating Takes Faith*. Springfield NJ: Behrman, 2004.

Zeitlin, Hillel. *Hasidic Spirituality for a New Era: The Religious Writings of Hillel Zeitlin*. Edited and translated by Arthur Green. New York: Paulist Press, 2012.

Zornberg, Avivah Gottlieb. *The Murmuring Deep: Reflections on the Biblical Unconscious*. New York: Schocken, 2009.

Index

b'apav, 205
Barukh of Medzibozh, 381
"Barukh She-amar," 92, 536
Beauty. See *Tiferet*
Be'er Hetev (Ashkenazi), 334–35
Beit Yosef (Karo), 255
belimah, 69
Ben Azzai, 34–36, 163,
    462nn25–26
Ben Porat Yosef (Jacob Joseph),
    351–53, 368–69
Ben Zoma, 34, 36, 462n31
Berakhot, 54, 309–10, 328–29
Berekhiah, Rabbi, 55–56
Berg, Philip. *See* Gruberger,
    Philip
Beri'ah, 273, 274–75, 276, 277–81,
    287–88, 536
berur, 502n28
Besht. *See* Ba'al Shem Tov
Bible, 10–23; Daniel and, 20–21,
    41–43; Ezekiel and, 12–16,
    458n6, 459n10; Gershom
    Scholem and, 22–23, 460n28;
    Hasidism and, 353; Isaiah and,
    10–12, 16; magic and, 295–98,
    504n2; Moses and, 16–20,
    459n16, 459n23. *See also*
    Psalms; Song of Songs; *specific
    books of*
Binah: about, 78, 114, 117, 118, 120,
    477n11, 479n26; *deveikut* and,
    137; *Ein Sof* and, 102–3, 104, 120,
    536; four worlds and, 275, 276–
    78; Hasidism and, 396; levels of
    soul and, 285, 288; Lurianic Kab-
    balah and, 231, 232–33; sexuality
    and, 196; sin and evil and, 220,
    250–52, 498n24
bittul ha-yesh, 360, 363, 365–66,
    374, 384, 404, 518n43, 536

Bloom, Harold, 115
Blumenthal, David, 44, 71, 129,
    216, 466n26, 470n19, 470n23
B'nei Mahshavah Tovah (Shapira),
    108
botzina d'kardenuta, 120–21, 536
boundaries of the universe, 72, 75
Brandwein, Yehuda, 448
Bratslaver Hasidism, 373–74,
    520n25
breaking the vessels, 225, 232,
    241–42, 244, 376–77, 494n7,
    543
Buber, Martin, 509n36, 514n1
Buddhism, Theravada, 281,
    501n10
Bunim, Simha, 385–87, 394,
    522n19, 523n29, 523–24n48
burning bush, 17–18
Buxbaum, Yitzhak, 6

"Cabalists, Mystics, and Wonder
    Workers" (Ausubel), 441–42
Cain, 249–51, 252
calendar, solar, 58–59, 61–63
Carlebach, Shlomo, 391, 408,
    448
cause of causes, 102, 279
Chabad Hasidism, 396–413;
    about, 396, 413, 526n39,
    527–28n56, 536; Dov Ber and,
    401–5; Lurianic Kabbalah
    and, 237–38, 496n20; Mena-
    hem Mendel Schneerson
    and, 406–13, 527n49, 527n54;
    messianism and, 397, 406–13;
    Shneur Zalman and, 396–402,
    404, 524n4, 525n17, 525n20,
    525n25, 525n28; Yosef Yitzhak
    Schneerson and, 405–6,
    526n37

derasha, 184, *536*
Deuteronomy, Book of, 51–52,
107, 259, 328, 337
deveikut, 130–46; about, 6, 66, 130–
31, 163, *536*; asceticism and, 267,
268; Ba'al Shem Tov and, 143–
45, 350, 482nn24–25, 482n29;
Ein Sof and, 107–8; Hasidism
and, 145–46, 356–61, 518n40,
518n44, 519n20; Isaiah Horowitz and, 140–41, 482n20; Judah
Loew and, 137–39; Maimonides
and, 131, 481n4; messianism
and, 311–12; prayer and ritual
and, 326, 330; Prophetic Kabbalah and, 162, 169; Rabbi
Elimelekh and, 145–46; *Reshit
Hokhmah* and, 140, 482n19;
sexuality and, 194, 201; *Shnei
Luhot ha-Brit*, 141–43; Shneur
Zalman and, 397–98; Torah
and, 187, 190; *tzorekh gavoha*
and, 157–58; Zohar and, 132–33,
134–37, 140–41, 481n10
De Vidas, Elijah, 139–40, 221–22,
223, 300, 482n19
dew of light, 89
diagram of the *sefirot*, 112–15, *113*,
477n6, 477n9, 479n26
Din, 114, 125, 219, 232, 479n26,
514n44, *536*. See also *Gevurah*
distortion of Jewish mysticism,
436–43
Divine Names: magic and, 298–300,
304–6, 505n17; in meditation,
263; Prophetic Kabbalah and,
162, 169, 172–76; in *Sefer Yetzirah*, 68, 123; *sefirot* and, 123, 190;
tzaddik and, 353. *See also* Four-
Letter Name of God
Divine need. See *tzorekh gavoha*

Divine Presence. See *Shekhinah*
Divrei Emet (Horowitz), 381–82,
516n8
Dodi. *See* Lakhah Dodi
Donmeh, 318
Dov Ber: Ba'al Shem Tov and,
347–50, 356, 516n12; Chabad
Hasidism and, 401–5, 524n4;
prayer and, 362–63; *shevirah*
and, 376–77; Shneur Zalman
and, 397; *tzaddik* and, 360;
tzimtzum and, 236–37
dreams, 246–47, 314–16
Dresner, Samuel, 352–53, 373,
395, 441, 443–45
Dubnow, Simon, 532n8
Dumah, 289, 503n31
du-partzufim, 195, 233, *537*
dybbuk, 293–94, 442, 504nn45–
46, *537*

ecstatic experiences, 161–62, 163,
168–71, 362, 402–5, 431. See
also *hitlahavut*
Ecstatic Kabbalah. *See* Prophetic
Kabbalah
Edom, 91, 316
ehad, 285, 329, 354
"Ein Keloheinu," 327, 485n5, *537*
Ein Sof, 99–109; about, 72, 99–102,
148, 190, 230, 474n4; four
worlds and, 279–80; Hasidic
masters and, 107–8, 476n25;
Isaiah Horowitz and, 106–7;
Lawrence Kushner and, 107–8;
Lurianic Kabbalah and, 225, 227,
229–33, 241, 495n11, 496n27;
Moshe Cordovero and, 105–6;
prayer and ritual and, 330;
sefirot and, 100–105, 110, 116–
18, 120–22, 474n1, 475n15

understanding of God, 30, 98; *Man is Not Alone*, 4, 429–30; *Man's Quest for God*, 434, 445; on *Merkavah* mystics, 163; *Moral Grandeur and Spiritual Audacity*, 430; *Mystical Element in Judaism*, 3–4, 432–33, 452, 477n8, 477n11, 478n15, 490n22, 500n20; on poverty, 389; on prayer, prophets and God's Presence, 430–34, 452, 528n1; on Temple, 63; on union with God, 3–4, 7

Heschel, Avraham Yehoshua, 428

Heschel, Susannah, 428

Hesed: about, 114, 117, 122, 124, 129, 280, 479n26, 538, 539; ritual and, 331, 334–35, 337, 512n18, 514n44; sin and evil and, 216, 247, 253; *tzorekh gavoha* and, 150

Hezekiah, King, 60, 296–97

Hiddushei Aggadot (Loew), 138–39

Hiddushei ha-Rim, 394, 523–24n48

higher consciousness, 21, 187, 367, 541

Hirsch, Samson Raphael, 326

hishtavut, 355–56, 382, 518n40, 539

History of the Jews (Graetz), 436–38, 440–41

hitlahavut, 201, 362–67, 519n10, 539

Hod, 114–15, 117, 335, 479n26, 514n44, 539

Hokhmah: about, 78, 113–14, 117–21, 477n6, 478n13, 479n26, 481n53, 535, 537,

539, 546; *Ein Sof* and, 102–5, 477n11; four worlds and, 276–78; Hasidism and, 392, 396, 536; Lurianic Kabbalah and, 231, 232–33; in prayer and ritual, 331, 334, 514n44; as root of the soul, 251, 288; sexuality and, 196

hokhmat ha-tzeiruf, 167, 539

Holocaust, 395, 417, 421–28, 445

Holy of Holies, 44, 54–55, 59, 104, 443–44, 458n6, 491n8

Holy Spirit, 82, 542

Horowitz, Aaron Ha-Levi, 401–2, 404

Horowitz, Isaiah, 495n15; *deveikut* and, 140–41, 143, 358; *Ein Sof* and, 106–7, 474n2; four worlds and, 275–81, 288; messianism and, 322; ritual and, 331–32, 341; *Shnei Luhot ha-Brit*, 106–7, 140–43, 151, 202, 275–81, 322–23, 330–32, 399, 474n2

Horowitz, Jacob Isaac, 323, 379–83, 385, 518n44, 521nn5–6

Horsley, Richard A., 467n22

Hoshanah Rabbah, 298–99, 539

House of Zadok, 61

Hovot ha-Levavot, 234

hukkim, 191–92, 490n30, 539

human body and the *sefirot*, 112–15, 117–18, 477n6, 477n8, 479n26, 479n28

ibbur, 264, 291–92, 293, 499–500n15, 539

Ibn Ezra, Abraham, 17, 164, 165

Ibn Gabbai, Meir, xii, 152–53, 155–56, 474n9, 489n17, 492n18

Idel, Moshe: on Abraham Heschel, 529n25; Ba'al Shem Tov teachings and, 514–15n1; eroticism and, 193; inverse Maggidism and, 293, 504n45; on Jewish mysticism, 439; on Lurianic Kabbalah, 496n23; magic and, 301, 505n17, 506n30, 521n7; messianism and, 508–9n33, 509n41; prayer and ritual and, 511n11, 513n36, 519n10; Prophetic-Ecstatic Kabbalah and, 170, 176, 487n24, 487nn26–27

Iggeret ha-Kodesh, 196–97, 491n10, 491n12

Iggeret ha-Reiyah (Kook), 419

image of God, 87–88, 91, 119, 238, 544

Imma, 287, 288, 539

incest, 27, 192

individual redemption, 419–20. *See also* redemption

Inge, Dean, 444

Insecurity of Freedom (Heschel), 431

inverse Maggidism, 293, 504n45

Irgas, Joseph, 497n42

Isaac, 114, 206, 337–38, 392–93

Isaac Meir Alter, 209, 394, 523–24n48

Isaac of Acre, 207, 267–69, 305–6, 518n40

Isaiah, 3, 10–12, 91, 296–97, 426, 504–5n4

Ishmael, 323, 337–38

Ishmael ben Elisha, 45–46, 54, 63, 422, 466n8, 469n36

Islam, 148, 318, 338, 508n29

Israel: *deveikut* and, 134, 135, 137–40; as God's crown, 89–91;

God's love of, 40, 193, 194–95; God's will and, 248; "Lekhah Dodi" and, 339; revival of, 324–25, 427; *Tzorekh Gavoha* and, 149–50, 154

Israel of Ruzhin, 371–72, 532n10

Isserles, Moshe, 97, 450, 474n1, 499n1

Iyyun circle, 228, 473n36

Jacob: Kalonymous Kalman Shapira and, 422–24; in messianic dream, 315–16; Mordecai Leiner and, 392–93; sin and, 216; *Tiferet* and, 114, 128–29, 481n56

Jacob Isaac of Przysucha (the "Yehudi"), 382–85, 393–94, 521n13, 522n23

Jacob Joseph of Polonnoye, 321, 349, 351–53, 368–69, 371, 380, 515n4, 517n21

Jacobs, Louis, 118, 349, 444–45; Chabad Hasidism and, 396, 525n28; Lurianic Kabbalah and, 224, 230, 495n11, 496n20

Jewish studies, 436–43, 448

Jewish survival, 445–46

Jewish Theological Seminary of America, 428, 439

Joseph, 115, 340, 422–24

Jubilees, Book of, 62–63, 539

Judah, 312–13

Judaism: development of, 63; Kabbalah and, 98, 474n2; magic and, 295, 504n2; mysticism and, 5, 98, 438–39, 440, 450, 458n6; numerology in, 58; sin and evil and, 208, 216–17

Judgment. See *Din*

Maggid of Mezeritch. *See* Dov Ber

"The Maggid of Rabbi Joseph Taitazek" (Scholem), 301-4

magic, 295-306; about, 295-96; automatic writing and, 301-5, 506n23; Ba'al Shem Tov and, 321; in Bible, 295-98; creative, 67, 296, 298, 303; God's Name and, 298-300, 304-5, 505nn16-17; Hasidei Ashkenaz and, 93, 473n31; Hasidism and, 521n7; Isaac of Acre and, 305-6; messianism and, 306-7, 506n30; Zohar and, 305

Magic of the Ordinary (Winkler), 305-6, 470n9

Magid, Shaul, 225, 353, 520n25

Maimonides, 33, 297, 462n31; Abraham Abulafia and, 161, 169; *deveikut* and, 131, 481n1; God and, 12, 17, 100, 142

mainline Kabbalah: about, 6-7, 98-99, 147, 149, 217, 226-27, 483n1; gap between humans and God and, 110; Moses Cordovero and, 176-77; mystics and God and, 54; prayer and ritual and, 326, 332, 338. *See also* Kabbalah

Malkhut: about, 104, 115, 117-18, 125-28, 478nn15-16, 481n53, 539, 541; *deveikut* and, 136-37; evil and, 247-48, 251; four worlds and, 275-80, 287-88; Lurianic Kabbalah and, 233; ritual and, 331, 338-39, 514n44; *Tiferet* and, 127-28, 148-49, 151-52, 157-58,

256-58, 513n36. See also *Shekhinah*

Man Is Not Alone (Heschel), 4, 429-30

Man's Quest for God (Heschel), 434, 445

Marcus, Ivan G., 90-91, 471n2, 472n17, 472n21

marriages, forbidden, 27-28

martyrdom, 82, 138, 262, 499n9

mashpia u'mekabbel, 491n10

masturbation, 195, 197, 491n15

Matrona, 478n15

Matronita, 247-48, 498n15, 541

Matt, Daniel C., 121, 137, 189, 191, 469nn38-39, 478-79n23, 501n14, 502n19

McGinn, Bernard, 3

meditation, 33, 92, 263-64; *deveikut* and, 141, 145, 162, 357, 359-60; Prophetic Kabbalah and, 162, 166-69, 174-76, 177, 487-88nn32-33; *sefirot* and, 110, 123, 226-27

Mei ha-Shiloah (Leiner), 391-94, 395

Meir, Rabbi, 136, 209

Menahem Mendel of Vitebsk, 361

Menahem Nahum of Chernobyl, 239, 322, 476n22, 511n12

Mendelssohn, Moses, 345, 440

Merkavah, 14, 33, 57, 327; Ezekiel's vision of, 60, 63, 72; Prophetic Kabbalah and, 163, 168, 485n5. See also *ma'aseh Merkavah*

Meroz, Ronit, 470n24, 475n17

Messiah ben David, 323, 510n45

Messiah ben Joseph, 323-24, 510n45

Reshit Hokhmah, 139, 518n40
restitution, 218, 433, 507n18
Righteous. See *tzaddik*
ritual and prayer. *See* prayer and
    ritual
ritual purity, 49, 466n24
Rosenthal, Gilbert, 217–18,
    495n15
Rosman, Moshe, 402, 403, 515n2,
    515n4, 517n21
ruah, 74, 275, 282–88, 290, 405,
    489n18, 542
Ruah ha-Kodesh, 82, 542
Rubenstein, Richard L., 474n8

Saadia Gaon, 445
Sabbateanism, 317–18, 346,
    514–15n1
Sabbetai Sevi (Scholem), 446–47,
    532–33n10
Sacks, Johathan, 254
Sacred Fire (Shapira), 421–27,
    530n30
sacred service, 56–57
Safed, 8, 223, 226–27, 265–67,
    500n22, 542
saffar, 68, 69
Samael, 205–7, 212, 216, 306–7,
    315–17, 320, 492n38, 506n30,
    542
Samuel bar Nahman, 55, 195
Samuel ben Kalonymus, 471n1
sanctity of Jewish people, 325,
    389, 401, 420
sapphire, 13, 15, 16, 70, 459n13
sappir, 15, 70, 78, 542
Sarah, 76, 123–24
Sarna, Nahum, 19, 459n20,
    459n22
Satan, 212, 245. *See also* Samael
Sava d'Mishpatim, 179–87,

489n9, 489n11, 489n15,
    489n17
Schachter-Shalomi, Zalman,
    199, 226, 408, 448, 524nn3–4
Schafer, Peter: mysticism in the
    Bible and Talmud, 458n6,
    459n10, 460n28, 461n10;
    Song of Songs and, 463–64n6;
    Temple and, 467–68nn22–23,
    467n14, 468nn31–32; *Unio
    liturgica* and, 510n3
Schechter, Solomon, 223, 438, 538
Schneerson, Menahem Men-
    del, 378–79, 406–13, 526n39,
    527n49, 577n54
Schneerson, Sholom Dov Ber,
    408, 525n17
Schneerson, Yosef Yitzhak, 405–
    6, 409–12, 526n37
Scholem, Gershom: automatic
    writing and, 301–4; Bibli-
    cal mysticism and, 22–23,
    460n28; *Ein Sof* and, 474n4,
    475n15; on evil, 245; Gnosti-
    cism and, 461n5, 464n8;
    Hasidism and, 514n1;
    Heikhalot mysticism and,
    464n9, 468n24; on Kabbalah,
    446–47, 486n22, 532–33n10;
    maggid and, 258; *Merkavah*
    and, 45, 465n20; messianism
    and, 321–22; mystical union
    and, 170, 488n22; on mysti-
    cism, 438–39, 446–47, 457n15,
    460n28; pantheism and,
    488n34
Schweid, Eliezer, 308–9
Second Temple, 59, 64
seder, 334–35, 514n50, 523n30
Seeker of Unity (Jacobs), 396,
    495n11, 496n20

Taitazek, Joseph, 301–4
Talmud, 27–38, 543–44; entering the *pardes* and, 32–38, 461n17, 462nn24–26, 462n31, 462–63nn36–37; Hasidism and, 384, 522n19; Mishnah and, 27–31; Rabban Yohanen ben Zakkai and, 31–32, 461n12; Temple and, 59; *tzorekh gavoha* in, 154–56, 484n27
Tanya (Shneur Zalman), 148, 237–38, 397, 399–401, 412
Tefillah, 485n2, 544
tefillin, 88, 90–91, 117, 128–29, 298–99, 492n21, 544
tehiru, 224, 544
Teitelbaum, Moshe, 482n25
Temple, 51–64; defilement of, 60–63, 467n22, 468n24, 468nn31–33, 469n36; mirror of divine order and, 56–60, 64, 467nn13–14; Prophetic Kabbalah and, 162–63; sexuality and, 194, 471n8; specialness of, 51–56, 466n3, 466n6, 466n8
ten, number, 68–71, 261
theodicy, 240
theosophy, 6–7, 458n10, 544
Theravada Buddhism, 281, 501n10
thirty-two paths of wisdom, 68–69
thoughts at the time of intercourse, 197
three knots of the Holy Name, 119–20
throne of God: descriptions of, 10–11, 13, 15, 17; *deveikut* and, 136; four worlds and, 275,

280–81, 371; *Heikhalot* and, 34–35, 38, 45–46; *Merkavah* and, 44, 464n10; Temple and, 56, 60, 468n32
Tiferet: about, 114–18, 122, 124, 127–29, 478n13, 478n16, 479n26, 481n53, 544; asceticism and, 257, 265; evil and, 248, 251; four worlds and, 275–78, 280; levels of soul and, 285, 288; light and, 136–37; Lurianic Kabbalah and, 233; prayer and ritual and, 331–34, 337–38, 339, 342, 512n18, 513n36; sexuality and, 198, 200, 205; Torah and, 182, 189–90; *tzorekh gavoha* and, 148–49, 151–52, 157–58, 483n1
Tiferet ha-Yehudi (Jacob Isaac the Yehudi), 384
Tigay, Jeffrey, 18
tikkun: about, 155, 217, 220, 450, 544; Abraham Isaac Kook and, 421; Lurianic Kabbalah and, 225–26, 227, 233, 241–42, 495n15; messianism and, 314, 507n18; sexuality and, 199–200; souls and, 292–93
Tikkunei ha-Zohar, 102, 116–18, 252, 274–75, 475n12, 502n22, 506n23, 544
Tikkun Leil Shavuot, 198–99, 340–41, 544
tikkun olam, 217–18, 544
Tikkunum. See *Tikkunei ha-Zohar*
Tirosh-Samuelson, Hava, 471n9, 477n8, 479n31
Tishby, Isaiah, 190, 244, 313, 479n32, 481n10, 532n11

CPSIA information can be obtained at www.ICGtesting.com
Printed in the USA
BVOW08s1047200616

452718BV00001B/19/P